Did Jesus Teach Salvation By Works?

The Evangelical Theological Society
Monograph Series

David W. Baker, Editor

Volume 4

Did Jesus Teach Salvation By Works?
The Role of Works in Salvation in the Synoptic Gospels

Did Jesus Teach Salvation By Works?
The Role of Works in Salvation in the Synoptic Gospels

Alan P. Stanley

Pickwick *Publications*
An imprint of *Wipf and Stock Publishers*
199 West 8th Avenue • Eugene OR 97401

DID JESUS TEACH SALVATION BY WORKS?
The Role of Works in Salvation in the Synoptic Gospels

The Evangelical Theological Society Monograph Series 4

Copyright © 2006 Alan P. Stanley. All rights reserved. Except for brief quotations in critical publications or reviews, no part of this book may be reproduced in any manner without prior written permission from the publisher. Write: Permissions, Wipf & Stock, 199 W. 8th Ave., Eugene, OR 97401.

ISBN: 1-59752-680-0

Cataloging-in-Publication data:

Stanley, Alan P.

Did Jesus teach salvation by works? : the role of works in salvation in the synoptic gospels / Alan P. Stanley.

Eugene, Ore.: Pickwick Publications, 2006
Evangelical Theological Monograph Series 4

xx + 416 p. ; 23 cm.

ISBN 1-59752-680-0   (alk. paper)

1. Bible. N.T. Gospels—Theology. 2. Bible. N.T.—Criticism, interpretation, etc. I. Title. II. Series.

BS2555.6 S65 2006

Manufactured in the U.S.A.

To Kathleen—
Who shares together with me in the gracious gift of life.

Contents

Figures / viii
Tables / viii
Foreword / xi
Preface / xiii
Abbreviations / xvii

1. Did Jesus Teach Salvation by Works? Is There Any Debate? / 1
2. The Role of Works in Salvation in Church History / 19
3. The Role of Works in Salvation in Judaism / 71
4. "Works" in the New Testament / 116
5. "Salvation" in the New Testament / 134
6. Requirements for Entering the Kingdom / 166
7. Attaining Eternal Life / 188
8. The Role of *Discipleship* in Salvation / 220
9. The Role of *Endurance* in Salvation / 242
10. The Role of *Treating Others* in Salvation / 260
11. The Role of *Judgment* in Salvation / 294
12. Summary, Conclusion & Some Final Thoughts / 315

Bibliography / 339
Subject Index / 363
Scripture Index / 379

Illustrations

Figures

1. Matthew's Perspective on Salvation / 175
2. Perfection—Ethical and Eschatological / 202

Tables

1. Thomas Aquinas and the Order of Salvation / 32
2. The *Via Moderna* and the Order of Salvation / 38
3. The Change in Relationship Brought About by Salvation in Paul / 164
4. Entering the Kingdom *versus* Not Entering the Kingdom in the Sermon on the Mount / 170
5. Surpassing Righteousness *versus* Doing the Father's Will in Matthew 5:20 and 7:21 / 171
6. Characteristics of Those Who Enter the Kingdom *versus* Those Who Don't / 174
7. Entering Life *versus* Entering the Kingdom in Matthew 5–7 / 179
8. The Negative and Positive Sides of Discipleship and Salvation—Some Examples / 232
9. The Outcome of Discipleship / 239
10. The Goal of Life's Tests from Two Perspectives / 250
11. Similarities between John 15 and Matthew 10 / 254
12. Outline of Matthew 5:21-26 / 262
13. Loving Your Enemies (Luke 6:27b-30) / 269

14. The Relationship between Enemy Love and "Son of God" / 272
15. The Relationship between Reward and
    Surpassing Righteousness in Matthew 5 / 274
16. A Comparison of the Slaves in Matthew 18:21-35 / 285
17. A Comparison of the
    Master's Responses in Matthew 18:31-35 / 286
18. Paul *versus* James / 310
19. "Save" in James 2:14 Restated as "Justified" in 2:24 / 310

Foreword

ONE of the more interesting things one can do in studying the New Testament is to consider the way in which different figures in the New Testament discuss the same area. Sometimes this is not easy. This becomes especially difficult when we become accustomed to a particular way of saying something. For the church, such a customary saying is that salvation is by grace alone through faith alone. Who has not read Ephesians 2:8-10 with a note of rejoicing at what God does by grace, while noting that salvation is not by works? But then one reads passages in the gospels where Jesus, Lord and Savior of the church, seems to indicate that works are associated with the judgment he will render to all. How does one put these two types of texts together?

It takes a skilled exegete and theologian to guide one through the options and analyze how one can make sense out of these two sets of emphases. What exactly is going on? Alan Stanley is well equipped to be such a careful guide. His work takes both types of passages seriously. His study works through the history of this discussion and negotiates the textual territory with clarity and discernment. He does not turn his back on the host of passages in the gospels that raise the issue (Matt 5:20, 21-26, 43-48 par.; 7:21-23; 10:22; 18:21-35; 19:17-21 pars.; 24:13 par.; 25:34-46; Luke 10:27-28). One by one he examines what is going on. In the process, he reveals the ultimate unity of affirmation coming from Paul and Jesus, even as they consider the same topic from different angles. He also shows how this unity is something the great figures in church history also affirmed, as well as how it compared to the Judaism of Jesus' time. The result is a New Testament study that is worth pondering, for in it one can appreciate that the canon exists for a reason. Stanley's study shows how different key New Testament figures address the same topic from distinct angles. The result solves a dilemma of a surface reading that looks to be contradictory and shows that the full-orbed teaching of salvation resolves itself in complementary teaching that results in the church's instruction, enrichment and edification. Another benefit is that we see how God's grace is even greater than we may have imagined, covering not only our justification, but our sanctification as well. Any work that shows the depth of God's great grace is worth commending. This is such a book.

Darrell L. Bock
Research Professor of New Testament Studies
Dallas Theological Seminary

Preface

THE subject of works and salvation is something that has interested me for a number of years and which I have thought a lot about on many different levels: personally, theologically and academically. It is of course a subject that always seems to create quite a stir and tensions can run high. Of especial interest to me have been Jesus' words in the Synoptic Gospels. I, probably like most, have been well endowed with a substantial diet of Paul's teaching on salvation. So much so that Jesus' teachings on the subject are so strikingly different as to appear some times completely contradictory. "Why?" I have often asked. I admit that this was probably the primary reason for wanting to write on this subject in the first place—basically I was curious. And so I wrote my doctoral dissertation on "The Relationship Between Works and Salvation in the Synoptic Gospels," which I completed in 2002.

However, since then I have been ministering as a Pastor and a Bible College Teacher. Naturally my thinking has developed in this area, though it has not changed. As I have continued to learn and study in the context of day-to-day ministry I have only grown in my conviction of the importance of this subject. I believe that the church needs to hear, accept and understand what Jesus says here. This is not something that can be relegated to academic debate. Eternal destinies are at stake.

Jesus' teaching is challenging. I know that many read the first three Gospels and feel more than mildly uncomfortable when confronted with His teaching on salvation. My hunch is that His words are disturbing because they are so clear. One must, it seems, do more than simply believe in order to be saved. One must do the Father's will, love one's neighbor, practise righteousness greater than that of the Pharisees, obey Jesus' commands, and so on. Even more disturbing are a couple of examples in John where people did believe in Jesus and yet are clearly not saved (John 2:23-24; 8:31-46; cf. also Acts 8:13, 20-23). What does all this mean? Could it mean that we have not properly understood the biblical doctrine of salvation? The church needs to be clear on this message.

It is not that these types of issues have not been written on in the past in some form or another. However Jesus, we are sometimes told, does not have much to say to us on the subject of salvation. For this we must turn to John or Paul. This to me seems odd especially since Jesus told His disciples to go and teach others to obey everything He had commanded them to obey (Matt 28:20). Presumably the message of salvation is in there somewhere. Solutions have been suggested as to the reason for the discrepancy between Jesus and the likes of Paul. However, in my mind the alternative proposals avoid a straightforward and plain reading of the text. Jesus says what He says on salvation and the role of works. Our job is to accept it and having accepted it, understand it. One of the major aims of this book is to help us understand the role of works in salvation as taught by Jesus. I believe that when we understand this relationship we will have a better grasp of why it is that Jesus' teaching emphasizes the role of works. I also believe—surprising as it may seem—that God's grace in salvation is magnified when we rightly understand this relationship.

That said, I am pleased to see that over the last three years or more there has been an increasing amount of literature challenging popular views concerning salvation equaling something akin to a decision. It is my sincere hope and prayer that this book in some way might contribute positively to what has already been written. It is my hope that Christians would recognize the need for urgency in their own Christian pilgrimage. It is my prayer that God's grace may be magnified when we properly understand the role of works in salvation. Ultimately it is my prayer that God may use this meager attempt in ways that would bring glory, honor and pleasure to Him.

As for acknowledgments, it seems appropriate that I write these thoughts while attending the fifty-seventh meeting of the Evangelical Theological Society at Valley Forge, Pennsylvania. It seems appropriate for two reasons. First, David Baker has so kindly accepted this work into the ETS Monograph Series. Second, the theme of this year's conference is "Christianity in the Early Centuries." Hence not only am I surrounded by many of today's evangelical scholars, but also by scholars and theologians from the distant past. I have been continually reminded of my indebtedness to exegetes, theologians, pastors, and professors, both those living now and those who lived long ago. I am grateful for all those who have dedicated their lives to the study of the Bible and have in turn in some way passed their learning on to me. If there is anything in this book that is worthy of note then it rests on the shoulders of scholars now living and those who have gone before. That which is deemed unworthy rests on my own shoulders.

I would like to say a word of thanks to the NT department at Dallas Theological Seminary especially to those who were there during the years

1998 to 2002. I am so thankful to each one of these men—Drs Buist Fanning, John Grassmick, Dave Lowery, Dan Wallace, Jay Smith, Darrell Bock, Harold Hoehner, and Hall Harris—who have demonstrated to me what it means to love God with one's heart *and* mind. I am grateful to them for modeling for me evangelical scholarship. They have shown me what it looks like to be guided first by the text.

Thank you to Drs Darrell Bock, Dave Lowery and Jeff Bingham—my doctoral readers. Each provided helpful and constructive comments at the dissertation stage back in 2001–2002. Their scholarship is well known to many, though it is their grace and tremendous congeniality toward me—both then and now—that I remember them for.

One always hesitates to single people out at the risk of missing others. However I would like to especially thank Dr. Harold Hoehner, Ph.D. chair during my time at Dallas, for his friendship both inside and outside of the classroom. With the help of email he continues to be a loyal and *patient* friend even though we live an ocean apart. I have appreciated his help and advice on many occasions ranging from questions of an academic nature to ministry related concerns to computer problems. Not to mention that he and his wife Gini kindly provided me with a place to stay when it came time to get this manuscript ready for print.

Closer to home, I want to express my appreciation to the elders at Buderim Gospel Chapel—Lindsay Cruickshank, Darryl McCulloch, Mal McKenzie, Bill Forward, and John Melville—for allowing me time away to write. I especially appreciate them for the great group of godly men that they are. They too are men that seek to be guided by the text. I am humbled to be involved with them week after week.

I owe a great deal of thanks to four people in particular. Tammy Venter provided ready and willing assistance with some problems early on; Colin Miles helped me in all sorts of ways in the final stages from computer help to layout suggestions; Yve Cruickshank kindly and meticulously proof-read the manuscript and saved me from many errors; Karen Fountain very graciously printed out the final manuscript while I was in Australia so as to save me money on postage. All four demonstrated nothing but Christian grace and kindheartedness in their willingness to help.

Thanks also to Heather Carraher at Wipf and Stock Publishers for her hard work in bringing this book to its completion.

Finally I would like to acknowledge my wife, Kathleen. She has been a true partner in ministry for more than a decade. A mother of two boys under four years of age—and one on the way—she has graciously allowed me time in the last few months to get this manuscript print ready. Even as I write we are on different sides of the world. She along with Luke and Jackson provide the world from which I minister. And what a world they provide. I am so blessed. To her this book is affectionately dedicated.

Alan P. Stanley
Sunshine Coast, Queensland, Australia
January 2006

Abbreviations

AB	Anchor Bible
ABD	*Anchor Bible Dictionary.* Edited by D. N. Freedman
ʿAbod. Zar.	ʿAboda Zara
ACW	Ancient Christian Writers
Ag. Ap.	Josephus, *Against Apion*
Ant.	Josephus, *Antiquities*
Apoc.	*Apocalypse*
Apoc. Abr.	*Apocalypse of Abraham*
ATJ	*Ashland Theological Journal*
b.	Babylonian Talmud
2–3 *Apoc. Bar.*	*Apocalypse of Baruch*
Bar	Baruch
B. Bat	Babaʾ Batraʾ
BAGD	Bauer, W., W. F. Arndt, F. W. Gingrich, and F. W. Danker, *Greek-English Lexicon of the New Testament and Other Early Christian Literature.* 2d ed. Chicago, 1979
BDAG	Bauer, W., F. W. Danker, W. F. Arndt, and F. W. Gingrich, *Greek-English Lexicon of the New Testament and Other Early Christian Literature.* 3d ed. Chicago, 2000
BDB	Brown, F., S. R. Driver, and C. A. Briggs, *Hebrew and English Lexicon of the Old Testament.* Oxford, 1907
BECNT	Baker Exegetical Commentary on the New Testament
Ber.	*Berakot*
Bib	*Biblica*
BSac	*Bibliotheca Sacra*
BJRL	*Bulletin of the John Rylands University Library*
CBQ	*Catholic Biblical Quarterly*
CGCS	Cambridge Greek Commentary Series
CSTJ	*Complexities of Second Temple Judaism.* Edited by D. A. Carson, P. T. O'Brien, and M. A. Seifrid
CT	*Christianity Today*
Did.	*Didache*

DJG	*Dictionary of Jesus and the Gospels.* Edited by J. B. Green, S. McKnight, and I. H. Marshall
DLNTD	*Dictionary of the Later New Testament and its Developments.* Edited by R. P. Martin and P. H. Davids
DPL	*Dictionary of Paul and His Letters.* Edited by G. F. Hawthorne, R. P. Martin, and D. G. Reid
EBC	*Expositor's Bible Commentary.* Edited by F. E. Gaebelein. Grand Rapids, 1976–88
ETS	Evangelical Theological Society
EvQ	*Evangelical Quarterly*
ExpTim	*Expository Times*
1–2 Esdr	Esdras
GTJ	*Grace Theological Journal*
HCD	*History of Christian Doctrine*
HTR	*Harvard Theological Review*
ICC	International Critical Commentary
Inst.	*Institutes of the Christian Religion*
JBL	*Journal of Biblical Literature*
JETS	*Journal of the Evangelical Theological Society*
JGES	*Journal of the Grace Evangelical Society*
JR	*Journal of Religion*
JSNT	*Journal for the Study of the New Testament*
JSNTSup	Journal for the Study of the New Testament, Supplement Series
JSOTSup	Journal for the Study of the Old Testament, Supplement Series
JT	*Journal of Theology*
JTS	*Journal of Theological Studies*
Jub.	*Jubilees*
J. W.	Josephus, *Jewish Wars*
Ker.	*Keritot*
Ketub.	*Ketubot*
LXX	Septuagint
Louw-Nida	Louw, J. P., and E. A. Nida. *Greek-English Lexicon of the New Testament Based on Semantic Domains.* New York, 1988
m.	*Mishnah*
Mak.	*Makkot*
Mek.	*Mekhilta de-Rabbi Yishmael*
Midr.	*Midrash*
MT	Masoretic Text

NAC	New American Commentary
NASB	New American Standard Version
NIBC	New International Biblical Commentary
NICNT	New International Commentary on the New Testament
NIDNTT	*The New International Dictionary of New Testament Theology.* Edited by C. Brown. 4 vols. Grand Rapids, 1975–85.
NIGTC	New International Greek Testament Commentary
NIV	New International Version
NovTSup	Novum Testamentum Supplements
NSBT	New Studies in Biblical Theology
NT	New Testament
NTS	*New Testament Studies*
OT	Old Testament
OTP	*Old Testament Pseudepigrapha*
PNTC	Pillar New Testament Commentary
Pr Azar	Prayer of Azar
Ps. Sol.	*Psalms of Solomon*
1QH	*Thanksgiving Hymns*
1QM	*War Scroll*
1QS	*Rule of the Congregation*
4Q393	*Communal Confession*
4Q504	*Words of the Luminaries*
Qid.	*Qiddušin*
Rab.	*Rabbah*
RSR	*Religious Studies Review*
S	*Sermones Predicabiles*
Sanh.	*Sanhedrin*
Str-B	Strack, H. L., and P. Billerbeck. *Kommentar zum Neuen Testament aus Talmud und Midrasch.* 6 vols. Munich, 1922–61
Selected Works	*Selected Works of John Calvin: Tracts and Letters*
Sent.	*Epithoma pariter et collectorium circa quattuor sententiarum libros*
Sermons	*Sermons on Selected Lessons of the New Testament*
Shab.	*Shabbat*
Šebu.	*Šebuʿot*
Sib. Or.	*Sibylline Oracles*
Sir	Sirach
SJT	*Scottish Journal of Theology*
SM	Sermon on the Mount

SNTSMS	Society for New Testament Studies Monograph Series
SP	Sermon on the Plain
STh	*Summa Theologica*
ST	*Studia Theologica*
T. Dan.	*Testament of Daniel*
T. Iss.	*Testament of Issachar*
T. Levi	*Testament of Levi*
T. Naph.	*Testament of Naphtali*
Tob	Tobit
T. Sanh.	*Testament of the Sanhedrin*
T. Sim	*Testament of Simeon*
Tab	*Tabletalk*
TCGNT	*Textual Commentary on the Greek New Testament*. B. M. Metzger. 2d ed. Stuttgart: German Bible Society, 1994.
TDNT	*Theological Dictionary of the New Testament*. Edited by G. Kittel and G. Friedrich. Translated by G. W. Bromiley. 10 vols. Grand Rapids, 1964–76.
Tg. Onq.	*Targum Onqelos*
Tg. Neof.	*Targum Neofiti I*
TheoEvan	*Theologia Evangelica*
Them	*Themelios*
TThom	*The Thomist*
TJ	*Trinity Journal*
TNTC	Tyndale New Testament Commentaries
TynBul	*Tyndale Bulletin*
WBC	Word Biblical Commentary
Wis.	Wisdom of Solomon
Luther, *Works*	*Luther's Works*. Edited by Jaroslav Pelikan and Helmut T. Lehmann. Philadelphia: Muhlenberg Press, 1955.
Arminius, *Works*	Arminius, J. *Works of James Arminius*
Wesley, *Works*	Wesley, J. *Works of John Wesley*
WesTJ	*Wesleyan Theological Journal*
WTJ	*Westminster Theological Journal*
WUNT	Wissenschaftliche Untersuchungen zum Neuen Testament
y.	Jerusalem Talmud
Zw	*Sämtliche Werke: Einzig vollständige Ausgabe der Werke Zwinglis unter Mitwirkung des Zwingli-Vereins Zürich her ausgegeben*. Corpus Reformatorum. Zürich: Theologischer Verlag, 1982–91.

1

Did Jesus Teach Salvation By Works? Is There Any Debate?

We are all familiar with Paul's reply to the jailor's question in Acts 16:30: "What must I do to be saved?"[1] Paul and Silas respond: "Believe on the Lord Jesus Christ and you will be saved" (v. 31). This response is repeated in his epistles—in Romans and Galatians as: "justified by grace through faith" (Rom 3:24, 28; 4:1-5; 5:1; 10:10; Gal 2:16; 3:11, 24), in Ephesians as: "by grace you have been saved, through faith . . . not by works" (2:8-9), in the Pastoral Epistles as: "saved . . . not according to our works" (2 Tim 1:9; cf. Titus 3:5), and so forth.

However Jesus' response to the same question is evidently quite different. A lawyer asks Jesus what he should do to inherit eternal life. Jesus puts the question back on the lawyer who understands the OT to teach that one is saved by loving God and one's neighbor. Jesus agrees and remarkably replies: "*Do* this and you will live" (Luke 10:25-28). Similarly, responding to a rich ruler's question on what he must *do* to receive eternal life, Jesus answers, "Sell your possessions and give to the poor" (Matt 19:21).

The jailor, the lawyer and the Rich Young Ruler all essentially asked the same question. However Jesus' answer to the question is clearly not the answer given by Paul.[2] And just as Paul's response can be traced and verified through his epistles, Jesus' two responses are in fact taken up and repeated in various ways in the Synoptic Gospels. To be saved Jesus lays down definitive conditions that must be fulfilled. "If you do not forgive men their sins, your Father will not forgive your sins" (6:14-15) and "He who endures to the end

---

[1] Whether the jailor has in mind full blown salvation from hell or merely salvation from physical harm is irrelevant here. What is important is that the answer concerns eternal salvation. See Joel B. Green, *Salvation*, Understanding Biblical Themes (St. Louis, Mo.: Chalice, 2003) 113–14.

[2] As noted by Joseph H. Hellerman, "Wealth and Sacrifice in early Christianity: Revisiting Mark's Presentation of Jesus' Encounter With The Rich Young Ruler," *TJ* (2000) 143–45.

will be saved" (10:22). Jesus tells his disciples in advance the criterion He will use to determine where people will spend eternity. In the final analysis, those who are not merciful will go away to eternal punishment while those who are merciful will go to eternal life (25:34-46).

So—did Jesus teach salvation by works? The role of works in salvation has always been a matter of tension and debate throughout the history of the church and remains so today.[3] Attempts to describe this role or relationship have inexorably given rise to alternative views. Endeavors to safeguard the priority of grace and faith have frequently seen "works" take a backseat role. Works, it is claimed, have little if any bearing on one's salvation. Works affect blessing either in this life or the next; however one's salvation remains unaffected by either their presence or their absence. "Once saved always saved" is the line often touted in this regard. However, this kind of thinking is unhealthy according to some. To leave works out of the salvation equation has the potential to lead one into licentiousness, not to mention a false sense of eternal security. Often touted here is the line, "One cannot simply, having professed faith, live as one wants and expect to be saved." Remarkably, regardless of where one stands on this debate, both sides believe the other is perverting the true gospel.

There is no hiding the fact that this book deals with a controversial topic. No matter what period of history we examine it seems that controversy is never too far away.[4] Of course one reason that this subject is such a hotbed for debate is its practical significance: quite simply, peoples' eternal destinies *may* be at stake.[5] The subject of works and salvation is never broached without some degree of conflict, emotion and passion. It only takes a quick perusal of the literature to see that we are dealing with an extremely sensitive issue.

Works Influence One's Eternal Destiny

In the Synoptic Gospels there are many passages that appear to teach a *direct* relationship between works and salvation. Simply put *the presence or absence of "works"*[6] *plays a significant role (in the final judgment) in determining where one spends eternity. That is, if works are present one can expect to spend eternity*

---

[3] I will look at how various individuals in church history have interpreted this relationship in chapter two.

[4] E.g., first century: Paul (and Jesus) versus the Judaizers; fifth century: Augustine versus Pelagius; sixteenth century: Luther versus Roman Catholicism; and most recently in the twentieth century (although perhaps not of the same magnitude as the aforementioned): MacArthur versus Hodges.

[5] Another very important reason (on all sides) is obviously a concern to be faithful to the teachings of Scripture.

[6] I will define the meaning of "works" in chapter four.

with God in heaven; if works are absent, one can expect to spend eternity without God in hell.

If this thesis[7] is correct, how do we reconcile this with what has become the hallmark of evangelical Christianity: "Salvation is by *grace alone* through *faith alone*"? Of course some might prefer to pose the question in another way[8]—"How does one reconcile Jesus' teaching on salvation with Paul's doctrine of justification by grace though faith *and not by works*?"[9] Yet even to pose the question in this way perhaps betrays more *our* understanding of where any incongruity lies than the Bible's understanding of where it might lie. The incongruity, we assume, must lie with Jesus. Yet why is it that Jesus must be reconciled to Paul as if Paul were the benchmark?[10] If anyone should be the benchmark, should it not be Jesus Himself?

For some no doubt my thesis will pose a threat to the theological heritage to which many evangelicals have become accustomed—also known as Paul's teaching on justification by grace through faith. However I take very seriously the words of Lewis Sperry Chafer, the founding president of Dallas Theological Seminary: "Only ignorance or reprehensible inattention to the

---

[7] I have deliberately left out the terms "salvation" and "justification" from this statement since both are often used synonymously conjuring up thoughts of a "conversion" in one's personal history. In chapter five I will examine the NT's use of these and other related salvation terms.

[8] Vis-à-vis the relationship between grace and works in Matthew, Petri Luomanen, *Entering the Kingdom of Heaven: A Study on the Structure of Matthew's View of Salvation*, WUNT, ed. Martin Hengel and Otfried Hofius, vol. 101 (Tübingen: Mohr, 1998) 3, poses the question this way: "Is God's grace the starting point which is followed by requirements directed to those who are already believers? Or should the priority be given to the final judgment, when grace would have only a subsidiary role?"

[9] This conflict is recognized and discussed by Hendrikus Boers, "Polarities at the Roots of New Testament Thought," in *Perspectives on the New Testament: Essays in Honor of Frank Stagg*, ed. Charles H. Talbert (Macon, Ga.: Mercer University Press, 1985) 55–75. Cf. also Karl E. Pagenkemper, "An Analysis of the Rejection Motif in the Synoptic Parables and its Relationship to Pauline Soteriology" (Ph.D. diss., Dallas Theological Seminary, 1991). At the end of the day whether the question is posed in relation to Paul or the Reformation amounts to little. Interpreters of Paul are now, and have been for half a century, calling into question Paul's doctrine of justification suggesting that Protestant exegesis has been informed too much by the Reformation (see chap. 2 for further discussion on this).

[10] In fact we see the same thing concerning discussions on Jas 2:24: "a man is justified by works and not by faith alone." Commentators seem to automatically assume that James is at odds with Paul. E.g., Peter H. Davids, *The Epistle of James: A Commentary of the Greek Text*, NIGTC, ed. I. Howard Marshall and W. Ward Gasque (Grand Rapids: Eerdmans, 1982) 130: James has come "closer than anywhere else in the epistles to directly contradicting Paul." Yet I have not as yet read a commentary on Romans 3–4 that even comes close to suggesting that Paul has contradicted James (and given the possibility that James wrote before Paul such a comment is not out of the question). This 'benchmark status' attributed implicitly to Paul perhaps reflects the Reformation's massive influence on NT interpretation over the last four hundred years.

structure of a right Soteriology will attempt to intrude some form of human works with its supposed merit into that which, if done at all, must, by the very nature of the case, be wrought by God alone and on the principle of sovereign grace."[11] It is certainly not my intention to be ignorant, reprehensible or inattentive—simply more informed. I believe—and we all should—that I have an obligation before God to "guide the Word of truth along a straight path" (2 Tim 2:15).[12]

The threat of this study to our evangelical heritage may turn out to be just that—a threat! Or it may not! Either way, the motivation behind this book is quite simple (and sincere): There are many passages, too many in my opinion, in the Synoptic Gospels that when taken *at face value* appear to teach a close relationship between works and salvation. What the exact nature of this relationship might be is the task before us. However, it is my conviction that it is inappropriate to render these passages inapplicable to the Church age or to exegete them in such a way that they do not impinge upon our traditional understanding of salvation. These passages, and their inherent theological problems, must be dealt with in the same way in which their words confront us (and the hearers who heard them) on the pages they appear—at face value![13]

The Need for This Book

Problem Passages

At the most recent annual conference for the Evangelical Theological Society, Steven Roy from Trinity Evangelical Divinity School suggested that more study was needed concerning "The necessity of sanctification/spiritual formation and the *consequences of failing to make progress in it.*"[14] We could easily rephrase Roy's statement into a question: "What is *the necessity of works for*

---

[11] Lewis Sperry Chafer, *Systematic Theology*, vol. 3 (Dallas: Dallas Seminary, 1948; reprint, Grand Rapids: Kregel, 1993) 371 (page citations are to the reprint edition). It is worth pointing out that Chafer equates "works" and "merit" thereby suggesting that the two are the same. However this is not always the case.

[12] Unless otherwise noted all biblical translations are my own.

[13] By saying that these passages need to be taken at "face value," I am not denying the use of figurative, hyperbolic or any other form of non-literal language in the Bible. I am merely suggesting that these texts deserve to be read and understood in light of their literary and historical context.

[14] Steven C. Roy, "New Wines and Old Wine Skins? The Relationship of Evangelical Thinking on Spiritual Formation and Theological Models of Sanctification," paper presented at the ETS (Valley Forge, Pa., 2005) (emphasis mine).

salvation and what are the consequences of failing to make progress in those works." In other words, what is at stake—salvation or something else?

There are passages in the Synoptic Gospels that appear to suggest that Jesus taught salvation by works.[15] These passages of course pose theological problems for many evangelical Christians. Both at a popular and scholarly level, much has been written on the role of works in salvation[16] under the guise of "Lordship Salvation,"[17] discipleship, and the place of rewards in relation to salvation.[18] However, there is a need for all these passages to be examined together and integrated into a biblical theology. To my knowledge there is no such study[19] devoted to the Synoptic Gospels.[20]

---

[15] There is a long history of debate, e.g., on Matthew's understanding of salvation. See Luomanen, *Entering the Kingdom of Heaven*, 7–32.

[16] On the scholarly front cf. esp. Luomanen, *Entering the Kingdom of Heaven*. There is no shortage of doctoral dissertations closely related to our subject. Cf. esp. Pagenkemper, "The Rejection Motif in the Synoptic Parables"; Homer Ausburn Page Jr., "An Investigation of the Concept of Reward in the Gospel of Matthew" (Ph.D. diss., New Orleans Baptist Theological Seminary, 1991); George Todd Wilson, "Entering the Kingdom in the Theology of Matthew" (Ph.D. diss., The Southern Baptist Theological Seminary, 1971); Caleb Tzu-Chia Huang, "Jesus' Teaching on 'Entering the Kingdom of Heaven' in the Gospel According to Matthew: (Interpretation of Selected Texts in Matthew's Gospel Including also Several Parables)" (Ph.D. diss., Concordia Seminary, 1986).

[17] See in particular John F. MacArthur Jr., *The Gospel According to Jesus* (Panorama City, Calif.: Word of Grace, 1988) and Zane C. Hodges, *Absolutely Free! A Biblical Reply to Lordship Salvation* (Grand Rapids: Zondervan, 1989). See chapter two for further bibliographic data on the Lordship salvation debate.

[18] See in particular Joseph C. Dillow, *Servant Kings: A Study of Eternal Security and the Final Significance of Man* (Miami, Fla.: Schoettle, 1992). See chapter two for further discussion on discipleship and the place of rewards in relation to salvation.

[19] A work that is strikingly close—and very recent; so recent I have not had time to interact fully with it—to this study on the relationship between works and salvation in Paul is, Paul A. Rainbow, *The Way of Salvation: The Role of Christian Obedience in Justification* (Waynesboro, Ga.: Paternoster, 2005).

[20] Although many do come close. At a popular level the question may validly be posed as to what the difference is between this book and the works of Zane Hodges and John MacArthur. There is no escaping the fact that there are of course many similarities and in some cases possibly overlap. However, there are in my mind three main differences; First, both Hodges and MacArthur state that central to their purpose is to clarify the nature of the gospel (Hodges, *Absolutely Free*, xiv; MacArthur, *The Gospel According to Jesus*, xiv–xv, 15, 17). My purpose is not to clarify the nature of the gospel, but to articulate the nature of the relationship between works and salvation in the Synoptic Gospels and, therefore, only examine those passages pertinent to this topic. In this respect this book is more restricted in its content. In actual fact many of the more significant passages I will discuss are not mentioned in either MacArthur or Hodges (e.g., Hodges does not discuss Matt 25:31-46, a very significant passage, and neither one discusses Matt 6:14-15; 10:22 or Luke 10:25-28). As a result both these works are inadequate (cf. Darrell L. Bock, "A Review of *The Gospel According to Jesus*," *BSac* 146 [1989] 21): MacArthur "has not produced an adequate theological synthesis." Second, on the

It may be helpful at this early stage to give an example of such a problem passage. Matthew 25:31-46 depicts a future time when the Son of Man will separate "the sheep" from "the goats." The scenario is simple: the separation will take place *on the basis of works* of mercy; the sheep go to eternal life and the goats to eternal punishment. Martin Luther, who for the most part seems to have steered clear of this passage, stated that "wie die meisten Evangelia fast allein den Glauben leren und treiben, Also lautet dis Evangelium von eitel werken, die Christus am Jüngsten tage anziehen wird, Damit man sehe, das er der selben wil auch nicht vergessen, sondern getrieben und gethan haben von denen, die da wollen Christen sein und in seinem Reich erfunden werden."[21] In more recent times on this passage Krister Stendahl has noted that Jesus "provides an interesting criterion for those who will be judged." He explains, "The usual way, I guess, of preaching on this text is to say that Jesus here pictures what will happen at the final judgment so that people can behave accordingly. At this level, however, an interesting *theological problem* arises as to how such a criterion accords with the doctrine of salvation by grace, *since here salvation seems to depend on works*."[22] Looking at the Gospels more generally, Thomas Schreiner writes: "The Lukan and Matthean emphasis on obedience may lead one to think that good works are necessary to merit entrance into the kingdom."[23] And Robert Shank on the parable of the unmerciful servant

---

other hand this study is wider in scope than Hodges or MacArthur. I will devote some space to attempting to understand the relationship between works and salvation in the rest of the NT as well as Judaism. Hodges and MacArthur have confined themselves to the NT and even then mostly to the Gospels. Third, although it is not my intent to write a complete biblical theology on the relationship between works and salvation in the New Testament it is my hope that I will at least be working towards one by tracing themes evident in the Synoptic Gospels through the rest of the NT. In sum, I would classify both the works of Hodges and MacArthur as systematic treatments of the essential aspects of the gospel and its implications. F. F. Bruce, *Hard Sayings of Jesus* (Downers Grove, Ill.: InterVarsity, 1983), also comes close to our study. However, while Bruce does discuss most of our "problem passages," he does not discuss all of them, and he does not approach them from a biblical theology. Furthermore, Bruce's book really only corresponds to my chapters six to eleven and then only in aspects.

[21] Martin Luther, *D. Martin Luther's Werke: Kritische Gesamtausgabe*, vol. 22 (Weimar: Hermann, 1929) 411, lines 16–20. For Luther's understanding on the relationship between works and salvation see chapter two.

[22] Kristen Stendahl, *Paul among Jews and Gentiles: And Other Essays* (Philadelphia: Fortress, 1963) 62–63, (emphasis mine). Stendahl also remarks on the Good Samaritan and the Rich Young Ruler (64), two passages that I will examine in chapter seven. Commenting on these passages, Stendahl, 65, writes: "In both narratives it would appear that the *doing*, works righteousness, is being stressed." Clearly Stendahl is aware of the theological problem that I myself have observed in these same passages.

[23] Thomas R. Schreiner, *The Law and Its Fulfillment: A Pauline Theology of Law* (Grand Rapids: Baker, 1993) 209. Cf. also Luomanen, *Entering the Kingdom of Heaven*, 7–13, who provides an overview of scholars who believe Matthew teaches salvation by works.

in Matthew 18:21-35, writes: "Jesus here teaches that the forgiveness of God . . . remains conditional, according to the individual's subsequent response to the gracious forgiveness which he has received."[24] Commenting on the Rich Young Ruler (see above), Jeannine Brown writes: "There is a relationship between eternal life and keeping the commandments."[25] Finally, John Gerstner could not be more palpable when he says; "Christ repeatedly makes good works a *condition* for salvation."[26]

Quite apart from anything else, these remarks appear to at least demonstrate the contention of this book: "the presence or absence of works plays a significant role in determining where one spends eternity."[27] There will obviously be some that will differ on my understanding of "significant role." Yet without wanting to over exaggerate my case in any way it does seem that scholarship in general supports this contention.[28] Even those who disagree are evidently hard pressed to dismiss the role of works in salvation entirely.[29]

Practical Need

It goes without saying that there is an inseparable link between theology and Christian living. In other words, if there are problems at the theological level there will be problems at the practical level. Since there is no consensus theo-

---

[24] Robert Shank, *Life in the Son: A Study of the Doctrine of Perseverance* (Springfield, Miss.: Westcott, 1961) 39.

[25] Jeannine K. Brown, *The Disciples in Narrative Perspective: The Portrayal and Function of the Matthean Disciples*, Academia Biblica, ed. Saul M. Olyan and Mark Allan Powell, no. 9 (Atlanta: SBL, 2002) 81–82.

[26] John H. Gerstner, *Wrongly Dividing the Word of Truth: A Critique of Dispensationalism*, ed. Don Kistler, 2d ed. (Morgan, Pa.: Soli Deo Gloria, 2000) 299. It should be noted that by salvation Gerstner does not mean here justification, a point on which I will later agree (see chap. 4).

[27] Although, it appears that the passage concerning the Sheep and the Goats (Matthew 25) did not lead Luther to the same conclusions as Stendahl, Schreiner, Shank, and Gerstner. Cf. comments by Walther Von Loewenich, *Luther als Ausleger der Synoptiker*, Forschungen zur Geschichte und Lehre des Protestantismus, ed. Ernst Wolf, ser. 10, vol. 5 (Munich: Kaiser, 1954) 199: "Man denkt, hier müsste sich Luther gründlich mit der Vorstellung des Gerichts nach den Werken auseinandersetzen, und man ist doch sehr enttäuscht, wenn man diese Predigt gelesen hat."

[28] With respect to the kind of comments that I have been making cf. also G. K. Beale, *The Book of Revelation: A Commentary on the Greek Text*, NIGTC, ed. I. Howard Marshall and Doanld A. Hagner (Grand Rapids: Eerdmans, 1999) 1138: "at the final judgment 'works' are considered a *necessary condition* for salvation" (emphasis mine).

[29] Even Dillow, *Servant Kings*, 136, observes that a number of NT passages speak of eternal life as presented "to the believer as something to be earned or worked for!" But when this is the case, according to Dillow, it is not salvation that is alluded to but the enjoyment of one's salvation. For a fuller discussion of Dillow's views on the relationship between works and salvation see chapter two.

logically among scholars on the role of works in salvation[30] there surely exists even more confusion at a practical level.[31]

There are significant practical implications depending on how one understands the relationship between works and salvation. Take for example the doctrine of *assurance*.[32] On what basis should an individual have assurance concerning their salvation? The answer will depend on how we understand the Bible's teaching on the role of works in salvation. Consequently, if five individuals hold as many views on the role of works in salvation, it is more than likely they will also hold as many views on assurance.[33] Closely related to the issue of assurance are the doctrines of *eternal security*, the nature of *perseverance* and the possibility of *apostasy*.[34] Can one who is a Christian lose their salvation? Certainly one's response to this will be influenced by one's interpretation of works in relation to salvation. Furthermore, the answer will undoubtedly affect how one lives and thinks about one's Christian responsibilities. Theology and life are interrelated.[35]

Then there are the issues surrounding *discipleship*. Can one be a bornagain Christian and yet not be a disciple? There are some that say yes and

---

[30] Cf. H. George Anderson et al., eds., "Justification by Faith" in *Lutherans and Catholics in Dialogue*, ed. Paul C. Empie and T. Austin Murphy, vol. 7 (Minneapolis: Augsburg, 1985).

[31] E.g., see John Piper, *The Pleasures of God: Meditating on God's Delight in Being God* (Portland, Ore.: Multnomah, 1991) 279–305, for his excellent response to a letter that questions the writer's point of conversion in light of the Lordship Salvation controversy. (Note that this letter has been omitted in Piper's 2001 edition of *The Pleasures of God*; the reason being that it has been taken up in his *The Purifying Power of Living by Faith . . . in Future Grace* [Sisters, Ore.: Multnomah, 1995]).

[32] For an excellent discussion on this subject see D. A. Carson, "Reflections on Christian Assurance," *WTJ* 54 (1992) 1–29.

[33] Cf. e.g., Thomas R. Schreiner and Ardel B. Caneday, *The Race Set Before Us: A Biblical Theology of Perseverance and Assurance* (Downers Grove, Ill.: InterVarsity, 2001) and Zane C. Hodges, *The Gospel Under Siege: Faith and Works in Tension*, 2d ed. (Dallas: Redención, 1981) esp. 9. Both Schreiner and Hodges understand the relationship between works and salvation differently. This understanding inevitably leads both of them to quite different views on assurance. For Schreiner's view on Christian assurance see *The Race Set Before Us*, 268–311; for Hodges' view see Hodges, *Absolutely Free*, 49–52, 174–75.

[34] From a Calvinist perspective on these subjects see G. C. Berkouwer, *Faith and Perseverance*, Studies in Dogmatics (Grand Rapids: Eerdmans, 1958). From an Arminian perspective see Shank, 1961. For a mediating position see I. Howard Marshall, *Kept by the Power of God: A Study of Perseverance and Falling Away*, 3d ed. (Carlisle: Paternoster, 1995); John Mark Hicks, "Election and Security: An Impossible Impasse?" (paper presented at the ETS, Colorado Springs, November 2001).

[35] For a treatment on the relationship between the "theology" of works and salvation and the "practicality" of living the Christian life see Ron Julian, *Righteous Sinners: The Believer's Struggle with Faith, Grace, and Works* (Colorado Springs, Colo.: NavPress, 1998).

suggest that "disciple" is synonymous with a "committed" Christian.[36] The difference between being a disciple and being simply a Christian ("uncommitted") is the difference between works and salvation. One's view here will determine how one understands Jesus in Mark 8:38 speaking to those who are ashamed of His words "in this wicked and adulterous generation." Is He speaking about uncommitted Christians or unbelievers? Surely Jesus' words here have enormous practical (not to mention eternal) consequence. Is Jesus' command to follow Him for every Christian or only for those who wish to enlist in the more stringent demands of discipleship? What happens to those who do not follow Him—in this life and the next?

Or take for example the matter of the *final judgment*. Who will be judged? What will it entail? What will be the criteria? Will salvation be at stake or the reception or loss of rewards? What exactly will be given "to each one according to his work" when the Son of Man comes in His glory (Matt 16:27)? And to whom will it be given?[37] These are serious questions with eternal ramifications[38] and are all influenced by how one interprets the role of works in salvation.

The Role of Works in Salvation in Judaism and Paul

The relationship between works and salvation in Judaism has also been variously debated over the course of the last century. In 1977 E. P. Sanders brought the debate to a level difficult for scholarship to ignore.[39] Contrary to centuries of Protestant exegesis, Sanders—according to some at least—has forcefully demonstrated that Judaism was never a religion based on works but on grace. His study has had such an impact that we might well wonder at the turn of another century whether we have reached a "most assured result of criticism" concerning the role of works in salvation in Judaism.[40] This conclusion inevitably led Sanders to consider Paul's understanding of the role of works in salvation in Judaism. Consequently the debate has become increasingly

---

[36] E.g., Dillow, *Servant Kings*, 150–56.

[37] See ibid. Dillow's work is directed toward answering this question.

[38] See, e.g., Craig L. Blomberg, "Degrees of Reward in the Kingdom of Heaven?" *JETS* 35 (1992) 159–72.

[39] See E. P. Sanders, *Paul and Palestinian Judaism: A Comparison of Patterns of Religion* (London: SCM, 1977).

[40] E.g., Colin G. Kruse, *Paul, The Law, and Justification* (Peabody, Mass.: Hendrickson, 1996) 24: "It is now widely agreed that first-century Judaism was not, in principle, a religion in which salvation was dependent upon merit accumulated by obedience to the law, but rather a religion based upon God's election and grace." Similarly, I. Howard Marshall, "Salvation, Grace and Works in the Later Writings in the Pauline Corpus," *NTS* 42 (1996) 340: "Sander's general view has been espoused by many scholars, so that it now seems to be the new orthodoxy, at least within the English-speaking world."

Pauline focused. Many scholars have challenged the traditional view of Paul, most notably the Pauline meaning of "righteousness" and "justification," the centrality of justification by faith in Pauline theology, the role of the Law and its relationship to Christians, and the antecedent of Paul's religion. This "new perspective"[41] on Paul raises the question as to what might the Gospels add to this debate and further, is Paul, as he has traditionally been interpreted, being understood correctly? Or should we be reading Paul along the lines of the new perspective?[42] The placement of Jesus (as with Paul) against his Jewish background is also important.

The Synoptic Gospels and Salvation

It has been suggested that the Synoptic Gospels have little to teach us on matters of salvation. Statements such as "John emphasized receiving the gift of eternal life by believing" whereas "the Synoptic writers emphasized discipleship training for the kingdom"[43] are representative of such a view. As a result it has become popular among some to think of John as the "benchmark" by which we might test other theories of salvation.[44] However, since all Scripture is profitable (1 Tim 3:16) it is hard to imagine that any NT writer would have imagined that his writings would stand as the benchmark for all others. Rather it is my contention that the Synoptic Gospels also contribute to our understanding of salvation—and to pit John against the Synoptics, or Paul against James for that matter, is to neglect to read Scripture in all its facets. As I hope to show in chapter five, salvation is multi-faceted and each facet is described by the NT writers, but rarely at once. Thus, in order to understand the *complete* picture of salvation one must read the Synoptic Gospels along with the rest of the NT.

Objections

It is only fair that I acknowledge the objections to writing this book. I am aware of three objections though there may be more:

---

[41] The term originates with James D. G. Dunn, "The New Perspective on Paul," *BJRL* 65 (1983) 95–122.

[42] Whether Paul is being understood correctly is an implication of this study (see chap. 3).

[43] Earl D. Radmacher, *Salvation*, Swindoll Leadership Library, ed. Charles R. Swindoll and Roy B. Zuck (Nashville: Word, 2000) 121. Cf. Charles C. Ryrie, *So Great Salvation: What it Means to Believe in Jesus Christ* (Wheaton, Ill.: Victor, 1989) 38–39: the Synoptic Gospels are essentially limited to teaching on the future millennial kingdom and since this was postponed, these books (presumably)—as far as I can surmise at least—have little bearing on soteriology for the church today.

[44] So Radmacher, *Salvation*, 127.

"The Synoptic Gospels Are Pre-Cross"

The first objection is that this study is dealing with teaching that occurred prior to the cross and thus deals with *Israel's* responsibility under the old covenant.[45] Hence, the passages we find difficult to reconcile with Paul are difficult precisely because they are dealing with a different era of salvation history.[46] Therefore the fault is not with Jesus or Paul; the fault is with their interpreters and their failure to properly demarcate between dispensations.[47]

This objection, as far as I can tell, only has merit if the Bible teaches two methods in God's salvific program: salvation by works under the old covenant and salvation by faith under the new. Yet this is something that the Bible demonstrably denies (e.g., see esp. Romans 4). Furthermore, it is not uncommon for NT writers addressing post-cross audiences (i.e., the church) to draw on pre-cross passages to illustrate their understanding concerning the role of works in salvation. For example, James, writing after the cross, draws on Jesus' words, spoken before the cross, to illustrate the relationship between works and salvation (cf. Jas 2:15-17 with Matt 25:44-46). Furthermore, as I hope to show in chapters six to eleven, Jesus' teaching—without exception—on the role of works in salvation can be found in NT writers following Pentecost. My point here is simply that if the application of pre-cross passages to the post-cross era took place for the NT writers then we should make use of it.

"Theological Sophistry"

Though not an explicit objection to *this* work, Joseph Dillow raises an issue in his book, *The Reign of the Servant Kings: A Study of Eternal Security and the Final Significance of Man*. Since I am at odds with his remarks concerning the role of works in salvation, his statement serves as a reasonable objection by all who would think the same way. Dillow asks:

> are they [those who see a connection between works and salvation] not introducing a serious heresy into the gospel? In order to become a Christian, one must not only believe on Christ, but he must also (1) hate his father, mother, wife, children, and his own life; (2) carry

---

[45] This objection has been voiced to me personally on more than one occasion.

[46] Cf. Robert N. Wilkin, *Confident in Christ: Living by Faith Really Works* (Irving, Tex.: Grace Evangelical Society, 1999) 201–2. Wilkin argues that since repentance isn't in John or Galatians it isn't a condition for salvation. I would plead: "What about the Synoptic Gospels, do they not matter?"

[47] E.g., Chafer, *Systematic Theology*, 3:292, on Matt 24:13 ("He who endures to the end will be saved") suggests that, "the address is to Israel. Had the passage been addressed to Christians, it, to be in keeping with Christian doctrine, would read, *He that is saved will endure to the end.*"

his cross; (3) be willing to follow Jesus around Palestine; and (4) give up everything. Can any amount of theological sophistry equate these four conditions with the simple offer of a free gift on the basis of believing? . . . If we are justified 'freely,' how can the enormous costs of being a disciple be imposed as a condition of that justification?[48]

Of course, Dillow would be entirely correct if conditions were being imposed upon Paul's justification by faith in Romans 3–4, Peter's call to conversion in Acts 2–3 or the Council's decree in Jerusalem in Acts 15. However this is definitely not the case! I recognize that this book places me right in the firing line of potential criticism though I unequivocally deny that I am contending for anything other than biblical truth.[49] This study concerns the role of works in salvation, not works in "justification" or conversion as we might commonly refer to it; the two are patently not always the same, as I shall duly demonstrate.[50]

"Back Loading the Gospel"

Again Dillow writes: "Back loading the gospel means attaching various works of submission as the means for achieving the final aim of our faith, final deliverance from hell and entrance into heaven."[51] In other words, he objects to those who teach that justification is by faith, but what counts at the door of eternity is works.[52]

Since Dillow has basically reiterated my argument for this study (see above) I will leave my response for the latter half of this book. For now I can only repeat: there are many passages in the Synoptic Gospels that teach an inseparable relationship between works and salvation. These passages in my opinion need to be squarely dealt with. It is not my intention to introduce "serious heresy into the gospel" or to engage in "theological sophistry." Our

---

[48] Dillow, *Servant Kings*, 154.

[49] Dillow directs his attack at "Experimental Predestinarians." However Dillow's suggestion that they have added conditions to *justification* is quite incorrect and runs contrary to their teachings. Cf. e.g., The Westminster Confession of Faith (1647): "good works, done in obedience to God's commandments, are the fruits and evidences [not the cause] of a true and lively faith . . . We can not, by our best works, merit pardon of sin [i.e., justification], or eternal life at the hand of God" (Philip Schaff, "The Westminster Confession of Faith, 1647" in *The Creeds of Christendom, with a History and Critical Notes* [New York: Harper, 1877; reprint, Grand Rapids: Baker, 1977] 3:633–34). It seems that Dillow, along with Chafer (see above), has equated works with merit. In chapter four I will make a distinction between *pre*-conversion works and *post*-conversion works. As a rule the latter are not viewed as being meritorious.

[50] See chapter five for my understanding of salvation in the NT.

[51] Dillow, *Servant Kings*, 11. Dillow also speaks of "front loading the Gospel," although "*back loading*" is probably a more apt objection to my work from his viewpoint.

[52] Cf. also Wilkin, *Confident in Christ*, 3–4, and his criticism of the thesis I am espousing.

exegesis must govern our theology not the other way round. Surely it is our duty to allow the results of our exegesis to reshape and even change, if necessary, our theology.

How to Proceed from Here

Theological Presuppositions

Rudolf Bultmann poses the question, "Is Exegesis without Presuppositions Possible?" He answers in the affirmative, providing that what we mean by presuppositions is predetermining the results of our exegesis. "In this sense, exegesis without presuppositions is not only possible but demanded," Bultmann claims. What he means is that exegesis must be without dogmatic prejudice; it must be without preconceived ideas in other words.[53] The exegete must be careful to hear what the text actually says rather than have it say what he or she wants to hear.[54] Surely this should be the ardent desire of every Christian, whether scholar, pastor or layman: to hear what *God* actually says; to be willing to refine and even change our ideas and theology as a result of either our own or someone else's.

Admittedly, we all have a tendency to interpret the Bible via our own presuppositions. I doubt that anyone is immune from the influence of church tradition and theological background, factors that often work powerfully to

---

[53] See Rudolf Bultmann, *Existence and Faith: Shorter Writings of Rudolf Bultmann,* trans. Schubert M. Ogden (London: Hodder and Stoughton, 1960) 289–90. Bultmann may push his notion of presuppositions further than most are willing to tolerate. He includes in his examples of prejudices, first, the presupposition that Matthew and John were disciples of Jesus therefore giving validity to the historicity of the Gospels; and second, that Jesus was conscious of his own messiahship. While some may disagree with these examples, I am personally of the opinion that even here Bultmann has a point. "All knowledge of a historical kind is subject to discussion" and therefore remains open. Of course the key words are "historical" and "open." In Bultmann's mind history is a closed continuum of which there is no outside divine intervention, thus ruling out miracles (291–92). It is my conviction that the Bible presents evidence to suggest that history is not a closed continuum (e.g., 1 Cor 15:3-8) and it is therefore the role of the exegete to accept its claims.

[54] It is unrealistic to expect anyone to approach the biblical text without some bias, theological or otherwise. But it is certainly possible to approach Scripture, in my opinion, with an honest awareness of our presuppositions and bias' and then using this awareness to carefully and honestly gauge their influence on our interpretations. Once this has been done we can make the necessary adjustments if we feel our exegesis has been unduly prejudiced by our own presuppositions. At this point we are letting our exegesis shape (or reshape) our theology. Cf. also D. A. Carson, *Exegetical Fallacies,* 2d ed. (Grand Rapids: Baker, 1996) 129: "But if we sometimes read our own theology into the text, the solution is not to retreat to an attempted neutrality, to try to make one's mind a tabula rasa so we may listen to the text without bias. It cannot be done, and it is a fallacy to think it can be. We must rather discern what our prejudices are and make allowances for them."

create deep-seated presuppositions. These presuppositions tend to have a blinding effect on our ability to see new things contrary to what we currently believe. The Bible affirms that tradition can be good and indeed necessary when it is in line with Scripture (e.g., 1 Cor 11:2, 23; 15:1-2; 2 Thess 2:15; 3:6). However, there is always the danger that tradition can end up replacing the very theology we wish to protect, a hole into which the religious leaders of Jesus' day all too easily fell (e.g., Mark 7:8-9). Sadly while these interpreters of Scripture believed in their own minds that they could see, the reality was that they were in fact blind (John 9:41).

Let's be honest, there is no easy solution to curtailing our presuppositions. It certainly must involve open (spiritual) eyes (cf. Ps 119:18) and a vigilant heart. In considering the procedure of this study it is my conviction that theological constructs and presuppositions must be resisted. We would all indeed do well at the outset of this book to agree to follow the advice of E. D. Hirsch who suggests that interpreters "must give every text its due and . . . avoid the external imposition of merely mechanical methods and canons of interpretation." Our interpretation, Hirsch continues, must be ground in "self-critical thinking" and be "tested against all the relevant data we can find."[55] We must continually hold our theological paradigms accountable to Scripture and always be prepared to revise them in light of our exegetical conclusions.[56] To borrow a phrase, we must not "place the 'cart' of systematic theology, as it were, before the 'horse' of contextual exegesis."[57] Where would the church be today if Luther had abandoned his unswerving commitment to Scripture in exchange for a millennium of tradition for example? May the Lord direct us all as we read and study His Word (Ps 119:35). May He revive our souls, make us wise, give joy to our hearts, and light to our eyes (Ps 19:7-8).

Definitions

The two terms most important to this study appear in its title—"works" and "salvation." It needs to be said that while useful and appropriate for a title, both these terms are more or less taken from popular usage. Admittedly they are prevalent in Paul (e.g., Eph 2:8-9) and James (e.g., Jas 2:14-26), but they scarcely appear elsewhere in the NT, especially together. Regardless of popu-

---

[55] E. D. Hirsch, *Validity in Interpretation* (New Haven: Yale University Press, 1967) 263–64. I would want to add—"as long as all relevant data includes the rest of the Bible."

[56] See Douglas J. Moo, "2 Peter and Jude" in *The NIV Application Commentary: From Biblical Text . . . To Comtemporary Life*, The NIV Application Commentary Series, ed. Terry Muck (Grand Rapids: Zondervan, 1986) 147–55, for a balanced and honest discussion on the relationship between theological frameworks and exegesis.

[57] Hellerman, "Wealth and Sacrifice in early Christianity," 145.

lar usage however we cannot assume a universal understanding for either of these words. So before we embark on our study proper these terms must be properly defined.

It probably goes without saying that defining these terms is not as straightforward as doing a simple word study on the Greek terms ἐργάζομαι and σῴζω or even their cognates. The relationship between these words is expressed in a *variety* of ways in the NT and none more so than the Synoptic Gospels where metaphors and parables are the prevalent mode of communication. Moreover, definitions cannot always be limited to words, even synonymous words. The NT writers often communicated conceptually. In fact, the terms "works" and "salvation" rarely occur in the Synoptic Gospels, at least in the traditional sense, and one needs to be careful against being anachronistic when discussing these terms by word use only in the first three Gospels.

How then should we objectively proceed in defining these two terms? First, by means of a simple word study, that is, examining the uses of ἐργάζομαι and σῴζω and their cognates. This is the most objective step. Second, by studying *words* which are synonymous to ἐργάζομαι and σῴζω. And third, by identifying *concepts and phrases* which can be considered to be synonymous with ἐργάζομαι and σῴζω. This last step is certainly the most subjective. However, I will attempt to show contextually in each case that the Synoptic Gospels do employ particular concepts and phrases pertinent to our understanding of "works" and "salvation."

Why Look at Only the Synoptic Gospels?

One may legitimately ask (and many have), "Why only look at the Synoptic Gospels, why not John?" First, the fourth Gospel is very different from the Synoptic Gospels, so much so that it warrants an individual study of its own.[58] Second, one has to select material based on its value for scholarship. The Synoptic material has value, in my opinion, because up until this point Jesus' teaching has been treated minimally in discussions on soteriology. There is enough material in the Synoptic Gospels to at least raise the question and, I believe, pursue an answer to the content of Jesus' soteriology. Third, that said, there is real value in seeing the big picture. Hence I will devote some space to what other NT authors have to say about the role played by works in salvation.[59]

---

[58] See George Eldon Ladd, *A Theology of the New Testament*, ed. Donald A. Hagner, rev. ed. (Grand Rapids: Eerdmans, 1993) 251–53.

[59] It is worth discussing briefly the issue concerning the authenticity of Jesus' words though it will not be a focus of this book since the results would not alter the conclusions in any way. It is worthwhile noting, however, that the fact that the majority of passages in question (see chaps. 6–11) constitute "hard sayings" speaks volumes regarding their authenticity. Why

Limitations Concerning the Scope of This Book

To the best of my knowledge there are at least two areas limiting the scope of this study.

Further Study in Judaism Required

In chapter three I will consider the role of works in salvation in Judaism in light of the debate instigated by E. P. Sanders. Ideally I need to carry out a thorough investigation of the Jewish literature in order to evaluate Sanders. However, this exercise alone would amount to more space and time than I have available. Furthermore, such an exercise would be unnecessarily repetitive since there has already been a multitude of articles and monographs written, not to mention some significant recent contributions to this debate. I shall focus more on understanding the nature of the debate and its significance for this study.

Significant Related Topics

I realize that this study may in fact pose more questions than it solves. Questions such as "How do rewards fit into the relationship between works and salvation?" "What about issues of eternal security and assurance?" "How does this study contribute to the Lordship Salvation debate?" "What is the relationship between justification and sanctification?" We might even include here the age-old question regarding our free will and God's sovereignty. The number of related topics is numerous and there are many areas to divert our attention. However each of these topics deserves its own treatment. Our subject is ambitious enough as it is. Pertinent side issues and implications will be footnoted and discussed at the appropriate place though I shall try hard to stay with the topic at hand: "What is the nature of the relationship between works and salvation in the Synoptic Gospels?"

Overview and the Way Ahead

With formalities out of the way and the task before us, there remains only one thing for me to do: present a brief overview of the chapters to follow. In chapter two I shall document the various views that have emerged throughout the history of the church on the nature of the relationship between works and salvation in the Bible. The point of the chapter is to 1) locate our study within its historical context; 2) gain an understanding of how various individuals throughout church history have understood the interplay between works

---

would the early church go to the bother of creating sayings that would only make their lives, not to mention their theology, more difficult?

and salvation in general; 3) identify what Scriptures have been significant in understanding this relationship; and perhaps most importantly 4) provide accountability for this study. This final point is worth elaborating. Biblical interpretation always occurs within the context of those who have gone before. Our predecessors—two thousand years of them—provide accountability and a framework from which we *should* be wary of straying. Without denying the place and need for original thought, the history of interpretation within the church, if taken seriously serves to protect against a 'lone ranger' type mentality that is prone to exegetical "mutations."[60] Of course church history does not prevent lone rangers or mutations though it does highlight them and in that sense keeps us all accountable.

In chapter three I shall outline and contrast the two positions that have emerged in post-Reformation scholarship on the relationship between works and salvation in *Judaism*. There are three purposes to this chapter: 1) to understand the historical backdrop against which Jesus walked and talked. How is Jesus similar or dissimilar to Judaism on the subject of works and salvation? 2) to evaluate E. P. Sander's thesis vis-à-vis Judaism as a religion of grace, and 3) to evaluate the subsequent backlash on Paul's, and to some extent the Gospels', understanding of works and salvation in Judaism.

Having considered in chapters two and three how *others* have understood the works-salvation relationship, in chapters four and five I shall work toward my own interpretation. Here I will examine how the Synoptic Gospels use the terms, "works" and "salvation." As already mentioned I shall not limit this aspect of the study to a simple word analysis but also investigate synonyms and concepts. In addition to looking at the synoptic material I shall also examine how other NT authors use these terms and what, if any, synonyms they employ.

In chapters six to eleven I shall discuss the crux of this book: the role of works in salvation in the Synoptic Gospels. I have identified key passages that articulate a clear relationship between works and salvation. In these chapters I will summarize these passages, deal only with pertinent exegetical problems, and attempt to explain the relationship between works and salvation. I must point out that it is my aim to understand this relationship from an "exegetical" standpoint. This does not mean that the theological is not important or that it will not be discussed. But it is not my aim to discuss questions that are not often raised in the text such as "loss of salvation," "eternal security," etc. While important, these sorts of questions come under the "significant related topics" discussed above. In these chapters I will also address other passages in

---

[60] I have taken this term from Christopher Hall, "What Evangelicals and Liberals Can Learn from the Church Fathers," plenary address at the ETS (Valley Forge, Pa., 2005).

the NT that fit within what we might call a "trajectory of thought" with the Synoptic passages.

In chapter twelve I shall revisit, reiterate and summarize the salient points of each chapter, particularly as they shed light on the question—"Did Jesus teach salvation by works? And what role do works play in salvation in the Synoptic Gospels?"

2

The Role of Works in Salvation in Church History

Throughout the history of the church various views have emerged on the role of works in salvation. The purpose of this chapter is to articulate eight of these views. But first an explanation as to what this chapter is not. This is not a complete history of the doctrine of the role of works in salvation.[1] Such a task would require multiple chapters. Second, it is not my aim in this chapter to critique or evaluate these various views. It is my hope that the latter half of this book will provide sufficient response by way of my own interpretation on the role of works in salvation. The point of this chapter is simply to provide a framework for where this study stands in church history on the interconnection between works and salvation and to gain an understanding of how various individuals throughout the history of the church have understood this relationship. Before outlining the various views, however, I will attempt to give a brief synopsis of the patristic period.

The Patristic Period: An Overview

In the first 350 years of the church discussions in the main concentrated on Christology and the Trinity. There is no sustained or properly defined soteri-

---

[1] For such treatments see Johann Heniz, *Justification and Merit: Luther vs. Catholicism* (Berrien Springs, Mich.: Andrews University Press, 1984) 95–248; Alister E. McGrath, *Iustitia Dei: A History of the Christian Doctrine of Justification*, 2d ed. (Cambridge: Cambridge University Press, 1998). On salvation in the early church see esp. Basil Studor, *Trinity and Incarnation: The Faith of the Early Church*, trans. Matthias Westerhoff and ed. Andrew Louth (Collegeville, Minn.: Liturgical, 1993). For general works on the history of doctrine see J. N. D. Kelly, *Early Christian Doctrines*, 5th ed. (New York: Harper, 1958; reprint, New York: Continuum, 2000); Hubert Cunliffe-Jones, ed., *HCD* (Philadelphia: Fortress, 1978). Cf. also H. George Anderson, T. Austin Murphy, and Joseph A. Burgess, eds., *Justification by Faith*, Lutherans and Catholics in Dialogue, vol. 7 (Minneapolis: Augsburg, 1985) 17–48.

ology,[2] although it is possible to present a brief synopsis on the relationship between works and salvation during this period.[3]

All of the church Fathers highlighted the need for works in the Christian life.[4] This is exacerbated by the fact that Paul's doctrine of justification by faith hardly receives a mention in the literature[5]—although there is no consensus as to the reason for this phenomenon. The issue is further complicated by different polemical backgrounds and the absence of any systematic treatment on the subject often leading to different emphases and apparent contradictions. Certainly antinomianism and libertinism were of a concern and perhaps provided the catalyst behind a works emphasis.[6] Whatever the reason however, works appear to be viewed rather innocently[7] in the patristic period. Origen (ca. 185–ca. 254) is representative:

> righteousness would be reckoned to a man, even if he has not yet produced works of righteousness. For faith which believes in the one who justifies is the beginning of being justified by God. And this faith, when it has been justified, is firmly embedded in the soil of the soul like a root that has received rain, so that when it begins to be cultivated by God's law, branches arise from it, which bring forth the fruit of works. The root of righteousness, therefore, does not grow out of the works, but rather the fruit of works grow out of the root of righteousness, that root, of course, of righteousness which God also credits even apart from works.[8]

Faith and works are inseparable. Cyril of Jerusalem (ca. 315–87) wrote: "True religion consists of these two elements: pious doctrines and virtuous actions. Neither does God accept doctrines apart from good works, nor are works, when divorced from godly doctrine, accepted by God."[9]

---

[2] See McGrath, *Iustitia Dei*, 17–23, for an overview of the church's soteriology in the pre-Augustinian era.

[3] For a helpful overview of the relationship between faith and works in the early church see Robert B. Eno, "Some Patristic Views on the Relationship of Faith and Works in Justification," *Recherches Augustiniennes* 19 (1984) 3–27.

[4] Otto W. Heick, *A History of Christian Thought*, vol. 1 (Philadelphia: Fortress, 1965) 49–51; Eno, "Patristic Views," 19–23.

[5] McGrath, *Iustitia Dei*, 19. Paul's words are mostly repeated by the Fathers with little exposition.

[6] Eno, "Patristic Views," 4.

[7] McGrath, *Iustitia Dei*, 23, notes, "If the first three centuries of the western theological tradition appear to be characterized by a 'works-righteousness' approach to justification, it must be emphasized that this was quite innocent of the overtones which would later [referring to Pelagius] be associated with it."

[8] Origen, *Commentary on the Epistle to the Romans*, 4.1.18.

[9] Cyril of Jerusalem, *Catechesis*, 4.2.

However justification by grace through faith is never denied.[10] Clement of Rome (d. 101?) asserted that we "are not made righteous by ourselves, or by our wisdom or understanding or piety or the deeds which we have wrought in holiness of heart, but through faith, by which Almighty God has justified all men from the beginning of the world."[11] Similarly, Polycarp (ca. 69–ca. 155): "by grace you are saved, not by works but by the will of God through Jesus Christ."[12] Ambrose (d. 397) wrote, "Let no one glory in his own works since no one is justified by his deeds, but one who is just has received a gift . . . It is faith, therefore, which sets us free by the blood of Christ."[13] All of the Fathers agreed: salvation is an unmerited gift.[14] (Although by the third and fourth centuries faith had become essentially "a synonym for orthodoxy"[15] and a first step in the salvation process).[16]

Problems seem to have arisen over pre and post-conversion sins.[17] The thinking on this is not entirely uniform although the tendency is to view *only* pre-conversion sins as forgiven at conversion (baptism). The phraseology appears particularly legalistic in the West.[18] Tertullian (ca. 160–ca. 225) is typical.[19] The baptized person is forgiven by faith,[20] delivered from death,[21] regenerated to eternal life,[22] and receives the Holy Spirit.[23] However, "one

---

[10] Although McGrath, *Iustitia Dei*, 23, notes that it is "inchoate and ill-defined."

[11] Clement, "First Epistle to the Corinthians," 32.4.

[12] Polycarp, "Epistle to the Philippians," 1.3.

[13] Ambrose, "Ambrose to Irenaeus," 83.

[14] Johann Heinz, *Justification and Merit*, 111; Eno, "Patristic Views," 23. However, note McGrath's qualification that the doctrine of justification was limited to the western church alone (see McGrath, *Iustitia Dei*, 3–4, for the factors behind this development). The Eastern emphasis is on deification (salvation by participating in the nature of the divine nature or "the imitation of God"), also a gift from God and according to His gracious work (see G. W. H. Lampe, "Christian Theology in the Patristic Period," in *HCD*, 49).

[15] Heinz, *Justification and Merit*, 112; cf. Eno, "Patristic Views," 20–21; Cyril of Jerusalem *Catechesis* 5.11–13.

[16] Cyril of Jerusalem *Catechesis* 5.11–13; Lampe, "Christian Theology," 81.

[17] See Eno, "Patristic Views," 26.

[18] See John Burnaby, *Amor Dei: A Study of the Religion of St. Augustine: The Hulsean Lectures for 1938* (London: Hodder and Stoughton, 1938) 236–37, on the differences between the Eastern and Western views on merit.

[19] See Heinz, *Justification and Merit*, 114–17, for Tertullian's teaching on merit.

[20] Tertullian, *On Baptism*, 1, 6, 7.

[21] Tertullian, *On Baptism*, 2.

[22] Tertullian, *On Baptism*, 2; cf. 5.

[23] Tertullian, *On Baptism*, 6, 8; but cf. 10: "sins are not forgiven, or the Spirit granted, except by God alone"; cf. Lampe, "Christian Theology," 61.

who renews his sins after baptism" "is appointed for the fire."[24] Tertullian can even say, "A good deed has God as its debtor."[25]

In sum the church Fathers all agreed on the primacy of God's unmerited grace for justification. However, they also equally affirmed the necessity for works following justification. Herein lies the tension although the Fathers do not seem to have had a problem expressing this tension[26] contending on the one hand that salvation is not by works yet in the same breath asserting that no one can be saved without them.[27]

Augustine[28]

It was not until the fourth and fifth centuries that the doctrine of soteriology was given a boost in the early church[29] thanks to Augustine of Hippo (354–430). Fundamental to Augustine's soteriology was his insistence that the plight of humanity is unfixable apart from divine intervention through the person and work of Jesus Christ. Man is therefore utterly dependent on God, a fact that led Augustine to stress the importance of grace in salvation. Hence Augustine affirmed the orthodox notion that salvation is by grace through faith.[30] On this he did not waver.[31] However, he also insisted, in line with his predecessors, that belief alone is not enough to secure eternal life.[32] He rejected the notion that salvation is by faith alone since Paul also rejected it (cf. 1 Cor 13:2; Gal 5:6; 1 Tim 1:5; 2 Tim 1:5; 3:8).[33]

---

[24] Tertullian, *On Baptism*, 8. Cf. Lampe, "Christian Theology," 61: "In his earlier days Tertullian was prepared to . . . allow that there could be a second penitence . . . after baptism: but never more. It would seem that the sins in question were apostasy, murder and adultery . . . Before he turned schismatic, however, he was prepared to speak more freely about the possibility of the post-baptismal sinner compensating for his offence and restoring his baptismal state of forgiveness by doing works of penance."

[25] Tertullian, *On Penance and Purity*, 2.

[26] E.g., Origen, *Commentary on the Epistle to the Romans*, 4.1.6, commenting on justification by works in James 2:21-22: "For it is certain that he who truly believes works the work of faith and righteousness."

[27] Eno, "Patristic Views," 21–23; cf. also Lamp, "Christian Theology," 156.

[28] For a valuable synopsis of Augustine's teaching on faith and works see Heinz, *Justification and Merit*, 121–36.

[29] Kelly, *Early Christian Doctrines*, 344. Even at this early stage a full-blown doctrine of salvation is sadly lacking (375–77).

[30] Cf. John R. Willis, *A History of Christian Thought: From Apostolic Times to Saint Augustine* (Hicksville, N.Y.: Exposition, 1976) 342–43.

[31] Eugene TeSelle, *Augustine The Theologian* (London: Burns & Oates, 1970) 178.

[32] Augustine, *Faith and Works*, 15.25.

[33] Gregory J. Lombardo, "*St. Augustine on Faith and Works*," ACW, ed. Walter J. Burghardt and Thomas Comerford Lawler, vol. 48 (New York: Newman, 1988) 5. Cf. G. Bavaud,

Augustine affirmed the need for both faith and works for salvation and at times spoke as though one or the other was preferred.³⁴ He suggested, for example, that Paul and the apostolic band agreed that eternal salvation would only be given to those who have lived good lives.³⁵ Faith is more than intellectual assent (Jas 2:19)³⁶ since saving faith "works through love" (cf. Gal 5:6).³⁷ This is classical Augustine. It follows that the person who professes faith yet has no works can have no assurance. Thus "let us diligently beware henceforth of giving men a false confidence by telling them that if only they will have been baptized in Christ, no matter how they will live in His faith, they will arrive at eternal salvation."³⁸ One must persevere in the "true doctrine of God."³⁹ "A Christian's life should harmonize with the sacred character of the sacrament of baptism, and that eternal life should not be promised to anyone

---

"La doctrine de la justification d'après Saint Augustine et la Rèforme," *Revue des études augustiniennes* 5 (1959) 24–26.

³⁴ Similarly, TeSelle, *Augustine*, 330, notes this tension in the late Augustine: "Ultimately salvation depends upon man's faithfulness, freely elicited—yet called forth by grace and sustained by grace."

³⁵ Augustine, *Faith and Works*, 14.22. It must be noted that Augustine's comments here are polemically motivated. They are a part of a fuller response to certain people who advocate salvation by faith alone even for those whose sins are notorious and flagrant and openly declare their intent to continue in such a state (see esp. ibid., 1.1; 13.20; 16.28; for Augustine's full response see 2.3–27.49). It should also be noted that much of his response is taken up with requirements for admittance to baptism, which for the most part was essential for salvation in Augustine's thinking.

³⁶ Cf. McGrath, *Iustitia Dei*, 30. But note Burnaby, *Amor Dei*, 78–80: "It cannot be denied that faith, in Augustine's general usage of the term, has the predominantly intellectual connotation of the definition which he gave at the end of his life—'to believe means simply to affirm in thought.'"

³⁷ Augustine, *Faith and Works*, 14.23; 16.27, 30; 21.38–39; 22.40; 27.49. Cf. McGrath, *Iustitia Dei*, 30: "The motif of *amor Dei* dominates Augustine's theology of justification." Hence "For Augustine, it is love, rather than faith, which is the power which brings about the conversion of man." For this reason McGrath points out that "it is unacceptable to summarise Augustine's doctrine of justification as *sola fide iustificamur* - if any such summary is acceptable, it is *sola caritate iustificamur*" (cf. though August Neander, *General History of the Christian Religion and Church*, trans. Joseph Toplady, 2d ed., vol. 4, [Boston: Crocker & Brewster, 1851] 510; cf. also Heinz, *Justification and Merit*, 121). This does not mean that Augustine denied the primacy of faith in justification. What needs to be understood is that faith and justification were the beginning of an indistinguishable process for Augustine (this would later be termed "sanctification" during the Reformation) and it is in this sense that justification could not be, for Augustine, by faith *alone*. For a fuller discussion on justification in Augustine see McGrath, *Iustitia Dei*, 23–36. See also Willis, *Christian Thought*, 343–44; L. Berkhof, *The History of Christian Doctrines* (Grand Rapids: Eerdmans, 1953) 206–7; Bavaud, "doctrine de la justification," 21–32.

³⁸ Augustine, *Faith and Works*, 26.48. Cf. also Eno, "Patristic Views," 18.

³⁹ Augustine, *Faith and Works*, 26.48.

who is either not baptized or not leading a good life."⁴⁰ It is true that one must be born again to enter the kingdom (John 3:5) but one's righteousness must also exceed that of the Scribes and the Pharisees (Matt 5:20).⁴¹ This does not mean, however, that a Christian will be without sin.⁴² Neither can we say that Augustine does not hold to the priority of faith.⁴³

The late Augustine (i.e., after 396/97)⁴⁴ understood δῶρόν in Ephesians 2:8 to refer to faith. The reason for the qualification in v. 9 ("not by works . . ."), he claimed, was to preclude any notion that faith is merited. This is not a denial of good works since works follow faith. This is typical Augustine.⁴⁵ Verse 8 simply establishes the priority of faith (cf. Rom 1:17).⁴⁶ Similarly, when Paul speaks of justification by faith apart from works (cf. Rom 3:28), this does not suggest that faith alone is sufficient in the absence of good works.⁴⁷ Elsewhere Paul states that "eternal life is given in return for good works" (see Rom 2:6; cf. Matt 16:27),⁴⁸ which raises the question: How can salvation be by grace (cf. also Rom 4:4; 6:23; 11:5-6)? The solution to the dilemma, for Augustine, is found in John 15:5 ("Apart from Me you can do

---

⁴⁰ Ibid.

⁴¹ In John 3:5 it is evident that by the kingdom Augustine meant the church here and now, while the kingdom in Matt 5:20 referred to the Church in the age to come (*City of God*, 20.9). See Augustine's *Faith and Works*, 26.48; cf. also 1.1; 14.23; 26.48; *The City of God*, 21.27; *The Retractions*, 1.18.4.

⁴² Augustine, *City of God*, 21.27. To be noted is that sin is unavoidable but the difference between a true Christian and a professing Christian is repentance and the desire to live a changed life (cf. *Faith and Works*, 22.41; also McGrath, *Iustitia Dei*, 28).

⁴³ Cf. Augustine *Faith and Works* 14.21: "When the Apostle says . . . man is justified through faith without works of the Law, he does not intend . . . to express contempt for the commandments and the works of justice by the profession of faith, but to inform anyone that he can be justified by faith even if he has not previously fulfilled the works of the Law; for they *follow when one has been justified*, and do not come before for one to be justified" (emphasis mine). See Bavaud, "doctrine de la justification," 24–26.

⁴⁴ See TeSelle, *Augustine*, 11–14, for his chronology of Augustine's works. TeSelle, 178, 185, notes that AD396–97 is a watershed in Augustine's thinking on predestination, grace, and the bondage of the will; related to this is his understanding on the relationship between faith and works (180–82). Augustine's subsequent teachings on faith and works, however, while elucidated, are a continuation of his earlier convictions on the subject (182; also Heinz, *Justification and Merit*, 123).

⁴⁵ E.g., Bavaud, "doctrine de la justification," 26: For Augustine, "Les bonnes oeuvres *futures* ne sont donc pas absentes de l'acte de la justification, puisqu'elles sont l'objet de son bon-propos."

⁴⁶ Augustine, *Grace and Free Will*, 7.17.

⁴⁷ Augustine, *Grace and Free Will*, 7.18; cf. also TeSelle, *Augustine*, 161.

⁴⁸ Augustine, *Grace and Free Will*, 8.19.

nothing").[49] The works necessary to reap eternal life are those that originate with God.[50] That is why Paul says in Ephesians 2:8, "Not as the outcome of works." By "outcome" he means works that originate from our own strength. Indeed verse 10 clarifies what kind of works are necessary, namely those that God (not man) has prepared in advance for us. All—faith, works, eternal life—are by God's grace,[51] a point often repeated throughout Augustine's later writings especially.[52]

Augustine makes a distinction between an individual who will be saved but only as through fire (1 Cor 3:15)[53] and an individual who claims to have faith but does not have works (Jas 2:14).[54] The difference can be explained by the choice one would make in a moment of crisis. Paul is speaking of the "carnal" man who would nevertheless choose Christ in a time of persecution. In spite of their carnality they "held on to Christ"[55] as their foundation. James, however, is speaking of a person who does not have Christ as his foundation. His affections "are so purely human that they are preferred to the love of Christ." It is all summed up for Augustine in Matthew 10:37: "He who loves father or mother more than Me is not worthy of me; and he who loves son or daughter more than Me is not worthy of Me."[56]

---

[49] Augustine, *Grace and Free Will*, 8.19–20.

[50] This is apparently the key difference between Augustine and Pelagius (cf. Lampe, "Christian Theology," 159–60, 166). Both Augustine and Pelagius agreed that no one could be justified apart from grace through faith and not by works. Both also agreed that works must follow justification. However, the difference between the two seems to lie in their understanding of free will and grace in relation to works. Similarly to the Greek Fathers Pelagius held to a very optimistic view of humanity. Man has free will and can, if he wants, obey God without sinning. Grace and free will cooperate and for this reason grace can be resisted (cf. Eno, "Patristic Views," 10–12). Augustine, on the other hand, taught that all good works originate from God. See McGrath, *Iustitia Dei*, 28, on the relationship between grace, works and eternal life. Esp. note McGrath's comment: "it is clearly wrong to suggest that Augustine excludes or denies merit." For Augustine, "eternal life is indeed the reward for merit - but merit is itself a gift from God, so that the whole process must be seen as having its origin in the divine liberality, rather than in man's works."

[51] Augustine, *Grace and Free Will*, 8.20. Cf. also, Kelly, *Early Christian Doctrines*, 367; Willis, *Christian Thought*, 347–50.

[52] Heinz, *Justification and Merit*, 123–24. See also Eno, "Patristic Views," 15–16; Willis, *Christian Thought*, 348, 353–54.

[53] Cf. also Augustine, *Faith and Works*, 15.24–25; 16.27.

[54] Cf. Augustine, *Faith, Hope and Charity*, 18.67–68.

[55] Augustine phrases things differently elsewhere although a similar meaning is apparent. The stipulation for being saved though as through fire is that one still "retains the Christian faith" (*Faith and Works* 1.1).

[56] Augustine, *City of God*, 21.26.

Augustine refutes the notion that those who have shown acts of mercy will be saved in spite of their sin clad lives (see Matt 6:14-15; Jas 2:13). "This kind of purely outward alms-giving is like being baptized without being justified." External acts of compassion are not enough they must be accompanied by a charitable spirit and a desire for a reformed life.[57] In Matthew 6:14 ("If you forgive men their offenses, your heavenly Father will forgive you your offenses") Augustine interprets your offenses[58] to refer to "small sins" since these words are addressed to those "already living in grace."[59] In any case Augustine recognizes that there is a condition that must be fulfilled (see also v. 15). James 2:13 affirms the same thing along with the parable of the unmerciful servant in Matthew 18:23-35. There are limits to God's mercy. "We must not imagine that any thoroughgoing scoundrel who remains utterly unreformed is likely to be received into" eternity.[60] However, no one knows "just what measure of unreformed immorality is compatible with God's mercy."[61]

Augustine's theology on works and salvation is best illustrated in his remarks on the rich ruler and the requirements that Jesus places upon him (Matt 19:21).

> Let them [Augustine's adversaries[62]] note carefully that He did not say that he had only to believe and be baptized—the sole requirement for eternal salvation according to their reasoning—but that He gave him precepts for the conduct of his life, precepts which certainly cannot be guarded and kept without faith. Just because the Lord seems to have been silent here about teaching faith, we shall most certainly not prescribe and maintain that only precepts for living well must be preached to men desiring eternal life. The two phases of instruction are mutually interrelated and connected . . . Although in Scripture one set of instructions sometimes is found without the other, either

---

[57] Augustine, *City of God*, 21.27.

[58] Note: this phrase is not in the Greek text. The text simply reads, "Your heavenly Father will not forgive you."

[59] Augustine, *City of God*, 21.27: "What, then, can 'your offenses' mean, if not 'the kind of sins from which even you who live in grace and holiness are not likely to be free'?"

[60] Augustine, *City of God*, 21.27. Augustine's reasoning here is evident in his observation of 1 Cor 6:9-10 (cf. also Gal 5:19-21) where fornicators and idolators, etc., will not possess the kingdom of God (*Faith and Works*, 12.18; 15.25).

[61] Augustine, *City of God*, 21.27. Thus Augustine concludes by distinguishing "three levels of living." One life is so evil that no amount of compassion will secure entrance into the kingdom, another life "good enough to make possible the obtaining of beatitude." There is a third life "which stands in need of merits of those whom they have befriended [cf. Luke 16:9] by their alms, in order that mercy may be obtained." It is this third life that remains somewhat ambiguous and Augustine finds it impossible to say just what services restitute for what sins.

[62] Augustine's adversaries teach that salvation is by faith alone irrespective of one's ensuing lifestyle (cf. Rom 3:8; 5:20). Cf. *Faith, Hope and Charity*, 18.67.

faith alone or good works alone instead of the complete doctrine,[63] it is to be understood that one cannot be without the other, because whoever believes in God ought to do what God commands and whoever does what God commands because He commands it necessarily believes in God.[64]

Clearly Augustine does not believe in salvation by works but simply a faith that manifests itself in some way. If the rich ruler had observed the commandments he would have demonstrated a manifesting faith in Christ.[65] But faith is first then works.

Augustine interprets Matthew 10:22 ("He who endures to the end will be saved") and other passages (cf. John 10:4;[66] 15:1-7[67]) to mean that continuance is necessary for ultimate salvation. For instance, Augustine finds it noteworthy that Jesus did not say, "He who begins will be saved."[68] Faith relates to the beginning while perseverance relates to the end. Both are a gift from God and both are necessary[69] for salvation.[70]

Augustine's understanding of works and salvation impacts his views on "the last judgment when Christ will come from heaven to judge the living and the dead"? All humanity, that is, "the saints" and "the wicked," will be subject to this judgment.[71] On why those who have done evil—and not those who believe—go to the resurrection of judgment (i.e., "eternal damnation"[72]) in John 5:29, Augustine explains that they either "never came alive

---

[63] Augustine often brings two passages together to demonstrate the Scripture's complete doctrine of faith and works in relation to salvation (e.g., John 3:5 and Matt 5:20 [see above]; John 17:3 and 1 John 2:3-4 [*Faith and Works*, 22.40]).

[64] Augustine, *Faith and Works*, 13.20; cf. also 15.25; 16.27. Note other similar statements, 7:11: "unless faith comes first in man himself, the good life cannot follow"; 14:21: "other apostolic letters of Peter, John, James, and Jude . . . firmly uphold the doctrine that faith does not avail without good works . . . Paul himself also does not approve any kind of faith whatever as long as it achieves belief in God, but only that . . . faith from which good works proceed through love [Gal 5:6]."

[65] See Augustine, *Faith and Works*, 16.27.

[66] Augustine, *Tractates on the Gospel of John*, 45.13.1.

[67] Augustine, *Tractates on the Gospel of John*, 41.1.4.

[68] Augustine, *Of the Agreement of the Evangelists Matthew and Luke in the Generations of the Lord*, 1 (Sermon 1).

[69] So also McGrath, *Iustitia Dei*, 28.

[70] Augustine, *On the Gift of Perseverance*, 2.2. Cf. also Lampe, "Christian Theology, 167; Kelly, *Early Christian Doctrines*, 369.

[71] Augustine, *The City of God*, 20.6; cf. also Augustine's comments on Matt 25:31-46 (*The City of God*, 20.5). Cf. Kelly, *Early Christian Doctrines*, 480–83.

[72] Augustine, *Faith and Works*, 23.42–3.

in the present first resurrection,⁷³ or, having come alive, they failed to abide in their new-gotten life unto the end."⁷⁴ On Jesus' criterion for eternal judgment between the sheep and the goats (Matt 25:31-46) Augustine observes that Christ "will not upbraid them because they did not believe in Him, but because they had not done good works."⁷⁵ In the last judgment then the decision as to who is saved will be made not on the basis of faith but works. Works will either express one's faith or its absence. Hence Christian works are all attributed to God's grace for "Then [at the judgment] will God crown not so much thy merits, as His own gifts."⁷⁶ This kind of thinking for all intents and purposes dissolved the idea of merit for the late Augustine.⁷⁷

In sum, according to Augustine, salvation is entirely a gracious gift from God apart from works; all boasting is precluded. His fixation with grace, however, does not mean that works do not play a role in the life of the justified.⁷⁸ Those who have been saved are now equipped by grace and obligated to obey God. Works are necessary to inherit eternal life, but even the ability to do good works originates with God. There is no such thing as works of our own.⁷⁹ Neither is there such a thing as justifying faith without effect. An absence of works indicates an absence of justifying faith. Faith and good works complement each other.⁸⁰

---

⁷³ By the "first resurrection" Augustine means *spiritual*, i.e., conversion (*The City of God*, 20.6–7).

⁷⁴ Augustine, *The City of God*, 20.2; cf. also *Faith and Works*, 23.42; Kelly, *Early Christian Doctrines*, 481.

⁷⁵ Cf. a similar remark on John 5:28-29: "Our Lord does not say those who have believed in the resurrection of life and, on the other hand, those who have not believed in the resurrection of judgment; He says: 'those who have done good'; 'those who have done evil.'" Augustine thus concludes: "Truly, the good life is inseparable from faith" (*Faith and Works*, 23.42).

⁷⁶ Augustine, "On the Same Words of the Apostle, Phil 3 . . ." 10 (Sermon 120).

⁷⁷ Gotthard Nygren, *Das Prädestinationsproblem in der Theologie Augustins* (Göttingen: Vandenhoeck & Ruprecht, 1956) 71: "Der Meritumgedanke ist untrennbar mit einer kausalen Betrachtung des menschlichen Willens - und Handlungslebens verbunden. Soll sinnvoll von Schuld bzw. Verdienst gesprochen werden, so muss der Beurteilte immer selber der tatsächliche Urheber der Zustände sein, die für ihn Schuld oder Verdienst mit sich bringen. Nun zeigte es sich aber, dass die Gnade eine Funktion des freien Willens nach der anderen übernimmt: die Bekehrung . . . die guten Vorsätze, die Kraft sie auszuführen, und den endlichen Sieg. Die Gnade, wie Augustin sie hier darstellt, scheint einfach jeden Gedanken an den freien Willen als selbständigen Faktor auf dem ursächlichen Gebiet auszuschalten und damit auch dem Meritumgedanken den Grund zu entziehen." See Heinz, *Justification and Merit*, 125, 129.

⁷⁸ Bavaud, "doctrine de la justification," 26: "Les bonnes oeuvres *futures* ne sont donc pas absentes de l'acte de la justification, puisqu'elles sont l'objet de son bon-propos."

⁷⁹ McGrath, *Iustitia Dei*, 28: "Eternal life is indeed the reward for merit - but merit is itself a gift from God."

⁸⁰ Eno, "Patristic Views," 18.

Thomas Aquinas (Thomism)

Thomism refers to "a history of the influence of the religious world-view of one theologian,"[81] Thomas Aquinas (1224/5–74).[82] In time Thomism (especially its soteriology) proved to be a precursor to the Council of Trent (1545–63). Thus Roman Catholicism "is inevitably Thomist in some of its viewpoints."[83]

Aquinas divides salvation into a beginning (the forgiveness of sins)[84] and an end.[85] In order to receive eternal life in Thomistic theology sin must be removed since it is a barrier to eternal life.[86] This is (the beginning of) justification[87] by which we are made "worthy of glory."[88] For justification to occur there needs to be an "infusion of grace"[89] followed by a movement of the will.[90] Thus according to Aquinas "justification occurs as, under the influence of grace, one moves towards God with faith in Christ."[91] Justification

---

[81] Thomas F. O'Meara, "Thomas Aquinas and Today's Theology," *Theology Today* 55 (1998) 48.

[82] Aquinas himself based his thinking on the very different ideas of Duns Scotus ('Scotism') (Alister E. McGrath, *Reformation Thought: An Introduction* [Oxford: Blackwell, 1988] 22). It is helpful, although unnecessary here, to understand the background behind the Thomist school, the factors that led to its development and its place within scholasticism and the medieval period in general. For a thorough treatment on the development of Christian thought during this period see Etienne Gilson, *History of Christian Philosophy in the Middle Ages* (New York: Random, 1955); on Thomism see esp. 361–83.

[83] O'Meara, "Thomas Aquinas," 47. See e.g., Catholic Church, *Catechism of the Catholic Church* (Mahwah, N.J.: Paulist, 1994) 751–52. For contrary positions on Aquinas' relationship to Catholic thought see John H. Gerstner, "Aquinas was a Protestant," *Tab* 18 (1994) 13–15, 52; Robert L. Reymond, "Dr. John H. Gerstner on Thomas Aquinas as a Protestant," *WTJ* 59 (1997) 113–21; Carl F. H. Henry, "Justification: A Doctrine in Crisis," *JETS* 38 (1995) 58.

[84] Stephen Pfurtner, *Luther and Aquinas on Salvation*, trans. Edward Quinn (New York: Sheed and Ward, 1964) 100–101.

[85] Ibid.

[86] Aquinas, *STh* I–II q. 114 art. 2.

[87] See Aquinas, *STh* I–II q. 113 art. 3; cf. also art. 6, 8. On justification in Aquinas see Brian Davies, *The Thought of Thomas Aquinas* (Oxford: Clarendon, 1992) 335–39.

[88] Aquinas, *STh* I–II q. 113 art. 10; q. 114 art. 5: "God gives grace to none but to the worthy, not that they were previously worthy, but that by his grace He makes them worthy." Cf. also III q. 46 art. 3.

[89] Aquinas, *STh* I–II q. 113 art. 7. Remission of sin and infusion of grace are the same "with respect to the substance of the act," (I–II q. 113 art. 6) although infusion of grace precedes the remission of sin *in nature*, but not in time.

[90] Aquinas, *STh* I–II q. 113 art. 6. There are 4 things required for the justification of the ungodly: (1) The infusion of grace; (2) the movement of freewill toward God; (3) the movement of freewill toward sin; (4) the remission of sin.

[91] Davies, *The Thought of Thomas Aquinas*, 335.

then is more than a declaration or imputation of righteousness—as Luther and Calvin would later argue—but it actually involves making one more righteous.[92] Although Aquinas' teaching on this point will eventually put him at odds with the Reformers after him[93] he does maintain that justification is a gift from God and not a result of works. In his thinking he by no means belittles the role of grace.[94]

Grace comes (from God) through the sacraments[95] of which there are seven (Baptism, Confirmation, the Eucharist, Penance, Extreme Unction, Order, and Matrimony).[96] If the sacraments are the only means of grace it follows that they are also necessary for salvation.[97] For Aquinas,

> a sacrament properly speaking is that which is ordained to signify our sanctification. In which three things may be considered; viz. the very cause of our sanctification, which is Christ's passion; the form of our sanctification, which is grace and the virtues; and the ultimate end of our sanctification, which is eternal life. And all these are signified by the sacraments. Consequently a sacrament is a sign that is both a reminder of the past, i.e., the passion of Christ; and an indication of

---

[92] Ibid., 337. Aquinas does state in his *Summa Theologica* that justification "is not successive, but instantaneous" (I–II q. 113 art. 7), although rather than suggest Aquinas is Protestant at this point (e.g., Gerstner) it is preferable to think of Aquinas as referring to the instant one becomes infused with grace predisposing the mind toward holiness (Reymond, "John H. Gerstner on Thomas Aquinas," 115).

[93] See McGrath, *Iustitia Dei*, 41. The basic difference between Aquinas and the Reformers at this point is the latter's distinction between justification and sanctification. Aquinas makes no distinction.

[94] Aquinas, *STh* I–II q. 114 art. 3, 5; Davies, *The Thought of Thomas Aquinas*, 338; cf. also O'Meara, "Thomas Aquinas," 54: "Aquinas is not a semi-Pelagian; only God can cause grace."

[95] Aquinas, *STh* III q. 61 art. 1: "God's grace is a sufficient cause of man's salvation. But God gives grace to man in a way which is suitable to him. Hence it is that man needs the sacraments that he may obtain grace."

[96] Aquinas, *STh* III q. 65 art. 1. These 7 were later listed and delineated at the Council of Trent (1545–63). According to Trent these sacraments belong to the "New Law" and are instituted by Jesus Christ (cf. Philp Schaff, *The Creeds of Christendom: With a History and Critical Notes*, vol. 2 [New York: Harper, 1919; reprint, Grand Rapids: Baker, 1977] 119). They are "necessary unto salvation" and the means by which people obtain "the grace of justification" each time they are celebrated (ibid., 120, cf. 121–98 for a full delineation of the sacraments; see also Roderick Strange, *The Catholic Faith* [Oxford: Oxford University Press, 1986] 81–99 for a discussion on "Sacramental Life" in the Catholic tradition). On Aquinas and the sacraments see Davies, 346–76; Charles A. Schleck, "St. Thomas on the Nature of Sacramental Grace," *TThom* 18 (1955) 1–30, 242–78.

[97] Aquinas, *STh* III q. 61 art. 1; cf. q. 65 art. 4.

that which is effected in us by Christ's passion, i.e., grace; and a prognostic, that is, a foretelling of future glory.[98]

Faith[99] too is not instantaneous but is something that 'unfolds.'[100] The acknowledgement of the existence of God is the first phase of faith and is what distinguishes Christians from others.[101] It is essential for man's salvation and "the beginning and ground of his whole relationship to God."[102] It "is the first foundation of things to be hoped for" (cf. Heb 11:6) so that "once faith is removed, man retains nothing that may be useful for the obtaining of eternal salvation."[103] At the other end of the spectrum is completed faith (fides formata). Completed faith manifests itself in hope and charity.[104] It is not enough "that the heart should believe, but also that external words and deeds should bear witness to the inward faith." In the same way, just as one's words and actions may demonstrate faith, so too "certain external words or deeds" may demonstrate an absence of faith.[105] This does not, however, insinuate a priority on works.[106]

At the final judgment[107] "all human affairs" will be taken into account and will have a direct bearing on one's final salvation. Admittance or exclusion is based on how one has conducted one's life while on earth (Matt 25:31,40)[108] and even though in regard to these affairs "a man neither merits

---

[98] Aquinas, *STh* III q. 60 art. 3.

[99] For Aquinas' understanding of faith see Davies, *The Thought of Thomas Aquinas*, 274–85.

[100] Aquinas, *STh* II–II q. 2 art. 6; q. 7 art. 2.

[101] Davies, *The Thought of Thomas Aquinas*, 275.

[102] Pfurtner, *Luther and Aquinas*, 62.

[103] Aquinas, *STh* II–II q. 12 art. 1; I–II q. 113 art. 4. See Benoit Duroux, "Aspects psychologiques de l' 'analysis fidei' chez S. Thomas d'Aquin," *Freiburger Zeitschrift für Philosophie und Theologie* 2 (1955) 156.

[104] Pfurtner, *Luther and Aquinas*, 65–66, n. 27: "The difference between this [unformed faith] and complete faith . . . consists, among other things, in the fact that the knowledge of salvation is not sufficiently effective in the whole conduct of life, that is, it does not impose itself on the subject's will with salutary effect" (cf. 68–85).

[105] Aquinas, *STh* II-II q. 12 art. 1.

[106] For an overview on the teaching of grace, works and faith in the medieval period see Karlfried Froehlich, "Justification Language in the Middle Ages," in *Justification by Faith: Lutherans and Catholics in Dialogue*, ed. H. George Anderson et al., vol. 7 (Minneapolis: Augsburg, 1985) 143–61.

[107] See John Finnis, *Aquinas: Moral, Political, and Legal Theory* (Oxford: Oxford University Press, 1998) 212, 327–31, on Aquinas and eternal judgment.

[108] Aquinas, *STh* III q. 59 art. 4.

or demerits, still in a measure they accompany his reward or punishment."[109] Aquinas' order of salvation is summarized below:[110]

Table 1: Thomas Aquinas and the Order of Salvation

1	2	3
Gratuitous infusion of grace	Moral cooperation: doing the best one can with the aid of grace	Reward of eternal life as a just due

Thus, for Aquinas, works are necessary for eternal life but only insofar as they are produced by grace working through faith.[111] Man, "by his natural endowments, cannot produce meritorious works proportionate to everlasting life." For the attainment of eternal life "a higher force is needed, viz., the force of grace. And thus without grace man cannot merit everlasting life."[112] (This does not mean that man can do no good work apart from grace; he can, but none deserving of eternal life). Grace is necessary to move the will[113] that in turn is necessary to do "works meritorious of everlasting life." Aquinas very much follows Augustine[114] here pointing out "that the will of man should be prepared with grace by God."[115] After all no man can come to the Father unless the Father draws him (John 6:44) and "Apart from Me you can do nothing" (John 15:5).[116] Man cannot prepare himself, he cannot draw himself,

---

[109] Aquinas, *STh* III q. 59 art. 6.

[110] Taken from Steven E. Ozment, *Age of Reform: an Intellectual and Religious History of Late Medieval and Reformation Europe* (New Haven: Yale University Press, 1980) 233.

[111] Cf. O'Meara, "Thomas Aquinas," 54: "Human beings do merit eternal life but only in a very modest way, for their actions are enabled by grace."

[112] Aquinas, *STh* I-II q. 109 art. 5: "As the gloss upon Rom. vi. 23, *The grace of God is life everlasting*, says, *It is certain that everlasting life is meted to good works; but the works to which it is meted, belong to God's grace*. And it has been said that to fulfill the commandments of the Law, in their due way, whereby their fulfillment may be meritorious, requires grace"; art. 7: "God is the First Mover"; q. 114 art. 2.

[113] Aquinas, *STh* I-II q. 109 art. 6: "Man's turning to God is by free-will . . . But free-will can only be turned to God, when God turns it" (cf. Jer 31:18); art. 9: "man needs the help of grace in order to be moved by God to act"; q. 113 art. 7: "For it is by grace that free-will is moved and sin is remitted."

[114] For the influence of Augustine on Aquinas see M. D. Chenu, *Introduction a l'etude de Saint Thomas d'Aquin* (Paris: Vrin, 1950) 44–51.

[115] Aquinas, *STh* I-II q. 109 art. 5.

[116] Aquinas, *STh* I-II q. 109 art. 6.

he cannot will himself, he cannot produce meritorious works necessary for eternal life himself;[117] he must have Divine grace.[118]

From this it is apparent that there is no such thing as a meritorious work unless it is preceded by grace. Works may proceed from man's free will[119] but not before they proceed from the grace of the Holy Spirit and this not before Divine ordination.[120] Thus the notion of merit[121] in Aquinas does not imply that God is our debtor for "it is right that His will should be carried out."[122] Furthermore, God grants eternal life on the basis of his justice (2 Tim 4:8) and so cannot be considered legalistic in the true sense of the term.[123] Therefore there is no such thing as a condign[124] merit in Thomism unless it

---

[117] Aquinas, *STh* I-II q. 109 art. 9: Even someone who has been justified by grace and thus can be said to "already possess grace needs a further assistance of grace in order to live righteously."

[118] On grace in Aquinas see Davies, *The Thought of Thomas Aquinas*, 262–73. Cf. also Thomas F. O'Meara, "Grace as a Theological Structure in the *Summa theologiae* of Thomas Aquinas," *Recherches de théologie ancienne et médiévale* 55 (1988) 130–53. Aquinas' thinking on grace underwent some development between his earlier and later writings. For a précis of this development see McGrath, *Iustitia Dei*, 104–7. Aquinas' *Summa Theologica* represents his mature thinking on the subject.

[119] By free will Aquinas is not meaning that man acts independent of God. Rather grace under-girds all our actions and hence he can envision God as causing and moving our will and yet without the will ceasing to be free. Cf. Davies, *The Thought of Thomas Aquinas*, 267.

[120] Aquinas, *STh* I-II q. 114 art. 1, 2, 4. Cf. Philip Watson, "Erasmus, Luther, and Aquinas," *Concordia Theological Monthly* 40 (1969) 754–56, for a discussion on the relationship between grace, free will, predestination, and merit in Thomas Aquinas. See also F. Earle Fox, "Biblical Theology and Pelagianism," *JR* 41 (1961) 172–76; Michael Lawler, "Grace and Free Will in Justification: A Textual Study in Aquinas," *TThom* 35 (1971) 601–30; Davies, *The Thought of Thomas Aquinas*, 158–69, 174–78.

[121] See Joseph P. Wawrykow, *God's Grace and Human Action: 'Merit' in the Theology of Thomas Aquinas* (Notre Dame, Ind.: University of Notre Dame Press, 1995) 1–33. Wawrykow reviews the secondary literature on merit in Aquinas and notes that merit is by and large a neglected aspect of Thomas' theology. Wawrykow critiques the literature for (1) a misunderstanding of Thomas' teaching on grace in relation to merit, (2) an inadequate consideration of the development of Thomas' teaching on merit (i.e., it did not remain static), and (3) a failure to understand merit within Thomas' larger theological framework. The result, according to Wawrykow, Thomas' teaching on merit has been distorted.

[122] Aquinas, *STh* I-II q. 114 art. 1. Cf. also McGrath, *Iustitia Dei*, 114.

[123] Aquinas, *STh* I-II q. 114 art. 1, 3. Wawrykow, *God's Grace and Human Action*, 32, suggests that the presence of clear juridical elements in Aquinas indicates a non-legalistic attitude toward merits. Cf. also Finnis, *Aquinas*, 328.

[124] In the Middle Ages the notion of merit came to be thought of in two senses. *Congruous* merit (*meritum de conguo*) refers to moral actions done prior to the infusion of justifying grace. These actions are considered congruous (appropriate) to merit justifying grace and thus place one in a state of grace. *Condign* merit (*meritum de condigno*) refers to moral actions done after justifying grace has been infused. That is, they are done while one is in a state of grace. By

originates with God. For the value of the merit does not depend on the power of man but on that of the Holy Spirit.[125]

When it comes to the issue of assurance it must be noted that for Aquinas there is a difference between certainty and security. "The certainty of hope is a *certitudo affectus*, not a *certitudo effectus*."[126] Yet the latter does not nullify the former. One can still be confident about one's salvation albeit not secure, for "a man hopes to obtain eternal life, not by his own power . . . but with the help of grace; and if he perseveres therein he will obtain eternal life surely and infallibly."[127] Anything to the contrary is not hope but presumption. Presumption is twofold. In lieu of their own moral aptitude one may trust in their own power for salvation[128] or conversely, but still erroneously, trust in God's power for salvation in the absence of any appropriate works.[129] Hope does not guarantee salvation.[130] Man's hope of eternal life does not rely on his own moral goodness "but on God's omnipotence and mercy, whereby even he that has not grace, can obtain it, so as to come to eternal life. Now whoever has faith is certain of God's omnipotence and mercy."[131] This is quintessential Thomas.[132]

Via Moderna (Nominalism)[133]

Both contemporary and modern critics have charged the *via moderna*, and principally that of William of Ockham (ca. 1285–1347) and Gabriel Biel (ca.

---

virtue of being in a state of grace these actions are now able to merit eternal life.

[125] Aquinas, *STh* I-II q. 114 art. 3.

[126] Pfurtner, *Luther and Aquinas*, 101.

[127] Aquinas, *STh* II-II q. 1 art. 3. Pfurtner, *Luther and Aquinas*, 104: "If by certainty of salvation we mean the unshakeable trust that God forgives my sins and effects my eternal salvation, as long as I cling to him with complete faith and firm hope, then we must say: Aquinas taught the certainty of personal salvation. This is of course a certainty of trust and confidence, not security of possession."

[128] Aquinas, *STh* II-II q. 21 art. 4.

[129] Aquinas, *STh* II-II q. 21 art. 4.

[130] Thus, Aquinas, *STh* II-II q. 18 art. 4: "That some who have hope fail to obtain happiness, is due to a fault of the free will in placing the obstacle of sin, but not to any deficiency in God's power or mercy." Cf. also q. 21 art. 2: "To sin with the intention of persevering in sin and through the hope of being pardoned, is presumptuous."

[131] Aquinas, *STh* II-II q. 18 art. 4.

[132] Pfurtner, *Luther and Aquinas*, 60.

[133] The medieval movement known as "nominalism" is now in recent scholarship being referred to as *via moderna* ("the modern way"). Nominalism embraces a number of theologians of two very diverse theological persuasions (generally Pelagian versus Augustinian) who nevertheless hold to a similar philosophy concerning epistemology. *Via moderna*, however, represents a soteriological strand (Pelagian orientation) within nominalism. Thus the term nominalism is

1420–95), with Pelagianism.[134] However this has now been challenged.[135] The disagreement has arisen over Ockham and Biel's use of *potentia absoluta* and *potentia ordinata*.[136] God's *absolute* power (*potentia absoluta*) refers to the infinite number of possibilities that He could have implemented to carry out His will. God's *ordained* power (*potentia ordinata*) refers to the limited number of possibilities that God did in fact choose. Ockham and Biel both use *potentia absoluta* and *potentia ordinata* in their writings. For example, Ockham believes *de potentia Dei absoluta* that man can merit God's favor.[137] The difficulty arises in deciding whether this is what Ockham actually believed to be the case concerning God's plan for salvation in which case *potentia absoluta* = *potentia ordinata* and the charge of Pelagianism is correct. Or does *potentia absoluta* merely reflect a hypothetical possibility and therefore not a true reflection of Ockham's beliefs, his beliefs being represented by *potentia ordinata*?[138] I am persuaded by the latter and henceforth will adopt this perspective.[139]

Closely associated with the notion of *potentia ordinata* is the belief that God has generously obligated himself by way of a covenant[140] to justify man on the condition that he "does his very best" (*facere quod in se est*).[141] That is, one is to have genuine contrition and love for God.[142] One is to detest sin and do good works. Both man and God have a role to play in justification—

---

more appropriately used to designate a philosophy while the term *via moderna* pertains to a theology and is therefore more apposite for our present discussion. See McGrath, *Iustitia Dei*, 166–72, for what we have essentially summarized here. Cf. Charles Trinkaus and Heiko A. Oberman, eds., *The Pursuit of Holiness in Late Medieval and Renaissance Religion*, "Nominalism and Late Medieval Religion" by William J. Courtenay, *Studies in Medieval and Reformation Thought*, ed. Heiko A. Oberman et al., vol. 10 (Leiden: Brill, 1974) 26–59.

[134] Particularly Heiko Augustinus Oberman, *The Harvest of Medieval Theology: Gabriel Biel and Late Medieval Nominalism* (Cambridge, Mass.: Harvard University Press, 1963).

[135] See esp. A. E. McGrath, "The Anti-Pelagian Structure of 'Nominalist' Doctrines of Justification," *Ephemerides Theologicae Lovanienses* 57 (1981) 107–19.

[136] Otherwise known as "the dialectic between the two powers of God." See Courtenay, *Medieval and Reformation Thought*, 37–43.

[137] Auguste Pelzer, "Les 51 articles de Guillaume Occam censurés, en Avignon, en 1326," *Revue d'histoire ecclésiastique* 18 (1922) 250–51.

[138] Cf. Courtenay, *Medieval and Reformation Thought*, 47.

[139] See Francis Clark, "A New Appraisal of Late Medieval Nominalism," *Gregorianum* 46 (1965) 733–65. McGrath, "The Anti-Pelagian Structure," 113, points out that Ockham maintained that there was only one power in God, *de potentia ordinata*; cf. also Ozment, *Age of Reform*, esp. 234.

[140] See McGrath, "The Anti-Pelagian Structure," 114–15.

[141] See Courtenay, *Medieval and Reformation Thought*, 47; Oberman, *Harvest of Medieval Theology*, 132–34; McGrath, *Iustitia Dei*, 83–91.

[142] See Biel, *IV Sent.* d. 16 q. 1 art. 2

"Draw near to God, and He will draw near to you" (Jas 4:8; cf. Luke 11:9).[143] From a human standpoint this means that everyone is capable of initiating his or her own salvation.[144] From God's standpoint He is obliged, according to the terms of the covenant, to accept human acts as meritorious of eternal life.[145] "It must be pointed out, however, that this obligation on the part of God is usually understood to arise as a consequence of his gracious decision to allow himself to be placed under obligation to man in this manner."[146]

Quite simply, for salvation to occur man must move from a state of sin to a state of grace for which there must be an infusion of grace. Natural man (outside the state of grace) cannot make this step but he can, by *facere quod in se est*, initiate the salvation process and come to the door of grace (Rev 3:20). There is no preparatory grace, no stirring from God that enables man to do his very best.[147] Grace is not the root but the fruit of man doing his very best.[148] If the *facere quod in se est* is "on account of God" (*propter deum*) then grace is immediately infused. This is the beginning of the process of justification.[149]

It must be pointed out that what is merited here is not eternal life, but a state of grace. This is what is known as a "congruent merit." *Facere quod in se est* done outside a state of grace acquired congruent merit, itself inadequate to merit salvation, but of the right kind to merit God's infused grace.[150]

---

[143] Ozment, *Age of Reform*, 234.

[144] The medieval period bears witness to a shift in emphasis on the relationship between works and salvation. For Augustine works played an important role in *final* justification at which point eternal life is bestowed. The priority of grace is assumed and works are an expression not a cause of grace. In the medieval period the discussion revolves around one's *initial* justification. Can one merit his initial justification? That most answered in the negative is due in no small way to the teaching of Augustine. McGrath, *Iustitia Dei*, 110, notes: "a distinction came to be drawn between the concepts of *merit* and *congruity*: while man cannot be said to merit justification by any of his actions, his preparation for justification could be said to make his subsequent justification 'congruous' or 'appropriate'." The important point for our present discussion is that "whenever a theologian of the twelfth century concedes merit prior to justification, the 'merit' in question is not merit in the strict sense of the term [*meritum de condigno*], but *meritum de congruo*" (ibid., 111). Hence the maxim *facere quod in se est* is understood both as a presupposition to and an expression of grace. "Man's justification must be seen as a divine *gift*, rather than a divine *reward*" (ibid., 112).

[145] Biel, *II Sent.* d. 27 q. 1 art. 3; McGrath, "The Anti-Pelagian Structure," 114–15.

[146] McGrath, *Iustitia Dei*, 112–13. Cf. also Euan Cameron, *The European Reformation* (Oxford: Clarendon, 1991) 84–85.

[147] Biel, *II Sent.* d. 28 q. 1 art. 3.

[148] Biel, *S I* 99 F. Oberman, *Harvest of Medieval Theology*, 141.

[149] See Oberman, *Harvest of Medieval Theology*, 146–84.

[150] See Biel, *IV Sent.* q. 9. Cameron, *European Reformation*, 85. Cf. McGrath, *Iustitia Dei*, 116: "According to Ockham, God rewards virtuous acts performed outside a state of grace

Although many have seen Pelagianism here this was not the intent of Ockham or Biel. Man's role in justification is to be thought of in light of God's covenant.[151] This was often illustrated by the medieval fiscal system.[152] In Medieval times when currency became scarce the king could designate a substitute currency either in the form of promissory notes or substitute money that could be fully redeemed at a future time. Naturally any substitute currency lacked the inherent value of normal currency, but because it had the backing of the king the substitute currency had ascribed to it a *nominal* value equal to that of the usual currency. In a similar way good works were viewed as substitute money. They had little inherent moral value and yet God had determined according to the terms of the covenant to treat these works with much greater value sufficient to merit the infusion of justifying grace. The difference between the nominalist and Pelagian understanding of works is that Pelagius ascribed a meritorious value to works apart from God. For Ockham and Biel they were nothing more than lead coins. The salient point from all this is summarized by McGrath: "man's disposition cannot be said to cause his justification on account of its own nature . . . but only on account of the value ascribed to it by God."[153]

By interpreting the relationship between works and justification within the confines of the covenant Ockham and Biel are able to avoid, in their own minds at least, an alliance with Pelagianism. For "the relationship between man's action and the divine response is a consequence of the divine ordination, rather than the nature of the entities in themselves."[154] The covenant is fundamental to *facere quod in se est*[155] precluding the possibility that justifying faith is a human work.[156]

---

with congruous merit. However, Ockham insists that this 'merit' carries with it no claim to eternal life, which arises only on account of merit *de condigno*. All that Ockham intends to convey by the notion of congruous merit is that man is capable of acting in such a way that God may bestow upon man a habit of grace." Cf. also Ozment, *Age of Reform*, 234: "If God rewards good works done in a state of grace with eternal life as a *just* due [i.e., condign merit], could he not also be expected to reward good works done in a state of nature with an infusion of grace as an *appropriate* due [i.e., congruous merit]? . . . Absolutely considered, it was not human activity, either outside or within a state of grace, that determined man's salvation; it was God's willingness to value human effort so highly" (emphasis mine).

[151] McGrath, *Iustitia Dei*, 77. Cf. also Clark, "Late Medieval Nominalism," 741–46.

[152] William J. Courtenay, "The King and the Leaden Coin: The Economic Background of 'Sine Qua Non' Causality," *Traditio: Studies in Ancient and Medieval History, Thought, and Religion* 28 (1972) 185–209, esp. 193–94.

[153] McGrath, *Iustitia Dei*, 88; cf. McGrath's discussion on merit, 109–19, esp. 115–18.

[154] Ibid., 89.

[155] See Oberman, *Harvest of Medieval Theology*, 132–34.

[156] McGrath, *Iustitia Dei*, 70–71.

From the moment a person is justified he is in a state of grace but this does not eliminate the need for *facere quod in se est*. Infused grace assists and perfects his or her love for God via the sacraments.[157] If a Christian falls into mortal sin he is responsible once again to do his very best.[158] Thus outside a state of grace one could initiate his or her salvation by *facere quod in se est* and merit God's infused grace (congruous merit). Once in a state of grace one could merit his or her eternal life by *facere quod in se est* (condign merit).[159] The order of salvation for the *via moderna* can be summarized as:[160]

Table 2: The *Via Moderna* and the Order of Salvation

1	2	3	4
Moral effort: doing the best one can on the basis of natural ability	Infusion of grace as an appropriate reward	Moral cooperation: doing the best one can with the aid of grace	Reward of eternal life as a just due

Certainly contemporary critics of Ockham and Biel believed, rightly or wrongly, these men to be teaching something akin to Pelagianism. For example, Gregory of Rimini,[161] a contemporary of Ockham and a predecessor of Biel, attacked Ockham for his Pelagian views and argued in true Augustinian[162] fashion that love for God and good works were impossible apart from grace.[163] It was Biel who then followed Rimini on the eve of the Reformation and defended Ockham against Rimini's attacks. Martin Luther then followed and took up Rimini's position leading the charge against the entire late medieval theology[164] accusing them all, excepting Rimini, of Pelagianism.[165]

---

[157] Oberman, *Harvest of Medieval Theology*, 153–54, 184.

[158] Biel, *II Sent.* d. 27 q. 1 art. 2.

[159] Ozment, *Age of Reform*, 236: "In the final analysis, earning by moral effort salvation as condign merit was only a higher form of earning by moral effort saving grace as semimerit."

[160] Taken from ibid., 234.

[161] See Oberman, *Harvest of Medieval Theology*, 196–206.

[162] See Heiko A. Oberman, *Masters of the Reformation: The Emergence of a New Intellectual Climate in Europe* (Cambridge: Cambridge University Press, 1981) 64–110, for a discussion on the Augustinian renaissance in the later Middle Ages.

[163] Ozment, *Age of Reform*, 41.

[164] Ibid., 42. See also Cameron, *European Reformation*, 111–35; Oberman, *Masters of the Reformation*, 64–110; B. A. Gerrish, *Grace and Reason: A Study in the Theology of Luther* (Oxford: Clarendon, 1962) 114–37.

[165] A fact that McGrath, *Iustitia Dei*, 197, attributes to "Luther's inadequate and ill-informed generalisations concerning the theology . . . of the late medieval church."

The Reformation

By the end of the Middle Ages the church was riding a penitential merry-go-round: a perennial cycle of sin, confession and pardon. Hence most agree, in Protestant circles at least, that the Reformation came as a breath of fresh air[166] convincing "many people that their souls were really saved *without* the paraphernalia of the sacramental and penitential system."[167] Soteriology lay at the heart of the Reformers' cause and none more so than an elucidation of the relationship between works and salvation. We will consider the Lutheran and Reformed positions independently.

Martin Luther

Martin Luther (1483–1546) made a "decisive break with the soteriology of the *via moderna* in 1515."[168] Later in life, recalling his conversion,[169] Luther wrote:

> At last, by the mercy of God, meditating day and night, I gave heed to the context of the words, namely, "In it the righteousness of God is revealed, as it is written, 'He who through faith is righteous shall live.'" There I began to understand that the righteousness of God is that by which the righteous lives by a gift of God, namely by faith . . . Here I felt that I was altogether born again and had entered paradise itself through open gates. There a totally other face of the entire Scripture showed itself to me. Thereupon I ran through the Scriptures from memory.[170]

That righteousness was imputed, not infused, a gift, not merited,[171] subsequently colored Luther's thinking on the Christian life, especially the relationship between works and salvation. Tenaciously drawing on Paul's state-

---

[166] Although cf. Oberman, *Masters of the Reformation*, 276–78.

[167] Cameron, *European Reformation*, 111; cf. 132–35; Ozment, *Age of Reform*, 374–75.

[168] McGrath, *Iustitia Dei*, 197. Although there are some aspects of Luther's early (1514–15) theology that correspond to the *via moderna* (e.g., the covenant framework of justification and *facere quod in se est*) (205–6). See Ozment, *Age of Reform*, 235–36, and Gerrish, *Grace and Reason*, 114–37, on Luther's critique of medieval soteriology.

[169] The year of Luther's conversion is a matter of debate spanning a period between 1513 and 1518–19. For the former see Heinrich Boehmer, *Road to Reformation: Martin Luther to the Year 1521*, trans. John W. Doberstein and Theodore G. Tappert (Philadelphia: Muhlenberg, 1946) 87–117. For the latter date see Uuras Saarnivaara, *Luther Discovers the Gospel: New Light Upon Luther's Way from Medieval Catholicism to Evangelical Faith* (Saint Louis, Mo.: Concordia, 1951) esp. 92–120.

[170] Luther, *Works*, 34:337.

[171] See Luther's denouncement of the scholastic theologians of the medieval period in his *Works*, 26:130–31.

ments concerning works and justification,[172] Luther in his *Prefaces to the New Testament* first published in 1522, stated that, "the gospel does not expressly demand works of our own by which we become righteous and are saved; indeed it condemns such works."[173] Similarly, in his *Preface to the Acts of the Apostles* some ten years later (ca. 1530–33), "that the true and chief article of Christian doctrine is this: We must all be justified alone by faith in Jesus Christ, without any contribution from the law or help from our works."[174]

However, it was not the doctrine of justification so much that captivated Luther—this he already knew from his Roman Catholic heritage. Rather it was the qualifier "by faith alone (*sola fides*) apart from works."[175] We are not justified "for our own merits and works but for our faith."[176] "Just as good fruits do not make the tree good, so good works do not justify the person."[177] For Luther works are inadequate for justification for several reasons.[178] (1) The doctrine of justification gives glory to God by denying man any ability whatsoever to achieve his own justification.[179] Hence those who pursue salvation by works "do not give glory to God."[180] (2) No one can fully obey the

---

[172] Gerrish, *Grace and Reason*, 104. Justification for Luther is the point that "we are delivered from sin and justified, and eternal life is granted to us" (Luther, *Works*, 26:132). For a good discussion on Luther's understanding of justification see Bernard Lohse, *Martin Luther's Theology: Its Historical and Systematic Development*, trans. and ed. Roy A. Harrisville (Minneapolis: Fortress, 1999) 258–66. See also Carl E. Braaten and Robert W. Jenson, eds., *Union With Christ: The New Finnish Interpretation of Luther* (Grand Rapids: Eerdmans, 1998), where Luther's traditional notion of justification as forensic is challenged.

[173] Luther, *Works*, 35:360.

[174] Luther, *Works*, 35:363. This is not to say that Luther equates Paul's "works of the law" with "works" in general, but he does make a logical assumption: if one cannot be justified by works of the law, human works must also be precluded. Cf. *Works*, 26:141, 333, 407: "If the Law of God is weak and useless for justification, much more are the laws of the pope weak and useless for justification."

[175] John D. Hannah, "The Meaning of Saving Faith: Luther's Interpretation of Romans 3:28," *BibSac* 140 (1983) 323. See also André Dumas, "Une fin créatrice de ses moyens: l'insouciance du Coeur," *Recherches de Science Religieuses* 68 (1980) 321–36. It was Luther's teaching on *sola fides* that attacked the heart of the Roman Catholic cycle of sin, confession and pardon. Instead of a believer perennially passing from a state of grace to sin via the sacraments, Luther showed that a believer was now a sinner (in practice) and righteous (in position) simultaneously (Cameron, *European Reformation*, 123).

[176] Luther, *Works*, 26:132.

[177] Luther, *Works*, 34:111.

[178] See Stephen Westerholm, *Israel's Law and the Church's Faith: Paul and His Recent Interpreters* (Grand Rapids: Eerdmans, 1988) 6–8, for points 1–3 of what follows. Westerholm gives a total of 6 reasons.

[179] Luther, *Works*, 26:66.

[180] Luther, *Works*, 26:229; cf. 127, 227.

Law[181] and thus faith in Christ is one's only recourse.[182] (3) Even our good works count for nothing unless they are done in faith. "That which is born of the flesh is flesh" (John 3:6)[183] and is therefore deplorable to God. (4) One cannot receive the Holy Spirit by keeping the Law for according to the Bible there is no blessing outside of the promise.[184] In fact to try and earn salvation through anything apart from the promise is to in effect accuse God of "lying in all His promises."[185]

Luther's persistent denigration of works led many of his contemporaries to accuse him of Antinomianism.[186] However, this is a misrepresentation. Certainly for Luther there is no greater truth than, "No flesh is justified by works of the Law" (Rom 3:20). Yet clearly works play a role for Christ himself says, "If you wish to enter life, keep the commandments" (Matt 19:17).[187] Luther resolves the tension between these two passages by affirming that while justification is by faith alone the faith that justifies is never alone (cf. Jas 2:20).[188] What governs Luther's understanding here is his distinction between justifying faith and human (i.e., false)[189] faith. The former is belief *in* God, the latter belief *about* God.[190] Human faith is a "dead faith" (2:17) for as soon as trials come it crumbles.[191] In short, it "is not a repentance to salvation."[192] Justifying faith on the other hand does not arise from human nature but is supernaturally given.[193] This kind of faith "works through love" (Gal

---

[181] Luther, *Works*, 26:273; cf. 398.

[182] Luther, *Works*, 26:274.

[183] Luther, *Works*, 26:139–40, 216.

[184] Luther, *Works*, 26:255.

[185] Luther, *Works*, 26:229.

[186] See Luther's discussion concerning his objectors on his exposition of Gal 3:10 (See his *Works*, 26:248–68). Cf. also Lohse, *Luther's Theology*, 178–84.

[187] Luther, *Works*, 44:298; cf. also 26:265; 51:285. On the relationship between law and Gospel in Luther see Charles P. Arand, *That I May Be His Own: An Overview of Luther's Catechisms* (Saint Louis, Mo.: Concordia, 2000).

[188] Luther, *Works*, 44:298; cf. 34:124: we are "not justified by obedience, nevertheless, faith produces obedience"; 176: "We say that justification is effective without works, not that faith is without works." See esp. Luther's discussion in his *Lectures on Galatians* on the relationship between faith and works (*Works*, 26:273). Luther can say that "works justify," but what he means is that "they show that we have been justified" (*Works*, 34:161).

[189] Cf. Luther, *Works*, 36:302.

[190] Cf. Hannah, "Saving Faith," 322–34.

[191] Luther, *Works*, 29:235.

[192] Luther, *Works*, 7:229; cf. 27:172, 291; 30:12.

[193] Cf. Luther, *Works*, 36:301, where faith comes from the Holy Spirit, and 29:235, faith comes from grace.

5:6)¹⁹⁴ *after* one is justified.¹⁹⁵ Therefore when Luther says that one is justified by faith alone, he does not mean by "human faith" which amounts to mere intellectual assent.

Once Luther is rightly understood on this point it is not even entirely correct to say that he rejects the necessity of good works in justification.¹⁹⁶ It must be remembered however that this necessity refers to post-conversion works not pre-conversion. Works inevitably follow justification; they do not cause it.¹⁹⁷ For even a good tree will produce fruit. Thus justification is "the beginning of obedience."¹⁹⁸ So while works must be absent prior to justification, this will inevitably not be the case post-justification. Good "works come from a person who has already been justified beforehand by faith, just as good fruits come from a tree which is already good beforehand by nature."¹⁹⁹ Abraham is a case in point. For Abraham circumcision was an external demonstration of the righteousness present in his faith. Similarly good works are "external signs which follow out of faith; like good fruit they demonstrate that a person is already inwardly righteous before God."²⁰⁰ This is not an optional occurrence for "if good works do not follow, it is certain that this faith in Christ does not dwell in our heart."²⁰¹ Thus "it is impossible for us to be born of our works, but rather, the works are born of us, so to speak."²⁰²

Luther is careful to avoid confusion here and understands the tension.²⁰³ "Works only reveal faith, just as fruits only show the tree, whether it is a good tree." Works indicate whether one has faith²⁰⁴ and thus provides confirmation of their election (2 Pet 1:10).²⁰⁵ They are "evidence to himself and to others

---

[194] Luther, *Works*, 27:291.

[195] Cf. Luther, *Works*, 26:260.

[196] Luther admits to obedience being "a partial cause of our justification" (*Works*, 34:165; cf. 163–66), 44:298: "it will be strongly objected that the works of the divine law commanded in the decalogue . . . do *not* justify" (emphasis mine).

[197] Cf. McGrath, *Iustitia Dei*, 200: "The good works of the justified demonstrate the believer's justification *by God*, and cannot be considered to cause it." For Luther's teaching on works see his "Treatise on Good Works," in *Works*, 44:15–114.

[198] Luther, *Works*, 34:163.

[199] Luther, *Works*, 34:111.

[200] Luther, *Works*, 35:374.

[201] Luther, *Works*, 34:111. Cf. 4:132: "the fruits of the Spirit are called evidences of faith which assure us of our election and call." See esp. Paul Althaus, *The Theology of Martin Luther*, trans. Robert C. Schultz (Philadelphia: Fortress, 1966), 247.

[202] Luther, *Works*, 34:113.

[203] Cf. Althaus, *Theology*, 248.

[204] To state it as briefly as possible: "Works are necessary in order to prove that we are righteous" (Luther, *Works*, 34:165).

[205] Luther, *Works*, 26:260; Lohse, *Martin Luther's Theology*, 265; Althaus, *Theology*, 246.

about him whether he has the true faith." For after justification even "Peter, Paul, and all other Christians have done and still do the works of the Law; but they are not justified by them."[206]

It must be noted that while Luther can speak of salvation as something unmerited as though it is an event in a person's life, what he often means is justification. In other words, justification "is the beginning of salvation."[207] However, Luther does not distinguish between justification and sanctification and so justification is *also* "a process[208] of becoming."[209] We "are justified daily."[210] Here Luther and Augustine agree. Justification is "an all-embracing process, subsuming the beginning, development and subsequent perfection of the Christian life."[211] Thus for Luther, understanding the relationship be-

---

[206] Luther, *Works*, 26:124.

[207] Luther, *Works*, 26:132.

[208] Cf. esp. Luther, *Works*, 25:433–34; 27:21–22; 32:208.

[209] McGrath, *Iustitia Dei*, 200; cf. also Cameron, *European Reformation*, 125–28. Note esp. Luther, *Works*, 34:152: "For we perceive that a man who is justified is not yet a righteous man, but is in the very movement or journey toward righteousness."

[210] Luther, *Works*, 34:167.

[211] In his understanding of justification as a process Luther is more Catholic than what is often thought. Later Protestantism would come to define justification as a *point in time* and the process of the Christian life as 'sanctification.' Unfortunately this later portrayal of justification has often been read back into Luther. One of the results of this is that modern scholarship has increasingly questioned the traditional (Protestant) understanding of Paul's doctrine of justification. NT interpreters have been criticized for reading Paul's doctrine of justification through the eyes of Luther (see chap. 3). Although there may be some merit to this, our own observations suggest any misunderstanding of Paul is not because we have read him through Lutheran spectacles but rather we have read him through *late Protestantism's portrayal of Luther*. We have failed to see that in Luther's view justification does not only occur at a particular point in time but also as a process, apparently a vestige from his Catholic heritage. (The essential difference between Luther and Catholicism is on their understanding of works and faith in relation to justification). A correct reading of Luther would indeed lead to a different reading of Paul than what modern Protestants are traditionally accustomed to (cf. e.g., Rom 2:13; 8:33; Gal 5:4-5). Lohse, *Martin Luther's Theology*, 260, says as much in his discussion on justification: "Luther defined it [justification] as a being declared righteous by God. On the other hand, he could define it as the event by which one is 'acquitted,' changed, and renewed by virtue of the divine promise and grace. In the latter instance, *justification is understood as a 'process' extending over all of life*, reaching its goal only in the resurrection" (emphasis mine). See also ibid., 262–64. Cf. McGrath, *Iustitia Dei*, 377–78; G. Bavaud, "La doctrine de la justification d'après Calvin et le Concile de Trent," *Verbum Caro* 22 (1968) 83–92. But note the criticisms from W. Robert Godfrey, "Reversing the Reformation," *Eternity* 35 (1984) 26–28; C. M. Gullerud, "U.S. Lutheran–Roman Catholic Dialog on Justification by Faith: An Examination," *JT* 24 (1984) 19–24. On the relationship between Protestantism and Roman Catholicism one should also read Daniel Olivier, *Luther's Faith: The Cause of the Gospel in the Church*, trans. John Tonkin (Saint Louis, Mo.: Concordia, 1982). Olivier presents a reevaluation of Luther from a Roman Catholic perspective.

tween works and salvation involves looking at the Christian life as a whole (in total).[212] What he means by this is that there are two aspects to the Christian life, one internal, the other external. The internal involves faith and the external, works. The internal refers to our justification before God; the external, to the fruit of our justification. It is here that Luther offers us his best insight into his understanding on the relationship between works and salvation:

> Works are necessary to salvation, but they do not cause salvation, because faith alone gives life. On account of the hypocrisy we must say that good works are necessary to salvation. It is necessary to work. Nevertheless, it does not follow that works save on that account, unless we understand necessity very clearly as the necessity that there must be an inward and outward salvation or righteousness. Works save outwardly, that is, they show evidence that we are righteous and that there is faith in a man which saves inwardly . . . Outward salvation shows faith to be present, just as fruit shows a tree to be good.[213]

Thus for Luther the relationship between works and salvation is articulated differently depending on the works in view. Pre-conversion works have no merit with respect to gaining eternal life or placating God.[214] Salvation is entirely by grace through faith. However, post-conversion works are inevitable and necessary. There is no such thing as justification without moral transformation. This is true to the extent that if works do not follow, one is surely not saved. Thus, we are justified by faith alone apart from works but the kind of faith that justifies is never without works.[215]

If there is any difference between Luther and Calvin (below) on this subject it is that Luther is seemingly the more cautious of the two in articulating a link between faith and works.[216] For example, according to Luther believers must understand the difference between being justified before God and being justified before men "so that they will not interchange and mix up

---

[212] Although James' statement on justification by works (Jas 2:24) clearly troubled Luther. He evidently understands this passage to speak of the "total Christian life" (Luther, *Works*, 34:125), understanding James to be speaking of the difference between being righteous and giving evidence to that righteousness (*Works*, 4:133). However, he appears to understand "justification" as used by James to signify the same thing as Paul and thus concludes the statement itself is false (*Works*, 4:134; cf. p. 96).

[213] Luther, *Works*, 34:165.

[214] I.e., Lohse, *Martin Luther's Theology*, 265: "When justification is at issue, 'works' should not be emphasized."

[215] For the same conclusions (above and below) on the relationship between faith and works in Luther see Gerrish, *Grace and Reason*, 105; Lohse, *Martin Luther's Theology*, 264–66; Althaus, *Theology*, 245–50.

[216] Ozment, *Age of Reform*, 374–80. Cf. Lohse, *Martin Luther's Theology*, 264–66, for his discussion on Luther's understanding of faith and works.

faith and love or life toward God and life toward men."²¹⁷ The temptation to add works to faith is a constant source of struggle for Luther. However, he insists that in spite of the 'exceeding difficulty' we must "clearly separate faith and love" and we must avoid all temptation to boast in our labors and works, even our ministry, before God.²¹⁸ Works do not make a person "either a believer or an unbeliever."²¹⁹ True righteousness consists of faith²²⁰ and in spite of the revelatory character of works with respect to the righteous and the wicked (cf. Matt 7:20), "All this remains on the surface" and can be deceptive concerning salvation.²²¹ Although such statements may seem at odds with others he makes, these are Luther's attempt to sever every conceivable connection between works and justification.²²²

It is not surprising that Luther's ability to separate faith and works on the one hand and yet enjoin them on the other has led to charges of inconsistency.²²³ However, one must remember that a systematic theologian Luther was not. He was an occasional writer.²²⁴ If Rome insisted that works contributed to one's salvation then Luther would ardently deny any affiliation between faith and works. If his objectors claimed that justification by faith leads to licentiousness then Luther would respond by affirming that works are an inevitable and necessary affiliate of faith. But faith's preeminence is always preserved.²²⁵ These two positions are outlined in his *Smalcard Articles* and serve as a fitting summary to Luther's thinking on the matter.

> I cannot change at all what I have consistently taught about this [how a person is justified], namely, that 'through faith' . . . we receive a different, new, clean heart and that, for the sake of Christ our mediator, *God will and does regard us as completely righ-*

---

²¹⁷ Luther, *Works*, 51:284.

²¹⁸ Luther, *Works*, 51:284.

²¹⁹ Luther, *Works*, 31:361. Cf. also 362: "Hence when a man is good or evil, that is effected not by the works, but by faith or unbelief."

²²⁰ Cf. Luther, *Works*, 44:33.

²²¹ Luther, *Works*, 31:362. For Luther's thinking on the relationship between works, salvation and assurance see Althaus, *Theology*, 446–58.

²²² Ozment, *Age of Reform*, 376. Cf. also Gerrish, *Grace and Reason*, 117–18; Lohse, *Martin Luther's Theology*, 266.

²²³ See Gerrish, *Grace and Reason*, 118. For an excellent handling of this apparent inconsistency see Althaus, *Theology*, 248–50.

²²⁴ Arand, *That I May Be His Own*, 147: "Luther was more an *ad hoc* theologian." Cf. also Gerrish, *Grace and Reason*, 7–8, 57, and note Lohse's warnings on 3–10, and his comments on 266 in relation to Luther's articulation of faith and works.

²²⁵ Ibid.

teous and holy. Although sin in the flesh is still not completely gone or dead, God will nevertheless not count it or consider it.

Good works follow such faith, renewal, and forgiveness of sin, and whatever in these works is still sinful or imperfect should not even be counted as sin or imperfection, precisely for the sake of this same Christ. Instead, the human creature should be called and should be completely righteous and holy . . . by the pure grace and mercy that have been spread over us in Christ. Therefore we cannot boast about the great merit of our works, where they are viewed apart from grace and mercy . . . Furthermore, we also say that *if good works do not follow, then faith is false and not true.*[226]

John Calvin

Along with Luther, the major Reformers by and large all agree on the relationship between works and salvation. All insist that salvation is by faith[227] and that good works are the product of salvation and not the producer[228] as summed up by G. Bavaud: "l'accomplissement des bonnes oeuvres est le signe d'une authentique justification."[229]

---

[226] Robert Kolb and Timothy J. Wengert, eds., *The Book of Concord: The Confessions of the Evangelical Lutheran Church*, trans. Charles Arand et al., *Smalcald Articles* by Martin Luther (Minneapolis: Fortress, 2000) 325 (emphasis mine).

[227] E.g., John Calvin taught that man is justified by faith apart from works. For his view on justification by faith see his *Inst.* 2.6–7; 3.11.2–3; 16.10–11; 17, 18.18.8–9. See also John H. Leith, *John Calvin's Doctrine of the Christian Life* (Louisville, Ky.: Westminster/John Knox, 1989) 87–94; Bavaud, "saint Augustin et la Réforme," 26–29, for Calvin's doctrine of justification.

[228] This is evident, e.g., in Huldrych Zwingli. For Zwingli's interpretation on the relationship between faith and works (Fides et opera) see, *Zw* 6.5:118.5–26.7. See also W. P. Stephens, *The Theology of Huldrych Zwingli* (Oxford: Clarendon, 1986) 154–69, for Zwingli's teaching on salvation, and esp., 158–59, for his understanding on the relationship between works and salvation. Zwingli observed that Christ said, "a good tree produces good fruit" (Matt 7:17), James, "faith without works is dead" (Jas 2:17), and Paul, "faith works through love" (Gal 5:6). All three, according to Zwingli, affirm true faith will produce works (*Zw* 6.5:125.13–18, 124.1–5). However, these works do not originate from ourselves but with God for He "würckt in im die liebe, den radtschlag und das werck . . . und ist in allem werck wol wüssend, das sin ding und werck nüt ist; das aber da beschicht, allein gottes ist" (2:237.16–18; cf. also 6.5:119.18: faith originates with the Spirit of God). This is the same as saying that "ergo bona opera fidei fructus sunt" (*Zw* 3:849.36–7; cf. also 6.5:119.10–11). In short, that which is not from God (cf. John 15:4; Jas 1:17) is from ourselves (Luke 6:43; 18:19; 1 Cor 15:10) (*Zw* 2:238.27–239.23) and that which is from ourselves is not from faith and an abomination to God (*Zw* 6.5:119.10–11, 17–18).

[229] Bavaud, "Saint Augustin et la Réforme," 26; cf. also 27: "Sur ce point, la Réforme est unanime: refus absolu de considérer l'amour de l'homme pour Dieu comme une cause du pardon des péchés."

However, in spite of this commonality, it is here that the Lutheran and Reformed positions diverge. The issue concerns the exact nature of the interconnection between works and salvation. Generally speaking, the Reformed position maintains a strong ethical emphasis with justification.[230] For example, for Zwingli (1484–1531) justification is determined "analytically" rather than "synthetically."[231] According to Heinrich Bullinger (1504–75) righteousness is not only imputed (*declararéue*) at justification but it is realized (*exerere*).[232]

John Calvin (1509–64) holds to a mediating view between Luther on the one hand and Zwingli and Bullinger on the other. Calvin clearly distinguishes between justification and regeneration.[233] Both are consequences of faith in Christ but in justification there is no hint of being *made* righteous. According to Calvin, in justification we are reconciled to God and in regeneration "we aspire to integrity and purity of life."[234] The important point for Calvin is that the two are distinct. To "be justified is something else than to be made new creatures."[235] (But it is also true that "we cannot be Christians without being new creatures").[236]

However for Calvin, as with Zwingli and Bullinger, the link between faith and works is still very much evident.[237] Salvation is a two-sided coin,[238] faith on the one side and works on the other. Justification by faith certainly does not repudiate the necessity for good works but it does lie "at the root of all godliness."[239] "La sanctification . . . est une conséquence du pardon des

---

[230] See McGrath, *Iustitia Dei*, 219–26. For the following discussion on Zwingli, Bullinger and Bucer see ibid., 220–21.

[231] Ibid., 220. See *Zw* 5.625.21–31; cf. also Stephens, *Theology of Huldrych Zwingli*, 160.

[232] Bullinger, Heinrich. *De gratia dei iustificante nos propter Christum, per solam fidem absq operibus bonis, fide interim exuberante in opera bona libri IIII* (Zurich: Froschoviana, 1554) 66.

[233] See Calvin's critique of Osiander in Calvin, *Inst.*, 3.11.6, or confounding justification and regeneration. See also McGrath, *Iustitia Dei*, 222.

[234] Calvin, *Inst.*, 3.11.1. See J. Boisset, "Justification et sanctification chez Calvin," in *Calvinus Theologus: Die Referate des Congrés Européen de recherches Calviniennes*, ed. W. H. Neuser (Neukirchen-Vluyn: Neukirchener, 1976) 131–48.

[235] Calvin, *Inst.*, 3.11.7. This is the major difference between justification in the Medieval and Reformation periods (McGrath, *Iustitia Dei*, 41).

[236] Calvin, *Selected Works*, 2:144.

[237] For Calvin's teaching on the role of works in the Christian life see Leith, *Christian Life*, 103–6.

[238] Cf. ibid., 87.

[239] Calvin, *Inst.*, 3.15.7; cf. Leith, *Christian Life*, 94: "justification by faith alone is the precondition of all aspects of the ethical life" (cf. 97–98).

péchés... un fruit de la foi justifinate."[240] Faith and works, although distinct, are clearly inseparable in Calvin's soteriology. For example,

> We deny that good works have any share in justification, but we claim full authority for them in the lives of the righteous. For, if he who has obtained justification possess Christ, and, at the same time, Christ never is where his Spirit is not, it is obvious that gratuitous righteousness is necessarily connected with regeneration. Therefore, if you would duly understand how inseparable faith and works are, look to Christ, who, as the Apostle teaches, (1 Cor. 1:30) has been given to us for justification and sanctification. Wherever, therefore, that righteousness of faith... is, there too Christ is, and where Christ is, there too is the Spirit of holiness, who regenerates the soul to newness of life. On the contrary, where zeal for integrity and holiness is not in vigour, there neither is the Spirit of Christ nor Christ himself; and wherever Christ is not, there is no righteousness, nay, there is no faith; for faith cannot apprehend Christ for righteousness without the Spirit of sanctification.[241]

In sum, for Calvin, "Christ regenerates to a blessed life those whom he justifies, and after rescuing them from the dominion of sin, hands them over to the dominion of righteousness, transforms them into the image of God, and so trains them by his Spirit into obedience to his will."[242]

It is here that we see the essential difference between Luther and Calvin. Luther, while articulating a root-fruit relationship between faith and works, is hesitant to attribute anything positive to the role of works.[243] Calvin, howev-

---

[240] Bavaud, "saint Augustin et la Réforme," 27.

[241] Calvin, *Selected Works*, 1:45; cf. 2:55; 3:144.

[242] Calvin, *Selected Works*, 1:45.

[243] Cf. Ozment, *Age of Reform*, 377: "*All Protestant* theologians shared the common problem of giving good works a constructive role within the believer's life without at the same time succumbing to the Pelagian covenant theology of the Middle Ages, in opposition to which Protestant theology had been born. On this issue Luther may be said to have been the more cautious; while he too recognized the commandments as a guide to Christian behavior and stressed them as emphatically as any other Protestant leader, he also resisted more firmly than any other the temptation to find either evidence of salvation where good works were present or indications of damnation where they were not. With remarkable consistency he spoke only of faith and unbelief in direct proximity with salvation and damnation...
"For Calvin, good works did not have the direct bearing on salvation that medieval theology taught; they attested divine favor and gave presumptive evidence of election, but they did not put one in a position to expect salvation as condign merit. On the other hand, Calvin's teaching... made good works and moral behavior the center of religious life and reintroduced religious anxiety over them. In Calvinism the presence or absence of good works came to be taken as a commentary on one's eternal destiny." Cf. also Lohse, *Martin Luther's Theology*, 264–65.

er, is unable to think of a saved person without them. For "a man will be said to be *justified by works*, if in his life there can be found a purity and holiness which merits an attestation of righteousness at the throne of God."[244] Calvin does not deny the priority of faith but merely holds to a prominent[245] view of works in the life of one who is justified by faith.[246]

We see this clearly in Calvin's comments on James' treatise on justification by works. Whereas Luther considered James' teaching on justification false on account of Paul, Calvin appears to have had little problem in integrating the two. For Calvin the tension is resolved by observing that the "faith" that James speaks of is not the faith of Paul and likewise the "justification" is not the same justification Paul speaks of. Concerning faith in James, it is *without works* (2:14), it is "worse than that of the devils" (v. 19) and finally it is "dead" (v. 24). This faith merely gives assent to the existence of God. Such a faith, according to Calvin, cannot justify. Concerning the term "justify" in James, Calvin interprets it to mean the "manifestation" of faith. In other words, "Those who are justified by true faith prove their justification by obedience and good works, not by a bare and imaginary semblance of faith. In one word, he is not discussing the *mode* of justification, but requiring that the justification of believers shall be *operative*. And as Paul contends that men are justified without the aid of works, so James will not allow any to be regarded as justified who are destitute of good works."[247] It is clear from Calvin's exposition here that the mere specter of faith does not justify, for a Christian always "manifests his justification by good works."[248]

The key word here is "manifestation." Justifying faith for Calvin will manifest itself *visibly* in good works.[249] This does not imply sinless perfec-

---

[244] Calvin, *Inst.*, 3.11.2.

[245] Cf. Leith, *Christian Life*, 105: For Calvin "The works of a Christian, although inadequate in themselves to be meritorious in the sight of God, are by God's grace far from valueless." Cf. Calvin, *Inst.*, 3.16.2.

[246] Although good works must flow from the heart for mere external works can still deceive. In the end only God knows the heart. Furthermore, our works are only pleasing to God on account of His boundless mercy through Christ (Calvin, *Selected Works*, 3:134–35; Calvin, *Inst.*, 3.14.9; see Leith, *Christian Life*, 103–4).

[247] Calvin, *Inst.*, 3.17.12 (emphasis mine). Calvin interprets Rom 2:13 (". . . the doers of the law shall be justified") to mean that if justification *was* to be sought through the law it would be those who fulfilled the law that would be justified, not the Jews who merely listened to the law. Since no one can perfectly obey the law the scenario remains hypothetical (*Inst.*, 3.17.13). Similarly Calvin understands Jesus' response to the rich ruler's request concerning eternal life in Matt 19:16-17 (*Inst.*, 3.18.9; see also 18.10).

[248] Calvin, *Inst.*, 3.17.12; cf. Calvin, *Selected Works*, 3:128, 247.

[249] Cf. Ozment, *Age of Reform*, 356: "The union of internal belief and external behavior would become the hallmark of Calvinism. Calvinists distinguished themselves, above all, by their fervent belief that religion not only changed inward perception, but also transformed

tion²⁵⁰ in this life but it does insinuate "progress."²⁵¹ Neither should the manifestation of works give rise to boasting; they are simply confirmatory.²⁵² Calvin describes good works as "proofs of God dwelling and reigning in us," "fruits of regeneration" and proof of the indwelling Holy Spirit and the means by which saints discern their election.²⁵³

Calvin recognizes many passages in Scripture that attribute the reception of eternal life to the basis of works. For example, "God will render to every one according to his works" (Matt 16:27; cf. also 5:12; 25:34; Luke 6:23; John 5:29; Rom 2:6; 1 Cor 3:8; 2 Cor 5:10). On these passages Calvin states:

> The passages in which it is said that God will reward every man according to his works are easily disposed of. For that mode of expression indicates not the cause but the order of consequence. Now, it is beyond a doubt that the steps by which the Lord in his mercy consummates our salvation are these, 'Who he did predestinate, them he also called; and whom he called, them he also justified; and whom he justified, them he also glorified' (Rom. 8:30). *But though it is by mercy alone that God admits his people to life, yet as he leads them into possession of it by the course of good works*, that he may complete his work in them in the order which he has destined, it is not strange that they are

---

public life and manners; beliefs could not sit idly in the mind, but must renew individuals and societies. Nothing stands out more prominently in the history of Calvinism than the enforcement of a high standard of individual and social sanctification." In contrast Luther paid less attention to such outward works.

²⁵⁰ Cf. Calvin, *Selected Works*, 3:134. Calvin defines perfection along with Augustine: "When we speak of the perfect virtue of the saints, part of this perfection consists in the recognition of our imperfection both in truth and in humility" (*Inst.*, 3.17.15).

²⁵¹ Cf. Calvin, *Inst.*, 3.17.15.

²⁵² Calvin, *Inst.*, 3.14.18-19: "when we exclude confidence in works, we merely mean, that the Christian mind must not turn back to the merit of works as an aid to salvation, but must dwell entirely on the free promise of justification. But we forbid no believer to confirm and support this faith by the signs of the divine favour towards him. For if when we call to mind the gifts which God has bestowed upon us, they are like rays of the divine countenance, by which we are enabled to behold the highest light of his goodness; *much more is this the case with the gift of good works, which shows that we have received the Spirit of adoption* . . . When believers, therefore, feel their faith strengthened by a consciousness of integrity . . . it is just because the fruits of their calling convince them that the Lord has admitted them to a place among his children" (emphasis mine). Cf. Ozment, *Age of Reform*, 379: "good works are presumptive evidence that one is among the elect."

²⁵³ Calvin, *Inst.*, 3.14.18–20. Cf. also The Westminster Confession of Faith written in 1647. The Confession states, "good works, done in obedience to God's commandments, are the fruits and evidences of a true and lively faith" (Philip Schaff, "The Westminster Confession of Faith, 1647," in *The Creeds of Christendom, with a History and Critical Notes* [Grand Rapids: Baker, 1977] 3:633). But elsewhere (in his denouncement of the Council of Trent) Calvin states that we should not base our assurance of salvation on works (Calvin, *Selected Works*, 3:146).

said to be crowned according to their works, since by these doubtless they are prepared for receiving the crown of immortality.[254]

According to Calvin, the term "reward" does not imply that works are a cause of our salvation for Scripture often states that the kingdom is bestowed as an inheritance (cf. Matt 25:34; Eph 1:18; Gal 4:30; Col 3:24). Therefore, even though eternal life is often promised as a reward for works it is received as an "inheritance," not because of works but because of God's adoption.[255] Thus while eternal life may be said to be "the recompense of works, it is bestowed by the gratuitous gifts of God."[256]

> Moreover, when Scripture intimates that the good works of believers are causes why the Lord does them good, we must still understand the meaning . . . viz. that the efficient cause of our salvation is placed in the love of God the Father; the material cause in the obedience of the Son; the instrumental cause in the illumination of the Spirit, that is, in faith; and the final cause in the praise of the divine goodness. In this, however, *there is nothing to prevent the Lord from embracing works as inferior causes*. But how so? In this way: Those whom in mercy he has destined for the inheritance of eternal life, he, in his ordinary administration, *introduces to the possession of it by means of good works*. What precedes in the order of administration is called the cause of what follows. For this reason, *he sometimes makes eternal life a consequence of works* . . . it [good works] is a kind of step to that which follows . . . In short, *by these expressions, the order rather than the cause is noted*.[257]

James Arminius (Arminianism)

Arminianism refers to the teachings espoused by James Arminius (1560–1609) that were refuted at the Synod of Dort in 1619.[258] Foremost among Arminius' heresies, according to the Synod of Dort, was his repudiation of the Calvinist teaching on predestination and apostasy.[259]

---

[254] Calvin, *Inst.*, 3.18.1 (emphasis mine).

[255] Calvin, *Inst.*, 3.18.2.

[256] Calvin, *Inst.*, 3.18.4.

[257] Calvin, *Inst.*, 3.14.21.

[258] For a history see A. W. Harrison, *The Beginnings of Arminianism to the Synod of Dort* (London: University of London Press, 1926); idem, *Arminianism* (London: Duckworth, 1937).

[259] Ibid., 9; R. Buick Knox, "The History of Doctrine in the Seventeenth Century," in *HCD*, 434.

Arminius, like the Reformers before him, contended that works play no part in one's salvation.[260] Man can only be justified by the grace of God apart from any form of works.[261] Faith is both the instrument of justification[262] and a gift.[263] The outcome of justification is "peace with God . . . and an assured expectation of life eternal."[264] For Arminius there are two aspects to justification. The first occurs at conversion "when all preceding sins are forgiven;—and through the whole life, because God has promised remission of sins to believers . . . as often as they repent and flee by true faith to Christ."[265] "But the end and completion of justification will be near the close of life, when God will grant, to those who end their days in the faith of Christ, to find his mercy absolving them from all the sins which had been perpetrated through the whole of their lives. The declaration and manifestation of justification will be in the future general judgment."[266]

Although Arminius affirms that justification is by faith, "and faith only," he also qualifies this by suggesting "there is no faith alone without works."[267] Works "come into the judgment of God so far only as they are testimonies of faith" and if there is any reward due it is only by God's grace.[268] No amount of "spiritual good" can be done or even desired, apart from grace. "This grace commences salvation, promotes it, and perfects and consummates it."[269]

Thus far Arminius is close to Augustine, Luther and Calvin. However he does not hold to the reformed teaching on the perseverance of the saints but rather acknowledges that it is "possible for believers to fall away from the faith."[270] There is no assurance for one to believe one will not fall away[271]

---

[260] See Robert Shank, *Life in the Son: A Study of the Doctrine of Perseverance* (Springfield, Mo.: Westcott, 1961) 3–9.

[261] Arminius, *Works*, 2:46–49, 406–7.

[262] Ibid., 2:49–51, 407.

[263] Ibid., 2:51–52, 723.

[264] Ibid., 2:407.

[265] Ibid.

[266] Ibid.

[267] Ibid., 2:701.

[268] Ibid., 2:729.

[269] Ibid., 2:700. Arminius disagreed with the Reformer's view on the relationship between grace and predestination. Arminius understood predestination to refer to the present life of the Christian, not the *final* outcome of perseverance. Arminius rejected the reformed doctrine of predestination because the corollary of it was that some were ordained to fall (*Works*, 2:274–75; see also Craig Alan Blaising, "John Wesley's Doctrine of Original Sin" [Ph.D. diss., Dallas Theological Seminary, 1979] 90).

[270] Arminius, *Works*, 2:725.

[271] Ibid., 2:726.

although those who "work out their salvation" need not fear.[272] If a believer does fall away it will not be on account of Satan, sin, the world or the flesh, but rather because he "willingly and of his own accord yield[s] to temptation, and neglect[s] to work out his salvation in a conscientious manner."[273]

Whether a believer can fall away (i.e., lose their salvation) hinges on one's understanding of the doctrine of eternal security. Those who agree with Arminius argue that eternal security is conditional upon the believer's perseverance. Robert Shank states, "There can be no question whether eternal life will endure. It cannot cease. But the point of many solemn warnings in the New Testament is that our privilege of *participating* in that eternal life is directly dependent on our continuing to abide in Him in whom, alone, that life is available to men. If we fail to abide in Him, the eternal life continues, but our participation in that life ceases. We share that life only as we continue to abide in Him 'who is our life.'"[274] For example, the condition of a steward (οἰκονόμος) being made "ruler over all" (Luke 12:44) in one of Jesus' parables is that "that servant" (ὁ δοῦλος ἐκεῖνος) be found faithful (vv. 42-43). However, if "that servant" (ὁ δοῦλος ἐκεῖνος) is unfaithful, the Lord "will cut him in pieces (διχοτομήσει) and will appoint his portion with the unbelievers" (v. 46).[275] The parable illustrates the necessity of continuing in faithfulness in order to maintain one's salvation (cf. also Matt 18:21-25; John 15:1-6).[276]

According to this view, Paul also teaches that salvation is conditional upon the believer's continuance (1 Cor 15:1-2; Col 1:21-23; 1 Tim 4:1, 16; 2 Tim 3:13-15).[277] Apostasy is a very real threat in the NT (e.g., 1 Tim 1:18, 19; 5:9-15; 6:9-10; Heb 6:4-6; Jude 4, 12; 2 Pet 2:20-21).[278] It is true that

---

[272] Ibid.

[273] Ibid. Although I. Howard Marshall, *Kept by the Power of God: A Study of Perseverance and Falling Away*, 3d ed. (Minneapolis: Bethany, 1995) 219, n. 25, notes that Arminian authors do not consider loss of salvation a very likely possibility.

[274] Shank, *Life in the Son*, 54. Similarly, "the New Testament affirms that eternal life in Christ is our present possession only on the condition of a present living faith, rather than as the irrevocable consequence of a moment's act of faith sometime in the past" (63). Cf. also Grant R. Osborne, "Soteriology in the Gospel of John," in *The Grace of God, The Will of Man*, ed. Clark H. Pinnock (Grand Rapids: Zondervan, 1989) 258.

[275] Cf. Shank, *Life in the Son*, 34–35. Shank argues the only way to get around this interpretation is to assume that there are two different servants in view, "one of whom proves faithful, and the other of whom proves unfaithful." However, ὁ κύριος occurs with the demonstrative pronoun ἐκείνους in Luke 12:43, 45 and 46 forbidding "any assumption that more than one servant is in view."

[276] Ibid., 38–48.

[277] Ibid., 66–70.

[278] Ibid., 173–79, 155–83, 235. Cf. also Osborne, "Soteriology," 254.

those who are the elect will persevere. However this amounts to nothing more than saying those who persevere are the elect.[279] Even John 10:28-29, a favorite for advocates of unconditional eternal security, is used by Arminians to promote conditional security. It is true that those whom the Father has given to Christ will never perish (vv. 28-29). However, this is governed by a condition, according to Shank, in v. 27: "My sheep hear My voice and I know them and they follow Me." The believer's security is dependent upon hearing and following (v. 27; cf. also 8:51).[280] Not all agree with Shank's interpretation, however, although no Arminian would argue that these verses teach absolute unconditional security as is often proclaimed.[281] Eternal security is "true only to the extent to which the believer 'abides' or 'perseveres' in God."[282]

A believer's eternal security is also conditional upon their continuance in holiness. Shank maintains that, "The New Testament writers do not contend that 'there is absolute safety and security for the Father's child even while he is sinning.'"[283] Those who manifest the desires of the flesh will not inherit the kingdom of God (Gal 5:21). For this reason Paul exhorts the Galatians not to become weary in doing good "for at the right time we shall reap [eternal life] *if* we do not give up" (6:9).[284] However, this does not mean forfeiture of salvation at the first act of sin, "but of an extended pattern of [deliberate][285] sinning."[286] The flip side of continuing in sin is continuing in obedience. If

---

[279] Shank, *Life in the Son*, 300.

[280] Ibid., 56–60. Similar arguments are mounted by Shank against John 5:24, another well-known verse championed by unconditional eternal security proponents (see 60–63).

[281] E.g., Osborne, "Soteriology," 250–51: commenting on John 10:27–29 Osborne notes that "Neither one (predestination and assurance) is absolute, i.e., accomplished apart from man's decision" (cf. also 254, 256). Osborne disagrees with Shank on his understanding of v. 27, preferring to read v. 27 as statements rather than conditions. Rather, according to Osborne, all one can say about vv. 27-29 is that "it is erroneous to read into this the impossibility of personal apostasy," a statement that Shank would also agree with as far as it goes. See also Gerald L. Borchert, *Assurance and Warning* (Nashville: Broadman, 1987) 121–22.

[282] Osborne, "Soteriology," 254.

[283] Shank, *Life in the Son*, 133.

[284] The participle ἐκλυόμενοι is translated as conditional by ibid., 134 (so also NASB and NIV). Shank also lists Rom 8:6, 12-14; 6:15, 16, 12 (sic), 23; Jas 1:12, 14-16 and 1 John 3:6-9.

[285] Shank seems to assume that habitual or repeated sinning is deliberate for he later writes, "that spiritual death is the inevitable consequence of habitual sinning as a *deliberate* pattern of behavior" (*Life in the Son*, 144, emphasis mine).

[286] Ibid., 135. "Similarly, Paul's warnings against 'sowing to the flesh' (Gal 6:8) and 'living after the flesh' (Rom 8:13) are warnings against, not single acts of sin, but continued deliberate patterns of behavior." Shank points out that the best means of preventing habitual sin developing in one's life "is a firm repudiation of every sin of which we become conscious, in humble contrition and confession before our High Priest" (136).

continual and deliberate sin results in the loss of salvation then obedience is a necessary condition for maintaining salvation. "Keeping His commandments is not optional for men who would enter into life. It is an essential aspect of saving faith."[287]

Some may wonder if this is not a threat to God's faithfulness.[288] However Arminians respond by declaring that God's faithfulness does not necessitate "a corresponding faithfulness in us." For example, the fact of God's faithfulness did not prevent the unbelief of some Jews and their subsequent severance (Rom 11:20-22). Neither will God's faithfulness "prevent a like calamity for individual Gentile believers who fail to continue to stand by faith" (cf. 2 Tim 2:12, 13).[289] Similarly, Judas is cited as the classical exception of an apostate in spite of the fact that Christ prayed for his preservation (John 17:12).[290] As for assurance, like Arminius, Shank believes that "No man who is not deliberately *persevering in the way of faith* has warrant for assuming that he has eternal life in Christ. No man who is not living in *obedient faith* has warrant for entertaining the hope of everlasting salvation."[291] Arminians walk a fine line between God's sustaining power and the need for Christian perseverance.

It is evident that salvation in this view is more than a point of conversion in the past but an ongoing reciprocal relationship between God and man. Eternal security is conditional upon the Christian's perseverance; perseverance is not guaranteed. Thus God is faithful to preserve His children by His grace *if* they continue in faith in Jesus Christ, but a believer can forfeit his or her salvation through unfaithfulness, apostasy or a pattern of continual and deliberate sin.

John Wesley (Wesleyan)

Following his conversion at Aldersgate[292] in 1738, John Wesley (1703–91) unequivocally affirmed salvation by grace (the source), through faith (the

---

[287] Ibid., 219: Conversely, "There is no saving faith apart from obedience."

[288] Cf. G. C. Berkouwer, *Faith and Persevrance*, Studies in Dogmatics (Grand Rapids: Eerdmans, 1958) 219–20, 222.

[289] Shank, *Life in the Son*, 171: "His faithfulness is no unconditional guarantee against either the possibility or the consequences of our own apostasy."

[290] Osborne, "Soteriology," 254.

[291] Shank, *Life in the Son*, 300.

[292] May 24, 1738, Aldersgate, is John Wesley's self-confessed moment of conversion. However, later comments made by Wesley himself concerning this event have given rise to speculation and various interpretations of this event. For differing views on the validity of Aldersgate as a "conversion" experience in Wesley's life see Kenneth J. Collins, "Twentieth-Century Interpretations of John Wesley's Aldersgate Experience: Coherence or Confusion?" *WesTJ* 24 (1989) 18–31. David L. Cubie, "Placing Aldersgate in John Wesley's Order of Salvation,"

sole condition),[293] apart from works.[294] Salvation though was not restricted to mere "deliverance from hell" or even "going to heaven . . . but a present deliverance from sin"[295] and a renewal of the image of God.[296] Grace includes both God's free unmerited favor toward man as well as His power working in us to will and to act according to His good pleasure.[297] Faith too is more than mere intellectual assent "but productive of all good works, and all holiness."[298]

Justifying faith, according to Wesley, is both "a divine ἔλεγχος that 'God was in Christ, reconciling the world unto himself'" (2 Cor 5:19) and "a sure trust and confidence that Christ died for *my* sins." Forgiveness is received through such faith.[299] However, an "immediate and constant fruit of

---

WesTJ 24 (1989) 32–53. Collins understands Aldersgate as Wesley's true conversion experience. Cubie, however, views the event as a continuation of Wesley's Christian life and Aldersgate as a call to ministry. The issues are complex but both agree that Aldersgate significantly impacted Wesley's subsequent teaching and was a cause for a spiritual awakening resulting in a heightened appreciation of the grace of God. Our discussion draws on Wesley's teaching post-Aldersgate.

[293] Wesley, *Works*, 5:8; 6:48; 8:47.

[294] Wesley, *Works*, 5:13, 58–64; 8:53–54. Cf. also Harald Lindstöm, *Wesley and Sanctification* (Stockholm: Nya Bokförlags Aktiebolaget, 1946) 88–91.

[295] Cf. also Wesley's view of justification. "The plain scriptural notion of justification is pardon, the forgiveness of sins" (*Works*, 5:57). Justification for the Reformers entailed a negative element (the forgiveness of sins) and a positive element (imputed righteousness). Wesley understands the former as justification and the latter (but rejecting the notion of imputation) as sanctification (Alister E. McGrath, "Justification in Earlier Evangelicalism," *Churchman* 98 [1984] 223; cf. also George R. Bolster, "Wesley's Doctrine of Justification," *EvQ* 24 [1952] 146–49). Cf. Wesley, *Works*, 5:56: Justification "is not the being made actually just and righteous. This is *sanctification*; which is, indeed, in some degree, the immediate fruit of justification, but, nevertheless, is a distinct gift of God, and of a totally different nature." Justification implies what "God does for us through his Son" while sanctification is what God "works in us by his Spirit." Cf. again McGrath, "Justification in Earlier Evangelicalism," 223: "It is evident that justification [for Wesley] is merely the gateway to the Christian life, and no more—the preliminary stage to the new birth in which generation takes place" (also Bolster, "Wesley's Doctrine," 152; Harmon L. Smith, "Wesley's Doctrine of Justification: Beginning and Process," *The London Quarterly and Holborn Review* 33 [1964] 121, 125; Charles W. Brockwell Jr., "John Wesley's Doctrine of Justification," *WesTJ* 18 [1983] 25). However, Wesley can also speak as though justification and sanctification are the same, although in these *rare* instances he is undoubtedly referring to final justification (see below); "the term *justified* or *justification* is used in so wide a sense as to include *sanctification* also; yet, in general use, they are sufficiently distinguished from each other" (*Works*, 5:56). Cf. also Lindström, *Wesley*, 83–84, 86.

[296] Wesley, *Works*, 8:47; cf. also Randy L. Maddox, "Responsible Grace: The Systematic Perspective of Wesleyan Theology," *WesTJ* 19 (1984) 16. For Wesley's understanding of salvation see Wesley, *Works*, 5:9–12; Lindström, *Wesley*, 105–25.

[297] E.g., Wesley, *Works*, 5:7–8; 9:103.

[298] Wesley, *Works*, 5:12. For a detailed explication of Wesley's understanding of faith see ibid., 8–9.

[299] Wesley, *Works*, 8:48; cf. also, 5:60–61.

this faith . . . is power over sin" (Rom 6)³⁰⁰ so that a believer is now able not to sin (1 John 3:5-6, 9).³⁰¹ (Wesley refutes the suggestion that habitual sin is in view in 1 John 3; rather it is voluntary).³⁰²

If salvation, for Wesley, is synonymous with present deliverance from sin, itself synonymous with holiness,³⁰³ the corollary is that good works will *inevitably* follow in a believer's life. Wesley maintains that, (1) good works *necessarily follow* justifying faith (Luke 6:43); (2) they originate ("spring out of") from justifying faith; and (3) they give evidence to true, justifying faith just as a tree is known by its fruit.³⁰⁴ If good works do not follow faith, "it is plain our faith is worth nothing; we are yet in our sins."³⁰⁵ Pre-conversion works contribute nothing to salvation but Wesley in no way denies the necessity for post-conversion works.³⁰⁶

In fact it is because of his emphasis on post-conversion works that Wesley labors over and over again to demonstrate that faith is the *only* condition of justification.³⁰⁷ Good works follow justification; they do not come

---

³⁰⁰ Wesley, *Works*, 5:214.

³⁰¹ Wesley, *Works*, 5:11, 215. For Wesley this is sanctification, and like justification is gained only by faith. See his *Works*, 6:47, 49, 52–53. Wesley understands both justifying and sanctifying faith as conviction (52), but that is where the commonality stops. The two are essentially different. Sanctifying faith is of the conviction that God has promised sanctification in the Holy Spirit; second, "what God hath promised he is able to perform"; and third, God "is able and willing to do it now" (52). Cf. also, idem, *The Repentance of Believers*, 5:165–66: "Believe that . . . He is able to save you from all the sin that still remains in your heart." Cf. Kenneth Collins, "A Hermeneutical Model for the Wesleyan Ordo Salutis," *WesTJ* 19 (1984) 29–30.

³⁰² Wesley, *Works*, 5:215, 227

³⁰³ Wesley, *Works*, 8:47: salvation, in this sense ("a present salvation from sin"), and holiness, are synonymous terms.

³⁰⁴ Wesley, *Works*, 8:47, 53–55; cf. also, 9:110–17; 5:452–54; see esp. 59.

³⁰⁵ Wesley, *Works*, 5:454; cf. also Bolster, "Wesley's Doctrine," 152.

³⁰⁶ E.g., Wesley, *Works*, 5:454: "We are justified without works of the law . . . but they are an immediate fruit of that faith whereby we are justified. So that if good works do not follow our faith . . . we are yet in our sins. Therefore, that we are justified by faith, even by faith without works, *is no ground for making void the law through faith; or for imagining that faith is a dispensation from any kind or degree of holiness*" (emphasis mine). Cf. also, *Works*, 5:12; 8:56; 9:47–52.

³⁰⁷ Wesley, *Works*, 8:47; cf. also 50–56; 5:8–16; 9:111. Note McGrath, "Justification in Earlier Evangelicalism," 221: "one must ask what Wesley understood by 'justification by faith'. It seems that he adopted the Arminian interpretation of justification, *propter fidem per Christum*, instead of the orthodox interpretation of justification, *propter Christum per fidem*: i.e., that man is justified because he believes, rather than faith as the instrument . . . through which man is justified. However, Wesley does not appear to have understood himself to differ from Protestant orthodoxy on this matter."

before.[308] Repentance "and fruits meet for repentance"[309] come before given opportunity.[310] By repentance, Wesley means "conviction of sin producing real desires" and a sincere resolve for reform. "Fruits meet for repentance" refers to "forgiving our brother" (Matt 6:14-15), "ceasing from evil, doing good" (Luke 3:4, 9), "using the ordinances of God" (Matt 7:7), "and in general obeying him according to the measure of grace which we have received" (25:29). However, for Wesley, these "fruits" cannot be termed "good works" for they do not spring from (and thus follow) faith.[311] This much is clear; faith alone justifies, not repentance or fruits meet for repentance.[312] The thief on the cross is a case in point.[313]

A distinctive teaching of Wesley is his doctrine of "double justification."[314] There are two types of justification, *initial* and *final*. Initial justification refers to "present forgiveness . . . and consequently acceptance with God" while final justification refers to "our acquittal at the last day."[315] He finds support in Hebrews 12:14: "Without holiness no one will see the Lord." Hence holiness, that is, good works,[316] is the "ordinary, stated condition of final justification."[317] Wesley thinks Paul probably refers to final justification when he says, "It is not the hearers of the law, but the doers of the law who shall be justified" (Rom 2:13). Jesus certainly does (Matt 12:36-37).[318] Thus while good works do not precede initial justification they *must* precede final justification for a believer to be acquitted. The tension is evident,[319] but it is

---

[308] Wesley, *Works*, 8:47, 53–55; 9:49–50.

[309] See Collins, "A Hermeneutical Model," 27–29, for a discussion Wesley's distinction between repentance and "fruits meet for repentance."

[310] Wesley, *Works*, 8:47, 57; 9:111.

[311] Wesley, *Works*, 8:47, 54.

[312] Wesley's order of salvation has been the subject of much discussion. What is clear is that for Wesley salvation was a process. See Lindstöm, *Wesley*, 105–25; Collins, "A Hermeneutical Model," 23–37.

[313] Wesley, *Works*, 8:55.

[314] Smith, "Wesley's Doctrine of Justification," 125; Cf. Brockwell, "John Wesley's Doctrine," 28; Lindström, *Wesley*, 119–20.

[315] Wesley, *Works*, 8:46; 5:56–58.

[316] Sanctification, holiness and good works are virtual synonyms for Wesley. Sanctification "implies a continued course of good works springing from holiness of heart" (Wesley, *Works*, 8:47).

[317] Wesley, *Works*, 8:56; cf. also 50; 47: "it is allowed, that entire sanctification goes before our justification at the last day." Also, 9:115: "It is undoubtedly true that nothing avails for our final salvation without καινὴ κτίσις . . . and consequent thereon, a sincere, uniform keeping of the commandments of God"; cf. 5:58.

[318] Wesley, *Works*, 5:57–58.

[319] For an articulation of this tension see Lindstöm, *Wesley*, 83–104, 213. Cf. Bolster, "John

no more apparent—for Wesley at least—than what exists between James and Paul. On reconciling the two apostles, Wesley points out that both are speaking of a different justification, a different faith, and a different works. Paul refers to initial justification, James to final. Paul refers to a living faith, James to dead. Paul refers to pre-conversion works, James to post-conversion.[320]

Because of Wesley's broad view of salvation, he can speak of *two* conditions to salvation. "I allow not only faith, but likewise holiness or universal obedience, to be the ordinary condition of final salvation."[321] Faith alone is the condition for *present* salvation. Obedience is the condition for *final* salvation.[322] Wesley recognizes the tension here[323] but clearly understands that these two conditions are not contradictory but complementary. Thus he responds to his objectors:

> Your last argument against justification by faith alone 'is drawn from the method of God's proceeding at the last day. He will then judge every man 'according to his works.' If, therefore, works wrought through faith are the ground of the sentence passed upon us in that day, then are they a necessary condition of our justification;' in other words, 'if they are a condition of our *final*, they are a condition of our *present*, justification.' *I cannot allow the consequence.*[324] All holiness must precede our entering into glory. But no holiness can exist, till, 'being justified by faith, we have peace with God, through our Lord Jesus Christ.'[325]

Wesley's Doctrine," 152: "good works must follow justification as surely as they cannot procure it."

[320] Wesley, *Works*, 9:116.

[321] Wesley, *Works*, 8:68.

[322] Ibid. It must be remembered that for Wesley, without faith no one can be holy. E.g., "without faith no man can be saved from his sins; can be either inwardly or outwardly holy. And . . . at whatever time soever faith is given, holiness commences in the soul." Furthermore, without God no one can have faith (see *Works*, 8:49; cf. also 5:7). Hence if there is any hint of salvation by works in Wesley it is effectively nullified by the aforementioned remarks.

[323] In spite of the tension Wesley creates between faith and works and initial and final justification, he works hard to defend salvation (initial) *by faith alone* in the face of those who insist that obedience is inherent to faith. Wesley seems to agree with his opponents' armory of Scripture in their assertions (e.g., Gal 5:6; Eph 2:8-10; Jas 2:22), in fact they support his faith/works and present/final argument, but "this is beside the question" to Wesley. It is their conclusion, i.e., salvation is not by faith alone, that he cannot tolerate. See Wesley, *Works*, 8:68–70.

[324] Cf. Wesley, *Works*, 8:47: "Now if by salvation we mean a present salvation from sin, we cannot say, holiness is the condition of it."

[325] Wesley, *Works*, 9:114 (emphasis mine). Wesley is quite lucid even though he walks a fine line between salvation and works. Cf. 115: (Initial) justification is by faith alone, i.e., there is no condemnation for those who are in Christ Jesus (Rom 8:1) provided they walk in Him (cf. Col 2:6; Rom 8:15). If they revert after the flesh, they would again be under condemnation.

Wesley's views impact his understanding of assurance. One can be assured of present salvation though not of future salvation. A pledge of faith in the past does not guarantee salvation in the future. Do not think, "I was justified once; my sins were once forgiven me."[326] This does not mean that Wesley neglects the witness of the Spirit. He doesn't.[327] But the Spirit's witness does not exist in a vacuum for "there can be no real testimony of the Spirit without the fruit of the Spirit."[328] The Spirit does not give assurance to decadent hearts. Assurance is twofold. The Holy Spirit testifies to us along with our own spirit, but the latter does not occur without walking after the Spirit.[329] This is not to imply the absence of sin,[330] but a believer is to repent,

---

"But this no way proves that 'walking after the Spirit' was the condition of their justification." Cf. also *Works*, 5:87–97. Furthermore, that Wesley holds to the primacy of faith is evident in his citation of the thief on the cross. He went to heaven without works but he did not go without faith. Never can it be the other way round (8:55).

[326] Wesley, *Works*, 5:95.

[327] See esp., Wesley, *Works*, 5:111–23, and 123–34, where Wesley defends the witness of the Holy Spirit as the Christian's basis for assurance.

[328] Wesley, *Works*, 125.

[329] Wesley, *Works*, 9:47; cf. 5:17–25. For an excellent discussion of my interpretation on Wesley's view of assurance see Mark A. Noll, "John Wesley and the Doctrine of Assurance," *BibSac* 132 (1975) 161–77, esp. 167–71. Noll describes Wesley's view as a twofold mix of Calvinism and Arminianism. Assurance comes from the immediate testimony of the Spirit and the believer's recognition of the fruit of the Spirit in his own life. (Though Wesley changed his thinking on this subject near the end of his life he still held to these essential 2 elements, see 171–73; cf. Lindström, 119). Cf. also Michael E. Lodahl, "'The Witness of the Spirit': Questions of Clarification for Wesley's Doctrine of Assurance," *WesTJ* 23 (1988) 188–97; Scott Kisker, "Justified but Unregenerate? The Relationship of Assurance to Justification and Regeneration in the Thought of John Wesley," *WesTJ* 28 (1993) 44–58.

[330] Wesley's doctrine of perfection has been confused with *sinless* perfection. First, Wesley adopts the term "perfection" in line with the NT (e.g., Heb 6:1). Second, he understood perfection to refer primarily to "perfect love." However, even this is unattainable: "go onto perfection. Yea, and when ye have attained a measure of perfect love . . . think not of resting there. That is impossible" (*Works*, 7:202). Wesley's writings do not reveal such a thing as sinless perfection. He does distinguish between inward (involuntary) and outward (intentional) sin. The Christian has no association with the latter (see 1 John 3:8-9) (*Works*, 5:146). Once a person is justified "he has the power both over outward and inward sin" (146–47). Yet one can be "carnal" and a "babe *in Christ*," the Corinthians being prime examples (147–50). So there is an already-not yet tension for Christians. Believers are a new creation but not completely (150–55). The reason is due to the existence of "two contrary principles"—flesh vs. spirit/nature vs. grace. This amounts to an undeniable difference between position and practice. If this were not so there would be no reason to pray and be on guard against evil (155–56). For some helpful discussions on this subject see Lindström, 117–19; Robert R. Drovdahl, "Myth of Becoming; Myth of Being," *Christian Education Journal* 13 (1992) 25–32; Geoffrey Wainwright, "Perfect Salvation in the Teaching of Wesley and Calvin," *Reformed World* 40 (1988) 898–909; D. Marselle Moore, "Development in Wesley's Thought on Sanctification and Perfection," *WesTJ* 20 (1985) 29–53; Johnson, W. Stanley, "Christian Perfection as Love for God," in *Christian*

believe and move on, assured that his *past* sins are forgiven.[331]

Salvation-Discipleship (also known as "Free Grace")[332]

While there is no discernible origin for this view, to my knowledge at least,[333] its proponents have become especially prominent as a result of the Lordship Salvation debate in the late 1980s and early 90s.[334] Fundamental to the view

---

Ethics: An Inquiry into Christian Ethics from a Biblical Theological Perspective, ed. Hynson, Leon O., and Lane A. Scott, Wesleyan Theological Perspectives, ed. John E. Hartley and R. Larry Shelton, vol. 3 (Anderson, Ind.: Warner, 1983) 97–113; David L. Cubie, "Perfection in Wesley and Fletcher: Inaugural or Teleological?" *WesTJ* 11 (1976) 22–37.

[331] Wesley, *Works*, 5:94–97. Cf. also 99–111, 112–34.

[332] This view has no specific title or originating proponent. It is close in practice to the Keswick model of sanctification but this label perhaps implies too much. Furthermore, those who identify themselves with what we are terming "salvation–discipleship" do not mention any Keswick affiliation. (For helpful overviews of Keswick theology see esp. J. Robertson McQuilkin, "The Keswick Perspective," in *Five Views on Sanctification* [Grand Rapids: Zondervan, 1987] 151–83; Steven Barabas, *So Great Salvation: The History and Message of the Keswick Convention* [Westwood, N.J.: Fleming H. Revell, 1952]; W. H. Aldis, *The Message of Keswick and Its Meaning* [London: Marshall, Morgan & Scott, n.d.]). Most, if not all, of the proponents of this view are dispensationalists although this does not mean that all dispensationalists hold to this view. Other labels may be just as suitable—"Once Saved, Always Saved," "The Partaker," etc.

[333] Certainly elements of this view have been around for sometime. In the mid-eighteenth century the Scotsman, Robert Sandeman, was strongly influenced by fellow countryman John Glas (see John Glas, *The Works of Mr. John Glas*, 5 vols [Perth: Morison, 1782]). In response to the teachings of the Reformation on works giving evidence to justification, Glas emphasized the simplicity of saving faith apart from works (cf. idem, 1:141–42). Sandeman perpetuated Glas' teaching highlighting intellectual assent as the essence of saving faith. Through his speaking and writing he emerged as the instigator of a new movement from which the name "Sandemanianism" transpired. For the Sandemanians "saving faith" amounted to "a bare intellectual conviction of the exact truth of the gospel message" (Williston Walker, "The Sandemanians of New England," in *Annual Report of the American Historical Association for the Year 1901*, 2 vols. [Washington: Government Printing Office, 1902] 1:139). For the teachings of Robert Sandeman see his *Discourses on Theron and Aspasio: Addressed to the Author* (Edinburgh: Sands, Murray, Donaldson, and Cochran, 1759; reprint, New York: Taylor, 1838). For a critique of Sandeman's teachings see Thomas Jacob South, "The Response of Andrew Fuller to the Sandemanian View of Saving Faith" (Ph.D. diss., Mid-America Baptist Seminary, 1993). Cf. also J. I. Packer, "History Repeats Itself," *CT* 33 (1989) 22.

[334] The concerns raised by the Lordship Salvation controversy are not new, however. The debate arose, or at least was brought to the fore, as a result of a decision made by the translators of the Revised Version of the King James Bible to translate Rom 10:9 to read "If thou shalt confess with thy mouth Jesus *as Lord* . . . thou shalt be saved." Before the revision it had read "*the Lord* Jesus." The controversy raised by this change is brought out in two articles that appeared in 1959 in the *Eternity* magazine entitled "Must Christ Be Lord To Be Savior?" The respective titles betray the view of their authors, Everett F. Harrison, "Must Christ Be Lord To Be Savior? No," *Eternity* 10 (1959) 14, 16, 48; John R. W. Stott, "Must Christ Be Lord To Be Savior? Yes," *Eternity* 10 (1959) 15, 17–18, 36–37. The issue was raised again a decade

is the teaching that people can be categorized into three groups.[335] One of the better-known proponents of this teaching is the founding president of Dallas Theological Seminary, Lewis Sperry Chafer.[336] In his book *He that is Spiritual*,

---

later by Charles C. Ryrie in his book *Balancing the Christian Life* (Chicago: Moody, 1969) 169–81. The debate subsequently continued although somewhat sporadically with increasing attention in the 1980s. See e.g., Walter J. Chantry, *Today's Gospel: Authentic or Synthetic?* (London: The Banner of Truth, 1970); T. Alan Chrisope, *Jesus is Lord: A Study in the Unity of Confessing Jesus as Lord and Savior in the New Testament* (Hartfordshire: Evangelical, 1982); G. Michael Cocoris, *Lordship Salvation—Is it Biblical?* (Dallas: Redencíon, 1983); Livingston Blauvelt Jr., "Does the Bible Teach Lordship Salvation?" *BibSac* 143 (1986) 37–45; Darrell L. Bock, "Jesus as Lord in Acts and in the Gospel Message," *BibSac* 143 (1986) 146–54. So the Lordship Salvation debate has been around for a while. However, in the last decade or so of the twentieth century the debate rose to an almost frenetic level instigated by John F. MacArthur Jr. and his book *The Gospel According to Jesus* (Panorama City, Calif.: Word of Grace, 1988). Zane C. Hodges quickly responded with *Absolutely Free!: A Biblical Reply to Lordship Salvation* (Grand Rapids: Zondervan, 1989) representing the other side of the debate. Hodges had expressed his views earlier in *The Gospel Under Siege*, although eight years on and *The Gospel According to Jesus* in the hands of Christians needing assurance, *Absolutely Free* carried with it added fervor. MacArthur and Hodges were viewed as two sides of the pendulum and various individuals have aligned themselves to either side or somewhere in between. The debate is essentially concerned with the essence of the gospel—What must one do to be saved? What does it mean to confess Jesus as Lord? What is the essence of saving faith? A second and related concern is the relationship between sanctification and justification—Do works necessarily follow salvation? Is there such a thing as a carnal Christian? Will every Christian persevere? The debate between MacArthur and Hodges spawned an unprecedented flurry of books, articles, dissertations, reviews, responses and counter responses not before seen in the days of Harrison and Stott. E.g., significant books including Ryrie, *So Great Salvation*; Robert H. Lescelius, *Lordship Salvation: Some Crucial Questions and Answers Including a Reply to "So Great a Salvation" by Charles Ryrie and "Absolutely Free" by Zane C. Hodges* (Asheville, N.C.: Revival, 1992); Joseph C. Dillow, *The Reign of the Servant Kings: A Study of Eternal Security and the Final Significance of Man* (Miami, Fla.: Schoettle, 1992); Curtis I. Crenshaw, *Lordship Salvation: The Only Kind There Is: An Evaluation of Jody Dillow's "The Reign of the Servant Kings" and Other Antinomian Arguments* (Memphis: Footstool, 1994). Articles and Reviews: S. Lewis Johnson Jr., "How Faith Works," *CT* 33 (1989) 21–25; Darrell L. Bock, "A Review of *The Gospel According to Jesus*," by John F. MacArthur, *BibSac* 146 (1989) 21–40; Zane C. Hodges, review of "A Review of *The Gospel According to Jesus*," by Darrell L. Bock, *JGES* 2 (1989) 79–83; Millard J. Erickson, "Lordship Theology: The Current Controversy," *SJT* 33 (1991) 51–55. Dissertations on the subject include Karl Edmond Pagenkemper, "An Analysis of the Rejection Motif in the Synoptic Parables and its Relationship to Pauline Soteriology (Eschatology)" (Th.D. diss., Dallas Theological Seminary, 1990); Charles C. Bing, "Lordship Salvation: A Biblical Evaluation and Response" (Th.D. diss., Dallas Theological Seminary, 1991); Donald Louis Ketcham, "The Lordship Salvation Debate: Its Nature, Causes, and Significance" (Ph.D. diss., Baylor University, 1995).

[335] Although I am not aware that anyone has stated it this way, it is apparent that this view certainly depends on this basic principle. Cf. Dillow's chapter on "The Carnal Christian," in *Servant Kings*, 311–31.

[336] Lewis Sperry Chafer, *He that is Spiritual: A Classic Study of the Biblical Doctrine of Spirituality*, rev. ed. (Philadelphia: Sunday School Times, 1918; reprint, Grand Rapids:

Chafer suggests three classes of men: "the natural man," "the carnal man," and the "spiritual man."[337] Chafer finds these three groups in 1 Corinthians and each is classified according to their ability to receive revelation. "The *natural man* (ψυχικὸς) does not receive the things of the Spirit of God . . . for they are spiritually discerned" (2:14). It is clear that the natural man is unregenerate. The next two classifications, however, are both Christians. "The *spiritual man* (πνευματικὸς) discerns all things" (v. 15a). And third, there are those who are *carnal* or *fleshly*, a description for which Paul reserves for the Corinthians. "Brothers I could not speak to you as spiritual (πνευματικοῖς) but as *fleshly* (σαρκίνοις), as babes in Christ" (3:1).

The difference between the spiritual man and the carnal man, according to Chafer, is as follows: The spiritual man has "no limitation on him in the realm of the things of God. He can 'freely' receive the divine revelation and he glories in it." "The 'spiritual' man is the *divine ideal* in life and ministry, in power with God and man, in unbroken fellowship and blessing."[338] The carnal Christian on the other hand "is born again and possesses the indwelling Spirit; but his carnality hinders the full ministry of the Spirit." He is "characterized by a 'walk' that is on the same plane as that of the 'natural' man . . . The objectives and affections are centered in the same unspiritual sphere as that of the 'natural' man."[339] In short the carnal Christian is controlled by the flesh whereas *he that is spiritual* is controlled by the Spirit. From this it follows that there are "two great spiritual changes which are possible to human experience." The natural man must become saved and the saved man—if he is fleshly—must become spiritual. "The former is divinely accomplished when there is real faith in Christ; the latter is accomplished when there is a real adjustment to the Spirit."[340]

These classifications are evident throughout the NT. For example, in the Gospels, according to this view, we find three classes of people—the unsaved,

---

Zondervan, 1967), 15–22. This view is certainly not original with Chafer, however. It is also found in C. I. Scofield, *The Scofield Reference Bible*. New York: Oxford University Press, 1967. Cf. also Ruth Paxson, *Rivers of Living Water: How Obtained—How Maintained: Studies Setting Forth the Believer's Possessions in Christ* (Chicago: Moody, 1918; reprint, Chicago: Bible Institute Colportage, 1941). Based on 1 Cor 3:1-4, Paxon's opening sentence states that "There are two kinds of Christians clearly named and described in Scripture" (9).

[337] Chafer, *He that is Spiritual*, 15–22. This notion of separate classes of Christians has been popularized in the latter part of the twentieth century. Cf. also Bruce Wilkinson, *Secrets of the Vine: Breaking Through to Abundance* (Sisters, Ore.: Multnomah, 2001). Wilkinson sees four classes of people in John 15:1-6.

[338] Chafer, *He that is Spiritual*, 22 (emphasis mine).

[339] Ibid., 21.

[340] Ibid., 22.

the uncommitted Christian,[341] and the (committed) disciple. On the distinction between a Christian and a disciple Joseph Dillow explains: "When Jesus calls a man to become a disciple, He is in no instance asking him to accept the free gift of eternal life. Instead, He is asking those who have already believed to accept the stringent commands of discipleship and find true life."[342] The difference between these two classes of Christians is evidently commitment. Likewise, "the conditions for becoming a disciple are different from those for becoming a Christian."[343] One becomes a Christian by faith alone in Christ alone. "But to become a disciple, something in addition to faith is needed, *works*."[344]

Hence the exact nature of the relationship between works and salvation can to a large extent be explained by the difference between discipleship and simply being a Christian (uncommitted). The former is by works, the latter by faith. Only when one confuses the demands for discipleship with the demands for simple salvation does one distort and introduce heresy into Jesus' soteriology.[345] For example, according to Zane Hodges the one thing the rich ruler lacked (Luke 18:22) was childlike faith (v. 17), not the need to divest himself of all his possessions for the sake of the poor. Jesus' invitation to sell up (v. 22) was "an invitation to discipleship," not salvation. The treasure in heaven that would have accrued for the ruler had he acted upon Jesus' request would have been reward, not eternal life. Faith precedes discipleship. For the rich ruler childlike faith would have secured eternal life; self-sacrifice would have secured reward in heaven.[346]

According to this view the two-fold classification between a (carnal/uncommitted) Christian and (spiritual/committed) disciple can be found else-

---

[341] The label "uncommitted" is inferred from J. Dwight Pentecost, *Design For Discipleship: Discovering God's Blueprint for the Christian Life* (Grand Rapids: Zondervan, 1971; reprint, Grand Rapids: Kregel, 1996) 12. He describes this class of Christian as one who has been "challenged and stimulated intellectually without making any personal commitment to the truth that He [Christ] was teaching or to the person of the teacher." Pentecost also uses the terms "curious" and "convinced [by the truth]" to describe the difference between these two classes of Christian. Similarly to Chafer, Pentecost believes that for the Christian there needs to be "a progression from the curious to the *convinced*" (13).

[342] Dillow, *Servant Kings*, 151. Cf. also Pentecost, *Design For Discipleship*, 14, "There is a vast difference between being saved and being a disciple."

[343] Dillow, *Servant Kings*, 154.

[344] Ibid., 154 (emphasis mine), see also 67. For a description of what a disciple is see ibid., 150–56, and Pentecost, *Design For Discipleship*, 10–17. Cf. also Zane C. Hodges, *Absolutely Free*, 168; idem., *The Gospel Under Siege*, 39–50.

[345] Cf. Dillow, *Servant Kings*, 154.

[346] Hodges, *Absolutely Free*, 186–88. For a similar interpretation see Dillow, *Servant Kings*, 64–67.

where in the New Testament—the Gospel of John, Hebrews and James, being prime examples.[347] In John 15 Jesus states that those who do not remain in Him can anticipate the same fate as unfruitful branches that are gathered up and burned (v. 6). According to Dillow this is a picture of a believer who has been deprived of his share in the future kingdom blessings.[348] He is saved but he is not a true disciple. The situation is similar in Hebrews.[349] From Hebrews 3:14 ("We have become *partakers* of Christ, if we hold fast the beginning of our confidence until the end"), Dillow takes the term "Partaker" to describe what the Gospels would call a disciple.[350]

> The Partaker . . . holds to the eternal security of the Christian but . . . believes the warning passages in the New Testament apply to true Christians. The Partaker is the Christian who perseveres in good works to the end of life. He is the faithful Christian who will reign with Christ in the coming messianic kingdom. He will be one of the servant kings. What is in danger, according to the Partaker, is not a loss of salvation but spiritual impoverishment, severe discipline in time, and a forfeiture of reward, viz., disinheritance in the future. For the Partaker the carnal Christian is not only a lamentable fact of Christian experience but is explicitly taught in the Bible as well.[351]

The key ingredient to being a partaker is obedience and perseverance.[352] The partaker is the one who enters God's rest (Heb 4). He builds with gold, silver and precious stones (1 Cor 3:12a). He walks in the light and has fel-

---

[347] See particularly ibid., 311–31.

[348] Ibid., 418–20. Dillow applies this paradigm (i.e., the carnal Christian will not enter the millennial kingdom) uniformly throughout the NT. Cf. also Robert Govett, *Entrance into the Kingdom: Or Reward According to Works* (Fletcher & Son, 1870; reprint, Miami Springs, Fla.: Schoettle, 1978) who argues similarly (although apparently unbeknown to Dillow since he does not appear in his bibliography); see also most recently, Paul N. Benware, *The Believer's Payday: Why Standing before Christ Should Be Our Greatest Moment* (Chatanooga: AMG, 2002); Robert N. Wilkin, *The Road to Reward: Living Today in Light of Tomorrow* (Irving, Tex.: Grace Evangelical Society, 2003).

[349] Cf. R. T. Kendall, *Once Saved, Always Saved* (Chicago: Moody, 1983) 219–28.

[350] This interpretation of "Partaker" however is not new with Dillow. See Hodges, *The Gospel Under Siege*, 82; but even earlier, G. H. Lang, *Firstborn Sons, Their Rights and Risks* (London: Samuel Roberts, 1936; reprint, Miami Springs, Fla.: Schoettle, 1984) 99.

[351] Dillow, *Servant Kings*, 20–21. Similarly, Kendall, *Once Saved*, 200, states that "partakers" "is not a reference merely to being saved but to a lively partaking of the very person of Jesus that makes Him real to us by the Spirit as He was to the disciples in the flesh" (cf. also Heb 3:6); also Wilkin, *The Road to Reward*, 90–91.

[352] On the issue of perseverance, ibid., 200–201, does not attribute a soteriological meaning to σῴζω in Matt 10:22 (cf. 24:13; Mark 13:13). Rather he thinks it refers to a "miraculous deliverance after a most severe kind of tribulation and persecution" (cf. Jer 30:7). By application one can be assured that if they endure to the end "he will not be hurt at all" (cf. Luke 21:18).

lowship with God (1 John 1:7).[353] He inherits the kingdom of God.[354] "The result is heaven *below*—partaking of Christ—and a reward in heaven above." Those who do not persevere cannot be renewed again to repentance (Heb 6:6), sadly for them "no sacrifice for sins is left (10:26) but only a fearful expectation of judgment and raging fire about to consume those who oppose [God]" (v. 27). Non-partakers can anticipate severe judgment, divine discipline, loss of reward, but not loss of salvation. They are forever saved for they have been "enlightened, they have tasted the heavenly gift and have become partakers of the Holy Spirit" (6:4).[355]

---

[353] Ibid.

[354] Ibid., 119–34. Kendall distinguishes between *entering* the kingdom of God (e.g., John 3:3) and *inheriting* the kingdom of God (e.g., Gal 5:21). The point is that one can enter the kingdom of God by faith but forfeit their inheritance by carnality. The kingdom of God, according to Kendall, *Once Saved*, 129, refers to "*heaven below*"; "*the life of God*"; "*the conscious presence of God*" while on earth. Hence, the warnings given by Paul concerning certain people who will not enter the kingdom of God "do not remotely relate to being saved but to . . . the *conscious presence of God*" (see 128–30). To inherit the kingdom of God is to be "filled with the Holy Spirit" (Eph 5:18); to "walk in the Spirit" (Gal 5:25); to adopt the "more excellent way" (1 Cor 12:31–13:13); to have "fellowship with the Father" (1 John 1:3, 7); "abiding in Christ" (1 John 3:6), etc. (see 132). Similarly, Dillow, *Servant Kings*, 62, also distinguishes between inheriting and entering: "not all [believers] will inherit the kingdom." However, while both agree that a believer can forfeit his inheritance (see 69), for Kendall "inherit" pertains to a believer's present experience on earth. Dillow, however, while allowing for present experience, seems to suggest that "inherit" mostly pertains to one's future kingdom experience in the millennium (see esp. 64, cf. 68, 109). "The inheritance in the Bible is either our relationship with God as a result of our justification [Kendall's meaning] or something in addition to justification, namely, a greater degree of glorification in heaven as a result of our rewards." Context must determine whether the present or the future is in view (90–91). Furthermore, inheriting the kingdom is not to be equated with entering it but, rather, with possessing and ruling it ("'to inherit the kingdom' is a virtual synonym for rulership in the kingdom and not entrance into it" [82]). "All Christians will enter the kingdom, but not all will rule there, i.e., inherit it" (62, see also 78). Thus when Paul says that certain people will not inherit the kingdom of God (1 Cor 6:9-10; Gal 5:19-21; Eph 5:5-6; cf. also Matt 25:34, 46) what he means is that they will not *reign* in the eschatological kingdom (68–69). Rather they will be found without proper attire (i.e., faithfulness on earth) at the wedding banquet in the millennial kingdom and subsequently bound and thrown into "the darkness outside" (τὸ σκότος τὸ ἐξώτερον) where there will be weeping and gnashing of teeth (Matt 22:1-14). These Christians will experience profound regret over their carnal and wasted lives and failure to persevere to the end (344–53). Hence "inheriting the kingdom is conditioned upon spiritual obedience and not faith alone" (cf. 2 Tim 2:11-13) (77, 87). For Dillow's entire discussion on the subject of inheritance see 61–110; cf. Kendall's discussion on 126–34, 155. Along similar lines cf. also Zane Clark Hodges, *The Hungry Inherit: Refreshing Insights on Salvation, Disicpleship, and Rewards* (Chicago: Moody, 1972) 96–107, esp. 105; and Govett, *Entrance into the Kingdom*, 168–70; Lang, *Firstborn Sons*, 84–92.

[355] Cf. Kendall, *Once Saved*, 175–83; Hodges, *The Gospel Under Siege*, 75–84.

James also testifies to two classes of Christians.[356] The uncommitted or carnal Christian is synonymous with the "hearers" of the Word (1:22) and "sinners" (5:20). These Christians are "deceived," their religion is "worthless" (1:26) and their "faith is dead" (2:26). Faith will not save this person from premature death (2:14).[357] However the Christian who is a "doer of the Word" will be blessed (1:25) and saved from death (5:19-20).[358]

Whether the category is committed or uncommitted, Christian or disciple, spiritual or carnal, partaker or non-partaker, the conclusion is the same: throughout the NT two classes of Christians can be found. The difference between the two is works, obedience and perseverance. Furthermore, since works do not impinge on a believer's salvation it naturally follows that faith alone is the only basis for assurance. Kendall categorically states, "*Whoever once truly believes that Jesus was raised from the dead, and confesses that Jesus is Lord, will go to heaven when he dies . . . Such a person will go to heaven when he dies no matter what work (or lack of work) may accompany such faith.*"[359] (Though this does not mean that everyone who professes faith is saved according to Kendall[360]). Thus at the final judgment when each believer is judged according to his or her works (Matt 16:27; cf. 12:36; 2 Cor 5:10; Rev 22:12), what is at stake is not their salvation status since justification by faith "shields us from the everlasting wrath of God in hell."[361] The issue is their reward status.[362] Faith may protect a believer from the fire of hell but it is not enough to secure rewards and an inheritance in heaven. A believer may squander his life on earth but at the peril of his enjoyment of heaven. "Loss of inheritance in heaven below means the loss of reward in heaven above."[363]

---

[356] Cf. Kendall, *Once Saved*, 170–72, 207–17.

[357] Cf. Zane C. Hodges, *Dead Faith: What Is It? A Study on James 2:14-16* (Dallas: Redención, 1987) 11–16, 21–22.

[358] Ibid., 12–13.

[359] Kendall, *Once Saved*, 19, cf. 20–33, 49–59. Cf. Dillow, *Servant Kings*, 271–310; Hodges, *Absolutely Free*, 50–52, 174–76.

[360] Kendall, *Once Saved*, 202, tempers his statement later: "But it has to be said that *not all* who initially make a profession of faith in Christ are saved . . . We do people no favor to grant them hope of being saved merely because they have made some kind of profession of faith. For true faith always included a change of mind—repentance" (emphasis mine). Kendall goes on to warn that we are never in a position to judge another's salvation, only our own. Similarly, Dillow, *Servant Kings*, 284 writes: "Only the individual can know if he has believed . . . Certainly the lack of fruit in a person's life raises the question, Does he posses the Spirit at all, or if he does, has he quenched Him? But just as the presence of fruit cannot prove a man is a Christian, neither can its absence deny it."

[361] Kendall, *Once Saved*, 168.

[362] See ibid., 159–84, on "The Judgment Seat of Christ."

[363] Ibid., 169.

Key points from this view are that there is a difference between being a Christian and a disciple. Works are required to be a disciple. Faith only is required to be a Christian.[364] One who is not a disciple has no works and misses out on fully experiencing God while here on earth. At the final judgment all believers will be judged on the basis of their works though at stake is not their salvation but temporal judgment and/or the reception or loss of future rewards. One who has not met the requirements of discipleship can expect to suffer loss of reward although he himself will be saved.

Summary

In summary, most of the views surveyed maintain some role for works in salvation, albeit in differing degrees. *Augustine* is the first major theologian to articulate a clear understanding between works and salvation. On the one hand salvation is by faith and this itself is God's gracious gift. However saving faith will always give evidence to its true nature (cf. Gal. 5:6) and for this reason Augustine cannot say that faith alone is enough to secure eternal life. Works are an integral part of salvation; so much so that he would never think of giving assurance to anyone whose life remained unchanged after their conversion. Thus Augustine delicately holds to the supremacy of grace and faith in salvation while also attributing an indispensable role to works.

In the Middle Ages *Thomas Aquinas* later proved to be a forerunner of the Council of Trent in that he understood salvation as a process of being made righteous for which there must be an infusion of grace via the sacraments. To be sure he believed justification to be a gift from God and grace to be indispensable but this is only the beginning. Justification does not necessarily result in eternal life. Grace is graciously given in order that works may be performed so that salvation (eternal life) may be merited. But while salvation is a reward Aquinas maintained that it is apart from works since the works themselves are only possible by grace.

Central to the teaching of the *via moderna* is the notion that God cannot draw near to man unless man first draws near to God (Jas 4:8). By *facere quod in se est* one can initiate one's own salvation at which point grace is ap-

---

[364] Although even here there seems to be some disagreement on the relationship between works and salvation as it relates to assurance. E.g., on the question of how one can have assurance Charles C. Ryrie, *So Great Salvation: What it Means to Believe in Jesus Christ* (Wheaton, Ill.: Victor, 1989) 143, suggests there are two ways. The first is objective based on the promises of Scripture, faith in Christ. The second is subjective: "Certain changes do accompany salvation, and when I see some of those changes, then I can be assured that I have received the new life." Dillow, *Servant Kings*, 309, on the other hand writes: "nothing more than looking to Christ is required, insofar as assurance of heaven is concerned." Cf. also Hodges, *The Gospel Under Siege*, 1,2, 51–72, for a similar view to Dillow.

propriately infused (thus called congruous merit). Eternal life is not merited at this point but one is now placed in a state of grace apart from which there can be no salvation. Once in this state of grace one must now continue by *facere quod in se est* and thus merit eternal life (condign merit). Crucial to understanding the relationship between works and salvation in this view is God's covenant. It is because God has obligated himself to ascribe meritorious value to works done in a state of grace that proponents of this view deny any allegiance to Pelagianism.

When it came to justification the Reformers stood united in condemning anyone who would attribute any salvific value to works. In short, for *Calvin* and *Luther* there is no relationship between works and justification. It is important to remember though that both Calvin and Luther were occasional writers and wrote according to the battles of the day. Luther especially writes variously on works according to what objectors he is contending with—Catholicism or Antinomianism. But both Luther and Calvin could think of salvation as a process. For Luther justification is a journey. One begins one's journey as righteous but at the same time cannot be said to be righteous. The difference is one of position versus practice. For Calvin, justification and sanctification are two parts of a chain distinguishable but inseparably linked. Hence both Luther and Calvin recognize that salvation while quite definitely occurring at a point in time can also be viewed entirely. It is because of this that they are able to see an inevitable relationship between works and salvation. Works do not cause salvation but they are the unavoidable result.

Arminius also denied any causal role to works viewing them only as a testimonial to justification. Arminians stress that salvation is an ongoing reciprocal relationship between God and man. God will faithfully and graciously preserve His children but on the condition that they continue in faith in Christ. Consequently a believer can forfeit his or her salvation through unfaithfulness, apostasy, or a pattern of continual and deliberate sin. This is the difference between Arminius and the Reformers: the former says that the apostate loses their salvation; the latter maintain they never had it.

Crucial to *John Wesley's* thinking is his doctrine of double justification. One's initial justification by faith will inevitably be vindicated by a final justification based on works. But faith first, then works. Works must be evident since without holiness no one will see the Lord (Heb 12:14). Underlying Wesley's thinking is his insistence that salvation is not just salvation from hell or the attainment of eternal life but also a perennial deliverance from sin. The end therefore matters as much as the beginning.

The *salvation-discipleship* view is unique in the sense that there is little if any relationship between works and salvation. Admittedly there may be some variance on this point but generally the relationship is not between works and salvation but between works and rewards—temporal or eternal. Fundamental to this view is the notion that salvation is synonymous with justification and saving faith amounts to intellectual assent. Thus works play no role in justification and so by definition they likewise play no role in salvation. However works do contribute to the level of one's Christian maturity and demonstrate that one is a disciple. Similarly the absence of works shows that one is not a disciple. Those who aren't disciples will still go into eternal life but without rewards.

The purpose of this chapter has been to articulate how various theologians, eight in total, have understood the role of works in salvation in the history of the church. The one constant in all the views examined is that all without exception attempt to uphold the priority of the grace/faith element in this relationship. The interesting and significant point is that in spite of this commonality, the role of works is viewed variously yet all claim to still hold to the supremacy of grace. In chapters six to eleven I will add my own articulation to this mix, but first, how scholars have understood the role of works in salvation in Judaism.

3

The Role of Works in Salvation in Judaism

Before I discuss the role of works and salvation in the Synoptic Gospels we must seek to understand the theological milieu to which Jesus addressed His teaching. The purpose of this chapter is to discuss and understand the relationship between works and salvation in Judaism and its implications for our present study.

A couple of caveats however are in order before we proceed. First, this discussion is part of a larger debate concerning the relationship of Paul to Judaism.[1] The issues are involved and complex. I shall only mention them here. They include the meaning of "righteousness" and "justification" in Paul, the centrality of justification by faith, the role of the Law, the antecedent of Paul's religion, and the nature of his conversion. Second, a complete study on the role of works and salvation in Judaism would be the length of this book thrice over. Quite simply I cannot do everything that needs to be done in one chapter.

However, we can enter into the debate by interacting with some key Jewish texts that have often been brought to bear upon this relationship. I will therefore begin by contrasting the two positions that have emerged on the role of works in Judaism from the time of the Reformation to the present followed by the reaction from scholars. I will then give my own reaction as well as discussing some key texts in the Jewish literature. I will conclude by outlining some implications for our study to come in the Synoptic Gospels.

---

[1] On the interconnectedness between our topic and Pauline theology cf. Stephen Westerholm, *Israel's Law and the Church's Faith: Paul and His Recent Interpreters* (Grand Rapids: Eerdmans, 1988) 142: "Clearly our review of the place of justification by faith in Paul's thinking about the law must begin with a discussion of the relation between salvation and 'works' in Judaism."

Contrasting Views on Judaism: Martin Luther to E. P. Sanders

Up until the last third of the twentieth century many scholars with few exceptions have agreed with Martin Luther's contrast between Pauline Christianity and Judaism: Paul taught salvation by faith whereas Judaism taught salvation by works. Yet for the remaining third of the century this contrast has been called into question. A "new perspective"[2] has arisen claiming that Judaism never taught salvation by works. No self-respecting Jew believed he could fully obey the Law. Paul either got his facts wrong or he did not say what four hundred years of scholarship supposed him to be saying. In short, "Paul claims that the works of the law cannot 'justify.' But who, the question is now being asked, ever thought they could?"[3]

The answer according to Luther is that Judaism thought they could. Yet many have critiqued Luther's reasoning since his understanding of Judaism had been so prejudiced by his own experience with Roman Catholicism. And while the protestant church has not read Judaism through the lens of Catholicism as Luther (supposedly) did, they have, it is suggested, read Paul through Luther. Comments such as: "the Pauline awareness of sin has been interpreted in the light of Luther's struggle with his conscience"[4] reveal the essence of the problem. It has been suggested that Paul's justification by faith provided Luther with the relief that he needed from his struggle. Hence it was only natural that Luther would view his own dispute with Catholicism as analogous to Paul's beef with Judaism. The result: it is claimed Luther interpreted first century Judaism through the lens of sixteenth century Catholicism. "To a remarkable and indeed alarming degree . . . the standard depiction of the Judaism which Paul rejected has been the reflex of Lutheran hermeneutics."[5] Although not the first to disagree with Luther, in 1977 E. P Sanders brought this debate to a level that could not be ignored. According to Sanders traditional readings of Paul seem "to owe more to Paul and Luther than to an analysis of Jewish texts."[6]

---

[2] The term originates with James D. G. Dunn, "The New Perspective on Paul," *BJRL* 65 (1983) 95–122, and appears virtually everywhere now in discussions on Paul and his relationship to Judaism.

[3] Westerholm, *Israel's Law*, 143.

[4] Krister Stendahl, *Paul among Jews and Gentiles and Other Essays* (Philadelphia: Fortress, 1963) 79.

[5] Dunn, "The New Perspective," 98–99.

[6] E. P. Sanders, *Paul and Palestinian Judaism: A Comparison of Patterns of Religion* (London: SCM, 1977) 296.

It is not my intention to provide any sort of comprehensive overview or survey of this debate,[7] simply the position of Luther and Sanders (and some intervening voices) and the reaction that this debate has spawned. As we shall see, this debate can be approached from two angles. One can argue from Paul or Judaism although many have done both to varying degrees.[8] We are concerned particularly with Sander's depiction of Judaism and although encroachment on matters Pauline is unavoidable, defending Paul is not our chief concern. Treatments on Paul's relationship to Judaism can be found elsewhere.[9] Our concern is with the relationship between works and salvation in Judaism.

Martin Luther's Position[10]

Luther defended what he termed "the chief article of the Christian faith, namely, that faith alone, without works, makes a man righteous."[11] "For if the doctrine of justification is lost, the whole of Christian doctrine is lost. And

---

[7] For a thorough treatment of the research on Rabbinic soteriology see Friedrich Avemarie, *Tora und Leben: Untersuchungen zur Heilsbedeutung der Tora in der frühen rabbinischen Literatur*, Texte und Studien zum Antiken Judentum, ed. Martin Hengel and Peter Schäfer, vol. 55 (Tübingen: Mohr, 1996) 11–49.

[8] The literature in general has been decidedly Pauline in focus with only general consideration given to Judaism (perhaps an indication that there is little left to achieve here). For the first major work since Sanders (and of greater size) on Second Temple Judaism see eds., D. A. Carson, Peter T. O'Brien, and Mark A. Seifrid, *CSTJ*, vol. 1.

[9] For an overview of Paul's relationship to Judaism as the background to Paul's thought see Donald A. Hagner, "Paul in Modern Jewish Thought," in *Pauline Studies: Essays Presented to Professor F. F. Bruce on his 70th birthday*, ed. Doanld A. Hagner and Murray J. Harris (Grand Rapids: Eerdmans, 1980) 143–65. For studies on Paul's teaching on Law and justification in Jewish thought there is a mass of literature. For helpful overviews see Douglas J. Moo, "Paul and the Law in the Last Ten Years," *SJT* 40 (1987) 287–307; Stephen Westerholm, *Israel's Law*, 1–101; Frank Thielman, *From Plight to Solution: A Jewish Framework for Understanding Paul's View of the Law in Galatians and Romans*, NovTSup, ed. C. K. Barrett, A. F. J. Klijn, and J. Smit Sibinga 61 (Leiden: E. J. Brill, 1989) 1–27; P. T. O'Brien, "Justification in Paul and Some Crucial Issues of the Last Two Decades," in *Right with God: Justification in the Bible and the World*, ed. D. A. Carson (Carlisle: Paternoster, 1992) 69–95; Thomas R. Schreiner, *The Law and Its Fulfillment: A Pauline Theology of Law* (Grand Rapids: Baker, 1993) 13–31; Donald A. Hagner, "Paul and Judaism: The Jewish Matrix of Early Christianity: Issues in the Current Debate," *Bulletin for Biblical Research* 3 (1993) 111–30; Colin G. Kruse, *Paul, The Law, and Justification* (Peabody, Mass.: Hendrickson, 1996) 27–53.

The literature in this area just keeps on coming. For a bibliography of most of the significant writing done in this area to date see Jay. E. Smith, "The New Perspective on Paul: A Select and Annotated Bibliography," *Criswell Theological Review* 2 (2005) 95–111.

[10] We are already familiar with Luther's overall position on the relationship between works and salvation (see chap. 2). We need only here to describe how he has understood this relationship within Judaism.

[11] Luther, *Works*, 34:90; 35:363.

those in the world who do not teach it are either Jews or Turks or papists or sectarians."[12] His opponents[13] on the other hand held that "'the article that faith alone saves and that good works are rejected shall not be preached or taught.'"[14] Hence Luther found himself in a controversy not too dissimilar from the apostle Paul. Luther saw "the same thing in the most holy fathers of the church, in pope, cardinals, and bishops" that he witnessed in his reading of Paul's description of the Jews: blindness, obduracy, and malevolence.[15] Whether it was the Jews or the papacy, the problem was the same. By relying on works both groups "retreat so much farther from Christ, from righteousness and salvation."[16]

From reading Romans and Galatians Luther had a very debased opinion of Judaism. He describes the Jews as "afflicted more widely than all the Gentiles" with the sickness of conceitedness.[17] "The Jews boast only about an Abraham who does works"[18] and "imagine that it is the will of God that they should worship God according to the commandment of the Law of Moses."[19] They "boast of the Law and of righteousness."[20] The Law is "good, holy, and righteous,"[21] and so they think "'If I obey the Law of Moses, I shall find God gracious to me, and so I shall be saved.'"[22] They insist "on the Law and circumcision as something necessary for salvation"[23] and by doing so are "denying grace" and take upon themselves "all the burdens of the Law."[24] Hence they know nothing of the grace of God but boast in their own heritage and privileges, proud of the fact that they are God's people. They believe that "they have fulfilled outwardly what the Law demands and forbids. For this reason they do not humble themselves, they do not despise themselves as sin-

---

[12] Luther, *Works*, 26:9.

[13] Luther's comments are directed especially at the papacy but include all "traitors and scoundrels (be they princes or bishops) who have appropriated the imperial name" (ibid., 34:67).

[14] Ibid., 34:90.

[15] Ibid., 47:177; see also 26:454.

[16] Ibid., 26:247.

[17] Ibid., 25:16.

[18] Ibid., 26:246.

[19] Ibid., 26:400.

[20] Ibid., 25:185.

[21] Ibid., 26:251.

[22] Ibid., 26:28.

[23] Ibid., 26:105.

[24] Ibid., 26:111.

ners. They do not seek to be justified, they do not cry out for righteousness, because they are confident that they already posses it."[25]

In Paul's depiction of Judaism then Luther saw in a mirror his own encounter with Catholicism and their "damnable doctrine of penance and works" whereby one is led to "seek salvation through his own works."[26] Even though his gripe was with Catholicism "*All* heretics and hypocrites imitate" Judaism.[27] Judaism and Catholicism merely represented "the self righteous of all ages."[28] The monk thinks, "'The works I am doing are pleasing to God. God will look upon my vows, and on their account He will grant me salvation.'" The Turk, "'If I live this way and bathe this way, God will accept me and give me eternal life.'"[29] Whether a Jew, Roman, Turk, bishop, priest, king, or prince, all are heretics if they subscribe to salvation by works and are unable to be saved because they do not consider "the[ir] spiritual goods and righteous works, worth nothing."[30]

Evidently the only difference between Judaism and Catholicism for Luther was that the former relied on 'works *of the Law*' for salvation whereas the latter relied on 'works.' Yet both sets of thinking amounted to the same thing—self-effort. "If the Law neither justifies nor makes alive, then works do not justify either."[31] The only difference then between first century Judaism and sixteenth century Catholicism was the quality of their works. Both groups "remain disciplinarians of works" and those who do such works "are not Christians."[32]

Dissenting Voices

In the nineteenth century **Ferdinand Weber** gave full expression to Luther's view that Judaism was the antithesis of Christianity. According to Weber "Jüdischer Soteriologie" teaches that "Gerechtigkeit vor Gott zu erwerben, ist die Uebung guter Werke"[33] and "Die Sühnung der Sünden geschieht endlich

---

[25] Ibid., 25:251.

[26] Ibid., 34:32.

[27] Ibid., 25:16 (emphasis mine).

[28] Ibid., 26:251.

[29] Ibid., 26:28.

[30] Ibid., 25:138.

[31] Ibid., 26:333.

[32] Ibid., 26:9–10.

[33] Ferdinand Weber, *Jüdische Theologie auf Grund des Talmud und verwandter Schriften* (Leipzig: Dörffling & Franke, 1897) 284 (microfiche). Weber appeals to such texts as *m. Pe'ah* 1.1: " . . . These are things the benefit of which a person enjoys in this world, while the principal remains for him in the world to come . . . [performance of] righteous deeds . . ."; Sir 29:11-13; *b. B. Bat* 8b; 9a; *b. Ketub.* 67b; *b. ʿAbod. Zar.* 17b (see 284–88). This is a revision

auch dem Wege der Ausgleichung böser Werke durch gute."[34] Weber's (and Luther's) views were given a further boost by one whose writings on Judaism have since been acclaimed as "simply the most important work on the history of the Jewish people . . . published in the 20th century",[35] **Emil Schürer**. According to Schürer "*the entire religious life of the Jewish people . . . revolved round these two poles: Fulfillment of the law and hope of future glory.*"[36] Religion is all about externalism. Obedience to the commandments is of the utmost importance since works are weighed and counted and in the end one's eternal destiny is determined "exactly in proportion to his works."[37] While not all Jews were this way inclined, admits Schürer, the "entire tendency" of Judaism demonstrates an agonizing attempt to fulfill the Law.[38] This view of Judaism continued well into the twentieth century, perpetuated first by **Hermann Strack** and **Paul Billerbeck**'s *Kommentar zum Neuen Testament aus Talmud und Midrasch*. In "Das soteriologische System der alten Synagoge"[39] "Die altjüdische Religion ist hiernach eine Religion völligster Selbsterlösung"[40] so that "Sühnung ist teils des Menschen, teils Gottes Werk."[41] However the real impetus came from **Rudolf Bultmann** who believed that Paul criticized the Jews for laboring under a blind illusion in their endeavors to fulfill the Law in order to attain salvation (cf. Rom 7).[42] Hence "the great error, the illusion, in

---

of his *System der altsynagogalen palästinischen Theologie aus Targum, Midrash und Talmud*, ed. Franz Delitzsch and Georg Schnedermann (1880); see 235–37, 290–92.

[34] Ibid., 330 (see 330–34). For Weber's complete treatment on Der soteriologische Lehrkreis in Judaism see 259–336.

[35] Jacob Neusner, *Ancient Judaism: Debates and Disputes* (Chico, Calif.: Scholars, 1984) 192.

[36] Emil Schürer, *A History of the Jewish People in the Time of Jesus Christ*, trans. Sophia Taylor and Peter Christie (New York: Scribner's, 1896) 4:93 (see 90–125). Concerning a correspondence between transgression and punishment, Schürer cites Weber, *m. ʾAbot* 5.8-9 and *m. Peʾah* 1.1. This correspondence originates, according to Schürer, from Lev 26 and Deut 28. He points to the pedantic expectations given in the literature giving rise to a false sense of piety and hypocritical externalism, e.g., *Shabbat, Erubin* and *Kelim* in the Mishnah. Schürer argues that obedience ensues in merit. *m. Mak.* 3.16: "The Holy One . . . wanted to give merit to Israel. Therefore he gave them abundant Torah and numerous commandments."

[37] Ibid., 4:182 (see 181–83).

[38] Ibid., 4:124, 125: "Life was a continual torment to the earnest man, who felt at every moment that he was in danger of transgressing the law."

[39] SB, 4:3-13. SB also cites *m. Mak* 3.16; *m. Peʾah* 1.1 (cf. Schürer). Cf. also Sir 15:17; *m. ʾAbot* 3.15: "In goodness the world is judged. And all is in accord with the abundance of deed[s]."

[40] Ibid., 4:6; cf. also 3:160–62.

[41] Ibid.

[42] Rudolf Bultmann, *Essays, Philosophical and Theological*, trans. James C. G. Greig, The Library of Philosophy and Theology (London: SCM, 1955) 37–41; cf. also 43. See also idem, *Existence and Faith: Shorter Writings of Rudolf Bultmann*, trans. Schubert M. Ogden (London:

which the Jews are involved," according to Bultmann, is that "man can gain his recognition in God's sight by what he does." It is in contrast to this that Paul presents his doctrine of justification by faith.[43]

Yet while Luther's understanding of Judaism remained largely untouched among the majority of scholars, there were a few dissenting voices. At the turn of the twentieth century **Claude Montefiore** argued that Paul was a Hellenistic Jew prior to his conversion (not rabbinic as many had thought) and it was this cold and calculating strain of Judaism that was the object of Montefiore's criticism.[44] In contrast the rabbinic Jew regarded the Law as a delight and given graciously by God for sanctification and all things good.[45] Boasting and self-righteousness were largely unheard of in rabbinic Judaism[46] since salvation was by God's grace.[47] Faith and works were not opposites[48] but a single whole.[49]

Hodder and Stoughton, 1960) 115.

[43] Bultmann, *Essays*, 45. In addition to SB Bultmann also cites 4 Ezra; *b. Shab.* 153a; *b. ber.* 28b: Rabbi Eliezer's disciples ask him: "Master, teach us the paths of life so that we may through them win the life of the future world. He said to them: Be solicitous for the honour of your colleagues, and keep your children from meditation, and set them between the knees of scholars, and when you pray know before whom you are standing and in this way you will win the future world."

[44] Cf. C. G. Montefiore, *Judaism and St. Paul* (London: Goschen, 1914) 13, 92–101, 126–27, 152–53. Montefiore does not note any Jewish texts directly.

[45] Montefiore criticized scholars for depicting Judaism based on Paul and then citing rabbinic literature as proof texts (ibid., 7, 22). His basic argument was that the Judaism of Paul in AD50 was not the rabbinic Judaism of AD300–500 (see 91) since, in his view, there was no great difference between rabbinic Judaism in AD500 and AD50 (87).

[46] Ibid., 35. Montefiore admits that there were probably exceptions. "In each generation there doubtless existed—and because they existed it is possible to say that Rabbininc Judaism produced them—some proud and self-righteous Jews, some anxious, scrupulous, timid and despairing Jews." However, this cannot be said to be the norm for Rabbinic Judaism. Cf. 154: "There are undoubtedly several Rabbinical utterances based upon this outward, inadequate, and mechanical conception of righteousness and character, and it is not surprising if the Christian commentators have fastened upon them with much satisfaction."

[47] Ibid., 30–36.

[48] Ibid., 77, notes that "The origin of the hard opposition between 'faith' and 'works' will always remain something of a puzzle. But it is much more a puzzle (so far as its development in the apostle's mind is concerned) if we think of him up till his conversion as a typical Rabbinic Jew."

[49] Ibid., 77, 121.

According to **George Foot Moore** salvation in Judaism was never by works[50] since perfect conformity to the Law was impossible.[51] Sin was a sign that one needed to repent not that salvation was lost.[52] Hence obeying the Law was not what made a man righteous but repentance.[53] One who is righteous strives to obey the Law but it is his *sincere intention* to obey and the "strenuous endeavor to accomplish it" that defines a righteous man, in spite of the fact that he may fall into grievous sin (e.g., King David).[54]

Contrary to Montefiore, **W. D. Davies** argued that Paul is not the antithesis of rabbinic Judaism (the distinction between rabbinic and Hellenistic Judaism is a false one).[55] Rather Christianity is the culmination of Judaism.[56] Paul's insistence that Christ had become the new Torah led him to emphasize faith over obedience but did not think of the two as antithetical (cf. e.g., Gen 15:6; Hab 2:14).[57] The real difference between Judaism and Christianity is over their evaluation of Jesus Christ. For Paul He is Messiah.[58]

---

[50] George Foot Moore, *Judaism in the First Centuries of the Christian Era: The Age of the Tannaim*, vol. 2 (Cambridge, Mass.: Harvard University Press, 1927) 94–95: "'A lot in the World to Come,' which is the nearest approximation in rabbinical Judaism to the Pauline and Christian idea of salvation, or eternal life, is ultimately assured to every Israelite on the ground of the original election of the people by the free grace of God, prompted not by its merits, collective or individual, but solely by God's love." Moore cites Deut 7:6-11; *m. Sanh.* 10.1: "All Israelites have a share in the world to come." In an early article, "Christian Writers on Judaism," *HTR* 14 (1921) 197–254, Moore criticized scholars for presenting a false picture of Judaism as the antithesis of Paul.

[51] Moore, *Judaism in the First Centuries of the Christian Era*, 1:467–68, 494–95; cf. also 3:150–55. Moore cites e.g., 1 Kgs 8:46; Ecc 7:20; Prov 20:9; *b. Sanh.* 101a; *b. ber.* 28b.

[52] Ibid., 1:474–93, 495.

[53] Ibid., 151.

[54] Ibid., 1:494–95. The difference then between Paul and Judaism is that for the former salvation is through faith in *Jesus Christ*, the latter through *Judaism*. However since Paul would be unable to convince his Jewish brethren of this (for they too taught grace and forgiveness) he wrote to dissuade his Gentile converts from Jewish propagandists who insisted that faith in Christ was not sufficient for salvation (3:151).

[55] W. D. Davies, *Paul and Rabbinic Judaism: Some Rabbinic Elements in Pauline Theology*, 4th ed. (Philadelphia: Fortress, 1980) vii–xi, xvii, xxiii–xxv, 1–16.

[56] Ibid., xxxv, 323.

[57] Ibid., 221–22. Though, according to Davies, many Jews did in fact rely on merit for their salvation (cf. e.g., *2 Bar.* 24.1; 44.14; *T. Levi* 13.5; *T. Naph.* 8.5; *Gen. Rab.* 35.2; *Exod. Rab.* 2.5; 15.3-5). That Paul was familiar with this doctrine can be seen from Rom 9:5 and 11:28. However Davies cautions that "It would be misleading to assert that the Doctrine of Merits and cognate ideas played a dominating part in first-century Judaism" (272; see his discussion on 268–72). Davies understands the general tenet of Judaism to teach that the Holy Spirit and faith are the source, not the result, of good works (cf. 219–21).

[58] Ibid., 324.

For **H. J. Schoeps** Paul's faith-works contrast "has always been unintelligible to the Jewish thinker."[59] Evidently Paul, influenced by Hellenistic Judaism (cf. Montefiore)[60] misunderstood and distorted the function of the Law within Judaism,[61] reducing it to a legalistic entity[62] and isolating it from its covenant context.[63] The Law was given not so one could *enter* the covenant but so one could *maintain* their place in the covenant and express their relationship to God.[64] Therefore, any "Christian who relied on Paul for information about the meaning and purpose of the Torah as an instrument of the Jewish covenant would receive a picture that was a complete travesty."[65] For Schoeps, the key difference between Paul and Judaism is that *Christ* has brought the era of the Law to an end.[66] It was not Paul's doctrine of salvation by faith that was new to Judaism[67] but that Jesus Christ was the Messiah and it is in Him that people must place their faith.

According to **Krister Stendahl** Luther's own struggle and subsequent relief through Paul's teaching on justification by faith has become paradigmatic for Western Pauline exegesis.[68] Western exegetes have been guilty of reading

---

[59] H. J. Schoeps, *Paul: The Theology of the Apostle in the Light of Jewish Religious History*, translated by Harold Knight (Philadelphia: Westminster, 1961) 202. As examples, Schoeps cites *b. Shab.* 31a: what counts at the judgment is fear of the Lord; and *Mek. Exod.* 15.1: "He who fulfills a commandment in faith merits highest praise before God."

[60] Ibid., 206.

[61] Ibid., 29: This is "explained by the fact that תּוֹרָה in the LXX picks up a more legalistic tone in the translation νόμος." Cf. also 213: "Paul succumbed to a characteristic distortion of vision which had its antecedents in the spiritual outlook of Judaic Hellenism." Also 206: "The tendency to establish a human claim over against God and to replace the Old Testament religion of grace by a human religion of merit is already observable in the LXX."

[62] Ibid., 213; νόμος in Paul is no more than a legalistic "sum of prescriptions" to be obeyed (188).

[63] Cf. ibid., 213.

[64] Ibid., 215: "The people maintain the covenant inasmuch as they observe the laws."

[65] Ibid., 200. "It must ever remain thought-provoking that the Christian church has received a completely distorted view of the Jewish law at the hands of a Diaspora Jew who had become alienated from the faith ideas of the fathers—a view which ignores that side of it connected with the *berith* as a sanctifying ordinance and which has reduced it to a matter of ethical self-justification and ritual performance. And still more astounding is the fact that church theology throughout Christian history has imputed Paul's inacceptability to the Jews to Jewish insensitivity, and has never asked itself whether it might not be due to the fact that Paul could gain no audience with the Jews because from the start he misunderstood Jewish theology" (261–62).

[66] Ibid., 171–74.

[67] Ibid., 206.

[68] Stendahl, *Paul among Jews*, 79.

Paul through *their* own troubled consciences.[69] "Faith and Works, Law and Gospel, Jews and Gentiles are read in the framework of late medieval piety" and religious legalism.[70] In contrast to this picture Stendahl suggests that Paul taught justification by faith in order to explain the relationship between Jews and Gentiles and the latter's inclusion into the messianic community, *not*, as Luther suggested, to explain how one is to be saved.[71]

To sum up, Luther's portrayal of Judaism and Christianity prevailed up until the twentieth century: the difference between the two was simply the difference between faith and works as alternative paths to salvation. Yet this supposition increasingly came under threat to the point where scholars were faced with two alternatives: either Judaism taught salvation by works or by grace.[72] Then E. P. Sanders came on to the scene.

E. P. Sander's Position

According to Sanders four hundred years of scholarship is wrong, Paul is not the antithesis of Judaism. Upon examination of the Jewish literature Sanders concludes that Judaism never taught salvation by works. On the contrary salvation was by God's gracious election.[73] Who then is to blame for this ap-

---

[69] In contrast, Stendahl cites Phil 3:6-15 (cf. Acts 22:3); 1 Cor 15:10; 2 Cor 5:11 (ibid., 12–14).

[70] Ibid., 85–86 (emphasis mine).

[71] Ibid., 3, 86.

[72] Concerning Pauline theology, however, the options are more than two. Either the Judaism that Paul knew was not rabbinic and took on some other poorer form such as Hellenistic Judaism (e.g., Montefiore). Or for whatever reason Paul distorted the Jewish understanding of the Law in relation to salvation (e.g., Schoeps). Or Paul means something different by "works of the Law" and "justification by faith" as many would traditionally understand these phrases. Rather than critiquing a works-righteousness mentality, Paul is critiquing Jewish exclusivity and their desire to hold on to national identity markers at the expense of Gentile inclusion into the covenant (e.g., Dunn). Or perhaps Paul was right in his critique of Judaism (e.g., Westerholm). See further below.

[73] Some of the key passages Sanders' lists to support his argument include: *T. Sanh.* 13.3; *Sifre Deut.* 26; *b. Šebu.* 13a; *b. Ker.* 7a; *Deut. Rab.* 2.24; 1QS3.18-25; 1QH6.8-10; 11.29-32; 15.13-19; 18.21-22: "I know it is for Thyself that Thou hast done these things, O God; for what is flesh [that Thou shouldst act] marvelously [towards it]? It is Thy purpose to do mightily and to establish all things for Thy glory"; *1 Enoch* 92.4-5: "He [God] will be gracious to the righteous and give him eternal uprightness, And He will give him power so that he shall be (endowed) with goodness and righteousness, And he shall walk in eternal light. And sin shall perish in darkness for ever, And shall no more be seen from that day for evermore"; *Jub.* 15.32-34; *Ps. Sol.* 9.16-19: "And now, Thou are our God, and we are the people whom Thou hast loved: Behold and show pity, O God of Israel, for we are Thine; And remove not Thy mercy from us, lest they assail us. For Thou didst choose the seed of Abraham before all the nations, And didst set Thy name upon us, O Lord, And Thou wilt not reject (us) for ever. Thou madest a covenant with our fathers concerning us; And we hope in Thee, when our soul

parent distortion? Ferdinand Weber receives the brunt of Sanders' criticism although Luther is ultimately to blame but still many others[74] receive a scolding along the way.[75] Luther's fault, according to Sanders, was in projecting his debate with Catholicism back on to first century Judaism "with Judaism taking the role of Catholicism and Christianity the role of Lutheranism."[76] The problem is that Paul became the major witness to Judaism.

Sanders, unlike Luther, examined the Jewish sources for himself. And while he readily admits that it is possible to cite *isolated* texts in support of Luther[77] his own study[78] reveals an all-persuasive view: "covenantal nomism." This "is the view that one's place in God's plan is established on the basis of the covenant and that the covenant requires as the proper response of man his obedience to its commandments, while providing means of atonement for transgression."[79] The important features of covenantal nomism are that

> (1) God has chosen Israel and (2) given the law. The law implies both (3) God's promise to maintain the election and (4) the requirement to obey. (5) God rewards obedience and punishes transgression. (6) The law provides for means of atonement, and atonement results in (7) maintenance or re-establishment of the covenant relationship. (8) All those who are maintained in the covenant by obedience, atonement and God's mercy belong to the group which will be saved. An important interpretation of the first and last points is that election

---

turneth (unto Thee). The mercy of the Lord be upon the house of Israel for ever and ever." See Sanders, *Paul and Palestinian Judaism*, 59–428.

[74] Ibid., 2–12, 33–59, critiques an illustrious list of NT scholars for misunderstanding Judaism (Schrenk, Bultmann, Billerbeck, Schürer, Wrede, and Bousset) a misunderstanding which he traces back to Weber and ultimately Luther.

[75] Ibid., 6–7: "the point of the question raised by Montefiore, Moore and others has not substantially influenced subsequent scholarship. Their point is that, *on matters which are essential to Rabbinic Judaism*, such as the way to salvation, the description of Judaism implicit in Paul's attack on 'works of the law' is wrong. Far from this view prevailing in New Testament scholarship, Paul's criticism of Judaism . . . is frequently taken to be accurate and to the point. In other words, there are broad and influential spheres of New Testament scholarship which have not taken up, one way or the other, the point raised by Montefiore and Moore" (cf. also 9).

[76] Ibid., 57.

[77] Ibid., 58.

[78] Ibid., 76–428.

[79] Ibid., 75; cf. also 81–84, 107, 180, 427. In ascertaining the relationship between works and salvation in Judaism, Sanders suggests that there would appear to be two alternatives: either salvation was attained by their own efforts, or that their own efforts were their response to God who had chosen Israel and given them the law. It is this second alternative that constitutes covenantal nomism (81).

and ultimately salvation are considered to be by God's mercy rather than human achievement.[80]

The key difference then between Sanders and Luther is how they understand the Law to function within Judaism. According to Luther obeying the Law *earns* one's salvation; according to Sanders it *maintains* one's salvation. The Law then was not for those on the outside of salvation (Luther) but for those on the inside (Sanders).[81] Rather than being a burden (Luther) the Law was regarded as a sign of God's gracious election and was to be obeyed with joy (Sanders).[82] The reason, according to Sanders, that Judaism paid so much attention to minutiae is that the Rabbis took their responsibility to obey seriously. The fact that the literature reveals teachings on transgression amounting to forfeiture of the world to come simply reveals how seriously they did in fact take their responsibility.[83]

Transgression and failure to obey however did not exclude anyone from the covenant for atonement was available through repentance.[84] Those excluded were those who deliberately rejected God and His covenant.[85] But

---

[80] Ibid., 422.

[81] Ibid., 420: Obedience "keeps an individual in the group which is the recipient of God's grace."

[82] Ibid., 110–11. Sanders suggests that the reason NT scholars have seen the commandments as burdensome is that to an outsider "the laws do seem complex, bewildering, inconsequential." However, we must understand them within a Jewish outlook. "To the Rabbis they could never appear inconsequential, since God had commanded them. Further, for people who lived in a community where many of the commandments were observed by daily routine, the biblical laws as interpreted by the Rabbis would not appear complex or difficult." Sanders compares this to the many rules and laws that exist at an international, national and local level. To anyone who would take the time to study and read all these laws they would appear nothing less than complex and quite formidable. Yet for the average law-abiding citizen, these requirements are not a burden and in fact many of us fulfill them each day without even giving them a second thought. Such was the case in Judaism.

[83] Ibid., 117–47. "The point is to encourage people to obey and not to transgress" (129). To reiterate, "homiletical exhortation should not be confused with basic belief" (181).

[84] Rabbinic Judaism, according to Sanders, readily acknowledged their inability to keep the Law. It was the intention to obey that was important. Ibid., 107–8: One who *intends* to obey acts "with sincere religious devotion. It is not a question of whether or not a man intends that his sacrifice, study or prayer fulfils the commandments to sacrifice, study and pray, but of whether or not what he does is done from pure religious motives and with a mind fixed on God. If so, the quantity of what a man does is of no account; what matters is his devotion" (cf. also 177, 180–82). "The intention and effort to be obedient constitute the *condition for remaining in the covenant*, but they do not *earn* it" (180).

[85] Ibid., 157, 173; cf. esp. 147: "The all-pervasive view is this: all Israelites have a share in the world to come unless they renounce it by renouncing God and his covenant. All sins, no matter of what gravity, which are committed within the covenant, maybe forgiven as long as a man indicates his basic intention to keep the covenant by atoning, especially by repenting of

they are not rejected because they did not earn it. They are excluded because they deny the promises of God. They exclude themselves.[86] Otherwise no amount of transgressions can exclude anyone from the covenant. God has provided for their forgiveness through the cycle of repentance and atonement. To maintain his place, one must simply indicate "his intention to remain in the covenant by repenting and doing other appropriate acts of atonement."[87] Repentance is not a work since it functions within the larger framework of God's "gracious election" and "assured salvation."[88] Within this framework the Law reflects God's desire for His people.[89] Hence "repentance is not a 'status-achieving' activity by which one initially courts and wins the mercy of God. It is a '*status-maintaining*' or 'status-restoring' attitude."[90]

What then of Paul's apparent denigration of the Jews in Romans and Galatians? According to Sanders, as a Jew prior to his conversion Paul never felt the Law to be an unattainable burden (cf. Phil 3:4-7). With his conversion to Christianity came a newfound understanding: *not* that obedience to the Law was unachievable and man's only solution was to be justified by faith in Christ (arguing from plight to solution). Rather, that God had sent His Son to provide salvation for both Jew and Gentile on the same basis, justification by faith in Christ. Since salvation now included Gentiles "works of the Law" could now be rendered obsolete, but not because they do not lead to righteousness but that they lead to the *wrong kind* of righteousness (arguing from solution to plight).[91]

According to Sanders there is some indication of covenantal nomism in Paul. Believers are expected to obey out of love for God. Works are the condition for remaining in the covenant but do not earn salvation (cf. Rom 11:22; 1 Cor 6:9-10; Gal 5:21). Repentance is required in cases of disobedience (2 Cor 12:21) while deliberate disobedience excludes one from salvation (Rom 11:22; 1 Cor 6:9-10; Gal 5:21).[92] In this regard "Paul is in perfect agreement" with Judaism.[93] Yet for the most part Sanders finds covenantal nomism an

---

transgression" Yet "Rejection of even one commandment with the intent to deny the God who gave it excludes one from the covenant" (135).

[86] See ibid., 147–57, on who is excluded from the world to come.
[87] Ibid., 157.
[88] Ibid., 181–82.
[89] Ibid.
[90] Ibid., 179; cf. 178:
[91] Ibid., 441–42.
[92] Ibid., 511–18.
[93] Ibid., 518.

inadequate description for understanding Paul primarily because one remains saved not because he is obedient but because he is united with Christ.[94]

The key difference then between *Paul and Judaism* is not that one taught salvation by works, the other salvation by grace (on this both are in agreement). The difference is in their understanding of righteousness.

> for to be righteous in Jewish literature means to obey the Torah and to repent of transgression, but in Paul it means to be saved by Christ. Most succinctly, righteousness in Judaism is a term which implies the *maintenance of status* among the group of the elect; in Paul it is a *transfer term*. In Judaism . . . commitment to the covenant puts one 'in,' while obedience (righteousness) subsequently keeps one in. In Paul's usage, 'be made righteous' ('be justified') is a term indicating getting in, not staying in the body of the saved. Thus when Paul says one cannot be made righteous by works of the law, he means that one cannot, by works of the law, 'transfer to the body of the saved'. When Judaism said that one is righteous who obeys the law, the meaning is that one thereby stays in the covenant. The debate about righteousness by faith or by works of the law thus turns out to result from different usage of the 'righteous' word-group.[95]

Hence according to Sanders Paul maligns Judaism for pursuing the wrong goal. The Jews pursue *righteousness* through *works of the Law*; Paul urges them to pursue *Christ* through *faith*. Judaism's problem is that they are ignorant concerning God's plan of salvation history. "They do not know that, as far as salvation is concerned, Christ has put an end to the law and provides a different righteousness from that provided by Torah obedience."[96] This explains why "works of the Law" only comes under attack "when it seems to threaten the exclusiveness of salvation by faith in Christ."[97] In sum, what Paul finds wrong with Judaism is not that they disagree about how to receive salvation (Judaism = grace; Paul = grace) or even the means of achieving their goal (Judaism = works of the Law; Paul = through faith). They disagree on the *goal* (Judaism = righteousness; Paul = Christ). In Sanders words, "*this is what Paul finds wrong in Judaism: it is not Christianity.*"[98]

---

[94] Ibid., 514, cf. 520. Sanders (549) coined the phrase "participationist eschatology."

[95] Ibid., 544.

[96] Ibid., 550.

[97] Ibid.: Sanders notes that in and of itself "works of the law" is not wrong. Paul's "fundamental critique" is that obedience to the Law is not compatible with being united to Christ. Hence "Doing the law, in short, is wrong only because it is not faith" otherwise it is a good thing (Rom 2:13).

[98] Ibid., 552.

Reaction to Sanders

Reaction to Sanders in General

While Sanders has had his fair share of critics no one disagrees that his contribution has been monumental.[99] His book has been hailed as "the most influential work of Pauline studies in recent times,"[100] and "a milestone in the history of Pauline scholarship."[101] It has been said that it "is no exaggeration to say that the entire flavor of Pauline studies has been changed, quite probably permanently, as a result" of Sanders' work.[102] Many agree that his work has brought about at least two timely cautionary notes. First, the Lutheran lens through which many have almost unwittingly read Paul has been called into question.[103] Second, many have accepted Sanders' assessment of Judaism as a religion based on grace[104] and with it have given a warning to those who wish to naively attempt to understand first century Judaism based on Paul.[105]

---

[99] G. B. Caird, review of *Paul and Palestinian Judaism: a Comparison of Patterns of Religion*, by E. P. Sanders, *JTS* 29 (1978) 543.

[100] Kruse, *Paul*, 35.

[101] Samuel Sandmel, review of *Paul and Palestinian Judaism: A Comparison of Patterns of Religion*, by E. P. Sanders, *RSR* 4 (1978) 160: "one of the very great works of New Testament scholarship of our time"; Nils A. Dahl, review of *Paul and Palestinian Judaism: A Comparison of Patterns of Religion*, by E. P. Sanders, *RSR* 4 (1978) 154; cf. W. Horbury, "Paul and Judaism," *ExpTim* 90 (1978–79) 118: a "very considerable achievement"; Thomas F. Best, "The Apostle Paul and E. P. Sanders: The Significance of Paul and Palestinian Judaism," *Restoration Quarterly* 25 (1982) 65, "a seminal work"; Hans-Martin Rieger, "Eine Religion der Gnade: Zur 'Bundesnomismus,' - Theorie von E. P. Sanders," in *Bund und Tora: Zur theologischen Begriffsgeschichte in alttestamentlicher, frühjüdischer und urchristlicher Tradition*, ed. Friedrich Avemarie und Hermann Lichtenberger, WUNT, ed. Martin Hengel und Otfried Hofius, vol. 92 (Tübingen: Mohr, 1996) 129: "grundlegenden Werk."

[102] Stephen Neill and Tom Wright, *The Interpretation of the New Testament: 1861–1986*, 2d ed. (Oxford: Oxford University Press, 1988) 424.

[103] E.g., Dunn, "The New Perspective," 106: "to start our exegesis here from the Reformation presupposition that Paul was attacking the idea of earning God's acquittal, the idea of meritorious works, is to set the whole exegetical endeavor off on the wrong track."

[104] Cf. Kruse, *Paul*, 24: "It is now widely agreed that first-century Judaism was not, in principle, a religion in which salvation was dependent upon merit accumulated by obedience to the law, but rather a religion based upon God's election and grace." Cf. also his own comments on 67, 69, 78–80, 225, 241.

[105] Cf. e.g., Best, "The Apostle Paul," 74: Sanders' work "has reminded us of the inadequacy of our traditional picture of Judaism;" Sandmel, review, 159; A. J. Saldarini, review of *Paul and Palestinian Judaism: A Comparison of Patterns of Religion*, by E. P. Sanders, *JBL* 98 (1979) 299; Brendan Byrne, *'Sons of God'– 'Seed of Abraham': A Study of the Idea of the Sonship of God of all Christians in Paul against the Jewish Background*, Analecta Biblica: Investigationes Scientificae in Res Biblicas, vol. 83 (Rome: Biblical Institute, 1979) 229.

Reaction to Sanders' Assessment of Paul[106]

While many agree with Sander's description of Judaism (see below) at least in principle, many disagree with his assessment of Paul.[107] Sanders' Paul, it is claimed, has become so detached from first century Judaism that his teaching would have come across as irrelevant and enigmatic.[108] This has led one scholar to suggest that Sanders has merely replaced the "Lutheran Paul" with an "idiosyncratic Paul."[109] Thus while many agree that Sanders has made a massive contribution to our understanding of Judaism, the burgeoning amount of literature subsequently published on Paul suggests that Sanders has left us no better off in our understanding of the apostle, perhaps more confused.[110] Hence given our new understanding of Judaism a number of scholars have attempted to explain and redefine Paul's critique of Judaism. In general, three main approaches have been explored.[111]

The first of these approaches is that Paul's criticism of justification by works of the Law is incoherent and inconsistent with Judaism's belief in salvation by grace. Paul has distorted the facts. His relationship to Judaism is anomalous.[112] Second, Paul is completely coherent when interpreted against God's covenant with Israel; it is his interpreters who have distorted his teachings. Paul's doctrine of justification by faith rather than being an attack on

---

[106] Once again, it is not my intention to engage in this debate from the side of Paul. However, a brief synopsis is necessary so that at least the debate can be seen in its entirety.

[107] In addition to his assessment of Paul's teaching, many have critiqued Sanders for devoting less than one-fifth of his book (*Paul and Palestinian Judaism*) to Paul (see most reviews). Hence his *Paul, the Law and the Jewish People* (Philadelphia: Fortress, 1983) is an attempt to rectify this imbalance.

[108] Cf. e.g., Schreiner, *The Law and Its Fulfillment*, 94–95, 98–99; cf. also J. C. Becker, *Paul the Apostle, the Triumph of God in Life and Thought* (Philadelphia: Fortress, 1980) 237; Byrne, '*Sons of God*', 233.

[109] Hence, Dunn, "The New Perspective," 100–101.

[110] Cf. the reviews of Sanders, by Dahl, 157, and Caird, 542–43.

[111] Cf. Thielman, *From Plight to Solution*, 20–25; R. Barry Matlock, "A Future For Paul," in *Auguries: The Jubilee Volume of the Sheffield Department of Biblical Studies*, ed. David J. A. Clines and Stephen D. Moore, JSOTSup, ed. David J. A. Clines and Philip R. Davies, vol. 269 (Sheffield: Sheffield Academic, 1998) 143–83; Robert Smith, "Justification in 'the New Perspective on Paul,'" *The Reformed Theological Review* 58 (1999) 16–30.

[112] E.g., Heikki Räisänen, *Paul and the Law* (Tübingen: Mohr, 1983; reprint, Philadelphia: Fortress, 1986) 188: "I cannot avoid the strong impression that Paul actually does give his readers a distorted picture of Judaism. He comes to misrepresent Judaism by suggesting that, within it, salvation is by works and the Torah plays a role analogous to that of Christ in Paulinism." Räisänen believes that Paul does indeed contrast grace with works and that in the apostle's view Judaism is pursuing the Law in order to attain salvation. But Paul was wrong (162–64). For Räisänen's complete discussion on his understanding of the antithesis between Paul and Judaism see 162–98.

salvation by works is an attack on Jewish exclusivity. There are at least three variations to this approach. (1) Paul criticizes Judaism for its adherence to covenantal nomism and its national identity markers ('works of the Law').[113] (2) Christ has replaced the Law as Israel's boundary marker.[114] (3) The cross marks the end of the exile for Israel. Jew and Gentile, now seen as a 'single family,' can partake together in the blessings of the covenant through faith in Jesus Christ.[115] In all three cases the difference between Paul and Judaism is not faith and Law as alternate paths to salvation but that with the coming of Christ the Law is now a barrier to Gentile inclusion into the covenant. The third approach is that Paul is understandable on his own terms[116] in spite of Judaism's teaching on grace.[117] By the way the same has also been said for the

---

[113] Dunn, "The New Perspective,"; idem, "Works of the Law and the Curse of the Law (Galatians 3:10-14)" in *Jesus, Paul and the Law: Studies in Mark and Galatians* (Louisville, Ky.: John Knox, 1990) 215-36. Dunn's main critique of Sanders is that he has not made use of his own conclusions on Judaism in interpreting Paul. The crux of Dunn's argument is that justification and 'works of the Law' in Paul are covenantal terms. Justification is "God's acknowledgement that someone is in the covenant—whether that is an *initial* acknowledgment, or a *repeated* action of God . . . or his *final* vindication of his people" ("The New Perspective," 103–6). 'Works of the Law' represented Israel's covenant markers (Sabbath keeping, circumcision, and dietary laws) by which one *demonstrated* (not *earned*) their place in the covenant. Hence when Paul claimed that no one could be *justified* by *works of the Law* what he meant was that no one could *maintain* their place in the covenant by being exclusively Jewish.

[114] Terrence Donaldson, *Paul and the Gentiles: Remapping the Apostle's Convictional World* (Minneapolis: Fortress, 1997).

[115] N. T. Wright, *The Climax of the Covenant: Christ and the Law in Pauline Theology* (Minneapolis: Fortress, 1992).

[116] Although this does not mean that all understand Paul's relationship to Judaism in the same way. Many scholars may legitimately fit under this approach (even Sanders, 12) although I am thinking particularly of Westerholm: it was Paul's estimation of the death of Christ as being for the sins of the world that caused him to completely replace works with grace as the way to salvation. Judaism however had no such theological grid and was more optimistic than Paul about man's ability to obey God (see esp. 148–50; a summarized version of Westerholm's view appears in his chapter on "Law, Grace and the 'Soteriology' of Judaism," in Peter Richardson and Stephen Westerholm, *Law in Religious Communities in the Roman Period: The Debate Over Torah and Nomos in Post-Biblical Judaism and Early Christianity*, Studies in Christianity and Judaism, ed. Peter Richardson, vol. 4 [Warerloo, ON: Wilfrid Laurier, 1991] 57–74); Kruse, *Paul*: Paul did not attack Judaism per se but his Jewish opponents who insisted on salvation by works (see esp. 67–69, 72; cf. also 80, 296); Mark A. Seifrid, *Christ, Our Righteousness: Paul's Theology of Justification*, NSBT, ed. D. A. Carson, no. 9 (Downers Grove, Ill.: InterVarsity, 2000) Paul rejected the "works of the Law" because they represented a false claim to righteousness, which could only be found wholly in Christ who justifies the ungodly; Schreiner, *The Law and Its Fulfillment*: Obedience to the law ('works of the law') could not bring salvation because one must obey the law perfectly which Paul concludes no one is able to do.

[117] Cf. e.g., Westerholm, *Law in Religious Communities*, 69: "That Jews pursue a righteousness based on law and requiring human deeds is thus Paul's Christian perception of what their conduct amounts to, in light of the gospel; it is not an attempt to portray, accurately and

Gospels (cf. Matt 23:4; Mark 7:6).[118] This last approach is perhaps not as far from Luther as has been proposed.[119]

Reaction to Sanders' Assessment of Judaism

> It must be admitted . . . that Sanders has made his principal negative case: that Christian scholars have distorted the reality of first-century Judaism. It is the great merit of Sanders' work to have drawn attention to the repeated efforts of Jewish scholars to correct this picture . . . After *Paul and Palestinian Judaism*, it should never again be possible to represent the view of first-century Judaism on a particular subject merely by citing the rabbinic passages mentioned at the appropriate spot in Strack-Billerbeck. To put the matter sharply, no work which handles first-century and rabbinic Judaism merely at the level of Strack-Billerbeck's *Kommentar* and Kittel's *Theological Dictionary of the New Testament* should be accepted for publication.[120]

While some may want to quibble with details of this statement, the three approaches to Paul I have mentioned above are all in general agreement with Sander's overall assessment of Judaism.[121] However, it is the third approach

---

objectively, the self-understanding of Contemporary Jews. Distortion enters the picture when the character of his writing as a Christian theology is forgotten, and the conclusion is drawn that Judaism itself distinguishes law from grace and opts for the former."

[118] Cf. Donald Hagner, *The Jewish Reclamation of Jesus: An Analysis and Critique of Modern Jewish Study of Jesus* (Grand Rapids: Zondervan, 1984) 171. Hagner accepts the authenticity of Judaism's belief in salvation by grace as well as the portrait presented in the Gospels. "In the final analysis, there is no necessity of a forced choice between the positive view of Pharisaism from the rabbinic literature and the (mainly) negative view from the Gospels" (189). He suggests that one way to explain the apparent anomaly is that the hyperbolic statements about the Pharisees make "it appear as though Pharisaism universally was corrupt." However, the real disagreement, according to Hagner, between the Pharisees and Jesus was not between outer and inner righteousness but that in Jesus was the kingdom of God (189–90). Similarly we could perhaps compare here those who have suggested that the difference between Paul and Judaism is not that of faith and works but that Jesus is the Messiah (e.g., Davies).

[119] See esp. Schreiner, *The Law and Its Fulfillment*; idem, "Israel's Failure to Attain Righteousness in Romans 9:30–10:3," *TJ* 12 (1991) 214–20; see also idem, "Is Perfect Obedience to the Law Possible? A Re-examination of Galatians 3:10," *JETS* 27 (1984) 151–60; Mark A. Seifrid, "Blind Alleys in the Controversy Over the Paul of History," *TynBul* 45.1 (1994) 73–95; also Hagner, "Paul and Judaism," 122.

[120] Best, "The Apostle Paul," 71.

[121] E.g., Westerholm, *Israel's Law*, 142: "it is misleading to represent Judaism as a religion of 'works-salvation'"; 150: to define Judaism as the antithesis of Paul is a "methodological error" and a "distortion" which Judaism knew nothing of (cf. also Schreiner, *The Law and Its Fulfillment*, 114). Donald A. Hagner, *The Jewish Reclamation of Jesus*, 171, notes that the Gospels also have played their part in misrepresenting Judaism (cf. Matt 23:4; Mark 7:6). "It IS REGRETTABLE, but true, that the Gospels are responsible for the consistently negative view of the Pharisees that has become so widespread among Christians, a view in which 'Pharisee'

that has been the most forthcoming in suggesting modifications. Generally speaking Sanders' representation of Judaism is regarded as overly simplistic.[122] For while Judaism may not have been a legalistic religion *in principle* it does not necessarily follow that there may not have been legalistic Jews *in practice*.[123] There have been many suggestions as to how a situation like this and the one Paul confronted might have come about. Colin Kruse suggests that, "the Jewish texts upon which our understanding of first-century Judaism rests reflect a spectrum of attitudes to the role of the Law in soteriology."[124] Sometimes obedience to the Law is stressed and sometimes God's grace and election. This is not to say that Law and grace are opposites but simply that from a human point of view "there is always a tendency among devout people to focus upon obligations at the expense of grace."[125] This does not deny that Judaism taught salvation by grace[126] but simply that such a phenomenon can happen and evidently did happen. Sanders, it seems, has assumed that what Judaism taught is what Jews practiced. Yet it has been observed that still after two thousand years of Christian writings and proclamation the careful articulation of grace has not prevented legalism from creeping into the church. Even the written doctrine of the Roman Catholic Church was at odds with what Luther observed happening in practice.[127] One can easily see then how

---

has become synonymous with 'hypocrite.'" See Hagner's discussion on "grace and works," (191–99).

[122] Jacob Neusner is especially critical. See esp. his *Judaic Law from Jesus to the Mishnah: A Systematic Reply to Professor E. P. Sanders*, South Florida Studies in the History of Judaism, ed. Jacob Neusner et al., no. 84 (Atlanta: Scholars, 1993) 49–78, 275–95. Cf. idem, *Judaism and Its Social Metaphors: Israel in the History of Jewish Thought* (Cambridge: Cambridge University Press, 1989).

[123] Kruse, *Paul*, 296: "While first-century Judaism may have taught that, *in principle*, inclusion among the people of God depended upon God's election and grace and not upon the observance of the law, *in practice* that teaching often degenerated into something else."

[124] Ibid.

[125] Ibid. Cf. also Hagner, *The Jewish Reclamation of Jesus*, 189. Caird, review, 539, criticizes Sanders for confining his understanding of legalism to soteriology. "But there are other broader senses of legalism, and Sander's argument does little to disperse the impression which the Mishnah regularly makes on non-Jewish readers, that the Rabbis were deeply preoccupied with legal minutiae, almost to the exclusion of other concerns."

[126] E.g., Kruse, *Paul*, 241: "That Paul says the Jews pursued the law for righteousness [in Rom 9:30-31] does not need to be construed in such a way as to imply that Judaism in his day was *by definition* a legalistic religion, or that pious Jews were all intent upon amassing merit by keeping the law . . . It was when obedience to the law was over-emphasized at the expense of God's saving grace that covenantal nomism degenerated into the legalism which the apostle attacked . . . In Paul's view, many Jews of his day . . . had fallen into the trap of believing justification could be attained by carrying out what the law required."

[127] Schreiner, *The Law and Its Fulfillment*, 115, 119.

legalism could have made its way into a grace-based religion such as Judaism. Donald Hagner articulates the same point.

> In its best theology, Judaism *is* a religion of grace. Often, however, its gracious foundations are tacitly assumed and often the law takes a place of overwhelming priority. It is not surprising if a religion whose heart lies in praxis rather than theory (theology) a religion dominated by nomism, where the covenant is more presupposed than articulated, inadvertently produces followers who fall into a legalistic mode of existence [cf. e.g., 4 Ezra] . . . A covenantal nomism will only remain 'covenantal' where very deliberate and explicit measures are taken to guard it as such; there will otherwise be a natural human tendency toward legalism.[128]

According to Hagner the Law began to assume a place of undue emphasis only after the exile.[129] Hence a certain amount of paradox between grace and works in Judaism can possibly be explained by the mere fact that Judaism represents continuity with the OT religion of grace yet began out of a renewed commitment to the Law.[130]

Along similar lines Stephen Westerholm has suggested that while Judaism may not have been ignorant of God's grace they did not share Paul's *exclusive* reliance on it.[131] Based on texts such as Leviticus 18:5,[132] Deuteronomy 30:15-18,[133] Ezekiel 20:11,[134] Westerholm suggests that at least in principle

---

[128] Hagner, "Paul and Judaism," 118–19; cf. also idem, "Salvation, Faith, Works," *Reformed Journal* 29 (1979) 26: "Sanders' accurate description of the true pattern of religion in Palestinian Judaism need not eliminate the probability that some of its adherents tended toward a legalism which sometimes had the effect of canceling out the gracious activity of God . . . Adherents of a religious faith seldom reflect the balance of its theology holistically conceived, but will often in practice stress a leading motif to the virtual exclusion of counterbalancing aspects that are really present in the theology."

[129] Hagner, "Paul and Judaism," 117.

[130] Ibid.: "It is a good question to what extent the rabbis or proto-rabbis of the first century assumed and articulated the grace that is foundational to the religion of their OT forebears . . . . one must note not only the lack of systematic thinking but the presence of . . . contradictory opinions."

[131] Westerholm, *Israel's Law*, 148, 150.

[132] "Keep my decrees and laws, for the man who obeys them will live by them. I am the Lord" (NIV).

[133] "See, I set before you today life and prosperity, death and destruction. For I command you today to love the Lord your God, to walk in his ways, and to keep his commands, decrees and laws; then you will live and increase, and the Lord your God will bless you in the land you are entering to possess. But if your heart turns away and you are not obedient, and if you are drawn away to bow down to other gods and worship them, I declare to you this day that you will certainly be destroyed. You will not live long in the land you are crossing the Jordon to enter and possess" (NIV).

[134] "I gave them my decrees and made known to them my laws, for the man who obeys them

both Paul (cf. Rom 2:13; 7:10; 10:5) and Judaism believed that keeping the Law could bring life. Hence "If Paul is wrong in considering the law a path to salvation, it is an error he shares with Leviticus, Deuteronomy, and Ezekiel."[135] Similarly Thomas Schreiner has described Judaism's soteriology as being "synergistic,"[136] that is, salvation by grace *and* works.[137]

Reaction to Sanders' Method

I will consider these claims—that Judaism was not as grace orientated as Sanders contends—in more detail momentarily, but first a brief synopsis regarding some reactions to Sander's method. In addition to his content Sanders' hermeneutic has also been heavily criticized.[138] His Judaism, according to some, goes beyond the texts[139] being influenced more by Christian the-

---

will live by them" (NIV).

[135] Westerholm, *Israel's Law*, 145–47.

[136] Cf. also Robert H. Gundry, "Grace, Works, and Staying Saved in Paul," *Bib* 66 (1985) 36. For evidence of the tension between grace and works in the Jewish writings see D. A. Carson, *Divine Sovereignty and Human Responsibility: Biblical Perspectives in Tension*, New Foundations Theological Library, ed. Peter Toon (Atlanta: John Knox, 1981) esp. 49–53, 68–74, 104–9. See Carson's critique of Sanders on 86–95.

[137] Schreiner, *The Law and Its Fulfillment*, 98: "Thus at the heart of legalism rests the delusion that human beings are good, and that their works can be sufficient." This is due to Judaism's optimism about man's ability to do good (94). Schreiner (115–19) uses the same evidence Sanders uses to argue for covenantal nomism "to support the idea that Palestinian Judaism was legalistic." He points out three elements from Sanders' work that suggests the presence of legalism in Tannaitic Judaism. (1) The vast number of laws and the associated minutiae documented in the Mishnah. "When people begin to stress complex and detailed prescriptions for obedience, then the primacy of grace is threatened, even if the specific laws are viewed as a divine gift." (2) The near absence of reference to the covenant in the Jewish literature. Sanders argues that the covenant is hardly mentioned because it is always presupposed. However, "when one combines the failure to mention the covenant with the emphasis on obeying the detailed prescriptions of the law, one has a recipe for legalism . . . Any theology that claims to stress God's grace but rarely mentions it and that elaborates human responsibility in detail inevitably becomes legalistic in practice, if not in theory." The fact remains that the notion that Judaism emphasized the covenant cannot be defended from the literature, whereas that legalism was a problem with the opponents of Paul and Jesus can. (3) "The rabbinic explanation of election." The rabbis explained that the covenant was offered to all nations but only Israel accepted it. And, second, Israel was chosen based on the meritorious work of their fathers. Both these explanations reveal a legalistic and boastful attitude. (The Rabbis give a third explanation, namely that God chose Israel for his name's sake). Paul, on the other hand gives no credit to merit of any sort on his explanation of Israel's election in Romans 9.

[138] Rieger, "Eine Religion der Gnade," 145–46; Beverly Roberts Gaventa, "Comparing Paul and Judaism: Rethinking our Methods," *Biblical Theology Bulletin* 10 (1980) 37–44.

[139] Jacob Neusner, *Paradigms in Passage: Patterns of Change in the Contemporary Study of Judaism*, Studies in Judaism, ed. Jacob Neusner et al. (Lanham, Md.: University Press of America, 1988) 175–95 (esp. 179–80). Cf. also Saldarini, review, 300; George Brooke, review

ology than anything found in the Jewish literature.[140] His covenantal nomism is supposed to be all-pervasive and yet the term "covenant" hardly appears in the literature.[141] This has led at least one scholar to accuse Sanders of being inconsistent. Sanders' Judaism has no room for merit soteriology yet this is also a concept that is relatively infrequent in the literature.[142]

Judaism: A Religion of Grace or Works?

As we have seen, scholars over the last third of the twentieth century and now into the twenty-first century have spilt much ink writing on the "New Perspective" which, while referring as much to Judaism as Paul, has mainly focused on the latter. True, reaction to Sanders' assessment of Judaism has not remained absent from the discussions but by and large the treatments have been very general. Certainly nothing has come close to Sander's 1977 voluminous effort in size, stature, or comprehensiveness. That is until recently. I

---

of *Paul and Palestinian Judaism. A Comparison of Patterns of Religion*, by E. P. Sanders, *Journal of Jewish Studies*, 30 [1979] 248–49). Sanders himself recognizes the infrequent appearance of the term "covenant" in the Jewish literature although contends that the concept of covenant is so much of an underlying conviction that it would have been superfluous to reiterate it (Sanders, *Paul and Palestinian Judaism*, 420–21).

[140] Note esp. Jacob Neusner, "Comparing Judaisms," *History of Religions* 18 (1978) 179–81: "Sanders does not come to Rabbinic Judaism to uncover the issues of Rabbinic Judaism. He brings to the Rabbinic sources the issues of Pauline scholarship and Paul." As a result "Sanders does not describe Rabbinic Judaism through the systematic categories yielded by its principal documents." Instead "what he has done . . . is to impose the pattern of one religious expression, Paul's, upon the description of another, that of the Tannaitic-Rabbinical sources." He "has not asked what is important and central in the system of Tannaitic-Rabbinic writings. All he wants to know is what, in those writings, addresses questions of interest to Paul." (I should point out that Neusner does not disagree with Sanders' assessment of Judaism, his critique concerns more his method [i.e., "systematic comparison"]). On this basis, Neusner concludes that, "in regard to Rabbinic Judaism, Sanders's book . . . is so profoundly flawed as to be hopeless and . . . useless in accomplishing its stated goals of systematic description and comparison." Cf. Rieger, "Eine Religion der Gnade," 148: "Folgt Sanders hier wirklich den Texten order mehr der Denkstruktur seiner Gegner . . . ?"

[141] Best, "The Apostle Paul," 72–73; cf. also Nicholas King, "E. P. Sanders, *Paul and Palestinian Judaism: A Comparison of Patterns of Religion*," *Bib* 61 (1980) 143; Brooke, review, 248–49.

[142] Ibid: Sanders "uses the argument from silence to cut" both ways. I should probably also note here Byrne's ('*Sons of God*', 232) criticism of Sanders vis-à-vis comparing Judaism, a religion still anticipating the age to come, with Paul for whom the age to come has already arrived in Jesus the Messiah. Hence "Paul represents a Judaism *one stage ahead* of Palestinian Judaism in the apocalyptic programme." For Paul righteousness has *already* been fulfilled in Christ and therefore not to be sought in works of the Law (cf. Rom 3:21). Therefore Paul's "'righteousness' language is precisely that of Judaism where he speaks of the righteousness appropriate to the time before the eschaton. Where he proclaims the arrival of the eschaton in Christ, he necessarily speaks of the failure of that righteousness and the availability of righteousness from a new source—God's gracious gift" (233).

am referring to two major contributions to this debate, the first by Friedrich Avemarie, *Tora und Leben: Untersuchungen zur Heilsbedeutung der Tora in der frühen rabbinischen Literatur*.[143] The second is the first volume of a two volume series: Justification and Variegated Nomism: *The Complexities of Second Temple Judaism*, edited by D. A. Carson and others.

I shall look at each of these contributions shortly. First it is evident from our discussion that although Sanders' conclusions have brought a much needed corrective to understanding the relationship between works and salvation in Judaism, there is growing consensus that his position has simply taken us to the other extreme of Weber and others. The likes of Westerholm and Schreiner have indicated a more moderate position and while many may disagree on particulars a growing number of scholars have come to similar conclusions. Mark Seifrid is one for example. He has suggested that rather than producing a harmonious theology, "the rabbis viewed salvation from (at least) . . . two independent perspectives." To put it another way "covenantalism" exists alongside "nomism" but not in the integrated way Sanders suggests.[144] Seifrid's conclusion is probably representative, broadly speaking, of scholarly opinion at the turn of the twenty-first century. Hence the pendulum seems to have swung from one extreme (Luther, Weber, etc.) to the other (Moore, Sanders, etc.) and perhaps is now settling somewhere in the middle. Avemarie and *CSTJ* represent this 'middle' or third position.[145]

Friedrich Avemarie: Tora Und Leben

The purpose of Avemarie's study is to examine "die Bedeutung der Tora und ihrer Gebote im soteriologischen Kontext [in der frühen rabbinischen Literatur]." In brief he concludes that the role played by the Law "in den frühen rabbinischen Heilsvorstellungen" is diverse.[146] Salvation can be on the

---

[143] Cf. also Friedrich Avemarie, "Erwählung und Vergeltung: Zur optionalen Struktur rabbinischer Soteriologie," *NTS* 45 (1999) 108–13.

[144] Mark Seifrid, "The 'New Perspective on Paul' and its Problems," *Them* 25 (2000) 5.

[145] Though in lumping them both together I am not suggesting they agree on all points or even agree on how to describe the relationship between works and salvation in Judaism. In fact as we shall see both agree that this relationship cannot be described as easily as either Weber or Sanders had thought. According to both, Judaism is much more complex. In this regard both can legitimately be located somewhere in the middle of the two (although of course we should bear in mind that *CSTJ* has been compiled by various authors and therefore exhibits a variety of conclusions).

[146] Avemarie, *Tora und Leben*, 3.

basis of grace or obedience to the Law.[147] That it is by the latter though is found "in allen Schichten der frühen rabbinischen Literatur."[148]

According to Avemarie the relationship between election and Law in rabbinic Judaism presents a "Spannung, die sich kaum auflösen lassen dürfte."[149] In Avemarie's mind Sanders does not adequately explain this tension. His "Modell liefert für jene Formulierungen ebensowenig eine befriedigende Erklärung wie das von Weber und Billerbeck."[150] Rather both views are open to criticism. Avemarie concludes, "Rabbinische Soteriologie basiert auf zwei konträren Prinzipien [i.e., Erwählung und Vergeltung or Gerechtigkeit und Barmherzigkeit], zwischen denen es kein festes Verhältnis gibt, so dass sie in immer wieder anderen Proportionen mit-, gegen- oder auch ohneeinander zur Geltung gebracht werden können."[151] *Mishnah Sanhedrin* 10.1 is a case in point where "die Heilsbedeutung der Zugehörigkeit zu Israel" is expressed: "All Israelites have a share in the world to come, as it is said, *Your people also shall be all righteous, they shall inherit the land forever; the branch of my planting, the work of my hands, that I may be glorified* (Isa 60:21)."[152] "Der Dissens in der Forschung bricht nicht darüber auf, dass es beide Vorstellungen, Heil durch Erwählung und Heil durch Vergeltung, bei den Rabbinen tatsächlich gibt. Das Faktum selbst wurde, soweit ich sehe, nie ernsthaft bestritten; die Bundesnomismus-Theorie von Sanders integriert die beiden Vorstellungen ebenso wie das vormals klassische System der rabbinischen Soteriologie nach Weber und Billerbeck, auch wenn das leicht übersehen werden kann."[153]

Leviticus 18:5 ("You shall therefore keep My statutes and My ordinances, by which the man who does them shall live, I am Yahweh") is a key text in the development of the notion that salvation or life could be attained by obedience to the Law.[154] The verb חיה ("to live") is interpreted in the rabbinic tradition to refer to either this life[155] or eternal life.[156] For the latter

---

[147] See ibid., 575–84; idem, "Erwählung und Vergeltung," 108–26.
[148] Avemarie, *Tora und Leben*, 382, and cf. 383–99, for a discussion on these texts.
[149] Ibid., 382.
[150] Ibid., cf. also idem, "Erwählung und Vergeltung," 108–13.
[151] Ibid., 126.
[152] Ibid., 110; cf. also idem, *Tora und Leben*, 43–44.
[153] Avemarie, "Erwählung und Vergeltung," 111.
[154] See Avemarie, *Tora und Leben*, 376–445.
[155] Ibid., 379–80: "nicht einfach das geschöpfliche Dasein des Menschen zwischen Geburt und Tod" but "Es ist Leben, das das alltägliche Dasein übersteigt . . . eigentliches Leben" and "eine Steigerung des irdischen Daseins, dessen Erfüllung in Wohlstand, Frieden, Gesundheit, Glück und der Abwesenheit von Not und Sorge ist"; cf. *m. ʾAbot* 2.7 A and B.
[156] Ibid., 377. How one can interpret "live" as eternal life can be seen from *Sifra* Aharé Mot 8.10 on Lev 18:5: "'. . . shall live': in the world to come. And should you wish to claim that the

interpretation *Sifra* Aharé Mot 8.10 reasons for example that the phrase "shall live" refers to "the world to come. And should you wish to claim that the reference is to this world, is it not the fact that in the end one dies? Lo, how am I to explain, '. . . shall live'? It is with reference to the world to come." The classic texts for which keeping "die Schrift" promises a long life are Exodus 20:12 ("Honor your father and mother that your days may be long in the land which Yahweh your God gives you") Deuteronomy 5:16 ("Honor your father and mother as Yahweh your God commanded you that your days may be prolonged and that it may go well with you in the land which Yahweh your God gives you") and 22:7 ("You shall let go the mother but the young you may take to yourself that it may go well with you and that you may live long").[157] In a similar way to Leviticus 18:5 "life" in these texts came to mean eternal life. For example Deuteronomy 22:7 understands *Targum Pseudo-Jonathan* as, "You shall surely send away the mother (first) and then take the young for yourself, in order that it may go well with you *in this world* and your days be lengthened *in the world to come*."[158] *Tosefta Hullin* 10.16 makes a similar argument vis-à-vis Deuteronomy 22:7.[159]

Hence it is not difficult to see how a relationship between obedience and "Leben in der kommenden Welt" eventually developed.[160] This present earthly life (i.e., as "eigentliches Leben") and eternal life are viewed as rewards or wages for obedience to God's commands.[161] "Gelegentlich werden in der rabbinischen Literatur 'Leben' und 'Lohn' sogar als austauschbare Begriffe gehandhabt" (cf. e.g., *m. Mak.* 3.15).[162] The Law is observed as the means to life.[163] Many texts articulate this relationship. Studying the Torah "provides for [your] eternal sustenance [in the World to Come]" (*y. Ber.* 7.1).[164] Rabbi

---

reference is to this world, is it not the fact that in the end one dies? Lo, how am I to explain, '. . . shall live'? It is with reference to the world to come." See Avemarie, *Tora und Leben*, 390–91, for his discussion on this text.

[157] Ibid., 377.

[158] See ibid., 378–79, for other references concerning the relationship between obedience to the Torah and life in the world to come.

[159] Ibid., 386–88.

[160] Ibid., 377; cf. also 104–17.

[161] Cf. ibid., 380. E.g., *Sifra* Aharé Mot 8:11 on Lev 18:5: "'I am the Lord your God': faithful to pay a reward." Cf. ibid., 391, on this text: "Der Mensch wird dann durch Gottes Gebote leben, wenn er sie hält und tut . . . Und wird dann der gehorsame Mensch in der künftigen Welt wieder zum Leben erweckt, so ist dies der Lohn, den ihm der gerechte Gott nicht vorenthält."

[162] Ibid. See 380–81 for more references.

[163] Cf. *m. 'Abot* 2.7: "[If] he has gotten teachings of Torah, he has gotten himself life eternal" (see ibid., 383–84).

[164] See ibid., 395–97.

Jacob comments on two of the aforementioned verses, Deuteronomy 5:16 and 22:7 respectively:

> There is no precept in the Torah, where reward is stated by its side, from which you cannot infer the doctrine of the resurrection of the dead. Thus in connection with honoring parents it is written, *That thy days may be prolonged, and that it may go well with thee.* Again in connection with the law of letting [the dam] go from the nest it is written, *'That it may be well with thee, and that thou mayest prolong thy days'*. Now, in the case where a man's father said to him, 'Go up to the top of the building and bring me down some young birds', and he went up to the top of the building, let the dam go and took the young ones, and on his return he fell and was killed—where is this man's length of days, and where is this man's happiness? But *'that thy days may be prolonged'* refers to the world that is wholly long, and *'that it may go well with thee'* refers to the world that is wholly good (*b. Hul.* 142a).[165]

Similarly, "You should observe My ordinances and (My) laws, which if a person practices them, he will live through them *in the future world;* I am the Lord" (*Tg. Onq.* Lev 18:5).[166] "And God called the firmament of heaven—Shamayim . . . for they [the heavens] weigh up (*shamim*) the deeds of men: if one is worthy, *The heavens declare his righteousness . . .* but if not, *The heavens shall reveal his iniquity*" (*Gen. Rab.* 22.6).

D. A. Carson: The Complexities of Second Temple Judaism

Turning now to the more recent *CSTJ*, the results in many ways are not that different from Avemarie. The stated intention of this work is "whether or not 'covenantal nomism' serves us well as a label for an overarching pattern of religion."[167] In fact the title of the volume betrays its conclusions—Judaism is complex. In the words of the editor, "The results are messy."[168] Judaism reflects an array of beliefs concerning the relationship between works and salvation in Judaism.[169]

It is not my aim here to summarize or review this valuable addition to the debate,[170] although a *sampling* of its results is in order especially as they

---

[165] Cf. ibid., 377, n. 18, for other references.

[166] See ibid., 377, for other references.

[167] D. A. Carson, "Introduction," in *CSTJ*, 1:5.

[168] Ibid.

[169] Philip S. Alexander, "Torah and Salvation in Tannaitic Literature," in *CSTJ*, 1:270: "either a theology of 'works-righteousness' or of 'grace,' or of any number of mediating positions in between."

[170] This has been aptly done by D. A. Carson, "Summaries and Conclusions," in *CSTJ*, 1:505–48.

relate to the topic of this chapter: the relationship between works and salvation in Judaism. But first a note: it must be kept in mind, as we are so often reminded throughout *CSTJ*, that given the range of results and complexity of Judaism's theology it is inappropriate even to make generalizations.[171] (Of course this fact alone is enough to dethrone Sanders' covenantal nomism as the 'reigning paradigm' for Palestinian Judaism). With this in mind I will simply focus in what follows on three "orientations" of Judaism, particularly pertinent to our study: i) grace, ii) works, iii) grace *and* works.

Grace in Judaism

Within Second Temple Judaism Sanders' covenantal nomism is certainly generally present,[172] even widespread. It is very evident in the prayers and Psalms.[173] Typical of Jewish prayers is a profound sense of unworthiness. There are many different kinds of prayers but common among them is the recognition that one is completely dependent upon God and can indeed depend upon Him because of His covenant. Petitioners recognize their sin, repent,[174] and on the basis of God's promises,[175] appeal to His mercy (penitential prayers).[176] The *Prayer of Manasseh* is one such example (vv. 7, 9-15) [177]

> Because you are the Lord, long-suffering, and merciful, and greatly compassionate; and you feel sorry over the evils of men. You, O Lord,

---

[171] Not to mention the fact that not even all the contributors to this volume agree.

[172] Most *CSTJ* contributors agree to some extent with Sanders though none completely.

[173] See Daniel Falk, "Psalms and Prayers," in *CSTJ*, 1:7–56.

[174] See Falk's discussion on the Psalms of Solomon, 1:46–47.

[175] E.g., Lev 26:40-42: "If they confess their iniquity and the iniquity of their forefathers, in their unfaithfulness which they committed against Me, and also in their acting with hostility against Me . . . or if their uncircumcised heart becomes humbled so that they then make amends for their iniquity, *then I will remember My covenant* with Jacob . . . and My covenant with Abraham as well, and I will remember the land"; Deut 30:1-10: "So it shall be when all these things have come upon you, the blessing and the curse which I have set before you [in chaps. 28–29], and you shall call them to mind in all the nations where the Lord your God has banished you, and you *return to the Lord your God and obey Him with all your heart and soul* according to all that I command you today . . . *then the Lord your God will restore you from captivity, and have compassion on you . . . if you obey the Lord your God . . . if you turn to the Lord your God with all your heart and soul*."

[176] Falk, "Psalms and Prayers," 1:8–17. Cf. e.g., Neh 9:6-37; 2 Chron 33:1-20. 4Q393 1-2.ii.2-4: "and what is evil [in your eyes] I have [done], so that you are just in your sentence, you are pu[re . . . when] you [jud]ge. Behold, in our sins w[e] were founded, [we] were [br]ought forth [ ] in impu[rity of . . .] and in [s]tiffness of neck"; 4Q504 4.6-7: [Do] "not reckon to us the sins of the former ones in all their wick[ed] dealings . . . but you, ransom us and forgive, [please], our iniquity and [our] s[in]" (cf. Ps 51); See ibid., 1:11–5, for further references.

[177] See ibid., 1:13–15.

according to the sweetness of your grace, promised forgiveness to those who repent of their sins, and in the multitude of your mercies appointed repentance as the salvation for sinners . . . Because my sins multiplied in number more than the sand of the sea, on account of the multitude of my iniquities . . . I do not deserve to lift up my eyes and look and see the height of heaven, because of the multitude of the iniquity of my wicked deeds . . . And now behold I am bending the knees of my heart before you; and I am beseeching your kindness. I have sinned, O Lord, I have sinned; and certainly I know my sins. I make supplication before you; forgive me, O Lord, forgive me! and do not destroy me with my transgressions; and do not be angry against me forever; and do not remember my evils; and do not condemn me and banish me to the depths of the earth! For you are God of the repenters. And in me you will manifest your grace; and although I am not worthy, you will save me according to the multitude of your mercies. Because of this (salvation) I shall praise you continually through all the days of my life.

Petitioners understand their needs, physical as well as spiritual (cf. e.g., 2 Macc 1:2-6) and pray accordingly for God's enabling based on His character and covenant (Amidah).[178] God is praised because He is righteous and faithful and man is not (Hodayot).[179] Even in the Psalms of Solomon[180] where there is a divergence of interpretations concerning its soteriology, the righteous are not defined by the absence of sin but a willingness to keep on returning to God (cf. Lev 26:40-5; Deut 30:1-5).[181]

First Esdras reflects a general pattern that could be described as covenantal nomism.[182] God's people do sin (1 Esdr 1:47-51). As a result God banishes them into exile (v. 23). They return and offer sacrifices, observe the Law, and admit their sin (5:49; 7:6-15; 8:74-80). God shows them mercy (vv. 74-80).[183] Indeed the covenant is vital in Israel's relationship to God. It is what keeps God from rejecting His people in spite of what sin may beset

---

[178] Ibid., 1:17–25.

[179] Ibid., 1:25–34.

[180] Ibid., 1:35–51.

[181] Ibid., 1:46–7, 49–50.

[182] Peter Enns, "Expansions of Scripture," in *CSTJ*, 1:74–77.

[183] Cf. ibid., 1:77: "The general picture presented in 1 Esdras . . . is not in any way surprising. It is the pattern demonstrated time and again in the pages of the Hebrew Scriptures. God has chosen a people for himself. If they sin, he will punish but not forsake them. They are his by election and they, or at least a 'root' or remnant, will remain so. Their own efforts, whether they are confession, oaths, or sacrifice, pertain to those who are already in, not the outsiders seeking entrance."

them (cf. also Pr Azar 1:11-12).[184] Deborah's speech in *Pseudo-Philo* offers but one of many examples: "And behold now the Lord will take pity on you today, not because of you but because of his covenant that he established with your fathers and the oath that he has sworn not to abandon you forever. Know, however, that after my departure you will start sinning again until the end of your days. On account of this the Lord will work wonders among you and hand over your enemies into your hands. For our fathers are dead, but the God who establishes the covenant with them is life."[185]

Works in Judaism

Pertinent to our discussion is the question: "Did Judaism believe that one could be saved by observing the Law?" Although by now it should be patently obvious that we cannot speak of Judaism in the singular, there is little doubt that the literature does bear witness to such a belief. And furthermore, texts of this nature are not confined to isolated instances as Sanders purports.

In spite of references to God's compassion and mercy in *Joseph and Aseneth*[186] it is difficult to escape the fact that "the author believes that salvation comes through obedience to the Torah."[187] Immortality is gained through eating the "blessed bread of life" (8.5; cf. v. 9; 15.5; 16.16; 19.5; 21.13-14, 21). And although the precise meaning of this expression is debated,[188] "'bread, cup, and ointment,' as enjoyed by Jews, provide life, immortality, and incorruption."[189]

Second Enoch reflects a strong emphasis on works-righteousness[190] for at judgment day "every deed of mankind" will be taken into account. "That is to say, each will be weighed in the balance, and each will stand in the market, and each will find out his own measure and (in accordance with that measurement) each shall receive his own reward" (44:5; cf. 49:2; 52:15).[191] What

---

[184] Ibid., 1:78, 81.

[185] *Pseudo-Philo* 30:7. See ibid., 1:89–90, for more references.

[186] Cf. e.g., *Joseph and Aseneth* 11:10: "But I have heard many saying that the God of the Hebrews is a true God, and a living God, and a merciful God, and compassionate and long-suffering and pitiful and gentle, and does not count the sin of a humble person, nor expose the lawless deeds of an afflicted person at the time of his affliction."

[187] See Craig A. Evans, "Scripture-Based Stories in the Pseudepigrapha," in *CSTJ*, 1:65.

[188] See C. Burchard, "Joseph and Aseneth," in *OTP*, 2:191.

[189] Ibid.

[190] See Richard Bauckham, "Apocalypses," in *CSTJ*, 1:153–56.

[191] Ibid., 1:154. In tension with this is the belief "that even before any person was in his mother's womb, individually a place I prepared for each soul, as well as a set of scales and a measurement of how long he intends him to live in this world, so that each person may be investigated with it. Yes, children, do not deceive yourselves; (for) ahead of the time a place has

is interesting is that in all seventy-two chapters of *2 Enoch* there is no reference to God's mercy.[192] Eternal life is based on works.[193] Similarly in *1 Enoch* 41.1 "the actions of people are weighed in the balance" (cf. 61.8). And in *The Apocalypse of Zephaniah* "it is necessary that the good and the evil be weighed in a balance" (8.5).[194]

This kind of trial evaluation receives attention also in the *Testament of Abraham*.[195] On his heavenly tour and escorted by the archangel Michael, Abraham sees two ways: the narrow way of the righteous leading to life and the broad way of sinners leading to destruction (A11; cf. also B9). He sees "two angels, with fiery aspect and merciless intention and relentless look" (A12.1) and "a wondrous man, bright as the sun, like unto a son of God" (v. 5) seated upon "a terrifying throne" (v. 4). The scene is one of "judgment and recompense" (v. 15) and "the wondrous man who sat on the throne was the one who judged and sentenced the souls" (v. 13). The "sins and righteous deeds" of "the entire creation" are recorded in a book and evaluated (vv. 17-18; 13.3). The "righteous deeds and the sins" are weighed "with the righteousness of God" (v. 10) and each one's work is tested by fire (v. 11). "And if the fire burns up the work of anyone, immediately the angel of judgment takes him and carries him away to the place of sinners, a most bitter place of punishment. But *if the fire tests the work of anyone* and does not touch it, this person is justified and the angel of righteousness takes him and carries him up to be saved in the lot of the righteous. And thus . . . all things in all people are tested by fire and balance" (vv. 12-14). Then there are those whose sins and righteous deeds are "equally balanced" (13.18). Abraham inquires regarding these, "'what is still lacking to that soul in order (for it) to be saved?'" (v. 3). Michael replies, "'If it could acquire one righteous deed more than (its) sins,[196] it would enter in to be saved'" (v. 4).[197] But note that even here Abraham is able to pray on behalf of this soul to see if God will heed his prayer (v. 5) which God indeed does (v. 6). The soul was saved because of Abraham's "righteous prayer" (v. 8) to which Abraham ascribes to God

---

been prepared there for each human soul" (*2 Enoch* 49.2-3).

[192] Ibid., 155–56.

[193] F. I. Andersen, "2 (Slavonic Apocalypse of) Enoch," in *OTP*, 2:96: "A blessed afterlife is strictly a reward for right ethical behavior."

[194] Although this does not mean that there is no room for God's mercy in salvation (see below).

[195] See Bauckham, "Apocalypses," 1:153–54, 158.

[196] But note Bauckham, 1:154: "this crudely arithmetical notion can hardly be intended literally. We should probably think of a process of just judgment on the overall quality of a person's whole life."

[197] Cf. also the *Apocalypse of Zephaniah*, 7:8.

the attribute of "boundless mercy" (v. 9). Abraham then feels encouraged to beseech God's compassion and mercy on behalf of other sinners as well praying for his own sin (vv. 10-11). In His "great goodness" God forgives both (vv. 14-15).

The Jewish historian Josephus recognizes a strong connection between keeping the Law and the resurrection.[198]

> the reward for such as live exactly according to the laws, is not silver or gold; it is not a garland of olive branches or of smallage, not any such public sign of commendation; but every good man hath his own conscience bearing witness to himself, and by virtue of our legislator's prophetic spirit, and of the firm security God himself affords such a one, he believes that God hath made this grant to those that observe these laws, even though they be obliged readily to die for them, that they shall come into being again, and at a certain revolution of things receive a better life than they had enjoyed before (*Ag. Ap.* 2.31 §§217–18).[199]

Similarly, concerning "those who depart out of this life" (by natural causes) "their souls are pure and obedient, and obtain a most holy place in heaven, from whence, in the revolution of ages, they are again sent into pure bodies" (*J.W.* 3.5 §374). Thus Josephus knows of a hope for his Jewish kin "that is predicated upon the conviction that God is in supreme control of the universe, and that, ultimately, unswerving loyalty to him expressed through obedience to the Law will have its reward."[200]

The relationship between Law and salvation in the Tannaitic literature has been noted as especially problematic for Sanders' thesis. Though this is not to say that rabbinic Judaism was a religion of works-righteousness anymore than it is to categorize it as a religion of grace. Quite simply, both views can be found.[201] Great caution is needed. One would hardly articulate the relationship between works and salvation in the Tannaitic literature as coher-

---

[198] Paul Spilsbury, "Josephus," in *CSTJ*, 1:257–58.

[199] Josephus verifies the strength of this statement by immediately going on to say: "Nor would I venture to write thus at this time, were it not well known to all by our actions that many of our people have many a time bravely resolved to endure any sufferings, rather than speak one word against our law" (*Ag. Ap.* 2.31 §219; cf. e.g., 2 Macc 6:18–7:40).

[200] Spilsbury, "Josephus," 1:258.

[201] Philip S. Alexander, "Torah and Salvation in Tannaitic Literature," in *CSTJ*, 1:270. We have already made mention of the fact that Sanders has been criticized for drawing an over simplistic view of Judaism (see above). Likewise ibid., 1:272, criticizes Weber for overemphasizing law and Sanders for overemphasizing grace. As a result "Sanders [and presumably Weber et al.] may also be in danger of distorting it [Judaism] by forcing it into a typology which it does not fit."

ent or systematic, much less definitive. To a large extent we must be prepared to leave the tensions as we find them.[202]

But certainly there is a close relationship between obedience and reward, disobedience and punishment. Mostly this relationship pertains to this life (cf. *m. 'Abot* 3.17; 4.9; 5.8-9) although apportionment after death is not absent (though the exact nature of what this entails is unclear).[203] For example, *mishnah 'Abot* 4.22: "Those who are born are [destined] to die, and those who die are [destined] for resurrection. And the living are [destined] to be judged—so as to know, to make known, and to confirm that . . . he is the one who is going to make the ultimate judgment . . . And know that everything is subject to reckoning . . . For . . . despite your wishes are you going to give a full accounting before the king of kings, the Holy One, blessed be he."[204]

Mercy and justice are presented in differing degrees of emphasis and are quite obviously in tension. On the one hand "God is just, requiting each exactly as he deserves; he justifies the innocent and convicts the guilty" (see *Sifre* 307 on Deut 32:4-6).[205] Yet on the other hand "Israel had two fine leaders, Moses and David, king of Israel. Their meritorious deeds could have sustained the whole world, yet they begged the Holy One, blessed be he, only on the basis of favor" (*Sipre* 26.1 on Deut 4:23-29).[206] The point is that if Moses and David had claim to such deeds yet still petitioned God's favor, how much more the rest of mankind. These two attributes stand together in *mishnah 'Abot* 3.15: "Everything is foreseen, and free choice is given. In goodness [mercy] the world is judged. And all is in accord with the abundance of deed[s]." Although this tension is never fully resolved mercy tends to prevail over justice.[207] That said though "it is doubtful that God's 'grace' or 'mercy' in Tannaitic theology is ever totally free."[208] Divine forgiveness is predicated upon repentance and good deeds. For example, Rabbi Eliezer says, "He who does even a single religious duty gets himself a good advocate. He

---

[202] Ibid., 1:268–69.

[203] Ibid., 1:285–86.

[204] For further discussion and references on the subject of reward and punishment in the Mishnah see ibid., 1:283–86.

[205] Cf. e.g., *Sifre* 307.3: "Just in the world to come as he pays back a completely righteous person a reward for the religious duty that he did in this world, so in this world he pays the completely wicked person a reward for every minor religious duty that he did in this world"; 4: "When someone dies, all the person's deeds come and are spelled out before him, saying to him, 'Thus and so did you do on such and such a day, and thus and so did you do on such and such a day.'" See ibid., 1:294, n. 75, for more references.

[206] See ibid., n. 76, for more references.

[207] See ibid., 1:286–88, 294–95.

[208] Ibid., 1:286–87.

who does even a single transgression gets himself a prosecutor. Penitence and good deeds are like a shield against punishment" (*m. 'Abot* 4.11). However intention counts. One cannot go through a deliberate cycle of sin-repentance-sin and expect to be forgiven (cf. *m. Yoma* 8.9).[209] Yet all in all it seems fair to view Tannaitic Judaism as "fundamentally a religion of works-righteousness."[210] There are no grounds for assuming the priority of grace over Law and there is little indication that God's forgiveness is given without the sinner doing his part (penance or good works).[211]

The picture is not a lot different in the Targums[212] although again caution is needed for "it is well nigh impossible to arrive at a synthesis of practically any doctrine in the Targumim."[213] Good works have their reward in this life and the next. "And you shall keep the commandments *of my law* and do them. I am the Lord, *who gives a good reward to those who keep the commandments of my Law*" (*Tg. Neof.* Lev 22:31). This is not to dispense with grace however, as seen elsewhere. For example, "do not say in your hearts, saying: 'it is because of *our merits* that *his Memra* has brought *us* in to possess this land,' . . . It is not because of *your merits* or the uprightness of *your* hearts that *you* are going in to possess their land" (*Tg. Neof.* Deut 9:4-5).[214]

Grace and Works in Judaism

Certainly no one seems to dispute the fact that God's grace is a central tenet of Judaism. The literature certainly testifies to this fact. The *Prayer of Manasseh* is exemplary. Yet even this prayer "raises the prospect of sinlessness."[215] "You, therefore, O Lord, God of the righteous ones, did not appoint grace for the righteous ones, such as Abraham, and Isaac and Jacob, those who did not sin against you; but you appointed grace for me, (I) am a sinner" (v. 8). The righteous and the sinner thus stand in contrast.

Yet still the notion that God has chosen Israel and that their destiny is in His gracious hands rather than their own appears throughout the literature.[216] "The question, however, is how a system of commandments fits into

---

[209] For this discussion see ibid., 1:286–88.

[210] Ibid., 1:300.

[211] Ibid., 300: still in tension with this is the doctrine of Israel's election that promises that God's people will not be forsaken regardless of their actions.

[212] See Martin McNamara, "Some Targum Themes," in *CSTJ*, 1:303–56.

[213] Ibid., 1:351.

[214] See ibid., 1:324–26.

[215] Falk, "Psalms and Prayers," 1:14.

[216] Cf. e.g., Robert A. Kugler, "Testaments," in *CSTJ*, 1:189–213.

this broader scheme."²¹⁷ In *Jubilees* for example (a book that Sanders treats at some length²¹⁸) there is some "ambiguity" between the role of obedience and election.²¹⁹ Clearly Israel's salvation is based on God's gracious choice for He will not abandon them "on account of all the evil which they have done to instigate transgression of the covenant" (1.5). He is "the Lord their God" and thus will "not forsake them" nor "be alienated from them" (v. 18). It is this fact that makes God merciful (v. 20) and allows Moses to pray: "they are your people and your inheritance, whom you saved by your great might from the land of the Egyptians" (v. 21).

Yet in spite of this obvious emphasis on grace and mercy, there are sins for which there is no forgiveness.²²⁰ Sanders deals with this ambiguity by suggesting, "salvation is not earned by obedience, although it may be forfeited by disobedience."²²¹ So while one enters the covenant by grace one can exclude oneself by *sinful* works. One could almost say that one's place in the covenant is on the basis of grace *and* works. In fact Sanders seems to say just that: "It is repeatedly emphasized that the *basis* of salvation is *membership* in the covenant *and loyalty* to it."²²² Yet does this statement not seem at odds with Sanders' over-all thesis of covenantal nomism? "Are *both* membership (i.e., election, covenant, 'getting in') *and* loyalty (i.e., obedience) the *basis* of salvation?"²²³ Although Sanders' words presumably say more than what he intends or believes, they do illustrate that even he is aware of the tension between grace and works present in some of the literature.

A similar tension is evident in the *Apocalypse of Zephaniah* where there is weighing of works, good and bad (8.5). Yet evidently God may still be merciful and compassionate to those who deserve torment. Zephaniah, being a case in point, sees the "manuscript" listing all his sins from his youth (7.1-7). But rather than wait for judgment he throws himself upon his face and prays to the Lord Almighty: "May your mercy reach me and may you wipe out my manuscript because your mercy has [co]me to be in every place and has filled every [p]lace" (v. 8). His plea is effective resulting in him being brought up "from Hades and the abyss" (v. 9). "This places the text firmly in the tradition

---

[217] Enns, "Expansions of Scripture," 1:94.
[218] Sanders, *Paul and Palestinian Judaism*, 362–85.
[219] Enns, "Expansions of Scripture," 1:94.
[220] See Sanders, *Paul and Palestinian Judaism*, 368–69, for references.
[221] Ibid., 371.
[222] Ibid., 367.
[223] Enns, "Expansions of Scripture," 1:94.

that holds that even the righteous can be saved only by the mercy of God in forgiving their sins" (cf. 2.8-9; 10.10-11; 11.1-6).[224]

Similarly, following Adam and Eve's transgression in the *Life of Adam and Eve* Adam begged the angels to let him "beseech God that he might have compassion and pity me, for I alone have sinned" (*Apoc.* 27.2; cf. 29.3). Adam is subsequently told by God that he must guard himself from "all evil" and he will be raised "at the time of the resurrection" and "shall be immortal forever" (28.4). They each go to great lengths to demonstrate their penance; mourning for seven days (*Vita* 1.1) fasting forty days (6.1) standing on a stone silently in the Tigris thirty-seven days (v. 2) and forty days in the Jordon (v. 3). "Perhaps the Lord God will pity us" (v. 3). Yet in spite of their efforts Adam still does not know whether God "shall be angry with us or turn to have mercy on us" (31.4). Evidently it is finally on account of God's mercy (*Apoc.* 37.2: "Blessed be the glory of the Lord over his works: he has had mercy on Adam") *and* their "vigorous repentance"[225] that Adam and Eve are pardoned. Certainly this story highlights God's mercy yet there is nothing to suggest that mercy alone provides assurance.[226]

The tension between grace and works is evident even in 4 Ezra.[227] Though purported by Sanders to be "the closest approach to legalistic works-righteousness which can be found in the Jewish literature of the period"[228] God's mercy is not absent. On the one hand the righteous contribute to their salvation. "For the righteous, who have many works laid up with you, shall receive their reward in consequence of their own deeds" (4 Ezra 8:33).[229] Yet the context calls into question to what extent this can be taken as axiomatic since immediately preceding God is said to be "merciful" to those "who have no works of righteousness" (v. 32). Likewise following: "in truth there is no one among those who have been born who has not acted wickedly, and among those who have existed there is no one who has not transgressed. For in this, O Lord, your righteousness and goodness will be declared, when you are merciful to those who have no store of good works" (vv. 35-6; cf. also 12:34; 14:34).[230] It seems that salvation in 4 Ezra is a matter of both works *and* grace. "God gives salvation to those members of his elect people who have kept the terms of the covenant and so merit the salvation promised in

---

[224] Bauckham, "Apocalypses," 1:158.
[225] Evans, "Scripture-Based Stories," 1:69.
[226] See ibid., 1:66–69.
[227] See Bauckham, "Apocalypses," 1:161–75.
[228] Sanders, *Paul and Palestinian Judaism*, 418.
[229] See ibid., 1:171–72, for more references.
[230] See ibid., 1:163–64, 173, for more references.

the covenant . . . Undoubtedly the result is a strong emphasis on the need to merit eschatological reward by difficult obedience to the Law."[231]

The situation is similar in *2 Baruch*,[232] a book written around the same time and occasion of *4 Ezra*.[233] In *2 Baruch*, like 4 Ezra, there is a strong emphasis on works-righteousness. "For the righteous justly have good hope for the end . . . because they possess with you a store of good works which is preserved in treasuries" (*2 Bar.* 14.12). Salvation is the reward for "works" (51.7) and those who keep the Law. The "coming world" (44.15) is given to those who "have preserved the truth of the Law" (v. 14). Those "who now act wickedly . . . shall suffer torment" (51.2) while "those who proved to be righteous on account of my law . . . may acquire and receive the undying world which is promised to them" (v. 3).

Yet salvation is ultimately attributed to God's mercy. "For if you do these things in this way, he shall continually remember you . . . he will not forever forget or forsake our offspring, but with much mercy assemble all those again who were dispersed" (78.6-7). In fact "who of those born can hope to arrive at these things, apart from those to whom you are merciful and gracious" (75.5). The tension between Law and mercy is seen in 84.8-11:

> And remember Zion and the Law and the holy land and your brothers and the covenant and your fathers, and do not forget the festivals and the sabbaths. And give this letter and the traditions of the Law to your children after you as also your fathers handed down to you. And ask always and pray seriously with your whole soul that the Mighty One may accept you in mercy and that he may not reckon the multitude of your sinners, but remember the integrity of your fathers. For if he judges us not according to the multitude of his grace, woe to all us who are born.

How are these (Law and mercy) to be reconciled? Simply that those who keep the Law have not withdrawn from mercy and vice versa (cf. 44.14).[234] The difference then between 4 Ezra and *2 Baruch* is that for the latter mercy is shown to those who keep the Law, albeit imperfectly,[235] the former to those

---

[231] Ibid., 1:173. Bauckham suggests that to choose between grace and works in *4 Ezra* is to present a false dichotomy unbeknown to the text. "To suppose that for 4 Ezra God gives the righteous eschatological salvation not because they are members of his elect people but because, regardless of their corporate affiliation, they have individually merited salvation, is to pose a false alternative" (ibid.).

[232] See ibid., 1:175–82.

[233] Both 4 Ezra and *2 Baruch* were written in response to the fall of Jerusalem in AD70.

[234] Ibid., 1:180-81.

[235] *2 Bar.* 85.15: "Then he will make alive those whom he has found, and he will purge them from sins, and at the same time he will destroy those who are polluted with sins."

who have no store of good works. Thus while it is true that God is merciful toward the righteous (in *2 Bar.*) it is "*because of their good works.*"[236] Salvation is "dependent on adherence to God and his Law."[237] This is not to minimize the importance of obedience or maximize the importance of grace in either of these writings however. Reward and grace are not necessarily antithetical. God graciously made a covenant with Israel and at the same time laid down demands as the condition for experiencing its blessings. Hence within the framework of the covenant, assurance of God's mercy may be given to those who obey the Law.[238]

The writings at Qumran, of which only a fraction existed in Sanders' time, certainly do not exhibit a clear-cut relationship between works and salvation. To express it most succinctly: salvation is by human effort and yet it is *alone* God's gracious gift. In the *Rule of the Community* covenant membership is defined among other things (cf. 1QS1–2) as not walking "in the stubbornness of his heart" (2.25) and to "freely volunteer to carry out God's decrees" (1.7). Membership is not by birth. Members can enter by choice and depart by virtue of their disobedience (2.25–3.3). The latter "shall not be justified while he maintains the stubbornness of his heart, since he regards darkness as paths to light" (3.3). Contrition and repentance is the means of reentrance (vv. 7-9). Upon reading these stipulations "A casual observer might be tempted to conclude from all this individualism that the Qumran community held to a straightforwardly merit-based understanding of salvation."[239] Against this individualism however stands "a strong doctrine of predestination."[240] For "Before they existed he [i.e., God] made all their plans and when they came into being they will execute all their works in compliance with his instructions, according to his glorious design without altering anything" (3.15-16; cf. also 11.11, 17-18). "Salvation, on this view, could never be a matter of human merit."[241]

---

[236] Ibid., 1:182.

[237] Ibid.

[238] Ibid.

[239] Markus Bockmuehl, "1QS and Salvation at Qumran," in *CSTJ*, 1:396 (see also 395 for other references).

[240] Ibid.

[241] Ibid., 1:397: "Here lies the paradox of Qumran's view of salvation: although the sons of light *freely choose* to belong to the covenant and thus to be saved, the very fact that they do so is itself an expression of the overruling grace of God, whose sovereign design disposes over both the saved and the damned."

Summary

In this chapter I have sought to understand the relationship between works and salvation in Judaism via the debate instigated by E. P. Sanders in 1977. Essentially three positions have emerged over the course of four hundred years, the most provocative occurring over the last twenty-five.

(1) Judaism = works. That Paul's justification by faith was an attack on Judaism's works-righteousness is traced back to Martin Luther. This view gained ascendancy through Ferdinand Weber in the nineteenth century and then the likes of Emil Schürer, Paul Billerbeck and Rudolf Bultmann in the twentieth century. Although embraced by the majority of twentieth century scholars (up until 1977 anyway) this view has not been without its critics, especially among Jewish scholars. Beginning with C. Montefiore and on to G. F. Moore, W. D. Davies, H. J. Schoeps, and K. Stendahl, Luther's depiction of Judaism was called into question. It was now being suggested that Judaism was in fact a religion of grace—not works—in spite of appearances to the contrary in Paul. This kind of thinking reached its climax in Sanders' work entitled, *Paul and Palestinian Judaism,* in 1977.

(2) Judaism = grace. Though Sanders' book certainly had its critics it was welcomed by many and quickly became the 'reigning paradigm,' generally speaking, for describing the relationship between works and salvation in Judaism. Most agree that Sanders' work has exposed a gaping hole in our understanding of Judaism. This has in turn spawned a great deal of investigation into 'traditional' interpretations of Paul and the apostle's own understanding of Judaism. It is now commonplace to speak of the "New Perspective" in Pauline studies. All now agree that Paul should not be used to describe Judaism. All agree that Weber and Billerbeck went too far in their analysis of Judaism. All agree that grace cannot be left out of any description of Judaism. All agree that Sanders has tipped the scales in the right direction. Doubtless Sanders has made a significant and valuable contribution.

(3) Judaism = works and grace. Now at the beginning of the twenty-first century most agree that Sanders has tipped the scales too far. Ironically he has been criticized for making the same error as Weber. Sanders criticized Weber and others, for characterizing Judaism as a religion of works but Sanders has simply tipped this characterization to the other extreme.[242] Instead of being a religion of works Judaism is now characterized as a religion of grace. Sanders' thesis, it is suggested, is overly simplistic. Many scholars over the last twenty-five years have critically chipped away at Sanders' claims (e.g., Hagner, Westerholm, Schreiner, Kruse, Seifrid) though none with more weight and

---

[242] Cf. Schreiner, *The Law and Its Fulfillment,* 115, 119; Seifrid, *Christ, Our Righteousness,* 15; Brooke, review, 248.

impact than Friedrich Avemarie (*Tora und Leben*) and D. A. Carson and others (*CSTJ*). These two studies have shown that Judaism is extremely complex and can be viewed as a religion of grace, works, or both. Avemarie finds in Judaism salvation by grace *and* works. Certainly the latter is present throughout the early rabbinic literature. But there is a tension between Erwählung and Vergeltung that is not easily reconciled, if at all. The conclusions in *CSTJ* resemble the nature of Judaism—complex. All we can say in summary is that Judaism runs the gamut on how it understands the relationship between works and salvation.

Conclusions

Before moving on to questions concerning the relationship between works and salvation in the Synoptic Gospels I must conclude with some of my own thoughts concerning the aforementioned discussions.

Works and Salvation in Judaism

I agree that Judaism cannot be characterized as a religion of works-righteousness—at least in principle. Paul evidently believed the same thing. After all he does go to great lengths in Romans 4 and Galatians 3 (cf. also Gal 2:16) to argue from the OT that justification was always by faith, never by works. This is important. For on the one hand he upholds Judaism (at least in the OT) as a religion of grace while on the other he chastises it for being a religion of works. What this shows, surely, is a disparity between theology and practice or belief and effect. Somewhere along the line Paul's opponents apparently parted company with their theology (unbeknown to them no doubt). When did this occur? We can only speculate. But in my opinion there are many things that could have either worked alone or together to bring about this shift. The Deuteronomic paradigm of 'obedience brings blessing' and 'disobedience brings cursing' is certainly capable of creating a works mentality (see typically Lev 26; Deut 28–29). Furthermore, though the Babylonian exile marked a low point in the history of Israel, along with it came a renewed commitment to remain faithful to God and His Law. It is more than likely that the Israelite desire to forever remain free from exile and divine judgment played a significant role in producing a mindset orientated towards works righteousness (cf. Ezra 9:1–10:17; 1 Esdr 8:74-80). We can even see how Sanders' covenantal nomism could have created a works mindset (see below). Irrespective of the reasons however, it seems clear that a shift did occur as represented in *2 Baruch*, 4 Ezra, *Psalms of Solomon*, and portions of Qumran. At the very least we can see how this literature could have engendered the same kind of criticism that we see from Jesus and Paul. In any grace-orientated religion where obedience is required there is always potential for some disjunction.

This perhaps explains the two instances in the Synoptic Gospels where the issue of salvation by works is encountered. The parable of the Good Samaritan (Luke 10:25) and the account of the Rich Young Ruler (Matt 19:16 pars.) both exhibit works-righteousness tendencies (see chap. 7). Whatever these two men may have believed about grace and election in theory, there is little doubt that they both presume some action is required on their part to obtain eternal life in practice. It is no surprise then that Judaism has been defended on the one hand concerning its reliance on grace yet accused on the other for teaching salvation by works. If we allow the picture presented in the Gospels and Paul to sit along side the Jewish literature, we may gain a better and more realistic understanding of Judaism in *theory* and in *practice*. I will discuss this more below.

However, it is my opinion that we do not only witness works righteousness tendencies in Jewish practice but their theology also betrays a works righteousness mentality. Heinous sins such as denying the covenant, perverting the Torah, reading heretical books, exclude the unrepentant from the world to come (*y. Pe'ah* 1.1, 31; cf. *b. Sanh.* 99a) as does wickedness in general (*y. Pe'ah* 1.1, 30). Those who perform "evil deeds" as Esau did will not enter the world to come (*b. 'Abod. Zar.* 10b). "He who performs mostly good deeds inherits the Garden of Eden, but he who performs mostly transgression inherits Gehenna" (*y. Pe'ah* 1.1, 32.a). These passages aside,[243] God's mercy may prevail where good deeds and sins hang in the balance (*y. Pe'ah* 1.1, 32.b). Rabbi Eleazar is of the opinion that God "tips the scale toward mercy, [even to the point of giving evildoers credit for good deeds they never performed]" (*y. Pe'ah* 1.1, 32.e).

This is not to say that we may, along with earlier tradition, type cast Judaism as a religion of works-righteousness. It seems clear now that Judaism is not a "one size fits all." In fact Carson's volume suggests that the most we can say now is that Judaism defies description. We may indeed be better off thinking of Judaism in the plural, that is, Judaism*s* rather than Judaism.[244] From this standpoint I consider Sanders' thesis to be too simplistic.[245] He has

---

[243] Cf. also *m. Sota.* 9.15: "Heedfulness leads to cleanliness, cleanliness leads to cleanness, cleanness leads to abstinence, abstinence leads to holiness, holiness leads to modesty, modesty leads to the fear of sin, the fear of sin leads to piety, piety leads to the Holy Sprit, the Holy Spirit leads to the resurrection of the dead, and the resurrection of the dead comes through Elijah, blessed be his memory, Amen" (cf. *b. 'Abod. Zar.* 20b).

[244] Cf. Jacob Neusner, *Judaic Law from Jesus to the Mishnah*, 50.

[245] Sanders' pattern does not fit all of Judaism. Cf. e.g., The *Testament of Moses* where "getting in" and "staying in" are both by God's grace.

fallen into the same trap it seems as Luther, Weber and many others who have attempted to stereotype Judaism. Apparently it cannot be done.

Covenantal Nomism

I have problems with Sanders' thesis vis-à-vis the relationship between works and salvation in Judaism at the practical level. His insistence that works do not earn salvation but *maintain* it may be all well and good in theory but I wonder how this doctrine may have worked in practice. It is not difficult to see how such thinking could lead to a salvation by works mentality.[246] Is it likely that someone would actually believe that they could maintain their salvation by works without thinking that salvation is apart from works? Doubtful! How does one maintain one's salvation by works and yet rely completely on God's grace for one's salvation? If salvation (or membership in the covenant) can be lost through sin then presumably salvation is not truly by grace. It may *begin* by grace but it certainly does not appear to *continue* by grace. Is this not what Paul was fighting against in Galatians (cf. e.g., Gal 3:1-5)? And is this not the reason that his Jewish opponents found justification by faith to be tantamount to antinomism?[247] To my way of thinking Sanders has not articulated the relationship between works and salvation satisfactorily.[248] It is an observable fact of life that reality does not always line up with theology.[249] Unbelievers are perhaps the quickest to point this out. But even

---

[246] Cf. also Hagner, "Paul and Judaism," 118: "we may still be confronted with a decided preoccupation with works, a preoccupation which by its very nature makes for human insecurity and thus prepares a promising ground for the nurture of legalistic tendencies."

[247] This seems the best way to understand Gal 2:17: "And if while seeking to be justified in Christ we are found also to be sinners, then is Christ a minister of sin?" In other words "the circumcision group" (v. 12) believed that since justification by faith in Christ meant dying to the Law (v. 19a) one had no means of controlling sin. Hence faith in Christ, so the logic goes, encourages sin. Peter is a case in point, breaking the Law and eating with Gentile sinners (vv. 11-14). However Paul responds by asserting that the opposite is in fact true (v. 18). If one were to go back to that which has been destroyed (κατέλυσα) i.e., the Law, he would in fact demonstrate himself to be a transgressor (παραβάτην) of the Law. Contrary to all logic, living under the Law makes sin inevitable (cf. Rom 7:7-25). The law simply cannot control sin. However one who has faith in Christ upholds (ἰστάνομεν) the Law (Rom 3:31).

[248] I am not the only one to make this observation. Enns, "Expansions of Scripture," 97: "it is not entirely clear how 'salvation' can be by grace but 'staying saved' is a matter of strict obedience . . . what meaning does 'election' have when it can so easily be undone by the actions of frail people whose very existence as a covenant people depends on grace/election to begin with?" Byrne, '*Sons of God*', 230: "Whatever be the fundamental case in *theory*—that is, that the covenant and God's mercy overarch the whole pattern of progress to salvation—if works are a condition of remaining 'in' the covenant community and if exclusion from that community means loss of salvation, then in *practice*—that is, from the point of view of one on the road from election to salvation—works *are* a means of gaining salvation."

[249] As Hagner, "Salvation, Faith, Works," 26, has observed: "Reality is more complex and less

believers know it is true. The apostle Peter is a case in point. He had been told by divine revelation that all foods were clean (Acts 10:15) and thus *theologically* understood that Gentiles were equal with Jews before God (v. 28). Yet in *practice* Paul scolds Peter for making Gentiles adhere to Jewish customs (Gal 2:14).

It also appears to me that Sanders has wrongly equated salvation with entry into the covenant ("getting in") or God's election.[250] Certainly this is one aspect of salvation but it is broader than this also encompassing the future (Joel 2:32). The same can be said for the NT, as I hope to demonstrate in chapter five. It may be more correct to say that *in some parts of Judaism it is true that no one became a member of the covenant by observing the Law but concerning salvation at the end of the age no one could be saved without having observed the Law.* This seems more in line with some of the evidence (e.g., *y. Pe'ah* above) and in fact comes close to what we shall observe in Jesus' teaching in due course.

Paul and Judaism

Nevertheless there is no question in my mind at least that Sanders has done NT scholarship a great service. Judaism should be understood on its own terms and not by its opponents. However, Sanders' refusal to let Paul be a witness, albeit secondary, creates an all too positive view of Judaism[251]—a view that in the end tends to focus more on theology and theory. A realistic picture must surely take into account Judaism in practice, and only those who had first hand encounters with Judaism can provide such adequate testimony (e.g., Paul and Jesus). By focusing on Jewish sources Sanders has rightly shown that it is dangerous to think of Judaism through Pauline glasses. However we should not conclude from this that Paul (or Jesus for that matter) has no value in contributing to our understanding of Judaism. Quite the contrary. Since Paul speaks as an "outside" observer He can rightly be considered an objective observer. Sure He views Judaism through a Christian lens (see below) but we must not forget that this lens is also *God's* lens (cf. e.g., Paul's salutations). Paul speaks for God! This is the same God whom Judaism theologizes about in literature and worships in practice. This commonality

---

consistent than our theologizing often allows."

[250] Enns, "Expansions of Scripture," 98, raises the same point and suggests, "It might be less confusing to say that *election* is by grace but *salvation* [in the age to come] is by obedience."

[251] Cf. Caird, review, 540: "adverse criticism is not primary evidence or unbiased evidence, but it is evidence; and when we attempt to decide whether it has genuine grounds, surely we are entitled to listen not only to what the Rabbis and others say about themselves, but also to what incidentally they betray about themselves."

together with his Jewish heritage makes Paul, along with the Gospels and Acts,[252] a valuable source for understanding Judaism's soteriology.

Granted we must recognize that by using Paul (or Jesus) we are reading a somewhat biased perspective. Paul's Christian perspective no doubt colored his thinking (cf. Gal 1:14; Phil 3:4-7 where Paul jumps out of this perspective).[253] We cannot expect his non-Christian opponents to portray themselves in the same (negative) light.[254] This does not mean we should discount Paul though—after all even Judaism is biased doubtless viewing themselves in a positive light—but it is something we must be aware of. Paul (with Jesus and Luke) is a credible observer of how Jews, at least the ones he encountered, (though cf. Rom 9:30–10:3) applied their theology. There seems no better way to gain a complete picture if we are to understand Judaism in its theology *and* practice.

Judaism and New Testament Christianity

Describing the relationship between works and salvation in Judaism may in many ways prefigure my own attempt to describe the same relationship in the Synoptic Gospels (see chaps. 6–11). Could we not speak of the same pattern—salvation is by grace yet maintained by works—in the NT? This is plausible but it is hardly likely given Paul's teaching in Romans 1:17. In the gospel "the righteousness of God is revealed from *faith to faith*; as it is written, 'But the righteous shall live by faith.'"[255]

Second, in spite of the fact that Judaism can speak of salvation by grace, it appears that it cannot speak of it in the same way as the NT. It is not that grace is missing in Judaism but that it is not exclusive whereas in Christianity it is. In Jesus' ministry grace is the initiator of the entire salvation process whereas in Judaism the starting point is election. Jesus' ministry entailed eating and drinking with sinners and thus signified His acceptance of them

---

[252] Cf. Horbury, "Paul and Judaism," 117.

[253] Though different in nature another example is that of Moses. In Exodus he is adamant that he is lacks eloquence and yet Stephen thinks otherwise in Acts 7:22 (Moses "was powerful in words"). Similarly we could also compare the meek and humble Paul of his epistles and the super-hero Paul of Acts.

[254] Similarly, we should not think that the opponents of Jesus or John were exactly as they have been portrayed in the NT. It is doubtful that the Pharisees would have described themselves as hypocrites as Jesus does in Matt 23. Likewise I'm sure John's opponents would not have thought of themselves as antichrists (1 John 2:18). Yet this does not make Jesus or John's depiction any less valid. Certainly Jews would not have agreed with Paul's assessment of the Law with respect to sin and death in Romans 7. Yet *God* surely agrees.

[255] Cf. Terrance L. Tiessen, *Who Can Be Saved? Reassessing Salvation in Christ and World Religions* (Downers Grove, Ill.: InterVarsity, 2004) esp. 253–54.

(Luke 5:27-32; 7:36-50; 14:15-24; 15:1-2; 19:1-10). This was something that the Jewish leadership frowned upon (Matt 11:19). In Judaism what mattered was being part of the elect (Luke 3:8; John 8:33, 39; 9:28; cf. Acts 3:25; Rom 2:19). Hence a major difference between Judaism and Jesus is the priority of election versus the priority of grace. Furthermore, within covenantal nomism repentance maintained one's salvation whereas in Jesus' ministry one must repent in order to enter the kingdom.

There is a third reason Sanders' covenantal nomism does not adequately describe the relationship between works and salvation in the NT: that is the presence of God's Spirit. Paul's view of post-conversion works is completely theocentric. Works belong to the "fruit of the Spirit" rather than human accomplishments (Gal 5:16-25; Rom 8:4-14). God's grace not only produces works within a believer (Titus 2:11-13) but also maintains his or her salvation, which evidently was not possible prior to the bestowal of the Spirit (cf. also Rom 15:15-16; 1 Cor 15:10; 2 Cor 3:3-18; 12:9-10).[256]

In fact the Spirit's role in the NT may account for more than is initially obvious. I am thinking mainly of the difference between personal and national salvation in the Jewish literature.[257] *Jubilees* for example shows that there are some sins for which there is no atonement and yet Judah committed such a sin and was forgiven (*Jub.* 41.24). Sanders cannot fully explain the incongruity[258] but according to Enns God graciously forgave him since without Judah the Jewish people would not continue. Had God not forgiven Judah He would have broken His covenant never to forsake His people.[259] We may take this further. New covenant believers *now* have the promise originally

---

[256] For more on this see Stephen Westerholm, "Letter and Spirit: The Foundation of Pauline Ethics," *NTS* 30 (1984) 229–48.

[257] Enns, "Expansions of Scripture," 79, may allude to this point though takes it no further.

[258] Sanders, *Paul and Palestinian Judaism*, 378.

[259] Enns, "Expansions of Scripture," 96–97: "Transgression . . . will result in individual punishment and forfeiture of one's individual covenant status. The fact of Israel's election, however, remains sure." Bauckham, "Apocalypses," 169, makes a similar point vis-à-vis God's faithfulness to His covenant and demand for obedience in 4 Ezra. The tension, for Bauckham, is explained by "the crucial role of the ten tribes in relation to God's faithfulness to his covenant with Israel. It is this that provides Ezra at last with a rationally coherent way of understanding how God can fulfill his covenant promises without relaxing the strict demand for observance of the Torah" for salvation. "The multitude of Abraham's descendents whom God had promised never to forsake will be found after all in the form of the ten tribes who have . . . remained faithful to the Torah." Concerning *2 Bar.* Bauckham notes not "all of ethnic Israel will be saved. With regard to humanity in general Baruch makes a clear distinction between righteous and sinners, of whom only the former will be saved." Thus for Ezra and Baruch: "if it is possible to be excluded from Israel's salvation through apostasy, then every individual's participation in that salvation is dependent on his or her continued faithfulness to the covenant through subjection to the Law" (179).

given to national Israel that God will never leave or forsake them (Heb 13:5 from Deut 31:6). The difference, I suspect, is God's presence in His people via the Holy Spirit (Rom 8:9; Eph 2:22). Under the old covenant God dwelt among His people via the Tabernacle and then via the Temple. Under the new covenant God still dwells inside the Temple—called His church (Eph 2:21; 1 Cor 3:16) and each member is a temple (6:19). The point is that what God promised national Israel vis-à-vis His permanent presence He now promises to NT believers who *individually* make up the church.

Finally we may ask what the difference is between the NT and Judaism concerning the relationship between works and salvation? For as we shall see in due course both articulate a close relationship between salvation and works (cf. Matt 25:34-46; John 5:29; Rom 2:6-7; Jas 2:14, 24). Yet why is Judaism criticized for it and NT readers urged in it? I suggest again that the answer may lie with the presence of the Spirit.[260] I shall discuss this more in chapter four but needless to say we are not far here from Augustine's observation: "Then [at the judgment] will God crown not so much thy merits, as His own gifts."[261] This it seems is a key difference between works under the old covenant regime and the new (see esp. 2 Cor 3:18).

Indeed this is why the kingdom is so central to Jesus' ministry for in it is revealed the good news (Mark 1:14-15) of God. In Paul this good news is the *power* ($δύναμις$) of God resulting in salvation (Rom 1:16; cf. 1 Cor 1:18, 24; 2 Tim 1:8-9). This power is the same power that raised Jesus from the dead (Eph 1:19) and is essentially synonymous with God's Spirit and indwells each believer (Rom 8:11; Eph 3:20). God's power however does not come through any human ability. In fact it comes through human weakness (2 Cor 12:9). This is equivalent to one who is poor in spirit being able to enter the kingdom (Matt 5:3). In contrast, the Law of Judaism was powerless ($ἀδύνατον$) to bring about salvation (Rom 8:3). Hence we see a strong connection between the kingdom in the Synoptic Gospels, and power and the Spirit in Paul. These three elements, I suggest, are what distinguishes Christianity from Judaism with respect to the relationship between works and salvation.

---

[260] Cf. Leonhard Goppelt, *Theology of the New Testament*, ed. Jürgen Roloff, trans. John E. Alsup, vol. 1 (Grand Rapids: Eerdmans, 1981) 123–24, and his discussion on merit in Judaism compared with Jesus. I am not saying here that Judaism knew nothing of divine assistance when it came to obedience to the Law (see Avemarie, *Tora und Leben*, 376–445).

[261] Augustine "On the Same Words of the Apostle, Phil 3 . . ." 10 (Sermon 120).

4

"Works" in the New Testament

WE are now in a position to examine in detail the relationship between works and salvation in the Synoptic Gospels. Before we do so, however, we must first define these two terms. This is the purpose of these next two chapters. In this chapter I shall discuss and define "works" and in chapter five I shall do the same with salvation. Discussing the nature of the relationship between these two terms will be the task of chapters six to eleven.

Nevertheless the task of defining these two words is not as straightforward as performing a simple word study on their corresponding Greek words. We cannot assume that there is a one to one correspondence with the English terms "works" and "salvation" and their Greek counterparts, that is, ἐργάζομαι, σῴζω and their cognates. It goes without saying that there is not always a one to one correspondence between words and phrases of different languages. On the other hand, to say that there is no connection between the two is probably going too far. We obviously assume some connection between the English and Greek otherwise the title of this book is gratuitous.[1] Therefore in order to avoid "gaps" I will examine the word groups of ἐργάζομαι and σῴζω along with synonymous words, phrases, and concepts.[2] Having established an understanding of these terms in the Synoptic Gospels I will take a brief look at "works" and "salvation" in the rest of the NT.[3]

---

[1] Cf. also Petri Luomanen, *Entering the Kingdom of Heaven: A Study on the Structure of Matthew's View of Salvation* (Tübingen: Mohr, 1998) 37–38.

[2] For a discussion on determining word meaning and the relationship between words and concepts see David Hill, *Greek Words and Hebrew Meanings: Studies in the Semantics of Soteriological Terms* (Cambridge: Cambridge University Press, 1967) 1–22, 294–300, esp. 18–22.

[3] For a complete diachronic word study of these terms see Georg Bertram, "ἔργον," in *TDNT*, 2:635–52, and Werner Foerster, "σῴζω," in *TDNT*, 7:965–1002.

Works in the Synoptic Gospels

Linguistic Usage

The verb ἐργάζομαι and its noun ἔργον[4] indicate activity[5] or a task to be performed (Mark 13:34). The meaning simply denotes "to do" or "carry out"[6] and occurs throughout the three Gospels (e.g., Matt 25:16; 26:10; Mark 21:28, Luke 13:14).[7] Whether the activity is positive or negative is determined by the context. In fact, often "works" that one would normally consider positive are deemed negative. In Matthew 7:23 "the workers" (οἱ ἐργαζόμενοι) of lawlessness[8] are those who perform many religious works in Jesus name[9] (v. 22; cf. Luke 13:27). The "works" include prophesying, casting out demons and performing miracles.[10] Though not negative in themselves, these works are judged inappropriate because they have not been performed according to the Father's will (v. 21).

Thus works are not measured according to man's criteria but God's. The woman who poured expensive perfume on Jesus' head is derided because of the apparent waste of the product. Yet in Jesus' assessment "she has done (ἠργάσατο) a good work (ἔργον)" (26:10). On the other hand, the Scribes and the Pharisees carry out what might appear to be "good" works. They wear phylacteries, take the most important seats at synagogues and greet people in the market places. Yet Jesus warns the crowds not to do "according to their works" (κατὰ δὲ τὰ ἔργα αὐτῶν) (23:3 cf. 5).[11] Evidently then, whether

---

[4] The words ἐνεργής, ἐνέργεια, ἐνεργέω, εὐεργεσία, εὐεργετέω do not occur in the Synoptic Gospels.

[5] When used intransitively the verb ἐργάζομαι connotes the idea of "work." Its transitive meaning is "to create, to produce, to perform" (F. Thiele, "Work," in *NIDNTT*, 3:1147. Cf. also Bertram, "ἔργον," 2:635–52.

[6] BDAG, 389. Similarly, ἐνεργέω means to operate or to be active (Matt 14:2) (BDAG, 335).

[7] Ibid., 389: "to engage in activity that involves effort." The term ἐργάτης is used to describe one who is engaged in agricultural work (Matt 20:1, 2, 8; cf. Luke 10:7) and thus provides an appropriate metaphor to describe those who are engaged in the work of the good news of the kingdom (Matt 9:37, 38; cf. 10:10).

[8] Lit. "Those who work lawlessness (οἱ ἐργαζόμενοι τὴν ἀνομίαν)."

[9] The phrase τῷ σῷ ὀνόματι is repeated three times in Matt 7:22.

[10] A similar idea is conveyed in Luke 13:27 with the noun ἐργάτης.

[11] Matthew adds to the discipleship dictum (cf. Mark 8:34-38; Luke 9:23-26) that at the return of the Son of Man "He will give to each one according to his τὴν πρᾶξιν" (Matt 16:27). The saying is significant though does not contain the traditional κατὰ τὰ ἔργα αὐτοῦ (ℵ* *f*¹ 1424 and some other mss, it vg^d sy and co contain τὰ ἔργα). However, κατὰ τὴν πρᾶξιν αὐτοῦ is the less frequent of the two phrases occurring nowhere outside Matt 16:27, whereas κατὰ τὰ ἔργα αὐτοῦ occurs eight additional times in the NT (Matt 23:3;

works are pious or otherwise is not the issue but rather the motive behind them.[12] Yet there are works that are to be seen by men so that God may be glorified (5:16 cf. 23:5). Furthermore, given that men can see works[13] suggests that works are more than (though may include) mere words (Luke 24:19). In Matthew 11:19 works provide a proof or demonstration (ἐδικαιώθη)[14] of something intangible, that is, wisdom.[15]

Synonyms

The four most important synonyms of ἐργάζομαι and ἔργον are the verbs ποιέω,[16] πράσσω, τηρέω, κατεργάζομαι. Of the four, ποιέω is by far the most prevalent in the Synoptic Gospels.[17]

Do (ποιέω)

This verb is used in a variety of ways in the NT being described as "A multivalent term, often without pointed semantic significance."[18] The term often portrays a simple doing activity[19] although the nature of this activity may be very broad (e.g., Mark 3:14).[20] From what we have observed so far then the common element between ἐργάζομαι and ποιέω is *activity*. Of the two ποιέω is broader semantically and so is easily able to encompass the notion

---

Rom 2:6; 2 Cor 11:15; 2 Tim 4:14; Rev 2:23; 18:6; 20:12, 13; cf. 2 Tim 1:9; 1 Pet 1:17). I will discuss Matt 16:27 further in chapter eleven.

[12] E.g., Matt 23:5: "They [the Scribes and the Pharisees] do all their works so that they may be seen (πρὸς τὸ θεαθῆναι) by men."

[13] Cf., BDAG, 390: "that which displays itself in activity of any kind."

[14] The term δικαιόω here certainly means to "demonstrate," "show," or "vindicate" (e.g., Luke 7:29; 10:29; cf. BDAG, 249; see also Jas 3:13). In other words works explain, prove, or demonstrate wisdom.

[15] Likewise, "the works of Christ" (τὰ ἔργα τοῦ Χριστοῦ) in Matt 11:2 presumably refer to Jesus' public ministry, i.e., teaching and miracles (cf. Matthew 8–9).

[16] The nouns ποίημα, ποίησις and ποιητής do not occur in the Synoptic Gospels.

[17] See Herbert Braun, "ποιέω," in *TDNT*, 6:478. In the Synoptic Gospels the verb ἐργάζομαι occurs six times (ἔργον 10 times) ποιέω approximately 220 times, πρώσσω six times and only in Luke, τηρέω seven times in Matthew and Mark, and κατεργάζομαι not at all.

[18] BDAG, 839; cf. 839–42, for the range of uses.

[19] E.g., Matt 1:24; 5:32, 46, 47; 7:12; 9:28; 12:2, 3, 12; 13:28, 58; 17:12; 18:35; 20:5, 15, 32; 21:15, 21, 23, 24, 27, 36, 40; 22:2; 26:12, 13, 18; 27:22, 23; Mark 3:4, 8; 5:32; 7:12, 13, 37; 9:39; 11:3, 5; 15:7; Luke 1:51, 68; 16:8. Ποιέω is often used to describe the activity of carrying out a command (e.g., Matt 8:9; 21:6; 23:23; 24:46; 25:40, 45; 26:19; 28:15; Luke 2:27; 4:23; 22:19).

[20] The action of the verb is often causative, meaning "to make" (e.g., Matt 3:3; 4:19; 5:36; 12:16; 17:4; 20:12; 21:13; 23:15; 26:73; 28:14; Luke 15:19) or "to bring about" (e.g., Mark 5:19, 20; 6:21; 10:35, 36; 15:8; Luke 1:25, 49; 18:7, 8).

of ἐργάζομαι. Hence for "works" to take place one must engage in *doing*.[21] For example, Jesus urges his hearers not to "do" (ποιεῖτε) "the works" (τὰ ἔργα) of the Scribes and the Pharisees (Matt 23:3). Kingdom participants are urged not to "do" (ποιεῖν) their righteousness before men (6:1).

Not surprisingly ποιέω occurs in some significant salvation passages.[22] For example, speaking on His requirements for entering the kingdom, Jesus concludes that it is not those who "call" (λέγων) Him Lord who will enter the kingdom of heaven, but only those who "do" (ποιῶν) the will of the Father in heaven (Matt 7:21).[23] Evidently then doing (ποιέω) involves more than just saying (λέγω). While doing the Father's will is not described as a "work" per se it certainly seems to have the same semantic force as ἐργάζομαι. In v. 23 "the workers (οἱ ἐργαζόμενοι) of lawlessness" are the same ones who "did (ἐποιήσαμεν) many miracles in your name" (v. 22).[24] That more than just passive acquiescence is in view is apparent in v. 24 where hearing (ἀκούει) *and* doing (ποιεῖ) Jesus' words avert one's house, figuratively speaking, from crashing down. The point is that ποιέω is more than, although clearly includes, "calling" (λέγων) "hearing" (ἀκούων, v. 26; cf. Luke 8:21) and "teaching" (ἐδίδαξαν, Mark 6:30).[25] Ποιέω involves activity and as such can appropriately be defined as a "work."[26]

One important note, "doing" for the synoptic writers is impossible apart from God. We see this especially in the SM where doing God's will is necessary to enter the kingdom (Matt 7:21) yet the doing is patently prefaced by 5:3: "Blessed are the poor in spirit." Significantly in 19:26 and parallels Jesus declares that it is *impossible* for anyone to enter the kingdom.[27]

---

[21] Just what the doing involves, i.e., the "manner of the action," is more specifically defined by a prepositional expression (BDAG, 841).

[22] See Matt 12:50; 18:35; 19:16; 25:40, 45; Luke 10:25, 28, 37. Cf. also Matt 3:8, 10; 7:17, 18, 19; 13:23, 26; 21:43; Mark 4:32, where ποιέω is associated with "repentance" and "fruit." In these contexts the meaning is "produce" or "grow."

[23] Cf. Matt 12:50; 21:31; Mark 3:35

[24] Moreover, in Matt 13:41 those who do not enter the kingdom are "those who do lawlessness" (τοὺς ποιοῦντας τὴν ἀνομίαν).

[25] The notion of contrast between verbal acknowledgement and practical demonstration is also seen in Matt 5:19 (ποιήσῃ is contrasted with λύσῃ); 23:3 (ποιήσατε is contrasted with λέγουσιν and synonymous with τηρεῖτε). Λέγω and ἀκούων (Luke 6:46, 47) and διδάξῃ (Matt 5:19) must be accompanied by ποιῶν.

[26] Cf. Col 3:23. See Braun, "ποιέω," 6:478, 481–82. Cf. also Matt 20:12a: μίαν ὥραν ἐποίησαν "they have *worked* for only one hour" (BDAG, 841).

[27] Note the use of ποιέω in Matt 19:16; Mark 10:17; Luke 18:18. The ruler wants to know what he must *do* to have eternal life and so Jesus tells Him—keep the commandments and sell up and give to the poor. His word to the disciples is that to enter the kingdom (and thus keep the commandments and give to the poor) is impossible apart from God.

Practice (πράσσω)

The basic meaning is "to do" or "to accomplish" something "through activity" and is often used without distinction from ποιέω.[28] In the Synoptic Gospels the verb is unique to Luke. Its usual meaning[29] is seen in 22:23 where the issue of Jesus' betrayal has been raised and the disciples "began to question among themselves as to which one of them it might be who would do (πράσσειν) this" (cf. 23:15, 41).

Keep (τηρέω)

The basic meaning is "to keep."[30] In spite of its few occurrences in the Synoptic Gospels, there are some significant uses that contribute to our understanding of "works." When asked by a rich ruler what he must do (ποιήσω) to receive eternal life, Jesus responds: τήρησον the commandments (Matt 19:16-17).[31] Quite clearly ποιέω and τηρέω are synonymous here, τηρέω functioning to define more clearly the activity of ποιέω. Another significant usage occurs in Jesus' derision of the Scribes and the Pharisees where Matthew connects the ideas of ποιέω, τηρέω and ἔργα (23:3).[32] Both texts express the idea of persistent obedience (cf. 28:20; Mark 7:9).[33]

Works in the New Testament

Johannine Literature

In the **Gospel of John** ἔργον refers to God's saving work or activity through Jesus Christ (cf. John 17:4).[34] Hence occurrences of the term "work" occur in contexts pertaining to the giving of sight (9:3-7) and eternal life (4:34-38; 5:17-21, 36-40; 6:27-29; 17:1-5). The Father is always the initiator of this work, never the Son (9:3-4; 10:32, 37). The work is God's because the Father is present in His Son (14:10) and as such Jesus' works testify not only to Himself but also to the union He has with His Father (10:38; 14:11; 15:24; cf. 5:36; 10:25). The work does not concern the moral or ethical realm per se

---

[28] Ibid., 860.

[29] In Luke 3:13 πράσσω means, "to take" or "collect" (also 19:23).

[30] BDAG, 1002. The noun τήρησις does not occur in the Synoptic Gospels.

[31] See chapter seven on this passage vis-à-vis keeping the commandments and salvation.

[32] The variants, ἀκούετε καὶ ποιεῖτε, ποιήσατε and τηρεῖτε each have little external support.

[33] BDAG, 1002.

[34] Gary M. Burge, *The Anointed Community: The Holy Spirit in the Johannnine Tradition* (Grand Rapids: Eerdmans, 1987) 89; cf. also Bertram, "ἔργον," 2:642–43.

but relates to salvation because 6:29 states that the *work of God is* "in order that you might believe" in Jesus Christ.

Yet Jesus' work(s) is never evil. It is always good (10:32) and so it not only demonstrates God's work in Jesus but also His work in believers.³⁵ Therefore just as the Father, Son and believers form an inseparable union in John's theology (14:20, 23; 17:21) so too do the works of the Father, Son and believers (14:12). So then, all good works whether performed by Jesus or His followers originate with God (3:21).³⁶ Likewise all evil works originate with the devil (8:39, 41, 44; cf. 1 John 3:8, 12; 2 John 11; 3 John 10).

The fulcrum of this teaching for believers occurs in John 15. Indubitably the point of this chapter is that a relationship with Jesus³⁷—expressed by "remain in Me"—is necessary in order to produce fruit (καρπὸν)³⁸ for apart from Him his disciples can do absolutely³⁹ nothing⁴⁰ (15:5).⁴¹ The disciples'

---

³⁵ Ibid., 2:642.

³⁶ Ibid., 2:643: "The works of God performed through Christ and those performed through believers cannot be separated from one another. They are the one work of God."

³⁷ Just what this relationship consists of is a matter of debate. The solution hinges on a number of key exegetical issues in John 15:1-6 that I cannot treat here since they deal significantly with the relationship between works and salvation. I will deal with this passage in chapter nine.

³⁸ There have been many suggestions as to the identity of "fruit" in John 15. Suggestions put forward include obedience, new converts, love, eternal life, or Christian character (see D. A. Carson, *The Gospel According to John* [Grand Rapids: Eerdmans, 1991] 517). The issue is not easily solved. It is tempting to identify fruit here as a moralistic behavioral demonstration based on other NT passages (cf. Matt 3:8; 7:20; Rom 6:22; Gal 5:22; cf. the *Net Bible: New English Translation* [Spokane, Wash.: Biblical Studies, 1998] 344, n. 8). However, it is my opinion that John 15:8 points to the identity of the "fruit" as *love*. Here we learn that the Father is glorified in the disciples producing much fruit. In 13:31-35 Jesus taught that God is "now" (νῦν) glorified in the Son, a reference to the anticipation of Jesus' death. These words occur in between the foot-washing incident and the giving of a new commandment to love one another, the foot-washing incident being an illustration of the new commandment. It is rather significant therefore, that in chapter 15 the glorification of the Father once again occurs in the immediate context of love (vv. 9-10). In fact, the latter part of v. 8 is reminiscent of 13:35 where "all men will know that you are my disciples, if you have love for one another." It seems therefore that the glorification of the Father and the production of fruit are in some sense tied to loving one another. Love is certainly an important theme in the Johannine literature (cf. 15:9, 10, 12, 13, 17; 1 John 2:10; 3:10, 11, 14, 18; 4:7, etc.). I cautiously suggest then that the fruit the disciples are to produce is love for one another (so also Francis J. Moloney, *The Gospel of John*, Sacra Pagina 4 [Collegeville, Minn.: Liturgical, 1998] 420–21). Although this certainly is not the last word since 14:12-17—a similar context to chaps. 13 and 15—also refers to the Father being glorified in the Son. Here glorification is specifically related to the future ministry of the disciples and the works that they will do as a result of answered prayer. This may broaden the definition of fruit to include the disciples' future ministry in some sense.

³⁹ The added οὐ plus οὐδέν in John 15:5 strengthens the negation (BAGD, 590).

⁴⁰ In this context οὐδέν refers to καρπόν, i.e., "apart from Me you can produce no fruit."

⁴¹ John's teaching here is reminiscent of Paul's teaching on union with Christ in Rom 6:1-14.

inadequacy apart from union with Jesus is also seen in 14:12: "Truly, Truly, I say to you, he who believes in Me will also do τὰ ἔργα that I do; and greater things than these will he do, because I go to the Father." In line with the notion of "work" in the Gospel of John these works allude to the saving acts[42] to be carried out by the disciples following Jesus' ascension to the Father. These works are possible because the disciples will be related to Jesus and the Father in a way that was not possible during Jesus' time on earth (cf. v. 20). It is this new relationship that makes "fruit"/"works" possible and is essential to understanding John's theology of works.

In *Revelation* works play a central role in the letters to the seven churches. The kind of letter received is governed by the kind of works being displayed (Rev 2:2, 19, 26; 3:1, 2, 8, 15) since they evidently testify to the spiritual condition of the Church (cf. 14:12-13). The works may be evil (cf. 2:6) or good (cf. 2:19). Yet while evil works are abhorred the presence of good works, though commendable, does not rule out the possibility of censure (2:2; cf. vv. 4-5). The works required are those fitting repentance (2:5; 9:20; 16:11) and longevity (2:5). The ostensible point is that works matter for they are the criteria (κατὰ τὰ ἔργα) by which God will judge all people (2:23; 18:6; 22:12; cf. 20:12-13?[43]).

Though the two are clearly not parallel the concepts are similar. The only reason Christians are able to live righteously (vv. 12-13) is because they have been united to Christ and subsequently have a new relationship to sin, i.e., they are dead to it. Similarly in John 15, one who remains in Christ has a new relationship to fruitfulness, i.e., one is now in a position to produce fruit.

[42] What are the greater works that Jesus speaks of? (I agree with and have summarized here, Carson, 495–97). Three Interpretations have been suggested: (1) Christians will do more spectacular works, e.g., miracles. However, the miracles in Acts never surpass the works that Jesus did in any sense (cf. e.g., raising Lazarus from the dead, the multiplication of bread and the turning of water into wine). (2) The *number* of works performed will be greater. E.g., on the day of Pentecost more people were added to the church than had become followers of Jesus during His entire three years of earthly ministry. Although this interpretation has more support than the first (and is in fact true) a third may be better. (3) The greater things are constrained by salvation-historical realities. That is, post-resurrection works are greater than works pre-resurrection since the former are performed in the power of the resurrected Lord. The "greater" then is a reference to the eschatological character of the works. What tips the balance in favor of this view over the second is that Jesus' going to the Father is associated with His glorification and hence the Holy Spirit being released (see esp. John 16:7). Cf. also 5:20-21: "For the Father loves the Son and shows him all that he does. And *greater things than these* (μείζονα τούτων) will he show him—ἔργα, that you may marvel." Verse 21 explains (γάρ) what these greater things (i.e., ἔργα) are: "For as the Father raises the dead and gives them life, *so also the Son gives life to whom he will.*" The works in view are salvific, the giving of life. This suggests that the "greater works" in 14:12 is the salvation with the Holy Spirit that these disciples were now able to bring to people only after Jesus had gone to the Father (so Acts 1–2; esp. 1:5-9; 2:1-4, 21-41).

[43] Based on the reference to "the dead, great and small (τοὺς νεκρούς, τοὺς μεγάλους καὶ τοὺς μικρούς)" (Rev 20:12) some have understood these verses to refer to God's judgment of

Acts

As in John, "work" in Acts can also refer to God's saving work (Acts 5:38; 13:2; 14:26; 15:38)[44] though the idea of human activity is not absent (7:22; cf. 9:36). There is an interesting phrase in 10:35 (ἐργαζόμενος δικαιοσύνην; lit. "working righteousness") occurring in the context of Peter's words to Cornelius and company. Peter asserts God's impartiality proclaiming that, "in every nation the one who fears Him and *works righteousness*[45] is right with Him." Then in 26:20 Paul expects his converts to "repent and turn to God, doing (πράσσοντας) works (ἔργα) worthy of repentance."

Here are two significant statements concerning the relationship between works and salvation.[46] It is worth making the following observations regarding the phrase ἐργαζόμενος δικαιοσύνην in 10:35. First, similar phraseology to Acts 10:35 occurs elsewhere (LXX Ps 14:2;[47] Heb 11:33;[48] Jas 1:20[49]). Second, it seems unlikely that Luke has in mind the commandments and requirements of God[50] since this could only be said of a Jew or a proselyte and Cornelius had not been circumcised (11:3). On the other hand C. K. Barrett suggests that it seems doubtful that Peter would have had in mind merely "being good."[51] Since this phrase is certainly a technical expression the answer

---

unbelievers on the basis of their works (e.g., John F. Walvoord, *The Revelation of Jesus Christ*, [Chicago: Moody, 1966] 306–8). However since the same wording occurs in Rev 11:18 for all believers (τοὺς μικροὺς καὶ τοὺς μεγάλους) and in 19:18 for all unbelievers (μικρῶν καὶ μεγάλων) it is also possible that the judgment includes the believing dead (cf. G. K. Beale, *The Book of Revelation: A Commentary on the Greek Text*, NIGTC, ed. I. Howard Marshall and Doanld A. Hagner [Grand Rapids: Eerdmans, 1999] 1032–34). An important verse in this matter is John 5:29—"And those who had done good went out into the resurrection of life and those who had done evil to the resurrection of condemnation"—which if parallel to Rev 20:12-13 would suggest a judgment for both believers and unbelievers on the basis of their works. (Although, I am aware that there is disagreement on seeing John 5:28-29 as a reference to a works judgment, most notably Zane C. Hodges, "Those Who Have Done Good — John 5:28-29," *Bib Sac* 136 [1979] 158–66. I will discuss this passage and the debate surrounding it further in chap. 11).

[44] Cf. Bertram, "ἔργον," 2:643.

[45] NIV: ἐργαζόμενος δικαιοσύνην = "do what is right."

[46] Crucial in understanding the relationship between works and salvation in Acts 10:35 is the meaning of "right (δεκτός) with God" since this is the result of ἐργαζόμενος δικαιοσύνην. In 26:20 the exact relationship between repentance and works needs to be explored.

[47] Πορευόμενος ἄμωμος καὶ *ἐργαζόμενος δικαιοσύνην*...

[48] οἱ διὰ πίστεως κατηγωνίσαντο βασιλείας, *εἰργάσαντο δικαιοσύνην*...

[49] ὀργὴ γὰρ ἀνδρὸς *δικαιοσύνην* θεοῦ οὐκ *ἐργάζεται*.

[50] Cf. Luke 1:6 where Zechariah and Elizabeth are said to be righteous (δίκαιοι) since they kept all ταῖς ἐντολαῖς καὶ δικαιώμασιν τοῦ κυρίου.

[51] C. K. Barrett, *A Critical and Exegetical Commentary on The Acts of the Apostles*, vol. 1, ICC, ed. J. A. Emerton, C. E. B. Cranfield, and G. N. Stanton (Edinburgh: T. & T. Clark, 1994)

probably lies somewhere in between. This appears to be the case in Psalm 14 (LXX) which as a whole refers generally to a life of moral integrity. We find the same thing in the epistle of James (e.g., 1:21).

Paul's statement in Acts 26:20 is less difficult since it is clear that the works in view are qualified by the phrase "worthy (ἄξια) of repentance." Furthermore given Luke's understanding of repentance it seems beyond doubt that the works he has in mind involve a life of moral veracity, abhorring evil, and obedience to God (cf. Luke 3:3, 8-14; Acts 3:19, 26; 5:31-32; 8:22).

Paul

Paul's most comprehensive statement on works appears in Ephesians 2:9-10. Here he states that salvation "is not from works" (οὐκ ἐξ ἔργων). Yet at the same time believers are "God's workmanship (ποίημα)[52] created in Christ Jesus for good works (ἔργοις ἀγαθοῖς) which God has prepared before hand (προητοίμασεν) in order that we might walk (περιπατήσωμεν) in them." If Paul had said nothing else about works these two verses would almost be enough. He articulates five significant truths in them.[53]

First, since salvation is by grace (v. 8) it cannot be of works (cf. Rom 11:6). The Ephesians adage is slightly different from Paul's earlier writings where he relentlessly insists that works *of the Law* (ἔργων νόμου)[54] play no part in one's *justification* (Rom 3:20, 28; Gal 2:16; cf. 3:2; Phil 3:9).[55] This demonstrates a later tendency in Paul to broaden his delineation on works until νόμου drops out altogether (2 Tim 1:9; Tit 3:5).[56]

Second, believers are God's ποίημα, a workmanship that He created. Elsewhere Paul refers to the community of believers as "the work of God" (τὸ

520.

[52] Cf. BDAG, 842.

[53] One should also see the most recent work by Paul A. Rainbow, *The Way of Salvation: The Role of Christian Obedience in Justification* (Waynesboro, Ga.: Paternoster, 2005) 79–96.

[54] As we have seen the phrase ἔργων νόμου is debated (see chap. 3). Most suggestions suffer from a certain amount of reductionism which is difficult to reconcile with the fact that Paul often speaks of the Law without further qualification (e.g., Rom 5:20; Gal 3:19) suggesting an entire entity. It seems best therefore to understand "works of the Law" as obeying the requirements of the Law. For this view see, Thomas R. Schreiner, *The Law and Its Fulfillment: A Pauline Theology of Law* (Grand Rapids: Baker, 1993) esp. 51–59; Douglas J. Moo, "'Law,' 'Works of the Law,' and Legalism in Paul," *WTJ* 45 (1983) 84–90.

[55] This is not to say that Paul never uses ἔργον by itself early on in his letters. However, invariably these occurrences are in the context of "works of the Law" (cf. e.g., Rom 3:27; 4:2, 6; cf. 3:28).

[56] The most likely explanation for this is that Paul uses "works of the Law" when Jews are the subject of discussion and "works" when either he is thinking of people prior to the time of Moses (cf. Rom 4; 9:10-12) or Gentiles (cf. Eph 2:9; 2 Tim 1:9; Tit 3:5) (Moo, 81).

ἔργον τοῦ θεοῦ) (Rom 14:20; 1 Cor 9:1). This is another way of saying that believers are the result of God's handiwork not their own. This truth alludes to a striking feature of Paul's theology of works: the difference between good and bad works is not the nature of the work per se but its *origin*. Good works are of divine origin produced by grace (2 Cor 9:8) and faith (1 Thess 1:3;[57] cf. Gal 5:6).[58] This theological insight appears more frequently and clearly in Paul than any other NT writer largely due to his almost exclusive use of ἐνεργέω.[59] Inherent to the meaning of this word group is the notion of power at work to bring about activity[60] (cf. esp. Eph 1:19-20). It is therefore perfectly apt in portraying good works as something impossible apart from God's power working within the believer (cf. Gal 2:8; Eph 3:20; Phil 2:13; Col 1:29; 1 Thess 2:13). (Even the unregenerate are unable to produce works apart from Satan's power [Eph 2:2; 2 Thess 2:7, 9; cf. Rom 7:5]).

This power is only available since God Himself indwells each believer (Phil 2:13) through His Spirit (Gal 5:16, 22-25; 2 Thess 2:13). The wonderful truth for the Christian is that this same power was operative in raising Christ from the dead (Rom 8:11; Eph 1:19-20; Col 2:12; cf. 2 Pet 1:3). It is therefore with confidence that Paul is able to motivate his Philippian readers to work out (κατεργάζεσθε) their salvation explaining (γάρ) that God is at work (ὁ ἐνεργῶν) in them to work (ἐνεργεῖν) in line with His good pleasure (Phil 2:12-13). However, although God is at work now the work is not yet complete (cf. 2 Tim 4:8) for this same power will eventually transform our lowly bodies into something akin to Christ's glorious body (Phil 3:21). Thus Paul's confidence is every believer's confidence for "He who began a good *work* in you will bring it to an end until the day of Christ Jesus" (Phil 1:6).

Third, even though salvation is not by works it is quite clearly *for* good works. Every believer has been created for this. More than once Paul asserts that Christians have been delivered from the unscrupulous in order that we

---

[57] The phrase τοῦ ἔργου τῆς πίστεως is most probably a genitive of production, i.e., "your work produced by faith" (cf. also Daniel B. Wallace, *GGBB* [Grand Rapids: Zondervan, 1996]) 106.

[58] Werner Georg Kümmel, *The Theology of the New Testament According to its Major Witnesses: Jesus-Paul-John*, trans. John E. Steely (Nashville: Abingdon, 1973) 229: Paul distinguishes between the plural "works" by which man cannot gain acceptance before God (e.g., Rom 13:12; Gal 5:19) and its singular "work" describing God's action in the Christian (e.g., 1 Cor 1:13; Phil 1:6; 2 Cor 9:8; Gal 6:4).

[59] Only occurring elsewhere in Matt 14:2; Mark 6:14; Jas 5:16. In Paul, see Rom 7:5; 1 Cor 12:6, 11; 2 Cor 1:6; 4:12; Gal 2:8; 3:5; 5:6; Eph 1:11, 20; 2:2; 3:20; Phil 2:13; Col 1:29; 1 Thess 2:13; 2 Thess 2:7. Cf. also Paul's use of ἐνέργεια in Eph 1:19; 3:17; 4:16; Phil 3:21; Col 1:29; 2:12; 2 Thess 2:9, 11; ἐνέργημα 1 Cor 12:6; 12:10; ἐνεργής 1 Cor 16:9; Phil 1:6.

[60] Cf. BDAG, 335.

might do good works (Tit 2:14; cf. Rom 6:1-14). This implies a distinction between pre-conversion and post-conversion works.[61] In Paul, as elsewhere, works may be good[62] or bad.[63] Both are variously described. Good works consist of obedience to God (Rom 15:18) and a "workman" is one who accurately handles the word of truth (2 Tim 2:15). On the other side various qualifiers accompany works: "flesh" (Gal 5:19) "darkness" (Rom 13:12; Eph 5:11) "unfruitful" (Eph 5:11) "evil" (Col 1: 21; 2 Tim 4:18; cf. Phil 3:2) and "lawless" (Tit 2:14a). For Paul the two types of works cannot coexist (cf. Rom 13:10).

Fourth, God has prepared these good works in advance. It is difficult to escape a predestinarian notion here.[64] Already in Ephesians God is praised for having chosen believers before the creation of the world "to be holy and blameless in His sight" (1:4). Since therefore believers are God's workmanship and good works only originate with Him it is no great stretch for Paul to think of these works as already in the mind and purpose of God before eternity.[65]

Fifth, good works are God's intention for the believer who has been saved by grace through faith in order that they might "walk in them." Paul's use of περιπατέω in the rest of Ephesians defines just what *kind* of works he has in mind[66]—according to their calling (4:1) no longer in the foolishness of their minds (v. 17; cf. 2:2) in love (5:2) as children of light (v. 8) and in wisdom (v. 15). For Paul then there is no such thing as an invisible work (1 Tim 5:25). Presumably this explains why the apostle always views works, as do the Synoptic Gospels, as an addition to the spoken word (2 Cor 10:11; Col 3:17; 2 Thess 2:17) for mere profession without good works may disguise one's spiritual condition (Tit 1:16).

In sum, although pre-conversion works count for nothing in Paul, post-conversion works clearly play an important part. One reason for this is the role of works at the eschatological judgment. First Corinthians 3:14-15 links works to rewards. Other passages appear to engender a "just deserts" mentality (cf. Rom 2:6-7, 10; 2 Cor 5:10; 11:15; Eph 6:8; Col 3:25; 2 Tim 4:14). Conduct plays a key role in determining who inherits the kingdom of God (Gal 5:19-21; 1 Cor 6:9-10; Eph 5:5). These passages have understandably

---

[61] This is a point well made by Rainbow, *The Way of Salvation*, 79–88.

[62] Cf. Rom 13:3; 2 Cor 9:8; Col 1:10; 2 Thess 2:17; 1 Tim 2:10; 5:10, 25; 6:18; 2 Tim 2:21; 3:17; Tit 2:7; 3:1, 8, 14.

[63] Cf. also Schreiner, *The Law and Its Fulfillment*, 52.

[64] As in Rom 9:23.

[65] Peter T. O'Brien, *The Letter to the Ephesians*, PNTC (Grand Rapids: Eerdmans, 1999) 181.

[66] BDAG, 803, observes Paul's use of περιπατέω is "always more exactly defined."

evoked many debates surrounding the relationship between works and salvation although no one denies that believers will stand before God one day in judgment. The question is: what exactly will this judgment entail?

Hebrews

The term ἔργον occurs eight times in Hebrews, its first four occurrences refer to God's acts of creation (Heb 1:10; 3:9; 4:3, 4, 10). The second four relate to human activity.[67] The works of humanity are dead (6:1) until one experiences the cleansing blood of Christ (9:14). Once cleansed, those who are saved can be confident that God will not neglect their work (τοῦ ἔργου ὑμῶν) demonstrated for His name (6:9-10). Clearly then for the writer of Hebrews good works are desirable for the converted. He therefore urges his readers to consider how they might provoke the practice of "good works" in one another (10:24)[68] although it is Jesus Christ who equips them to do good in the first place (13:21).[69]

The notion of activity is also present in the terms "endurance" (ὑπομονή)[70] and "holding fast" (κατέχω, κρατέω). Endurance is needed (10:36) to run the race of faith effectively (12:1). However, it is Jesus Christ, the quintessential model of endurance (12:2-3) who provides the stamina for the race (cf. 13:21). In Hebrews (and in the rest of the NT)[71] endurance is in the main doctrinally rather than ethically motivated. In other words the recipients of this brief word of exhortation (13:22) are urged to hold fast to

---

[67] The five warning passages (Heb 2:1-4; 3:7–4:11; 5:11–6:12; 10:19-39; 12:14-29) also fit within our discussion on the relationship between works and salvation although they deserve a fuller treatment than I can give in this book. For a treatment of these passages see Scot McKnight, "The Warning Passages of Hebrews: A Formal Analysis and Theological Conclusions," *TJ* 13 (1992) 21–59; Bruce R. Compton, "Persevering and Falling Away: A Reexamination of Hebrews 6:4-6," *Detroit Baptist Seminary Journal* 1 (1996) 135–67; Wayne Grudem, "Perseverance of the Saints: A Case Study from Hebrews 6:4-6 and the other Warning Passages in Hebrews," in *The Grace of God, the Bondage of the Will*, ed. T. Schreiner et al., vol. 1 (Grand Rapids: Baker, 1995) 133–82; John A. Sproule, "Parapesontas in Hebrews 6:6," *GTJ* 2 (1981) 327–32; Harold W. Attridge, *A Commentary on the Epistle to the Hebrews*, Hermeneia, ed. Helmut Koester (Philadelphia: Fortress, 1989) 168–77. I will give some attention to 3:6, 14, in chapter nine.

[68] In addition to the noun form, the verb εἰργάσαντο together with δικαιοσύνην occurs in Heb 11:33 (but see my discussion on Acts 10:35 above).

[69] P. H. Davids, "Faith and Works," in *DLNTD*, 368.

[70] Note e.g., the action words surrounding ὑπομονη the two times it occurs in Heb 10:36: ὑπομονῆς γὰρ ἔχετε χρείαν ἵνα τὸ θέλημα τοῦ θεοῦ ποιήσαντες κομίσησθε τὴν ἐπαγγελίαν; 12:1: ὄγκον ἀποθέμενοι πάντα καὶ τὴν εὐπερίστατον ἁμαρτίαν, δι᾽ ὑπομονῆς τρέχωμεν τὸν προκείμενον ἡμῖν ἀγῶνα. The verb ὑπομένω occurs in 10:32; 12:2, 3, 7.

[71] See chapter nine for an explication of the biblical view of endurance.

their original confession whereby they placed their trust and hope in Jesus Christ (cf. 4:14; 10:23).

James

"Works" is a key theme in James.[72] They are the proof of a tested faith (Jas 1:2-4).[73] One who has received the "implanted word" (v. 21) is said to be a "doer of work" (ποιητὴς ἔργου)[74] in contrast to a "forgetful hearer" (ἀκροατὴς ἐπιλησμονῆς) (v. 25). His most comprehensive understanding of works though appears in 2:14-26.[75] On the basis of his humanitarian illustration in vv. 15-16 and other such examples many have suggested that here works equal mercy.[76] After all true religion is "to visit orphans and widows in their affliction" (1:27a) and Christians are to show no partiality (2:1-7) and love their neighbor (v. 8). These statements converge appropriately into a warning in v. 13: "For judgment is without *mercy* to one who has shown no mercy; yet mercy triumphs over judgment."

Doubtless James certainly has in mind works of mercy. However his illustration of Abraham and Isaac (vv. 21-23) does pose a problem for this view.[77] Furthermore, the epistle as a whole clearly shows that James is interested in a comprehensive obedience. Christians must bridle their tongue (v. 26), keep themselves morally pure (v. 27b), keep sin in check (v. 15), be quick to hear, slow to speak, and slow to anger (v. 19), and put away all "filthiness and rank growth of wickedness" (v. 21) (NRSV). They are to be doers of the word (v. 22) not just doers of mercy. It seems clear that James is concerned with a "perfect and complete" lifestyle in general "lacking in nothing" (v. 4; cf. 3:1-12, 13b).

There is also evidence to suggest that endurance (NRSV: "perseverance") is closely associated with works in James (cf. Hebrews). For just as the man who endures (ὑπομένει) testing will be blessed (μακάριος) in James 1:12 so

---

[72] The noun ἔργον occurs in Jas 1:4, 25; 2:14, 17, 18, 20, 21, 22, 24, 25, 26; 3:13; the verb ἐργάζομαι in 1:20; 2:9; the noun ποιητής in 1:22, 23, 25; 4:11; and the verb ποιέω in 2:8, 12, 13, 19; 3:12, 18; 4:13, 15, 17; 5:15.

[73] BAGD, 308. Lit. Jas 1:4 reads: "perseverance must have its perfect work (ἔργον)."

[74] NRSV: "a doer that acts."

[75] I will revisit the meaning of this passage in chapter eleven.

[76] E.g., Peter H. Davids, *The Epistle of James: A Commentary of the Greek Text*, NIGTC, ed. I. Howard Marshall and W. Ward Gasque (Grand Rapids: Eerdmans, 1982) 119–34; Roy Bowen Ward, "The Works of Abraham: James 2:14-26," *HTR* 61 (1968) 283–90.

[77] Although James' use of the plural ἔργων has posed difficulties for some, a suitable solution is not too hard to find. James' flow of argument has dictated his use of the plural in 2:21-22. He uses the plural "works" six times before he gets to v. 21. Therefore we should probably think of "works" and "work" as interchangeable (cf. John 6:28, 29; BAGD, 308).

the "doer of work" in v. 25 will also be blessed (μακάριος) in what he does (ποιήσει)."[78] In James then "endurance" and "doing" are broad examples of "works." Whereas his teaching on orphans and widows, love, mercy, the tongue, present particular examples of the works he has in mind.

Yet James knows of two kinds of works, the aforementioned and those that flow out of an unwise heart (cf. 3:14-16). "The anger of man does not *work* (ἐργάζεται) the righteousness of God" (1:20) and to show partiality is to *work* (ἐργάζεσθε) sin (2:9). James' division of works is without a doubt encapsulated in his depiction of earthly (ἐπίγειος) wisdom versus heavenly (ἄνωθεν) wisdom in 3:14-18.

This leads us to the subject of wisdom in James. In 3:13 James asks, "Who is wise (σοφός) and understanding (ἐπιστήμων) among you?" The answer is that from (ἐκ) their "good conduct" (καλῆς ἀναστροφῆς) they will demonstrate (δειξάτω) their works (ἔργα) in the humility of wisdom (σοφίας) (cf. Deut 4:5-6 LXX). The term δείκνυμι (in Jas 3:13 it is an imperative) means to *prove* or *explain*.[79] Thus wisdom is proved or explained by one's good conduct and will manifest itself in works (= good conduct). Furthermore, James uses the same term (δείκνυμι) in 2:18 in his treatise on faith and works. This suggests that "works" are the outflow or explanation of one's faith (2:18) and wisdom (3:13).

Therefore in piecing together various strands of thought we can say that for James "endurance" and "doing" combine to form a conglomeration termed "works." These works are exemplified by the numerous illustrations that James offers throughout his epistle.[80] The powerhouse[81] behind this con-

---

[78] Andrew Chester and Ralph P. Martin, *New Testament Theology: The Theology of the Letters of James, Peter, and Jude* (Cambridge: Cambridge University Press, 1994) 50.

[79] BDAG, 172.

[80] Nowhere does James use the expression "works of the Law" as in Paul. On this basis some have suggested a difference in the content of works between the two authors (e.g., Luke Timothy Johnson, *The Letter of James*, AB [New York: Doubleday, 1995] 242). However, Doug Moo has pointed out that there is no real difference between Paul and James in principle. He cites Rom 9:10-11 as the major proof text where "works" refers to anything that is done, whether good or bad (Douglas J. Moo, *James*, rev. ed., TynNTC [Grand Rapids: Eerdmans, 1987] 101–2). Both views have merit although any solution seems incidental to James' teaching on works. It is much more significant that the difference between Paul and James lies not in the type of works they describe but their perspective in relation to conversion. I will devote some space to Jas 2:14-26 and his teaching on justification by works compared with Paul's justification by faith in chapter eleven.

[81] The similarities between the function of wisdom in James and the function of the Holy Spirit in Paul are striking. E.g., James compares the fruit of demonic wisdom with the fruit of heavenly wisdom (Jas 3:15-18) in language reminiscent of Paul's comparison between the works of the flesh and the fruit of the Spirit in Gal 5:19-23. Furthermore, in Paul the person who has the Spirit has the enabling to endure suffering (Rom 8:18-27, esp. v. 25: ὑπομονῆς)

glomeration is wisdom.[82] And furthermore, just as earthly wisdom and its malevolent manifestations (e.g., 4:1-3) come from the devil (3:15; cf. 4:7) so too the wisdom that is from above can only come from God (1:5).

1–2 Peter and Jude

In 1 Peter 1:17 work is the basis for God's judgment since He judges impartially "according to each one's work" (κατὰ τὸ ἑκάστου ἔργον). Similarly in 2 Peter 2:8 and Jude 15 all works will be subject to divine judgment. Hence Peter urges his readers to "conduct" (ἀναστράφητε) themselves in fear for the time of their sojourn (1 Pet 1:17). These two words (ἔργον and ἀναστροφὴν) occur again in 2:12, the only other place ἔργον occurs in 1 Peter (again in the context of God's judgment). Peter views these terms as synonymous[83] although he prefers ἀναστροφή and its verb ἀναστρέφω[84]—probably because it more appropriately fits in with his portrayal of his readers as Christian sojourners[85] and their responsibility in an unrighteous society.[86]

What is in view is a way of life, Christian or otherwise.[87] Christian conduct (ἀναστροφή) is exemplified by the ἀγαθοπο word group.[88] Believers are to "do good" (1 Pet 2:15, 20; 3:6, 17; 4:19; cf. 1 Pet 2:12; 3:2, 16). They are to be holy (1 Pet 1:15; 2 Pet 3:11) and to fear God (1:17; 3:2).[89] And they

---

obey God, and resist the works of the flesh that lead to death (Rom 7:6; 8:4-11; Gal 5:16). Similarly the person in James who has wisdom has the enabling to endure trials and so receive the crown of life (Jas 1:12). Conversely he is able to resist the desire (the NIV has "evil desire," the Greek just "desire") that leads to death (Jas 1:14-15). For a defense of the thesis that there are parallels between the function of wisdom in James and the Holy Sprit in the NT, see J. A. Kirk, "The Meaning of Wisdom in James: Examination of a Hypothesis," *NTS* 16 (1969) 24–38.

[82] Donald E. Gowan, "Wisdom and Endurance in James," *Horizons in Biblical Theology* 15 (1993) 145–53, makes a similar connection. His thesis is that wisdom in James is the divine power that makes endurance possible under testing; cf. also R. F. Chaffin, "The Theme of Wisdom in the Epistle of James," *ATJ* 29 (1997) 23–49.

[83] 1 Pet 2:12: τὴν ἀναστροφὴν ὑμῶν ἐν τοῖς ἔθνεσιν ἔχοντες καλήν, ἵνα ἐν ᾧ καταλαλοῦσιν ὑμῶν ὡς κακοποιῶν ἐκ τῶν καλῶν ἔργων ἐποπτεύοντες δοξάσωσιν τὸν θεὸν ἐν ἡμέρᾳ ἐπισκοπῆς.

[84] The noun ἀναστροφή occurs another seven times in the Petrine epistles (1 Pet 1:15, 18; 3:1, 2, 16; 2 Pet 2:7; 3:11) and the verb ἀναστρέφω twice (1 Pet 1:17; 2 Pet 2:18).

[85] Cf. Moses Chin, "A Heavenly Home for the Homeless: Aliens and Strangers in 1 Peter," *TynBul* 42 (1991) 96–112.

[86] Cf. Leonhard Goppelt, *Theology of the New Testament: The Variety and Unity of the Apostolic Witness to Christ*, ed. Jürgen Roloff, trans. John E. Alsup, vol. 2 (Grand Rapids: Eerdmans, 1982) 161–78.

[87] Cf. BDAG, 73.

[88] Cf. also Peter's use of ποιησάτω ἀγαθόν (1 Pet 3:11) and ἀγαθός (esp. 2:18; 3:13).

[89] The expression reads: τὴν ἐν φόβῳ ἁγνὴν ἀναστροφήν.

are to do and be these things "in Christ" (3:16; cf. Jude 16–19)[90] for there is such a thing as futile ἀναστροφῆς (1:18). Peter's concern is that this kind of (good) conduct has an impact on the unsaved. By doing good one may silence the ignorance of foolish men (2:15) save a husband (3:1) and cause people to glorify God in the eschaton (2:12). The impact may be personally directed; one may receive praise from the authorities (2:14) find favor with God (v. 20) become a member of Abraham's progeny (3:6)[91] maintain a good conscience (vv. 16-17) and grow in dependence upon God (4:19). Or the impact may be negative resulting in the humiliation of others (3:16).

Summary and Conclusions

(1) Central to the meaning of "works" is the notion of activity.

(2) Furthermore, "works" properly defined involve more than, though do not preclude saying (λέγω) hearing (ἀκούω) and teaching (διδάσκω).[92]

(3) The exact nature of the activity is often specified by the context while the appropriateness of the activity in relation to God is determined by a divine-criteria. What may appear to be "good works" in the eyes of men are often not so in the eyes of God.

(4) Yet works are definitely important since they provide a tangible and external proof or demonstration of something intangible and internal. However, once again this presumably is a demonstration that only God can

---

[90] In Jude the men who have committed ungodly works are described as following their *own* (ἑαυτῶν) *natural* (ψυχικοί) desires and do not have the Spirit. The point is that their works are not done *in Christ*.

[91] 1 Pet 3:6 is suggestive of a relationship between works and salvation: ὡς Σάρρα ὑπήκουσεν τῷ Ἀβραάμ κύριον αὐτὸν καλοῦσα, ἧς ἐγενήθητε τέκνα ἀγαθοποιοῦσαι καὶ μὴ φοβούμεναι μηδεμίαν πτόησιν (cf. John 8:39). Invariably Bible translations and commentators have viewed this relationship as conditional in some sense. However Greg Forbes, "Children of Sarah: Interpreting 1 Peter 3:6b," *Bulletin for Biblical Research* 15 (2005) 105–9, argues that Peter's teaching on salvation as a whole suggests that the participles—ἀγαθοποιοῦσαι and μὴ φοβούμεναι—should be taken as result. Forbes assumes, apparently, however that what Peter has in mind in this verse is equivalent to Paul's justification by faith and thus of course has problems with the conditional translation. Yet he does not appear to consider the interrelationship between works and *final* or *eschatological* salvation, which is a predominant theme in 1 Peter (see 1 Pet 1:4-5, 9; cf. vv. 7, 9, 13; 2:12; 4:7, 13, 18; 5:1, 4, 6, 10). In fact the following verses argue, in my opinion and I shall discuss these further in chapter ten, that there is in fact a conditional aspect to salvation. But Peter is not talking here of justification as it were but final salvation: "The one who desires to love life and see good days should keep his tongue from speaking evil and his lips from speaking deceit. Turn from evil and do good; seek peace and pursue it" (3:10-11).

[92] One aspect I have not looked at is the fact that the NT understanding of works does not preclude the presence of sin (e.g., Gal 6:1; Jas 3:2; 1 John 1:8). In other words, "works" does not equal sinless perfection. Indeed the very presence of commands presupposes this fact.

evaluate for people tend to be inaccurate assessors of works. In other words, works can deceive.

(5) An implication of this is that neither the Synoptic Gospels nor the rest of the NT makes any effort to quantify works. There is much that is said about quality, "good works," "evil works," etc. The NT as a whole presents a graphic picture of what these various works look[93] like—apparently so that one might understand the nature of the activity to be sought or avoided. Yet quantitative qualifiers appear to be lacking. But even when they are present[94] it is characteristic for quantitative terms to defy precise measurement.[95]

(6) One reason that NT writers may avoid quantifying works is that it is not the nature of the work per se that is important to God but rather the origin of the work. This might explain the close association between words such as " to witness" (μαρτυρέω), "to demonstrate" (δείκνυμι), and "works" (cf. esp. the Gospel of John and James).

(7) Hence what makes the difference between valuable and valueless works is one's relationship to Jesus Christ (John 14–15). The works of the unsaved are dead (Heb 6:1) whereas God will not neglect those works performed for Christ's sake (v. 10). The Gospel of John presents an inseparable link between believers' works and their relationship to God and Jesus Christ. (The same can be said for unbelievers and their relationship to the devil). Underlying John's theology is his maxim: "apart from me you can do nothing" (John 15:5). This is a truism that every NT author without exception agrees with albeit stated in different ways (see esp. Matt 5:3; 19:26; Mark 10:27; Luke 18:27; Acts 1:8; Eph 2:10; Phil 2:13; Heb 13:21; Jas 1:5; 1 Pet 3:16; implied in Jude 16–19). Yet due to their infrequency, Paul being the exception, such statements are barely perceptible though they are there and are fundamental[96] to understanding the NT's view of works.[97]

(8) Hence what the NT writers are agreed upon is that, whether regenerate or unregenerate, works do not originate from one's natural enabling. Paul makes a significant contribution here maintaining that a believer can

---

[93] According to 1 Tim 5:25, works whether good or bad are never invisible.

[94] E.g., in Acts 9:36 Tabitha is described as a woman πλήρης ἔργων ἀγαθῶν.

[95] E.g., Tabitha was not said to be a woman "full of *fifty* good works *per day*."

[96] Somewhat similar to this is our frequent mention of our plans for the day, week, year, etc. We often speak about such plans, especially day to day plans, without any reference to God although our unspoken assumption is (at least it should be) "Lord willing." Similarly the NT writers clearly understand that apart from God believers can do nothing however to state this every time activity is exhorted would border on being superfluous.

[97] Cf. e.g., Michael J. Townsend, "Christ, Community and Salvation in the Epistle of James," *EvQ* 53 (1981) 115–23. Townsend's point is that James' theology of works presupposes the presence of Jesus Christ even though this is not explicitly stated. See also Sophie Laws, "The Doctrinal Basis for the Ethics of James," *StudEvan* 7 (1973) 299–305.

perform good works by virtue of the fact that God indwells him or her through the power of His Spirit that raised Christ from the dead. This is Paul's confidence.

(9) The preceding two points go a long way to explaining the various emphases in the NT on works. Sometimes they are of the utmost importance (Jas 2:14-26) while other times they receive scant attention. Yet the NT writers have not left us a systematic treatise on works. Their discussions, as we saw with Luther in chapter two, are driven by the situation of their readers. Generally speaking if pre-conversion matters are the topic of discussion works take a back seat (e.g., Acts; parts of John,[98] Romans and Galatians). However, if post-conversion issues are at stake then there tends to be an increased emphasis on works (e.g., the Pastorals, James; 1 Peter).[99] The fact that there is a range of emphases in the Synoptic Gospels is merely reflective of the various occasions and problems the writers were dealing with.

(10) Finally the NT writers know of an eschatological judgment that will occur based on works. Questions remain though concerning the exact nature of this judgment and just what is at stake—rewards or eternal salvation.

(11) It is possible then to posit a general definition of works but recognizing that each NT author must be understood against his own historical and theological context. That said, *works are assorted activities, good and bad, performed by people that invariably demonstrate before God the nature of their internal condition.*[100] *It is therefore not the works by themselves that are important but rather the condition of the heart they reflect.*

---

[98] The Gospel of John is often touted as honing in on faith and yet it is not lacking in emphasis on works. However, as we have seen even to believe is a work in John which seems to reflect his rather unique portrayal of works as completely originating with God.

[99] Cf. also a similar observation by Davids, "Faith and Works," 369: "The stress in the various pieces of literature could be arranged on a continuum according to the situation of the author and the church or churches addressed. The more evangelistic the document is, the more the emphasis is on faith [and hence less on works]. The more pressure the community is experiencing . . . the more the emphasis is on works."

[100] The idea that "works" are things done in order to *earn* something is not completely discernible from this study. More evident, as I have noted, is the idea that works are an external reflection of an internal reality.

5

"Salvation" in the New Testament

There is perhaps no more readily used and theologically rich term in the Christian language than the term "salvation."[1] Unfortunately for all its significance there is no universal agreement concerning its meaning in the NT, let alone the Synoptic Gospels.[2]

Salvation in the Synoptic Gospels

Linguistic Usage[3]

Save (σώζω)[4]

The basic meaning is to save or rescue from danger, either physical or spiritual.[5] The Synoptic Gospels are especially replete with examples of σώσω describing salvation from physical danger and imminent death (Matt 24:22; 27:40, 49; Mark 3:4; 13:20; 15:30; Luke 6:9; 23:37). Many of these examples are usually very obvious from the context.[6] For example, the disciples,

---

[1] For a thorough treatment of salvation in the NT see E. M. B. Green, *The Meaning of Salvation* (Philadelphia: Westminster, 1965).

[2] A similar observation is made by ibid., 7, at the very outset of his work: "The concept of salvation is clearly central to Christianity, although it is often either neglected or misunderstood."

[3] The verb σώζω occurs forty-six times in the Synoptic Gospels (47 if we include Mark 16:16). Σωτηρία occurs four times in the Gospel of Luke (and once in the shorter ending of Mark). Σωτήρ and σωτήριον both occur twice in Luke. Σωτήριος does not occur in the Synoptic Gospels.

[4] On how salvation is portrayed in the Gospels see Green, *The Meaning of Salvation*, 119–35.

[5] See BDAG, 982; Cf. also J. Schneider, "Redemption," in *NIDNTT*, 3:205; Werner Foerster, "σώζω," in *TDNT*, 7:966, 989.

[6] Contra Zane C. Hodges, *Dead Faith: What Is It? A Study on James 2:14-16* (Dallas: Redención,

fearful of drowning, cry out to Jesus to save (σῶσον) them in the midst of a storm (Matt 8:25; cf. 14:20). Especially striking are the occurrences of σῴσω in contexts of sickness and disease (9:21; Mark 5:23; 6:56; Luke 8:36, 48, 50) and Jesus' formulaic response: "Your faith has healed (σέσωκέν) you" (Matt 9:22; Mark 5:34; 10:52; Luke 17:19; 18:42). However even here it is likely that physical healing also involves spiritual deliverance since Peter states in the book of Acts that Jesus healed (ἰώμενος) all who had been oppressed by the devil (Acts 10:38).[7] Another instance is where Jesus is confronted by a paralytic and responds first with the words, "your sins are forgiven" (Mark 2:5). Though there may a direct cause between sin and sickness (e.g., 2 Chron 7:14; Pss 41:4; 103:3; 147:3; Isa 19:22; 38:16-17; Jer 3:22; Hosea 14:4; cf. Luke 13:1-5; John 9:1-3) there is no explicit connection here. Rather Jesus' response illustrates the implicit connection between sin and sickness and ultimately death, a result of the curse in Genesis 2:16-17. We should therefore not be so quick to separate the physical from the spiritual (cf. Mark 3:4).[8] After all every healing Jesus performed was a testimony to the fact that the kingdom of God (= salvation: see below) had arrived in His person and work (Matt 11:2-5; cf. Isa 26:19; 29:18; 35:5-6; 42:7).[9]

1987) 12: "In some places its (σῴζω) sense is obvious, and in some it is not." While there is some truth to this statement I have found that context is usually a good indicator to whether physical deliverance is in view or not. Cf. Matt 8:25; 9:21, 22; 14:30; 24:22; 27:40, 42, 49; Mark 3:4; 5:23, 28, 34; 6:56; 10:52; 13:20; 15:30, 31; Luke 6:9; 8:12, 36, 48, 50; 17:19; 18:42; 23:35, 37, 39; John 11:12; 12:27; Acts 4:9; 14:9; 27:20, 31; (1 Tim 2:15?). This is not to say that spiritual deliverance isn't in view in some of these cases, but the context emphasizes physical deliverance.

[7] See John T. Carroll, "Sickness and Healing in the New Testament Gospels," *Interpretation* 49 (1995) 130–42. I. H. Marshall, "Salvation," in *DJG*, 722, suggests three reasons why physical salvation in the Gospels may have taken on a spiritual meaning. First, stories concerning physical salvation may have been used in the early church with symbolic significance. E.g., as the disciples cried out in the boat for Jesus to save them from the storm, so too people are asked to cry out to Jesus to save them from the storms of life. Second, the phrase often translated "your faith has healed you" occurs once in Luke 7:50 outside of a healing context and applied to a woman forgiven of her sins. It "is quite probable that early Christians were led to see healing as symbolic of salvation and to draw the parallel between healing by faith and salvation by faith." Third, the line between the physical and the spiritual in the ancient world was often blurred. Thus, sometimes it may have been difficult to distinguish between physical and spiritual healing. Cf. also Gerald G. O'Collins, "Salvation," in *ABD*, 5:910; Green, *The Meaning of Salvation*, 112–18; and Thiele, "Work," 3:211–12.

[8] In addition to the above, note Green, *The Meaning of Salvation*, 112: "We suffer today from a false distinction between the . . . physical and the spiritual. The Christian Church has sometimes behaved as though only the spiritual element in man was the subject of God's concern. The actions of Jesus as recorded in the Gospels give the lie to this, and show that God's salvation concerns the whole man."

[9] Ibid., 112–13.

There are a few significant instances where σώσω is used to refer to spiritual or eternal salvation. Inherent in the name "Jesus" is that "He will *save* His people from their sins" (Matt 1:21). In an incident totally unrelated to physical healing Jesus assures a sinful woman that "your sins are forgiven" (Luke 7:48) and only a moment later reaffirms this comment by proclaiming "Your faith has saved (σέσωκέν) you" (v. 50). Clearly forgiveness of sins and salvation are synonymous here. The purpose for which Satan snatches away the Word from people's hearts is in order that they might not be "saved" (σωθῶσιν) (Luke 8:12). Luke understands Jesus' promise of salvation to Zacchaeus within the framework of saving (σῶσαι) the lost (19:10). Bemused by Jesus' assessment on the probability of the wealthy entering the kingdom of God, the disciples anxiously ask, "Who then can be *saved*" (Matt 19:25; Mark 10:26; Luke 18:26).[10] These examples are enough to show that σώσω in the Synoptic Gospels cannot be limited to physical salvation,[11] and going by the examples given Luke uses the verb in a more spiritual sense than Matthew and Mark[12] (cf. also Luke 13:23).

In some cases both meanings may be present. For example, the sarcasm evident in the remark from the religious leaders at the cross—"He *saved* others, He cannot *save* himself" (Matt 27:42; Mark 15:31; Luke 23:35)—probably contains a double meaning.[13] From the point of view of those who spoke these words a more physical connotation was probably intended. While the understanding of the Gospel writers and their readers is no doubt more spiritual (cf. also v. 39).

Having established the meaning of σώσω, we must now investigate further and look at its various temporal perspectives. Some examples: it is clear that eschatological salvation is in view in Matthew 10:22b: "He who endures to the end, this one *will* be saved (οὗτος σωθήσεται)" (cf. 24:13; Mark 13:13). Presumably the person from whom the devil snatches the word misses out on present salvation (Luke 8:12). Certainly the woman whose sins Jesus forgave experienced salvation in the present (7:48, 50).[14] In some

---

[10] W. C. Van Unnik, "L'usage de σωζειν 'sauver' et des dérivés dans les Évangiles synoptiques," in *Sparsa Collecta: The Collected Essays of W. C. Van Unnik*, SNT, ed. W. C. Van Unnik et al., vol. 1 (Leiden: Brill, 1973) 21. I will discuss more the equation between the kingdom of God/ heaven and salvation below (see Green, *The Meaning of Salvation*, 100–102).

[11] Cf. I Howard Marshall, "Salvation, Grace and Works in the Later Writings in the Pauline Corpus," *New Testament Studies* 42 (1996) 721. Mark 16:16, though probably not authentic, certainly is a reference to eternal salvation ("He who believes and is baptized will be *saved*").

[12] Allan Martens, "Salvation Today: Reading Luke's Message for a Gentile Audience," in *Reading the Gospels Today*, McMaster New Testament Studies, ed. Stanley E. Porter, (Grand Rapids: Eerdmans, 2004) 105–8.

[13] Cf. also O'Collins, "Salvation," 5:910.

[14] Cf. A. George, *Études sur l'oeuvre de Luc* (Paris: Gabalda, 1978) 309–16. George lists a

cases though it is not at all clear whether the salvation in view is present or eschatological (e.g., Matt 19:25; Mark 10:26; Luke 18:26).[15] In fact it is quite possible that some instances of σώσω entail both present *and* future salvation (e.g., Luke 13:23). In such instances we should not be too concerned about trying to nail down a time reference. We do an injustice to the Gospel writers' understanding of salvation when we impose time restrictions. This is a matter that I will take up in some detail shortly.[16]

Salvation (σωτηρία, σωτήρ, σωτήριον)

The Gospel of Luke is the only synoptic writer to use the remainder of the σώσω word group.[17] For Luke God is the provider of salvation and is especially central. Jesus Christ appears as the mediator of salvation that was promised long ago. These elements are present in Mary's exaltation of God her Savior (σωτῆρί) (1:47). For "He has given help to His servant Israel remembering His mercy, just as (καθὼς) He spoke to our fathers beforehand, to Abraham and to his seed forever" (vv. 54-55). Therefore, integral to God being Savior is His mercy and His covenant.

The link between the ancient promises and salvation in Luke is also seen in Zacharias' praise of God. God is to be praised "because He has visited and made redemption (λύτρωσιν) for His people and has raised a horn of salvation (σωτηρίας) for us in the house of His servant David, just as he spoke through the mouth of his holy prophets from long ago" (vv. 68-70). This salvation (σωτηρίαν) involves physical[18] deliverance from Israel's enemies and from the hands of all those who hate them (v. 71; cf. v. 74). And included again is the notion of "mercy" and "covenant" (v. 72). Also involved is that God's people might "serve Him in holiness and righteousness before Him all our days" (v. 75). This is the other side of salvation, the first being salvation from enmity (and death, v. 79) the second being salvation to serve God in holiness, righteousness and peace (also v. 79). Salvation (σωτηρίας) is defined in v. 77 where part of Jesus' mission is proclaimed: "to give knowledge

---

number of salvation passages according to "le salut eschatologique," "le salut présent corporel," "un salut présent non corporel," "salut présent ou eschatologique?"

[15] Cf. also ibid., 315–16.

[16] I will discuss the debatable use of σώζω in Mark 8:35 in chapter eight.

[17] On salvation in Luke see esp. George, *Études sur l'oeuvre de Luc*, and his chapter on "le vocabulaire de salut," 307–20; and Green, *The Meaning of Salvation*, 125–31.

[18] Although salvation here may well be physical (BDAG, 986) there is no reason to rule out spiritual deliverance from spiritual enemies. In Luke especially it appears that the physical dimension, while very real and important, represents also the spiritual (cf. e.g., Luke 4:18-19); see esp. Martens, "Salvation Today," 105–8.

of salvation to His people." The content (ἐν) of this salvation is "the forgiveness of their sins."

The angel announced to the Shepherds that a Savior (σωτήρ) had been born and ascribes Him the title of "Messiah" (χριστός) Israel's promised deliverer, and "the Lord" (κύριος) the LXX rendering for Yahweh in the Old Testament (2:11). Simeon, a man waiting for the Lord's Messiah (τὸν χριστὸν κυρίου) (v. 26) proclaims, "My eyes have seen your salvation (τὸ σωτήριόν σου)" (v. 30). This salvation "has been prepared [by God] in the presence of all peoples" (v. 31) and is further described as "a light" to the Gentiles and "the glory of your people Israel" (v. 32).

John the Baptist preached a "baptism of repentance for the forgiveness of sins" (3:3). Using Isaiah 40:3-5 the idea of forgiveness and deliverance is captured in the imagery of "every ravine will be filled and every mountain and hill will be made low" (v. 5a). The idea of repentance and righteousness is apparent in "the crooked will become straight and the rough roads smooth" (v. 5b). The quote ends: "And all flesh will see the salvation of God (τὸ σωτήριον τοῦ θεοῦ (v. 6). The passage highlights two aspects of salvation: (1) salvation is from sin to righteousness, and (2) God is the provider.

Jesus' encounter with Zaccheus sums up well how Luke understands salvation. Zaccheus eagerly responds to Jesus' call with a promise to be charitable (19:8). Jesus responds to the man's repentant attitude by assuring him that "Today, salvation (σωτηρία) has come to this house" (v. 9). Two explanations are given for this response. First, this man "is a son of Abraham" (v. 9b). Second, "the Son of Man came to seek and to *save* the lost" (v. 10). We see here then four elements important to Luke's understanding of salvation. (1) Salvation is always *from* something (here being lost). (2) Conversely salvation involves being delivered *to* something (here generous giving).[19] (3) Furthermore, salvation is something that has come from God and (4) can be experienced in the present, *today*.

Synonyms

Deliver (ῥύομαι)

The verb occurs three times in the Synoptic Gospels. We see its basic meaning in the final petition of the Lord's Prayer "*deliver* us from the evil" (Matt 6:13). Similarly, in Luke's Benedictus (a passage replete with salvation terms) deliverance is from the hand of Israel's enemies (1:74). Yet like salvation the idea of rescue and deliverance is only one side of its meaning.[20] Deliverance

---

[19] Martens, "Salvation Today," 106: "Salvation, for Luke . . . is essentially *liberation*."

[20] David J. Bosch, "Evangelism and Social Transformation," *TheoEvan* 16 (1983) 47–48,

is *from* (ἐκ) Israel's enemies *to* serve (λατρεύειν) God "in holiness and righteousness" (v. 75). That ῥύομαι is synonymous with σώσω is evident in Matthew 27:42-43 where Jesus' accusers cynically conclude that "He cannot save (σῶσαι) Himself" (v. 42) yet perhaps God will rescue (ῥυσάσθω) Him. Hence God is always the provider and man is always the object of salvation.[21]

Redemption (λυτρόω, λύτρον, λύτρωσις, ἀπολύτρωσις)

The basic meaning is that one is set free or rescued from an oppressive or captive situation[22] and so is synonymous with σώζω.[23] The NT notion of redemption is very much rooted in the Exodus event (cf. Acts 7:25). (1) Exodus tells the account of Israel's salvation (or deliverance or redemption) *from* servitude under Pharaoh *to* servitude under Yahweh (19:1-15).[24] (2) Israel's salvation is rooted in God's covenant (cf. 2:23-25; 3:7-10, 16-22; 6:2-9). (3) Redemption (גָּאַל) implies personal relationship.[25] Note for example the relational overtones in Exodus 6:7 following Yahweh's declaration that He will *redeem* His people in verse 6: "I will take you for *My people* and I will be *Your God* and you shall *know* that I am Yahweh *your God* who has brought you from under the burdens of the Egyptians."

The prophets often viewed God's dealings with Pharaoh and deliverance of Israel as paradigmatic of a time when He would deliver His people from oppression once and for all (cf. Isa 41:14; 43:14; 44:24; cf. 43:16-18). Since Israel had not yet found herself in a place of deliverance by the first century her expectation was still ripe. In a variety of terms reminiscent of the Exodus Zacharias depicts Israel's salvation at the advent of Jesus. In Jesus he acknowledges that God "has visited (ἐπεσκέψατο) and made redemption (λύτρωσιν) for His people" (Luke 1:68).[26] The term ἐπεσκέψατο indicates

---

seems to make the same observation.

[21] Wilhelm Kasch, "ῥύομαι," in *TDNT*, 6: 1002; cf. also Schneider, "Redemption," 3:202.

[22] BDAG, 117, 605–6.

[23] Cf. e.g., Ps. 7:2 LXX: κύριε ὁ θεός μου ἐπὶ σοὶ ἤλπισα σῶσόν με ἐκ πάντων τῶν διωκόντων με καὶ ῥῦσαί με. Ceslas Spicq, *Theological Lexicon of the New Testament*, trans. and ed. James D. Ernest (Peabody, Mass.: Hendrickson, 1994) 2:424.

[24] The key passage in Exodus is 19:4-6 where the Sinaitic negotiations formalize Israel's new status as "servants" (3:12; 7:16; 8:1 [MT 7:26] 20 [MT v. 16]; 9:1, 13; 10:3, 7, 26). See Eugene H. Merrill, "A Theology of the Pentateuch," *A Biblical Theology of the Old Testament*, ed. Roy B. Zuck (Chicago: Moody, 1991) 32.

[25] BDB, 145.

[26] Although redemption, like its synonym σώζω, also has a future aspect, "for the full realization of redemption will only come with the parousia" (Luke 21:28) (C. Brown, "Redemption," in *NIDNTT*, 3:199).

God's concern over the oppression of His people and occurs in the LXX in Exodus 3:16. The context is replete with covenant language. The covenant-keeping God (Yahweh) of Abraham, Isaac and Jacob has *visited* (ἐπέσκεμμαι) His people and will deliver them into a land flowing with milk and honey according to His promise (v. 17) (cf. also 4:31; 13:19; 32:34; 38:25). The term λύτρωσιν indicates God's salvation (σωτηρία: Luke 1:69, 71, 77) and deliverance (ῥύομαι: v. 74) from that oppression. The salvation of Israel is something long anticipated (v. 70) since it is grounded in God's covenant program (vv. 72-73). And as we have already seen God's redemption also implies deliverance into a new relationship with God (vv. 74-75, 77).[27] The prophetess Anna speaks of this hope for Israel "to all who were awaiting the redemption (λύτρωσιν) of Jerusalem" (2:38; cf. Isa 52:9). Later two individuals on the road to Emaus are disillusioned over Jesus' death since they too had hoped that He was the one to deliver (λυτροῦσθαι) Israel (Luke 24:21) from their oppression. Quite clearly in Luke Jesus is Israel's Redeemer according to the covenants of the promise.

A host of debatable issues surround the ransom saying in Mark 10:45 (par. Matt 20:28) where Jesus sums up the purpose of His coming.[28] However we are not told who the beneficiaries of this ransom are or from what they have been ransomed.[29] What is apparent though is that while no one is able to give anything in exchange (ἀντάλλαγμα) for his own soul (Mark 8:37; cf. Ps 49:7-9) Jesus claims that He is able to give His life as a substitute (ἀντὶ)[30] for others and redeem their souls. Without His ransom there would be no possibility of redemption, a subject developed further in the NT epistles.

The Manifold Nature of Salvation

While we must begin with an understanding of σῴζω, this is hardly enough to understand salvation in the NT but especially the Synoptic Gospels.[31] The

---

[27] From the perspective of a first century Jew Israel's salvation was thought of many times in physical terms. Since the time of the Babylonian captivity foreign oppression had been a constant companion. However, this does not suggest that deliverance was always confined to the physical realm (e.g., Luke 1:77; cf. Ps 130:8; Spicq, 2:424). Like σῴζω the physical doubtless took on spiritual overtones.

[28] See e.g., C. K. Barrett, "The Background of Mark 10:45," in *New Testament Essays: Studies in Memory of Thomas Walter Manson 1893–1958*, ed. A. J. B. Higgins (Manchester: Manchester University Press, 1959) 1–18.

[29] F. Büchsel, "λύω," in *TDNT*, 4:343; cf. 344.

[30] See M. J. Harris, "Prepositions and Theology in the Greek New Testament," in *NIDNTT*, 3:1179–80.

[31] Although evidently it is enough for Joseph C. Dillow, *The Reign of the Servant Kings: A Study of Eternal Security and the Final Significance of Man* (Miami: Schoettle, 1992) esp. 111–33. I am much more persuaded by O'Collins, "salvation," 5:907: "Even if it does not always

three Gospels employ many metaphors and phrases that encompass the biblical notion of salvation.[32] I will not focus on all of them for the task could potentially become endless and in the end redundant. I shall therefore only focus on a few to grasp Jesus' understanding of salvation. My approach will be to take a passage that uses a variety of terms and phrases that are demonstrably synonymous *in some sense* with σῴζω and look at how these synonyms are used elsewhere in the Synoptic Gospels to develop a comprehensive picture of salvation. The conversation between Jesus and the Rich Young Ruler[33] illustrates the various ways salvation can be described (Matt 19:16-22; Mark 10:17-22; Luke 18:18-23).[34]

Eternal life

The opening question from the ruler provides the framework for the dialogue that follows. The question pertains to the reception of eternal life (Matt 19:16; Mark 10:17; Luke 18:18). It is worded differently in Matthew[35] from Mark and Luke[36] although Jesus' subsequent comment concerning entering the kingdom suggests that the intent is still the same (Matt 19:23-24; Mark 10:23-24; cf. v. 15; Luke 18:24-25; cf. v. 15). The question is important for it anticipates an answer: how one can have eternal life. In the mind of this young Jewish man eternal life was undoubtedly eschatological[37] that is, life

---

use a formally salvific terminology, the Bible introduces on practically every page the theme of salvation. . . . To express the comprehensive nature of salvation, the OT and NT employ a rich variety of terms with different nuances according to their contexts." Indeed, if our understanding of salvation was only limited to the use of σῴζω we would gain very little from the Gospel of John since the word group is sparsely represented (Schneider, "Redemption," 3:216).

[32] Cf. Green, *The Meaning of Salvation*, 117.

[33] Thomas R. Schreiner and Ardel B. Caneday, *The Race Set Before Us: A Biblical Theology of Perseverance and Assurance* (Downers Grove, Ill.: InterVarsity, 2001) 81–83, have also recognized the significance of this passage and its contribution to our understanding of salvation.

[34] This exercise, at this stage, is more descriptive than exegetical to show that salvation is variously described and therefore multi-dimensional. Although there will inevitably be some overlap here I will leave the interpretation of this passage as it relates to the relationship between works and salvation until chapter seven.

[35] "What good thing should I do in order that I might *have* (σχῶ) eternal life?"

[36] "What good thing should I do in order that I might *inherit* (κληρονομήσω) eternal life?"

[37] W. D. Davies and Dale C. Allison, Jr., *A Critical and Exegetical Commentary on The Gospel According to Matthew*, vol. 3, ICC, ed. J. A. Emerton, C. E. B. Cranfield, and G. N. Stanton (Edinburgh: T. & T. Clark, 1997) 42.

in the age to come[38] reserved for the righteous (Matt 25:46).[39] Presumably then eternal life is the subject of the ensuing dialogue[40] (cf. Matt 19:29; Mark 10:30; Luke 18:30).[41]

Enter Into the Life

In Matthew Jesus rephrases the ruler's question as a desire (θέλεις) to "enter (εἰσελθεῖν) into *the life*" (19:17). The article (τὴν) is clearly anaphoric pointing back to ζωὴν αἰώνιον in v. 16 making these two phrases synonymous. However, the same construction (τὴν ζωήν) also occurs in 7:14; 18:8, 9. Hence the article is also probably *par excellence* pointing to the *true* life as opposed to any other kind (cf. Luke 12:15; 16:25).[42] The dropping of "eternal" probably focuses the man's attention on the quality of life as well as the quantity.[43] Jesus wants him to know that eternal life is something to be enjoyed and experienced now in addition to something to be anticipated in the life beyond (cf. e.g., John 17:3). This in all probability is why Matthew rephrases the ruler's question from "have" (σχῶ) to "enter" (εἰσελθεῖν) indicating that Jesus is shifting the man's perception of eternal life from one of a bulk purchase to a "pilgrimage."[44] To enter into *the life* (τὴν ζωήν) is to escape the eternal fire of Gehenna (18:8-9). But it is not something to be merely had or inherited. One must enter through the small *gate* (ἡ πύλην) and travel the narrow *way which leads* (ἡ ὁδὸς ἡ ἀπάγουσα) to *the life* (τὴν ζωήν)" (7:14).[45] Eternal life is thus a road to be traveled.

---

[38] David Hill, *Greek Words and Hebrew Meanings: Studies in the Semantics of Soteriological Terms* (Cambridge: Cambridge University Press, 1967) 188, 191–92. For Judaism's understanding(s) of the life hereafter see George W. E. Nickelsburg Jr., *Resurrection, Immortality, and Eternal Life in Intertestamental Judaism*, Harvard Theological Studies, vol. 26 (Cambridge, Mass.: Harvard University Press, 1972); see also Rudolf Bultmann, "ζάω," in *TDNT*, 2:856–57, 859.

[39] Cf. also Dan 12:2-3; *Pss Sol* 3:12; 13:11; 14.10; *1 Enoch* 58:2.

[40] Cf. George Eldon Ladd, *The Presence of the Future: The Eschatology of Biblical Realism* (Grand Rapids: Eerdmans, 1974) 196, 205, 207.

[41] Contra Zane C. Hodges, *Absolutely Free!: A Biblical Reply to Lordship Salvation* (Grand Rapids: Zondervan, 1989) 186–88; Robert Govett, *Entrance into the Kingdom: Or Reward According to Works* (Fletcher & Son, 1870; reprint, Miami, Fla.: Conley & Schoettle, 1978) 130.

[42] Cf. Bultmann, "ζάω," 2:863–64. Cf. also the two ways in Matt 7:13-14.

[43] Cf. Craig L. Blomberg, *Matthew*, NAC, ed. David S. Dockery, vol. 22 (Nashville: Broadman, 1992) 296: "In light of the synonyms [eternal life = kingdom = saved] eternal life must have both temporal and qualitative aspects to it"; Hill, *Greek Words*, 189.

[44] Davies and Allison, *Matthew*, 3:43.

[45] Similarly in John, Jesus is the "door" by which one must "enter" (εἰσέλθῃ . . . εἰσελεύσεται) (10:7, 9) to be saved. However He is also "the way" (ἡ ὁδός) (14:6).

To Be Perfect

Matthew again modifies the ruler's understanding of eternal life to include the notion of perfection (v. 21). That Jesus understands perfection and eternal life to be synonymous is evident in the double use of the phrase "if you desire" (εἰ θέλεις) in vv. 17[46] and 21. Furthermore, the word τέλειος only occurs elsewhere in Matthew in 5:48 where Jesus' command to be perfect is surely not limited to a select few who follow Him.[47] We see then that the Rich Young Ruler's original question is re-expressed as a desire to enter into *the life* and to *be perfect*. Admittedly this would not have been what the rich ruler originally had in mind but Jesus is reshaping his preconceived Jewish notions of eternal life. In effect He is helping the young man to understand exactly what it is that he is asking. Eternal life is a pilgrimage beginning with an *entrance* and ending with *perfection*. I will hold off on discussing further Matthew's use of τέλειος until chapter seven. My point here is simply that Jesus understands salvation to be a *pilgrimage*.[48]

Treasure in Heaven

Having answered the ruler's question Jesus then assures him that he will have what he asked for—eternal life—if he does what He has asked him to do. Once again the term "eternal life" is not used, it is rephrased ("*treasure in heaven*") (Matt 19:21b; Mark 10:21b; Luke 18:22b) into yet another synonym.[49] Jesus' teaching elsewhere on this phrase points to continuity between life now and the life to come. Treasure in heaven consists of deeds of love now (Luke 12:33; cf. Matt 6:19-21). The point is that there are imperishable blessings associated with eternal life.[50] This is why Jesus compares the kingdom of heaven to a "treasure hidden in a field" which when found is worth more than the total amount of one's possessions. Anyone who realizes the true value of this treasure will "go" (ὑπάγει) and "sell" (πωλεῖ) all he has just to acquire it (13:44). Hence the kingdom of heaven is of inestimable value. Therefore when Jesus promises the man "treasure in heaven" He is again emphasizing the quality of eternal life. But this time He puts the young man's understand-

---

[46] In Matt 19:17 the phrase includes δὲ.

[47] Davies and Allison, *Matthew*, 3:47.

[48] I am borrowing the term from ibid., 3:43.

[49] Robert H. Stein, *Luke*, NAC, ed. David S. Dockery, vol. 24 (Nashville: Broadman, 1992) 458; Blomberg, *Matthew*, 298; although cf. Darrell L. Bock, *Luke 9:51–24:53*, BECNT, ed. Moisés Silva, vol. 3B (Grand Rapids: Baker, 1996) 1481: "more than eternal life is meant"; cf. also Govett, *Entrance into the Kingdom*, 131: reward beyond eternal life.

[50] Cf. Bock, *Luke 9:51–24:53*, 1167, 1481.

ing to the test by asking him to "go" (ὑπάγει) and "sell" (πώλησόν)⁵¹ all he owns (τὰ ὑπάρχοντα).

Come Follow Me

Jesus expects the reception of eternal life to ensue in a life of discipleship.⁵¹ The command to "come" (δεῦρο) and "follow" (ἀκολούθει) (Matt 19:21; Mark 10:21; Luke 18:22) should come as no surprise to the wealthy youth who has since learned that eternal life consists of a pilgrimage. However some have suggested that Jesus' command to follow Him poses an *additional* demand of discipleship on the young man that goes beyond the faith requirement for salvation.⁵² Although much could be said here I wish at this point to *limit* the discussion⁵³ to five reasons why entering into discipleship is synonymous with entering into eternal life.⁵⁴

(1) In one instance Jesus states that in order to become a disciple one must *renounce* (ἀποτάσσεται) all his possessions (Luke 14:33). Yet Zacchaeus promised to give away half of his possessions to the poor and payback four-fold anyone he had defrauded (19:8)⁵⁵ and is said to have received *salvation* (v. 9).

---

⁵¹ Note the connection between the parable in Matt 13:44 where the man who realizes the inestimable worth of the kingdom "goes" (ὑπάγει) and "sells" (πωλεῖ) all he owns.

⁵² Δεῦρο and ἀκολουθέω are often used in the Synoptic Gospels to designate a call to discipleship (e.g., Matt 4:19; 8:22; 9:9; 16:24 par.); Bock, *Luke 1:1–9:50*, 461; Stein, *Luke*, 170; Davies and Allison, *Matthew*, 1:399; Craig S. Keener, *A Commentary on the Gospel of Matthew* (Grand Rapids: Eerdmans, 1999) 475.

⁵³ E.g., Zane C. Hodges, *Absolutely Free*, 181–90, esp. 187: "Jesus knew that for this young man, trust in His Person would have to precede trust in His promise of heavenly reward. But once he had obtained the gift of life, a gift that was absolutely free, the goal of heavenly treasure *could still be reached* by self denying discipleship to the Son of God." See Michael J. Wilkins, *Following the Master: A Biblical Theology of Discipleship* (Grand Rapids: Zondervan, 1992) 25–34, for a survey on the various models of discipleship.

⁵⁴ I am tempted to include here a full discussion on discipleship for it clearly relates to our current topic: Jesus' understanding of salvation. However given that any discussion must consider fully the *conditions* for discipleship, conditions that could be understood as *works*, I will leave this discussion for chapter eight. For the moment then I shall confine (and restrain) myself to a brief discussion on why Jesus' call to discipleship can be understood as a call to salvation.

⁵⁵ Some may want to quibble with the fact that Zacchaeus did not renounce *all* his possessions. However it must be noted that Zacchaeus' promise would have more than likely amounted to a full renouncement had he ever needed (and he may have needed to—we don't know) to follow through on his commitment. Furthermore, Zacchaeus took the initiative in this encounter with Jesus (contra the Rich Young Ruler). Jesus' response in Luke 18:9 explains that salvation has come to Zacchaeus' house *because* he is a son of Abraham. In Luke it is clear that Zacchaeus was a son vis-à-vis his fruitful repentance (see 3:8; John 8:39). There are two

(2) When Jesus says to the follower who wishes to return home to bury his dad: "let the dead bury their own dead" (Matt 8:21-22; Luke 9:59-60) the dead who are to do the burying are almost certainly the spiritual dead.[56] Hence the choice is not between remaining saved and following but between salvation and eternal death.[57]

(3) Mark uses ὑμᾶς to refer to a disciple (9:41) whereas its parallel in Matthew 10:42[58] has τῶν μικρῶν (10:42).[59] Evidently then Jesus refers to his disciples as *little ones*.[60] This is confirmed by the fact that Matthew qualifies "little ones" with "because (εἰς)[61] he is My disciple." The term μικρός[62] in Matthew can mean little (26:39, 73; 13:32) insignificant and unimportant (11:11; 13:32) or children (18:6, 10, 14). Since the context of 10:42 is familial (cf. v. 35-37) Jesus seems to be comparing disciples to children.[63] In Matthew 18 Jesus states that one must become like *children* (παιδία) in order to enter the kingdom of heaven (v. 3). (These children are referred to as μικρῶν in vv. 6, 10 and 14). In other words one must become like a *disciple* to be saved.

(4) In John 12:46 Jesus states "Everyone who *believes* in Me does not remain in darkness." Whereas in John 8:12 the one who *follows* Jesus does not walk in darkness.[64] Thus to believe and follow are one and the same—at least in John.

---

conclusions we can draw from this. First, salvation is not conditional upon a *literal* giving up. The important thing is the priority of a person's heart. Second, salvation is bestowed upon Zacchaeus and his house due to his repentance.

[56] Martin Hengel, *The Charismatic Leader and His Followers*, ed. John Riches, trans. James C. G. Greig (Endinburgh: T .& T. Clark, 1996) 8; Davies and Allison, *Matthew*, 2:56: "the buriers of the dead are those who have rejected Jesus and his proclamation."

[57] Ibid.

[58] Kurt Aland, *Synopsis of the Four Gospels*, 10th ed. (Stuttgart: Biblia-Druck, 1993) 159 (§ 167); Robert H. Gundry, *Mark: A Commentary on His Apology for the Cross* (Grand Rapids: Eerdmans, 1993) 510.

[59] Davies and Allison, *Matthew*, 2:228.

[60] Michael J. Wilkins, *The Concept of Disciple in Matthew's Gospel: as Reflected in the Use of the Term Μαθητής*, NovTSup, ed. C. K. Barrett and A. F. J. Klijn (Leiden: E. J. Brill, 1988) 131; Davies and Allison, *Matthew*, 2:228–29; D. A. Carson, "Matthew," in *EBC* (Grand Rapids: Zondervan, 1984) 258–59; cf. Christopher D. Marshall, *Faith as a Theme in Mark's Narrative*, SNTSMS, ed. G. N. Stanton, vol. 64 (Cambridge: Cambridge University Press, 1989) 154–59.

[61] The use of εἰς here is probably causal (Davies and Allison, *Matthew*, 2:226; Carson, "Matthew," 259).

[62] See BDAG, 650.

[63] Insignificance is certainly in view also since child-likeness and humility are synonymous in Matt 18:4 (cf. also 11:11).

[64] See W. Bauder, "Disciple," in *NIDNTT*, 1:482.

(5) Jesus' response to His disciples concerning the difficulty of entering the kingdom of God and the disciples' subsequent response concerning salvation suggests that Jesus had invited the ruler to be saved. The disciples, believing that God only blessed the rich,[65] anxiously ask, "Who then can be *saved*?" (Matt 19:25; Mark 10:26; Luke 18:26). Clearly the disciples' question is a response to the difficulty that wealth poses for entering the kingdom.[66]

Jesus is not known for confining Himself to singular expressions and there is no reason why His call to discipleship need exclude a call to salvation (whether it is understood as a conversion or a pilgrimage).[67] The post-resurrection church certainly came to intermingle discipleship expressions with evangelistic.[68] By the time of the great commission the term μαθητής had evidently lost its "literal"[69] connotation (Matt 28:19-20).[70] In Acts μαθητής came to apply to all believers until the term "Christian" (χριστιανός) came into vogue[71] suggesting that subsequent converts to Christianity regarded their new relationship to Christ in some sense similar to that of the first disciples and the earthly Jesus.[72]

---

[65] Ernest Best, *Disciples and Discipleship: Studies in the Gospel According to Mark* (Endinburgh: T. & T. Clark, 1986) 21. For reflections of this thinking in the OT see esp. Ps 112:3; Prov 13:18; cf. Ps 1:1-3; Prov 10:15, 16; 15:6. See further Friedrich Hauck and Wilhelm Kasch, "πλοῦτος," in *TDNT*, 6:318–32. I will discuss the implications of this further in chapter seven.

[66] Schreiner and Caneday, *The Race Set Before Us*, 82: That the disciples have understood entrance into the kingdom and salvation as synonymous concepts is seen in Jesus' reply: "With men this is impossible, but with God all things are possible" (Matt 19:26; Mark 10:27; Luke 18:27).

[67] That both conversion and pilgrimage are in view is evident from the tense sequence in Matt 16:24; Mark 8:34; Luke 9:23: ἀρνησάσθω (Matt has ἀπαρνησάσθω -aorist). . . ἀράτω (aorist). . . and ἀκολουθείτω (present). Discipleship begins with a decision to deny self and take up one's cross and emerges in following. Hence entrance and journey (note also the phrase καθ' ἡμέραν) are involved but not separated for following Jesus emerges from denying oneself and taking up one's cross (Bock, *Luke 1:1–9:50*, 852; Davies and Allison, *Matthew*, 2:671).

[68] Cf. Hengel, *The Charismatic Leader*, 88: "discipleship became an expression of existence in faith."

[69] Dillow, *Servant Kings*, 150–51, suggests that being a disciple of Jesus involved literally following Him around Israel and therefore no one can be a disciple today unless they are physically present with Jesus in Israel (cf. Hengel, *The Charismatic Leader*, 61–63).

[70] Hans Kvalbein, "Go therefore and make disciples . . . The Concept of Discipleship in the New Testament," *Them* 13 (1988) 52; cf. Hengel, *The Charismatic Leader*, 88.

[71] Acts 11:26; 26:28; cf. 6:1 [cf. 5:14]; 6:2 [cf. 4:32]; 6:7; 9:1 [cf. v. 2] 10, 25 (=Saul's followers) 26, 36, 38; 11:29; 13:52; 14:20, 21, 22, 28; 15:10; 16:1; 18:23, 27; 19:1 [cf. v. 2] 9, 30; 20:1, 30 [?]; 21:4, 16).

[72] Kvalbein, "The Concept of Discipleship," 49.

Kingdom

Not convinced by the connection between Jesus' demand to sell all and the promise of treasure in heaven, the ruler leaves with his wealth. Jesus turns toward His disciples and explains that it was the man's wealth that was preventing him from getting his desire—eternal life. Once again this is rephrased as "the *kingdom* of heaven" (Matt 19:23) or its equivalent "the *kingdom* of God"[73] (Matt 19:24; Mark 10:23, 24, 25; Luke 18:24, 25). The issues surrounding the kingdom are too numerous and complex to discuss here.[74] My point is that the kingdom is in some sense synonymous with eternal life and hence salvation.[75] This can be seen from a number of passages.[76]

The prophet Isaiah brought *good news* (MT: בָּשַׂר, LXX: εὐαγγελίζω) to Israel anticipating a time when God would exercise His kingly rule by saving them from the hands of their enemies (Isa 40:9-11; 52:7-10; 61:1-11; cf. Ps 40:9-10 [39 LXX]; 96:1-13 [95 LXX]).[77] Jesus, like Isaiah before Him, was able to proclaim the fulfillment of God's *good news* (τὸ εὐαγγέλιον τοῦ θεοῦ) but this time the anticipation was over. The time had been fulfilled (πεπλήρωται ὁ καιρὸς) the kingdom of God had arrived (ἤγγικεν cf. Matt 21:34)[78] and was available to all who would repent and believe in this *good news* (τῷ εὐαγγελίῳ) (Mark 1:14-15; Luke 16:16). To enter the kingdom one must have simple faith (Matt 18:3; Luke 18:16-17). Similarly faith is needed to receive forgiveness of sins (Luke 5:20) and *salvation* (Luke 17:19).[79] Presumably this is why it is difficult for the rich to enter the kingdom causing the disciples to wonder "who then can be *saved*?" (Matt

---

[73] That these two phrases are equivalent is shown by their parallel uses between the Gospels (e.g., Matt 13:11 and Mark 4:11 and Luke 8:10; Matt 19:23 and Mark 10:23 and Luke 18:24) and here within the passage of the Rich Young Ruler (Matt 19:23, 24).

[74] See e.g., W. Willis, ed., *The Kingdom of God in 20th-Century Interpretation* (Peabody, Mass.: Hendrickson, 1987); Gösta Lundström, *The Kingdom of God in the Teaching of Jesus: A History of Interpretation from the Last Decades of the Nineteenth Century to the Present Day*, trans. Joan Bulman (Edinburgh and London: Oliver and Boyd, 1963).

[75] Green, *The Meaning of Salvation*, 100–102.

[76] E.g., Ladd, *The Presence of the Future*, 195–217. Among the many passages Ladd discusses he includes Matt 18:23-25; 25:34, 46; Mark 10:17-30.

[77] See C. E. B. Cranfield, *The Gospel According to Saint Mark*, CGCS, ed. C. F. D. Moule (Cambridge: Cambridge University Press, 1959) 35.

[78] Herbert Preisker, "ἐγγύς," in *TDNT*, 2:331.

[79] It is clear that physical salvation is experienced by the tenth leper since all the lepers had already been made clean in Luke 17:14. If spiritual (or a more complete) salvation is not in view we may well ask along with Ladd, *The Presence of the Future*, 212: "Are we to suppose that the other nine were not really healed?" Cf. also Bock, *Luke 9:51–24:53*, 1405: "What the man receives here the others do not."

19:23-25 par.).[80] To enter the kingdom is the antithesis of being thrown into Gehenna (Mark 9:47 par.) which is the same as being lost (Matt 5:30). To be lost (ἀπόλλυμι) then is to be outside the kingdom (Matt 10:6-7) and so too *salvation* (Matt 10:28; Luke 9:24-25; cf. Matt 8:25). Conversely one who is in the kingdom experiences reconciliation with God (cf. Matt 8:11-12; 22:1-14; 25:1-12; Mark 14:25; Luke 13:29; 14:16-24; 22:30).[81]

The temporal element of the kingdom is also important. The first three Gospels reveal an indelible tension between the 'not yet' future occurrence of the kingdom (e.g., Matt 19:28; 25:34; Mark 14:25; Luke 14:15; 22:30)[82] and its 'now' present occurrence.[83] The fulfillment of time has brought about the arrival of the kingdom (Mark 1:15; Matt 12:28; Luke 11:20[84]) in the person of Jesus (17:21)[85] and is open to anyone who will repent (Matt 3:2;

---

[80] Cf. van Unnik, "L'usage de σωζειν 'sauver,'" 1:21.

[81] Ladd, *The Presence of the Future*, 208.

[82] See George, *Études sur l'oeuvre de Luc*, 309.

[83] For an extensive discussion on these passages see G. R. Beasley-Murray, *Jesus and the Kingdom of God* (Grand Rapids: Eerdmans, 1986) 71–218.

[84] The presence of the kingdom hinges on one's understanding of the phrase "the kingdom of God *has come upon you / come near.*" The phrase ἔφθασεν ἐφ' ὑμᾶς is debated. However, the evidence favors the arrival of the kingdom, i.e., "come upon you" (Bock, *Luke 9:51–24:53*, 1080). (1) The normal meaning of φθάνω when linked with the preposition ἐπὶ means "to come upon someone," "to overtake" (BAGD, 856; LXX Dan 4:24, 28; 1 Thess 2:16). (2) The context suggests arrival (esp. Matt 12:29). Exorcism means that Satan's house has been plundered and he has been bound. Jesus' parable would lose its force if the kingdom had not arrived. (3) The personal object (ὑμᾶς) of the preposition ἐπὶ indicates arrival (cf. BAGD, 288–89). (4) Other passages indicate the presence of the kingdom (e.g., 5:3, 10). However, a spatial kingdom is not in view here (cf. vv. 25, 26, 28). The imagery is of a battle between Jesus and Satan suggesting that the kingdom has come in authority and power.

[85] Being asked by the Pharisees when the kingdom of God was coming, Jesus responds: "The kingdom of God is not coming with apocalyptic observation; nor will they say, 'Here it is!' or 'There!' for behold, the kingdom of God ἐντὸς ὑμῶν ἐστιν." This phrase is debated. Is the kingdom present or still coming? On the phrase ἐντὸς ὑμῶν ἐστιν there are three options (see Bock, *Luke 9:51–24:53*, 1414–18). (1) The kingdom is *inside you*. However, the Pharisees are the last group of people that Jesus would say has the kingdom in them (cf. Luke 11:52). (2) More likely is the interpretation *within your grasp*. In other words, whether the kingdom comes depends on the Pharisees' response. However, one may wonder why Jesus did not give his stock response: "Repent, for the kingdom of God is near" (cf. 5:31-32; 11:29-32). (3) *In your midst* fits the context better than (2). The Pharisees learn that the kingdom is present in Jesus. They don't need to look around for it—it's right there in front of them.

A. J. Mattill, *Luke and the Last Things: A Perspective for the Understanding of Lukan Thought* (Dillsboro, N.C: Western North Carolina, 1979) 190–207, esp. 198–201, argues that the kingdom of God in Luke 17 is future based on context. E.g., the future tense in vv. 21 and 23 (ἐροῦσιν; cf. also future verbs in vv. 24b, 26, 30, 31, 33, 34, 35, 36, 37) and 17:22-37 clearly refers to the future. Against this however is the emphatic use of the present ἐστιν (contra ibid., 198, who suggests it is "unemphatic"). Luke then switches to the future ἐλεύσονται in v. 22.

4:17; 10:7).[86] One can therefore enter and experience the kingdom today (e.g., Matt 5:3, 10; Luke 23:42-3). However, the present and future do not always stand adventitiously together. Sometimes both perspectives are in view simultaneously.[87] There is continuity between the sowing of seed (Mark 4:26) its growth (vv. 27-28) and its harvest (v. 29). Likewise there is no interruption between the minuteness of the mustard seed and the grand haven that it becomes (vv. 31-32). Other times the kingdom's progress is described in a variety of ways and seems to have no fixed point in time. The point is that it comes in separate yet inseparable stages (cf. Matt 3:2; 4:17; 6:10; 11:12; 12:28).[88]

(The story of the rich ruler offers a salient example of the present and future being welded together. Eternal life has a future reference while the invitation to enter into the life is present. Perfection suggests an eschatological reference although the present may also be in view. "Treasure in heaven" pertains to the future although the storing of treasure begins on earth. The dialogue back and forth between Jesus and His disciples is very general with respect to time. However, the story takes on a decidedly future orientation in its references to the eschatological renewal associated with the Son of Man and the future inheritance of eternal life).

The temporality of the kingdom is due to its dynamic nature. The majority of scholars today agree that the kingdom is not limited to a sphere of God's rule but includes the idea of God's power at work through the presence of Jesus Christ.[89] It is God acting to defeat His enemies and bringing His people to salvation[90] (cf. Deut 9:26; Ps 47; cf. also Esth 13:15 [LXX]). The OT notion of salvation and Jesus' understanding of the kingdom are synonymous. Thus Isaiah could proclaim: "How beautiful on the mountains are the

---

Furthermore, the word *kingdom* is never used in vv. 22-37 to describe what is clearly a future period. What is significant is that Luke's description of this period seems to involve some necessary observation (cf. v. 20 with vv. 24, 30).

[86] In what sense had the kingdom come near (ἤγγικεν)? This phrase always occurs in the context of repentance (cf. Matt 3:2; 4:17; 10:7; Mark 1:15; Luke 10:9, 11). For the hearers the kingdom is near because all have an opportunity to enter (cf. Mark 12:34). Cf. also John M. McDermott, "Jesus and the Kingdom of God in the Synoptics, Paul, and John," *Eglise et Théologie* 19 (1988) 75: Jesus "probably wished to indicate the effect of the kingdom's proximity, namely, the conversion for which Jesus calls."

[87] Ibid., 76.

[88] Cf. Carson, "Matthew," 101; McDermott, "Jesus and the Kingdom of God," 72: While there is tension between the present and future rule of God in Judaism Jesus proclaimed both aspects together.

[89] See Darrell L. Bock, "The Kingdom of God in New Testament Theology," in *Looking into the Future: Evangelical Studies in Eschatology*, ed. David. L. Baker (Grand Rapids: Baker, 2001) 45–48.

[90] I. Howard Marshall, "Preaching the Kingdom of God," *ExpTim* 89 (1976–77) 15.

feet of those who *bring good news*, who proclaim peace, who bring good tidings, who proclaim *salvation*, who say to Zion, 'Your God *reigns*'" (Isa 52:7; NIV). Hence when Jesus came He was able to express His mission in a variety of ways, the kingdom of God being only one of them (Luke 4:43) without discrepancy. Elsewhere His mission is patently soteriological. He was called (καλέσαι) to help *sinners* not the righteous (Mark 2:17). He came (ἦλθεν) not to serve but to be served and to give His life as a *ransom* for many (Mark 10:45). He came (ἦλθεν) also to seek and *save* that which was lost (Luke 19:10). He was anointed (ἔχρισέν) to preach the *gospel* to the poor and was sent (ἀπέσταλκέν) to preach a message of liberty to those in bondage (4:18-19). It was God's purpose (δεῖ) that He suffer, die and rise again (Matt 16:21 par.). Following the resurrection the person of Christ replaced the concept of the kingdom.[91] Jesus is now thought of as King. He is called "Christ" (lit. anointed) and "Lord" and the term "kingdom" is replaced by "eternal life"[92] in John's Gospel.[93] The point is that in the Synoptic Gospels the kingdom and salvation should not be divorced.[94]

Saved

We have already seen that the disciples understand the encounter between the ruler and Jesus as a matter concerning *salvation*. In contrast to the Rich Young Ruler the disciples have left all and *followed* Jesus (Matt 19:27; Mark 10:28; Luke 18:28). Consequently they have what the rich man desired but forfeited, that is, blessings in this life[95] and *eternal life* in the age to come

---

[91] There is a noticeable shift in kingdom language outside of the Synoptic Gospels. E.g., the term βασιλεία does occur in the rest of the NT (some 40 times) although relatively infrequent compared to the Synoptic Gospels (over 100 times). However, the thrust of the kingdom message changes significantly after the Synoptics. The phrase "kingdom of God" is still the most frequent (John 3:3, 5; Acts 1:3; 8:12; 14:22; 19:8; 28:23, 31; Rom 14:17; 1 Cor 4:20; 6:9-10; 15:15; Gal 5:21; Col 4:11; 2 Thess 1:5; Rev 12:10; cf. also Eph 5:5 ["kingdom of Christ and of God"]). The phrase "kingdom of heaven" or "repent for the kingdom of God is near" never appears outside the Synoptics. Instead we read of the "kingdom of the Lord" (2 Pet 1:11; Rev 11:15) the "kingdom of Christ" (Eph 5:5; Rev 11:15) or the "kingdom of the Son" (Col 1:13). The kingdom is something that believers have been called into (1 Thess 2:12).

[92] In other words, "*what is expressed in the rest of the New Testament by the Gospel of free grace is expressed in the teaching of Jesus by the proclamation of the kingdom of God*" (Marshall, "Preaching the Kingdom," 15).

[93] Ibid.

[94] Brenda B. Colijn, "Salvation as Discipleship in the Gospel of Mark," *ATJ* 30 (1998) 13.

[95] Matthew does not mention a time frame for when the disciples can expect to receive these things although the verbs (λήμψεται ... κληρονομήσει) are future. On the other hand Mark and Luke both make it clear that there will be blessings in the present age for the disciples and eternal life in the future age. Matthew may be implying that all these are received in the

(Matt 19:29; Mark 10:30; Luke 18:30). The story has then come full circle beginning and ending with eternal life. The various terms and phrases in between merely describe the different facets of eternal life. Salvation is capable of being described and understood in a variety of ways. Evidently the young man could have asked his question in a number of ways: "What must I do to enter into the life–be perfect–have treasure in heaven–follow Jesus–enter into the kingdom of heaven/God–be saved?" It all amounts to the same thing—"What must I do to receive eternal life?"[96]

Our study leads us to an important conclusion: salvation in the Synoptic Gospels is a *pilgrimage* and therefore can be described in an assortment of ways depending on what part of the pilgrimage is in view. It can be viewed as present, future, or both together.[97] It can be thought of as an entering into a life of spiritual blessing in the earthly here and now or entering into the life hereafter, or both. The point is that salvation in the Synoptic Gospels is understood *comprehensively* or *totally* as opposed to a particular point in time.[98] This is something that other NT interpreters have also recognized.

Thomas Schreiner and Ardel Caneday observe two dimensions to salvation existing in an already-not yet tension.[99] Salvation according to Schreiner and Caneday is both "prospective" and "retrospective." A number of state-

---

future age although his lack of comment may be intentional suggesting that a present-future timeframe is in view. This would fit with his idea that eternal life is a pilgrimage from entering life to perfection.

[96] Schreiner and Caneday, *The Race Set Before Us*, 82: "Interpreting these terms (eternal life, the kingdom of heaven, salvation, perfect and treasure in heaven) to refer to different realities confounds the story incredibly"; also Warren Carter, *Households and Discipleship: A Study of Matthew 19–20*, JSNTSup, 103, ed. Stanley E. Porter (Sheffield: Sheffield Academic, 1994) 117–18.

[97] Cf. Green, *The Meaning of Salvation*, 102, 117; John G. Stackhouse Jr. (ed.) *What Does It Mean to Be Saved: Broadening Evangelical Horizons of Salvation* (Grand Rapids: Baker, 2002) 63, 137; Joel B. Green, *Salvation,* Understanding Biblical Themes (St. Louis, Mo.: Chalice, 2003) esp. 113–15, 127–33.

[98] Cf. Dillow, *Servant Kings*, 132: "Salvation is a broad term." However, he goes on to say, "only with difficulty can the common meaning of 'deliver from hell' be made to fit into numerous [NT] passages. It commonly means 'to make whole,' 'to sanctify,' 'to endure victoriously,' or 'to be delivered from some general trouble or difficulty [sic].'" Taken on its own I agree with this conclusion although Dillow's contention that deliverance from hell is not present in numerous salvation passages is perplexing in light of my own study. The reason that deliverance from hell is not often in view in Dillow's thinking is because he—I assume—recognizes (as his study shows, 111–33) that the majority of salvation passages do not comply with Paul's teaching on justification by faith. E.g., on Phil 2:13 he writes: "A salvation which can be achieved by labor is hardly the justification-by-faith-alone kind of salvation offered elsewhere." Hence the term salvation in Phil 2:13 must mean something other than deliverance from hell.

[99] See esp. Schreiner and Caneday, *The Race Set Before Us*, 46–86; cf. Green, *Salvation*, 127–30.

ments articulate his point: "Both the present and future dimensions of salvation should be viewed as two aspects of an indivisible whole. Almost inevitably the impression that separable parts are intended will tend to creep into readers' minds, but we must fix in our minds from the beginning that *wholes instead of parts are in view*."[100] "Salvation is not merely a past reality; it is also our future destiny."[101] "Almost all Christians think of salvation exclusively in terms of the past. Believers often say, 'I have been saved' . . . most evangelical Christians do not use the word *salvation* as it is usually used in the Bible, where the term denotes our future salvation."[102] "We conclude that it is wrong to conceive of salvation exclusively in terms of the past . . . We are already saved, yet our salvation has not yet been completed or consummated."[103]

Along similar lines Gerald Borchert writes: "Those who define salvation merely in terms of justification . . . need to see the multidimensional nature of salvation. Justification or beginning the pilgrimage with Christ is not the only meaning of being saved in the New Testament. Being saved also refers to the process of becoming holy or to sanctification. In addition, being saved refers to the final experience of joining Christ in heaven. It is not all over when one joins Christ in justification. There is far more to salvation than an initial yes to Christ and a public profession of faith in Christ."[104]

Also worth quoting here is the seventeenth century English puritan preacher Jeremiah Burroughs: "conversion must not be only at one instant at first. Men are deceived in this, if they think their conversion is finished merely at first; you must be in a way of conversion to God all the days of your life."[105]

Viewing salvation this way may be a problem for some. If it is, Joel Green suggests it is "because of the caricatures of the message of salvation we have encountered, or which have been inflicted on us. Threats of hellfire and damnation come to mind. Turn or burn . . . we should not confuse these

---

[100] Ibid., 47 (emphasis mine).

[101] Ibid.

[102] Ibid., 48.

[103] Ibid., 52. Cf. also Mark A. Seifrid, *Christ, Our Righteousness: Paul's Theology of Justification* (Downers Grove, Ill.: InterVarsity, 2000) esp. 172–86; cf. Frederick Dale Bruner, *Matthew: A Commentary* (Dallas: Word, 1990) 659: "We sometimes think in the church that when . . . we have received forgiveness of sins . . . the whole drama is over. We sometimes think that the whole history of salvation has reached its destination when people reach initiation. But in the Gospel of Matthew this is not so . . . this forgiveness is the beginning . . . but—alarmingly—not necessarily the ending, of the drama." Similarly, see esp. Paul A. Rainbow, *The Way of Salvation: The Role of Christian Obedience in Justification* (Waynesboro, Ga.: 2005).

[104] Gerald, L. Borchert, *Assurance and Warning* (Nashville: Broadman, 1987) 206–7.

[105] Jeremiah Burroughs, *The Rare Jewel of Christian Contentment* (London: Peter Cole, 1648; Edinburgh: Banner of Truth, 1964; Reprint, 1979) 143.

with the focus of the biblical theme of salvation . . . Salvation is a 'way,' a journey, a life-path, and not only or merely a point in time or a destination we seek."[106]

I agree with Schreiner, Caneday, Borchert, Burroughs, and Green.[107] The ongoing nature of salvation can be seen throughout the NT.[108] And yet churches today, for some reason, appear oddly oblivious to the idea that salvation is a process in any sense of the word. Rather most probably think of salvation as a one-time decision,[109] as I once thought myself. But as we have already seen in chapter two this idea is not one that has come from our church forebears—Augustine, Luther or Calvin, and certainly not Wesley. Furthermore, we have just seen that it did not come from Jesus and as we *shall* see it has not come from the NT epistles. This leaves a period spanning approximately the last two hundred years for this notion to have made its way in through church doors. Regardless of its origins though, the idea that salvation is a decision has largely been taken up by the "Salvation-Discipleship" camp, the last view surveyed in chapter two.

So it is to the NT that we now turn. I should point out that this will not be an exhaustive study on salvation in the NT. I simply hope to demonstrate what I have already shown in the Synoptic Gospels: salvation[110] is multifaceted and when all its facets are comprehensively in view it can legitimately be understood as a pilgrimage.[111]

---

[106] Green, *Salvation*, 2.

[107] For more discussion in this area see esp. Scot McKnight, *Turning to Jesus: The Sociology of Conversion in the Gospels* (Louisville, Ky.: Westminster John Knox, 2002); Stackhouse, *What Does It Mean To Be Saved*.

[108] Cf. also Rudolf Bultmann, *Theology of the New Testament*, trans. Kendrick Grobel, vol. 2 (London: SCM, 1955) 157–202; Kümmel, *The Theology of the New Testament*, 141–46, 325–33; Hans Conzelmann, *An Outline of the Theology of the New Testament*, The New Testament Library, ed. Alan Richardson et al., trans. John Bowden (London: SCM, 1969) 356–58; Karl Hermann Schelkle, *Theology of the New Testament: Salvation History—Revelation*, trans. William A. Jurgens (Collegeville, Minn.: Liturgical, 1971) 2:205–9; Donald Guthrie, *New Testament Theology* (Downers Grove, Ill.: InterVarsity, 1981) 592; Leon Morris, *New Testament Theology*, (Grand Rapids: Zondervan, 1986) 320; George Eldon Ladd, *A Theology of the New Testament*, ed. Donald A. Hagner (Grand Rapids: Eerdmans, 1993) 482–84; G. B. Caird, *New Testament Theology*, ed. L. D. Hurst (Oxford: Clarendon, 1994) 118–35; Green, *Salvation*.

[109] See Stackhouse, *What Does It Mean to Be Saved*, notably 47, 56, 64–66, 97–100, 106, 116–18, 181; McKnight, *Turning to Jesus*, 5–15. McKnight's last description is perhaps the one with which many are familiar—"personal decision."

[110] That σῴζω and its cognates can refer to physical salvation is well known. We are only interested in how the NT authors understand salvation in its soteriological sense.

[111] Ibid., 3: "conversion is a process, and we should recognize that what one person might think of as less-than-a-full-conversion may be an early dimension in the process of conversion."

Salvation in the New Testament

Johannine Literature

"The theological distinctiveness of John's Gospel does not come to expression in σώζω or σωτηρία,"[112] replaced instead by "life" (ζωή) or commonly "eternal life" (αἰώνιος ζωή).[113] That the two are synonymous however is seen in the purpose for Christ's coming. He came (ἦλθον) to *save* the world (John 12:47; cf. 3:17); He came (ἦλθον) in order that they might have *life* abundantly (10:10). The purpose of John's Gospel is therefore expressed: "These things are written in order that you might believe that Jesus is the Christ the Son of God, and that by believing you might have *life* in his name (20:31)."

John's use of life enables him to explicate both the qualitative[114] and quantitative nature of salvation in Jesus Christ. Qualitatively life is a present possibility for those who believe in Jesus.[115] "Truly Truly I say to you, whoever hears My word and believes in the One who sent Me has (present tense: ἔχει) eternal life" (5:24a; cf. also 3:36; 6:47; 17:3). Such a person "has passed (perfect tense: μεταβέβηκεν) from death to life" (5:24b). The present and perfect tense both stress the present reality of this life (cf. 1 John 3:14). In as much as this life is a present reality it is to be thought of as surpassing the life of this world. "This is *true* life, in order that you might know the only true God and the One whom He sent, Jesus Christ" (17:3). True life constitutes a relationship with the Father and the Son (cf. 2:23-24; 5:12; 1 John 1:3; 5:20). In contrast the physical earthly life in this world is transitory (John 12:25a; cf. 1 John 2:17) whereas eternal life (John 12:25b; cf. 8:23) is of another quality altogether.[116]

However the quantitative element of life is not lost in John. Life is something that believers have been saved *to*. Whoever has life has passed from death to life (5:24; 1 John 3:14). His sins have been propitiated (4:10). And

---

[112] Foerster, "σώζω," 7:995.

[113] Schneider, "Redemption," 3:216. The ζω– word group occurs 163 times in the Johannine writings compared to 12 uses of the σω– word group. For John's understanding of "life," see esp. G. R. Beasley-Murray, *Gospel of Life: Theology in the Fourth Gospel* (Peabody, Mass.: Hendrickson, 1991) 1–14; see also Raymond E. Brown, *The Gospel According to John*, AB, vol. 29 (Garden City, N.Y.: Doubleday, 1970) 1:cxv–cxxi; Rudolf Schnackenburg, *The Gospel According to St John*, vol. 2 (New York: Crossroad, 1982) 352–61; Hill, *Greek Words*, 192–201.

[114] Schnackenburg, *The Gospel According to St John*, 2:353–55, stresses the qualitative nature of life in John.

[115] Beasley-Murray, *Gospel of Life*, 3–4; Brown, *The Gospel According to John*, 1:cxvii.

[116] Schnackenburg, *The Gospel According to St John*, 353.

although this life can be a present reality, to have life is to anticipate a future that endures beyond death.[117] This is implied in the phrase οὐ μὴ ἀπόλωνται εἰς τὸν αἰῶνα[118] (John 10:28) where life is expected to continue beyond this present age (cf. 3:16; 17:12). Likewise those who have life "will live forever" (ζήσει εἰς τὸν αἰῶνα) (6:51, 58; 8:51, 52; 11:26; cf. 4:14).[119] John makes an explicit connection between ἀπόλλυμι and τῇ ἐσχάτῃ ἡμέρᾳ (6:39, 40, 54; 11:24-26; 12:48). What this shows is that life in John lasts beyond physical death (cf. 6:50-51, 58; 8:51; 10:28; 11:25-26).[120]

This qualitative-quantitative element of salvation is also seen in John's use of μένω,[121] often used synonymously for life (see esp. 6:53-58).[122] The term implies a continuing residency.[123] Therefore one who remains has an enduring living relationship with the Father and the Son. In 1 John 2:10-11: "The one who loves his brother *remains* in the light" whereas "the one who hates his brother is in the darkness." Two alternatives therefore exist; one can either remain or be in darkness, which in Johannine theology is to be void of life (cf. John 12:46; 1 John 3:6). The point is that salvation or life in John is "both enduring and present."[124]

In Revelation the noun σωτηρία occurs three times (7:10; 12:10; 19:1). In all three occurrences it is salvation *belonging* to God (subjective genitive) not salvation *in* God (objective genitive). Final *salvation* is in view and in each instance the meaning conveys victory.[125] There are two sides to this salvation: positively it consists of *vengeance, glory, power* and the *kingdom* of God and the *authority* of His King (τοῦ χριστοῦ). Negatively it consists of *judgment* and *casting out of the devil*. For the recipients too there is a positive and a negative depending on what side of salvation one stands. For

---

[117] Beasley-Murray, *Gospel of Life*, 5.

[118] Lit. "Shall not perish into the age."

[119] Schnackenburg, *The Gospel According to St John*, 353.

[120] Ibid., 361.

[121] The term is crucial for understanding Jesus' words in John 15 (see further chap. 9).

[122] Note the synonyms in John 6:53-58:
v. 53 "Unless you eat the flesh of the Son of Man and drink his blood, you have no *life* in yourselves"
v. 54 "He who eats my flesh and drinks my blood has *eternal life*"
v. 56 "He who eats my flesh and drinks my blood *remains* in me, and I in him"
v. 57 "As the living Father sent me, and I live because of the Father, so he who eats me, he also shall *live* because of me."
v. 58 "he who eats this bread shall *live forever*"

[123] The noun μονή of the verb μένω occurs only in John 14:2, 23 where residency is the focus.

[124] F. Hauck, "μένω," in *TDNT*, 4:576.

[125] Foerster, "σῴζω," 7:998.

those in cahoots with the devil their destiny is *destruction* (ἀπώλειαν: cf. the Gospels' use of ἀπόλλυμι above) (17:8) and the *second death* (20:15) while the destiny for those who overcome (νικάω)[126] is *life* (2:7, 11; 3:5 cf. 2:17, 26; 3:12, 21; 21:7).

Acts

In Acts σώζω and σωτηρία are used to define the central proclamation of the early church although carryover from the synoptic tradition is evident (e.g., Acts 4:9; 14:9; 27:20, 31, 34). However the prevalent use is soteriological but non-descript and general. One who calls upon the name of the Lord will be *saved* (σωθήσεται) (2:21). *Salvation* (σωτηρία) is in no one else except Jesus Christ (4:12). It is a gift of God (8:20; 11:17; cf. 15:11) and can be experienced immediately since "each day the Lord was adding those who were being saved" (2:47; cf. also 11:14-15).

However, the primary thrust of salvation in Acts is *conversion* (ἐπιστροφὴν) for which Luke uses a wide variety of terms and phrases. Conversion marks one's *turning to God* (9:35; 11:21; 14:15; 15:19; 26:20). A Christian may recollect this time (15:3) as the point where he or she became spiritually receptive (28:17) and *called* on the Lord (22:16) *turning* from darkness to light and from the power of Satan to God (26:18). It is the moment a sinner *repents* (2:38; cf. 5:31; 17:30) *believes* (4:4; 5:14; 13:48; 16:31; 11:21) and is invariably *baptized* (2:38; 22:16; cf. 8:36, 38; 10:47-48; 16:33). Theologically a number of significant things happen at one's conversion. A person is *justified* (13:39) and *sanctified*[127] (20:32). He or she receives the *forgiveness of sins* (2:38; 5:31; 10:43; 13:38; 26:18; cf. 3:19; 22:16) the *Holy Spirit* (8:15, 17; 10:44-6; 11:15; 15:8; 19:2) *eternal life* (13:46, 48; cf. 11:18) and is *added* to the community of disciples (2:47; 11:24).

Present salvation receives little attention in Acts although it is clearly there (cf. 2:47 above). Luke's figurative use of ὁδός (road, way)[128] to characterize the Christian message (e.g., 13:10, 12; 16:7; 18:25, 26) *and* its community (e.g., 22:4) implies a specific *way* of life and the presence of salvation.[129] Salvation is also present in the form of God's rule, that is, *kingdom of God* (cf. 8:12; 19:8; 20:25; 28:23, 31). In a few instances it is eschatological

---

[126] Note 1 John 5:4: "whoever is born from God *overcomes* (νικᾷ) the world: and this is the victory (ἡ νίκη ἡ νικήσασα) which has overcome (νικήσασα) the world—our faith."

[127] Note the use of ἁγιάζω here is a perfect passive (ἡγιασμένοις).

[128] Cf. also Luke's use of ὁδός in discipleship contexts in Luke 8:27–10:52 (e.g., 8:27; 9:33; 10:32, 52) whereas in Matthew and Mark it is virtually absent (Best, *Disciples and Discipleship*, 19).

[129] G. Ebel, "Walk," in *NIDNTT*, 3:942.

(1:3, 6; 14:22) although evidently future salvation is not Luke's focus (1:7; cf. 3:21; 20:32; 24:15, 25).

Paul[130]

Paul is able to speak of past salvation as the salvation, which has "come to pass with the reception of the Gospel."[131] This is clear in Titus 3:5 where it is "not because of works which we have done in righteousness but according to His mercy God has *saved* (aorist: ἔσωσεν) us by the washing of regeneration and the renewal of the Holy Spirit" (Tit 3:5; cf. 2 Tim 1:9). Paul says the same thing but positively in Titus 3:7: "that *having been justified* (aorist passive: δικαιωθέντες) by His grace we might become heirs according to the *hope of eternal life*." Hence salvation and justification are presented as past realities anticipating the hope of eternal life.[132]

However, Paul typically uses the σω- word group to refer to future or eschatological salvation[133] (e.g., 1 Cor 3:15; 2 Tim 4:16). Believers are saved *from*[134] God's wrath (Rom 5:9, 10; 1 Thess 5:9; cf. 1:10),[135] death (2 Cor 7:10), and destruction (Phil 1:28; 2 Thess 2:10). They are saved "*into* (εἰς) possession of the glory of our Lord Jesus Christ" (2 Thess 2:13-14; cf. Phil 3:20-21; 2 Tim 2:10) and "His heavenly kingdom" (4:18). This eschatological salvation is nearer now than when we first believed (Rom 13:11-12) and coincides with the Day of the Lord (1 Cor 5:5). Future salvation is also in view in the phrase *inheriting the kingdom of God* (1 Cor 6:9; 15:50; Gal 5:21)[136] being *made worthy of the kingdom of God* (2 Thess 1:5) and *eternal life* (Rom 2:7-8; 6:22-23;[137] Gal 6:8).[138]

When Paul does speak of past or present salvation he usually employs other terms such as *justification, reconciliation, redemption,* or *sanctification*.[139]

---

[130] See Green, *The Meaning of Salvation*, 152–89, for an excellent treatment of salvation in Paul.

[131] Foerster, "σῴζω," 7:994; see also Green, *The Meaning of Salvation*, 153–54.

[132] Similarly Paul appears to use σῴζω as a synonym for "convert" in Rom 11:15 and 1 Cor 9:22 (C. E. B. Cranfield, *The Epistle to the Romans*, vol. 2, ICC, ed. J. A. Emerton, C. E. B. Cranfield [Edinburgh: T. & T. Clark, 1979] 561).

[133] Foerster, "σῴζω," 7:992; Green, *The Meaning of Salvation*, 153, esp. 179–89.

[134] For a detailed treatment see ibid., 154–61.

[135] In 1 Thess 1:10 Jesus ῥυόμενον believers from the coming wrath.

[136] Contra Zane C. Hodges, *The Hungry Inherit: Refreshing Insights on Salvation, Discipleship, and Rewards* (Chicago: Moody, 1972) 96–107; Dillow, *Servant Kings*, 61–91.

[137] Cf. Rom 6:21: τὸ γὰρ τέλος ἐκείνων θάνατος and v. 22: τὸ δὲ τέλος ζωὴν αἰώνιον.

[138] Foerster, "σῴζω," 7:993, n. 115.

[139] Although even here there are exceptions where he may refer to the future. Cf. e.g.,

Justification and reconciliation are clearly distinguished from salvation in Romans 5:9-10.[140] We *were reconciled* (κατηλλάγημεν) and are *now justified* (δικαιωθέντες νῦν) but we *will be saved* (σωθησόμεθα). Similarly in 6:22 we *were redeemed* (ἐλευθερωθέντες) from sin and the end (τέλος) is eternal life. The decadent Corinthians have already been *sanctified* (ἡγιάσθητε) and *justified* (ἐδικαιώθητε) (1 Cor 6:11; cf. 1:2).

There are instances where Paul's use of σῴζω is ambiguous and it is difficult to locate a time element (e.g., Rom 10:9, 13; 1 Cor 10:33; 15:2; 1 Tim 1:15; 2:4). In these instances a comprehensive understanding of salvation is probably in view.[141] This seems right since Paul can speak of salvation in the past, present, future, or all three. In Philippians he urges his readers to continually work out (present tense: κατεργάζεσθε) their own *salvation* (Phil 2:12). In Romans 1:16 "the gospel is the power of God for *salvation*." (In Romans salvation cannot be confined to the past or the present).[142] Salvation is evidently something that keeps going on in the present. People are in two groups: they are either perishing or *being saved* (present passive: σῳζομένοις– 1 Cor 1: 18; 2 Cor 2:15) suggesting that the way to salvation (σωτηρία) or destruction (ἀπώλεια) is still open.[143] Salvation is a present possibility for now is the day of salvation (2 Cor 6:2). Paul states in Ephesians that we have been saved although the perfect tense (σεσῳσμένοι) suggests that salvation has implications for the present (Eph 2:5, 8)[144] born out by the presence of the term "walk" (περιπατήσωμεν) in v. 10 (cf. 2:2; 4:1, 17; 5:2, 8, 15). What is clear is that for Paul the salvation that has been experienced in the past cannot be divorced from the present or the future. For *in hope we*

δικαιωθήσονται in Rom 2:13 (δικαιούμενοι in 3:23 is present) ἀπολύτρωσιν in 8:23; καταλλαγὴ in 11:15 (parallel with ζωὴ ἐκ νεκρῶν); ἁγιάσῃ in Eph 5:26; cf. Seifrid, *Christ, Our Righteousness*.

[140] Foerster, "σῴζω," 7:992.

[141] Ibid.

[142] Although there is probably more in view here than eschatological salvation as in Rom 5:9, 10; 8:24 (cf. 10:9, 13; 11:14).

[143] Foerster, "σῴζω," 7:992. Similarly, Anthony C. Thiselton, *The First Epistle to the Corinthians*, NIGTC, ed. I. Howard Marshall and Donald A. Hagner (Grand Rapids: Eerdmans, 2000) 156, points out that the Corinthians are *on their way to salvation*. Cf. also J. Héring, *The First Epistle of Saint Paul to the Corinthians* (London: Epworth, 1962) 8: "It is highly characteristic of Paul's soteriology that he does not speak of 'the saved' (which would be 'σεσῳσμένοι') but of those who are being saved (σῳζομένοις). Salvation is not yet gained in its totality, in so far as the . . . 'future age', has not appeared"; see also Green, *Salvation*, 129.

[144] Peter T. O'Brien, *The Letter to the Ephesians*, PNTC (Grand Rapids: Eerdmans, 1999) 169.

were saved (aorist passive: ἐσώθημεν) the hope being "the redemption of our body" (8:23).[145]

Hebrews

In Hebrews the term σωτηρίας is invariably final or future for angels are sent to serve "those who are about to inherit salvation" (μέλλοντας κληρονομεῖν σωτηρίαν) (Heb 1:14). Here salvation is tied to the "the powers of the age to come" (6:5) "the good things to come" (10:1) "the world to come" (2:5) and "the city that is to come" (13:14). To inherit is to receive the promise, which in Hebrews is future (10:36; cf. 6:12; 9:15). This future salvation is variously alluded to as *glory* (2:10) *eternal* (5:9) *hope* (6:11 cf. v. 9) *perfection* (6:1) an *unshakeable kingdom* (12:28) and *complete* (7:25). It is this salvation that Christians wait for when Christ comes a second time (9:28).

However, while σωτηρίας is still future it clearly has a past and a present although it is described in ways other than σωτηρίας. In 12:1 the writer refers to the Christian life as a race[146] (ἀγῶνα).[147] The readers have had their beginning (τῆς ἀρχῆς: 6:1a) but they are to press on to perfection (τελειότητα: v. 1b) which is ultimately their end (cf. the use of τέλος in 3:14; 6:11)[148] that is, their final salvation. The race begins (cf. ἀρχῆς) with

---

[145] Schneider, "Redemption," 3:214. In Gal 5:5 believers await the *hope of righteousness* (δικαιοσύνης). In Rom 10:10 δικαιοσύνη and σωτηρία are synonymous. "For with the heart he believes to *righteousness* and with the mouth he confesses to *salvation*" (Foerster, "σῴζω," 7:993).

[146] Others have described it as a pilgrimage; cf. esp. Ernst Käsemann, *The Wandering People of God: An Investigation of the Letter to the Hebrews*, trans. Roy. A. Harrisville and Irving L. Sandberg (Minneapolis: Augsburg, 1984) 17–48.

[147] Cf. Luke's use of the verb ἀγωνίζεσθε in Luke 13:24 ("*strain every nerve to enter* [BDAG, 17] through the narrow door") and Paul's use of the verb with the noun in 1 Tim 6:12 ("ἀγωνί ζου the good ἀγῶνα of faith: take hold of *eternal life*"). Here it is significant that Paul appears to equate ἀγῶνα with eternal life (cf. also 1 Cor 9:25; 2 Tim 4:7).

[148] The τελ– word group plays a significant role in Hebrews. Perfection is applied to both Christ and believers. When applied to Christ perfection speaks of His position as well as His practice. Christ was made perfect by means of (διά) suffering (Heb 2:10). His perfection indicates a learned obedience (practice) in the face of suffering (5:8) which then equipped Him to become the source of eternal salvation to all who obey Him (v. 9). His perfection is then to be thought of as vocational indicating His complete suitability as a Savior (cf. 2:18; 4:14-15). Perfection is a term also applied to believers concerning their *position* as well as their *practice*. Concerning position Christ's sacrifice has already made believers perfect (10:14; 12:23) i.e., their consciences have been cleansed from sin (9:14) something that the Law was unable to achieve (7:11, 19; 9:9; 10:1). However, although believers are perfect in their position before God the readers of Hebrews are urged to be perfect in their practice (6:1). Here the term is virtually synonymous with ἁγιάζω (cf. 10:14; R. Schippers, "Goal," in *NIDNTT*, 2: 63-64) although its eschatological overtones are greater. Evidently the readers of Hebrews are not yet perfect (5:11-14) although it is a goal the writer wants them to reach (6:1). It is therefore

hearing the gospel, placing one's *faith* (4:2-3; cf. v. 6) and *confidence* in Jesus Christ (3:14) *repentance from dead works* and *faith in God* (6:1) and *coming to God* (7:25). Those who begin the race have *entered God's rest* (4:3) become *partakers of the Holy Spirit* (6:4) tasted the *powers of the age to come* (v. 5) been *sanctified* (10:10, 29) *made perfect forever* (10:14; 12:23) and have come to the *heavenly Jerusalem* (12:22).

However while the race has begun it is not yet finished and continues until the end. Participants who have been sanctified are in the process of being sanctified (10:14) and will be sanctified (12:10). They have been made perfect, are presently enjoying that perfection (τετελείωκεν)[149] and yet are urged to press on to perfection (6:1). Clearly they have entered God's rest since they continue to enter (present tense: εἰσερχόμεθα) (4:3). However this does not prevent the writer from exhorting his readers to enter (v. 11) since the promise to enter still stands (vv. 1, 9). Similarly it is never said that these readers have come to God, yet it is assumed since they are to keep on coming (present tense: προσερχομένους) (7:25). They have tasted the powers of the age to come and come to the heavenly Jerusalem yet they still seek the city that is to come (13:14).

It is important then to understand that salvation in Hebrews is a now but not yet experience. The "good things" of the new covenant have arrived (9:11)[150] yet there are still "good things" to come (10:1). Salvation has begun and so is now present but it is not yet a future reality. For this reason race imagery is apt for these fledgling participants who are tempted to throw away their confidence (10:35). For although they have put their faith and confidence in Jesus the writer still urges them to hold firmly to that first confession of faith (4:14; cf. chap. 11) and confidence until the end (3:14).[151] They are

---

apparent that perfection begins here in this life although there is an eschatological element to perfection which suggests that one is not completely perfected until one's salvation is complete in eternity (cf. 3:14; 6:8, 11; cf. also 7:28; 9:11). For a full discussion on perfection in Hebrews along the same lines which I have presented here, see David Peterson, *Hebrews and Perfection: An Examination of the Concept of Perfection in the 'Epistle to the Hebrews'*, SNTSMS, ed. R. McL. Wilson and M. E. Thrall, vol. 47 (Cambridge: Cambridge University Press, 1982).

[149] Note the perfect tense. Perfection is achieved in the past but presently experienced (ibid., 167).

[150] At Heb 9:11 the external evidence is split between γενομένων ἀγαθῶν ("the good things *which have come*"; P46, B, D*, 1739) over μελλόντων ἀγαθῶν ("the good things *about to come*"; ℵ A D² 33 1881 maj. lat). On the whole however the γενομένων reading is to be preferred being the earlier and more diverse. Scribes may have been influenced by 10:1 (μελλόντων ἀγαθῶν). See Bruce M. Metzger, *TCGNT*, 2d ed. (Stuttgart: German Bible Society, 1994) 598.

[151] Cf. Harold W. Attridge, *A Commentary on the Epistle to the Hebrews*, Hermeneia, ed. Helmut Koester (Philadelphia: Fortress, 1989) 22: "Faith is connected with the summons to maintain things such as boldness, hope, and the 'initial reality' . . . provided by participation

in need of endurance (10:36) and so are urged to run with endurance (12:1). They are to be patient not lazy (6:12) and hold unswervingly to their hope (10:23). In their suffering (see esp. 12:4-11) they are urged to leave the *beginning* (ἀρχῆς) things of Christ and press on to *perfection* (τελειότητα) (6:1). Hence Jesus Christ is their paradigm for they are to fix their gaze on Him who was *made perfect* through suffering and therefore is the quintessential *beginner* (ἀρχηγὸν) and *perfector* (τελειωτὴν) of their faith (12:2; cf. also 2:10).

James

The first occurrence of σώζω occurs in James 1:21: "Therefore, laying aside all uncleanness and surplus wickedness in humility, receive the implanted word which is able to *save* your souls (ψυχὰς)." According to Zane Hodges "to save the soul" is a standard and normal way of saying "to save the life."[152] He concludes that salvation for James is the "preservation of the physical life from death."[153] We have seen that σώζω can refer to physical salvation,[154] however we also saw that the context is usually very clear when this is the case.[155] In addition to 1:21 the term also occurs in 2:14; 4:12; 5:15, 20. The last two references (5:15, 20) can be debated so I will leave them out (it matters little to our discussion). In the immediate context of 1:21 the Word (λόγον) has power to "give birth" (or "regenerate"; ἀπεκύησεν)[156] (v. 18) and save souls (v. 21). The contrast between *birth* and *salvation* suggests a contrast between the beginning of salvation and the end.[157] This seems especially the case since the intervening verses (vv. 19-20) deal with matters subsequent to regeneration—listening, anger, righteous living. Eschatological salvation is certainly in view in 4:12 where God, by virtue of His being "lawgiver and judge," "is able to save (σῶσαι) and destroy (ἀπολέσαι)." James has drawn on Matthew 10:28, "fear Him who is able to destroy both soul and body *in hell*."[158]

---

in Christ."

[152] Zane C. Hodges, *The Epistle of James: Proven Character Through Testing*, ed. Arthur L. Farstad and Robert N. Wilkin (Irving, Tex.: Grace Evangelical Society, 1994) 61.

[153] Hodges, *Dead Faith*, 12.

[154] See BAGD, 798.

[155] Cf. Matt 8:25; 9:21, 22; 14:30; 24:22; 27:40, 42, 49; Mark 3:4; 5:23, 28, 34; 6:56; 10:52; 13:20; 15:30, 31; Luke 6:9; 8:12, 36, 48, 50; 17:19; 18:42; 23:35, 37, 39; John 11:12; 12:27; Acts 4:9; 14:9; 27:20, 31; (1 Tim 2:15?).

[156] Douglas J. Moo, *James*, rev. ed., TynNTC (Grand Rapids: Eerdmans, 1987) 81.

[157] Ibid.: "the salvation [in 1:21] is regarded as future: 'receiving the word' leads to deliverance in the day of judgment."

[158] Buist M. Fanning, "A Theology of James," in *A Biblical Theology of the New Testament*, ed.

The most debated reference is found in 2:14: faith without works cannot save. Yet there is good reason to see along with 1:21 and 4:12 eschatological or final salvation. (1) There are observable points of contact between James and 1 Peter[159] (e.g., 1 Pet 1:9)[160] (2) and especially Matthew[161] where eschatological salvation is clearly in view (e.g., Jas 2:15-17 cf. Matt 25: 44-46). (3) The use of δύναται in v. 14 orientates the discussion toward the future.[162] (4) The entire epistle is set within the context of eschatological hope (1:12; 5:7-8 cf. 4:10) and judgment (4:11-12; 5:9, 12). (5) James' warnings to the rich are eschatological in nature (1:10-11; 5:3). (6) In particular the immediate context of 2:14 is judgment (v. 13).[163] No one point settles the matter but taken overall it seems best to understand salvation in James as salvation from eschatological judgment.[164]

1–2 Peter and Jude

Peter addresses his readers as "aliens" (παρεπιδήμοις) (1 Pet 1:1; cf. v. 17). Perhaps it is no coincidence that the word παρεπίδημος connotes pilgrimage for their salvation is also a pilgrimage.[165] It began with their *election* (v. 1) according to the foreknowledge of God (v. 2). Consequently God[166]

Roy B. Zuck (Chicago: Moody, 1994) 425.

[159] See Andrew Chester and Ralph P. Martin, *New Testament Theology: The Theology of the Letters of James, Peter, and Jude* (Cambridge: Cambridge University Press, 1994) 10–11, for examples.

[160] The phrase σωτηρίαν ψυχῶν is clearly future in 1 Pet 1:9 for it is described as the τὸ τέλος τῆς πίστεως. Significantly it occurs in the context of trials (cf. 1:6-7 with Jas 1:2-4, 12).

[161] See Massey H. Shepherd, "The Epistle of James and the Gospel of Matthew," *JBL* 75 (1956) 40–51; Davids, *The Epistle of James*, 47–50. The fact that James never cites Jesus explicitly is not in itself evidence against literary or conceptual affinity. James' readers would not need explicit citation if they already knew the source.

[162] Although by itself this does not argue that eschatological salvation is in view. Cf. Martin Dibelius, *James: A Commentary on the Epistle of James*, trans. Michael A. Williams and rev. Heinrich Greeven, Hermeneia, ed. Helmut Koester (Philadelphia: Fortress, 1976) 152: "Is faith able to save him, once that time comes?"

[163] We might also note here James 3:1 where James states that teachers will receive the "stricter judgment," perhaps suggesting that the preceding discussion on salvation and justification by works is the *less* strict judgment.

[164] BAGD, 452; Schneider, "Redemption," 3:216; Peter H. Davids, *The Epistle of James: A Commentary of the Greek Text*, NIGTC, ed. I. Howard Marshall and W. Ward Gasque (Grand Rapids: Eerdmans, 1982) 120; Rainbow, *The Way of Salvation*, 213–23; contra Hodges, *Dead Faith*, 15: "heaven or hell is not the issue anywhere in these verses [Jas 2:14-26]."

[165] See esp. Moses Chin, "A Heavenly Home for the Homeless: Aliens and Strangers in 1 Peter," *TynBul* 42 (1991) 96–112; cf. BDAG, 775 ("sojourners").

[166] In the Catholic epistles God is the initiator of salvation while Christ is the means (1 Pet

has given them *new birth* (ἀναγεννήσας) (v. 3; also v. 23) and *redeemed* (ἐλυτρώθητε) them from their former way of life (v. 18). However their redemption only begins their pilgrimage for they have been born into a *living hope* (ἐλπίδα) (v. 3). The meaning of "living" is explained by the phrase "through the resurrection of Jesus Christ"[167] indicating the present reality of their new birth. Hope anticipates their future salvation (cf. v. 13).[168] However before this future salvation is realized they must "grow up into (εἰς) *salvation*" (2:2). Hence their present salvation eventually culminates in their final salvation. This final salvation consists in "the salvation of your souls" (σωτηρίαν ψυχῶν). This is the end or *goal* (τέλος) of their faith (1:9; cf. 4:17-18). It is what the prophets searched for (1:10) and it is where Peter's readers are to set their hope (ἐλπίσατε) (1:13). It is Peter's focus[169] that salvation is more than new birth or redemption (cf. 2 Pet 3:13, 15). Believers are also heirs (3:7) who anticipate an imperishable *inheritance* kept in heaven for them and a *salvation* (σωτηρίαν) prepared to be revealed in the last time (1:4-5). Elsewhere this salvation is described as *the grace that is to be brought to you at the revelation of Jesus Christ* (v. 13); *the grace of life* (3:7); *the glory to be revealed* (5:1); an *eternal glory* (5:10)—hence believers will receive the *crown of glory* (v. 4).

Summary

(1) The basic meaning of salvation, whether referring to σῴζω or its various synonyms is deliverance.

(2) Fundamental to the notion of salvation is a change in relationship. Salvation is never one sided.[170] The Israelites were delivered *from* slavery to Pharaoh *to* slavery to God. People in Jesus' day were saved from sickness to health, from enmity to peace, from one's own self to following Christ. In John and the epistles people are saved from a relationship with the devil to a relationship with God; from sin to righteousness; from death to life. Numerous examples could be given[171] but here is a smattering from Paul.

1:3) meaning that both can rightly be called Savior (Jude 1:25; cf. 2 Pet 1:1; 2:20; 3:2, 18; Jude 1:3).

[167] Edouard Cothenet, "Le réalisme de l'espérance chrétienne selon 1 Pierre," *NTS* 27 (1981) 565.

[168] Ibid., 564–65.

[169] Schneider, "Redemption," 3:215; cf. Foerster, "σῴζω" in *TDNT*, 7:995; cf. also Jude 25.

[170] See esp. Stackhouse, *What Does It Mean To Be Saved*.

[171] See esp. Amy L. Sherman, "Salvation as Life in the (New) City, in *What Does It Mean To Be Saved: Broadening Evangelical Horizons of Salvation*, ed. John G. Stackhouse Jr. (Grand Rapids: Baker, 2002) 137–52.

Table 3: The Change in Relationship Brought About by Salvation in Paul

Saved from . . .	Saved to . . .
Dead in your trespasses and sins (Eph 2:1).	For *good* works (Eph 2:10).
In which you formerly walked (v. 2a).	That we should *walk* in them (v. 10; 4:1).
According to the age of this world (v. 2b).	In the ages *to come* (2:7; cf. 1:14).
The ruler and authority (v. 2c).	In *Christ* Jesus (2:6, 7, 10, 13, 20); in the *Lord* (v. 21).
Of the air (v. 2d).	And raised us and seated us with Him in the *heavenly places* (v. 6).
The spirit at work (v. 2e).	Sealed in Him with the *Holy Spirit* (1:13).
In the sons of disobedience (v. 2f).	Sons *of God* (Gal 3:26; 4:6).
In which we also all lived formerly (v. 3a).	*Made us alive* together with Christ (Eph 2:5; cf. Rom 8:11).
In the desires of our flesh doing the will of the flesh and the mind (v. 3b).	Those who are of Christ Jesus have crucified the flesh with its passions and *desires* (Gal 5:24).
We were by nature children of wrath (v. 3c).	Children of *light* (Eph 5:8); of *God* (Rom 8:16; 9:8); of the *promise* (9:8; Gal 4:28).

(3) It is significant that the NT rarely (though not exclusively) uses the salvation word group to refer to the past event of regeneration; however, it has been traditional to think of salvation as the point at which one enters the Christian life.[172] Words such as conversion, justification, redemption, are often equated to salvation. While there is some legitimacy in this, it is only one facet of salvation. The NT writers understand salvation to be multi-faceted describing it from a variety of temporal perspectives and in a variety of ways. For example, the beginning may be described as entering the kingdom, life, justification, sanctification, salvation, redemption, reconciliation, conversion, etc. The present as discipleship, following Jesus, life, eternal life, perfection, salvation, etc. Its end is hope, justification, sanctification, glory, salvation, inheritance, kingdom, eternal life, perfection, etc.

(4) The NT confirms what we have seen in the Synoptic Gospels and particularly in the account of the Rich Young Ruler: salvation is a pilgrimage and as such it has a beginning, middle and an end—a past, present and a future. This is referred to in various ways: Jesus urges people to *follow* Him; John's readers are to *remain*; Acts speaks of *The Way*; Paul's readers have en-

---

[172] This is being addressed in the literature. I have mentioned in this chapter most recently esp. Green, *Salvation*; Stackhouse, *What Does It Mean To Be Saved?*; McKnight, *Turning to Jesus*; Schreiner and Caneday, *The Race Set Before Us*.

tered into a *walk*; the readers of Hebrews are urged to *run the race*; and Peter addresses his readers as *pilgrims*.[173]

Conclusion

In this chapter I have attempted to define "salvation" in the Synoptic Gospels and the rest of the NT. I have not limited my study to the salvation word group for synonyms and expressions are also important. My conclusions have doubtless challenged some traditional perceptions. Clichés such as "once saved always saved" reveal an incorrect notion of salvation as equaling nothing more than a verbal profession of faith. This is not biblical. The NT understands salvation as something much more dynamic and perhaps less clear cut than many of us would like. If nothing else we have seen that salvation terminology needs to be interpreted in its proper biblical context rather than importing theological meanings that may or may not apply. These comments will remain immediately relevant as we now turn to discuss Jesus' teaching on "What must one do to be Saved" and the *relationship* between works and salvation in the Synoptic Gospels.

---

[173] I am pleased to see that Green, *Salvation*, 127–33, has made strikingly similar observations to what I have made here; see esp. 132.

6

Requirements for Entering the Kingdom

"Unless your righteousness exceeds that of the scribes and the Pharisees, you will in no way ever enter into the kingdom of heaven" (Matt 5:20).

"Not everyone who says to me, 'Lord, Lord,' will enter into the kingdom of heaven, but only he who does the will of My Father who is in heaven" (Matt 7:21).

"I tell you the truth, unless you change and become like little children, you will never enter the kingdom of heaven" (Matt 18:3).

Introduction

WE are now at a point where we can look closely at Jesus' teaching on the relationship between works and salvation. More specifically, what are His requirements for salvation and what part do works play in these requirements? Before going any further however, I will first recap. In chapter two we saw that there have been at least eight different ways of explaining the relationship between works and salvation throughout the history of the church. In the following chapters I will present my own understanding of this relationship.

In chapter three I discussed the relationship between works and salvation in Judaism within the framework of the debate generated by E. P. Sanders in 1977. In light of that discussion it is my understanding that Judaism could speak of salvation by either works or grace or a mixture of both. However it must be kept in mind that salvation need not always mean election and entrance into the covenant as Sanders suggests. It can mean entrance into the age to come and this is where works are often the point of focus. On the surface the Synoptic Gospels demonstrate similarities with Judaism. After all, in the judgment of the Sheep and the Goats in Matthew 25:31-46, eternal destinies are determined by works. In 5:20 Jesus says that only those who have exceeding righteousness will enter the kingdom (5:20). The Jewish lawyer can only have eternal life if he demonstrates mercy (Luke 10:25-37). And so on. Yet in spite of the superficial similarities between Judaism and Jesus, there are obvious differences since Jesus repeatedly condemned the Jewish leadership for their emphasis on works. I hope to highlight these differences in the remaining chapters.

In chapters four and five I defined "works" and "salvation." "Works" constitute activities, good and bad, and are a reflection of one's internal condition. NT "salvation" is multifaceted and in the Synoptic Gospels is best thought of holistically or in the sense of a pilgrimage. This does not mean that the evangelists cannot speak of certain aspects of salvation to the neglect of other aspects. But overall it is important that we treat salvation in the Gospels as a way of life rather than a one-time conversion experience.

Now that I have defined these two terms it is time to discuss the *relationship* between them. My approach will be to look at a number of central passages in the Synoptic Gospels in which works and salvation clearly exist in relationship to each other. Although there will be none—presumably—who will disagree with what I have identified as "works" in these passages, I am *sure* there will be disagreement as to whether all these passages legitimately discuss salvation. This being the case I shall devote necessary space to argue that these passages do indeed address salvation. Furthermore, I shall add brief excurses to those issues that have given rise to significant debate in the area of works and salvation. However my main concern is to address those passages that indicate a *direct* relationship between works and one's eternal destiny. My intention is not to be polemical or intransigent. I recognize that the topic with which I am dealing is delicate and needs to be discussed sensitively.

The path ahead for the rest of this study will give rise to many questions that reflect more than just academic interest. For instance, what does Jesus mean in saying that God will treat unforgiving people in the same way they treat others? There are two instances where men ask Jesus in effect what they must do to be saved. In each case Jesus neglects to speak of faith in His person. Why? Jesus tells His disciples that only those who endure to the end will be saved. Does He mean physical salvation, spiritual salvation, salvation for another dispensation? Behavior toward others is clearly a high priority for Jesus. So much so that an absence of love and compassion towards one's fellow man or woman is tantamount to being absent from the kingdom. Does this suggest a judgment for believers on the basis of works? If so, how are we to understand the clear NT passages that teach salvation by faith? What about issues concerning discipleship? Just what is at stake when Jesus teaches that people must give up all they have if they want to become a disciple? Does this mean that one is not saved if one does not give up everything, hate mother and father, even one's own life? Or is one merely not a disciple—but still a Christian? These are only some of the questions that arise in these passages.

My approach will be to begin by discussing those passages in which Jesus gives *His* answer to what one must do to enter the kingdom and eternal life (chap. 7). These passages are important since Jesus spells out what exactly is required for one to be "saved."

Discipleship is an important topic in the Synoptic Gospels and we cannot avoid it here especially since there are some who view the conditions of discipleship as "works." We must therefore devote some time to the relationship between discipleship and salvation. We will then move on to discuss specific passages that articulate a relationship between works and salvation. I will discuss the relationship between *endurance, treatment of others, judgment* and salvation.

At the outset of each chapter I will begin by summarizing the passage(s) within its context and then attempt to *understand* the relationship between works and salvation. My treatment will be exegetical. That is, I will not be so concerned about questions relating to assurance and eternal security—unless they arise from the text—as about trying to understand how works relate to salvation. In each of the forthcoming chapters I will also trace trajectories of thought throughout the NT. This will not only serve to show that the NT as a whole is in agreement with Jesus' teaching on works and salvation but that the NT authors more than likely drew on His teaching perhaps more than is sometimes suggested.

I am not unaware that some will disagree with my conclusions. Ideally I would interact on every debatable point if it were not for the fact that such a task would require at least three times the space. I shall choose my battles but my primary aim is to present my own explanation and interpretation of the relationship between works and salvation in the Synoptic Gospels and give Jesus' answer to the question—"What must I do to be saved?"

The Kingdom in the Sermon on the Mount

Central to Jesus' ministry is His proclamation of the kingdom, the fulfillment of Israel's prophetic hopes (cf. Matt 13:16-17; Mark 1:15). Although Jesus taught the presence of the kingdom (cf. Matt 5:3, 10; 11:12; 12:28; Luke 4:21; 16:16; 17:21) it is clear that believers also await its consummation (cf. Matt 25:34; Luke 21:31; 22:28-30; 23:42). At the core of kingdom teaching is the idea that God is ruling in the person of Jesus Messiah (Matt 11:2-6; Luke 17:20-21).[1]

---

[1] In addition to the references and what I have said in chapter five concerning the kingdom see also Scot McKnight, *A New Vision For Israel: The Teachings of Jesus in National Context*

Matthew 4:17 summarizes Jesus' ministry illustrating the importance of the kingdom: "From that time on Jesus began to preach, 'Repent, for the *kingdom* of heaven is near'" (cf. also v. 23). Jesus begins by urging a group of fishermen to relinquish their jobs and family associations and *follow* Him, which they do (vv. 18-22).[2] Although His subsequent ministry resulted in large crowds *following* Him presumably this did not consist of forsaking job and family ties (v. 25; cf. also 8:1).[3] It is upon seeing these crowds that Jesus makes His way up a mountain to teach (5:1). The sermon begins with the audience (crowds and disciples)[4] being told to whom the *kingdom* belongs (vv. 3, 10). They are told who will enter (εἰσέλθητε) (5:20) and who will not enter (εἰσελεύσεται) (7:21) and are urged to enter (εἰσέλθατε) themselves (vv. 13-14). The difference between the one who enters and the one who doesn't is the difference between eternal life (τὴν ζωὴν)[5] (v. 14) and eternal destruction (ἀπώλειαν)[6] (v. 13b); between a good tree producing good fruit (καρποὺς καλοὺς) and a rotten tree producing bad fruit (καρπους πονηροὺς) (v. 17); between one who does God's will and one who merely makes a confession to do God's will (vv. 21-23); between a wise (φρονίμῳ) man who does what Jesus says and a foolish (μωρῷ) man who does not;

(Grand Rapids: Eerdmans, 1999) 70–155.

[2] Ἠκολούθησαν αὐτῷ (Matt 4:20, 22); for discussion on this passage and its role in Matthew see Warren Carter, "Matthew 4:18-22 and Matthean Discipleship: An Audience-Orientated Perspective," *CBQ* 59 (1997) 58–75.

[3] Idem, *Matthew and the Margins: A Socio-Political and Religious Reading*, JSNTSup, ed. Stanley E. Porter, vol. 204 (Sheffield: Sheffield Academic, 2000) 127: "here the verb (ἀκολουθέω) denotes physical movement. Missing are Jesus' call and a costly response" (cf. also BDAG, 36).

[4] There is some debate as to the people to whom the SM was addressed. Matt 5:1 mentions that Jesus "beholding the *crowds* went up on to the mountain and sat down and *His disciples* came to him. Verse 2 goes on to say that, "He began to teach them, saying . . ." Some have argued that Jesus withdrew from the crowds to train his disciples (e.g., Robert H. Gundry, *Matthew: A Commentary on His Handbook for a Mixed Church under Persecution*, 2d ed. [Grand Rapids: Eerdmans, 1994] 66). However μαθηταὶ need not refer to the 12 (cf. e.g., 8:21; 10:24-25) although even if the disciples are distinguished from the crowds (cf. 23:1) this does not exclude the possibility that Jesus taught with both groups in mind. Certainly 7:28–8:1 seems to indicate as much. Cf. also W. D. Davies and Dale C. Allison Jr., *A Critical and Exegetical Commentary on the Gospel According to Matthew*, vol. 1, ICC, ed. J. A. Emerton, C. E. B. Cranfield, and G. N. Stanton (Edinburgh: T. & T. Clark, 1988) 421–22; Eduard Schweizer, *The Good News According to Matthew*, trans. David E Green (Atlanta: John Knox, 1975) 79; and esp. Graham N. Stanton, "The Origin and Purpose of Matthew's Sermon on the Mount," in *Tradition and Interpretation in the New Testament: Essays in Honor of E. Earle Ellis*, ed. Gerald F. Hawthorne and Otto Betz (Grand Rapids: Eerdmans, 1987) 188.

[5] BDAG, 430.

[6] Ibid., 127.

between the security of a house built on rock and the instability of one built on sand (vv. 24-27).

Table 4: Entering the Kingdom *versus* Not Entering the Kingdom in the Sermon on the Mount

Entering the Kingdom	Not Entering the Kingdom
Entering into eternal life (7:14)	Eternal destruction (7:13)
Like a good tree producing good fruit (7:17a)	Like a bad tree producing bad fruit (7:17b)
Those who do God's will (7:21b)	One who professes to do God's will (7:21a, 22-23)
Those who do what Jesus says (7:24a)	Those who do not do what Jesus says (7:26a)
Like a wise man (7:24b)	Like a foolish man (7:26b)
Like the stability of a house built on a rock (7:24c-25)	Like the destruction of a house built on sand (7:26c-27)

Unifying the whole sermon,[7] 5:20 states that in order to enter the kingdom one's righteousness must exceed that of the scribes and the Pharisees. The sermon in its entirety is an articulation of what this exceeding righteousness looks like.[8] This righteousness is embodied in the words of Jesus in vv. 21-47 who now authoritatively transcends the Law. Above all to exceed in righteousness is to be perfect (τέλειοι) as God is perfect (5:48). Surpassing righteousness consists of internal purity in *addition* to external observance (6:1-18), an undivided commitment to God and His kingdom (vv. 19-34) and proper treatment of others (7:1-12). I shall discuss this more fully shortly.

In short the SM is addressed *to those following Jesus, committed or otherwise,* and addresses *the kind of righteousness required to enter the kingdom and the respective consequences for those who have or lack this kind of righteousness.*[9]

---

[7] Craig L. Blomberg, *Matthew*, NAC, ed. David S. Dockery, vol. 22 (Nashville: Broadman, 1992) 105.

[8] For a good summary of the various interpretations on the SM see Darrell L. Bock, *Luke 9:51–24:53*, BECNT, ed. Moisés Silva, vol. 3A (Grand Rapids: Baker, 1996) 936–43.

[9] For a not too dissimilar line of interpretation see D. A. Carson, "Matthew," in *EBC*, ed. Frank E. Gaebelein and J. D. Douglas, vol. 8 (Grand Rapids: Zondervan, 1984) 127–28.

Surpassing Righteousness (Matt 5:20)[10]

Evidently there are two kinds of righteousness. Jesus implies that the Pharisees were righteous (5:20) but this will not get them into the kingdom (cf. 23:23). The mere appearance of righteousness will not admit anyone into the kingdom (6:1; 23:28). The righteousness must be God's (6:33,[11] 21:32) as opposed to man's righteousness (9:13; cf. Rom 10:3). Jesus defines the righteousness needed to enter the kingdom in more detail in Matthew 5:21-48, otherwise known as the antitheses. Irrespective of one's interpretation of this passage[12] Jesus is clearly presenting Himself as the new authority on the Law (cf. 7:29) not abolishing it but transcending it (5:17-19).[13] Since Jesus is now the fulfillment of the Law and since the Law revealed God's will for people's lives, people must now look to Him for God's will. They must get in line with Jesus. They must submit to Him (6:33) rather than relying on formal obedience to the Law (cf. chap. 23).

Furthermore, there is an obvious connection between 5:20 and 7:21 that is helpful. Those who have exceeding righteousness *will enter the kingdom of heaven* (εἰσελεύσεται εἰς τὴν βασιλείαν τῶν οὐρανῶν) and thus are the same as those who do the Father's will (θέλημα) since they too *will enter the kingdom of heaven* (εἰσελεύσεται εἰς τὴν βασιλείαν τῶν οὐρανῶν). The similarity between the two sayings is easily evident:

Table 5: Surpassing Righteousness *versus*
Doing the Father's Will in Matthew 5:20 and 7:21

	Matthew 5:20	Matthew 7:21
Entry requirement stated negatively		"Not everyone who says to me, 'Lord, Lord.'"

---

[10] The meaning of "righteousness" in Matthew has received much discussion and is far more complex that what I have made it appear to be here. See Benno Przybylski, *Righteousness in Matthew and His World of Thought*, SNTSMS, ed, R. McL. Wilson, vol. 41 (Cambridge: Cambridge University Press, 1980).

[11] Note the possessive pronoun construction—δικαιοσύνην αὐτοῦ—in Matt 6:33.

[12] See Hans Dieter Betz, *The Sermon on the Mount: A Commentary on the Sermon on the Mount, Including the Sermon on the Plain (Matthew 5:3–7:27 and Luke 6:20-49)* Hermeneia, ed. Adela Yarbro Collins (Minneapolis: Fortress, 1995) 200–214, for the issues.

[13] D. J. Moo, "Law," in *DJG*, 457.

Entry requirement stated negatively	"Unless your righteousness exceeds that of the scribes and the Pharisees."	"But only he who does the will of My Father who is in heaven."
Outcome concerning the kingdom	"You will in no way ever enter into the kingdom of heaven."	"Will enter into the kingdom of heaven."

There are two things to note. First, the clear eschatological character of 7:21 points to 5:20 also being eschatological.[14] Second, to do the Father's will is to have the surpassing righteousness necessary to enter the kingdom[15] (cf. also 12:50; Heb 10:36; 1 John 2:17).[16] They are one and the same. What then is the Father's will? God's will for others is expressly stated only twice in Matthew. In 9:13 and 12:7,[17] Jesus cites Hosea 6:6: "I desire (θέλω) *mercy* and not sacrifice." We may therefore deduce a connection between mercy, God's will[18] and therefore presumably righteousness. With this in mind it is significant that Jesus derides the Pharisees for failing to observe the *weightier matters of the Law*: justice, *mercy*, and faithfulness (23:23). Externally they appear *righteous* (δίκαιοι) yet on the inside they are full of hypocrisy and *lawlessness* (ἀνομίας) (v. 28). It is exactly those who are lawless who do not do the Father's will and enter the kingdom in 7:23. Hence they are not able to enter the kingdom of heaven (23:13). In 24:12 ἀνομίαν is associated with the love of many growing cold. Evidently then a key difference between the righteousness of the Pharisees and that of those who will enter the kingdom is the presence or absence of internal qualities such as mercy and love.[19] Indeed

---

[14] Charles H. Talbert, *Reading the Sermon on the Mount: Character Formation and Decision Making in Matthew 5–7* (Colombia: University of South Carolina Press, 2004) 65.

[15] Cf. also Ulrich Luz, *Matthew 1–7: A Commentary*, trans. Wilhelm C. Linss (Minneapolis: Augsburg, 1989) 445. See Przybylski, *Righteousness in Matthew*, 105–15, and his discussion on the relationship between "doing the Father's will" and "righteousness" in Matthew.

[16] Hebrews 10:36 states that "you have need of endurance in order that having done (ποιήσαντες) the *will of God* you will receive the promise." Similarly, 1 John 2:17: "the one who does the *will of God* remains forever."

[17] On God's will in Matthew see also 6:10; 12:50; 18:14; 21:34; 26:42.

[18] Cf. also Petri Luomanen, *Entering the Kingdom of Heaven: A Study on the Structure of Matthew's View of Salvation* (Tübingen: Mohr, 1998) 98: "for Matthew the love command presents the core of God's will."

[19] Cf. D. Flusser, "A New Sensitivity in Judaism and the Christian Message," *HTR* 61 (1968) 127: "Christianity surpasses Judaism, at least theoretically, in its approach of love to all men"; and J. Klausner, "Christian and Jewish Ethics," *Judaism* 2 (1953) 22. Cf. also Donald Hagner, *The Jewish Reclamation of Jesus: An Analysis and Critique of Modern Jewish Study of Jesus* (Grand Rapids: Zondervan, 1984) 169.

at the final judgment this is what separates the sheep, which are described as *righteous* (δίκαιοι) (25:37, 46) from the goats. Only those who have shown mercy to others will inherit the kingdom (v. 34) and go into eternal life (v. 46).[20] Similarly 1 John 3:10 states that "In this is manifest the children of God and the children of the devil: everyone who does not practice *righteousness* (δικαιοσύνην) is not from God, and the one who does not *love* his brother." Hence there appears to be a strong connection between righteousness and qualities such as love and mercy.[21] I shall discuss the relationship between these qualities and one's eternal destiny in due course (see chap. 10).

---

[20] We almost need at this point to jump ahead to our discussion on the Good Samaritan in the next chapter. The parable illustrates the same truth: those who show mercy do God's will and those who do God's will enter the eschatological kingdom. Based then on our understanding of Matt 7:21 and the connection with Matthew's use of Hos 6:6 it is theologically legitimate for Jesus to promise the lawyer (eschatological) eternal life if he loves (shows mercy) to his neighbor. Cf. John R. Donahue, "Who Is My Enemy? The Parable of the Good Samaritan and the Love of Enemies," in *The Love of Enemy and Nonretaliation in the New Testament*, ed. William M. Swartley, Studies in Peace and Scripture, ed. Ben C. Ollenburger and Willard M. Swartley (Louisville, Ky.: Westminster John Knox, 1992) 145.

[21] This seems to be confirmed by Matt 5:48 ("therefore you be perfect as your heavenly Father is perfect"). Verse 48 appears as a summary of vv. 21-47 and therefore defines the greater righteousness of v. 20 (so also Przybylski, *Righteousness in Matthew*, 85–87; cf. Betz, *The Sermon on the Mount*, 204–5). But the content of perfection appears to be mainly spelled out in vv. 43-47, "love your enemies and pray for those who persecute you" (cf. too vv. 21-42; see also Col 3:14: "over all these things [put on] *love*, which is the bond of *perfection* [τελειότητος])." This is also the view espoused by, Patrick J. Hartin, "Call to Be Perfect through Suffering (Jas 1:2-4) The Concept of Perfection in the Epistle of James and the Sermon on the Mount," *Bib* 77 (1996) 477–92; cf. also E. Brown, "The Meaning of Perfection in Matthew," *Unitarian Universalist Christian* 53 (1998) 24–30. Note also Ulrich Luz, *Matthew 1–7*, Ulrich. *Matthew 1–7: A Commentary*, trans. Wilhelm C. Linss. (Minneapolis: Augsburg, 1989) 270: "the higher righteousness of the disciples is . . . primarily a qualitative intensification of the life before God—*measured on love*" (emphasis mine). However, having said this I am not suggesting that Matthew's righteousness is synonymous with love and mercy (see S. McKnight, "Justice, Righteousness," in *DJG*, 411–16). If Matthew wanted to equate the two surely he would have been better to stick with "Be merciful, even as your Father is merciful" as Luke did in 6:36. Przybylski, *Righteousness in Matthew*, 87, is probably right in suggesting that τέλειος offered Matthew a more comprehensive meaning of righteousness than οἰκτίρμων and therefore the former was more appropriate as a conclusion to Matt 5:21-47. Przybylski also notes that ἐλεημοσύνη and δικαιοσύνη can sometimes be used interchangeably in the LXX (99–101). However, with regard to Matthew, Przybylski concludes (on the basis of 6:1) that ἐλεημοσύνη and ἔλεος is simply *one aspect* of δικαιοσύνη. My point is not that mercy and righteousness are synonymous but that the former appears to be a key factor in what distinguished the righteousness of the Pharisees and that of those who enter the kingdom of heaven. Cf. esp. 23:23: "Woe to you, scribes and Pharisees—hypocrites. For you give a tenth of mint and dill and cummin, and have neglected the weightier things of the Law—justice, mercy, and faithfulness. *These things you ought to have done* without neglecting these others." On 5:20 Betz, *The Sermon on the Mount*, 192, writes: "the shortcomings of the scribes and Pharisees come to one point, that their teaching and practice of the Torah do not lead to the 'surplus' necessary

Before we go on we may helpfully join together a few key strands of thought:

> To enter the kingdom one must surpass the Pharisees' righteousness (5:20)
>
>> The Pharisees appear *righteous* (23:28)
>>
>> But the Pharisees lack *love and mercy* (23:23)
>>
>> The Pharisees are full of *lawlessness* (23:28)
>
> To enter the kingdom one must do God's desire/will (7:21)
>
>> God's desire/will is to show *mercy*, etc. (9:13; 12:7)
>
> Those who fail to enter the kingdom fail because they didn't do God's will (7:21)
>
> Those who fail to do God's will are called "workers of *lawlessness*" (7:23)

Table 6: Characteristics of Those Who Enter the Kingdom *versus* Those Who Don't

Those Who Enter the Kingdom . . .	Those Who Don't Enter the Kingdom . . .
Do God's will	Don't do God's will
Are righteous beyond mere appearances	May appear righteous (cf. Matt 7:22) but lack internal righteousness
Are loving and merciful	Their love has grown cold
Are lawful (cf. Rom 8:4)	Are workers of lawlessness

Returning to Matthew's use of righteousness, it is significant that whenever he speaks of "the righteous" (οἱ δίκαιοι) in relation to eternity it is in the eschatological sense (13:43, 49; 25:46; cf. 5:6).[22] I have already suggested that Jesus' teaching on the kingdom in the SM is primarily eschatological

---

at the large judgment." What I am saying is that a large component (if not the component) of this surplus appears to be matters relating to love and mercy. Certainly Jesus' critique relates to internal matters (23:25-28).

[22] Przybylski, *Righteousness in Matthew*, 103, also makes this observation.

and this would seem to confirm it. Significant too is the fact that it is *not* "the righteous" that Jesus *calls* but "sinners" in 9:13. Is this then a contradiction in terms? But rather than contradicting Matthew's notion that only the righteous participate in eternity it is more likely that since Jesus' *call* relates particularly to conversion[23] (4:21; cf. also Luke 5:32) Matthew is merely looking at salvation from different perspectives. Sinners are called and converted at the front end but it is those who are righteous who enter into the future kingdom and life.[24] We might diagram this as follows:

Figure 1: Matthew's Perspective on Salvation

Conversion	Eternity
Sinners	Righteous
Matthew 9:13	*Matthew 5:20*

Somewhere along the way converted sinners evidently become righteous and therefore eligible to enter the kingdom. That there is such a close relationship between righteousness and eternity should not surprise us for Paul also taught that those who practice the works of the flesh would not inherit the kingdom of God[25] (Gal. 5:19-21; cf. 6:8a; cf. also 1 Cor 6:9-10; Eph 5:51). On the other hand those who sow in the Spirit will reap eternal life (Gal 6:8b). Likewise for Jesus those who practice such things will not enter the kingdom of God (cf. Matt 5:21-22, 29b, 30c).[26]

Doing the Father's Will (Matt 7:21-23)

In v. 15 Jesus warns against the presence of false prophets (ψευδοπροφητῶν). From Matthew's eschatological discourse we know that many (πολλοὶ) false prophets (ψευδοπροφῆται) will come *in Jesus' name* (ἐπὶ τῷ ὀνόματι) (24:5, 11) doing "great signs and wonders" (v. 24). They will try and deceive many (vv. 4, 11, 24). Hence in 7:15 Jesus warns his audience: "Pay attention" (προσέχετε) (cf. 24:4: βλέπετε). Deception is a very real possibility

---

[23] See also Talbert, *Reading the Sermon on the Mount*, 33.

[24] The suggestion that "enter" is the same as participate or experience (so Joel Marcus, "Entering into the Kingly Power of God," *JBL* 107 [1988] 663–75) is well taken, especially since the kingdom is often misunderstood as a physical realm rather than God's rule.

[25] Cf. also Luke 13:27: "workers of *unrighteousness*" (ἐργάται ἀδικίας) will be refused entry into the kingdom (Matt 13:49 makes a distinction between those who are evil and those who are righteous).

[26] Joel B. Green, *Salvation,* Understanding Biblical Themes (St. Louis, Mo.: Chalice, 2003) 115–18; 116: "conversion entails *autobiographical reconstruction.*"

since these false prophets will come in sheep's clothing thus appearing as God's people.[27] They are not easy to spot.[28] However their true identity is not seen in their outward appearance but in their inner character—wolves.[29] They are in fact "counterfeit Christians."[30] Yet their "fruit"[31] will betray their true nature and thus provide a means of guidance by which God's people can distinguish between true and false prophets. It is a well-known principle, as we saw in chapter four: one's external behavior will betray one's internal commitment (7:16-20).

Verses 21-23 continue in a similar vein although it is likely that Matthew is now broadening the application to include more than just false prophets[32] (note πᾶς ὁ in v. 21).[33] It is important to note that vv. 15-20 address recognition (vv. 16, 20: ἐπιγνώσεσθε) while vv. 21-23 address judgment,[34] specifically eschatological judgment.[35] God is the ultimate judge. Only He will cut down and throw into the fire those who produce bad fruit (v. 19).[36] This may alleviate some of the tension between 7:1-6 (μὴ κρίνετε) and vv. 15-20.[37]

Just as the appearance of righteousness is not enough to enter the kingdom (5:20) neither is a mere confession, that is, "Lord, Lord" (κύριε κύριε)[38] (25:44; though cf. Rom 10:9). Confession must be coupled with doing God's

---

[27] God's people are often identified as sheep (cf. e.g., Num 27:17; Ps 100:3; *1 Enoch* 89:12–90:42; cf. also Ezek 34; Matt 2:6 (Carter, *Matthew and the Margins*, 188).

[28] Ibid., 189.

[29] On the distinction between sheep as God's people and wolves as wicked see *1 Enoch* 89:12-27.

[30] Davies and Allison, *Matthew*, 1:704.

[31] Ibid., 1:305 (on Matt 3:8) "It could also be put down to the implicit equation, 'good fruits' = 'good works' or 'deeds.'"

[32] Certainly this is the case in Luke 13:26-27.

[33] I am not convinced that Matt 7:21-23 has only false prophets in view (as Carter, *Matthew and the Margins*, 188–92). Certainly there are connections (see Davies and Allison, *Matthew*, 1:693–94) however, the use of πᾶς ὁ suggests a broadening of application. I am inclined to think that vv. 21-23 may be a reference to all who would fit the same kind of category as false prophets, i.e., have the appearance of sheep but inside are wolves (cf. Luz, *Matthew 1–7*, 444; Luomanen, *Entering the Kingdom of Heaven*, 97). For taking vv. 15-20 and vv. 21-23 as two distinct groups (i.e., false prophets and charismatic prophets) see David Hill, "False Prophets and Charismatics: Structure and Interpretation in Matthew 7:15-23," *Bib* 57 (1976) 327–48. Betz, *The Sermon on the Mount*, 539, also sees two groups.

[34] On the abuse of this passage in the history of the church see Luz, *Matthew 1–7*, 446–49.

[35] On this passage and the last judgment see Betz, *The Sermon on the Mount*, 542–43.

[36] Note that ἐκκόπτεται and βάλλεται (Matt 7:19) occur in the passive tense. Carter, *Matthew and the Margins*, 190: "God, not disciples, carries out the judgment."

[37] See Davies and Allison, *Matthew*, 1:706; Carter, *Matthew and the Margins*, 190.

[38] McKnight, *A New Vision for Israel*, 114: "Confession is not adequate" for entrance into the kingdom; Betz, *The Sermon on the Mount*, 546.

will, which seems to be marked primarily by love and mercy. Certainly it does not consist of prophesying, casting out demons, and performing miracles (Matt 7:22)—in totality anyway. But at the same time it is clear that Jesus does not condemn such charismatic acts (cf. 4:23-25; 10:7-8). Rather they are rejected because they are not done in a spirit of love and mercy, that is, they are not done according to "the will of My Father."[39] This is surely confirmed by the fact that their actions are tantamount to works of *lawlessness* (οἱ ἐργαζόμενοι τὴν ἀνομίαν) which as we have seen is associated with the love of many growing cold (24:12). In other words where there is lawlessness love will be non-existent.[40] Conversely where the law is being fulfilled there will be love (Rom 13:10, etc.).

God demands righteousness at the last judgment.[41] Since works are merely a reflection of one's relationship with God (Matt 7:15-20) they are a legitimate criteria which God, not man, may use to judge at the end of the age (cf. 25:31-46). Jesus' words in 7:21 are a reminder to *all* "that a mere confession—even the right confession—does not guarantee salvation unless followed by the right behavior."[42] Matthew of course is not the only one to teach that works confirm one's faith (see esp. Jas 2:14-26).[43]

The Relationship between Surpassing Righteousness, Doing the Father's Will, and Entering the Kingdom

In order to understand the link between surpassing righteousness and entering the kingdom in Matthew 5:20 we must understand Jesus' teaching on the kingdom. We know who the recipients of the kingdom are—"those who are poor in spirit" (οἱ πτωχοὶ τῷ πνεύματι) (Matt 5:3) and "those who are persecuted on account of righteousness" (οἱ δεδιωγμένοι ἕνεκεν δικαιοσύνης) (v. 10). We know what one must do to enter the kingdom (εἰσέλθητε) (v. 20) and we are told who will not enter (εἰσελεύσεται) (7:21). But what is the nature of the kingdom?

Certainly Matthew's use of εἰσέρχομαι ("will enter") in 7:13, 21, is eschatological. "The narrow gate" (τῆς στενῆς πύλης) in v. 13 is an escha-

---

[39] Cf. also Carter, *Matthew and the Margins*, 191–92: "these external actions are not part of a lifestyle committed to doing the will of my Father. These miraculous deeds are not matched by other merciful and transformative actions of the type envisioned throughout the sermon. They lack an integrity between inner commitment and external actions (6:1-18). Miracles alone are not sufficient to enter the reign."

[40] Cf. BDAG, 1100.

[41] Betz, *The Sermon on the Mount*, 190.

[42] Luomanen, *Entering the Kingdom of Heaven*, 97.

[43] Along these lines concerning the role of works at the judgment see Donald G. Bloesch, *The Last Things: Resurrection, Judgment, Glory* (Downers Grove, Ill.: InterVarsity, 2004) 68–70.

tological metaphor for eternal life (cf. 4 Ezra 7:6-14).[44] The construction εἰς τὴν ἀπώλειαν in the NT refers to eternal destruction (Acts 8:20; Rom 9:22; 1 Tim 6:9; Heb 10:39; Rev 17:8, 11) and the phrase "the life" (τὴν ζωὴν) in Matthew refers to eternal life (Matt 18:8, 9; 19:17). In 7:22 "in that day" (ἐν ἐκείνῃ τῇ ἡμέρᾳ) is clearly an eschatological concept[45] (cf. 24:19, 22, 29, 36; 26:29) since many *will* say (7:22) and Jesus *will* confess (v. 23). His confession too is reminiscent of other judgment scenes in Matthew (13:41; 25:41). The sermon finishes with eschatological judgment (7:24-27).[46] This suggests that Jesus' perception of the kingdom in the SM, including 5:20, is chiefly an eschatological concept[47] (cf. 6:10)[48] although its presence is still seen in 5:3, 10.[49]

It is also apparent that Jesus' invitation to enter the kingdom in 7:13 suggests a close link between *eternal life* and the *kingdom*. For all intents and purposes the two are synonymous[50] as the following table shows:

---

[44] J. Jeremias, "πύλη," in *TDNT*, 6:923.

[45] See Gerhard Delling, "ἡμέρα," in *TDNT*, 2:948–53.

[46] Cf. Davies and Allison, *Matthew*, 1:697.

[47] Cf. Betz, *The Sermon on the Mount*, 190; G. R. Beasley-Murray, *Jesus and the Kingdom of God* (Grand Rapids: Eerdmans, 1986) 178; Leonhard Goppelt, *Theology of the New Testament: The Variety and Unity of the Apostolic Witness to Christ*, ed. Jürgen Roloff, trans. John E. Alsup, vol. 2 (Grand Rapids: Eerdmans, 1981) 226–27; BDAG, 168.

[48] Further evidence that Matt 5:20 concerns the eschatological kingdom is that the "righteous" never enter the kingdom in the present only the future (see 13:43; 25:46). Sinners enter *now* (see 21:31).

[49] Matthew 5:3, 10 forms an inclusio around vv. 4-9 with the phrase αὐτῶν ἐστιν ἡ βασιλεία τῶν οὐρανῶν. The intervening promises are marked by future passives (–θησονται). This suggests that the future aspect of the kingdom is certainly in view here (cf. v. 12). It is difficult to imagine that Matthew (Jesus) has in mind persecution as a means of entering the kingdom *now* (v. 10). That said however, Matthew's use of ἐστιν in contrast to –θησονται seems significant and deliberate. "The natural conclusion is that, though the full blessedness of those described in these beatitudes awaits the consummated kingdom, they already share in the kingdom's blessedness so far as it has been inaugurated" (Carson, "Matthew," 132; cf. also Davies and Allison, *Matthew*, 1:446; Beasley-Murray, *Jesus and the Kingdom of God*, 174–80).

[50] Contra Robert Govett, *Entrance into the Kingdom: Or Reward According to Works* (Fletcher & Son, 1870; reprint, Miami Springs, Fla.: Schoettle, 1978) entrance into the kingdom of heaven and the reception of eternal life are distinct (see esp. 134–35). However this distinction is clearly not tenable in light of Jesus' words in Matt 5:29b, 30b ("It is better for you to lose one part of your body than for your whole body to be thrown/go into hell"). This is surely a negative commentary on v. 20, the surpassing righteousness being contrasted with a man looking at a woman for the purpose of desiring her (πρὸς τὸ ἐπιθυμῆσαι αὐτήν) and the kingdom of heaven being contrasted with hell. Quite clearly, to enter the kingdom of heaven is to not go to hell or to enter into life.

Table 7: Entering Life *versus* Entering the Kingdom in Matthew 5–7

Matthew 5:20	Matthew 7:13-14	Matthew 7:21
"You will in no way ever *enter* (εἰσέλθητε) into the *kingdom* of heaven."	"*Enter* (εἰσέλθατε) through the narrow gate . . . small is the gate and narrow the road that leads to *life*."	"Will *enter* (εἰσελεύσεται) into the *kingdom* of heaven."

However it is the "kingdom" that unifies the sermon[51] (and indeed Jesus' entire ministry) and not "life." This is important for the kingdom, or the presence of God's rule, implies the necessity for obedience, submission, trust, and generally complete commitment.[52] Presumably this is why Jesus couples the need for repentance with the reception of the kingdom (Matt 3:2; 4:17, 10:7; Mark 1:15; see esp. Matt 6:20-24, 33). But those who enter the kingdom are not necessarily always characterized in such terms.

The Poor in Spirit (Matt 5:3)

The term πτωχός occurs in the LXX[53] to denote those who first and foremost lack material wealth.[54] Hence they are needy,[55] dependent on other people,[56] helpless, weak and unable to defend themselves.[57] They are usually unskilled and unwanted,[58] often depicted as being oppressed and exploited.[59] They can also be described as humble.[60] It is precisely these qualities which God seems to find endearing, especially their defenselessness and inability to assist themselves (cf. e.g., LXX Job 29:12). Thus we see in the Psalms particularly that πτωχός becomes a more general term denoting an impoverished quality or condition, maybe both,[61] to which God is especially responsive.

---

[51] See Carson, "Matthew," 127–28.

[52] Cf. Leonhard Goppelt, *Theology of the New Testament*, ed. Jürgen Roloff, trans. John E. Alsup, vol. 1 (Grand Rapids: Eerdmans, 1981) 77–78; Hagner, *The Jewish Reclamation of Jesus*, 169–70.

[53] In the MT the poor are usually described as עָנִי.

[54] Cf. LXX Esth 1:20.

[55] Cf. LXX 1 Sam 2:8; Pss 9:18; 34:10.

[56] Cf. LXX Exod 23:11; Lev 19:10; 23:22; Deut 24:19; Esth 9:22.

[57] Cf. LXX Ps 9:23, 30; Prov 2:22.

[58] Cf. LXX 2 Kgs 24:14; Prov 19:7.

[59] Cf. LXX Amos 2:7; 4:1; 5:11; 8:4; Isa 3:14-15; 10:2; Ezek 18:12; 22:19.

[60] Cf. LXX 1 Sam 2:7; 22:28; Isa 29:19.

[61] Sometimes it is difficult to tell which is being emphasized, a spiritual quality or a physical condition, or both. Πτωχός may not always denote financial hardship but may simply

God is on the side of the poor[62] since they have no one else to help them (cf. LXX Ps 71:4, 12). He will not forsake them (LXX Ps 41:17). The verb πτωχεύω is used to describe one who is in need of God's forgiving compassion.[63] One who is in a state of being poor (πτωχός) financial, physical, spiritual, or otherwise recognizes one's dependence on God[64] and appears to be most likely to be receptive to His good news (LXX Isa 61:1). God identifies Himself with the poor[65] and how one responds to the poor indicates one's attitude toward God.[66]

The situation is similar in the NT. The gospel is targeted at the poor since they are presumably the most receptive to it (Matt 11:15; Luke 4:18; 14:13; cf. also Matt 19:23-24 par.). They are the object of Jesus' concern (Matt 19:21) and dependent upon the provision of others (Rom 15:26; Gal 2:10). Although they are often oppressed (Jas 2:2-3, 6) πτωχός is an endearing quality in God's sight (Luke 6:20; Jas 2:5). Certainly there are financial connotations to being *poor* although at times the term is totally divested of any financial association (e.g., 2 Cor 8:9; Rev 3:17).[67]

Hence in Matthew 5:3, the qualifier "in spirit" indicates that Matthew is interpreting πτωχοὶ in relation to spiritual realities[68] (cf. Jas 2:5). One who is not poor in spirit has a hard heart (cf. 1QM14:7). Thus as the psalmist so often recognized, it is those who are utterly helpless that quickly recognize their need for God. It is these kinds of people to whom the kingdom belongs. "For this is what the high and lofty One says—he who lives forever, whose name is holy: 'I live in a high and holy place, but also with him who is con-

---

indicate one's plight, financial or otherwise (cf. e.g., LXX Pss 68:30; 69:6).

[62] Cf. e.g., LXX Pss 9:35; 11:6; 13:6; 24:16; 33:7; 68:30; 69:6; 71:13; 106:41; 139:13.

[63] E.g., LXX Ps 78:8: "Do not remember the lawlessness of our fathers; let your compassion come quickly to us *for we have become very poor.*"

[64] E.g., LXX Ps 87:10: "My eyes have grown weak from *poverty.* I cried out to you Lord all day, I spread out to you my hands" (cf. also LXX Ps 108:22).

[65] Presumably God identifies Himself with *all* the poor. Jesus is commissioned to take the gospel to the poor (e.g., Luke 4:18) and commands others to give to the poor (e.g., Matt 19:21). It is difficult to imagine that only some poor are in view here. However though God might identify with all the poor it is evidently only those who are "poor *in spirit*" who may have a relationship with Him. But it is the materially poor who have a greater chance of recognizing their spiritual poverty.

[66] E.g., LXX Prov 14:31: "The one who slanders the poor (πένητα) provokes the One who made him and the one who honors Him shows mercy to the *poor* (πτωχόν)" (cf. also 17:5; 19:17). This also seems to be a key ingredient to Matt 25:31-46, the separation of the Sheep and the Goats.

[67] For a helpful and extensive overview of poverty in the Bible that takes into account more than the term πτωχός see J. David Pleins, "Poor, Poverty," in *ABD*, 5:402-14; Thomas D. Hanks, "Poor, Poverty," in *ABD*, 5:414-24.

[68] H.-H. Esser, "Poor," in *NIDNTT*, 2:824.

trite and lowly in spirit, to revive the spirit of the lowly and to revive the heart of the contrite'" (Isa 57:15) (NIV).

Hence one thing we may *not* say regarding those who enter the kingdom is that they do so because they are able. God does *not* help those who help themselves! It is surely not insignificant that the SM, recognized for its rigorous demands and high ideals, begins with a promise to those who are helpless and dependent upon God. Surpassing righteousness and entry into the kingdom cannot be gained apart from complete and utter dependence upon God.[69]

Those Persecuted for Righteousness (Matt 5:10)

Without exception the NT authors view persecution, tribulation and suffering, as a right of passage to eternity. Disciples are told that through many tribulations they must enter into the kingdom of God (Acts 14:22; cf. Matt 24:29-31). It is their endurance in persecution (πᾶσιν τοῖς διωγμοῖς) that makes the Thessalonians worthy of the kingdom of God (2 Thess 1:4-5). The readers of the book of Hebrews are told that their sufferings are necessary to share in God's holiness (Heb 12:10; cf. v. 11). Similarly for James one who endures in trials will receive the crown of life (Jas 1:2-4, 12). Whatever trials Peter's readers may have been facing or are about to face they are reminded that they are "receiving the goal of your faith, the salvation of your souls" (1 Pet 1:9). In Revelation it is the martyrs who reign with Christ in His kingdom (20:4; cf. also 1:9; 2:9-10; 7:14-7).[70]

Hence persecution on account of one's allegiance to Christ is not to be disdained (John 15:20–16:4; Rom 12:14; 1 Cor 4:12; 1 Pet 3:14). It is to be expected (cf. Gal 4:29; 1 Thess 3:3; Phil 1:29; 2 Tim 3:12). Why is this? Presumably Jesus' own experience provides the pattern (1 Pet 2:21; cf. Heb 2:10; 5:8-9; 7:28). So therefore Matthew's readers are told that righteousness is necessary to enter the kingdom but at the same time warned that they might be persecuted for it (ἕνεκεν δικαιοσύνης).

So, just what is the relationship between entering the kingdom and being persecuted? To put it another way, how can persecution rightly be understood as an *entry requirement* into the kingdom? After all, persecution is

---

[69] Cf. also H. M. Ridderbos, *Matthew*, Bible Student's Commentary, trans. Ray Togtman (Grand Rapids: Zondervan, 1987) 101–2. "Blessed are the poor in spirit" would fit into the same line of thinking as John 15:5; Acts 1:8; Eph 2:10; Phil 2:13; Heb 13:21; Jas 1:5; 1 Pet 3:16; Jude 16–19, as discussed in chapter four.

[70] Of course it is not the persecutions themselves that provide the right of passage but one's endurance in the midst of persecution (cf. Matt 10:22-23; Luke 21:12-19; I will discuss this more in chap. 9).

not something that one can be commanded to do like being poor in spirit for example. And what about those who live in places where there is no persecution? Are they excluded from the kingdom simply on the basis of their geographical location?

Understanding the relationship between persecutions and entering the kingdom lies in recognizing that the series of beatitudes are a description of the *repentant* lifestyle of a *follower* of Jesus in His *kingdom* (cf. Matt 4:17-25).[71] In other words the repentant are those who first and foremost acknowledge and recognize their dependence upon God ("poor in spirit") (5:3). Furthermore those who are repentant mourn over their sin (5:4; cf. 2 Cor 7:9-10)[72] they are "meek" (Matt 5:5; cf. Ps 37:11)[73] and "hunger and thirst for righteousness" (Matt 5:6; cf. Ps 107:5-9).[74] These inward attitudes lead to changes in behavior of the heart (cf. 2 Cor 7:11) such as "mercy" (Matt 5:7), purity of heart (v. 8), and peaceable relationships (v. 9).[75] It is at this point that the last

---

[71] There has been plenty of discussion surrounding the function of the beatitudes. Are they entry requirements for the kingdom, implied imperatives, the indicative prior to the imperative, promises to those who have already entered the kingdom, etc? The structure is significant: a description followed by a promise. The promise essentially is the kingdom (Matt 5:3, 10). The description therefore is of those to whom the kingdom *belongs* and *will* be given. That being so, prior to this point in Matthew to whom is the kingdom given? It is given to those who repent (3:2; 4:17). It is surely significant that in vv. 17-25 various followers are mentioned in light of the command to repent and enter the kingdom. Therefore I understand the beatitudes to be a *description* of repentant followers of Jesus. To put it another way, one who is repentant will be poor in spirit, mournful over their sin, meek, etc. Theirs is the kingdom. The converse is also true. Of course repentance is not limited to the beatitudes. Both 5:20 and 7:21 describe people who will enter the kingdom. The entire sermon then describes truly repentant followers of Jesus (Talbert, *Reading the Sermon on the Mount*, 144). Jesus therefore begins the SM by describing what repentance is and thus by implication what a true follower and kingdom participant looks like.

[72] Isaiah applies the language of restoration to those who mourn (πενθοῦντας) (LXX 61:2-3). They will be called "priests" and "servants" (λειτουργοὶ) (LXX v. 6).

[73] Talbert, *Reading the Sermon on the Mount*, 51–52, sees meekness and poor in spirit as synonymous. I view meekness as being a *further* development of being poor in spirit and mourning over one's sin. Matthew's phrase concerning the meek is taken from Ps 37:11 ("but the meek will inherit the land and enjoy an abundance of peace"). In this Psalm meekness is understood to be trusting and delighting in the Lord (vv. 3-5) being patient in the Lord (vv. 1, 7-9, 34) and generally not trying to take things into one's own hands but leaving it to God. The meek take refuge in God (v. 40). A helpful way to describe the difference, as I see it, between poor in spirit and meekness is to think of them as two sides of a coin. Poor in spirit is the negative side of the coin and describes one who recognizes their inherent inability to please God. Meekness is the positive side of the coin and describes one who therefore does not *try* to please God.

[74] In Revelation it is said that God's people will never "hunger" (πεινάσουσιν) for the Lamb will be their shepherd (Rev 7:16; cf. John 6:35).

[75] Talbert, *the Sermon on the Mount*, 48, observes that the beatitudes demonstrate that one's

beatitude concerning persecution is given and clearly is intended as a kind of a bookend to the list since it finishes with the same words as the first beatitude—"for theirs is the kingdom of heaven" (ὅτι αὐτῶν ἐστιν ἡ βασιλεία τῶν οὐρανῶν) (v. 10b cf. v. 3b). The point seems to be that a repentant lifestyle (described in vv. 3-9) will be noticed (cf. vv. 13-14) and thus will inevitably result in persecution of some kind.[76] This may not be full blown persecution. It may come in the form of insults and false accusations (v. 11). Jesus stops His list here presumably because persecution in any form is the final and true test of living out these beatitudes. In other words, beatitudes one to nine may be in place but the onset of persecution may in fact produce a different result (cf. Luke 8:13).

Become Like a Child (Matt 18:3)

The entrance requirements for entering the kingdom are not limited to "righteousness" and doing "the will of My Father" (in addition to 5:20; 7:21; cf. 18:3; 19:13-15, 23-24; 21:31; 23:13; Mark 9:47; 10:15, 24-25; Luke 18:17, 24-25). Striking is the relationship expressed in all three Gospels between entering the kingdom and becoming like a child (18:1-4; 19:13-15; Mark 10:13-15; Luke 18:15-17).[77] We shall look at Luke's version in the context of the Rich Young Ruler in chapter seven (cf. also Matt 19:13-15; Mark 10:13-15). Here we will look briefly at Matthew 18.

Only in Matthew does Jesus associate *children* with *humility* (see vv. 1-5). The analogy is apt. One commentator writes, "Note their vulnerability in a violent and dangerous world subject to imperial violence (2:8, 9, 11, 13, 14, 20, 21), hunger (14:21; 15:38), sickness, including paralysis (8:6; 9:2), death (9:18), and demon possession (15:26; 17:18)."[78] Children exemplify the "poor in spirit" (5:3) and indeed counter any claims that the kingdom might belong to those who think they have any ability to enter it. It does not belong to those who think they are great (18:1) and that is Jesus' point. Whatever the disciples believed greatness to look like (cf. 16:16-19, 22-23;

---

relationship to God (Matt 5:1-6) expresses itself in one's relationship with others (vv. 7-9). We might think of Romans 1–11 (relationship to God) and 12–16 (relationship to others) by way of example.

[76] This is the exact point that Paul makes to Timothy: "everyone who wants to live a godly life [i.e., the kind of life described in the beatitudes] in Christ Jesus will be persecuted" (2 Tim 3:12). Similarly Paul tells the Christians at Thessalonica that their persecutions are *evidence* of their place in God's kingdom (2 Thess 1:4-5).

[77] See Judith M. Gundry-Volf, "The Least and the Greatest: Children in the New Testament," in *The Child in Christian Thought*, ed. Marcia J. Bunge (Grand Rapids: Eerdmans, 2001) 36–42.

[78] Carter, *Matthew and the Margins*, 362. See also the background study on children in antiquity, by Gundry-Volf, "Children in the New Testament," 31–36.

17:4, 24-27)[79] it was certainly not what Jesus had taught them (cf. 16:23b). Kingdom participants are not great in the world's eyes. They are poor in spirit (5:3) meek (v. 5) merciful (v. 7) persecuted (v. 10) and reproached (v. 11). They are tired and weighed down by burdens (11:28; cf. 9:36). They consist of the powerless and insignificant: servants (20:26; 23:11) and slaves (20:27), tax collectors and prostitutes (21:31). They stand in contrast to societies' "political elite"[80] and Jesus Himself is the paradigm (20:28). However when judgment day comes the humble will be exalted and the exalted will be humbled (23:12;[81] cf. 11:23; 18:4). There is no indication that exaltation will take place in this life (cf. esp. 11:20-24; Jas 4:10-12).[82]

Jesus' disciples must *turn* (στραφῆτε) and *become* (γένησθε) as children, that is, they must be humble.[83] The turning surely consists of turning from their preconceived notions of greatness. However even here in a context we might consider more akin to Paul's grace/faith doctrine than Matthew's works dominated SM, morality and purity are not far from view (18:6-9). In fact Matthew seems to express a close relationship between being humble like a child (v. 4) and purging oneself of sin (vv. 6-9).[84] For apparently no one may enter (εἰσελθεῖν) into life (τὴν ζωὴν) (cf. 7:14; 19:16-17; 25:46) that is, the kingdom (18:3)[85] if they have not first taken care of whatever causes them to

---

[79] See Carter, *Matthew and the Margins*, 362.

[80] Ibid.

[81] The future passives (ταπεινωθήσεται, ὑψωθήσεται) indicate eschatological judgment and that it will be God doing the humbling and exalting (Ibid., 455; Davies and Allison, *Matthew*, 3:279).

[82] Certainly the scribe of 1 Pet understood 5:6 ("Be humble therefore under the mighty hand of God in order that He might exalt you in time") to mean eschatological judgment. Some manuscripts (A P 33 vg) have added ἐπισκοπῆς (i.e., "in the time of visitation" when Christ returns).

[83] There is some debate on what exactly Matt 18:3 means by becoming as a child since a child is not normally thought of as humble (see Davies and Allison, *Matthew*, 2:757–58, for the options; cf. also Ulrich Luz, *Matthew 8–20: A Commentary*, trans. James E. Crouch, Hermeneia, ed. Helmut Koester [Minneapolis: Fortress, 2001] 427–28). However, in light of the clarification in v. 4 ("whoever *therefore* [οὖν] humbles himself *as a child*") I much prefer Donald A. Hagner, *Matthew 14–28*, WBC, ed. David A. Hubbard and Glenn W. Barker, vol. 33B (Dallas: Word, 1995) 518: "Any further stipulation of the symbolism of a child's humility leads to unwarranted allegorizing"; cf. also Luz, *Matthew 8–20*, 428–29; Craig A. Evans, Jesus' Ethic of Humility, *TJ* 13 (1992) 127–38; along with my own discussion below.

[84] Daniel Patte, "Jesus' Pronouncement About Entering the Kingdom Like a Child: A Structural Exegesis," in *Semeia*, ed. Daniel Patte (Chico, Calif.: Scholars, 1983) 30, equates the two. Though I am not sure that this is indeed the case I cannot deny that Matthew makes the connection extremely close with his three entrance sayings (Matt 18:3, 8, 9).

[85] Cf. Matt 18:3: οὐ μὴ εἰς ἔλθητε εἰς τὴν βασιλείαν τῶν οὐρανῶν / v. 8b: εἰσελθεῖν εἰς τὴν ζωήν / v. 9b: εἰς τὴν ζωὴν εἰσελθεῖν.

sin. The destiny of those who do not attend to sin, understood as what causes one's own sin[86] as well as others', is "the eternal fire"/"the Gehenna of fire" (vv. 8-9; cf. esp. 5:28-29).[87]

However since this passage (esp. 18:6-9) is about eschatological matters Matthew is not thinking of Paul's initial justification,[88] that is the beginning of salvation. This is for prostitutes and tax collectors. But the end of salvation is for the *righteous* (again cf. 25:31-46 and see fig. 1 above). Second, since Matthew appears to almost equate receiving Jesus (18:5) with entering the kingdom (v. 3)[89] it is possible that childlike humility has more to do with the beginning of salvation, and the eradication of sin with eschatological salvation (vv. 8-9). It is difficult to say though childlike humility certainly characterizes the "poor in spirit" (5:3) and tax collectors and prostitutes (21:31)[90] who posses the kingdom presently (21:31). However, once again the presence of the kingdom can never be divorced from its eschatological component.[91]

Surpassing Power

At this point it may be helpful to tie a few strands of thought together to some of our findings in chapters three and four. We asked in chapter three, what the difference was between the NT and Judaism concerning the relationship between works and salvation? As we saw in Judaism and now as we have seen in Jesus' teaching concerning the kingdom, there is no difference per se in the relationship. For both exhibit a close connection when *final* salvation is

---

[86] Note, "if your hand your foot causes *you* (σε) to stumble" (Matt 18:8; cf. v. 9).

[87] Cf. *b. Yoma* 87a: "'whosoever causes the community to sin, no opportunity will be granted him for repentance', lest he be in *Gan Eden* and his disciples in Gehinnom, as it is said: *A man that is laden with the blood of any person shall hasten his steps unto the pit; none will help him.*"

[88] For a discussion on the differences and similarities between Matthew's view of salvation and Paul's see Przybylski, *Righteousness in Matthew*, 106–7. Both Matthew and Paul agree that salvation is a gift of God (cf. esp. Matt 1:21; 26:28).

[89] I should point out however that this is not a connection made in the commentaries. But cf. Daniel Patte, "Jesus' Pronouncement About Entering the Kingdom Like a Child: A Structural Exegesis," *Semeia* 29 (1983) 29: "'entering the kingdom' is thus defined as equivalent to 'receiving Jesus.'" Blomberg, *Matthew*, 272, thinks that most likely the present form of the kingdom is in view (cf. Matt 5:19; 11:11).

[90] The present tense of προάγουσιν may indicate that tax collectors and prostitutes are presently entering the kingdom (so Carter, *Matthew and the Margins*, 425) in which case the emphasis is on the initial stage of salvation. However it is also possible that the entering is at the final judgment (e.g., NASB). I prefer the former because of the present tense along with Matt 23:13. Beasley-Murray, *Jesus and the Kingdom of God*, 179–80, leaves the time of entry open, though leans towards the present.

[91] However, if in fact Matthew does have in mind entering the kingdom now in 18:1-5 and in the future in vv. 6-9 this would be close to John 5:24-29 where faith is emphasized up front (v. 24) but works receive the emphasis at the judgment (vv. 28-29).

in view. However we also noted that Judaism is criticized for its articulation of works and salvation whereas Jesus is not. Why is this? I suggested that the answer might well lay with the Holy Spirit.

Indeed we discovered this to be true concerning our discussion on works in chapter four. Jesus declared that apart from Him fruit bearing was impossible (John 15:5). Though never stated in the same way, the NT testifies to this fact, whether it be said as "poor in spirit" (Matt 5:3) "with man this is impossible" (19:26 pars.) "God is the One who works in you both to will and to act according to His good pleasure" (Phil 2:13) or God "equip[ping] you in every good work so that you might do His will" (Heb 13:21). All these statements amount to the same thing: surpassing righteousness may be needed to enter the kingdom but it cannot and will not originate within any human being apart from God's enabling.[92]

The apostle Paul terms this enabling, "power." The gospel is the *power* (δύναμις) of God resulting in salvation (Rom 1:16; cf. 1 Cor 1:18, 24; 2 Tim 1:8-9). This power is exceedingly great (τὸ ὑπερβάλλον μέγεθος τῆς δυνάμεως αὐτοῦ) (NIV: "incomparably great") since it is the same power that raised Jesus from the dead (Eph 1:19). This "all-surpassing power" (NIV) (ἡ ὑπερβολὴ τῆς δυνάμεως) is from God and not from us (2 Cor 4:7). It is indeed synonymous with God's Spirit and indwells each believer (Rom 8:11; Eph 3:20). Furthermore, it is at its greatest when believers are at their weakest (2 Cor 12:9; cf. Matt 5:3).

What does this tell us concerning the requirements for entering the kingdom? Though we are not told in the SM *how* surpassing righteousness is to be attained (we are just told that it is to be), it is without a doubt that this surpassing righteousness—doing the Father's will, being loving and merciful—is only made possible by surpassing power.

Summary

(1) Central to Matthew's SM is the kind of righteousness required to enter the kingdom as stated in 5:20, itself analogous to doing the Father's will in 7:21. Based on a couple of references taken from Hosea 6:6 it is evident that righteousness and the Father's will are tantamount to showing love and mercy. While righteousness cannot be simply defined as love or mercy these are certainly qualities that separated the insufficient righteousness of the

---

[92] See Green, *Salvation;* Talbert, *Reading the Sermon on the Mount*, 32–43, 58, 65; Terrance L. Tiessen, *Who Can Be Saved? Reassessing Salvation in Christ and World Religions* (Downers Grove, Ill.: Intervarsity, 2004) 230–58. I am thinking in particular of Tiessen's points concerning God's "efficacious grace" in sanctification, 250–57.

scribes and the Pharisees with the exceeding righteousness necessary to enter the kingdom. They are at the core.

(2) Hence while Matthew (and Jesus) does in fact teach a close relationship between salvation (i.e., entering the kingdom) and works, we must remember that the salvation in view is *eschatological*. Instead of "works" however it is perhaps more accurate to speak of "righteousness" (Matt 5:20; 13:43, 49; 25:46).

(3) However, lest anyone confuse this kind of salvation with the kind of justification by works Paul condemns, we must make two careful caveats. First, Paul condemns those who attempt to be justified by their own striving. Jesus' entire teaching in the SM is to be received with a qualification: SM living cannot be achieved by striving in one's own effort but by complete dependence upon God. Only those who are poor in spirit can enter the kingdom (5:3). They cannot do it themselves (v. 5; Ps 37). It is not those who are righteous who join with Jesus up front—at conversion; it is the prostitutes and tax collectors, those weighed down by burdens, the powerless in society as exhibited in Jesus' call to become humble like a child (18:3-4). Hence the exceeding righteousness of 5:20 will only be exhibited in those people who recognize their utter dependence upon God (cf. also 19:26b par). There is no such thing as meritorious righteousness. Such righteousness is man-centered and Pharisaic and is not according to the Father's will. No one will enter the kingdom relying on his or her own righteousness.[93] Second, Paul condemns pre-conversion works. Jesus evidently describes a kind of righteousness that is only possible within a relationship with God, that is, post-conversion.

(4) What this shows is that Jesus is able to consider salvation from different perspectives. Sinners may be called up front and the righteous turned away but it is only those who are righteous that enter the future kingdom and workers of lawlessness who are turned away. However one interprets this phenomenon—sinners becoming righteous and righteous becoming sinners—it is evident that one's conduct evidently plays a role in determining one's eternal destiny. Confession must be accompanied by doing the Father's will (7:13-14, 21; cf. Jas 2:14-26).

---

[93] Is the SM "righteousness" (Matt 5:20) God's *gift* to man or God's *demand* on man? I see it as the latter. First, to see Paul's gift of righteousness here is to read Paul into Matthew (so also, Talbert, *Reading the Sermon on the Mount*, 64). Second, vv. 21-48 define righteousness in terms of demand. Third, "righteousness" is possessive ("your") (Betz, *The Sermon on the Mount*, 190). However this is not to say that SM righteousness occurs apart from God. Only those who are poor in spirit (Matt 5:3), who mourn (v. 4), are meek (v. 5), and hunger and thirst for righteousness (v. 6), meet God's demand for righteousness. Otherwise it is impossible (19:26a). Hence those who exhibit SM righteousness and thus enter the kingdom do so *only* by God's enabling (v. 26b). SM righteousness is to be ours and yet it can't be ours apart from God (cf. McKnight, "Justice, Righteousness," 414; Goppelt, *Theology of the New Testament*, 2:227–28).

7

Attaining Eternal Life

A man came to Jesus and asked, "What good thing should I do in order that I might have eternal life"... Jesus said... "If you desire to enter into life, keep the commandments... if you desire to be perfect, go sell your possessions and give to the poor, and you will have treasure in heaven." (Matt 19:17b, 21 pars.)

A certain lawyer stood up in order to test Jesus asking, "What having done will I inherit eternal life?" And Jesus said to him, "What is written in the Law"... And he answered, "Love the Lord your God from your whole heart and with all your soul and with all your strength and with all your mind and your neighbor as yourself"... And Jesus said to him, "You have answered correctly—Do this and you will live." (Luke 10:25-28)

The Rich Young Ruler

THE account of the Rich Young Ruler (Matt 19:16-30; Mark 10:17-31; Luke 18:18-30) is well known though perhaps uncomfortably so. We are all familiar with Jesus' words to the wealthy young man, "sell everything you have and give to the poor" (Mark 10:21; Luke 18:22). Of course this is enough to cause us more than mild discomfort but it's really Jesus' next words that unsettle our souls: " *and* you will have treasure in heaven." Not surprisingly then, at least one commentator remarks, "No one can take comfort from this story; it is profoundly disturbing."[1] Perhaps our disturbance has caused us to "wriggle" out of the clear demands Jesus' words present. Joseph Hellerman suspects so. He suggests that the Apostle Paul's teaching on justification has done more to influence interpretations on this passage, not to mention our own social and worldview, than any cultural factors inherent in the text. As a result interpretations, he suggests, conveniently "preserve both our Protestant theological traditions *and* our opulent Western lifestyle."[2]

---

[1] Paul Barnett, *The Servant King: Reading Mark Today* (Sydney: AIO, 1991) 206.

[2] Joseph H. Hellerman, "Wealth and Sacrifice in early Christianity: Revisiting Mark's

Leaving this discomfort aside for a moment—discomfort with the text and interpretations of the text—we might well ask what this story has to teach us today. The meeting is an evangelistic opportunity since the ruler's first words concern how he might have eternal life (Matt 19:16; Mark 10:17; Luke 18:18). Does this story then have anything to say to us regarding evangelism and the gospel? What about the man's failure to heed Jesus' call and sell his possessions? Though it has been argued that this failure resulted not in the absence of eternal life but discipleship,[3] the whole tenor of the account does not give this impression. We are quite clearly left with the sense that this "sad" (λυπούμενος) (Matt 19:22; Mark 10:22)[4] ruler did not receive what he asked for because he did not like the answer he received. What then does this story have to teach us concerning the *content* of the gospel? What are we to say to someone who might ask, "What must I do to be saved"?

Clearly these questions are more than academic for the *eternal* lives of people depend on them. However before answering such questions we must first look more closely at the account itself. I shall begin by giving an overview.

Overview

The encounter between the Rich Young Ruler[5] and Jesus occurs in the triple tradition. There are differences here and there though the basic story line remains the same. A rich man asks Jesus, addressing him as "Good Teacher" in Mark (10:17b) and Luke (18:18b) and "Teacher" in Matthew (19:16b), what he must do to receive eternal life. Evidently the man is under the impression that he must *do* (ποιέω) something to secure his eternal destiny, a point made explicit in Matthew suggesting that a *good thing* is what is required (Matt 19:16b).[6]

Presentation of Jesus' Encounter With The Rich Young Ruler," *TJ* (2000) 143–45.

[3] See chapter five; most notably, Zane C. Hodges, *Absolutely Free!: A Biblical Reply to Lordship Salvation* (Grand Rapids: Zondervan, 1989) 186–88; see also, Robert Govett, *Entrance into the Kingdom: Or Reward According to Works* (Fletcher & Son, 1870; reprint, Miami, Fla.: Conley & Schoettle, 1978) 130.

[4] Luke (18:23) describes the ruler as περίλυπος, a word that was used to describe Jesus' overwhelming sorrow to the point of death in the Garden of Gethsemane (Matt 26:38 pars.; cf. also Mark 6:26).

[5] Only Matthew (19:20) indicates that the man is young (νεανίσκος) while only Luke (18:18) says that he is a ruler (ἄρχων). All three make clear that the man is wealthy: Matt 19:22; Mark 10:22 (κτήματα πολλά); Luke 18:23 (πλούσιος σφόδρα).

[6] Cf. Matt 19:16b: τί ἀγαθὸν ποιήσω ἵνα σχῶ ζωὴν αἰώνιον; Mark 10:17b: τί ποιήσω ἵνα ζωὴν αἰώνιον κληρονομήσω; Luke 18:18b: τί ποιήσας ζωὴν αἰώνιον κληρονομήσω.

Jesus picks up on this and probes further the intent of the man's inquiry before giving him an answer to his very important question. Noting the ruler's use of "good" and perhaps some underlying motives (cf. John 2:25) Jesus asks, "Why do you ask Me concerning what is good?" (Matt 19:17a).[7] In all three Gospels Jesus makes the same affirmation: God alone is good (Mark 10:18b; Luke 18:19b; cf. Matt 19:17b).[8]

Having established that God alone is the true standard of goodness Jesus then sets about answering the rich man's question—"how do I get eternal life?" This is made explicit in Matthew: "If you desire to enter into *life*[9] keep the commandments" (v. 17c).[10] Jesus then lists the commandments He has in mind, reciting the second table of the Decalogue pertaining to man's relationship to man—though He leaves out the command concerning coveting (Matt 19:18-19; Mark 10:19; Luke 18:20; cf. Exod 20:12-16; Deut 5:16-20).[11]

The Rich Young Ruler is emphatic in his reply. "*All these things* (πάντα ταῦτα)[12] I have kept" (Matt 19:20; Mark 10:20; Luke 18:21). Mark and Luke add "from (my) youth" indicating the extent of the man's obedience. As good as this obedience is though it is not good enough. He still lacks something. Matthew's (19:20b) ruler asks, "what do I still lack" (τί ἔτι ὑστερῶ), whereas Mark and Luke have Jesus affirming that something is still lacking (Mark 10:21: ἕν σε ὑστερεῖ; Luke 18:22: ἔτι ἕν σοι λείπει). Presumably what the ruler thinks he lacks (as in Matthew) and what Jesus knows he lacks (as in Mark and Luke) concerns the one thing needed to have/inherit eternal

---

[7] Since the ruler in Mark and Luke addresses Jesus as good Jesus questions the young man as to the reason for this address (Mark 10:18a; Luke 18:19a).

[8] Mark 10:18b and Luke 18:19b both have οὐδεὶς ἀγαθός εἰ μὴ εἷς ὁ θεός. Cf. Matt 19:17b: εἷς ἐστιν ὁ ἀγαθός. Note the scribal activity in Matthew 19:17 which leans toward greater explicitness. The majority text has clearly been influenced by Mark and Luke: τί με λέγεις ἀγαθόν; οὐδεὶς ἀγαθός εἰ μὴ εἷς ὁ θεός. The western tradition (lat) has added ὁ θεός and e has added ὁ πατήρ.

[9] For this use of "life" in Matthew see 7:14; 18:8, 9.

[10] Mark (10:19a) and Luke (18:20a) are less direct: "You know the commandments."

[11] There are differences in the order of the commandments between each of the evangelists as well as between the evangelists and the Old Testament. Matthew's order is murder, adultery, stealing, false witness, honoring father and mother; he adds the love command (6 commandments). Mark has the same order as Matthew but adds, "do not defraud" in between false witness and father and mother (6 commandments). Luke has adultery, murder, stealing, false witness, and honoring father and mother (5 commandments). All three Gospels depart from the order of Exodus and Deuteronomy, which both begin the second table with honoring father and mother, murder, adultery, stealing, false witness, and *coveting*. Matthew and Mark have added the love command and "do not defraud."

[12] In Mark 10:20 ταῦτα πάντα is preceded by διδάσκαλε.

life.¹³ Indeed this appears to be what is meant by Jesus' reply in Matthew, "if you *desire* to be perfect" (εἰ θέλεις τέλειος εἶναι).¹⁴

Jesus now spells out what it is that the ruler lacks. In order to have true wealth, that is, treasure in heaven,¹⁵ he must sell all he has¹⁶ and give the proceeds to the poor. Jesus then issues the man with a call to follow Him (Matt 19:21; Mark 10:21; Luke 18:22). However, the ruler finds himself unable to do the *one thing* he still lacks and goes away grieving. The explanation (γάρ) for the man's grief is evident: he was very rich (v. 23; cf. Matt 19:22; Mark 10:22).

With the Rich Young Ruler having now left the scene the discussion turns to the disciples. The rich man's refusal to part with his wealth allows Jesus to instruct His disciples on how difficult it is for those who have wealth to enter the kingdom (Matt 19:23; Mark 10:23; Luke 18:24; cf. Matt 5:20; 7:23; 18:3).¹⁷ Such a scenario is analogous to a camel trying to "pass through" (διελθεῖν, Matt/Mark) or "enter" (εἰσελθεῖν, Luke) the eye of a needle except that the camel has a higher chance of success (Matt 19:24; Mark 10:25; Luke 18:25).¹⁸ The implication is that it is not only difficult but also quite impossible (cf. Matt 19:26; Mark 10:27; Luke 18:27).

Evidently the disciples hear this as new teaching for they express great astonishment (Matt 19:25; Mark 10:26). In their minds it seems that if the rich are unable to enter the kingdom then it must be shut up to everyone, hence their response, "*Who* then can be saved (σωθῆναι)" (Matt 19:25; cf.

---

¹³ So too Walter W. Wessel, "Mark," in *EBC*, ed. Frank E. Gaebelein and J. D. Douglas, vol. 8 (Grand Rapids: Zondervan, 1984) 715; cf. also Warren Carter, *Matthew and the Margins: A Socio-Political and Religious Reading*, JSNTSup, ed. Stanley E. Porter, vol. 204 (Sheffield: Sheffield Academic, 2000) 389; D. A. Carson, "Matthew," in *EBC*, ed. Frank E. Gaebelein and J. D. Douglas, vol. 8 (Grand Rapids: Zondervan, 1984) 423.

¹⁴ Cf. Matt 19:17b: εἰ δὲ θέλεις εἰς τὴν ζωὴν εἰσελθεῖν (cf. 5:48; 7:13-14).

¹⁵ It is suggested by some that "treasure in heaven" is a reference to something extra than eternal life. However I have argued in chapter five that this phrase refers to eternal life.

¹⁶ Matthew has "sell your τὰ ὑπάρχοντας" (19:21); Mark has ὅσα ἔχεις πώλησον (10:21) and Luke adds πάντα ο. ε. π. (18:22).

¹⁷ Only in Mark do the disciples express amazement at this point. This gives Jesus an opportunity to repeat His assertion but without mentioning riches. "How hard it is to enter the kingdom of God." It is not surprising therefore that scribes inserted τοὺς πεποιθότας ἐπὶ τοῖς χρήμασιν (10:24).

¹⁸ The camel was considered to be the largest animal in Israel (cf. Matt 23:24; Otto Michel, "κάμηλος," in *TDNT*, 3:593), while the eye of the needle represented the smallest thing imaginable (BAGD, 828). The two images therefore emphasize the impossibility of the wealthy entering the kingdom. The Talmud (dated later than the NT) brings out the impossibility of such a scenario. *b. Ber.* 55b: "a man is never shown in a dream a date palm of gold, or an elephant going through the eye of a needle." Thus not even in a dream—where the impossible is generally possible—could an elephant go through the eye of a needle.

Mark 10:26; Luke 18:26)?[19] The answer is that on the one hand "no one" can be saved for Jesus too thinks this is impossible with men. Yet on the other hand everyone *can* be saved since *all things* (πάντα) are possible with God (Matt 19:26; Mark 10:27; cf. Luke 18:27). God can get the camel through the eye of the needle so to speak. He can do what people cannot. He can get a rich person, and indeed any person, into the kingdom (cf. Luke 19:1-10).

However rather than spurring confidence in the disciples Jesus' words incite doubt. In each Gospel Peter is the spokesman and emphatically asserts (ἰδοὺ ἡμεῖς) that the Twelve[20] have indeed left everything to follow (ἠκολουθήσαμέν) Jesus (cf. Matt 4:20, 22; Mark 1:18-20).[21] The intent behind his question is brought out by Matthew 19:27, "What then will there be for us?" The question is a natural one. Peter is most likely recalling Jesus' exhortation to the ruler—"sell what you have and *follow* (ἀκολούθει) Me." In light of the impossibility of entering the kingdom Peter looks for reassurance. Maybe Jesus will respond in the same way as He did to the ruler—"still one thing you lack"? Thus contrary to how we might sometimes read Peter's words, his question actually reflects a great deal of insecurity over their *own* salvation rather than any great deal of confidence.

However Jesus quickly alleviates his disciples' insecurity, affirming (ἀμὴν λέγω ὑμῖν)[22] (Matt 19:28; Mark 10:29; Luke 18:29) that everyone[23] who has left (ἀφῆκεν) everything—and so includes the Twelve (cf. Matt 19:27; Mark 10:28-ἀφήκαμεν; Luke 18:28-ἀφέντες). The leaving is comprehensive (Matt 19:29; Mark 10:29; Luke 18:29).[24] The reason (ἕνεκεν)[25] for the leaving is for Jesus' name (Matt), for Jesus and the gospel (Mark), for the

---

[19] Warren Carter, *Households and Discipleship: A Study of Matthew 19–20*, JSNTSup, 103, ed. Stanley E. Porter (Sheffield: Sheffield Academic, 1994) 124, notes that the disciples have understood very well Jesus' comment concerning wealth as a hindrance to the kingdom, hence their astonishment.

[20] Note the presence of ἡμεῖς in all three Gospels and the plurals, ἀφήκαμεν (Matt/Mark), ἀφέντες (Luke), and ἠκολουθήσαμέν in the triple tradition indicating that Peter is speaking for the Twelve.

[21] Matthew 19:27 and Mark 10:28: ἰδοὺ ἡμεῖς ἀφήκαμεν πάντα; Luke 18:28 has ι. η. ἀφέντες τὰ ἴδια. ι. η. The perfect tense indicates that this took place some time ago and still continues.

[22] BDAG, 53.

[23] Matthew 19:29 states the promise positively—"*everyone* who has left . . ." (πᾶς ὅστις ἀφῆκεν) whereas Mark (10:29) and Luke (18:29) state it negatively—"there is *no one* who has left . . ." (οὐδείς ἐστιν ὃ ἀφῆκεν). The point is the same: there will be no one excluded from eternal life who has met this condition.

[24] Matthew and Mark include brothers, sisters, fathers, mothers, children, fields, whereas Luke has houses, *wives*, brothers, *parents*, and children.

[25] Ibid., 334.

kingdom of God (Luke). But the reward far outweighs the sacrifice. The disciples—and "everyone. . ."—will not be disappointed.[26] All such people will receive eternal life in the age to come. But clearly there are gains in this age as well.[27] This is made clear in Mark 10:30 (νῦν ἐν τῷ καιρῷ τούτῳ) and Luke 18:30 (ἐν τῷ καιρῷ τούτῳ) though it is left somewhat ambiguous in Matthew (Matt 19:29).[28]

We should not miss the fact that this story ends on the same note on which it started—eternal life—thus forming an inclusio. Only Matthew (19:30) and Mark (10:31) end with the saying: "the many who are first will be last and the last first." The saying is somewhat ambiguous[29] but seems to summarize the irony of the situation[30] with general application. The Rich Young Ruler who had everything appeared to be first and the disciples who had left everything appeared to be last. However the reverse is in fact true. The last *will* be first and the first *will* be last.

The Relationship between Keeping the Commandments, Selling All, and Eternal Life

I have discussed this passage in chapter five at some length with respect to the different ways in which salvation is presented. To briefly recap: though debated it is my opinion that many synonyms occur in this pericope—eternal life, life, perfect, treasure in heaven, follow, kingdom of heaven/God, saved—to present one concept. That one concept is salvation. It is viewed from various temporal perspectives although overall the passage presents a *holistic* view of salvation.

Though there is much that could be gleaned from this passage I shall confine myself to four questions. The first three questions are interpretive, the last concerns application. 1) What is the relationship between keeping

---

[26] The reason (ἕνεκεν) for the leaving is for Jesus' name (Matt), for Jesus and the gospel (Mark), and for the kingdom of God (Luke).

[27] Most agree that the reward in this age refers to the family of believers who more than make up for blood ties disciples have left. Carson, "Matthew," 426; Cater, *Matthew band the Margins*, 393; Darrell L. Bock, *Luke 9:51–24:53*, BECNT, ed. Moisés Silva, vol. 3B (Grand Rapids: Baker, 1996) 1490; Robert H. Gundry, *Mark: A Commentary on His Apology for the Cross* (Grand Rapids: Eerdmans, 1993) 566.

[28] Only Matthew makes reference to the Son of Man sitting upon His glorious throne in the new age (τῇ παλιγγενεσίᾳ) along with the Twelve on their thrones judging the tribes of Israel (Matt 19:28).

[29] See Carter, *Matthew and the Margins*, 393.

[30] Thus I take the δέ as conjunctive. See W. D. Davies and Dale C. Allison Jr., *A Critical and Exegetical Commentary on the Gospel According to Matthew*, vol. 3, ICC, ed. J. A. Emerton, C. E. B. Cranfield, and G. N. Stanton (Edinburgh: T. & T. Clark, 1997) 60–61, for the various options and issues.

the commandments and entering into life? 2) What does Matthew mean by "perfect"? 3) Why does the young ruler have to sell all to receive eternal life? 4) What application does this passage have for the gospel message today?

Keeping the Commandments and Entering Into Life

Only in Matthew's account does Jesus say, "If you desire to enter into life keep the commandments" (19:17; cf. Luke 10:26-28). The "commandments" (τὰς ἐντολάς) refer to the Mosaic Law (cf. e.g., 22:36 par.).[31] Does Jesus then require obedience to the Law as a means to enter eternal life?[32] Why did Jesus ask if the young man had kept the commandments?[33] A number of options are possible. One line of reasoning is that Jesus quizzes the ruler on the commandments because this is good evangelism strategy. In other words the relationship between keeping the commandments and entering into life has more to say about *method* than *content*. Jesus' method is to initiate a discussion to draw the ruler out knowing that obedience to the Law is not in fact a means to eternal life.[34] Certainly Jesus does go on to expose the rich man's lack. However the Rich Young Ruler does not confess his lack, in fact he replies by saying that he has indeed kept all these commandments (Matt 19:20; Mark 10:20; Luke 18:21). Should we not then expect Jesus—in Matthew's Gospel at least—to allow this man to enter into life (cf. Matt 19:17)? But He doesn't. Evidently keeping the commandments is not enough after all.

A second and similar option is that Jesus' mention of the commandments is intended to expose the ruler's selfishness with regard to others. It is certainly significant that Jesus only cited commandments pertinent to societal relationships of which "the procurement and use of wealth" would have been a central issue.[35] Hence the ruler's claim to have obeyed all these command-

---

[31] D. J. Moo, "Law," in *DJG*, 451.

[32] It is clear that Jesus means enter into *eternal* life here given Matthew's use of "enter" and "life" elsewhere. In 7:13 Jesus says *enter* (εἰσέλθατε) through the narrow gate, which in v. 14 is "life"—as opposed to eternal destruction (ἀπώλειαν) (see John 17:12). In Matt 8:8-9 Jesus says that it is better to *enter* (εἰσελθεῖν) life maimed rather than be thrown into the eternal fire (τὸ πῦρ τὸ αἰώνιον) (v. 8) and the Gehenna of fire (τὴν γέενναν τοῦ πυρός) (v. 9).

[33] This question is made difficult by the fact that Jesus stands on the dividing line of salvation history with one foot on the side of the old covenant and one foot in the new. There is an obvious tension that is not easily explained. On the one hand Jesus can be portrayed as endorsing the Law (e.g., Matt 5:18-9; 8:4; 23:23) while on the other hand transcending it (5:21-48; 12:8). See ibid., 459.

[34] Ibid., 454, suggests this as a possibility. Cf. R. C. H. Lenski, *The Interpretation of St. Luke's Gospel* (Columbus, Ohio: Wartburg, 1946) 914–15: Perhaps Jesus strategically uses the Law to lead this young man to the gospel.

[35] Carter, *Matthew and the Margins*, 388.

ments "is exposed by his considerable wealth."[36] The ruler's excess wealth would thus imply someone else's shortfall. His greed inevitably meant that his *neighbor* had to go without. "This man's abundance means greed, violence and oppression. He has impoverished, not loved, his neighbor."[37] This line of interpretation is found in *The Gospel of the Nazaraeans* §1:

> Another rich man said to him, "Master, what good thing shall I do to live?" He said to him, "O man, fulfil the law and the prophets." He replied, "I have done that." He said to him, "Go sell all that you possess and distribute it to the poor, and come, follow me." But the rich man began to scratch his head and it did not please him. And the Lord said to him; "How can you say, 'I have fulfilled the law and the prophets', since it is written in the law: You shall love your neighbor as yourself, and lo! many of your brethren, sons of Abraham, are clothed in filth, dying of hunger, and your house is full of many goods, and nothing at all goes out of it to them."[38]

I would also add a third option concerning method and strategy: Jesus wants to simply point out to the ruler that his failure to obey the second table of commandments is evidence that he has failed to obey the first. In other words, the ruler has failed to love others and thus he has failed to love God (cf. 1 John 4:20). Significant in this regard is Matthew's addition to the commandments, "love your neighbor as yourself" (cf. Luke 10:26-27).

There indeed is merit to these strategies. God's demands certainly should cause one to humbly acknowledge his or her dependence upon Him (e.g., Matt 5:3-4; John 15:5) and after all, Jesus does go on to tell His disciples that the only hope anyone has of entering the kingdom is by God's grace (Matt 19:26; Mark 10:27; Luke 18:27). Furthermore, the ruler's failure to sell all his possessions and give the money to the poor does indeed seem to suggest that maybe he is not as obedient as he might think he is. However we are still left with questions. For instance, Jesus does not criticize the young man for his claim to have kept the commandments. In fact the very mention of "one thing" still lacking seems to imply that *all other things* have been fulfilled—just one more to go! Second, to suggest that Jesus was engaging in good evangelistic strategy may have more of a ring of modern day evangelism than first century evangelism. Third, we have to assume that Jesus actually

---

[36] Ibid.

[37] See Carter, *Matthew and the Margins*, 388. Cf. also G. Schrenk, "ἐντολῇ," in *TDNT*, 2:548; W. Mundle, "Command," in *NIDNTT*, 1:335.

[38] *The Apocryphal New Testament: A Collection of Apocryphal Christian Literature in an English Translation*, ed. J. K. Elliott (Oxford: Clarendon, 1993) 10–11. Cf. Isa 5:8-10; 10:1-3; Ezek 22:6-31; 27; Amos 2:6-7; 5:10-12; 8:4-8; Carter, *Matthew and the Margins*, 388, for other references.

expected this man to sell his possessions. Strategy or no strategy the ruler was to give up all he had to follow Jesus (cf. Matt 13:44). Certainly there may be evangelistic strategy involved here but it does not seem at all clear how it is working.

It is possible that a less sophisticated reason exists concerning Jesus' question regarding the commandments. It has been suggested that Jesus was simply giving the traditional *Jewish* response to a *Jewish* man wanting to enter into eternal life.[39] The possibility therefore exists for this man to enter life through keeping the commandments.[40] Certainly there were those in Judaism who appear to have believed this (cf. Rom 7:10).[41]

Leaving aside the mention of the Mosaic Law for a moment—to which I shall return below—we cannot deny that Jesus demanded obedience to enter into *eschatological* life.[42] In Matthew 7:21 Jesus said that "only those who *do* (ποιῶν) the will of My Father" will enter the kingdom of heaven. The Father's will in Matthew is expressed in 5:20 as "surpassing righteousness," which itself is defined and described in vv. 21-48 as not getting angry[43] with a brother, not looking lustfully at a woman, loving one's enemy, etc.[44] In other

---

[39] D. J. Harrington, "The Rich Young Man in Matthew 19:16-22: Another Way to God For Jews?" in *The Four Gospels*, ed. F. Van Segbroeck et al., vol. 2 (Leuven: Leuven University Press, 1992) 1429: "The 'Jewish' character of this episode has been distorted by assuming that the conversation [between the rich man and Jesus] concerns Christians (whereas for Matthew it concerns Jews)."

[40] Ibid., 1431.

[41] Contra E. P. Sanders, *Paul and Palestinian Judaism: A Comparison of Patterns of Religion* (London: SCM, 1977); but see Davies and Allison, *Matthew*, 3:43, n. 30, lists Deut 30:11-20; Lev 18:5; Prov 6:23; Mal 2:4-5; Bar 3:9; *Ps. Sol.* 14.2; Rom 7:10; 4 Ezra 14:30; *m. ʾAbot* 2.7 in addition to the references we have cited in chapter three above.

[42] By 'eschatological' I mean the same as Paul's "glorified" (Rom 8:30) as opposed to his "justified." Justification occurs at the *front* end of salvation whereas glorification occurs at the *back* end of salvation.

[43] Given the well-known and documented connections between James and the SM, it is interesting that James describes anger as *surpassing* wickedness (περισσείαν κακίας) (Jas 1:20).

[44] At first this may seem quite impossible for "who has not felt anger in his heart at some time and is thus, on the authority of Jesus, a murderer (Mt. 5.21-22)?" (Joseph C. Dillow, *The Reign of the Servant Kings: A Study of Eternal Security and the Final Significance of Man* [Miami, Fla.: Schoettle, 1992] 175). However this line of interpretation views anger, e.g., as a momentary event that if taken literally will disqualify everyone from the kingdom. However there are at least three good reasons why we should not understand Jesus' words this way. First, the entire tenor of the SM is to get away from legalistic righteousness (6:1-18). Second, the present tense verbs (e.g., ὀργιζόμενος in 5:22; βλέπων in v. 28; σκανδαλίζει in v. 30; ἀγαπᾶτε in v. 44; ἔσεσθε in v. 48) suggest a pattern of life rather than momentary lapses. In this case Jesus would be saying something like, "anyone who is *constantly* or *habitually* angry [the idea is certainly also without repentance] with his brother will be liable to judgment" (cf. 1 John 3:15). This

words, Jesus demands very real and concrete obedience[45] in order for one to enter into the kingdom and thus eternal life (see esp. 25:34-46). (I shall discuss these passages Matthew 5–7 in more detail in the next chapter). In a strikingly similar fashion Paul warns that flagrant disobedience to God will not admit anyone into the kingdom (1 Cor 6:9-10; Gal 5:19-21; Eph 5:5). Likewise John writes, "This is how we know who the children of God are and who the children of the devil are: Anyone who does not *do* (ποιῶν) what is *righteousness* (δικαιοσύνην) is not from God and anyone who does not love his brother" (1 John 3:10).

What this shows is a clear trajectory of thought within the New Testament concerning a close relationship between *practical righteousness and eschatology*.[46] When viewed like this Jesus' question to the Rich Young Ruler concerning the commandments really poses no more of a problem than Paul's words in Romans 2:13: "it is not the hearers of the Law who are justified before God, but the doers (ποιηταί) of the *Law* will be justified (δικαιωθήσονται)" (cf. also *m. 'Abot* 1:17).[47] Furthermore, given that the Rich Young Ruler's request is future[48] (cf. esp. Matt 19:29 par.) Jesus could be asserting the need for obedience to inherit eternal life *in the future* (cf. Matt 7:21; 25:46; Jas 1:22-25).

In case this sounds something close to salvation by works we should remember two things: first, Jesus does not expect anyone to obey the commandments to enter into a relationship with Himself for he did "not come to call the righteous, but *sinners*" (Matt 9:13; Mark 2:17; Luke 5:32). However He does say that it will be the righteous who will enter the kingdom (e.g.,

---

seems to be the intent of John's words, e.g., in 1 John 2:6: "Whoever claims to live in him must walk (περιπατεῖν) (*as a pattern of life*) as Jesus did" (cf. 1:6). Third, Jesus makes it very clear in Matt 5:27-30 that a failure to deal seriously with sin leads to hell (γέενναν).

[45] "Therefore everyone who hears these words of mine and *does* (ποιεῖ) them will be like a wise man who built his house upon the rock and the rain came down . . . and fell upon that house, and it did not fall for it was established upon the rock" (Matt 7:24; cf. Jas 1:22-25).

[46] In addition to the references already given see also Matt 13:41; 16:27; Luke 6:37; 14:14; John 5:29; Rom 2:5-8; 1 Cor 6:9-10; 2 Cor 5:10; Gal 5:19-21; 6:8-9; Eph 5:5; 1 Tim 4:16; 6:18-19; Heb 10:36; Jas 1:12; Rev 20:12-13; 21:7-8, 27; 22:12, 15.

[47] It is quite possible that Paul is speaking here of an eschatological justification. The verb "justify" is future (-θήσονται) and the context is eschatological judgment (Rom 2:5). For this interpretation see James D. G. Dunn, *Romans 1–8*, Word Biblical Commentary, ed. David A. Hubbard and Glenn W. Barker, vol. 38A (Dallas: Word, 1988) 97–98; Paul A. Rainbow, *The Way of Salvation: The Role of Christian Obedience in Justification* (Waynesboro, Ga.: Paternoster, 2005) 165–67; though contra Douglas Moo, *The Epistle to the Romans*, New International Commentary on the New Testament, ed. Gordon D. Fee (Grand Rapids: Eerdmans, 1996) 147–48.

[48] See G. R. Beasley-Murray, *Jesus and the Kingdom of God* (Grand Rapids: Eerdmans, 1986) 176–77.

Matt 5:20; 13:43, 49; 25:34-46). Second, Jesus told his disciples that it is impossible for *anyone* to enter the kingdom. We may conclude from this that any righteousness that admits anyone into eternity is due completely to the work of God and His grace (cf. esp. Gal 5:22-23; 6:8). This is a theological truism, as we have already seen in chapter four, regardless of what New Testament author we read. Whether it be stated as "Blessed are the poor in spirit" (Matt 5:3), "God caused it to grow" (1 Cor 3:6), "God is the One who works in us to will and to act according to his good purpose" (Phil 2:13), or "good behavior *in Christ*" (1 Pet 3:16), it all amounts to the same thing—"apart from me you can do nothing" (John 15:5).[49] The works of the unsaved like the Rich Young Ruler are dead (Heb 6:1) whereas God will not neglect those works performed for Christ's sake (v. 10). It is this conclusion that led Augustine to say that at the judgment God will merely "crown not so much thy merits, as *His own gifts*."[50] And similarly John Calvin, while eternal life is "the recompense of works, it is bestowed by the *gratuitous gifts of God*."[51] Thus, according to Calvin, "There is nothing to prevent the Lord from embracing works as inferior causes" and so making "eternal life a consequence of works."[52]

What then of Jesus' mention of the *Law*? In order to answer this we must first understand Jesus' own relationship to the Law. In Matthew Jesus clearly presents Himself as the fulfillment of the Law (Matt 5:17-20). In Mark it is clear that Jesus has exclusive authority and thus is capable of superseding the Law (Mark 2:27; 7:19; 12:33). In Luke it appears that the authority of the Law as it was in the Old Testament has ceased with Jesus' inauguration of the kingdom (Luke 16:16).[53] In all three of these Gospels then Jesus in some sense 'transcends' the Law.[54] Hence the issue *now* is not really one's relationship to the Law but one's relationship to Jesus.

---

[49] See also Acts 1:8; Eph 2:10; Heb 13:21; Jas 1:5; and Jude 16–19.

[50] Augustine "On the Same Words of the Apostle, Phil 3 . . .", in *Sermons on Selected Lessons of the New Testament*, A Library of Fathers of the Holy Catholic Church, Anterior to the Division of the East and the West, 2 vols. (Oxford: John Henry Parker, 1844) 10.

[51] John Calvin, *Institutes of the Christian Religion*, trans. Henry Beveridge (Grand Rapids: Eerdmans, 1975) 3.18.4 (emphasis mine).

[52] Ibid., 3.14.21.

[53] Moo, "Law," 458–60.

[54] The question of Jesus' relationship to the Law is a difficult one. Much of the difficulty comes from the fact that Jesus stands on the dividing line of salvation history with one foot on the side of the old covenant and one foot in the new. Hence there is an obvious tension that is not easily explained. On the one hand Jesus can be portrayed as endorsing the Law (e.g., Matt 5:18-9; 8:4; 23:23) while on the other hand it is clear that He transcends it (5:21-48; 12:8). For a helpful discussion on the relationship between Jesus and the Law see ibid., 459.

With this is mind we should probably think of this in a similar sense to what Paul referred to as the "law of Christ" (Gal 6:2; cf. 1 Cor 9:21; Jas 1:25; 2:8, 12). Admittedly it was the Mosaic Law that Jesus was referring to when speaking with the Rich Young Ruler but the key is that Jesus takes the ruler *beyond* the Law—and thus *surpasses* it—to *Himself*. In the end what is clear is that it is Jesus' own demand that determines the ruler's eternal destiny—not the Law.[55] Jesus Himself declared that the Law was still valid but only in as much as it is "caught up in, and re-applied"[56] by Him (Matt 5:17-20).[57] Furthermore, if entering into life was dependent upon keeping the commandments the Rich Young Ruler would have not been excluded since Jesus gives no indication that He is dissatisfied with the young man's claim—"all these things I have kept" (19:20a). The "one thing" that the rich ruler lacks is taken up by Jesus himself, worded elsewhere as "love your neighbor as yourself" (cf. Luke 10:27). It is no surprise to find that this command essentially defines the "law of Christ" in Paul (Gal 6:2) and the "*kingly* (βασιλικὸν) law" in James (Jas 2:8). "Therefore love is the fulfillment of the law" (Rom 13:10). In the final analysis then, what excludes the ruler from entering the kingdom is not the demands of the Mosaic Law but his reluctance to depart with his wealth—and thus *love* the poor—and follow Jesus[58] (cf. 6:24). In demanding that the young man follow Him Jesus is placing Himself beyond the commandments and thus the Law. What we have here then appears to be another example (in addition to Matt 5:21-48) of *surpassing* righteousness. In asking the young man to sell all he has Jesus surpasses the commandments of the Mosaic Law and directs the ruler's attention toward 'perfection' (cf. v. 48). This is indeed where we shall now turn our attention.

What Does Jesus Mean - "If You Desire To Be Perfect"?

By presenting the young man with the possibility of being perfect (τέλειος) it appears that Jesus is actually giving a promise (Matt 19:21) in *addition* to eternal life.[59] The first requirement—keep the commandments—is given in

---

[55] Ibid., 454; Jeannine K. Brown, *The Disciples in Narrative Perspective: The Portrayal and Function of the Matthean Disciples*, Academia Biblica, ed. Saul M. Olyan and Mark Allan Powell, no. 9 (Atlanta: SBL, 2002) 82.

[56] Moo, "Law," 459.

[57] This is very similar to Paul's mention of the Mosaic commandments in Rom 13:9. Clearly the commands are still valid for Paul *but* only in as much they are caught up and re-applied in the one rule (λόγῳ), "love your neighbor as yourself."

[58] Petri Luomanen, *Entering the Kingdom of Heaven: A Study on the Structure of Matthew's View of Salvation* (Tübingen: Mohr, 1998) 155: "In practice, the salvation of the [rich] young man is not endangered by his failure to keep the commandments but by his improper understanding of the person of Jesus as well as his unwillingness to join the band of Jesus' followers."

[59] Harrington, "The Rich Young Man," 1425–32; Robert Govett, *Entrance into the Kingdom:*

order that the ruler might have *eternal life*. The second requirement—sell up and give to the poor—is given in order that the ruler might be *perfect*. Such an interpretation has led some to the conclusion that there are two types of believers.[60] However this is unlikely for a number of reasons. First, the parallel between "eternal life" (v. 17) and "perfect" (v. 21) (see fig. 2 below) dismisses "any notion of a superior level of discipleship."[61] Second, obedience to this command would result in "treasure in heaven" (v. 21), which logically must be the same or at least the result of perfection (v. 21). I have argued in chapter five that the phrase "treasure in heaven" is synonymous with eternal life. Third, the only other place Matthew uses τέλειος is in 5:48 where it appears to be a quality for all rather than a select group.[62] In fact it is at the heart of 'surpassing righteousness.' Jesus is not talking about 'sinless' perfection but rather He is speaking in the context of love. In the immediate context this is certainly true (vv. 41-47) but also the wider (vv. 21-42).[63] Since these verses describe the greater righteousness required to *enter the kingdom* (v. 20)[64] then so too must τέλειος. This makes good sense of course since love is the fulfillment of the Law. We are therefore not far from Paul's declaration in Gal 5:6: that the only thing that counts is "faith working itself out through *love*" or Eph 5:1-2: "Be imitators of God . . . and walk in *love*" or 1 John 4:7: "Everyone who *loves* has been born of God and knows God." Perfection in Matthew then is clearly a requirement to enter the kingdom and not a higher level of attainment.[65] Fourth, the most convincing reason for adopting this interpretation however is that "Jesus' comment after the withdrawal of the young man (19:23) implies that in the last analysis the young man's

---

Or Reward According to Works (Fletcher & Son, 1870; reprint, Miami, Fla.: Conley & Schoettle, 1978) 130–31. See Luomanen, *Entering the Kingdom of Heaven*, 152–54, for a discussion on the various ways in which Jesus' offer to the Rich Young Ruler to be perfect has been handled.

[60] Cf. though Harrington, "The Rich Young Man," 1425–32: the distinction is not between two types of believers but between Jews and believers. Govett, *Entrance into the Kingdom*, 127–52, argues that perfection pertains to the eschatological millennial kingdom in contrast to eternal life.

[61] Carter, *Households and Discipleship*, 121, n. 1.

[62] Luomanen, *Entering the Kingdom of Heaven*, 152; Davies and Allison, *Matthew*, 3:47.

[63] John Piper, *'Love Your Enemies': Jesus' Love Command in the Synoptic Gospels and in the Early Christian Paraenesis*, SNTSMS, ed. R. McL. Wilson and M. E. Thrall, vol. 38 (Cambridge: Cambridge University Press, 1979) 146.

[64] Cf. G. N. Stanton, "SM/Plain," in *DJG*, 740, 744.

[65] Piper, *'Love Your Enemies,'* 147: "'perfection' is not something *more* than what is needed to enter life."

reluctance to take heed of the second advice results in his exclusion from the kingdom of heaven."[66]

What then does it mean to be *perfect*?[67] I have basically already answered the question: perfection is a synonym for eternal life and a requirement for entry into the kingdom. There exists a relationship between perfection and love in the SM[68] along with entering the kingdom. Certainly the same is emphasized here especially since the command to sell all would no doubt be viewed as an act of love.[69] However most seem to think that the concept of perfection in Matthew (5:48; 19:21) is broader and thus "whole-hearted obedience to Jesus Christ" is in view.[70] The latter is certainly evident although I am of the opinion that love is at the core.[71] Regardless of its ethical dimension however we cannot escape the impression that Matthew also appears to be in some sense equating being perfect with eternal life. This is seen from the two statements:

If you desire to *enter into life* (v. 17)
(εἰ δὲ θέλεις εἰς τὴν ζωὴν εἰσελθεῖν)

If you desire *to be perfect* (v. 21)
(εἰ θέλεις τέλειος εἶναι τέλειος)

Thus to "enter into life" (εἰς τὴν ζωὴν εἰσελθεῖν) and "to be perfect" (εἶναι τέλειος) are parallel and thus presumably synonymous.

---

[66] Luomanen, *Entering the Kingdom of Heaven*, 152; Piper, *'Love Your Enemies,'* 147: "it is apparent from [Matt] 19:22-24 that what the youth refused to do did not merely keep him from perfection, but also blocked the way to eternal life."

[67] For an excellent discussion on Matthew's concept of perfection in relation to the Rich Young Ruler and the enemy love command see ibid., 145–49.

[68] Also, Davies and Allison, *Matthew*, 3:48; Piper, *'Love Your Enemies,'* 146.

[69] Cf. *b. B. Bat.* 9a: According to Rabbi Assi "Charity is equivalent to all the other religious precepts combined."

[70] Davies and Allison, *Matthew*, 3:48; cf. R. T. France, *Matthew*, TNTC, ed. Leon Morris (Grand Rapids: Eerdmans, 1989) 129–30; Craig S. Keener, *A Commentary on the Gospel of Matthew* (Grand Rapids: Eerdmans, 1999) 205.

[71] Also Piper, *'Love Your Enemies,'* 148: τέλειος "is a restatement in radical form of what Mt really intended when he added the love command to the list of Old Testament commandments in 19:19 . . . That the young man thought he had fulfilled this absolute command, even though he loved his possessions so much, shows that he completely misunderstood God's ultimate intention of the Old Testament commandments. In order to expose the root problem behind this misunderstanding, Mt lets Jesus confront the youth with the staggering demand for perfection—perfection which consists first in selling one's possessions and giving them to the poor, i.e., obedience to the love command."

I conclude then that there is both an *ethical* and *eschatological* dimension to perfection. Complete perfection (i.e., as God is perfect) is not fully attained until eternity although it begins here on earth (cf. Heb 6:1; Jas 1:4).[72] We are to be like God and His Son now but this will not be realized until eternity (Phil 3:21; 1 John 3:2). Until then it is a process (cf. also Rom 8:29; 2 Cor 3:18). The ethical culminates in the eschatological.[73] Thus it would be more correct to say that perfection begins *here on earth* but finds its end in eternity (see fig. 2).

Figure 2: Perfection—Ethical and Eschatological

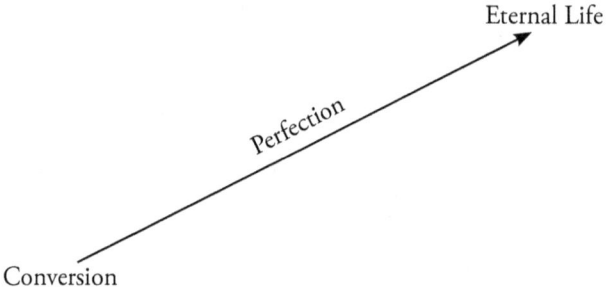

Selling All to Have Eternal Life?

Clearly Jesus understands the young man's failure to sell all as a failure to enter the kingdom, and thus eternal life.[74] Yet this raises a huge question: is this then the Gospel for Jesus—"Sell all you have and you will be saved" (cf. Acts 16:31)? Apparently the Rich Young Ruler did not think so. His gospel stated, "Accumulate as much wealth as you can and you will be saved." This is indicated by two reasons. First, all three Gospel writers give the reason (γάρ) for the young man's disappointment. Matthew (19:22) and Mark

---

[72] Also Peter H. Davids, *The Epistle of James: A Commentary of the Greek Text*, NIGTC, ed. I. Howard Marshall and W. Ward Gasque (Grand Rapids: Eerdmans, 1982) 70, on τέλειοι in Jas 1:4: "the incremental character of the process"; "a pattern of eschatological perfection." In Jas 1 trials are to be embraced because they produce endurance and endurance in turn, if allowed to finish its work, produces *perfection* (τέλειοι), otherwise defined as not lacking in anything (v. 4). The person who endures is therefore the one who receives the *crown of life* (v. 12). Thus perfection begins where trials begin (here on earth) but has its end in eternity.

[73] Hence I agree with Carter, *Matthew and the Margins*, and his assessment, 389: "To be perfect is a synonym for 'have eternal life' ([Matt] 19:16) and 'enter life' (19:17). It is to imitate God in indiscriminate loving which benefits the other (5:43-48)."

[74] Cf. Gerhard Kittel, "ἀκολουθέω," in *TDNT*, 1:214: "ἀκολούθει μοι is an answer to the question concerning ζωὴ αἰώνιος."

(10:22) both explain that he had many possessions while Luke (18:23) adds "he was *extremely* rich" (πλούσιος σφόδρα). Especially noteworthy is the fact that a scribe has added the phrase "those who have *confidence* in riches" (τοὺς πεποιθότας ἐπὶ χρήμασιν) in Mark 10:24. Presumably the scribe has understood the ruler to be placing his confidence in riches to enter the kingdom. However second and even more telling than the explanation of the man's wealth is the disciples' reaction to things. Evidently they too had been infected by the same prosperity theology.[75] In response (note the aorist participle ἀκούσαντες in Matt 19:25 and Luke 18:26) to Jesus' assertion that it is impossible for the rich to enter the kingdom[76] they exclaim, "Who then can be *saved*?" (Matt 19:25; Mark 10:26; Luke 18:26).

A little background is important at this point.[77] Based on a select reading of the Old Testament some Jews believed that wealth signified God's blessing. If you had wealth then you were considered pious.[78] The Pentateuch taught that wealth came from God (Deut 8:18). People such as Abraham (e.g., Gen 13:2), Isaac (e.g., 26:12-15) and Jacob (e.g., 30:43) confirmed such a belief. One of Job's comforters, Eliphaz, believed that piety and wealth were connected (Job 4:7).[79] Psalm 112:3 exclaimed, "wealth and riches are in His house, and His righteousness endures forever." Proverbs 13:18: "He who ignores discipline comes to poverty and shame, but whoever heeds correction is honored."[80] Passages like these (cf. also Deut 28:1-14) spurred the belief that wealth and blessing accompanied each other[81] while poverty was a sign of sin and disobedience (cf. vv. 47-48). Hence Eliphaz believed that the ungodly would come to financial ruin (Job 15:4, 29). Even in the NT people assumed a relationship between godliness and success (cf. Luke 13:1-5; John 9:1-2).[82] Although not all of Judaism followed this line of thinking[83] (cf. e.g., Sir 31:3-

---

[75] Davies and Allison, *Matthew*, 3:53; Carter, *Matthew and the Margins*, 391.

[76] Mark omits any remark concerning the difficulty of the rich entering the kingdom although note the variant reading which is surely inauthentic (see above) (Mk 10:24). However v. 25 makes clear that it is the rich that are in view: "It is easier for a camel to pass through the eye of a needle *than the rich* to enter into the kingdom of God." It is v. 25 that the disciples respond to.

[77] See, e.g., Carter, *Households and Discipleship*, 131–38.

[78] Hellerman, "Wealth and Sacrifice in early Christianity," 148.

[79] Ibid.

[80] Cf. also Ps 1:1-3; Prov 10:15, 16; 15:6; Friedrich Hauck and Wilhelm Kasch, "πλοῦτος," in *TDNT*, 6:318-32.

[81] P. H. Davids, "Rich and Poor," in *DJG*, 703: the "prosperity-theology equation."

[82] Hellerman, "Wealth and Sacrifice in early Christianity," 148.

[83] The rabbis, e.g., viewed wealth as a curse (see C. Boerma, *The Rich, The Poor—and the Bible* [Philadelphia: Westminster, 1978] 25). *Ahiqar* 137: "[Do not *amass*] wealth lest you pervert your heart"; 207: "Let not the rich man say, 'In my riches I am glorious'"; *Ps. Sol.*

10), some did. Among those who believed that riches were an expression of God's salvation was the hierarchy of the Sadducees.[84] We can only speculate who this rich ruler might have been, but since he was young we would not expect him to be a Synagogue ruler or a religious leader. It may be that this man then was a well-respected and pious member of society.[85]

Given this background we might well imagine the thought processes going on inside the disciples' minds. "If the rich cannot enter the kingdom—and we know that wealth is a sign of God's blessing on the pious and so that leaves out the poor—*what* (τίς)[86] *sort of person can be saved?*[87] Their reaction is understandably one of astonishment and bewilderment.[88]

This piety-prosperity link is crucial for explaining Jesus' request to the Rich Young Ruler to sell up and give to the poor. Jesus is in effect asking the ruler to give up that which he is placing his *confidence* in for salvation.[89] This is important for what might at first glance appear to be a kind of salvation by "works" in fact turns out to be salvation by trusting completely in Jesus *alone*. Jesus is asking the Rich Young Ruler to give up his confidence in riches and place his confidence in Him.[90]

Implications for Understanding and Preaching the Gospel

Before discussing some important implications from this passage let me first recap. Jesus did not expect the Rich Young Ruler to obey the Law per se in order to enter life, however He did expect him to obey *Jesus* ("the law of Christ"). This was a genuine offer not merely some evangelistic strategy to get the ruler to see his need for Jesus. Furthermore, we should not understand

---

5.16-17: "Happy is (the person) whom God remembers with a moderate sufficiency; for if one is excessively rich, he sins. Moderate (wealth) is adequate—with righteousness; for with this comes the Lord's blessing." See Walter C. Kaiser Jr., "The Old Testament Promise of Material Blessings and the Contemporary Believer," *TJ* 9 (1988) 151–69; see also Hellerman, "Wealth and Sacrifice in early Christianity," 148–49; Carter, *Households and Discipleship*, 138–43.

[84] See F. Hauck and W. Kasch, "πλοῦτος," in *TDNT*, 6:318-32.

[85] Bock, *Luke 9:51–24:53*, 1476.

[86] Cf. BDAG, 1007.

[87] Cf. esp. Brown, *The Disciples in Narrative Perspective*, 83.

[88] The adverbs used to describe the disciples' amazement (ἐξεπλήσσοντο) are striking: σφόδρα (Matt 19:26) and περισσῶς (Mark 10:26).

[89] Carter, *Households and Discipleship*, 123: "Jesus' command to sell his wealth and give to the poor aims to transfer the allegiance of his heart."

[90] Furthermore, if selling one's possessions is a universal mandate for gaining eternal life we are hard pressed to explain the salvation of Zacchaeus in Luke 19:1-10 who promised to give away *half* of his possessions.

enter here to mean something akin to Paul's point of justification or conversion. Jesus has in mind the eschatological age to come.

Now on to the implications: first, only those who place their undivided confidence in Jesus receive salvation. In fact 'undivided confidence in Jesus' is another way of saying justifying faith according to the apostle Paul. In the midst of defending justification by faith in Romans 3:21-4:25 Paul gives what is probably the clearest articulation of 'justifying faith' in the New Testament. In Romans 4 Paul expounds Genesis 15:6 ("Abraham believed God and it was credited to him as righteousness") and for the most part is concerned to show that this righteousness was credited apart from works. However near to the end of the chapter Paul describes what kind of belief (ἐπίστευσεν) Abraham exercised—and thus what kind of belief is needed to justify (Rom 4:18). First, it was *not weak* (ἀσθενήσας) (v. 19). Second, he did *not doubt* (οὐ διεκρίθη) God's promise (v. 20). Third, his faith was *strengthened* (ἐνεδυναμώθη) (v. 20). Fourth, he was *absolutely sure* (πληροφορηθεὶς) that God had the power (δυνατός) to do what He had promised (v. 21). This is the kind of faith that brings glory to God (v. 20) and trusts in God's promise concerning His Son without wavering. Abraham's faith was strong but what made it strong was the strength of the Object. We should not miss pointing out that in vv. 18-21 the promise is mentioned three times (vv. 18, 20, 21).[91] The Rich Young Ruler's failure to sell his possessions reflected his lack of confidence in Jesus' *promise* concerning treasure in heaven.

That we are on the right track here is supported by the context in which the Rich Young Ruler appears. Prior to all three accounts Jesus declares that the kingdom belongs to those who are like (τοιούτων) children (τὰ παιδία) (Matt 19:14; Mark 10:14; Luke 18:16). Since "kingdom" is the link word between the two scenes I am inclined to think that the attitude of the Rich Young Ruler is a negative illustration of "such as these" (τοιούτων) entering the kingdom.[92] What the young man 'lacked' was the ability to single-mindedly place his security in Jesus. This is what is needed. This is the message of Jesus' gospel.

The context of Luke 18 is even more definitive. A single theme can be traced through the chapter. God will *justify* (ἐκδίκησιν) those who persevere

---

[91] Romans 4:18 (οὕτως ἔσται τὸ σπέρμα σου), v. 20 (τὴν ἐπαγγελίαν τοῦ θεοῦ) and v. 21 (ὃ ἐπήγγελται).

[92] See also, Stephen Fowl, "Receiving the Kingdom of God as a Child: Children and Riches in Luke 18ff," *New Testament Studies* 39 (1993) 153–58. Fowl views the Rich Young Ruler (Luke 18:18-30), the disciples' response (vv. 24-30), the blind man near Jericho (vv. 35-43), and Zacchaeus (19:10) as positive and negative examples of receiving the kingdom like a child. "The childlike nature . . . inheres in each character's sudden, single-minded attraction to a particular object of person. Further, such attraction leads these characters to abandon or circumvent anything which threatens to keep them from the focus of their affections" (158).

in prayer (Luke 18:1-8). Those who beg for *mercy* (ἱλάσθητί μοι) will also find themselves *justified* (δεδικαιωμένος); those who exalt themselves will be humbled and those who humble (ταπεινῶν) themselves will be exalted (vv. 9-14). Thus in order to enter the kingdom one must become like a child (vv. 15-17). Following the account of the Rich Young Ruler Jesus meets a blind man who begs for *mercy* (ἐλέησόν με) and is healed because of his *faith* (ἡ πίστις σου σέσωκέν σε) (vv. 31-34). The theme of the chapter is clearly: what must one do to be saved? To put it another way, what must one do to be justified (vv. 1-8), receive God's mercy (vv. 9-14), enter the kingdom (vv. 15-17), attain eternal life (vv. 18-30), and be healed (vv. 31-34)? The answer is that one must pray, beg for mercy, be humble, and trust in Jesus.

Luke 19:1-9 continues the theme of salvation and functions to answer the disciples' question, "who then can be *saved*?" The two men being compared are the same in status: one is a ruler (ἄρχων) (18:18) who was rich (πλούσιος) (v. 23), the other a tax collector (ἀρχιτελώνης) (cf. vv. 9-14) who was also rich (πλούσιος) (19:2). But that is where the similarity stops.[93] In response to Jesus' command the tax-collector responds with joy (χαίρων) (v. 6) while the Rich Young Ruler responds with grief (περίλυπος) (18:23). The rich ruler refuses to give his wealth to the poor (πτωχοῖς) (18:22) whereas the tax-collector promises to give away *half* of his possessions to the poor (πτωχοῖς), the other half presumably going to pay back four times what he may have defrauded people (19:8). Jesus promised "treasure in heaven" to the ruler (18:22) and the tax collector receives "salvation" (σωτηρία) today (19:9). It therefore seems quite clear that the tax collector did what the Rich Young Ruler did not and therefore received what the Rich Young Ruler did not. Hence the disciples receive the answer to their question: "who then can be saved (σωθῆναι)?" The answer is that God is able to save anyone, even a wealthy tax collector. By God's grace the camel is able to pass through the eye of a needle.

The second implication concerns the nature of faith. (I shall discuss this in more detail in an excursus in chapter ten though it is appropriate that I begin the discussion here with some brief comments). Why did the ruler have to sell all? This needs to be understood against the background of piety and prosperity teaching in some parts of Judaism as discussed above. The requirement to sell all is certainly not a requirement for everyone. However, I would have to say that one who is trusting in riches to save him or her may well indeed be confronted with the same requirement the Rich Young Ruler

---

[93] Also the ruler was νεανίσκος (Matt 19:20) while the tax collector was ἡλικίᾳ μικρὸς (Luke 19:3).

faced.⁹⁴ Nothing may take the place of Jesus as the object of one's confidence and trust. After all, "there is no other name under heaven given among men by which we must be saved" (Acts 4:12). It can be no other way since *nothing* may take the place of Jesus as the object of one's confidence and trust for salvation.

So could the young man not just *say*, "I trust you"? Presumably the answer to this question has something to do with the fact that Jesus knows what's in a person's heart (John 2:25). Yet it is more than this since Jesus' idea of faith is not merely a verbalized faith but a demonstrated or *seen* faith. We know from the Gospels that Jesus is able to recognize faith precisely because it is recognizable.⁹⁵ We see this where four friends bring their paralytic friend to Jesus for healing. Mark adds that Jesus *saw* (ἰδὼν) their *faith* (πίστιν) (Mark 2:5 par.). Faith is no faith unless it is acted out (cf. e.g., Matt 8:5-13 par.; 9:20-22 par.; 15:21-28; Mark 10:46-52 par.; Luke 7:36-50; 17:15-19). Thus James declares, "I will *demonstrate* (δείξω) from (ἐκ)⁹⁶ my works my *faith* (πίστιν)" (Jas 2:18; cf. 3:13).

The third implication concerns the danger of wealth.⁹⁷ The Synoptic Gospels take a dim view of wealth not because it is evil but because it is viewed as a hindrance to having a relationship with God. Jesus declares that the kingdom belongs to those who are poor (Luke 6:20) in contrast to the rich (v. 24).⁹⁸ Wealth causes unfruitfulness (Mark 4:18-19; Luke 8:14). Those who are secure in their wealth will receive their due in the life hereafter (12:16-21). One may have comfort in this life but eternal separation from God awaits them in the next (16:19-31). Indeed it is impossible to serve both God and mammon (Matt 6:24).⁹⁹

---

⁹⁴ This giving up must either take place in one's attitude (cf. e.g., Matt 6:25-34 par.) or physical abandonment (the Rich Young Ruler); Scot McKnight, *A New Vision For Israel: The Teachings of Jesus in National Context* (Grand Rapids: Eerdmans, 1999) 191.

⁹⁵ See ibid., 166–68, for the various images used in the Gospels to depict faith; cf. also R. T. France, "Faith," in *DJG*, 223–26.

⁹⁶ Luke Timothy Johnson, *The Letter of James*, Anchor Bible, ed. William Foxwell Albright and David Noel Freedman, vol. 37A (Garden City, N.Y.: Doubleday, 1995) 270; BDAG, 297: of the source, from which something flows. Works are the inevitable *outflow* of faith for James.

⁹⁷ The lesson from the Rich Young Ruler is not only applicable to those who have wealth. For in moving the discussion from the ruler to the disciples Jesus moves the discussion beyond wealth to family relationships. In doing so Jesus' challenge becomes relevant to everyone since though all may not be wealthy all do have families (Ernest Best, *Disciples and Discipleship: Studies in the Gospel According to Mark* [Endinburgh: Clark, 1986] 18).

⁹⁸ Luke 6:20 refers to financial poverty, at least in some sense, since "woe to the rich" in v. 24 hardly means *spiritually* rich.

⁹⁹ See Davies and Allison, *Matthew*, 3:705; cf. Kaiser, "The Old Testament Promise," 161. See also Gerald D. Kisner, "Jesus' Encounter with the Rich Young Ruler and Its Implications

Fourth, Jesus expects obedience from anyone wanting to enter into life at the end of the age. In Matthew this is called "surpassing" righteousness or being "perfect" as your heavenly Father is perfect (cf. Eph 5:1-2) and is ultimately fulfilled in loving one's neighbor as oneself (cf. Gal 5:6; 1 John 4:7). In short, Jesus expects that anyone who will enter into life at the end of the age will have demonstrated a practical outworking of righteousness here on earth.

Fifth and following on from this is an implication concerning Jesus' statement concerning the impossibility of entering the kingdom. Are we to take from this declaration that all that was asked of this young man was nothing more than an *impossible* demand designed to expose his need for a Savior? We should bear in mind here—and cast our thoughts back to chapter four—that it is not at all uncommon for the writers of the New Testament to demand things of their readers, which their readers are unable to do. For instance, Paul asks the impossible of his readers at Philippi, "work out your salvation with fear and trembling" (Phil 2:12). However he explains the power and motivation for doing the impossible in v. 13: "for (γάρ) God is the one who works in you to will and to act according to his good purpose." Similarly, Jesus expects his hearers (and readers) to put into practice His words in the SM (Matt 7:24, 26), however He also expects them to admit that they can't (5:3). In other words, the requirements—indeed any of the Biblical commands—are real and expected *but impossible* apart from divine enablement (John 15:5). Indeed the divine enablement constitutes the life raising power of the Spirit over the flesh (Rom 8:11; Eph 1:19-20).

This point bears reiterating. The requirements being placed upon this rich young man, while genuine, were quite impossible apart from God. That is, there is no indication here whatsoever that this young ruler was being asked to earn his salvation in any way shape or form.

Excursus on the View that the Rich Young Ruler Missed Out on Discipleship and *Not* Salvation

Zane Hodges maintains that Jesus' request to sell all and give to the poor is in fact a call to discipleship, not salvation. He writes, "Clearly these words are an invitation to discipleship and to immense self-sacrifice" (i.e., not eternal life).[100] Hodges claims that the subsequent command to follow puts an *ad-*

---

for Theology and Development," *Journal of Religious Thought* 49 (1992–93) 81–86; Luke T. Johnson, *Sharing Possessions: Mandate and Symbol of Faith*, Overtures to Biblical Theology, ed. Walter Brueggemann and John R. Donahue, vol. 9 (Philadelphia: Fortress, 1981); Scot McKnight, *A New Vision for Israel: The Teachings of Jesus in National Context* (Grand Rapids: Eerdmans, 1999) 187–93.

[100] Zane C. Hodges, *Absolutely Free! A Biblical Reply to Lordship Salvation* (Grand Rapids:

ditional demand of discipleship on the young man that goes beyond the faith requirement for salvation.[101] In chapter ten I will address the relationship between discipleship and salvation from the wider context of the Synoptic Gospels and the rest of the NT. However I can say here that the immediate context does not indicate that any additional demand is being placed on this young man.

First, the opening question provides the framework for the ensuing dialogue. Jesus' closing words confirm that the subject of discussion has not changed. What is at stake is eternal life.[102]

Second, Jesus' response indicates that the young ruler missed out on salvation, not something additional. If Jesus' invitations to sell, give and follow are distinct from entering eternal life why then does Jesus say that it is difficult for the rich to *enter* the kingdom in His response to His disciples? A plain reading of the passage surely indicates that the difficulty refers to the ruler's refusal to sell all he has. If something more than salvation was in view would we not expect Jesus to say something other than "enter." Perhaps even, to fit Hodges' thinking at least, "How difficult it is for the rich to *inherit* the kingdom."[103] Clearly Jesus understands the ruler's failure to sell all and follow as a failure to *enter* the kingdom.[104] If this is correct, and most (even Hodges!) agree that entering the kingdom and salvation are the same, then we are at a loss to understand how both can be the same and yet the rich ruler misses out on the kingdom but receives salvation. The inconsistency is patent.

Third, the disciples' response indicates that the ruler missed out on being saved. Hodges writes, "How fortunate that one's entrance into the king-

---

Zondervan, 1989) 186.

[101] E.g., Hodges, *Absolutely Free*, 181–90, esp. 187: "Jesus knew that for this young man, trust in His Person would have to precede trust in His promise of heavenly reward. But once he had obtained the gift of life . . . the goal of heavenly treasure *could still be reached* by self denying discipleship to the Son of God." See Michael J. Wilkins, *Following the Master: A Biblical Theology of Discipleship* (Grand Rapids: Zondervan, 1992) 25–34, for a survey on the various models of discipleship.

[102] Cf. George Eldon Ladd, *The Presence of the Future: The Eschatology of Biblical Realism* (Grand Rapids: Eerdmans, 1974) 196, 205, 207. Contra Hodges, *Absolutely Free*, 186–88; Govett, *Entrance into the Kingdom*, 130.

[103] This would be a more defensible phrase from Hodges' point of view. See e.g., Zane Clark Hodges, *The Hungry Inherit: Refreshing Insights on Salvation, Discipleship, and Rewards* (Chicago: Moody, 1972) 96–107; Joseph C. Dillow, *The Reign of the Servant Kings: A Study of Eternal Security and the Final Significance of Man* (Miami, Fla.: Schoettle, 1992) 61–91.

[104] Cf. Kittel, "ἀκολουθέω," 1:214: "ἀκολούθει μοι is an answer to the question concerning ζωὴ αἰώνιος"; David Hill, *Greek Words and Hebrew Meanings: Studies in the Semantics of Soteriological Terms*, SNTSMS, ed. Matthew Black, vol. 5 (Cambridge: Cambridge University Press, 1967) 192: "According to the teaching of Jesus, entrance into the Kingdom . . . is made possible by discipleship."

dom of God [i.e., *salvation*] did not depend on his discipleship . . . Indeed, the disciples themselves could not help wondering if they could really measure up, in the long run, to such standards. If eternal life had depended upon doing so, the disciples could have felt no assurance that they really possessed it or ever would."[105] Yet the disciples did wonder, they did momentarily lack assurance. This is obvious from their question, "Who then can be *saved*?" The Twelve give unmistakable evidence that they understand entering the kingdom and salvation to be one and the same thing. Otherwise why did they ask about being saved? Clearly their question is a response to the difficulty that wealth poses for entering the kingdom.[106] It seems very clear that the disciples explicitly interpret 'entering the kingdom,' and thereby implicitly 'following Jesus,' as *salvation*.

Fourth, the disciples receive assurance that their own commitment to Jesus will ensue in eternal life. The disciples have done what the rich man failed to do (*followed* Jesus) and so are assured of what the rich man desired—*eternal life*.[107] If the ruler's failure to sell and follow meant anything more (or less as the case may be) than forfeiture of salvation we would not have expected the terms *enter* and *saved* to appear in the following dialogue between Jesus and the Twelve. In this context entering the kingdom is synonymous with entering discipleship.[108] Jesus responds by telling His disciples that those who have left all for His sake will not be lacking; to which the disciples reply—we have! Jesus then gives them assurance that they will have *eternal life*!

In closing, I find it odd that the kingdom is described as something of inestimable value (so Matt 13:44) and yet evidently, according to Hodges' interpretation, Jesus is not.[109] Is it reasonable to expect that Jesus, self-confessed embodiment of the kingdom (Luke 17:21),[110] would have taught that it was worth making sacrifices for the kingdom but *not* for Himself? Surely if one would give up all one owned for the kingdom (Matt 13:44) one would

---

[105] Hodges, *The Hungry Inherit*, 72–73.

[106] Thomas R. Schreiner and Ardel B. Caneday, *The Race Set Before Us: A Biblical Theology of Perseverance and Assurance* (Downers Grove, Ill.: InterVarsity, 2001) 82: That the disciples have understood entrance into the kingdom and salvation as synonymous concepts is seen in Jesus' reply: "With men this is impossible, but with God all things are possible" (Matt 19:26; Mark 10:27; Luke 18:27).

[107] Hellerman, "Wealth and Sacrifice in early Christianity," 159: "Peter and the disciples have done precisely what Jesus demanded of the RYR [Rich Young Ruler]."

[108] Brenda B. Colijn, "Salvation as Discipleship in the Gospel of Mark," *ATJ* 30 (1998) 12.

[109] I'm sure this is not what Hodges would believe though. However, as I put the pieces together in my own mind I cannot see the connections amounting to anything less.

[110] Darrell L. Bock, "The Kingdom of God in New Testament Theology," in *Looking into the Future: Evangelical Studies in Eschatology*, ed. David. L. Baker (Grand Rapids: Baker, 2001) 45: "Jesus' presence means the kingdom's presence."

also give up all they owned for Jesus? Are not the two—Jesus and the kingdom—essentially one?

The Good Samaritan

The parable of the Good Samaritan arises from a discussion with a certain lawyer (νομικός τις) and Jesus. Testing Jesus the lawyer asks, "Teacher, what having done will I inherit eternal life" (Luke 10:25). Jesus replies in turn by asking the lawyer to give his own reading of the Law (τῷ νόμῳ) (v. 26). The lawyer answers in effect, "Love God fully and love your neighbor as yourself" (v. 27). The answer is enough to satisfy Jesus—"you have answered correctly"—and presumably settles the matter for He responds: "*This do and you will live* (τοῦτο ποίει καὶ ζήσῃ)" (v. 29). In other words, love God and your neighbor and you will live (ζήσῃ) *eternally.*

The lawyer has his answer but feels the need to vindicate (δικαιῶσαι)[111] himself and asks Jesus to explain just who exactly is his neighbor (πλησίον) (v. 29). Jesus replies with a parable, commonly known as the Good Samaritan. The parable is well known and its point apparently straightforward. A man goes down (κατέβαινεν) from Jerusalem to Jericho and is attacked by robbers and left for dead (v. 30). A priest is also on his way down (κατέβαινεν) but upon seeing (ἰδὼν)[112] the helpless victim crosses the street (ἀντιπαρῆλθεν denotes the opposite side[113]) and continues on his way (v. 31). A Levite repeats the scene (v. 32) and a Samaritan shortly follows. The Samaritan is the last person on earth the lawyer would have expected to help but rather than cross to the opposite side of the road, the Samaritan goes to (*προσελθὼν* in contrast to *ἀντι*παρῆλθεν) the injured man and attends to his wounds (vv. 34-35).

Jesus returns to the point of the parable by again asking the lawyer to answer his own question: identify the neighbor (πλησίον) (v. 36 cf. v. 29). Again the lawyer answers correctly: it was the man who showed (ὁ ποιήσας) mercy on him (v. 37a). And again Jesus leaves the man with a command to go and *do* (ποίει; cf. v. 28) likewise, that is, show the same mercy to everyone in need (v. 37).

Hence the parable ends with a twist.[114] Since Leviticus 19:18—cited by the lawyer and affirmed by Jesus—says, "Love your neighbor as yourself" the

---

[111] The first question arises because the lawyer is trying to *test* (ἐκπειράζων) Jesus. The second question now arises because he is trying to *justify* (δικαιῶσαι) himself.

[112] Cf. also Luke 10:32, 33.

[113] BDAG, 90.

[114] See John R. Donahue, "Who Is My Enemy? The Parable of the Good Samaritan and the Love of Enemies," in *The Love of Enemy and Nonretaliation in the New Testament*, ed. William

lawyer would have expected the neighbor to be the injured man. This would then be the type of person the lawyer is to love as himself (v. 27). However, Jesus phrases the question in such a way—"which one of these three . . . ?"—indicating that a neighbor is not just someone in need but someone who cares for someone in need.[115] The lawyer then not only discovers who his neighbor is but that he himself is to be a neighbor. Thus there are neighbors who are benefactors (the Good Samaritan) and neighbors who are beneficiaries (the injured man). But everyone is a neighbor. The crucial point is that the lawyer has a visual of what it means to "love your neighbor as *yourself*."[116]

Interpretive Issues

As straightforward as this parable may appear it has not escaped debate.[117] Even its title is debated.[118] One of the most important issues concerns the unity of the discussion between Jesus and the lawyer (vv. 25-28) and the parable that follows (vv. 30-36).[119] This is exasperated by the fact that the

---

M. Swartley, Studies in Peace and Scripture, ed. Ben C. Ollenburger and Willard M. Swartley (Louisville, Ky.: Westminster John Knox, 1992) 143-45.

[115] Georges Crespy, "The Parable of the Good Samaritan: An Essay in Structural Research," trans. John Kirby, *Semeia* 2 (1974) 34 (originally published as "La parabole dite: 'Le bon Samaritain.' Recherches structurales," *Etudes théologiques et religieuses* 48 [1973] 61-79): The parable's *object* becomes the *subject*.

[116] Many have observed a lack of coherence between the lawyer's question (who is my neighbor) and Jesus' response. Jesus does not appear to answer the lawyer's second question, "who is my neighbor" (Luke 10:29). It has been suggested that the lawyer is in the role of the victim and the Samaritan's mercy is a demonstration of love towards one's enemy. The point of the parable is then *not* just go and show mercy *as* the Good Samaritan did, but to go and show mercy *to* the Samaritans (i.e., to one's enemies). For this interpretation see Norman H. Young, "The Commandment to Love Your Neighbor as Yourself and the Parable of the Good Samaritan (Luke 10:25-37)," *Andrews University Seminary Studies* 21 (1983) 265-72. However, the apparent incompatibility of the answer of v. 37 to the question in v. 29 makes perfect sense if understood as an answer to both the lawyer's questions but especially the first question relating to the reception of eternal life.

[117] For an overview of the parable's history of interpretation see Robert H. Stein, "Interpretation of the Parable of the Good Samaritan," in *Scripture, Tradition, and Interpretation*, ed. W. Ward Gasque and William Sanford LaSor (Grand Rapids: Eerdmans, 1978) 278-85.

[118] The term "Good" does not occur in the parable. Some have reacted to the title "Good Samaritan" since it inevitably predetermines the point of the parable: the point being to imitate the example of the Samaritan who showed mercy. In fact that this is the point of the parable is a matter of some debate. E.g., Robert W. Funk, "The Good Samaritan as Metaphor," *Semeia* 2 (1974) 74-81, argues that the lawyer, and hence the reader, are not to identify with the Samaritan but with the "man in the ditch." Cf. also Robert Farrar Capon, *The Parables of Grace* (Grand Rapids: Eerdmans, 1988) 58-67. Farrar entitles his chapter on the 'Good Samaritan' as "The First of the Misnamed Parables."

[119] Cf. Rudolf Bultmann, *The History of the Synoptic Tradition*, trans. John Marsh (New York:

answer given in v. 37 ("the one who showed mercy") is incongruent with the question raised in v. 29 ("who is my neighbor?").[120] This of course has implications for how one understands the point of the parable.[121] Furthermore, this parable has been subject to many allegorical interpretations throughout its history.[122] For a time Adolf Jülicher's pioneering insights into parables (i.e., parables were not allegories), served as the standard for interpretation. However Jülicher's work, carried out in the late nineteenth century, has now

---

Harper and Row, 1963) 178: the connection between Jesus' dialogue with the lawyer and the ensuing parable is artificial.

[120] Cf. Adolf Jülicher, *Die Gleichnisreden Jesu* (Tübingen: Mohr, 1910; reprint, Darmstadt: Wissenschaftliche Buchgesellschaft, 1963) 596.

[121] Depending on how one understands the unity between the lawyer's neighbor question and Jesus' response two somewhat different interpretations result. For example, Jesus has already said to the lawyer—"Do this and you will live" (Luke 10:28) vis-à-vis loving God and loving his neighbor. One would expect then that Jesus' second command ("Go and you do likewise" [v. 37]) would parallel His first. In other words, "Go and love your *neighbor*"—as opposed to "Go and *be a neighbor as the Samaritan* did." The lawyer has just identified the Samaritan as a neighbor so it would make sense that what Jesus is saying is, "Go and show love to the Samaritan (or someone similar)." For this interpretation see Bastiaan Van Elderen, "Another Look at the Parable of the Good Samaritan," in *Saved by Hope: Essays in Honor of Richard C. Oudersluys*, ed. James I. Cook (Grand Rapids: Eerdmans, 1978) 109–19. Cf. also, Young, "The Commandment to Love," 265–72. Young argues that Jesus is telling the lawyer to go and love his enemies of whom the Samaritan would be a representative. For the more traditional interpretation see the short article by, Robert S. Clucas, "The Neighbour Questions," *TheoEvan* 17 (1984) 49–50. My own opinion is that both *applications* are to be followed. Both *interpretations* are valid although it seems likely that Jesus is telling the lawyer to *be a neighbor* as the Samaritan was a neighbor. For the command "Go and you do (ποίει) likewise" (v. 37b) follows so closely to the lawyer's answer—"the one who showed (ὁ ποιήσας) mercy upon him" (v. 37a). By telling the lawyer to go and do as the Samaritan did he is telling him to show mercy to everyone in need, *including* Samaritans (cf. 6:27-28, 35-36). See Stein, "Interpretation of the Parable of the Good Samaritan," 287–90, for a convincing defence of this interpretation; also Crespy, "The Parable of the Good Samaritan," 46–48.

[122] See Leslie W. Barnard, "To Allegorize or not to Allegorize," *ST* 36 (1982) 1–10, esp., 4–5; cf. also Stein, "Interpretation of the Parable of the Good Samaritan," 278–84. Origen, e.g., understood the Good Samaritan to represent Jesus Christ while the injured man represents all those who have voluntarily sinned. His injuries represent sins. The priest represents the Mosaic Law and the Levite stands in for the prophets. Only Jesus can bring life to the injured sinner. Even the donkey and the inn have meaning. The donkey represents Christ's body upon which the sins of humanity are laid while the inn is the church where sinners can go for help. For Augustine the injured man is Adam, the robbers are the devil and his angels, the priest and the Levite represent the ministry of the old covenant and the Good Samaritan is Jesus. The innkeeper is the apostle Paul.

been called into question[123] and subsequently borderline allegorical interpretations of the Good Samaritan still persist[124] today.[125]

The Relationship between Doing the Law and Eternal Life

Perhaps these interpretive issues have clouded the (more important) theological issue in the passage—Jesus' answer to how one is saved and the role of works in his answer. Regardless of the reasons this topic has rarely even been raised with respect to this parable.[126] One almost wonders if it is an issue; although we can hardly imagine a gospel message with the words, "*Do* this and you will be saved." The relationship between works (identified here as "doing" [ποιέω]) and salvation (i.e., "eternal life") is patent in the discussion between Jesus and the lawyer. The lawyer asks, "What shall I *do* (ποιήσας) to inherit eternal *life* (ζωὴν)?" (v. 25).[127] Jesus throws the question back on the lawyer (v. 26). The lawyer answers: "Love God and your neighbor" (v. 27). Jesus says, "Correct! *Do* (ποίει) this and you *will live* (ζήση)" (v. 28). One writer on this passage has observed that the lawyer's question is flawed. "*Doing* and *inheriting* are not compatible terms. The gospel is good news freely available. It is not a matter of 'go and do.'"[128] Another has said: "The parable of the Good Samaritan . . . seems to promote a kind of works righteousness worthy of St. James rather than Paul's disciple Luke. Its punch lines . . . both say: 'Go and do!'"[129] However we are still left with, and puzzled by Jesus' own assessment

---

[123] See G. B. Caird, *The Language and Imagery of the Bible* (Grand Rapids: Eerdmans, 1980) 161–63.

[124] Funk, "The Good Samaritan as Metaphor," 74–81, in contrast to Jülicher, takes Luke 10:25-37 to be a metaphor rather than an example story.

[125] E.g., more recently: Mike Graves, "Luke 10:25-37: The Moral of the 'Good Samaritan.'" *Review and Expositor* 94 (1997) 272–74, suggests that the injured man represents the suffering Christ and the Samaritan represents the Gentiles in place of the Jews who have been ousted because of their rejection of Jesus. The parable then shows what it means to minister to the Lord and by extrapolation to others who are suffering. S. Willis, "The Good Samaritan: Another View," *ExpTim* 112 (1999–2000) 92: the Samaritan represents Jesus' compassion to lost sinners. The command to "go and do likewise" is a command to see your neighbor (i.e., Jesus presumably) as the one who can give eternal life; see also J.-Y. Baziou, "Quand le salut vient à l'Église par l'étranger," *Spiritus* 170 (2003) 45–54: the Samaritan is Christ and the inn is the church.

[126] Though cf. Stephen F. Noll, "The Good Samaritan and Justification by Faith," *Mission and Ministry* 8 (1990) 36.

[127] In fact the lawyer's question literally reads: "What *having done* shall I receive eternal life" (Luke 10:25).

[128] Graves, "Luke 10:25-37," 272; cf. also Capon, *The Parables of Grace*, 62–67.

[129] Noll, "The Good Samaritan," 36.

of the situation. For He not only gives the lawyer top marks for his understanding of the Law but advises him, "*Do* this and you will *live*." The future indicative ζήση together with its link to eternal ζωὴν in v. 25 indicates that Jesus means, "will live eternally."[130] Evidently in responding to the lawyer's reading of the Law, Jesus has, in line with later rabbinic tradition, applied the promise of "life" in Leviticus 18:5 to eternal life.[131] There is no suggestion from Jesus that the lawyer is on the wrong track by thinking he must do something. In fact Jesus repeats the command at the end of the parable: "Go and you *do* (ποίει) likewise" (v. 37). If this seems odd we might also think of His words in the SM, "Not everyone who says to Me, 'Lord, Lord,' will enter the kingdom of heaven, but the one who *does* (ὁ ποιῶν) the will of My Father who is in heaven" (Matt 7:21). It appears that Jesus does in fact seem to think that *doing* and *eternal life* is compatible.

However, it is possible that the lawyer, like the Rich Young Ruler (cf. esp. 19:16, 20), was thinking of the *one* thing he might do to inherit eternal life (note the *aorist* participle ποιήσας in Luke 10:25). Jesus responds by showing that loving your neighbor does not consist of one act but a continual doing (note the *present* tense verb ποίει in vv. 28, 37). It seems then that the lawyer "had a major act of benevolence, pilgrimage, or some act of devotion in mind." By doing it, he would be assured of eternal life.[132] But even though we may now console ourselves with the possibility that the lawyer was wrong in his understanding of how to inherit eternal life we are still left with Jesus' response. Jesus may have corrected the lawyer's "misdirected concept of eternal life"[133] but He has not alleviated the tension present between doing and eternal life. For by employing the present tense He simply exhorts the lawyer "to perform these acts of love repeatedly and continually"[134] and then he will live. With this new information we may now be in a worse dilemma!

The key point of course is that it is not merely a right reading of the Law that results in eternal life. It is the *doing* of the Law, specifically here summed

---

[130] Also, BDAG, 425; William Richard Stegner, "The Parable of the Good Samaritan and Leviticus 18:5," in *The Living Text: Essays in Honor of Ernest W. Saunders*, ed. Dennis E. Groh and Robert Jewett (Lanham, Md.: University Press of America, 1985) 30.

[131] See esp. Stegner, "Leviticus 18:5," 30–32 (including extra-biblical references); cf. also Craig S. Keener, "Luke," in *The IVP Bible Background Commentary: New Testament* (Downers Grove, Ill.: InterVarsity, 1993) 217. Also see my discussion on the relationship between Leviticus 18:5 and eternal life in chapter three along with Friedrich Avemarie, *Tora and Leben: Untersuchungen zur Heilsbedeutung der Tora in der frühen rabbinischen Literatur*, Texte und Studien zum Antiken Judentum, ed. Martin Hengel and Peter Schäfer, vol. 55 (Tübingen: Mohr, 1996) 376–445.

[132] Van Elderen, "Another Look," 111.

[133] Ibid.

[134] Ibid.

up in loving God and one's neighbor. This is brought out first by the twofold use of ποιέω in the present tense (vv. 28, 37) as opposed to the lawyer's question posed in the aorist tense (v. 25). That doing and not merely reading is the link to eternal life is also brought out by Luke's use of the priest and the Levite (vv. 31-32). Both presumably know the Law but fail to *do* it. The Samaritan, however, is an outsider when it comes to matters of the Law, but he nevertheless fulfills the requirement (cf. esp. Rom 2:12-16).

But what explains this relationship between doing and eternal life, bearing in mind that "doing" here is defined as loving God and one's neighbor and showing mercy to those in need? Two points appear significant. First, it is most probable that what the lawyer has in mind concerning eternal life is the resurrection of the righteous at the end of the age (cf. Dan 12:2). In Rabbinic writings post dating the Good Samaritan the end of the age was spoken of as the world to come.[135] The question is therefore eschatological in nature. So too presumably is Jesus' promise "you will live," that is, live "in the glory of the life to come" (cf. Sir 48:11).[136] I shall not discuss this point any further here for I have already discussed the relationship between doing (ποιέω) and eschatological salvation in chapter six with respect to Matthew 7:21-23. I shall discuss this relationship more concerning 25:31-46 in chapter eleven. Needless to say, it is of some significance that future salvation is often closely related to works not only in the Synoptic Gospels but elsewhere in the NT (cf. e.g., John 5:28-29; Rom 2:5-8; Jas 2:14-26).

The second point concerns the relationship between loving one's neighbor and loving God.[137] Evidently the lawyer (and others like him) did not think he had a problem with loving God with his whole heart, soul, strength, and mind (cf. Luke 18:11-12). This is inferred from the fact that his question concerns his neighbor and not God.[138] The lawyer's question is tantamount to asking, "Who do I have to show love to?" and by implication, "Who do I *not* have to show love to?" This is confirmed by Luke's narrative comment: "and trying to *justify* (δικαιῶσαι) himself he said to Jesus . . ." (10:29). Whatever

---

[135] *b. Ber.* 28b speaks of "life of the future world"; *b. Sota* 7b speaks of inheriting "the world to come"; cf. also *m. ʾAbot* 2.7; 4.16; 5.19; my chapter three; and Bock, *Luke 9:51–24:53*, 1023, for further references.

[136] BDAG, 425.

[137] For the combining of the two love commands see *T. Iss.* 5.2; 7.6-7 ("I acted in piety and truth all my days. The Lord I loved with all my strength; likewise, I loved every human being as I love my children. You do these as well, my children, and every spirit of Beliar will flee from you, and no act of human evil will over power you. Every wild creature you shall subdue, so long as you have the God of heaven with you, and walk with all mankind in sincerity of heart"); *T. Dan.* 5.3.

[138] Van Elderen, "Another Look," 112.

this expression may reveal about the lawyer's intention[139] it seems clear that he was at least attempting to find the minimal requirement for obeying the love command. This brings about the twist in the parable that follows. By telling the man that he is to be a neighbor to all (v. 37)[140] Jesus is in effect saying that *everyone* is his neighbor.[141] The doing (ποιέω, vv. 28, 37) of the neighbor command, coupled with loving God, will lead to eternal life (vv. 25, 28).[142]

But this still leaves the question of how loving one's neighbor can be the means of attaining eternal life, remembering that we are primarily thinking of eternal life in the future. Nothing more is said about loving God in this passage but when Jesus says, "Do this (τοῦτο) and you will live" (v. 28) He clearly means love *both* God and neighbor. We may then assume with good reason that Jesus' lesson on being a neighbor is also a lesson on what it means to love God.[143] In Jeremiah God associates King Josiah's neighborly concern with knowing Him. "He defended the cause of the poor and needy . . . Is that not what it means to *know* Me?" (Jer 22:16). John says as much in his first epistle. "If anyone says that 'I love God' and hates his brother he is a liar" (1 John 4:20a). The reason that he is a liar is because love for a brother is evidence of loving God. The absence of the former simply implies the absence of the latter. Evidently then God does not consider love for Him to be authentic unless it is expressed in love toward others. The point is that this love must be practiced (ποιέω) as shown by the Good Samaritan (cf. esp. 1 John 3:17; see Jas 1:27). This is central to explaining the relationship between *doing* and eternal life in this passage.

How then can Jesus say, "*Do* this and you will live"? The answer is that in order to inherit eternal life one must love God and this will *inevitably* be reflected in love for others. To put it in a nutshell, loving God and loving one's neighbor are synonymous.[144] There is somehow an identity between

---

[139] See Bock, *Luke 9:51–224:53*, 1027–28, for options.

[140] Following the traditional interpretation.

[141] Ibid., 1028: "The lawyer is looking for the *minimum* obedience required, but Jesus requires *total* obedience."

[142] Cf. Crespy, "The Parable of the Good Samaritan," 37–38.

[143] Cf. Peter Rhea Jones, "The Love Command in Parable," *Perspectives in Religious Studies* 6 (1979) 225: "the second love command assumes the first, making both *theocentric*."

[144] See esp. Gustavo Gutiérrez, *A Theology of Liberation: History, Politics, and Salvation*, ed. and trans. Caridad Inda and John Eagleson (Maryknoll, N.Y.: Orbis, 1973) 189–212.

God and neighbor.[145] This is not so much mystical as it is biblical.[146] We see this concept of identity in other contexts. Jesus says to His disciples in Luke 10:16, a few verses prior to the Good Samaritan, "The one who hears you *hears Me*, and the one who rejects you *rejects Me*. And the one who rejects Me *rejects the One who sent Me*." The reason some are judged righteous and worthy of eternal life at Matthew's sheep and goat judgment is that acts of mercy toward Jesus' brothers are in fact representative of one's attitude toward Jesus Himself (Matt 25:40). Conversely absent acts of mercy represent an absence of love for Jesus: "Whatever you did not do for one of the least of these, you did not do for *Me*" (v. 45; cf. also Acts 9:4). Thus an "action towards another is at the same time an action towards God."[147] The reasons for this identification between the divine and man (cf. esp. John 14) are beyond the scope of our discussion but needless to say this identification is central to understanding the relationship between *doing* and eternal life in Luke 10:25-37.[148]

Summary

The Rich Young Ruler: the key to understanding the relationship between works and salvation in Jesus' encounter with the Rich Young Ruler is a proper understanding of a pervasive attitude toward wealth and salvation in Judaism at the time. For the young man to sell all he had would be tantamount to placing undivided confidence in Jesus to save him. This fact alone demonstrates that what Jesus was asking of this ruler was no more than simple trust in His person. This then is nothing more than a traditional evangelical gospel

---

[145] For a discussion see Jean-Claude Ingelaere, "La 'parabole' du Jugément Dernier (Matthieu 25:31-46)," *Revue d'Histoire et de Philosophie Religieuses* 50 (1970) 56–59; and see Gutiérrez, *A Theology of Liberation*, 189–212, esp. 196–203.

[146] I use the word "synonymous" but I do not mean that one can simply love God by loving those in need. That would be similar to saying, "I have works and *therefore* I have faith" (cf. Jas 2:18)—"I love those in need, therefore I love God." I have said above that love for God will be "reflected in love for others." One cannot love others unless they love God *first*.

[147] Ibid., 202.

[148] The victim's relationship to God in the Good Samaritan is left unstated but in other passages where there is identity between the divine and man it is apparent that such a union exists only between believers and God and Jesus. (The identity of the "brothers" in Matt 25:31-46 may be an exception but I shall discuss this further in chapter 11). This is an important point. If I were to postulate a reason for this it would have to be related to the NT concept of God indwelling the believer (cf. e.g., John 14:23; Rom 8:9-11; 1 Cor 3:16; 2 Cor 6:16). This concept doubtless goes back to the notion of God dwelling inside the Tabernacle (cf. John 1:14), then the Temple, and now in believers and the church, God's new *temple* (Eph 2:21). Thus Jesus could say when He was here on earth: "the one who has seen *Me* has seen the *Father*" (John 14:9). It is this sort of relationship that explains the correlation between loving God and loving one's neighbor.

appeal, though asked in a completely non-traditional and non-evangelical way.

Jesus' use of the Law vis-à-vis entering life is more difficult to understand although solutions are not too hard to find. Part of the difficulty is in understanding Jesus' relationship to the Law and its application for believers today. Part of the solution may lie in the fact that Jesus is merely giving the stock Jewish answer for anyone wanting to enter life. The other part of the solution may lie in Jesus' evangelistic strategy of which we can only really speculate. Either way it is certain that what counts in the end is not obedience to the Law but the demand of Jesus. It is also worth noting the emphasis Jesus places on ethics given that salvation and eternal life are primarily eschatological. This is something we shall see repeatedly throughout the NT.

The Good Samaritan: the relationship between "doing" (ποιέω) and "eternal life" is evident in the parable of the Good Samaritan. While this may smack of works-righteousness other texts in the Synoptic Gospels also suggest a close relationship between ποιέω and salvation (esp. Matt 7:21-23; 25:31-46). Once again this can be explained by the fact that future salvation is in view. However, the crucial point in understanding the role of "works" in this passage is that in Jesus' thinking loving your neighbor is synonymous with loving God (cf. esp. 1 John 4:20a). Another way of saying this is to say that love for others is a *reflection* of love for God. The identification of God and Jesus with people, especially God's people, is a well-known concept. Close at hand in fact is Luke 10:16: "The one who hears you hears Me, and the one who rejects you rejects Me."

8

The Role of *Discipleship* in Salvation

In many ways this chapter provides a break in thought in our discussion on the relationship between works and salvation. However it is important for two reasons. First, it is "popular" to make a distinction between Jesus' call to conversion and His call to discipleship. I have argued in chapter five that the two are the same although both can also be thought of as a process of which conversion is merely one aspect and eternity is the completion. However since many view Jesus' call to discipleship as a form of "works" it is appropriate that we discuss it further. Second, Jesus' understanding of discipleship, I suggest, provides a coherent explanation of why there is such a close relationship between works and salvation in the Synoptic Gospels. I include this chapter here rather than say two chapters earlier or nearer to the end of the book because it takes into account passages already discussed and will provide some framework for understanding the passages yet to be discussed.

Background

Although it is common to think of a disciple as a pupil[1] the use of the term μαθητής in the ancient Greco-Roman world suggests that *more* than a pupil is in view.[2] Certainly the relationship may have been academic consisting of

---

[1] Cf. W. Bauder, "Disciple," in *NIDNTT*, 1:482; Hans Kvalbein, "Go therefore and make disciples . . . The Concept of Discipleship in the New Testament," *Themelios* 13 (1988) 49.

[2] K. H. Rengstorf, "μαθητής," in TDNT, 4:417–18. For the historical development of the term μαθητής in the Greco-Roman world and Judaism see ibid., 4:416–41; Michael J. Wilkins, *The Concept of Disciple in Matthew's Gospel: As Reflected in the Use of the Term Μαθητής*, NovTSup, ed. C. K. Barrett, A. F. J. Klijn, and J. Smit Sibinga, vol. 59 (Leiden: Brill, 1988) 11–125.

learning a certain skill[3] or just plain education.[4] However the term was often applied more broadly to devotion and commitment.[5] Even in the context of learning commitment and adherence to the teacher and his philosophies was foremost in view.[6] We see a similar trend in Judaism. While the relationships varied the common thread was commitment and devotion to a renowned leader, teacher or sect;[7] this is not to say that learning is not in view in these contexts, it is. But that inherent in being a disciple is the idea of devotion.

This continued until the time of Jesus to the point where the notion of learning receded into the background and "religious commitment and imitation"[8] best describes the disciples' relationship.[9] The Pharisees and John the

---

[3] E.g., Plato, *Euthydemus*, 276.A.7, speaks of disciples being taught the skill of writing. They are described in this context as learners (μανθάνω) (see 275.D.5; 276.A.2, 4). Cf. also Plato, *Laws*, 796.A.8, speaks of disciples being taught wrestling.

[4] E.g., Aristotle, *Metaphysics*, 5.986b.22: Parmenides was said to be Xenophanes' disciple in the study of metaphysics.

[5] E.g., Herodotus, 4.76–77, tells of Anacharsis' devotion to Greek culture (τῆς Ἑλλάδος μαθητὴς γένοιτο); Plato, *Protagoras*, 343.A.6, describes people who are "lovers and disciples of the Spartan culture."

[6] E.g., Isocrates, *Busiris*, 28.1–29.9: (the context is the piety of the Egyptians) "On a visit to Egypt he [Pythagoras] became a μαθητὴς of the religion of the people, and was first to bring to the Greeks all philosophy, and more conspicuously than others he seriously interested himself in sacrifices and in ceremonial purity, since he believed that even if he should gain thereby no greater reward from the gods, among men, at any rate, his reputation would be greatly enhanced. And this indeed happened to him. For so greatly did he surpass all others in reputation that all the younger men desired to be his μαθητάς, and their elders were more pleased to see their sons staying in his company than attending to their private affairs. And these reports we cannot disbelieve; for even now persons who profess to be μαθητάς of his teaching are more admired when silent than are those who have the greatest renown for eloquence."

[7] Josephus, *Ant.*, 13.289, speaks of Hyrcanus being a disciple (in context = adherent; see BDAG, 609) of the Pharisees; Josephus, *Ant.*, 15.367–71, speaks of disciples who refused to submit to taking an oath of loyalty to Herod on account of their commitment to Pollion the Pharisee and Samaias. Cf. Philo, *Sacrifices*, 7.1–10; 64.10; 79.10.

[8] Michael J. Wilkins, *Following the Master: A Biblical Theology of Discipleship* (Grand Rapids: Zondervan, 1992) 77–78.

[9] Note esp. Dio Chrysostom, *On Homer and Socrates*, 1–5: Dio is making a case for Socrates being a disciple of Homer even though Socrates was never associated with Homer since Homer had long since died. His point is that since Socrates was a "zealous follower" (ζηλωτήν) he must therefore have been a disciple. He writes, "Then, if a zealot (ζηλωτής) he would also be a disciple (μαθητής). For whoever is zealous for any one surely knows what that person was like, and by imitating (μιμούμενος) his acts and words he tries as best he can to make himself like him. But that is precisely, it seems, what the disciple (μαθητής) does—by imitating his teacher and paying heed to him he tries to acquire his art . . . However, if you shrink from calling Socrates a disciple (μαθητήν) of Homer, but would prefer to call him just a zealot (ζηλωτὴν δὲ μόνον) it will make no difference to me." Note also Dio Chrysostom, *Kingship* 1.38.6: "it stands to reason that practically all the kings among Greeks or barbarians who

Baptist both had their disciples but it is clear that more than learning is in view.[10] These disciples were committed to a way of life (e.g., Mark 2:18). Certainly no pharisaic disciple would have considered his relationship to be merely academic when asked to trap Jesus in His sayings (Matt 22:15-16) a mission designed to lead to His arrest (21:46) and death. Jesus' own disciples demonstrated their commitment to Him by breaking with their Mosaic traditions and heritage (12:1-2). The point is that the nature of a disciple's relationship impacted his life (Luke 5:33). This is not to say that teaching and learning were not important (cf. Matt 11:1; Luke 11:1; cf. John 18:19) but theory was only valuable insofar as it led to a change in lifestyle. More than pupils then, Jesus' disciples were *adherents*.[11] Furthermore, just as the disciples were more than students Jesus was more than a ῥαββι (Matt 26:25; Mark 9:5; 11:21; 14:45; John 1:49; 4:31; 6:25; 9:2; 11:8). He was κύριος (Matt 12:8; John 8:67-69) and indeed θεός (20:28). Hence He did more than teach (Matt 5:1-2; Mark 8:21-22; 9:31; Luke 11:1; John 8:28). He called for people's allegiance to His person (Matt 11:37-39) and submission to His authority and rule (8:21-22). He called people to break with their pasts, suffer as He would suffer, and follow Him.[12]

Among true disciples of Jesus different stages of discipleship are apparent. Stage one: believers in Christ and occasional companions (e.g., John 2:2, 11-12; 3:22; 4:1-27, 31). Stage two: abandonment of jobs and permanent followers (e.g., Matt 4:18-22; 9:9). Stage three: training for apostleship (e.g.,

---

have proved themselves not unworthy of this title ['like Zeus in counsel'] have been disciples and ζηλωτάς [=enthusiast, adherent, loyalist: BDAG, 427; cf. Acts 22:3] of this god." Cf. also Diodorus, *The Library of History*, 2.20.1; Plutarch, *That a Philosopher Ought to Converse Especially With Men in Power*, 776.E.

[10] Cf. Wilkins, *Following the Master*, 85.

[11] Ibid., 27, 39; BDAG, 609; cf. Martin Hengel, *The Charismatic Leader and His Followers*, ed. John Riches and trans. James C. G. Greig (Edinburgh: T. & T. Clark, 1981) 86; and see again Dio Chrysostom, *Kingship*, 1.38.6.

[12] Ernest Best, *Disciples and Discipleship: Studies in the Gospel According to Mark* (Endinburgh: Clark, 1986) 7: "[Jesus'] call is not one to accept a certain system of teaching . . . nor . . . a philosophical position . . . It is a call to fall in behind Jesus and go with him." Warren Carter, "Matthew 4:18-22 and Matthean Discipleship: An Audience-Orientated Perspective," *CBQ* 59 (1997) 58–75, esp. 69–75: the essence of discipleship entails living within the social and economic structures of society and yet without being devoted to these structures. The disciples' participation in society has now been redefined and reframed by God's reign and their new loyalty to Jesus. To follow Him thus entails wholehearted commitment to doing and obeying God's will.

Matt 4:19; cf. John 17:18).[13] Stages two and three were not required of everyone. Jesus did not invite everyone who had faith in Him to follow Him.[14]

Some were even told to *go* rather than *follow* (e.g., Luke 7:50; 17:19; cf. Mark 5:18-19, 34; Luke 8:48; but cf. 18:42-43). Fewer still were called to stage three (cf. Acts 1:26; 15:2).[15] However, irrespective of the stage one was always a "disciple."[16] The term "disciple" simply described their allegiance: they were followers of Jesus, not of John or the Pharisees.[17]

The Concept of Discipleship in the New Testament

What then does it mean to be a disciple *of Jesus*? In short it means to be like Him.[18] Indeed this may be the point of Jesus' words in Luke 6:40:[19]

---

[13] These stages are taken from, A. B. Bruce, *Training of the Twelve* (Edinburgh: T. & T. Clark, 1871; reprint, Grand Rapids: Kregel, 1971) 11–12.

[14] See Hengel, *The Charismatic Leader*, 61–63, 71–74. On this basis Hengel concludes that to follow Jesus was *not* a condition for salvation. It applied only to specific individuals of Jesus' choosing.

[15] Cf. BDAG, 122.

[16] E.g., Jesus' disciples accompanied Him to the wedding at Cana (John 2:2) before they received their call to stage two. Those who went on to stage three were chosen from stages one and two (cf. Luke 6:13).

[17] Wilkins, *Following the Master*, 37. There is nothing in the way disciples are described that indicates that a disciple has something extra to a *mere* believer, like commitment. It is clear that all disciples are not believers. However there is nothing to dismiss the conclusion that *all* believers are disciples (unless the argument is made that the demands made on disciples imply a works mentality, yet I will argue against this shortly). The term μαθητής can refer to a student/teacher relationship (Matt 5:1; 9:11, 14, 19; 10:24, 25; Luke 6:40); the twelve or a portion thereof (Matt 8:23; 9:37; 10:1; 11:1; 12:1, 2; 13:36; 14:15, 19, 22, 26; 15:2, 12, 23, 32, 33, 36; 16:5, 13, 20, 21, 24; 17:16, 19; 18:1; 19:10, 13, 23, 25; 20:17; 21:20; 23:1; 24:1, 3; 26:1, 8, 18, 26, 35, 36; 27:64; 28:7, 8, 13, 16; Mark 2:23; 3:7, 9; 4:34; 5:31; 6:1, 35, 41, 45; 7:2, 5, 17; 18:1, 4, 6, 10, 27, 33, 34; 9:14; 9:18, 28, 31; 10:10, 13, 24, 46; 11:14; 12:43; 14:14, 32; 16:7; Luke 6:1; 7:11; 8:22; 9:14, 16, 18, 40, 43; 10:23; 11:1a; 12:1, 22; 16:1; 17:1, 22; 18:15; 20:45; 22:11, 39; John 2:2, 11, 12, 17, 22; 3:22; 4:2, 8, 27, 31, 33; 6:3, 12, 16, 22, 24; 9:2; 11:7, 8, 12, 54; 12:16; 13:5, 22; 16:29; 18:1, 2, 19; 20:10, 18, 19, 20, 25, 26, 30; 21:1, 2, 4, 8, 12, 14); a select group from the twelve (Matt 17:6, 10, 13; 21:1, 6; 26:17, 19, 40, 45, 56; Mark 11:1; 13:1; 14:12, 13, 16; Luke 9:54; 19:29; 22:46; John 6:8; 12:4; 13:23; 16:17; 18:15, 16, 17, 25; 19:26, 27; 20:2, 3, 4, 8; 21:7, 20, 23, 24); general reference not pertaining to the twelve (Matt 8:21; John 6:60, 61, 66; 7:3); general reference to believers belonging to Christ by virtue of their commitment to Him (Matt 9:10; 10:42; 12:49 [cf. v. 50]; 13:10; Mark 2:15, 16; Luke 5:30; 6:13, 17, 20 [cf. Matt 5:1]; 8:9; 10:23; 14:26, 27, 33; 19:37, 39; John 4:1; 8:31; 9:27, 28a; 13:35; 15:8; 19:38 (?)); disciples of John the Baptist (Matt 11:2; 14:12; Mark 2:18; 6:29; Luke 7:18; 11:1b; John 1:35, 37; 3:25) the Pharisees (Matt 22:16) and Moses (John 9:28b).

[18] Ibid., 41–42; cf. Best, *Disciples and Discipleship*, 3.

[19] Wilkins, *Following the Master*, 42; cf. Darrell L. Bock, *Luke 1:1–9:50*, BECNT, ed. Moisés Silva, vol. 3A (Grand Rapids: Baker, 1996) 613.

"A disciple is not more than His teacher but everyone who is fully trained (κατηρτισμένος)[20] *will be like* His teacher." Either way, it is evident that to be a disciple is to be like Jesus since Jesus called people to take up their cross (like Him) give up their life (like Him) and follow *Me*. As the Son of Man came to serve so disciples must also serve (Mark 10:43-45).[21] Although the term μαθητής never appears outside the Gospels and Acts we find the same concept in the epistles.[22] Paul encourages his readers to be *imitators* (μιμητής) of Christ (cf. 1 Cor 11:1; 4:16; Eph 5:1; 1 Thess 1:6; 2:14).[23]

In fact terms infrequently used to describe disciples in the Gospels are frequently employed to refer to believers elsewhere in the NT.[24] In the Gospels Jesus' *brother* (ἀδελφός) and *sister* (ἀδελφή) are those who obey God.[25] The Twelve are called "brothers" (Matt 28:10). In the epistles *brothers* becomes the norm for addressing believers in Christ.[26] The term *child* (τέκνον, μικρός or παιδίον) in the Gospels occasionally describes someone who has faith in Jesus.[27] Outside the Gospels however believers are frequently referred to as children.[28] Since the noun *slave* (δοῦλος) and its verb *to serve* (δουλεύω) are used many times in the Gospels to refer to a worker under authority (cf. Matt 8:9; Luke 7:2) they are often employed to describe the relationship between God and man.[29] Not surprisingly they are also frequently used to describe

---

[20] NASB. Cf. 1 Cor 1:10; 1 Thess 3:10; Heb 13:21; 1 Pet 5:10 where the sense is to be made complete (BDAG, 526).

[21] Best, *Disciples and Discipleship*, 3.

[22] Wilkins, *Following the Master*, 42: "This [that discipleship = being conformed to the image of Christ] establishes a link between explicit discipleship sayings in the Gospels and Acts with similar concepts in the rest of the New Testament." For a defense of this see esp. ibid., 291–310.

[23] Hengel, *The Charismatic Leader*, 62, suggests that it is possible to see an "overarching connection" between the Gospels' use of μαθητής and Paul's μιμητής "in the sense that they both refer to the believer's unconditional sharing of a common destiny with Christ." See esp. Philo *Sacrifices* 64.14 and 65.3 for a connection between μαθηταὶ and μιμεῖσθαι, and Dio Chrysostom *On Homer and Socrates* 4.

[24] This fact rings of authenticity. In other words, if the church had imposed their own teaching concerning discipleship onto Jesus' lips we would expect to find the same frequent terminology and expressions in the epistles. However what we find instead is the concept of discipleship and the *infrequent* terminology carried over from the Gospels.

[25] Matthew 12:50; Mark 3:35; Luke 8:21; cf. Matt 28:10; John 20:17.

[26] Cf. Rom 16:1, 23; 1 Cor 1:1; 7:15; 9:5; 16:12; 2 Cor 1:1; Phil 2:25; Col. 1:1; 4:7, 9; 1 Thess 3:2; Phlm 1, 2; Jas 2:15; 1 Pet 5:12; 2 Pet 3:15 (BDAG, 18).

[27] Cf. Matt 9:2; 18:3, 6; 19:14; Mark 2:5; 10:14, 15, 24; Luke 18:16, 17.

[28] The term τέκνον is frequently employed. Cf. Rom 8:16; 9:8; 1 Cor 4:14, 17; 2 Cor 6:13; Gal 4:19, 31; Eph 5:1; Phil 2:15; 1 Tim 1:2; Heb 2:13; 1 John 3:2.

[29] Cf. Luke 17:7-10; cf. 1:38, 48; 2:29.

the nature of God's kingdom.³⁰ In the rest of the NT those who are engaged in the Lord's work are often described as *slaves*.³¹ Hence they are often portrayed in a *serving* capacity³²—although these terms also apply to believers in general.³³ The term also describes a believer's relationship to God. In the Gospels one cannot serve (δουλεύειν) two masters (Matt 6:24; Luke 16:13). The epistles teach that all human beings alike are slaves to something. Either someone is a slave to sin and its schemes³⁴ or to God and His righteousness (Rom 6:16-22). In John 15:13-15 Jesus calls His disciples *friends* (φίλος) (cf. also 11:11). Jesus has a reputation for being a *friend* of tax collectors and sinners (Matt 11:19; Luke 7:34). While the noun φίλος is rarely used outside the Gospels John does refer to believers as friends in his third epistle (3 John 15). John uses the verb φιλέω to describe the disciples' *love* for Jesus (John 16:27; 21:15-17). Paul declares that if anyone does not *love* the Lord a curse be on him (ἤτω ἀνάθεμα) (1 Cor 16:22). He also speaks of those who *love* him in the faith (Tit 3:15).³⁵

Thus, although the term μαθητής does not appear outside of the Gospels and Acts, the concept is readily seen throughout the entire NT. We have already noted this same phenomenon in chapter five concerning salvation but we can now see that it equally applies to discipleship. Jesus urges people to *follow* Him; John urges readers to *remain* in Him; Luke's readers are people of *The Way*; Paul's readers have entered into a *walk*; the writer of Hebrews urges his readers to *run the race*; and Peter's readers are on a *pilgrimage*.³⁶ Hence all who are believers in Christ are disciples.³⁷

The Reality of Discipleship

While the term μαθητής describes one's allegiance/adherence to a teacher/teaching the term itself does not function as a commentary on one's salvation. This must be determined by the context. In fact disciples come in all sorts of spiritual shapes and sizes. They are constantly in need of instruction (Matt 16:21; Mark 4:10; 7:17; Luke 11:1) to which there may be varying responses

---

³⁰ Cf. Matt 13:27-28; 18:23-32; 21:34-36; 22:3-10; 25:14-30; Luke 19:15.

³¹ See Murray J. Harris, *Slave of Christ: A New Testament Metaphor for Total Devotion to Christ*, NSBT, ed. D. A. Carson, no. 8 (Downers Grove, Ill.: InterVarsity, 1999).

³² Cf. Acts 16:7; Rom 1:1; Phil 1:1; 2:2; Col 4:12; 2 Tim 2:24; Titus 1:1; Jas 1:1; 2 Pet 1:1; Jude 1:1; Rev 1:1.

³³ Cf. Acts 2:18; 1 Thess 1:9; 1 Pet 1:16; Rev 1:1; 2:20; 7:3; 19:5; 22:3, 6.

³⁴ Cf. Gal 4:3, 8; Titus 3:3; Heb 2:15.

³⁵ See Wilkins, *Following the Master*, 291–310.

³⁶ Cf. also Best, *Disciples and Discipleship*, 5.

³⁷ Although, as I have pointed out this does not mean that all disciples are believers.

from acceptance (John 6:67-69) to complaining (John 6:60-61) resistance (Mark 9:32) anxiety (Luke 18:26) and complete bewilderment (John 14:22). It is not uncommon for disciples to be severely lacking in faith (Matt 17:17, 20; Mark 4:40) spiritual insight (6:52; 7:18; 8:17-21) commitment (Matt 8:21) and a mind that is set on the things of God (Mark 8:33). Yet sometimes disciples do get things right. Jesus' disciples refused to leave Him after others had (John 6:67-68) and at times showed remarkable insight into His person (Mark 8:29; John 6:69; 16:30). They believed (John 2:2; 16:30) and Peter risked life and limb to demonstrate his commitment to Jesus (Matt 14:28-29). However this does not mean that disciples aren't fearful (Mark 10:32;[38] John 20:19) even to the point of secrecy (19:38). They may be daring one minute (18:10) and cowardly the next (vv. 15-18, 25-27). They can be arrogant (Mark 9:34) and make laudable promises they later do not fulfill (Mark 10:38-39; John 14:37). Peter denied knowing Jesus (Mark 14:66-72) Judas betrayed Him (John 6:70-71; 18:2-5) all His disciples eventually left Him (Mark 14:50) and others simply stopped following Him (John 6:66). In short disciples are a mixed bag. The Twelve did not even measure up to Jesus' call to discipleship all of the time.[39] Disciples may be saved or unsaved, committed or uncommitted.[40] Hence while the conditions for discipleship may paint an *idealistic* picture, the Gospels as a whole paint a *realistic* picture.

We see a good example of this especially in Matthew 8:19-27 where two men who desire to *follow* (ἀκολουθέω) Jesus are told that they must accept the lofty demands of discipleship and leave their homes and families behind (vv. 19-22). Jesus leaves the scene and gets into a boat. Matthew records that His disciples were *following* (ἠκολούθησαν) Him (v. 23). Matthew's use of ἀκολουθέω in v. 23 is important for it is his way of connecting vv. 19-22 with vv. 24-27 and thereby tying the two passages together into the theme of discipleship.[41] While in the boat the disciples are overwhelmed by a great

---

[38] Note: "And those who followed (ἀκολουθοῦντες) were afraid."

[39] This has also been observed by Jeannine K. Brown, *The Disciples in Narrative Perspective: The Portrayal and Function of the Matthean Disciples*, Academia Biblica, ed. Saul M. Olyan and Mark Allan Powell, no. 9 (Atlanta: SBL, 2002) 40: "Who the disciples as a character group show themselves *to be* in the narrative might be quite different from what all disciples *should be* according to Jesus" (see also 73).

[40] Wilkins, *Following the Master*, 43–44, makes a similar observation: "Some ministries refer to those only with advanced commitment as 'disciples.' This implies that those with less commitment are not disciples. Instead, we should call all believers disciples and those with advanced commitment something like 'mature disciples.'" See also Darrell L. Bock, "A Review of *The Gospel according to Jesus*," *BSac* 146 (1989) 34–37.

[41] W. D. Davies and Dale C. Allison Jr., *A Critical and Exegetical Commentary on the Gospel According to Matthew*, vol. 2, ICC, ed. J. A. Emerton, C. E. B. Cranfield, and G. N. Stanton (Edinburgh: T. & T. Clark, 1991) 71.

storm. Jesus sleeps and the disciples panic, "Lord, save us, we are perishing" (v. 25). Now awake, Jesus responds, "Why do you doubt, men of *little faith*" (v. 26). Evidently these twelve disciples still have a lot to learn about the person of Jesus (v. 27). But this is the "reality" of discipleship. Sometimes disciples have "little faith." And yet this does not take away from the ideal of discipleship expressed in Jesus' call to the two men in vv. 19-27.

These two passages in Matthew 8 illustrate well the point I am making. We must be careful to distinguish between the *call* to be a disciple and the *reality* of being a disciple. Since many define discipleship only as the conditions laid down by Jesus in the Gospels it is not surprising that "disciple" has become virtually synonymous with "committed Christian." Yet as we have seen this was patently not the case with the Twelve and neither is it the case for the rest of the NT.

Christians are all *children* and yet we are told to "walk as children of light" (Eph 5:8) to be obedient (1 Pet 1:14) to remain in Christ (1 John 2:28) and to love other brothers (3:10). We are all *slaves* and yet we are urged to "not become subject again to a yoke of slavery (δουλείας)" (Gal 5:1; cf. also 1 Cor 7:23). All believers are *brothers* and yet there are evidently strong as well as weak brothers (8:9-13). The definitive mark of a Christian is works (Jas 2:14-26) but this does not mean that Christians don't stumble in all sorts of ways (3:2). One becomes a disciple at 'conversion' but one also spends the rest of one's life becoming a disciple, that is, an imitator of Jesus. To put things another way, disciples are not only defined by the indicative but also by the imperative; not only by their position but also by their practice; not only by their call but also by their conduct. Discipleship is as much about reality as it is about ideality. The ideality is that disciples are called to complete commitment to Jesus Christ. The reality is they often fall short. Discrepancies often exist in the lives of disciples. Inconsistency abounds more than we would like.[42] Yet this is the reality of discipleship. The point is that *all* believers are disciples and all are involved in becoming the disciples Jesus calls them to be. It is a process[43] of becoming like Jesus[44] and *every* believer is involved since God has predestined every believer to be "conformed to the

---

[42] See e.g., Warren Carter, *Matthew: Storyteller, Interpreter, Evangelist*, rev. ed. (Peabody, Mass.: Hendrickson, 2004) 215–27. Carter (217–18, 222–23, 224) describes the traits *true* (i.e., their position) of disciples and the traits required of disciples (i.e., their required practice).

[43] Cf. Brenda B. Colijn, "Salvation as Discipleship in the Gospel of Mark," *ATJ* 30 (1998) 11: Discipleship is "salvation in action." I happen to agree with Hodges, *Absolutely Free*, 69: "regeneration brings with it immense capacities and staggering possibilities. But all these capabilities come, so to speak, not in their ripened maturity, but in the form of a 'seed' which requires cultivation."

[44] Wilkins, *Following the Master*, 42.

image of His Son so that He might be the first-born among many *brothers* (ἀδελφοῖς)" (Rom 8:29).

The Call to Discipleship

I have argued in chapter five that Jesus' call to discipleship constitutes a call to salvation thought of as both an *initiation* and a *pilgrimage*.[45] However to suggest this is often not popular[46] and we must wonder why it is that for some the demands of discipleship appear as such an intrusion on the gospel. The evidence from the Gospels suggests that the two are not contradictory. It will be helpful at this point if we separate Jesus' call to discipleship into two categories, *general* and *specific*, the latter being an expression of the former.

"General" Conditions

During His earthly ministry Jesus laid down general conditions for being His disciple. A host of expressions are commonly used: *come after Me* (Matt

---

[45] Joseph C. Dillow, *The Reign of the Servant Kings: A Study of Eternal Security and the Final Significance of Man* (Miami, Fla.: Schoettle, 1992) 150–51, suggests that being a disciple of Jesus involved literally following Him around Israel and therefore no one can be a disciple today unless they are physically present with Jesus in the land of Israel. Some observations are in order. (1) While Dillow's point is in some sense true (cf. Hengel, *The Charismatic Leader*, 61–63; though cf. Scot McKnight, *A New Vision For Israel: The Teachings of Jesus in National Context* [Grand Rapids: Eerdmans, 1999] 171) we must wonder why the early church considered themselves to be disciples (e.g., Acts) in the *absence* of the earthly Jesus. (2) If discipleship is a literal phenomenon why then is it applied to Christians at all today—as it is indeed applied by Dillow himself? (3) The phrase καθ' ἡμέραν in Luke 9:23 transforms the call to discipleship into a metaphor for commitment to Jesus and thus suggests more than a literal phenomenon (contra Zane C. Hodges, *Absolutely Free!: A Biblical Reply to Lordship Salvation* [Grand Rapids: Zondervan, 1989] 72) (cf. Matt 26:55; Mark 14:49). Yet Jesus' disciples didn't even fall into this category if taken literally. Rather the phrase is simply pointing to the longevity of the commitment required. Discipleship is not a one-time affair. Best, *Disciples and Discipleship*, 8: by qualifying "take up your cross" with "daily" Luke "has turned it [καθ' ἡμέραν] completely into a metaphor" (also Joel B. Green, *The Gospel of Luke*, NICNT, ed. Gordon D. Fee [Grand Rapids: Eerdmans, 1997] 373).

[46] The evidence that Hodges marshals in support of a distinction between a disciple and a Christian comes exclusively from outside the Synoptic Gospels and mostly that of John (see e.g., Zane C. Hodges, *The Gospel Under Siege: Faith and Works in Tension* [Dallas: Redención, 1992] 35–45). His reasons for denying any affiliation between discipleship and salvation are that the conditions for discipleship conflict with John's view of salvation. I cannot take the time or space to go into John's soteriology; my point here is simply that the use of the term μαθητής in the Synoptic Gospels does not support Hodges' contention.

16:24; cf. Mark 8:34[47]) *deny himself* (Matt 16:24; Mark 8:34) *take*[48] *up his cross* (Matt. 10:38; 16:24; Mark 8:34; Luke 14:27) *hate*[49] *his mother and father* (Luke 14:26) *lose his life* (Matt 10:39; 16:25; Mark 8:35; Luke 9:24; 14:26). It is significant that in each case these conditions are addressed to either the "crowds" (Luke 14:25) the Twelve (Matt 10:1; 16:24; Luke 9:23) or both (Mark 8:34). Hence they are *general* conditions offered to *all*.

Furthermore, since these conditions are general the exact nature of the condition in most cases is not made explicit. Rather what discipleship entails is born out by the tenor of Jesus' ministry as a whole and especially His interaction with individuals. We shall look at specific instances shortly. What we can tell from these general conditions though is that the call to discipleship is if nothing else a call to fall in line with Jesus—*follow Me* (Matt 10:38; 16:24; Mark 8:34; Luke 9:23).[50] In other words, Jesus does not call anyone to do what He has not already done. He denied Himself, took up His cross, and gave up His life (Phil 2:6-8). Thus "The rule of discipleship is: Jesus. As Jesus was, so the disciple must be."[51] I have already said as much above.

The various discipleship manifestos present a comprehensive portrait of what it means to follow Jesus.[52] One's self, family, indeed one's very life, must all take a back seat to following Jesus. To follow Jesus is the positive side of self-denial. Self-denial denotes 'leaving behind' whereas following suggests 'moving forward' (cf. Matt 4:20, 22). Although ἀκολουθέω always applies to the earthly Jesus[53] its figurative sense is not absent.[54] First, it does not make sense that one could only be worthy of Christ if he or she were literally following Him (Matt 10:38; cf. 22:8). Second, there are those who did

---

[47] Mark has ἀκολουθεῖν for Matthew's ἐλθεῖν. Among other manuscripts ℵ A B has copied in ἐλθεῖν but this is certainly due to Matthew's reading for it is hard to imagine a scribe omitting ἐλθεῖν in favor of the more difficult ἀκολουθεῖν since the word occurs again at the end of Mark 8:34.

[48] Various terms are used here: λαυβάνει ' (Matt 10:38); ἀράτω (16:24; Mark 8:34); βαστάζει (Luke 14:27).

[49] "Hate" should not be understood as "detest" (e.g., Luke 1:71; 6:22) but as a degree of love (as in Matt 10:37). The point is that one must love Jesus *more than* his or her family. Cf. Josephus, *Ag. Ap.*, 2.27: "Honour to parents the Law ranks second only to honour to God."

[50] On what it meant to follow Jesus see Hengel, *The Charismatic Leader*.

[51] Best, *Disciples and Discipleship*, 3.

[52] For how scholars have described this portrait, see e.g., James D. G. Dunn, *Jesus Remembered*, vol. 1, Christianity in the Making (Grand Rapids: Eerdmans, 2003) 543–611; Carter, "Matthew 4:18-22 and Matthean Discipleship," 58–75; idem, *Matthew: Storyteller*, 217–18, 222–23, 224; Brown, *The Disciples in Narrative Perspective*, 59–120.

[53] Rev 14:4 is the exception; Hengel, *The Charismatic Leader*, 62; C. Blendinger, "Disciple," in *NIDNTT*, 1:482.

[54] Kittel, "ἀκολουθέω," in *TDNT*, 1:214.

not follow but clearly demonstrated following-like commitment (e.g., Luke 19:1-9). Third, John equates "follow" and "believe" in John 8:12 and 12:46 respectively (see chap. 5). Fourth, the phrase "take up your cross" is clearly figurative since discipleship "is not a short journey to the place of execution."[55] This is not to take away from the historical context[56] but as we have already seen the post-resurrection church integrated the concept of discipleship into their teachings. This suggests that it was not one's external following that true following represented (cf. Matt 8:10, 19; Mark 3:7) but *internal* commitment to Jesus.[57]

In light of this brief overview I suggest that the essence of Jesus' call to discipleship also constitutes His call to conversion,[58] that is, *repentance* and *belief* in the gospel (Mark 1:15; cf. Luke 13:3; 15:7; Acts 2:38).[59] *Repentance* involves turning *from* whatever it is that is preventing one from turning *to* (i.e., believing in) the gospel.[60] It is the negative side of conversion. One who is repentant is persuaded (πείθω) that their way of life is wrong and God's way is right (Luke 16:31).[61] They must make a comprehensive turn in both their attitudes and actions (Matt 3:8; Luke 3:8-14). The *whole* person is involved not just the mind (cf. Matt 23:26; also *Jub.* 1:15, 23). Although

---

[55] Best, *Disciples and Discipleship*, 8.

[56] In addition to Hengel's *The Charismatic Leader* see McKnight, *A New Vision for Israel*, 176–96, for understanding the historical background of following Jesus.

[57] Cf. Kittel, "ἀκολουθέω," in *TDNT*, 1:213–14.

[58] McKnight, *A New Vision For Israel*, 164–76.

[59] Remember that we are speaking primarily here of *initial* salvation as opposed to eschatological salvation. For the latter see e.g., Matt 5:20; 10:22; 25:34, 46.

[60] Cf. James D. G. Dunn, *Jesus' Call to Discipleship*, Understanding Jesus Today, ed. Howard Clark Kee (Cambridge: Cambridge University Press, 1992) 20: repentance literally means, "*turn around,' and head in a quite new direction*" (cf. Isa 55:7; Jer 3:12, 14, 22; Hos 6:1). Cf. though Zane C. Hodges, *Harmony With God: A Fresh Look at Repentance* (Dallas: Redención, 2001). Hodges argues that since Acts 16:31 (and John's Gospel) declares belief as the only means of salvation, repentance is not a condition for eternal life. For a similar argument see Robert N. Wilkin, *Confident in Christ: Living By Faith Really Works* (Irving, Tex.: Grace Evangelical Society, 1999) 201–3. (Though interestingly Dillow, *Servant Kings*, 21, n. 31, considers repentance as a part of conversion; apparently in contrast to Hodges and Wilkin). I find Hodges' argument difficult to fathom especially in light of 17:30b: God "commands all men everywhere to repent!" (cf. also 20:21). Nevertheless I can only reply by asking, "what about the Synoptic Gospels—do they not have a say on the matter?" Both the Rich Young Ruler and the Jewish lawyer asked very similar questions to that of the Philippian jailer (see v. 29). Should these passages not also have a bearing on how we understand what one must do to be saved? Hodges evidently thinks not; I disagree. Why should the Philippian Jailor scenario hold sway, or serve as a benchmark, over these other two scenarios? Furthermore, the epistles endorse everything that Jesus taught concerning salvation (as I am indeed attempting to demonstrate).

[61] In contrast cf. Luke 18:9.

the term "repent" or "repentance" rarely occurs in the Gospels[62] we see the concept illustrated in a variety of ways.[63] The prodigal son, having become persuaded in his mind[64] that being with his father was better than going it alone (Luke 15:17) returned to his father admitting he was wrong (vv. 18-21).[65] In contrast to the Pharisee who was persuaded (πεποιθότας) by his own righteousness (18:9) the tax collector felt grief[66] over his sin, which led him to beg for mercy[67] (18:13). Zacchaeus responded to Jesus' invitation to come down from his tree (19:5-6). Then being identified as a sinner he turned (σταθείς) to Jesus and promised to give half his possessions to the poor and make restitution for his unscrupulous affairs (19:7-9). Repentance then is more than a change of mind. It begins with being *persuaded* that my way is wrong and God's way is right. But true persuasion can never remain in the mind; it must result in life-changing decisions.[68]

Belief is the positive side of repentance; it is turning *to* (God).[69] But it is more than cognitive assent.[70] Negatively faith involves *not* fearing (Mark 5:36; Luke 8:50) not doubting (Mark 11:23; cf. Jas 1:6) or not believing in anyone but Jesus (Mark 13:21). Positively it means to submit to Jesus' authority (Matt 8:8-10, 13) have confidence in His ability to help (9:22-24) trust in God's word (Luke 8:12, 13) and His promises (Mark 11:23; Luke 1:45; 24:25).

---

[62] Μετανοέω: Matt 3:2; 4:17; 11:20, 21; 12:41; Mark 1:15; 6:12; Luke 10:13; 11:32; 13:3, 5; 15:7, 10; 16:30; 17:3, 4; μετάνοια: Matt 3:8, 11; Mark 1:4; Luke 3:3, 8; 5:32; 15:7; 24:47. Πιστεύω occurs well over one hundred times and πίστις over twenty in the four Gospels.

[63] Dunn, *Jesus' Call to Discipleship*, 21–25; McKnight, *A New Vision for Israel*, 172–76; Christopher D. Marshall, *Faith as a Theme in Mark's Narrative*, SNTSMS, ed. G. N. Stanton, vol. 64 (Cambridge: Cambridge University Press, 1989) 51.

[64] Luke 15:17: εἰς ἑαυτὸν δὲ ἐλθών.

[65] That the prodigal son illustrates repentance is seen from the context (i.e., Luke 15:7, 10).

[66] Beating one's chest (Luke 18:13; cf. 23:48) was a sign of grief (BAGD, 767).

[67] Luke 18:13: ἱλάσθητί μοι τῷ ἁμαρτωλῷ.

[68] Marius Reiser, *Jesus and Judgment: The Eschatological Proclamation in Its Jewish Context*, trans. Linda M. Maloney (Minneapolis: Fortress, 1997) 254: "for Jesus the ultimate consequence of repentance was discipleship."

[69] Dunn, *Jesus' Call to Discipleship*, 25; James R. Edwards, *The Gospel According to Mark*, PNTC, ed. D. A. Carson (Grand Rapids: Eerdmans, 2002) 47; McKnight, *A New Vision for Israel*, 166–72.

[70] Cf. Marshall, *Faith*, 50, 54–56, suggests that cognitive assent is conveyed by πιστεύειν ὅτι (cf. Mark 11:23-24) rather than πιστεύειν ἐν as in 1:15.

Table 8: The Negative and Positive Sides of Discipleship and Salvation—
Some Examples

	Negative Terms	Positive Terms
Discipleship conditions	Deny yourself Hate his father and mother . . . even his own life	Take up your cross Follow Me Come to Me
Conversion conditions	Repent	Believe
Other terms and expressions	Turn *from* "I am *persuaded* that I am wrong" Hate the one Despise the other	Turn *to* "I am *persuaded* that God is right" Love the other Devoted to one

By now it should be clear that repentance and belief involves more than, though does not exclude the mind. In Mark 1:14-15 repentance and belief are to be exercised in the context of the "good news" and the arrival of the "kingdom of God." One must therefore believe in God's promise of salvation and submit to His rule[71] embodied in the person of Jesus.[72] And what else is the essence of becoming a disciple if it is not "a call first and foremost *to recognize the reality of God's rule.*"[73]

> In short, the repentance Jesus called for was not just a matter of saying 'sorry' . . . What Jesus called for was *conversion*, for a turning around of heart and will and life, as well as a change of mind. He called for a conversion which was the end of self-serving and self-justification, a recognition of the delusiveness of adult independence and material possessions, a realisation of where a person's true worth and long-term good lies. He called for a conversion to *God*, a yielding of life in and from its innermost values and purpose to God's direction . . . what he called for was a submission to the rule of God before all other claims on affection or commitment.[74]

---

[71] Dunn, *Jesus' Call to Discipleship*, 9–19, 27–28, 30; E. M. B. Green, *The Meaning of Salvation* (Philadelphia: Westminster, 1965) 102.

[72] Marshall, *Faith*, 46–48.

[73] Dunn, *Jesus' Call to Discipleship*, 30.

[74] Ibid., 24–25.

"Specific" Conditions

That which Jesus 'generally' called for among the crowds and His disciples He applied 'specifically' to certain individuals.[75] Discipleship terms are rarely used except for "follow," but these encounters present a comprehensive picture of what it means to be a disciple. In Matthew 8:19-22 and Luke 9:57-62 Jesus is confronted by three would-be followers. The first is a scribe[76] (Matt 8:19-20=Luke 9:57-58) and claims that he will "follow" (ἀκολουθήσω) Jesus *anywhere* (ὅπου ἐάν). Jesus warns this would-be disciple that following Him would not guarantee him a roof over his head. Animals have a place to dwell but the Son of Man has *nowhere* (οὐκ ἔχει ποῦ) to lay His head. By linking the words ὅπου and ποῦ Jesus tailor-makes His response so that it penetrates to the very core of the scribe's profession.[77]

Matthew refers to the second would-be follower as another of Jesus' disciples[78] (Matt 8:21-22=Luke 9:59-60). But before following Jesus he asks to be allowed to first (πρῶτον) return home and bury his father—evidently assuming Jesus would provide him with a special exemption.[79] Jesus replies, "Let the dead bury their own dead" (see chap. 5). The reply indicates that Jesus understands that this disciple is committed to more than just providing his father with a decent burial. His request in fact unveils a deeper commitment to Jewish Law and custom.[80] The obligation to bury one's family members was established by Abraham vis-à-vis his dead wife in Genesis 23.[81] Only in the OT did sinners not receive a burial (Deut 28:25-26; 1 Kgs 14:10-11; Jer 16:4).[82] Josephus states that the Law has provided for the decent burial of the dead and "the funeral ceremony is to be undertaken by the nearest relatives."[83] To neglect this responsibility was to violate the fifth commandment.[84] Hence Jesus' response is not so much a critique of burial per se (cf.

---

[75] Brown, *The Disciples in Narrative Perspective*, 40.
[76] Luke 9:57 is nondescript: "τις."
[77] Davies and Allison, *Matthew*, 2:42.
[78] Luke 9:59 simply has ἕτερον.
[79] Cf. *m. Ber.* 3.1: "One whose dead is lying before him [awaiting burial] is exempt from the recitation of the *Shema*, and from [wearing] phylacteries."
[80] See Darrell L. Bock, *Luke 9:51–24:53*, BECNT, ed. Moisés Silva, vol. 3B (Grand Rapids: Baker, 1996) 979–80.
[81] E. P. Sanders, *Jesus and Judaism* (Philadelphia: Fortress, 1985) 253.
[82] Elizabeth Bloch-Smith, "Burials," in *ABD*, 1:785.
[83] Josephus *Ag. Ap.* 2.26; cf. also Tob 6:15.
[84] D. A. Schlatter, *Der Evangelist Matthäus: seine Sprache, sein Ziel, seine Seibständigkeit: Ein Kommentar zum ersten Evangelium* (n.p., 1948; reprint, Stuttgart: Calwer Verlag, 1963) 288.

Matt 14:12) but a challenge to make a break with his Jewish tradition,[85] which would thereby indicate an authentic commitment to Jesus.

In a third scenario (Luke 9:61-62) another man says, "I will follow you, Lord. But first (πρῶτον) let me return to say good-bye to my family." Jesus replies, "No one who puts his hand to the plough and looks behind is fit for the kingdom of God." The scene is reminiscent of Elijah calling Elisha in 1 Kings 19:19-21. Elijah finds Elisha plowing with oxen. Elijah goes to him and throws his cloak around him. Elisha asks if he may first say good-bye to his mother and father to which Elijah agrees. Elisha then returns home taking his yoke of oxen and plowing equipment with him and destroys the lot. Then he followed (ἐπορεύθη ὀπίσω) Elijah and became his *disciple*.[86]

Each of these scenarios makes the same point that we have already observed in the account of the Rich Young Ruler in chapter seven. The lesson in each case is not so much wealth, a place to sleep, burying a father, or saying farewell to family, but that each of these represent, or at least *potentially* represent, a barrier to following Jesus. This is tantamount to not trusting in Jesus and His word. Hence Jesus responds to would-be followers differently in order to expose the priority of their heart. The point is that Jesus must come first (Matt 10:37; Luke 14:26; cf. Deut 33:9; Josephus, *Ag. Ap.* 2.27). Loyalties cannot be divided. Works are not so much the issue but *trust*.

An Important Principle

Having considered specific examples and defined the general conditions of discipleship we are led to the following conclusion. *Where large crowds or the Twelve are present Jesus lays down general conditions for becoming a disciple. Yet when Jesus is addressing an individual the conditions are specific and varied.*[87] In other words, *Jesus personalized the cost of discipleship according to what He knew to be the priorities of a person's heart*[88] (cf. John 2:25). What Jesus calls for amongst the masses takes on a specific form with individuals. No two cases

---

[85] Hengel, *The Charismatic Leader*, 14: There "is hardly one logion of Jesus which more sharply runs counter to the law, piety and custom than does Mt 8.22 = Lk 9.60a"; Sanders, *Jesus and Judaism*, 25.

[86] LXX 1 Kings 19:21: καὶ ἐλειτούργει αὐτῷ ("and he served him"); the MT has שָׁרַת ("attendant, servant, assistant") (cf. Gen 39:4; Exod 24:13; 33:11; Num 11:28; Josh 1:1; 2 Kgs 6:15). However the Hebrew term occurs predominantly in cultic contexts concerning, e.g., service in the tabernacle or temple (e.g., Exod 28:25, 43; 29:30; 30:20; Num 3:6, 31; Deut 10:8; 21:5; 1 Sam 2:11, 18; 3:1; Ezek 40:46; 42:14; 43:19; 44:11, 12, 15, 16, 17, 19, 27, etc.).

[87] Wilkins, *Following the Master*, 28, 36: when the crowds are the object of instruction the purpose is *evangelism*, i.e., that they might become disciples. When disciples are on the receiving end the goal is *growth* as a disciple.

[88] Ibid., 110.

are alike. The reason for this presumably is that individuals by their nature each have something that they find security and comfort in. If something is preventing one from trusting in Jesus it must go. The young ruler trusted in wealth. The disciple who wanted to bury his dad trusted more in Jewish tradition than he did in Jesus. The demands that Jesus made on these individuals may appear radical but in each case it can be shown, I believe, that the priorities of their heart—wealth and tradition—represent an alternate avenue of trust to Jesus and His word. In each case *eternal destinies are at stake*. Wealth and tradition are alternative avenues to eternal life but they are the wrong avenues. For this reason they must be displaced. Jesus is the only avenue.

Thus not all are asked to sell their possessions (cf. Luke 18:22 and 19:8) only those who trust in wealth. Evidently not all are asked to leave their homes and family (Mark 5:19; cf. Luke 8:14).[89] There is nothing sinister about burial (Matt 14:12) but there is everything wrong with holding onto old traditions (Mark 7:5-13). Saying goodbye to one's family is acceptable (1 Kgs 1:20) but not if it will render a person unfit for the kingdom. The scenario may vary but the lesson is the same: all are asked to trust completely in Jesus and take Him at His word.[90] Hence to the degree that wealth, family, religion, or anything else, keeps one from trusting in Jesus is the degree to which Jesus confronts each individual and demands these things be put aside.

Excursus on the Nature of Saving Faith

The whole concept of giving up is no doubt bothersome for some. "Does this mean I have to give up . . .?" From our examination the issue is really not about "giving up."[91] Rather the issue is, "What is the object of my faith?"

---

[89] McKnight, *A New Vision for Israel*, 187, suggests the possibility that "only those followers whose families objected to Jesus' mission had to leave their families behind" (see 179–87, for his discussion on Jesus and family); see also Warren Carter, *Households and Discipleship: A Study of Matthew 19–20*, JSNTSup, 103, ed. Stanley E. Porter (Sheffield: Sheffield Academic, 1994) 123, n. 2.

[90] Ibid., 123: "What applies to all disciples is the call to follow Jesus."

[91] Concerning Jesus' invitation to the Rich Young Ruler Joseph H. Hellerman, "Wealth and Sacrifice in early Christianity: Revisiting Mark's Presentation of Jesus' Encounter With The Rich Young Ruler," *TJ* (2000) 143–64, suggests—on the basis of the connection between Jesus' command to the ruler and His response to the disciples—that the invitation entailed making "his wealth available to the members of Jesus' alternative community, that is, to his potential new family of fellow believers." This is indeed what the early church did (cf. Acts 2:44-45; 4:32-37) (see esp. 156–64). Hellerman, presumably, is suggesting that is what all believers should be doing and that the story of the Rich Young Ruler should not be reduced to a *personalized* incident. I do agree with Hellerman in that all believers should be selling and giving based on passages such as Rom 12:13 (the word κοινωνοῦντες, which also occurs

It can only be in *one* of two places, Jesus or something else.[92] This is an important point: *faith in Jesus cannot exist where there is trust in something else* (cf. esp. Matt 6:20-24).[93] This was the problem for the Rich Young Ruler. He could not trust in Jesus *and* money at the same time (6:24). The same is true for the son who wanted to bury his father (8:21-22 par.). He could either follow Jesus and become a member of the saved or bury his father and remain a member of the dead, that is, the unsaved (see chap. 5). In both cases a choice had to be made if eternal life was to be received. To choose one was to in effect reject the other. To interpret these passages in any other way is to misunderstand the nature of faith in the Gospels.

For instance, we know from the Gospels that Jesus is able to recognize faith precisely because it is recognizable.[94] Take for example Mark's narrative comment after some men had gone to a lot of effort to deliver their paralyzed friend to Jesus: "Jesus *seeing* (ἰδών) their *faith* (πίστιν)" (Mark 2:5 par.). Over and over in the Gospels faith expresses itself (cf. Matt 8:5-13 par.; 9:20-22 par.; 15:21-28; Mark 10:46-52 par.; Luke 7:36-50; 17:15-19). James affirms the same thing about faith: "I will *prove/demonstrate* (δείξω)

---

in Acts 2:44 and 4:32, is translated "share" by the NIV); Gal 6:10, etc. However it is also clearly based on the examples that we have considered, that Jesus personalized the cost of discipleship for each individual according to what was in their heart. Carter, *Households and Discipleship*, 123 (and esp. n. 2) "The recognition of wealth as that which rules his heart enables the audience [of Matt] to understand why the command to sell one's wealth is not applied literally in the Gospels to all who would be disciples." This does not detract from Hellerman's interpretation of the Rich Young Ruler—but Jesus asked the ruler to sell all *because* wealth was the priority of his heart. However Matt 8:18-22 (par.) demonstrates, e.g., that other people have different priorities and thus Jesus confronts each would-be disciple according to the priority of their heart. This too is Carter's point: "The command to the man to sell all arises *from his commitment to wealth* and his need to be freed from it if he is to enter eternal life" (emphasis mine).

[92] The epistle of James is instructive here. James teaches that there is no alternative to faith. One has faith or one doesn't. The one who has faith does not doubt (Jas 1:6; cf. Matt 21:21). The one who doubts is a "double-minded (δίψυχος) man" (Jas 1:8). The "double-minded" man in James is a "sinner" (ἁμαρτωλοί) (4:8) and an "adulterer" (μοιξαλίδες) (v. 4). To be an "adulterer" is to be a friend with the world and an enemy of God (v. 4). We can see then for James that to lack this kind of faith (cf. 2:14-26) is tantamount to being a "sinner" = "adulterer" = "an enemy of God" = "double-minded man." In James such an individual is not saved.

[93] Although the disciples on occasion are rebuked for their *little* faith (Matt 8:26; 14:31; 16:8; Luke 12:28). However it is the object of faith that is important not the size (17:20; Mark 11:22; Luke 17:5-6). Therefore when the object is anything but Jesus, as with the Rich Young Ruler and others, faith is *absent* (cf. Matt 13:58: "their *lack* of faith" [NIV] is actually "their *unbelief*" [ἀπιστίαν]; cf. also Mark 6:6. Note also 4:40: Jesus questions His disciples as to the presence of any faith; cf. Luke 8:25).

[94] See McKnight, *A New Vision For Israel*, 166–68, for the various images used in the Gospels to depict faith; cf. also R. T. France, "Faith," in *DJG*, 223–26.

from (ἐκ)[95] my works my *faith* (πίστιν)" (Jas 2:18; cf. 3:13). The same can be said of repentance. Jesus called people to "produce *fruit worthy of repentance* (καρπὸν ἄξιον τῆς μετανοίας)" (Matt 3:8 par.). Similarly Paul exhorted people to *repent* and to do *works worthy of repentance* (ἄξια τῆς μετανοίας ἔργα) (Acts 26:20). The point is that faith, or repentance, cannot be reduced to an intellectual phenomenon.[96] Certainly it begins in the mind. But there will be expression since the very nature of faith is confidence in the words of Jesus.

Therefore we must keep in mind that while there are instances in the Gospels where individuals are called to specific actions, these actions are not required of all. But *all* are required to submit to the general conditions of discipleship given by Jesus to the crowds and His disciples. What this will entail for each individual will vary according to one's spiritual nemesis. For example, if someone is trusting in wealth, family or religious tradition to gain eternal life, they must displace these *wrong* objects of faith for the *right* object of faith—Jesus. This must be the case; for the essence of the gospel is to trust in Jesus! This means relinquishing all *other* avenues of trust, whether it is money, family or tradition.[97]

Conclusion

It is popular to see a distinction between discipleship and salvation (when viewed as a conversion) in the Gospels. However based on our own study

---

[95] Luke Timothy Johnson, *The Letter of James*, AB, ed. William Foxwell Albright and David Noel Freedman, vol. 37A (Garden City, N.Y.: Doubleday, 1995) 270; BAGD, 235: of the source, from which something flows. Works are the inevitable *outflow* of faith for James.

[96] Contra Hodges, *The Gospel Under Siege*, 21: "faith . . . is nothing more than a response to a divine initiative" (cf. also Wilkin, *Confident in Christ*, 3–15). Later on Hodges seems to equate the faith of demons in Jas 2:19 with the faith of men. "Men and demons may even believe the same truth (that there is one God)" (*The Gospel Under Siege*, 28). Admittedly the faith of demons here is dead faith but in Hodges' view this is still saving faith; e.g., "The dangers of dying faith are real. But they do not include hell" (32). In his *Absolutely Free*, 30, Hodges defines faith as, "the *inward conviction* that what God says to us in the gospel is true. That—and that alone—is saving faith." Evidently for Hodges saving faith is nothing more than an intellectual profession akin to that of the demons. However, such an understanding of saving faith does not comply with the rest of the NT (cf. Rom 1:5; Gal 5:6; Jas 2:1). Take e.g., John 2:23 and 8:31. Idem, *The Gospel Under Siege*, 38, states that, "John knows nothing about a faith in Christ that is not saving." He argues that the Greek construction πισ- + εἰς of 8:31 is always used for saving faith but he fails to include 2:23 in his list (see ibid., 37) which indubitably refers to *non*-saving faith. See also William G. Bjork, "A Critique of Zane Hodges' *The Gospel Under Siege*: A Review Article," *JETS* 30 (1987) 461.

[97] It seems to me that this relinquishment must either take place in one's attitude (cf. e.g., Matt 6:25-34 par.) or physical abandonment (the Rich Young Ruler); McKnight, *A New Vision for Israel*, 191.

and by way of conclusion I would like to suggest that two fundamental misunderstandings exist among those who hold to such a dichotomy. First, the concept of salvation in the Synoptic Gospels has not been *fully* understood[98] which has in turn led to a misunderstanding of its entry requirements and the nature of saving faith. On the other side it appears that the concept of discipleship has also been misunderstood as an overly arduous commitment[99] that has in turn led to placing it into a separate category outside of salvation. However two passages challenge both these misunderstandings.

In response to the first misunderstanding Luke 13:23-24 is instructive. Jesus replies to a question concerning people being saved (σωζόμενοι). He proclaims, "*strain every nerve* (ἀγωνίζεσθε)[100] to enter (εἰσελθεῖν) through the narrow door" (cf. Matt 7:13-14). The context of this saying is clearly eschatological (Luke 13:25-30) so future salvation is in view.[101] Since this is the only time ἀγωνίζομαι occurs in the Synoptic Gospels[102] it is difficult to say exactly *how* one is to "strain every nerve" but if Paul is any indication we should not think too specifically.[103] According to the apostle everyone who ἀγωνιζόμενος for an imperishable crown exercises self-control in *all things* (πάντα) (1 Cor 9:25). Paul urges Timothy to train himself for godliness for it is to this end that ἀγωνιζόμεθα (1 Tim 4:7-10). Godliness is again the context of 1 Timothy 6:12 where Paul exhorts Timothy to "ἀγωνίζου the good ἀγῶνα of faith." This entails fleeing from things that are contrary to godliness and pursuing righteousness, godliness, faith, love, endurance, and humility (cf. 5:3–6:16). Evidently by the end of his life Paul is the quintessential example of someone who has τὸν καλὸν ἀγῶνα ἠγώνισμαι and now subsequently awaits "the crown of righteousness" (2 Tim 4:7-8). Hence

---

[98] In addition to the references already cited in chapter five note Colijn, "Salvation as Discipleship," 20: "Many . . . think that salvation means 'accepting Christ as personal Savior' (language that is foreign to the NT)."

[99] E.g., Hodges, *The Gospel Under Siege*, 40–41: "Can a man who trusts Christ for eternal life but fails to 'hate' his father and mother go to heaven? If the answer to this is 'no,' then it is perfectly clear that 'hating' one's father and mother is a *condition* for ultimate felicity . . . Heaven cannot be reached except by the most strenuous self-denial and loyalty to Christ." Cf. also Dillow, *Servant Kings*, 168: the Christian in 1 John 3:6-9 "does not sin *even one time, not at all*" (emphasis mine).

[100] BDAG, 17; cf. esp. 1 Cor 9:25; 1 Tim 4:10; 6:12; 2 Tim 4:7.

[101] John Nolland, *Luke 18:35–24:53*, WBC, ed. David A. Hubbard and Glenn W. Barker et al., vol 35c (Dallas: Word, 1993) 734: "The time of effort is now, but the time of entry is . . . in the eschatological future." Cf. also Green, *The Gospel of Luke*, 530; Bock, *Luke 9:51–24:53*, 1233, n. 6.

[102] Ἀγωνίζομαι occurs in John 18:36; 1 Cor 9:25; Col 1:29; 4:12; 1 Tim 4:10; 6:12; 2 Tim 4:7.

[103] See Ethelbert Stauffer, "ἀγών," in *TDNT*, 1:137.

for someone to *strain every nerve* to enter through the narrow door is to live a godly life,[104] at least in Paul and there is nothing to suggest otherwise in Luke.[105] Mere *seeking* will not be enough (Luke 13:24b). Indeed those who are refused entry into the kingdom are "workers of *unrighteousness*" (ἐργάται ἀδικίας) (Luke 13:27).[106] But remember that the context here is future salvation not something akin to Paul's "justification." Hence this fits into the link we have observed between ethics and eschatology in the NT. This does not deny the priority of God's grace and mercy in one's salvation (18:13-14). Though this passage does not speak to how this striving is to occur (cf. Matt 5:20). But that it is not by one's own effort is plain (Luke 18:17, 27). One more observation: "if the door is narrow that leads to life then is the door of discipleship narrower still?"

In reply to the second misunderstanding concerning discipleship being misunderstood as an overly arduous commitment we turn to Matthew 11:28-29. Here we have two invitations to discipleship. Jesus invites *all* (πάντες) those who are weary and burdened.

Table 9: The Outcome of Discipleship

Invitation to Discipleship	Result
"Come to Me"[107] (v. 28a)	"Rest" (v. 28b)[108]
"Learn (μάθετε) from Me" (v. 29a)	"Rest" (v. 29b)

One might expect that the results of *learning* might be different from *coming*; however they are the same. Both the one who comes and the one who learns

---

[104] I. Howard Marshall, *The Gospel of Luke: A Commentary on the Greek Text*, NIGTC, ed. I. Howard Marshall and W. Ward Gasque (Grand Rapids: Eerdmans, 1978) 565: "moral effort is necessary in order to enter the kingdom." Cf. Green, *The Gospel of Luke*, 530.

[105] Although cf. Bock, *Luke 9:51–24:53*, 1234: "The idea is . . . to labor hard at listening and responding to his [Jesus'] message."

[106] In contrast to those who are δίκαιοι who will inherit the kingdom prepared for them (Matt 25:34) and go into eternal life (v. 46).

[107] The same words occur in Jesus' call to discipleship in Luke 14:26: "If anyone comes to (ἔρχεται πρός Με and does not hate his own father . . . he cannot be My disciple."

[108] Who are the weary and burdened? (1) Those suffering under the heavy demands of the Pharisees? (2) Those suffering from the rigors of discipleship? (3) Those suffering under the burden of sin? There is perhaps more support for option 1 given the context and background of the day (cf. Matt 11:12 [if the phrase βιασταὶ ἁρπάζουσιν means that "*violent men* are *trying to attack* the kingdom of heaven"; see BAGD, 109]); 12:1-14; 23:4). However support could also be gathered for views two (10:1-23, 37-39) and three (v. 28; 11:21-24). Probably the best solution is to leave the identity non-specific since Jesus did invite *all* (πάντες) who are weary (Davies and Allison, *Matthew*, 2:288; cf. also D. A. Carson, "Matthew," in *EBC*, ed. Frank E. Gaebelein and J. D. Douglas, vol. 8 [Grand Rapids: Zondervan, 1984] 278).

find *rest* (ἀνάπαυσιν) (v. 29; cf. Exod 33:14). Hence "The 'yoke of Jesus' is the yoke of discipleship."[109]

How though is *rest* reconciled with the costly nature of discipleship? The answer is in the paradoxical nature of discipleship (cf. the beatitudes) "The one who finds his life will lose it and the one who loses his life for my sake will find it" (Matt 10:39).[110]

Both these passages—Luke 13:23-24 and Matthew 11:28-29—warn us on the one hand against understating or minimizing Jesus' understanding of salvation[111] and its requirements and on the other hand overstating or exaggerating His understanding of discipleship and its requirements.

I conclude this discussion on discipleship by quoting Scot McKnight. Writing on the nature of conversion to Jesus, McKnight has defined the essence of Jesus' call to discipleship and conversion in basically the same manner in which I have done. His approach and content differs although we do appear to be on the same page.

> The various images for repentance [I have discussed this in terms of discipleship][112] may be synthesized into two categories: internal [in our study = 'general conditions for discipleship'] and external [i.e., 'specific' in our study] or self-denial [i.e., 'general'] or world-denial [i.e., 'specific']. Under the category of internal repentance fall the expressions 'repentance,' 'self-denial,' and 'taking up the cross'; under external repentance are the terms 'selling all,' 'leaving all,' and 'hating all else.' The former concern self-crucifixion and the latter, world-crucifixion. The two categories are integrally related, however; the first leads to the second, though the second does not necessitate the first. That is, internal repentance is not just a private affair but manifests itself in external ways.[113]

---

[109] Graham N. Stanton, "Salvation Proclaimed: Matthew 11:28-30: Comfortable Words?" *ExpTim* 94 (1981–82) 7.

[110] Ibid., 8. See also Ralph P. Martin, "Salvation and Discipleship in Luke's Gospel," *Interpretation* 30 (1976) 366–80, esp. 378–80.

[111] Worth reading in this regard is John G. Stackhouse, Jr. (ed.) *What Does It Mean To Be Saved: Broadening Evangelical Horizons of Salvation* (Grand Rapids: Baker, 2002) esp. 115–36.

[112] I am in agreement with McKnight, *A New Vision for Israel*, 166–76. "There are two dimensions of conversion in Jesus' teachings: a positive movement toward Jesus and a negative movement away from sinfulness and unfaithfulness. The positive movement is best expressed in the concept of faith, while the negative movement finds its most lucid description in repentance" (176).

[113] Ibid., 173.

Excursus on Mark 8:35 and Parallels

It would be amiss on any discussion concerning discipleship not to mention Mark 8:35 and parallels: "Whoever desires to *save* (σῶσαι) his ψυχὴν will lose it, and whoever will loose his ψυχὴν on account of Me and the gospel will *save* (σώσει) it." Zane Hodges contends that ψυχὴν refers to physical life and *save* is something akin to true enjoyment of life.[114] However this interpretation is unlikely for the following reasons.

First, the reference to forfeiting one's ψυχὴν in Mark 8:36 certainly loses its force as a statement about physical life since the promise of longer life would hardly serve as an appropriate comparison to the "whole world." The NT writers are not in the habit of encouraging their readers (esp. in times of trial) with the hope of holding onto their physical lives (cf. e.g., 2 Cor 4:7–5:5; 1 Pet 1:3-9).

Second, in Mark 8:37 Mark cites Psalm 49:8-9a (MT)—"A man cannot ransom himself or give to God the price of his life, for the ransom of their life (ψυχῆς LXX 48:8) is costly." The life in view is qualified in the next verse: "and he (it) ceases forever that he should continue to live forever and never see the pit" (vv. 9b-10). It may be that in its original context this statement did not conjure up thoughts of immortality but it surely would have in Jesus' time.

Third, Mark 8:38 places these statements within the framework and perspective of the Second Coming of Christ when one's eternal destiny is determined (cf. Matt 25:31-46).

Fourth, Matthew 10:39 ("Whoever finds his ψυχὴν will lose it, and whoever loses his ψυχὴν on account of Me will find it") parallels Mark 8:35. Clearly what this person will find is eternal life. Earlier in Matthew 10:28 Jesus says: "Do not be afraid of those who kill the body (σῶμα) but are *unable* to kill the ψυχὴν. But be afraid of the one who is *able* to destroy both ψυχὴν and body (σῶμα) in Gehenna."

In conclusion, Hodges' claim that ψυχή refers to physical life in these passages is simply unfounded.[115]

---

[114] Zane Clark Hodges, *The Hungry Inherit: Refreshing Insights on Salvation, Discipleship, and Rewards* (Chicago: Moody, 1972) 73–77.

[115] On Mark 8:35 and pars. cf. Karl-Wolfgang Tröger, "ψυχή," in *TDNT*, 9:642–43: "there is no explicit ref. to martyrdom here. The grouping [of Mark 8:34-35] with the prediction of the passion and resurrection of the Son of Man shows already that the saying of Jesus will retain its validity even beyond physical death."

9

The Role of *Endurance* in Salvation

The one who endures to the end will be saved
(Matt 10:22, 24:13; Mark 13:13)

Endurance in Context

THESE words occur twice in Matthew, once in Mark and a variation occurs in Luke 21:19 although clearly Luke is working with the same tradition. Matthew's two sayings occur in related but distinct contexts. The first of them, 10:22, occurs in Matthew's missionary discourse. Jesus instructs His disciples to take the message of the kingdom "to the lost sheep of the house of Israel" (vv. 6-7). However their mission is inevitably dangerous. Not all will welcome them or their message (v. 14). In fact they will experience severe opposition (v. 16). They will be arrested, flogged (vv. 17-19), hated (v. 22), and persecuted (v. 23). Nevertheless they are not to worry (v. 19) or be afraid (vv. 26, 31). They are to remain faithful and committed to their mission (vv. 32-33, 37-39). It is a life long task (v. 23) and they are to *endure* until the end (v. 22).

The second saying occurs in Matthew's eschatological discourse. There are similarities. Though chapter 24 may be more eschatological, chapter 10 is not void of eschatological matters (vv. 23b; 32b, 33b, 39, 41, 42b). Conversely chapter 24 is not void of matters pertaining to the present age (vv. 2, 4-23). Again in chapter 24 the disciples are warned that arrest and persecution await them (v. 9) as they preach "the gospel of the kingdom." Here the field of mission is widened to the entire world (v. 14) and not just the people of Israel. Hence those who will hate them are also widened to include "all nations" (v. 9). The disciples are warned that in addition to persecution many will be led into sin (v. 10) and many false prophets will arise who will deceive many people (v. 11). Lawlessness will increase and "the love of many will grow cold" (v. 12). In contrast (δὲ) though "the one who endures to the end will be saved" (v. 13).

The saying in Mark is not too dissimilar. The eschatological discourse provides the context. As in Matthew 10, the disciples are warned that they will be arrested and flogged (vv. 9, 11) as they take the gospel to *all nations* (v. 10). As in Matthew 10:22, Jesus warns that the disciples will be hated by all but it is the one who endures until the end that will be saved (v. 13).

Luke's eschatological discourse is less eschatological than either Matthew or Mark with the focus very much on the destruction of Jerusalem (note esp. Luke 21: 7, 20-24). However even in Luke the catastrophe of AD 70 prefigures the end (cf. vv. 22, 24b, 25-28, 36).[1] Mention of the gospel or the kingdom is absent although missionary activity is not completely missing since persecution will turn into an opportunity for testimony (v. 13). Hence Luke's endurance saying involves many of the same elements as Matthew and Mark: mission, suffering, hatred, and death (v. 16). Luke's saying (in v. 19) differs however in two respects. First, he uses the noun (ὑπομονή) instead of the verb (ὑπομένω). Second, salvation (i.e., σωτηρία) per se is not promised but the possession of their lives/souls (κτήσασθε τὰς ψυχὰς ὑμῶν) (but cf. Matt 10:39).

The Relationship between Endurance and Salvation

In order to discuss the relationship between endurance and salvation I must first make a few comments concerning the nature of these two terms as they occur in these passages.

The Nature of Salvation

Although the exact nature of the salvation in Matthew and Mark is not spelled out it is clear that neither evangelist is speaking of physical salvation from death. In Matthew's missionary discourse Jesus warns that there will be death as a result of the disciples' mission (10:21; see also Mark 13:12; Luke 21:16). The disciples are expressly warned in Matthew 24:9: "They will kill you." Yet Jesus warns the disciples to not be afraid of their opponents who *kill* the body (10:28). Since death is a very real possibility and in some cases evidently a forgone conclusion Jesus cannot be saying that one who endures until the end will be saved from physical death (cf. Rev 2:10).[2] Eternal—and not physical—salvation is in view.

---

[1] See Darrell L. Bock, *Luke 9:51–24:53*, BECNT, ed. Moisés Silva, vol. 3B (Grand Rapids: Baker, 1996) 1675.

[2] Also, R. T. France, *Matthew*, TNTC, ed. Leon Morris (Grand Rapids: Eerdmans, 1989), 184; Craig L. Blomberg, *Matthew*, NAC, ed. David S. Dockery, vol. 22 (Nashville: Broadman, 1992) 175; contra Robert N. Wilkin, *Confident in Christ: Living by Faith Really Works* (Irving, Tex.: Grace Evangelical Society, 1999), 266, n.5: "[Matt 10] Verse 22 shows that the 'salvation' of verse 12 refers to surviving the Tribulation alive, not to deliverance from hell."

This seems very clear although many do argue that salvation here refers to surviving until the end of the Tribulation.[3] Under this view these texts apply to another dispensation as well as another people, the Jews alive during the end-time Tribulation. The implication is that these verses are not instructive concerning Jesus' soteriology. However, not only do these verses not apply to physical deliverance but also I am not convinced that Jesus' promises concerning endurance and salvation can be relegated to a specific dispensation or people group. While the eschatological discourses (Matthew 24; Mark 13; Luke 21) certainly do have an end-time referent this does not mean that the present is not in view. These passages are apocalyptic in genre and as with other apocalyptic texts the present and the future often co-exist in a typological manner (cf. e.g., 4 Ezra 3:1-2).[4] Hence the tribulation to befall Jerusalem represents the tribulation to befall the end of the world before the Son of Man returns. Matthew 10 stands as Jesus' missionary manifesto to the twelve disciples (vv. 1-5) and so His promise concerning endurance applies to them and to each subsequent disciple generation, not just the one at the end (so 28:19-20).

With respect to the nature of salvation there is no doubt, in my mind at least, that it is eschatological and spiritual, in short: future salvation from sin is in view.[5] The eschatological meaning is suggested by the future tense (σωθήσεται) in 10:22; 24:13; and Mark 13:13, along with the reference to the Son of Man's return in Matthew 10:23; 24:27-31; Mark 13:26-27. The salvation is certainly deliverance from sin since Jesus speaks in His missionary discourse of eternal destruction (Matt 10:28), eternal judgment (vv. 32-33), the gain or forfeiture of eternal life (v. 39), and eschatological reward (vv. 41-42). (I shall show in chapter 10 that reward in Matthew is equivalent to receiving the kingdom or eternal life [cf. 25:34, 46]). Furthermore, eschatological judgment is in view throughout Matthew's eschatological discourse (24:40-41, 51; 25:10, 30, 31-46).

Luke's endurance saying is more complex since he omits the term σώζω and the phrase εἰς τέλος, his discourse is less eschatological than either Matthew or Mark, and preceding the saying are the words: "And a hair from your head will not be destroyed (ἀπόληται)" (Luke 21:18), thus hinting at a *physical* deliverance. However even here it is hard to imagine physical deliverance being in view since only two verses prior we read that some will

---

[3] Ibid., 266.
[4] Bruce W. Jones, "More about the Apocalypse as Apocalyptic," *JBL* 87 (1968) 326; John J. Collins, *The Apocalyptic Imagination: An Introduction to Jewish Apocalyptic Literature*, 2d ed. (Grand Rapids: Eerdmans, 1998) 51–52.
[5] Thomas R. Schreiner and Ardel B. Caneday, *The Race Set Before Us: A Biblical Theology of Perseverance and Assurance* (Downers Grove, Ill.: InterVarsity, 2001) 149.

be put to death (Luke 21:16). Evidently then Jesus did not intend the statement concerning their hair to be taken literally. This is simply another way of saying that their lives will not be eternally destroyed.[6] Hence although κτήσασθε τὰς ψυχὰς ὑμῶν in v. 19 could be a reference to physical life[7] it seems most unlikely in light of v. 16. Therefore one who endures (lit. ἐν τῇ ὑπομονῇ) in Luke gains "redemption" (Luke 21:28) and "the (eschatological) kingdom of God" (v. 31) when the Son of Man returns (v. 27).[8]

The goal or termination point of this endurance is "to the end" (εἰς τέλος). It is possible to understand εἰς τέλος as "until the end of one's life"[9] (cf. Rev 2:10) or in an eschatological sense, that is, "until the Son of Man's return"[10] (cf. Matt 10:23). While I am inclined to see the eschatological sense primarily in view (see v. 23) the end of one's life[11] is surely not precluded as if only those who are alive when Christ returns will be saved.[12] The same can be said of 24:13 although there may be less ambiguity here since τέλος refers to the eschatological end in vv. 6 and v. 14. This is also the case in Mark 13:13 (cf. v. 7). The phrase is significant for as we saw in chapter five "many Christians have formulated salvation almost exclusively in terms of the beginning, namely, conversion in one's personal history, not in terms of consum-

---

[6] I. Howard Marshall, *The Gospel of Luke: A Commentary on the Greek Text*, NIGTC, ed. I. Howard Marshall and W. Ward Gasque (Grand Rapids: Eerdmans, 1978) 769: "spiritual safety"; contra Leon Morris, *Luke*, rev. ed., TNTC, ed. Leon Morris (Grand Rapids: Eerdmans, 1988) 325.

[7] John Nolland, *Luke 18:35–24:53*, WBC, ed. David A. Hubbard and Glenn W. Barker et al. vol 35c (Dallas: Word, 1993) 998: "Luke thinks concretely of the saving of life in the midst of danger (he thinks of deliverance in concrete situations)."

[8] Marshall, *The Gospel of Luke*, 770: salvation = "eternal life"; Joel B. Green, *The Gospel of Luke*, NICNT, ed. Gordon D. Fee [Grand Rapids: Eerdmans, 1997] 738, n. 36: "an implicit reference to the resurrection."

[9] So Robert H. Gundry, *Mark: A Commentary on His Apology for the Cross* (Grand Rapids: Eerdmans, 1993) 771. "Continually" (as in Luke 18:5) is unlikely (W. D. Davies and Dale C. Allison Jr., *A Critical and Exegetical Commentary on the Gospel According to Matthew*, vol. 2, ICC, ed. J. A. Emerton, C. E. B. Cranfield, and G. N. Stanton [Edinburgh: T. & T. Clark, 1991] 187).

[10] Robert H. Mounce, *Matthew*, NIBC, ed. W. Ward Gasque, vol. 1 (Peabody, Mass.: Hendrickson, 1985) 95; contra France, *Matthew*, 183.

[11] Robert H. Gundry, *Matthew: A Commentary on His Handbook for a Mixed Church under Persecution*, 2d ed. (Grand Rapids: Eerdmans, 1994) 193–94. It may be telling that Luke does not include the phrase εἰς τέλος since his focus is not on the end of the age. Cf. Craig A. Evans, *Luke*, NIBC, ed. W. Ward Gasque (Peabody, Mass.: Hendrickson, 1990) 309; Bock, *Luke 9:51–24:53*, 1674–75.

[12] Blomberg, *Matthew*, 175; cf. also D. A. Carson, "Matthew," in *EBC*, ed. Frank E. Gaebelein and J. D. Douglas, vol. 8 (Grand Rapids: Zondervan, 1984) 250, 499; Warren Carter, *Matthew and the Margins: A Socio-Political and Religious Reading*, JSNTSup, ed. Stanley E. Porter, vol. 204 (Sheffield: Sheffield Academic, 2000) 238, 472.

mation."¹³ Furthermore, the use of the future tense ("will be saved") indicates that salvation is not a one-time event but a pilgrimage¹⁴ that includes "beginning, process and consummation."¹⁵

The Nature of Endurance¹⁶

The meaning of endurance is not too hard to define since the context in each instance leaves plenty of clues. This is especially the case in the three eschatological discourses. Jesus warns His disciples not to be deceived since (γάρ) many will be (Matt 24:4-5; cf. Mark 13:5-6; Luke 21:8). Apparently deception will be spurred on by troubled times, for example, wars, famines, earthquakes, and persecution. People will be looking for "The Deliverer" and as a result will fall prey to those who claim to have the right credentials (i.e., ἐγώ εἰμι ὁ χριστός) to deliver them from these perilous times (Matt 24:5-9; cf. Mark 13:6-9; Luke 21:8b-12). Similarly many will be led into sin (σκανδαλισθήσονται) and be deceived by false prophets (Matt 24:10a, 11b; cf. Mark 13:22). Hatred will be rampant and "the love of many will grow cold" (Matt 24:10b, 12b; cf. Mark 13:13a; Luke 21:17). Once again "tribulation" (θλῖψιν), death and being hated on account of Jesus is what is responsible for spurring on this spiritual and ethical denigration. However Jesus urges His disciples not to respond to these perilous times in such a way. Rather they are to *endure* (ὑπομένω) (Matt 24:13; Mark 13:13; cf. Luke 21:19). Evidently one who endures will *not* be deceived or be led into sin. They will *not* hate or grow cold in their love for one another.

In Matthew's missionary discourse Jesus follows His promise concerning endurance with another promise followed by a warning:¹⁷ "Therefore whoever (πᾶς . . . ὅστις) confesses (ὁμολογήσει) in Me before men, I also will confess (ὁμολογήσω) before My Father in heaven. But whoever (ὅστις) denies Me before men, I also will deny him before My Father in heaven" (Matt 10:32-33). In context this means that when these disciples ap-

---

¹³ Schreiner and Caneday, *The Race Set Before Us*, 147.

¹⁴ Ibid., uses the term "continuum."

¹⁵ Ibid.

¹⁶ Wilkin, *Confident in Christ*, 133, argues from the outset that endurance is a "work" and therefore contradictory to the gospel. However this is incorrect reasoning since he begins by theologizing and drawing conclusions based on the nature of the gospel rather than the nature of endurance. Logically his argument follows that since endurance is a work it can have no part in the gospel. However, his understanding of endurance is skewed right from the start, which of course throws doubt on his conclusions. As far as I can tell Wilkin makes no serious attempt to understand what NT endurance really is. Rather his only definition appears to be based on a modern day triathalon analogy for which he provides absolutely no scriptural support.

¹⁷ Schreiner and Caneday, *The Race Set Before Us*, 153.

pear before hostile authorities (cf. vv. 17-20) they should not fail to publicly confess Jesus.[18] Those who fail to confess will find that Jesus likewise will not acknowledge them on judgment day.

Excursus on Peter's Denial

The warning to those who deny Jesus raises the question as to Peter's denial and his subsequent restoration. Why is it that Peter appears to be exempt from the warning issued in vv. 32-33? After all the language between Peter's denial and Jesus' warning is remarkably similar. Matthew says that Peter "*denied before* all" (*ἠρνήσατο ἔμπροσθεν* πάντων) (26:70). Two more times Peter makes the same denial (vv. 72, 74; cf. John 13:38; 18:25, 27) and Matthew records it using the same word used in the warning at 10:33. The verbal similarities are impossible to miss. Jesus warns those who *denied* Me *before* men (*ἀρνήσηταί* με *ἔμπροσθεν* τῶν ἀνθρώπων). There is no doubt that Peter fits the category of Jesus' warning in vv. 32-33—three times!

However that Peter committed the very same denial that Jesus warns against and yet was subsequently restored is in fact the key to understanding the warning. The warning evidently only applies to those who *continue* in a state of denial; Judas being a prime example. Peter on the other hand was clearly repentant in both word and action. He wept bitterly (ἔκλαυσεν πικρῶς)[19] recalling his promise to die for Jesus only to have denied Him three times (26:75). The next time Peter saw Jesus he couldn't get to Him fast enough, stopping his fishing expedition and jumping over the side of the boat to get to Him (John 21:7). At what was an excruciating question and answer session for Peter, Peter nevertheless three times affirms his complete love for Jesus (vv. 15-17). Clearly this shows that Jesus' warning against denial does not have to be permanent and is indeed conditional upon the person's response. The case of Peter illustrates that there is room for repentance and restoration.

The Nature of Endurance Continued

The link with ὁμολογήσω in 7:23 is unmistakable which means that Jesus' warning in v. 33 is a reference to those who fail to enter the eschatological kingdom (cf. 25:12).[20] This warning is followed up by three discipleship sayings concerning one's family (10:37), cross (v. 38), and life (v. 39); and three further sayings concerning one's response to Jesus and His messengers (vv.

---

[18] Davies and Allison, *Matthew*, 2:215–16.

[19] Cf. Isa 22:4 LXX where the same expression is used of God weeping bitterly (πικρῶς κλαύσομαι) over the destruction of Israel.

[20] Ibid., 2:216.

40-42). All are introduced by either a relative pronoun (cf. vv. 32-33) or a substantival participle (cf. v. 23b) indicating that each one provides further amplification on the nature of endurance in v. 23b.[21]

Endurance: A Condition or Evidence of Salvation?

If what we have seen above is correct with respect to salvation, these passages patently teach salvation *via* endurance. Thomas Schreiner and Ardel Caneday speak directly to the issue: "Jesus denotes a condition for salvation but does not use the word *faith*. He says that salvation will belong only to 'the one who perseveres.' This kind of talk worries many evangelicals because it sounds like salvation by works to them."[22] While "condition" may appear to be an unnecessarily loaded term it is important to note that these texts that speak of endurance say nothing about endurance being a *demonstration*—an expression that may be more palatable theologically—of salvation. Jesus does not say, "The one who endures to the end *will demonstrate* he is saved." Of course the reason for this is that Jesus is not talking about *initial* salvation—in which case the term "demonstrate" would be entirely appropriate. Jesus is talking about *future* or *final* salvation. He is not looking at an event already occurred but an event *still yet to occur*. Thus He cannot speak of endurance as a demonstration of something that has not yet occurred; there is nothing to demonstrate for it is still future. It may help then to ask the question: "If endurance is not present will one be saved in the end?" The answer is clearly no.[23] Looking at things then from a purely exegetical standpoint it is difficult to escape the fact that these passages do teach that endurance is a *condition* to (final) salvation.[24]

It is unfortunate that the term "condition" carries with it all sorts of negative connotations, for Jesus does not mean condition here in the sense of gaining merit or favor. He simply means that one must continue in their *already existing* relationship with God if they are to be finally saved, that is, to be admitted into heaven. Thus when we look at the big picture of salva-

---

[21] See Schreiner and Caneday, *The Race Set Before Us*, 154–57.

[22] Ibid., 147.

[23] John Piper, *'Love Your Enemies': Jesus' Love Command in the Synoptic Gospels and in the Early Christian Paraenesis*, SNTSMS, ed. R. McL. Wilson and M. E. Thrall, vol. 38 (Cambridge: Cambridge University Press, 1979) 76, defines "condition" as: "without which it [salvation] does not occur or exist."

[24] Schreiner and Caneday, *The Race Set Before Us*, 151–52: "Jesus' words indicate that perseverance to the end is the necessary condition. Perseverance is a means that God has appointed by which one will be saved . . . if we want to be saved in the final day. It is really this simple!" Contra Wilkin, *Confident in Christ*, 132: "According to the Bible . . . perseverance is not a condition of getting into God's kingdom."

tion as a *whole* we could legitimately speak of endurance being a "constituent part" or "intrinsic aspect" of salvation. We will see this more clearly when we look at the rest of the NT's teaching on endurance shortly. How we define "salvation" will determine whether we use "condition" or "constituent part" to describe the relationship between endurance and salvation.

Endurance in the Rest of the New Testament

The NT as a whole teaches that perilous times may have either a positive or a negative effect on one's relationship to God (cf. e.g., Matt 13:21; Rev 2:3). This is seen very clearly in James 1:2-15 and is helpful in explaining the relationship between endurance and salvation. James uses the term πειρασμοῖς (NIV: "trials") in 1:2-4, 12, to describe the *positive* effect of trials. The one who endures (the noun ὑπομονὴ occurs in vv. 3-4 and the verb ὑπομένει in v. 12) will be perfect and complete (v. 4) and ultimately will receive the "crown of *life*" (v. 12). In vv. 13-15 he describes the *negative* effect of trials by using the verb πειράζω (NIV: "tempt").[25] Those who do not endure but give in to their own "desire" are drawn into sin. The result for those who do not endure is not life but *death*. For James then trials sort out believers[26] from unbelievers (cf. also Rev 2:10-11; 3:10-12). For Peter trials (πειρασμοῖς) (1 Pet 1:6) are achieving for his readers the goal (τέλος) of their faith, the salvation of their souls (v. 9).

In line with this is the fact that the noun πειρασμός and the verb πειράζω connote the idea of testing.[27] Therefore although the NIV for example translates πειρασμός in James 1:2-4, 12 and 1 Peter 1:7 as "trials" and the term πειράζω in James 1:13-15 as "tempt," we need to remember that the two words are in fact the same. While the words "trial" and "tempt" may at the end of the day convey the correct meaning the theological idea is much richer if we bear in mind that the words actually mean, "test." Of course this makes things very intriguing for James states that God does not "test" (πειραζόμενος) anyone (v. 13). However James has just asserted that we should respond to "tests" (πειρασμοῖς) with joy. Furthermore the Bible

---

[25] Louw & Nida §88:308: "to endeavor or attempt to cause someone to sin."

[26] That James is making a distinction between believers in 1:12 and unbelievers in vv. 13-15 hinges on how one interprets "the crown of life" (τὸν στέφανον τῆς ζωῆς). I take it to mean "the crown *which is* life" (genitive of apposition), i.e., "eternal life." This is contrasted with "eternal death" in v. 15 (cf. Rom 6:23). Further support for this is found in Jas 2:5 where the phrase ἐπηγγείλατο τοῖς ἀγαπῶσιν αὐτόν clearly refers to *all* believers. The same phrase occurs in 1:12 designating those who receive the crown of life. One thing is sure; "the crown of life" is not physical since one who endures trials is not guaranteed preservation from physical death (cf. 5:6; Rev 2:10).

[27] I.e., Louw & Nida, §27:46: "to try to learn the nature or character of someone or something by submitting such to thorough and extensive testing."

is explicit: God does *test* people (cf. e.g., Gen 22:1; John 6:6; 6:13). On the face of it then James appears to be contradicting himself. On the one hand God does bring tests into believers' lives (Jas 1:2-4) and yet on the other hand He does not (v. 13). The way ahead is not as difficult as it might seem. The key is in the *goal* of the tests. The OT asserts that God *tested* Israel to bring about God-ward obedience (e.g., Gen 22:12; Exod 20:20; Deut 8:2; Jud 2:22; 3:4; 2 Chron 32:31; Zech 13:9); God never tests to lead people away from Him into sin. This is what James means when he says that God "does not test anyone" (1:13). However Satan does test people and his testing is always to lead people *away* from God into sin (cf. e.g., Matt 4:1; 1 Cor 7:5; 1 Thess 3:5; cf. Matt 19:3; 22:18). We can see the difference in the two tests in the table below:

Table 10: The Goal of Life's Tests from Two Perspectives

Tests From God (Jas 1:2-4, 12)	Tests from Satan (Jas 1:13-15)
Positive Testing Examples: Gen 22:12; Exod 20:20; Deut 8:2.	Negative Testing Examples: Matt 4:1; 1 Cor 7:5; 1 Thess 3:5.
The Goal Endurance (Jas 1:3), perfect and complete (v. 4), life (v. 12).	The Goal Seduction (Jas 1:14), sin (v. 15a), and death (v. 15b).

This is helpful for our present discussion on endurance for one's response to tests demonstrates their true allegiance. A positive response demonstrates allegiance to God; a negative response demonstrates allegiance to Satan.

Both James and Peter affirm that trials are a *test* of one's faith (esp. Jas 1:3; 1 Pet 1:7). The genuineness of one's faith is determined by how one responds to these tests. It is no surprise then that the "great tribulation" (θλῖψιν μεγάλην) in Revelation (see Rev 2:22) is referred to as "the hour of testing" (τῆς ὥρας τοῦ πειρασμοῦ) and is designed to *test* (πειράσαι: infinitive of purpose[28]) those dwelling upon the earth (Rev 3:10). Those who endure, that is, who keep God's commands and faith in Jesus (14:12), are the same ones who will reign with Christ (20:4; cf. 2 Tim 2:12). They receive the crown of life (Rev 2:10) and will not be hurt by the second death (v. 11). However there will be those who do not repent in spite of intense tribulation (9:20-21). Satan will have deceived them with his *tests* and their fate will be eternal separation from God (20:7-15).

---

[28] Robert W. Wall, *Revelation*, NIBC, ed. W. Ward Gasque (Peabody, Mass.: Hendrickson, 1991) 84.

Endurance is also an important quality for Paul. He could boast in tribulation (θλῖψις) because it produced endurance (ὑπομονὴν) (Rom 5:3). It is by means of endurance that believers await the hope of their final salvation (8:25; cf. 15:4). Such endurance indicated to him that the Thessalonians had a share in God's kingdom (2 Thess 1:4-5). This explains his otherwise enigmatic saying in Romans 2:7 concerning those who demonstrate endurance (ὑπομονὴν) in good works receiving eternal life on the day of judgment. Paul urges Timothy to continue (ἐπίμενε) in faith, doctrine, godliness, and the Word (cf. 1 Tim 4:1-16a) for by doing so he will save himself and his hearers (v. 16b). However in line with Paul's teaching on works only originating with God and His Spirit (see chap. 4) we should also note that endurance is not something that people are able to drum up, it comes from God (Rom 15:5; 2 Thess 3:5)

The evidence certainly points to the fact that in the early church the presence of endurance was a defining mark of genuine faith. This is the reason evidently the writer to the Hebrews was concerned about his readers. Apparently on account of persecution and suffering (cf. 12:4) these fledgling believers were entertaining thoughts of turning back to Judaism (see 7:11-19; 9:9-10; 13:9),[29] a decision that would be tantamount to apostasy (cf. 3:12; 4:11; 6:6; 10:35). The writer openly states that what his readers need is endurance (ὑπομονῆς). Only then will they receive the promise (v. 36; cf. 6:12; 11:9). They must hold fast (κατάσχωμεν) to the hope of the gospel for *only* those who do so are part of Christ's house (3:6). In fact there is the faint suggestion that the writer is drawing on Jesus' teaching on endurance and salvation. Verse 14 states that "we have become partakers (μέτοχοι) (cf. 6:4) of Christ *if* we hold fast our beginning confidence until the *end* (τέλους)" (note the use of τέλος in Matt 10:22; cf. also Heb 6:11).[30] This involves holding fast (κατέχωμεν) to their confession (ὁμολογίαν) (10:23; cf. 4:14; note the use of ὁμολογήσει in Matt 10:32). Yet their endurance (ὑπομονῆς) is

---

[29] Harold W. Attridge, *A Commentary on the Epistle to the Hebrews*, Hermeneia, ed. Helmut Koester (Philadelphia: Fortress, 1989) 13.

[30] I do not agree with Joseph C. Dillow, *The Reign of the Servant Kings: A Study of Eternal Security and the Final Significance of Man* (Miami, Fla.: Schoettle, 1992), 216 concerning his interpretation of "partakers" (μέτοχοι) in Heb 3:14. According to Dillow partakers constitute Christians who will partake in the millennial kingdom while "non-partakers" (still Christians) will be excluded. They are partakers by virtue of their perseverance (see chap. 2). However, the same Greek word is used in 6:4 to describe someone who has been enlightened, tasted the heavenly gift, the good Word of God, the powers of the age to come, and have become "a *partaker* (μετόχους) of the Holy Spirit." Interestingly though Dillow does not translate μετόχους in v. 4 as "partakers" but as "sharers." Yet such a description in light of v. 6 (these partakers will not be renewed again unto repentance) can only apply to a carnal Christian *according to Dillow* (see ibid.). I ask therefore, how can a "partaker" be a partaker of kingdom blessings in 3:14 yet a carnal Christian—though still a partaker—in 6:4?

not just a matter of continuing in their confession, it involves eradicating sin (12:1).[31] It involves enduring (ὑπομένετε) their present suffering from God's perspective (v. 7) so that they might share in His holiness (v. 10).

Thus Paul, Hebrews, James, Peter, and Revelation, all demonstrate a strong relationship between endurance and future eternal salvation. The reason being that while one may at first receive the gospel with joy, times of *testing* may indeed prove their faith to be false, or genuine. Jesus anticipated this: "And the [seed] that fell upon rocks represent those who when they hear receive the Word *with joy* but they have no root. They *believe for a time but in the time of testing* (πειρασμοῦ) they fall away" (Luke 8:13).

Now as to the exact nature of the relationship between endurance and salvation it seems clear that endurance does not cause salvation but rather is a *demonstration* of it.[32] This is most clearly seen in 2 Thessalonians 1:4-5: " . . . your endurance and faith (τῆς ὑπομονῆς ὑμῶν καὶ πίστεως) in all your persecutions and tribulations in which you are enduring (ἀνέχεσθε) is *evidence* (ἔνδειγμα) of the righteous judgment of God with the *result* that you are considered worthy (εἰς τὸ καταξιωθῆναι: infinitive of result[33]) of the kingdom of God for which you are suffering." The evidential nature of endurance is also seen in Hebrews 3:14: "We have *become* (γεγόναμεν) partakers of Christ *if* we hold fast (κατάσχωμεν) our beginning confidence until the end." The perfect tense of γεγόναμεν indicates that one has become a partaker (cf. 6:4) in the past and continues to be a partaker but only if one holds fast. That holding fast does not cause one to become a partaker is clear since becoming a partaker happens *prior* to holding fast (γεγόναμεν). The only possible explanation is that holding fast provides evidence now that one has already become a partaker in the past.

Therefore, taking the NT teaching on endurance as a whole I believe we are certainly justified in understanding endurance as a necessary component for salvation. If endurance looks *back* onto salvation that has already occurred then it is clearly a *demonstration* of that salvation. If endurance looks *forward* to salvation yet to occur then it is clearly a *condition* for salvation. This second point needs explaining though. It is a condition because salvation hasn't occurred yet. It may have occurred in terms of a past conversion experience but it hasn't occurred in the sense of final entry into heaven. At this point

---

[31] Note Rev 14:12: "Here is the endurance (ὑπομονή) of the saints: those who keep the commandments of God and have faith in Jesus."

[32] I am aware that this appears to contradict what I have said above concerning Matt 10:22, however I will explain the difference shortly.

[33] D. Edmond Hiebert, *The Thessalonian Epistles: A Call to Readiness* (Chicago: Moody, 1971) 285; cf. also Charles A. Wanamaker, *The Epistles to the Thessalonians*, NIGTC, ed. I. Howard Marshall and W. Ward Gasque (Grand Rapids: Eerdmans, 1990) 223.

we must remember that entry into heaven cannot occur without initial conversion and thus it is quite incorrect to say that endurance is an addition to the gospel. Faith and endurance are not separate entities,[34] the one implies the other as the article–noun–καί–noun construction in 2 Thessalonians 1:4 shows: τῆς ὑπομονῆς ὑμῶν καὶ πίστεως. Here faith and endurance are governed by only one article and joined by a single καὶ suggesting an *inseparable* relationship between the two.[35]

The only way the Hebrew readers will inherit the promise is by *faith* and *patience* (Heb 6:12). In Revelation 14:12 John writes: "Here is the endurance of the saints: those who keep the commandments of God and have *faith* in Jesus" (τὴν πίστιν Ἰησοῦ here an objective genitive). The point I am making is very important for endurance cannot be considered a "work" especially not in the sense that Paul thinks of works in Ephesians 2:9.

Once again, it is not faith *plus* endurance. Rather endurance "explains and amplifies the gospel's call for belief by making the point that no one who will be saved in the end can ignore the requirement of *persistent faith*" in Jesus Christ.[36] This point is aptly made in the epistles.[37] Colossians 2:6: "*As* you received Christ Jesus as Lord, in Him walk" (cf. 1:4-8). Believers have been reconciled to God only "*if* you continue (ἐπιμένετε) in the faith established and firm and not moving from the hope of the gospel which you heard" (v. 23). Similarly in 1 Corinthians 15:1-2: "I make known to you brothers the gospel which I preached to you, which also you received, in which also you stand, through which also you are saved—*if* you hold firmly (κατέχετε) to the word which I preached to you." Hebrews 4:14: "Let us hold fast (κρατῶμεν) the confession." 10:23: "Let us hold fast (κατέχωμεν) the confession of hope without wavering."

---

[34] Wilkin, *Confident in Christ*, 133, fails to recognize the link between faith and perseverance. He argues that perseverance can only be a condition for eternal salvation if it is synonymous with faith, which he claims it is not. Wilkin considers perseverance a work and therefore contradictory to Eph 2:9. Wilkin however seems to misunderstand that the fundamental nature of perseverance is *continuing faith* in God (cf. esp. 1 Cor 15:1-2; Col 1:23).

[35] The construction here comes close to Granville Sharp. The construction requires the two nouns to be *personal*, singular and non-proper names. Faith and endurance cannot therefore be completely identical since the nouns are impersonal. However there is nothing grammatically to suggest the two nouns cannot be united albeit distinct. Furthermore there are ample examples of impersonal constructions in the NT where the nouns are closely related (see Daniel B. Wallace, *Greek Grammar Beyond the Basics: An Exegetical Syntax of the New Testament* [Grand Rapids: Zondervan, 1996] 286–88).

[36] Schreiner and Caneday, *The Race Set Before Us*, 153.

[37] So too, G. C. Berkouwer, *Faith and Perseverance* (Grand Rapids: Eerdmans, 1958) 9–36: perseverance is synonymous to continuity in one's confession of faith in Christ.

We see the same concept articulated in John's Gospel. Faith is central to John (20:31). Opportunities abound for people to believe in Jesus (cf. 2:11, 23; 3:1-12; 4:39-42, 50, 53; 5:1-18; 6:14, 60, 66).[38] Some do, some don't, and some appear uncertain. Some believe on account of signs, others on account of His words. Some leave Him; one betrays Him. Some Jews believed in Jesus (8:31) but turn out to be sons of Satan. The disciples believed at Cana (2:11) although Philip (14:9), the beloved disciple (20:8), and Thomas (vv. 25-29), either lost or grew in their faith somewhere along the way. Peter boldly refuses to leave Jesus (6:68) though his subsequent denial casts doubt on his profession (18:17, 25, 27). It is impossible to say for sure at what point these men were "converted."[39]

The volatility of faith in John's Gospel provides the background for understanding Jesus' words in John 15:4: "Remain in Me and I will remain in you." This is a call to continue believing.[40] The saying and context is especially close to the endurance saying in Matthew 10:23. Jesus warns against eternal punishment (John 15:6; cf. Matt 10:15, 28, 33; cf. also Matt 3:10; 13:40), hatred from the world (John 15:18-19; cf. Matt 10:22) and persecution for Jesus' sake (John 15:20-21; cf. Matt 10:22a, 23a). Treatment of Jesus is tantamount to treatment of the One who sent Him (John 15:21a-24; cf. Matt 10:40). The disciples will receive help from the Holy Spirit (John 15:26; cf. Matt 10:19-20) and will testify to Jesus (John 15:27; cf. Matt 10:18). Note also that in Matthew 10:24b Jesus declares that, "a slave (δοῦλος) is not above his master." In John 15:15 Jesus says to His disciples: "No longer do I call you *slaves* (δοῦλους) . . . but I have called you friends." These parallels are summarized in the table below.

Table 11: Similarities between John 15 and Matthew 10

Themes	John 15	Matthew 10
Eternal Destruction	"If anyone does not remain in Me, he is like a branch that is thrown outside and is withered, and they gather them together and they throw them into the fire and it is burned" (v. 6).	"Be afraid of the one who is able to destroy both soul and body in hell" (v. 28; cf. vv 15, 33).

---

[38] Cf. R. Alan Culpepper, *Anatomy of the Fourth Gospel: A Study in Literary Design* (Philadelphia: Fortress, 1983) 88–89.

[39] Cf. ibid., 89, 104; also Richard V. Peace, *Conversion in the New Testament: Paul and the Twelve* (Grand Rapids: Eerdmans, 1999).

[40] Culpepper, *Anatomy of the Fourth Gospel*, 55–66; cf. also J. Carl Laney, "Abiding is Believing: The Analogy of the Vine in John 15:1-6," *BSac* 146 (1989) 55–66.

Hatred on account of Jesus	"If the world *hates* you, you know that it hated Me first" (v. 18).	"You will be *hated* by all men on account of Me" (v. 22).
Persecution on account of Jesus	"If they *persecuted* Me they will persecute you also" (v. 20).	"Whenever they *persecute* you in one city, flee to another" (v. 23a; cf. v. 22a).
Union between the Father and the Son	"He who hates Me hates my Father also" (v. 23).	"He who receives you receives Me, and he who receives Me receives the One who sent Me" (v. 40).
Help from the Holy Spirit in witnessing	"When the Comforter comes whom I will send to you from the Father . . . He will testify concerning Me" (v. 26).	"When they arrest you do not be anxious about what you might say for it will be given to you in that hour what you should say" (vv. 19-20).
Testimony	"And you also *testify* for you have been with Me from the beginning" (v. 27).	"You will be brought before governors and kings on account of Me as a *testimony* to them and to the Gentiles" (v. 18).
Slaves	"No longer do I call you *slaves* because the *slave* does not know what his *master* does" (v. 15).	"A *slave* is not above his *master*" (v. 24).

These parallels are striking and suggest a parallel in meaning between the passages. That is, to endure until the end and be saved is tantamount to remaining in Jesus the Vine. Failure to endure until the end and thus not be saved is a failure to remain in the Vine and thus to be thrown into the fire and burned. All this to say that just as failure to endure will result in no future salvation so too the failure to remain will result in eternal destruction (John 15:6).

Excursus on John 15:1-6

Unfortunately I cannot treat John 15:1-6 in full here. The passage is debated: does vv. 1-6 teach that Christians who do not remain lose their salvation?[41] Do they merely experience divine discipline now and loss of rewards later?[42]

---

[41] Raymond E. Brown, *The Gospel According to John: Introduction, Translation, and Notes*, vol. 2, xiii–xxi, AB, ed. William Foxtwell Allbright and David Noel Freedman, vol. 29A (Garden City, N.Y.: Doubleday, 1970) 675–76.

[42] Dillow, *Servant Kings*, 409–12.

Or do vv. 1-6 concern disciples who believed but never continued in their faith and can therefore expect eternal judgment.[43] Very briefly the main issues (see also the commentaries) are:

First, the meaning of αἴρει in v. 2. The word can denote either "take away/remove," or "lift up." Both meanings have been argued for here and both meanings occur in John.[44] Those who argue for "lift up" maintain that it was common practice to lift fallen vines "into position with meticulous care and allowed to heal."[45] The implication is that *fruitless* Christians are lifted up and encouraged and put it into a position where they can produce fruit. "If after this encouragement, they do not remain in fellowship with Him and bear fruit, they are cast out" (v. 6).[46] The problem with this interpretation is that it relies more on historical background than on the context of the passage.[47] Furthermore, if the use of αἴρει in John's Gospel bears any weight then priority should probably be given to the meaning "take away" since it is this meaning that occurs—without exception—from chapter 11 onward (11:39, 41, 48; 16:22; 17:15; 19:15, 31, 38; 20:1, 2, 13, 15). Finally, vv. 2 and 6 appear to be saying the same thing[48] for the one who does not remain (v. 6) is clearly the one who does not produce fruit (vv. 4-5). And the one who does not produce fruit is also the one who is cut off (v. 2). There is no indication that vv. 2 and 6 are concerned with a different process. The terms in v. 6—ἐβλήθη, ἐξηράνθη, συνάγουσιν, and βάλλουσιν together with the imagery of fire and burning—hardly create a picture of an "encouraged" Christian.

Second, the meaning of μένω in vv. 4-10 is debated.[49] I have already shown in chapter five that μένω in 6:56 is synonymous with eternal life (cf. v. 27; 8:35; 14:10). 8:31 is also significant ("If you *remain* in my word, then you are truly disciples of mine"). Jesus is talking to people who had "believed in him" (v. 30) though this does not exempt Jesus from designating them

---

[43] J. Carl Laney, "Abiding is Believing," 55–66.

[44] For the meaning "take away" see John 1:29; 2:16; 10:18; 11:39, 41, 48; 16:22; 17:15; 19:15, 31, 38; 20:1, 2, 13, 15; for "lift up" see 5:8, 9, 10, 11, 12; 8:59; 10:24.

[45] R. K. Harrison, "Vine," in *The International Bible Encyclopedia*, ed. Geoffrey W. Bromiley, vol. 4 (Grand Rapids: Eerdmans, 1988) 986; Dillow, *Servant Kings*, 409–12.

[46] Ibid., 409.

[47] See C. H. Dodd, *The Interpretation of the Fourth Gospel* (Cambridge: Cambridge University Press, 1968) 136. There is in fact a play on the two verbs αἴρει and καθαίρει in John 15:2. The latter verb provides a link to the adjective καθαροί in v. 3. This play on words and literary link may indicate that Jesus' reason for choosing αἴρει was more for communication purposes than historical accuracy.

[48] Contra. Dillow, *Servant Kings*, 411–12.

[49] John uses μένω more than any other NT author: forty times in his Gospel, twenty-seven times in his epistles. This is sixty-seven times compared with 118 times in the NT.

"sons of the devil" (v. 44). In other words, these so-called believers have not *remained* in Jesus' word and are therefore not truly disciples—they belong to the devil. What then does it mean to remain in Christ? I suggest that Jesus is urging his disciples to endure in their belief in Him in the same way that He urges His disciples in His missionary discourse (Matt 10) to endure (see above; cf. 1 John 2:27-28).

Third, the fire imagery in John 15:6 suggests eternal rather than temporal judgment. Jesus' words are reminiscent of Ezekiel 15 (cf. also 19:12). In Ezekiel the people of Jerusalem are compared to useless wood that is thrown onto the fire as fuel (vv. 4, 6). Here Ezekiel stresses the finality of the judgment for Jerusalem for if the wood "was not useful for anything when it was whole, how much less can it be made into something useful when the fire has burned it and it is charred?" (v. 5). The Synoptic Gospels also speak of fire in reference to eternal punishment (Matt 3:8-12). Those who do not produce *fruit* are "cut down and thrown into the fire" (v. 10). Similarly in 13:24-30, 36-43 at the end of the age the weeds, that is, the "sons of the evil one," are tied in bundles and burned. Their destiny is the fiery furnace where there will be weeping and gnashing of teeth.[50] Finally extra biblical literature often associates fire with eternal punishment at the end of the age (cf. e.g., *Apoc. Abr.* 15.6; *Sib. Or.* 1.100-3; 2.292-310; Josephus *Ant.* 18.14; *J. W.* 2.163; 3.374-75).[51]

In conclusion it is my understanding that those who do not remain are *not* believers. The question is, were they ever believers? In other words, did they lose their relationship with Jesus by not remaining or did they never have it? John's theology seems to point toward the latter. John has a category for false belief, that is, faith that does not save (e.g., esp. 2:23-25; 8:30-46). Most instructive in this regard are John's comments in his first epistle concerning those who had now left the community of believers and yet were once part of that community (see 1 John 2:19). John's language strongly suggests that these people were never believers to begin with but it is only with the benefit of hindsight that John is able to make this deduction. He now is able to say that these people were never true believers—in spite of first impressions. For if they were sincere in their faith they would have *remained* (μεμενήκεισαν), the pluperfect tense of the verb suggesting that past commitments and professions would have needed to stand the test of time.

---

[50] See J. Lunde, "Heaven and Hell," in *DJG*, 310–11.

[51] Cf. also Rom 11:20 where Paul explains that the branches (i.e., Jews) were broken off because of *unbelief*. Paul urges his readers to therefore consider the "kindness and severity of God" for those who persist in unbelief will be cut off while those who persist (ἐπιμένῃς) in God's kindness will not.

Endurance in the Rest of the New Testament (continued)

I should also point out that the Bible does not ignore the ethical side of endurance as if continuing in faith without works was enough (1 Tim 4:16; Rev 14:12). James presents Job as the quintessential example of endurance (Jas 5:11). Job is an interesting choice for at first glance he actually appears to be anything but a model of endurance. For as soon as suffering hit he cursed the day of his birth wishing he'd never been born (3:1-12; 10:18-19). He longed to die, was discouraged and miserable (3:13-26; 6:2; 7:3). He was weary, despairing and unhappy (7:7). He complained (v. 11; 23:2) and despised his life and the futility of it (9:21; 10:1). He asked God to relieve him of his suffering (13:21). He dared to question God and even blamed Him for his predicament (1:21; 16:7-14; 19:21; 23:14-16; 27:2; 30:11). We might well wonder if Job represents the quintessential example of impatience (6:11; 21:4). Jesus is another One who is presented as an example of endurance. The writer to the Hebrews declares that He "endured the cross" (ὑπέμεινεν) (Heb 12:2; cf. also v. 3) and yet while on the cross He questioned God as to why He had forsaken Him (Matt 27:46). Prior to the cross He was overwhelmed with sadness (26:38) and asked God if He might be relieved of His assignment (v. 39).

From our brief look at these two *pillars* of endurance we can say fairly confidently I believe that endurance does not preclude such feelings as weariness, helplessness and despair in the midst of suffering. Endurance is not a matter of exhibiting 'superman' type qualities. We distort the biblical concept of endurance by imposing on it—not to mention imposing on others and ourselves—expectations that even Jesus and certainly Job did not meet. Suffering is a reminder of the reality of living in a fallen world and it is not easy or pleasant. Yet both Job and Jesus are apt illustrations of endurance. Both remained faithful to God and obedient in spite of the pressures that beset them.[52] Job never gave up on God (6:10; 13:15; 14:14-17; 16:19-21; 17:9; 19:25-27; 23:10-12), he never sinned (1:22; 2:10; cf. 6:30; 7:20; 23:11-12; 27:2-6) and he always spoke what was right concerning God (42:7, 8; cf. 9:2-20; 12:10-25; 26:6-14; 28:23-28).[53] With respect to Jesus He affirmed His commitment to God by submitting nevertheless (πλὴν) to God's will rather than His own (Matt 26:39b). Through all this He was obedient (Heb 5:8). Both aspects are inherent to endurance: not giving up on God and obedience.

---

[52] BDAG, 1039: endurance is maintaining "a belief or course of action in the face of opposition."

[53] Cf. also H. A. Fine, "The Tradition of a Patient Job," *JBL* 74 (1955) 28–32.

"Here is the endurance of the saints: those who keep the commandments of God and have faith in Jesus" (Rev 14:12).

10

The Role of *Treating Others* in Salvation

Whoever says, "You fool!" will be answerable to the Gehenna of fire. (Matt 5:22c)

Love your enemies and pray for those who persecute you in order that you might become sons of your Father. (vv. 44-45a; cf. Luke 6:35)

In anger his master handed him over to be tortured until which time he could pay back all he owed. Thus also my Father in heaven will do to you, if you do not each forgive his brother from your heart. (Matt 18:34-35)

THESE three (four including Luke 6:35) passages have one thing in common: one's eternal destiny is associated with how one treats others. That is, "hate," "love," and "forgiveness" have a bearing on where one spends eternity. There is no doubt that this is the case in Matthew 5:22 although admittedly one could perhaps argue that vv. 44-45 and 18:35 refer to something else other than eternal salvation.[1] Though I will argue all the above passages speak of eternal salvation I am not unaware that this leaves us with somewhat of a theological conundrum. That is, God's treatment of people in eternity is evidently *dependent* upon one's treatment of others here on earth.

Anger in Matthew 5:21-26

In 5:21-48 Matthew defines the surpassing righteousness of v. 20 needed to enter into the kingdom (see chap. 6). This righteousness is defined by six antitheses, each introduced by "You have heard that it was said . . . but I say to you . . ." (vv. 21a, 22a, 27a, 28b 31a, 32a, 33a, 34a 38a, 39a, 43a, 44a). There are variations to the first part of each saying: "You have heard that it was said

---

[1] E.g., Joseph C. Dillow, *The Reign of the Servant Kings: A Study of Eternal Security and the Final Significance of Man* (Miami, Fla.: Schoettle, 1992) 348, 368, 384. Oddly enough Dillow (175) *appears* to dismiss any notion that Matt 5:22 is referring to eternal salvation in spite of the phrase "Gehenna of fire."

to the ancients" (v. 21a), "and it was said" (v. 31a), "*Again* you have heard that it was said *to the ancients*" (v. 33a), but the gist is the same. The phrase "But I say to you" (ἐγὼ δὲ λέγω ὑμῖν) however contains no variation. This observation is significant. The issues surrounding this section of Scripture with respect to Jesus' relationship to the Law are complex and too involved for this study.[2] Yet without trying to minimize the debate or simplify the issues the fundamental point, irrespective of one's interpretation,[3] seems to be "Jesus' role as sovereign interpreter of the law"[4] (cf. 7:29). With Jesus as the Fulfiller of the Law (5:17) the emphasis is now on what *He* (note that in each case the ἐγὼ is emphatic) says and not on what *was* said. *He* is the *new* Authority.

In v. 21 Jesus cites the sixth commandment as it was said "to the ancients" (τοῖς ἀρχαίοις):[5] "You shall not murder" (Exod 20:13)[6] and follows up with the penalty for murder: "*he will be liable[7] to judgment*" (ἔνοχος ἔσται τῇ κρίσει). However Jesus does not leave matters there as if the act of murder was all one could be held accountable for. He authoritatively (ἐγὼ δὲ λέγω ὑμῖν) elaborates[8] the sixth commandment in v. 22 by giving a general principle (πᾶς ὁ . . .):

General principle: Everyone who (πᾶς ὁ) is *angry* (ὀργιζόμενος) with his *brother*[9] (ἀδελφῷ = neighbor)[10] will also "*be liable to judgment*" (ἔνοχος ἔσται τῇ κρίσει).

---

[2] For my own understanding of Jesus and the Law see Douglas J. Moo, "Jesus and the Authority of the Mosaic Law," *JSNT* 20 (1984) 3–49.

[3] For the views on Jesus' relationship to the Law see ibid., 4. For the views on Jesus' relationship to the Law in the Antitheses see ibid., 40, n. 109.

[4] Craig L. Blomberg, *Matthew*, NAC, ed. David S. Dockery, vol. 22 (Nashville: Broadman, 1992) 106.

[5] BDAG, 137; Moo, "Jesus and the Authority of the Mosaic Law," 17.

[6] On whether Jesus is citing written or oral tradition or both see ibid., 18.

[7] BDAG, 338: ἔνοχος = "guilty."

[8] The δέ is not to be taken as contrastive as if Jesus was abrogating the Law. In line with Him being the Fulfiller of the Law (Matt 5:17) it is better to view Him elaborating (or transcending) the Law (Warren Carter, *Matthew and the Margins: A Socio-Political and Religious Reading*, JSNTSup, ed. Stanley E. Porter, vol. 204 [Sheffield: Sheffield Academic, 2000] 144).

[9] Scribal tradition dating back to the second century (e.g., ℵ² D L W Θ 33 it) has added εἰκῇ ("without cause") no doubt to bring the offense more in line with the penalty. Certainly we cannot imagine scribes omitting the word, which would in effect make the saying more demanding. The text reading has good support from P64 ℵ* B. See *TCGNT*, 11.

[10] Ἀδελφός in Matthew can refer to disciples of Jesus or blood brothers. However in each instance the context is usually a very clear indicator (spiritual brothers = Matt 12:48, 49, 50; 18:15, 21, 35; 23:8; 25:40; 28:10; blood brothers = 1:2, 11; 4:18, 21; 10:2, 21; 12:46, 47; 13:55; 14:3; 17:1; 19:29; 20:24; 22:24, 25). The SM instances contain the most ambiguity (5:22, 23, 24, 47; 7:3, 4, 5). However these verses are quite different to those denoting blood

Two specific examples (ὃς δ' ἂν ... ὃς δ' ἂν ...) follow:

First example: "Whoever (ὃς δ' ἂν) calls his brother (ἀδελφῷ) a numbskull (ῥακά)[11] *will be liable to the council* (ἔνοχος ἔσται τῷ συνεδρίῳ)."

Second example: "Whoever (ὃς δ' ἂν) calls his brother a fool (μωρέ) *will be liable to the Gehenna of fire* (ἔνοχος ἔσται εἰς τὴν γέενναν τοῦ πυρός)."

Jesus then gives two applications[12] (οὖν)[13] for His hearers in vv. 23-26 lest they end up being liable to judgment:

First application: A *religious* setting concerning a *brother* (vv. 23-24).
Second application: A *secular* setting involving an *opponent* (vv. 25-26).

The principle of v. 22 is therefore applied to *every* area of life (religious and secular) and *every* kind of relationship (brother and opponent).

Table 12: Outline of Matthew 5:21-26

General principle:	Everyone who is angry with his brother will be liable to judgment.
First example:	Whoever calls his brother numbskull will be liable to the council.
Second example:	Whoever calls his brother a fool will be liable to the Gehenna of fire.
First application:	Religious: before offering a gift at the altar reconcile with your brother who has something against you.
Second application:	Secular: before going to court reconcile with your opponent.

---

brothers. Each one occurs in a *relational* context. They are also governed by Jesus' instructions to always be on best terms with those who are brothers. Since Jesus clearly places no restriction on which people, people are to love, these references surely take on a more general connotation in the sense of "neighbor" whether spiritual or familial (so BDAG, 19: "without ref. to a common nationality or faith *neighbor*"; W. Günther, "Brother," in *NIDNTT*, 257–58). Contra D. A. Carson, "Matthew," in *EBC*, ed. Frank E. Gaebelein and J. D. Douglas, vol. 8 (Grand Rapids: Zondervan, 1984) 149; Robert H. Mounce, *Matthew*, NIBC, ed. W. Ward Gasque, vol. 1 (Peabody, Mass.: Hendrickson, 1985) 45, who both limit "brother" here to a Christian.

[11] BDAG, 903. May also be translated "empty-head" or "fool."

[12] Or illustrations (Hans Dieter Betz, *The Sermon on the Mount: A Commentary on the Sermon on the Mount, Including the Sermon on the Plain [Matthew 5:3–7:27 and Luke 6:20-49]*, Hermeneia, ed. Adela Yarbro Collins [Minneapolis: Fortress, 1995] 222; Carson, "Matthew," 149).

[13] Note also the link words ἀδελφός, ἀδελφῷ in Matt 5:23, 24, and τῷ κριτῇ and ὁ κριτής in v. 25.

In the first application one should not continue to offer a gift at the altar if he remembers that his brother (ἀδελφός) has something against him (v. 23). He should rather go and be reconciled (διαλλάγηθι) to his brother and then offer his gift (v. 24). The underlying assumption is that failing to rectify the situation in this way could result in this worshipper getting angry with his brother and judging him to be a ῥακά or a μωρέ. This of course would have eternal consequences (cf. v. 22c).

In the second application one should make friends (εὐνοῶν) quickly with their opponent. Since the scene is a judicial one (cf. the par. in Luke 12:57-59[14]) the idea is "settle the case quickly with your plaintiff."[15] Failure to rectify the dispute "on the way" (to court) could ultimately result in being thrown into prison (v. 25) and kept there until the appropriate debt is paid (v. 26).[16]

The Relationship between Anger and Salvation in Matthew 5:21-26

There is some debate on whether the crimes and punishments in v. 22 are given in ascending order.[17] There may be something to be said for the fact that ῥακά is less severe than μωρέ.[18] To label someone ῥακά was to insult their intelligence and tantamount to being called an "empty-head."[19] Whereas the label μωρέ is unique to Matthew, elsewhere designating those who are excluded from the kingdom (7:26; 23:17; 25:2, 3, 8). If this is the case here Matthew may be thinking of someone making a judgment "against a brother's membership in the kingdom,"[20] a serious offense indeed (cf. 7:1-2). However, the general tenor of the passage along with the entire Sermon suggests that one is not to think of incremental offenses (even though this may be the case). Such thinking is expected from the scribes and the Pharisees but certainly not Jesus.

---

[14] Betz, *The Sermon on the Mount*, 226.

[15] BDAG, 409.

[16] Matthew 5:56 has been used to support the Roman Catholic doctrine of purgatory (see A. Michel, "purgatoire," in *dictionnaire de théologie catholique: contenant l'exposé des doctrines de la théologie catholique leurs preuves et leur histoire*, ed. A. Vacant, E. Mangenot, and É. Amann, vol. 13 [Paris: Letouzey et Ané, 1936], 1171). However the point is not that one can earn their way back from judgment but that God's judgment is certain (cf. Matt 5:22) (Carson, "Matthew," 150).

[17] Mounce, *Matthew*, 45: the penalties are in ascending order but not the offenses.

[18] See Robert H. Gundry, *Matthew: A Commentary on His Handbook for a Mixed Church under Persecution*, 2d ed. (Grand Rapids: Eerdmans, 1994) 84.

[19] BDAG, 903.

[20] Gundry, *Matthew*, 84–85; cf. Carter, *Matthew and the Margins*, 145.

The question on whether Matthew is depicting an increasing scale of judgment is more difficult. "The council" (τῷ συνεδρίῳ), a common reference to the local council (Matt 10:17; Mark 13:9) such as the Sanhedrin, will judge those who label their brother ῥακά (Matt 26:59; Acts 5:21).[21] On the other hand, the one who calls his brother μωρέ will be subject "to the Gehenna of fire" (v. 22). Gehenna (γέεννα) originally referred to a valley of ill repute in South Jerusalem (2 Kgs 23:10). Though a garbage dump in Jesus' day it had come to symbolize the place of eternal fire where the wicked would be eternally condemned (*1 Enoch* 27.1-2; 54.1-6; 90.26; *2 Bar.* 85.13; *4 Ezra* 7:26-36).[22] It is this latter meaning that Matthew is thinking of (cf. Matt 8:29; 13:42, 50; 23:15, 33; 25:41; Mark 9:43-47; Luke 12:5).[23] On the evidence then it appears that these two offenses are judged on an ascending scale, one earthly and the other heavenly[24] although it is completely possible that τῷ συνεδρίῳ is a reference to God's council and therefore parallels the reference to Gehenna.[25]

Absolute certainty on this question is impossible. However the issue needs to be viewed in light of the surpassing righteousness of 5:20, which in my mind makes the debate over ascending judgments somewhat irrelevant. The point is that anger, whether it be of the ῥακά variety or the μωρέ kind, *if not dealt with* will eventually lead to eternal destruction, that is, Gehenna (cf. v. 26;[26] 18:34). Hence even allowing for an ascending scale of judgment, 5:20 lets no one off the hook. Clearly anger is not surpassing righteousness; and one who lacks surpassing righteousness, for example, anger—be it murder, ῥακά or μωρέ—will not enter the kingdom of heaven.[27] The consequences are eternal.

---

[21] BDAG, 967; although see Craig S. Keener, *A Commentary on the Gospel of Matthew* (Grand Rapids: Eerdmans, 1999) 184, for references to the contrary.

[22] Joachim Jeremias, "γέεννα," in *TDNT*, 1:657–58; Carter, *Matthew and the Margins*, 145; cf. David C. Sim, *The Gospel of Matthew and Christian Judaism: The History and Social Setting of the Matthean Community*, Studies of the New Testament and its World, ed. John Barclay, Joel Marcus, and John Riches (Edinburgh: T. & T. Clark, 1998) 135–39.

[23] Jeremias, "γέεννα," 1:658.

[24] So Gundry, *Matthew*, 84–85.

[25] Blomberg, *Matthew*, 107; Keener, *A Commentary on the Gospel of Matthew*, 184; Ulrich Luz, *Matthew 1–7: A Commentary*, trans. Wilhelm C. Linss (Minneapolis: Augsburg, 1989) 283, argues that there is an increase in judgment but it is qualitative rather than quantitative.

[26] Betz, *The Sermon on the Mount*, 229: Matt 5:26 = eschatological judgment.

[27] Note also the present tense (ὀργιζόμενος) in Matt 5:22. The thought is most probably something along the lines of: "anyone who is *constantly* angry with his brother will be liable to judgment." Contra Dillow, *Servant Kings*, 175, who seems to view v. 22 as potentially a momentary event: "who has not felt anger in his heart at some time and is thus, on the authority of Jesus, a murderer (Matt 5.21-22)?" However, it seems incongruous to the tenor

It is of course striking that Matthew views anger as being just as culpable as murder. The reason is surely along the lines that because murder originates with anger "anger is murderous in principle."[28] Insulting someone by labeling him or her "numbskull" (Matt 5:22) may appear innocent enough but there is no doubt that the seeds of murder fester within (esp. 15:19; cf. Sir 28:11). Jewish tradition associates the spirit of anger with murderous intent (*T. Sim.* 2:6-13; *T. Dan.* 1:3–2:5).[29] It was anger that led Cain to kill his brother Abel (Gen 4:5-8). Two centuries prior to Jesus it was observed that just as "the vapor and smoke of the furnace precede the fire; so insults precede bloodshed" (Sir 22:24). This fits with the general tenor of the SM: the conjunction of inner motive with outward actions.[30]

The two scenarios presented in Matthew 5:23-26 are governed by v. 22: "everyone who is angry (ὀργιζόμενος) with his brother (ἀδελφῷ) will be liable to judgment (κρίσει)." This principle is unpacked first in vv. 23-24 with ἀδελφός as the link word and then in vv. 25-26 with κριτῇ and κριτής as the link word. The term for anger—ὀργή—however is not used again. This is significant for in its place Jesus urges reconciliation (διαλλάγηθι) and friendship (εὐνοῶν). Anger is contrary to surpassing righteousness. Rather it is, according to James 1:20-21, *surpassing* (περισσείαν) wickedness. Reconciliation and friendship is the righteousness necessary to enter into the kingdom.[31] This is a rather interesting and significant point for it is not so much anger that hinders one from entering the kingdom but *unresolved* anger.[32]

The worshipper who remembers his brother has something against him must rectify the relationship before continuing to offer his gift (Matt 5:23-24) otherwise his worship is futile (cf. 15:8-9; Mark 12:33). Since one's attitude toward God is reflected in one's treatment of others (Matt 22:37-40; Luke 10:27; 1 John 4:17) to continue to worship without restoring the human relationship would be tantamount to abrogating the divine relationship.[33]

---

of the entire SM to reduce unrighteousness to momentary flaws and thus make righteousness into some kind of legalistic system where a momentary lapse excludes one from the *millennial* (in Dillow's view) kingdom and vice versa.

[28] Carson, "Matthew," 148; Betz, *The Sermon on the Mount*, 220: "The goal must be to imagine a behavior that gains control over anger and thereby eliminates the root cause of murder."

[29] Cf. Josephus, *Ag. Ap.*, 2.30: "the mere intention of doing wrong to one's parents or of impiety against God is followed by instant death."

[30] Moo, "Jesus and the Authority of the Mosaic Law," 18.

[31] Sirach 28:5: "If a mere mortal harbors wrath, who will make an atoning sacrifice for his sins?"

[32] Hence Dillow (above) misses the point vis-à-vis momentary anger.

[33] Betz, *The Sermon on the Mount*, 223.

One's worship of God cannot be divorced from one's relationship with others (see Deut 27). It's that simple!

In the second scenario (Matt 5:25-26) the term εὐνοεῖν suggests that whatever the nature of the dispute the relationship has turned sour and needs repairing.[34] One's relationship with God, as we have seen elsewhere will manifest itself in one's relationship with others. This is central to understanding the relationship between murder/anger and judgment/Gehenna.

Anger in the Rest of the New Testament

In his epistle James makes the same point as Matthew. "The anger (ὀργή) of man does not produce the *righteousness* (δικαιοσύνην) of God" (Jas 1:20). James is in all likelihood drawing on SM material here for he urges his readers to do away with *surplus wickedness* (περισσείαν κακίας). Given the well-known connections between James and the SM presumably we are to draw a connection between James' use of περισσείαν and Matthew's use of περισσεύσῃ. If this were the case, doing away with surplus wickedness would constitute having surpassing *righteousness* (δικαιοσύνην). This would then enable James' readers to "receive the implanted word, which is able to *save your soul* (σῶσαι τὰς ψυχὰς ὑμῶν)"[35] (v. 21). Anger is to have no place among Paul's readership (Rom 1:19; Eph 4:31; Col 3:8; 1 Tim 2:8; Titus 1:7) for vengeance belongs to the Lord; He will repay (Rom 12:19).[36]

---

[34] Ibid., 228: "the basic reason for going to court is emotional and thus related to anger (ὀργή)."

[35] James' dependence on Matt is well known and esp. the SM (see Massey H. Shepherd, "The Epsitle of James and the Gospel of Matthew," *JBL* 75 [1956] 40–51; Leonhard Goppelt, *Theology of the New Testament: The Variety and Unity of the Apostolic Witness to Christ*, ed. Jürgen Roloff and trans. John E. Alsup, vol. 2 (Grand Rapids: Eerdmans, 1982) 199–208. Peter H. Davids, *The Epistle of James: A Commentary of the Greek Text*, NIGTC, ed. I. Howard Marshall and W. Ward Gasque (Grand Rapids: Eerdmans, 1982) 47–48, observes twenty five parallels from the SM. Cf. also R. W. Wall, "James, Letter of," in *DLNTD*, 554). If in fact Jas 1:20 is drawing on Matt 5:20, 22, it is not out of the way to suggest that James' "save your soul" is equivalent to Matthew's entering the kingdom (cf. esp. Jas 2:8). We might compare the two passages as follows:

Matt 5:20:
   "Unless your *righteousness* (δικαιοσύνη)
      Surpasses (περισσεύσῃ) that of the Scribes and the Pharisees
         You will in no way enter into *the kingdom of God* (τὴν βασιλείαν τῶν οὐρανῶν)."

Jas 1:20-21:
   "The wrath of man does not work the *righteousness* (δικαιοσύνην) of God.
      Therefore put off all filth and *surpassing* (περισσείαν) wickedness, and in humility receive the implanted word,
         Which is able *to save your souls* (σῶσαι τὰς ψυχὰς ὑμῶν)."

[36] Sirach 27:30–28:11.

Evidently the repayment is in line with Matthew's SM teaching. Those who are angry (θυμοί) will not inherit the kingdom of God (Gal 5:20-21; cf. Matt 5:20: "will not enter the kingdom of heaven"). Those who are characterized by murder (φόνος) (Rom 1:29; as in Matt 5:21) are presently experiencing the wrath (ὀργή) of God (Rom 1:18).[37]

Enemy Love in Matthew 5:43-48 and Luke 6:27-35

Matthew 5:43-48 is the last of the antitheses and continues the theme of relationships (cf. vv. 38-42). In v. 43 Jesus cites the love command of Leviticus 19:18: "You shall love your neighbor" and adds, "You shall hate your enemy." The addition does not appear in the OT (though cf. Ps 139:21-22). It is possible that the saying merely represents the converse of loving "fellow Jews" (cf. Lev 19:17).[38] However the OT never puts limits on neighborly love (v. 34) and so the saying cannot even be regarded as "a fair extrapolation" of the OT attitude toward one's neighbor.[39] It seems more likely that the saying represents the Jewish interpretation of the matter (cf. MT 2 Sam 19:7; Luke 10:29).[40] If this is the case Jesus gives the *correct interpretation* in vv. 44-48.[41] One is to love, not hate, one's enemy. Debate surrounds the precise origin of this command[42] although it is more than likely it originated with Jesus without any prior influence.[43] To love their enemies for Matthew's readers meant praying for their persecutors (cf. vv. 10-12).[44]

---

[37] Note too 1 John 3:15: "Everyone who hates his brother is a murderer (ἀνθρωποκτόνος) and you know that every murderer does not have eternal life remain in him."

[38] R. T. France, *Matthew*, TNTC, ed. Leon Morris (Grand Rapids: Eerdmans, 1989) 128.

[39] Moo, "Jesus and the Authority of the Mosaic Law," 22.

[40] Str-B 1:353: "Das Ganze wird eine populäre Maxime sein, nach der der Durchschnittsisraelit in Jesu Tagen sein Verhalten gegen Freund und Feind eingerichtet hat" (see also 368). Betz, *The Sermon on the Mount*, 304: "an interpretive comment stating the improper interpretation of Lev 19:18." Cf. also Donald Hagner, *The Jewish Reclamation of Jesus: An Analysis and Critique of Modern Jewish Study of Jesus* (Grand Rapids: Zondervan, 1984) 144–50.

[41] Ibid., 309.

[42] See William Klassen, "'Love Your Enemies': Some Reflections on the Current Status of Research," in *The Love of Enemy and Nonretaliation in the New Testament*, ed. William M. Swartley, Studies in Peace and Scripture, ed. Ben C. Ollenburger and Willard M. Swartley (Louisville, Ky.: Westminster John Knox, 1992) 1–31.

[43] John Piper, *'Love Your Enemies': Jesus' Love Command in the Synoptic Gospels and in the Early Christian Paraenesis*, SNTSMS, ed. R. McL. Wilson and M. E. Thrall, vol. 38 (Cambridge: Cambridge University Press, 1979) 56–65; W. D. Davies and Dale C. Allison, Jr., *A Critical and Exegetical Commentary on The Gospel According to Matthew*, vol. 1, ICC, ed. J. A. Emerton, C. E. B. Cranfield, and G. N. Stanton (Edinburgh: T. & T. Clark, 1997) 552.

[44] On prayer for one's enemies in Judaism see *b. Ber.* 10a; *Midr. Pss.* 41.8; 104.27; Str-B

The purpose (ὅπως γένησθε; see below) for Jesus' command is given in v. 45: "in order that you might become *sons of your Father* who is in heaven." The reason (ὅτι) for this is that God "causes the sun to shine upon both the evil and the good and sends rain on both the righteous and the unrighteous." Love for enemies is therefore grounded in the love of God. SM readers are to love and pray for their enemies because even God demonstrates love toward His enemies—those who are "evil" (πονηρούς) (cf. vv. 11; 13:38-39) and "unrighteous" (ἀδίκους). To rejoice on account of persecution is to demonstrate the character of the prophets (5:12) but to pray for one's persecutors is to demonstrate the character of God (v. 48).[45] Hence God's love for His enemies not only provides the basis for the believers' love for enemies but the pattern for it.[46]

Jesus spells out the implications (γάρ) of *not* loving one's enemies in vv. 46-47. Verse 46 concerns love and v. 47 concerns greeting, a manifestation of love.[47] Both verses patently make the same point:[48] *if you only love those whom it is easy to love then you are no different from an unbeliever*. To love those who love in return (e.g., the good and righteous of v. 45) is to act no differently from the tax collectors (v. 46). Rather than demonstrating the character of God such a person aligns himself with the character of a tax collector. To put it in another way, to love those who love in return is to identify with sinners (9:10-11; 11:19), not the Father. What reward can such a person expect (τίνα μισθὸν ἔχετε)? "The answer can only be: none."[49] Verse 17 refutes any notion that Leviticus 19:18 applied only to Jews. One is not to greet their brothers (ἀδελφούς) only (μόνον). Again, such actions do not betray the character of God but the character of Gentiles (ἐθνικοί), namely those outside the believing community (see esp. Matt 6:7, 32; 18:17; cf. 10:5; 28:19).

Luke includes a fuller version of this tradition[50] in his SP though his basic point is the same as Matthew: "Love your enemies" (Luke 6:27, 35).[51]

1:370–71.

[45] Carson, "Matthew," 159.

[46] Piper, *'Love Your Enemies,'* 62.

[47] Blomberg, *Matthew*, 115.

[48] Note the synonymous structure: Matt 5:46: ἐάν ... τοὺς ... τίνα ... οὐκὶ καὶ οἱ ... τὸ αὐτὸ ποιοῦσιν / v. 47: ἐάν ... τοὺς ... τί ... οὐκὶ καὶ οἱ ... τὸ αὐτὸ ποιοῦσιν.

[49] Betz, *The Sermon on the Mount*, 318.

[50] Although verbal and conceptual parallels of Luke 6:29-30 are present in Matt 5:39-40 (see Kurt Aland, *Synopsis of the Four Gospels: Greek-English Edition of the Synopsis quattuor Evangeliorum. With the Text of the Revised Standard Version*, 10th ed. (Stuttgart: Biblia-Druck, 1993) 67 (§80); cf. Piper, *'Love Your Enemies,'* 53–65.

[51] Ibid., 136.

On the whole Matthew's account is more theological whereas Luke's is more applicational. Verses 27b-30 (cf. Matt 5:39-40) can be subsumed under *love* (i.e., the manifestation[52] of it) and *enemy* (i.e., the object of love).[53]

Table 13: Loving Your Enemies (Luke 6:27b-30)

Love	Enemy
Do good	People who hate you
Bless (εὐλογεῖτε)[54]	People who curse you
Pray	People who abuse you
Offer the other cheek	People who insult you[55]
Do not withhold giving clothes	People who take your clothes
Give	People who demand things from you
Don't demand borrowed things back	People who borrow and don't return

Clearly Luke's enemies include a wider and less aggressive range of people than Matthew's.[56] Also Luke's enemies tend toward the economic sphere.[57] Potentially any and every person could be an enemy for Luke.[58] Luke's point

---

[52] William Klassen, *Love of Enemies: The Way to Peace*, Overtures to Biblical Theology, ed. Walter Brueggemann and John R. Donahue, vol. 15 (Philadelphia: Fortress, 1984) 86: illustrations.

[53] For a treatment on these sayings in Matthew and Luke, in addition to the commentaries see Walter Wink, "Neither Passivity nor Violence: Jesus' Third Way (Matt. 5:38-42 par.)," in *The Love of Enemy and Nonretaliation in the New Testament*, ed. William M. Swartley, Studies in Peace and Scripture, ed. Ben C. Ollenburger and Willard M. Swartley (Louisville, Ky.: Westminster John Knox, 1992) 104–12. Cf. Richard A. Horsley, "Ethics and Exegesis: 'Love Your Enemies' and the Doctrine of Nonviolence," in *The Love of Enemy and Nonretaliation in the New Testament*, ed. William M. Swartley, Studies in Peace and Scripture, ed. Ben C. Ollenburger and Willard M. Swartley (Louisville, Ky.: Westminster John Knox, 1992) 85–88.

[54] The idea seems to be to seek God's best for one's enemy; cf. Hermann W. Beyer, "εὐλογέω," in *TDNT*, 2:754–63; Darrell L. Bock, *Luke 1:1–9:50*, BECNT, ed. Moisés Silva, vol. 3A (Grand Rapids: Baker, 1996) 589.

[55] Lit. "to the one who strikes you on the cheek" = "a formal insult" (Horsley, "Ethics and Exegesis," 86; Wink, "Neither Passivity nor Violence," 105.

[56] Although see Horsley, Richard A. "Ethics and Exegesis: 'Love Your Enemies' and the Doctrine of Nonviolence," in *The Love of Enemy and Nonretaliation in the New Testament*, ed. William M. Swartley, Studies in Peace and Scripture (Louisville, Ky.: Westminster John Knox, 1992) 76–89.

[57] Klassen, *Love of Enemies*, 76, 86.

[58] Horsely, "Ethics and Exegesis," 85–89: personal enemies.

is made clear in a summary statement in v. 31: Treat others in the same way you would want them to treat you.[59]

Luke at this point begins to track again with Matthew. What credit (χάρις; cf. Matt μισθὸν/περισσὸν) is it if you show love or do good (cf. Matt "greet") to those who love or do good to you. Even sinners (cf. Matt "tax collectors"/"Gentiles") do that (vv. 32-33). Luke extends his argument to lending and receiving (v. 34). Verse 35a is the positive application of vv. 32-34: "love your enemies, do good and lend expecting nothing in return." Verse 35b is similar to Matthew in concept. Luke expands the motivation for loving one's enemy to include "your reward (μισθός) will be great" along with "you will be sons of the Most High" (cf. Matt "sons of your Father in heaven"). Similar to Matthew, Luke too grounds (ὅτι) the command to love one's enemies in God's kindness (χρηστός) to those who don't deserve it (the evil and ungrateful). However Luke does not elaborate on how God is kind, just that He is. Since for both Matthew and Luke God's love is the pattern for enemy love they both conclude, "Be like your Father." Matthew 5:48: "Be perfect *as* your heavenly Father is perfect." Luke 6:36: "Be merciful *just as* your Father is merciful."[60]

The Relationship between Enemy Love and Salvation in Matthew 5:43-48 and Luke 6:27-35

There is much that could detain us here: source, tradition, and redaction issues, background questions, not to mention the origin of the enemy command and its association to Leviticus 19:18: "love your neighbor."[61] These issues however are quite secondary to our discussion, which I shall largely confine to the relationship between treatment of others and salvation. I shall devote most of the discussion to the expressions "sons of the Father" (Matt), "sons of the Most High" (Luke) and the term "reward" (μισθός). I will argue that in each case what Matthew and Luke have in mind is tantamount to eschatological salvation.

The Nature of the ὅπως Clause in Matthew 5:45

Matthew expresses the relationship between love and being "sons of the Father" with ὅπως (Matt 5:45). Luke's saying is straight forward simply stating, "*and you will be* (καὶ ἔσεσθε) sons of the Most High" (Luke 6:35). The construction ὅπως plus various inflections of γίνομαι always denote *purpose* in the NT (Acts 20:16; 25:26; 2 Cor 8:14; Phil 1:6; Heb 9:15) and

---

[59] Lit. "And just as you desire that men might do to you do to them likewise."

[60] See Piper, *'Love Your Enemies,'* 146, for further discussion on Matt 5:48/Luke 6:36.

[61] See e.g., Swartley, *The Love of Enemy*, 1–176; Piper, *'Love Your Enemies.'*

suggests that Matthew 5:45 should be understood in the same way.[62] The purpose then of enemy love is sonship. Of course this raises the question as to the meaning of sonship.

The Meaning of "Sons of the Father/Most High" in Matthew 5:45/Luke 6:35

"Son" (υἱός) is a familial term denoting relationship to a mother (Matt 1:21; 20:20-21) or father (Matt 13:55; Mark 10:46; Luke 1:13). However the term is not limited to family relationships and is often used to denote group membership (Acts 23:6; Eph 3:5; Heb 2:6). Yet regardless of the relationship, inherent in being a son is the notion of identity. The son's identity is defined by virtue of whatever family or group the son belongs to. Associated with sonship and identity is also character. These three aspects—sonship, identity, and character—are intertwined in the NT. In other words, if a *central* character is evil then all those who are evil are identified as his sons. Likewise if a *central* character is righteous then all those who are righteous are identified as his sons. For example, Jesus can regard the scribes and the Pharisees as "sons of those who murdered the prophets" (Matt 23:31) because they themselves have already begun to plot Jesus' demise (cf. 21:38-39, 45-46; 22:15). Believers are called "sons of Abraham" because Abraham believed in God (Gal 3:6-7). Yet Jesus could not regard the Jews who believed in Him as "children of Abraham" because they did not do the works of Abraham (John 8:39). Rather they did the works of their "father" and desired the desires of their "father," the devil (vv. 41, 44). Similarly everyone who loves has been "born" (γεγέννηται) from God precisely because God is love (1 John 4:7-8). The "children of God" and the "children of the devil" are so called because sin is part of the devil's character and not of God's (3:8-10).[63] The point is that the identity and character of the "son" is tied to and defined by the identity and character of the father, be it those who murdered the prophets, Abraham, the devil, or God. This is the essence of sonship and it is evident in Matthew 5:45 and Luke 6:35.

Matthew and Luke both follow the promise of sonship with an explanation (ὅτι)[64] of God's kindness. Both make the same point: God is kind to

---

[62] BDAG, 718; Betz, *The Sermon on the Mount*, 315; Carter, *Matthew and the Margins*, 155; Leon Morris, *The Gospel According to Matthew*, PNTC, ed. D. A. Carson (Grand Rapids: Eerdmans, 1992) 131; cf. F. Blass and A. Debrunner, *A Greek Grammar of the New Testament and Other Early Christian Literature*, trans. and rev. Robert W. Funk (Chicago: University of Chicago Press, 1961) 186–88 (§369).

[63] See BDAG, 1024–27, for further references.

[64] The ὅτι seems to function as the grounds for why enemy love is appropriate for disciples but since it follows immediately after the sonship clause it also serves to explain what sonship

those who don't deserve it. The basic argument in both passages then runs as follows:

Table 14: The Relationship between Enemy Love and "Son of God"

> The *command*: disciples are to love their enemies.
>
> The *purpose* of obeying this command: **enemy lovers might become sons of their Father.**
>
> The *reason* why an enemy lover becomes a son of God: **God also loves His enemies.**[65]

Hence to be an enemy lover is to emulate the character of God, which in turn makes one a son.[66] This explains why Matthew exhorts his readers to "be perfect *as* (ὡς) your heavenly *Father* is perfect" (Matt 5:48) and Luke, "be merciful *just as* (καθὼς) your *Father* is merciful" (Luke 6:36).[67]

The next question is whether the promise of sonship is for now[68] or the future?[69] In my mind neither can be ruled out and we should probably understand sonship here to be now-but-not-yet.[70] That the present is not absent is evident since disciples *already* call God their Father (Matt 6:9). Often in

---

is, i.e., emulating the character of the Father.

[65] A connection between being a "man of peace" and a "son of God" appears in 1 Chron 22:9-10 but there is no connection between the two in extra biblical literature. Jesus' statement appears unique. There are however similarities. Parallels to Matthew's beatitude in 5:9 are found in 1 Macc 6:49, 58; 11:51; 13:37; 14:11; 2 Macc 1:4. The just man is described as a child of God in Wis. 2:13, 16; 5:5. In the Mishnah peace on earth is associated with benefit in the world to come. *m.* Pe'ah 1:1: "These are things the benefit of which a person enjoys in this world, while the principal remains for him in the world to come: . . . [acts which] bring peace between a man and his fellow." See Klassen, *Love of Enemies*, 75.

[66] Cf. *b. Qid.* 36a: according to Rabbi Judah, "when you behave as sons you are designated sons; if you do not behave as sons, you are not designated sons."

[67] Piper, *'Love Your Enemies,'* 62: "The saying in both Mt and Lk affirms that sonship of God depends on acting like God: God is kind to his enemies; therefore anyone who wants to be a son of God must do the same."

[68] E.g., Gundry, *Matthew*, 98; John Nolland, *Luke 1–9:20*, WBC, ed. David A. Hubbard and Glenn W. Barker, vol. 35A (Dallas: Word, 1989) 300, on Luke's saying: "To be a son of God here is not a verdict of the future judgment . . . It is rather the present manifestation in the believer through love of enemy"; cf. Robert H. Stein, *Luke*, NAC, ed. David. S. Dockery, vol. 24 (Nashville: Broadman, 1992) 209.

[69] BDAG, 1025; Betz, *The Sermon on the Mount*, 313.

[70] Carter, *Matthew and the Margins*, 155: present and future (eschatological) dimensions; cf. Davies and Allison, *Matthew*, 1:554: Realized eschatology; Jan Lambrecht, "The Sayings of Jesus on Nonviolence," *Louvain Studies* 12 (1987) 305.

the SM God is described as "your Father" (ὁ πατήρ σου/ὑμῶν) suggesting it to be presently the case (5:16, 48; 6:1, 4, 6, 8, 14, 15, 18, 26, 32; 7:11; see also Luke 6:36). This accords with other NT passages affirming the present status of a believer's sonship (cf. John 1:12; Rom 8:14-15; Gal 3:26-27; 4:5-6; Eph 1:5).

However it is also clear from the NT that there is a status of sonship *yet to be realized* (Rom 8:19, 23; 9:26; Rev 21:7).[71] This also seems to be the case in Matthew's SM. The connection between Matthew 5:45 and v. 9 ("Blessed are the peacemakers for they *will be* called sons of God") is the most notable. Since v. 9 promises an eschatological blessing of sonship on peacemakers and v. 45 promises sonship to those who love their enemies—an alternate way of expressing peacemakers—it seems likely that v. 45 also anticipates eschatological sonship. We must also remember that enemy love constitutes the surpassing righteousness necessary to enter into the *eschatological* kingdom (5:20). It is therefore unthinkable that the promise of sonship is not in some sense tied to one's entrance into the kingdom.[72] Furthermore, sonship is closely associated with reward (μισθὸν) in v. 46, which I shall argue below is also eschatological. Thus the phrase "sons of your Father in heaven" certainly applies to the present in the same sense that being perfect in v. 48 applies to the present. However there is quite clearly a stage of sonship yet to be realized just as there is a stage to perfection yet to be realized.[73] The same argument may not apply in all areas to Luke's SP although reward and sonship are both future (ἔσται . . . ἔσεσθε) in 6:35, a passage not devoid of an eschatological context (vv. 21, 23, 25, 37-38).

The relationship between enemy love and salvation can therefore be summed up quite simply: the one "who does not love his enemy will not enter into the Kingdom of God."[74]

The Meaning of Reward in Matthew

There is no doubt that "reward" (μισθός) in Matthew's SM refers to eschatological reward.[75] This is clear from Matthew 5:12. Those who are persecuted are to rejoice because (ὅτι) their reward is great *in heaven*. However exactly what the reward consists of is not specified. Matthew only tells us who will

---

[71] Davies and Allison, *Matthew*, 1:458–59.

[72] Piper, *'Love Your Enemies,'* 197, n. 24.

[73] Cf. ibid., 87: "The disciple who obeys Jesus' command of enemy love . . . would have already begun to live as he will live in the consummated Kingdom, and therefore his behavior would be now a sign of how it will be then."

[74] Ibid., 60–61. Cf. Sir 28:6: "Remember the end of your life, and set enmity aside; remember corruption and death."

[75] See Betz, *The Sermon on the Mount*, 152.

receive it and who won't. Those who won't are those who parade their righteousness before others to see (6:1, 2, 5, 16) while those who will are those who take a humble attitude towards their piety and seek after God (6:4, 6, 18: ἀποδώσει σοι).[76] In other words in the context of the SM it is only those who exhibit the surpassing (περισσεύσῃ) righteousness of 5:20 who will be rewarded. The link should not be missed between *περισσεύσῃ* in v. 20 and τί περισσὸν ποιεῖτε in v. 47b. The latter verse parallels v. 46b: τίνα μισθὸν ἔχετε and thus makes μισθὸν and περισσὸν synonymous[77] pointing toward περισσεύσῃ righteousness. The parallels in wording and structure can be seen clearly below in vv. 46b and 47b and show that "reward" and "surpassing" are clearly synonymous suggesting therefore also a link with v. 20 and entrance into the kingdom.

Table 15: The Relationship between Reward and Surpassing Righteousness in Matthew 5

> If you love those who love you, what *reward* (μισθὸν) do you have? Do not also the tax collectors do the same thing (οὐχὶ καὶ οἱ τελῶναι τὸ αὐτὸ ποιοῦσιν) (Matt 5:46b)?
>
> If you greet your brothers only, what *surpassing* (περισσὸν) thing do you do? Do not also the Gentiles do the same thing (οὐχὶ καὶ οἱ ἐθνικοὶ τὸ αὐτὸ ποιοῦσιν) (Matt 5:47b)?
>
> Unless your righteousness *surpasses* (περισσεύσῃ) that of the Scribes and the Pharisees you will in no way enter the kingdom (Matt 5:20).

Those who merely greet their brothers have no surpassing righteousness—"What surpassing (περισσὸν) thing do you do?" The expected answer (οὐχὶ) is, no surpassing thing! When put like this, it is clear the people who love only those who love them must also lack surpassing righteousness. Except it is not termed as "surpassing thing" but "reward?" What then is the reward they lack? It must be entrance into the kingdom. Quite clearly then entering the kingdom and reward are in some sense synonymous since "surpassing" and "reward" are synonymous. The question is; does this reward consist of something in *addition* to entrance into the kingdom? The connection between vv. 20, 46b and 47b suggest not. Matthew's use of the term μισθός elsewhere also suggests the same conclusion.

---

[76] Cf. James I. McDonald, "The Concept of Reward in the Teaching of Jesus," *ExpTim* 89 (1978–79) 271.

[77] E. M. Sidebottom, "'Reward' in Matthew 5. 46, etc.," *ExpTim* 67 (1956–57) 219.

The theme of persecution, mission activity and reward are present in 5:11-12 and 10:40-42. The parallels are plainly apparent. Both contexts anticipate persecution on account of Jesus in the midst of missionary work (cf. 5:13-16).[78] Furthermore in both passages Matthew views this scenario as analogous to the prophets. As the prophets were persecuted so the disciples could expect persecution (v. 12).

Apart from the link between v. 46 and surpassing righteousness in v. 20 Matthew 5 offers little further help concerning the nature of reward. In 10:40-42 however the parallel sayings—"the one who receives *you* receives Me" (ὁ δεχόμενος ὑμᾶς ἐμὲ δέχεται) (v. 40a) and "the one who receives a prophet" (ὁ δεχόμενος προφήτην) (v. 41a)—make it likely that the prophet probably refers to the missionary disciples since "you" in v. 40a and prophet in v. 41a seem to be synonymous.[79] It may well be that the righteous (ὁ δεχόμενος δίκαιον) in v. 41b are the same as well, although this is far from certain. The important point is that those who receive (δεχόμενος) the missionaries also *will* receive (λήμψεται) a reward. Therefore since receiving a missionary is synonymous with receiving the kingdom message (v. 14), Jesus (v. 40a), and God (v. 40b) surely this suggests that the reward is nothing more than the kingdom of heaven proclaimed in v. 7.

This line of interpretation is further confirmed by the fact that the reward is a "*righteous* reward" (μισθὸν δικαίου) (v. 41b). In Matthew's last judgment scene it is the *righteous* (οἱ δίκαιοι) who will inherit the kingdom and enter into eternal life (25:34, 37, 46; cf. also 13:43, 49). Therefore 5:20 no doubt sets the pattern: those who are (surpassingly) righteous enter the kingdom; the kingdom is their reward.

Second, "whoever gives a drink (ποτίσῃ) of cold water to one of these little ones" (ἕνα τῶν μικρῶν τούτων)[80] also finds a parallel with the last judgment. Those who inherit the kingdom and enter into eternal life are those who give a drink (ἐποτίσατε) (25:35) to one of the least of Jesus' brothers (ἑνὶ τούτων τῶν ἀδελφῶν μου τῶν ἐλαχίστων) (v. 40), who incidentally turn out to be Jesus (ἐμοὶ ἐποιήσατε). The parallel with 10:40a should be obvious: "the one who receives *you* receives *Me*."[81] Matthew's last

---

[78] Eung Chun Park, *The Mission Discourse in Matthew's Interpretation*, WUNT, ed. Martin Hengel and Otfried Hofius, vol. 81 (Tübingen: Mohr, 1995) 157–58.

[79] Ibid. For the identification of "apostles" and "prophets" see *Did.* 11.3-6.

[80] Evidently scribes also noticed the parallel between Matt 10 and 25:31-46 since they inserted ἐλαχίστων τ. (D and latt), and μ. τ. τῶν ἐλαχίστων (1424 and a few other manuscripts).

[81] I shall discuss this passage (Matt 25:31-46) and its relationship to Matt 10 below but for now it is enough to acknowledge the similarities between the two.

judgment in chapter 25 therefore appears to be an explication of the reward in 10:40-42.[82]

Finally, since the ending of every one of Matthew's four other discourses (7:24-27; 13:47-50; 18:32-35; 25:31-46) clearly refer to eschatological judgment with respect to one's eternal destiny, we should also expect the same here in 10:40-42.[83]

In conclusion to this very brief study on reward in Matthew, it seems quite clear that the reward Matthew has in mind in the SM is no more than entrance into the kingdom of heaven (5:20; 7:23; cf. 25:34). In the context of the whole SM it could not be anything else. After all those who do not receive the reward are "pagans" (5:47; cf. 6:7) and "hypocrites" (vv. 2, 5, 16). Since Matthew's "hypocrites" do not enter the kingdom of heaven (23:13) and are condemned to hell (vv. 15, 33; 24:51) we can only assume that the "reward" they miss out on in the SM is salvation. What else could it be? Thus salvation in the Sermon is variously described (cf. chap. 5) as the kingdom of heaven (5:20; 7:21), treasure in heaven (6:20; cf. 19:21), and life (7:14). We may add to this list "reward"[84] and "sons of your Father in heaven"—at least in the context of the Synoptic Gospels.[85] Reward is merely another aspect of this salvation but the evidence suggests that it is something that every believer will receive and is *not* an addition to entering the kingdom.[86]

One final note; the fact that the SM reward is the *same*[87] as the reward in Matthew 10 but received for different reasons—that is, in the SM reward

---

[82] Park, *The Mission Discourse*, 162.

[83] Frederick Dale Bruner, *Matthew: A Commentary* (Dallas: Word, 1990) 663, for this observation; cf. also William R. G. Loader, *Jesus' Attitude towards the Law: A Study of the Gospels*, WUNT, ed. Martin Hengel and Otfried Hofius, vol. 97 (Tübingen: Mohr, 1997) 256; Charles H. Talbert, *Reading the Sermon on the Mount: Character Formation and Decision Making in Matthew 5–7* (Colombia, S.C.: University of South Carolina, 2004) 143.

[84] As I stated in chapter five I am not suggesting that these terms are synonymous and can merely be exchanged one for the other. Rather the variety of terms indicates the multi-faceted nature in which eternity is described. The beatitudes are a case in point describing the various blessings (Matt 5:4-9) of the kingdom (vv. 3, 10) (Piper, *'Love Your Enemies,'* 60).

[85] Ibid.; cf. p. 76 on the relationship between reward and sonship in Matt 5:46-47 and Luke 6:32-33: "if you do not obey the command to love your enemies, you will have no reward at all . . . To love your enemies is to receive the reward of sonship; not to love your enemies is to be denied the reward of sonship. The fulfilment of Jesus' love command is a condition for sonship of the heavenly Father."

[86] H. Preisker, "μισθός," in *TDNT*, 4:700, equates reward and kingdom. Cf. also David K. Lowery, "A Theology of Matthew" in *A Biblical Theology of the New Testament*, ed. Roy B. Zuck and Darrell L. Bock (Chicago: Moody, 1994) 63: reward is synonymous with enjoying being in God's presence (cf. Matt 5:8).

[87] The reward in Matt 10:40-42 must be the same as that in the SM because of the connection between 5:11-12 and chapter 10. Matthew's readers would have hardly understood μισθός in

is received for righteousness and in 10:40-42 for receiving missionaries (tantamount to receiving Jesus as in 25:35-45)—is not a contradiction. To put it another way, that the SM reward is received for "works" but the Matthew 10 reward is received for "faith" in effect is not at odds. This merely asserts what we have observed in 7:21-23: confession and doing God's will; faith and works; surpassing righteousness and receiving Jesus must complement each other. This leads us to an important point concerning the relationship between works and salvation in Matthew. *Evidently Matthew expects those who receive Jesus to also exhibit the surpassing righteousness of the SM.* Matthew 10:40-42 asserts that all one must do to receive this reward is to receive Jesus and His message. This being the case, the one who receives Jesus will obviously also exhibit surpassing righteousness and do the will of God.[88]

John Piper brings this part of our discussion to a fitting summary and conclusion:

> To become a son of God and to enter into the Kingdom of God are closely related events. One cannot be a son of God and be excluded from his Kingdom, nor can one be included in the Kingdom of God and be denied sonship. Sonship of God is a blessing which all those and only those enjoy who will enter the Kingdom of God. This is confirmed by the Matthean form of the beatitudes where to be called the sons of God (5:9) is one of the blessings of belonging to the Kingdom of heaven (5:3, 10). Consequently the reward spoken of in Jesus' rhetorical questions (Matt 5:46f par) is nothing less than entering into the kingdom of God. Accordingly the fulfilment of Jesus' love command is in some sense a condition for entering into the kingdom of God.[89]

Excursus on Reward in the New Testament

Probably the main, and certainly most "popular," passage concerning the function of rewards in the NT is 1 Corinthians 3:1-15. Based on v. 15—"if anyone's work will be burned up, he will suffer loss, but he himself will be saved and thus as through fire"—many have understood Paul to be speaking of carnal Christians (cf. vv. 1-3) who will be saved "by the skin of their teeth."[90] However a *careful* reading of this passage indicates that Paul does not

---

5:12 to be a different μισθός from the other SM references.

[88] Goppelt, *Theology of the New Testament*, 2:228–29: reward for Jesus is not the same as righteousness by works.

[89] Piper, *'Love Your Enemies,'* 76–77.

[90] For a critique of this view see Brian Borgman, "Rethinking a Much Abused Text: 1 Corinthians 3:1-15," *Reformation and Revival* 11 (2002) 71–93, esp. 86–91.

have in mind all Christians but people such as himself and Apollos—"ministers (διάκονοι) through whom you believed" (v. 5).

The tasks of these ministers are described in language reminiscent of growing a garden but the focus is on *growth*. Paul planted and Apollos watered (v. 6). The point is that there is no difference between the two since as ministers they are both one (v. 8a). Paul then states that, "each one will receive his reward according to his own labor (κόπον)" (v. 8b). The phrase "each one" refers not to the Corinthians but Paul and Apollos since Paul explains (γάρ) in v. 9: "*we* are God's fellow workers (συνεργοί)" but "*you* are God's building (οἰκοδομή)." Clearly Paul makes a distinction between himself and Apollos ("God's fellow workers") and the Corinthians ("God's building"). He changes the imagery from growing a garden to constructing a building but the focus is still on growth. But Paul and Apollos as 'gardeners' and 'builders' are *separate*, here at least, from the Corinthians who are the garden and the "building."

This becomes clearer as Paul goes on to describe the tasks of *builders*. In v. 10 he describes himself as a "wise ἀρχιτέκτων (*architect*)" who laid a foundation but there are others who have built upon it. He warns that each one must take care how he builds. Those who have to be careful how they build are those like Paul and Apollos, and presumably other ministers (διάκονοι) who are involved in this building process. The Corinthians themselves however do not seem to be involved in the process of building since *they are* the building. Thus vv. 12-15 likewise is limited to διάκονοι, gardeners and builders, not the Corinthians who are the result of *labor* (κόπου). The people in view in vv. 12-15 are those who *build* (ἐποικοδομεῖ) (v. 12) the church (see Eph 4:10-16). The *work* (τὸ ἔργον) that will be manifest and tested by fire (1 Cor 3:13) is therefore the work of the *builder* (note v. 14a: εἴ τινος τὸ ἔργον μενεῖ ὃ ἐποικοδόμησεν). It is not, and indeed cannot be, the *building*.

This is not to say though that the Christians at Corinth, and indeed all Christians, are not involved in the building process in some way. In fact Paul encourages them in their *labor* (κόπος) in 15:58. Hence perhaps we should not be too strict in determining who and who will not be at this judgment. However, irrespective of *who* is there, what is clear is that this is not a judgment to decide who have lived *carnal* lives so to speak and those who have lived *fruitful* lives. This is a judgment concerning solely those who have been involved in the building of the church. Hence the one who will receive or lose his reward (vv. 14b-15) refers especially to people like Paul and Apollos—διάκονοι![91] This is made clear in 4:6 where Paul states that "these things,

---

[91] Ibid., 85: "The passage has a special focus, the judgment of those who labor in God's field and build on God's building. It has, as it were, *a ministerial emphasis*" (emphasis mine); see

brothers, I have applied to *myself and Apollos* for your sakes."[92] Presumably this is why Paul is so concerned not to *labor* (κόπος) in vain (Gal 2:2; 4:11; Phil 2:16; 1 Thess 3:5).

An objection to this view however may be that even though Paul does apply this teaching to himself and Apollos he does so *for your sakes* (1 Cor 4:6). After all why devote so much space to a judgment that the Christians at Corinth may not even participate in? Do these two facts not suggest that the Corinthians will be up for reward as well? Perhaps. However the context of 1 Corinthians 3 is vital for understanding Paul's words in 4:6: "for your sakes." The reason Paul has applied this passage to himself and Apollos is because of the divisions that were infecting the Corinthian church (1:11). The cause of these divisions was due to the fact that not all agreed on who was the best teacher. They were making judgments about these men based on worldly values—eloquence, wisdom, persuasive words, etc. (2:1-5; 4:3). Hence some were following Paul and some were following Apollos (1:12; 3:4). Paul's point in these early chapters then is expressed in 1:10—he is appealing for unity. It is in this context that Paul makes his appeal. He does this by reminding the Corinthians that these men whom they are dividing over are merely "servants" (διάκονοι) (3:5a). Furthermore, God has determined their area of service (3:5b; 4:1b); they are God's servants and should be regarded as such (4:1a). In and of themselves they are nothing (3:7a). They are weak in themselves. Their power to speak comes from God (2:1-5). They do not speak according to the world's values but God's (2:6-16). Hence God is the One who produces the results (3:7b). He is therefore the One to receive the praise—not His servants. *Therefore* (ὥστε), Paul says, "judge nothing before the time; wait until the Lord comes" (4:5a). It is the Lord who will judge these men—not the Corinthians (4:5b). He will judge Paul (4:4). He will judge Apollos (cf. 4:6a). Furthermore, He will judge according to what is in each one's heart, the things that God values, not according to what the world sees and values. "And then the praise will come to each one from God" (4:5c). It is in the midst of all this that chapter 3 sits. What is its point? It is that God

---

also David E. Garland, *1 Corinthians*, BECNT, ed. Robert W. Yarbrough and Robert H. Stein (Grand Rapids: Baker, 2003) 104–21, esp. 104, 117–19.

[92] For a similar argument see F. W. Grosheide, *Commentary on the First Epistle to the Corinthians*, NICNT, ed. N. B. Stonehouse (Grand Rapids: Eerdmans, 1953) 88: "Vs. 15 does not speak of all men in general but of teachers only." Cf. also Jay Shanor, "Paul as Master Builder: Construction Terms in First Corinthians," *NTS* 34 (1988) 461–71; more recently Borgman, "Rethinking a Much Abused Text," 71–93, esp. 82–85. One should also see Craig A. Evans, "How are the Apostles Judged? A Note on 1 Corinthians 3:10-15," *JETS* 27 (1984) 149–50: judgment takes place during the Day of the Lord. For the background of Paul's building imagery as a reference to teachers see J. Duncan M. Derrett, "Paul as Master-builder," *EvQ* 69 (1997) 129–37.

will appraise these servants for how they have served. "That appraisal awaits God's final judgment. God alone, not the Corinthians or anyone else, is the ultimate arbiter."[93]

So we can see that chapter 3 has nothing to do with judgment concerning "carnal Christians." The judgment concerns ministers and their ministry. Other NT writers probably allude to this same judgment. James 3:1 warns, "Let not many become teachers, my brothers, knowing that you will receive greater judgment." Could it be that the "greater judgment" for *teachers* is indeed outlined for us in 1 Corinthians 3. Other passages speak similarly about judgment for those in ministerial type positions. The writer of Hebrews urges his readers, "Obey your leaders and submit, for they keep watch over your souls *as those who will give an account*" (13:17; cf. also Mark 12:38-40; 1 Pet 5:3).

In 1 Corinthians 3 those ministers who gain a reward[94] are those who have used lasting building materials—gold, silver, costly stones—that is, the message of Christ crucified (1:18-25). Whereas those who lose their reward will be those who have built with perishable materials—wood, hay or straw—that is, human wisdom (1:18-25; 3:18-20). Each one's work will be shown for what it is. What then is the "work"? It certainly refers to the *methods* used in ministry. However it may also refer to the *objects* of the ministry, that is, the people themselves. In 9:1 Paul refers to the Corinthians as his "work." Indeed, elsewhere Paul describes his Christian readers as his joy and crown (1 Thess 2:19-20; Phil 4:1). They are his boast (2:16).[95] Thus the people who have received ministry may constitute part of the "work." If this is the case, presumably Paul has in mind "true" versus "false" converts[96] since some "work" will go up in flames but other "work" won't. The connection

---

[93] Garland, *1 Corinthians*, 104; cf. also 119.

[94] The reward is specified in 1 Cor 4:5 as praise from God.

[95] Along similar lines cf. ibid., 119.

[96] Also holding this view was the nineteenth-century scholar and preacher Robert Lewis Dabney, Discussions, ed. C. R. Vaughan, vol. 1 (Richmond: Presbyterian Committee of Publication, 1890–92) 553: "The building reared on this foundation by various hands is the church of Jesus Christ, taken generally; and the gold, silver, precious stones, are genuine and regenerate persons introduced into the church by the labors of wise and faithful ministers, while the wood, hay, stubble, represent spurious converts, and unconverted professors of religion, introduced into the church by less judicious laborers." Cf. Borgman, "Rethinking a Much Abused Text," 83, n. 38: "This ['work'] may well include genuine converts in contrast to spurious converts." Borgman though does not make the link between "work" in 3:13 and 9:1. If this view is correct however Paul cannot be saying that converts will be the sole criteria for which ministers will be evaluated—otherwise Jesus' ministry will go up in smoke. Ministry methods will also be taken into account and "the motives of men's hearts" (1 Cor 4:5). Thus there may be at least three criteria used—ministry methods, genuine versus false converts and motives.

between methods and the people being ministered to is not hard to see. The message of Christ crucified on the cross results in true converts (1:21; 2:5b) whereas ministry constituting human wisdom results in false converts (v. 5a). Worldly methods will be found to have produced "worldly Christians" whereas Christ-centered-cross-saturated ministry will be found to have produced *true* Christians.

With regard to the application of this passage, Gordon Fee helpfully writes:

> This text has singular relevance to the contemporary church. It is neither a challenge to the individual believer to build his or her life well on the foundation of Christ, nor is it grist for theological debate. Rather, it is one of the most significant passages in the NT that warn—and encourage—those responsible for 'building' the church of Christ. In the final analysis, of course, this includes all believers, but it has particular relevance . . . to those with teaching/leadership responsibilities. Paul's point is unquestionably warning. It is unfortunately possible for people to attempt to build the church out of every imaginable human system predicated on merely worldly wisdom, be it philosophy, 'pop' psychology, managerial techniques, relational 'good feelings,' or what have you. But at the final judgment, all such building (and perhaps countless other forms, where systems have become more important than the gospel itself) will be shown for what it is: something merely human, with no character of Christ or his gospel in it.[97]

Finally, one may of course take the passages referring to the reception of various "crowns" as applying to rewards (1 Cor 9:25; 2 Tim 2:5; 4:8; Jas 1:12; 1 Pet 5:4; Rev 2:10; 3:11). However in all of these instances there is nothing to suggest that the crown is anything more than eternal life. Some of these passages even give some qualification indicating that all Christians receive these crowns. Most notably 2 Timothy 4:8 states that the "crown of righteousness" will be given "to all who have loved His appearing." Admittedly those who receive the crown of life in James 1:12 are those who endure. However the crown is promised "to those who love" God, which in James is *all* those whom God has chosen (2:5).[98]

---

[97] Gordon D. Fee, *The First Epistle to the Corinthians*, NICNT, ed. Gordon D. Fee (Grand Rapids: Eerdmans, 1997) 145.

[98] Cf. Craig L. Blomberg, "Degrees of Reward in the Kingdom of Heaven?," *JETS* 35 (1992) 163–64; Schreiner and Caneday, *The Race Set Before Us*, 83–86, 114.

Enemy Love in the Rest of the New Testament

John Piper has observed that the early church[99] also followed Jesus in linking enemy love with eternal salvation. This does not take away from the priority of God's work in salvation (see e.g., Matt 18:21-35 and discussion below) but merely takes seriously what Jesus said in the SM/P concerning enemy love and future reward.[100] Paul teaches that anyone who practices (πράσσοντες: present tense stressing ongoing enmity) enmity (ἔχθραι) will not inherit the kingdom of God (Gal 5:20-21). Peter's readers are exhorted to love their enemies[101] with the incentive that they "might inherit (κληρονομήσητε; cf. 1:4) a blessing" (1 Pet 3:9). Just what this blessing is, is explained and confirmed (γάρ) further in vv. 10-12 (citing Psalm 34:13-17) as peace, life, seeing good days, and being seen by God. Not surprisingly those who inherit this blessing—and thus love their enemy—are called "righteous" whereas those who don't are called "evil" (1 Pet 3:12).[102] According to Peter then one must refrain from getting back at their enemies if they are to inherit their blessing, which is tantamount to eschatological salvation[103] (cf. 1:4).[104]

Once again, as we have repeatedly observed elsewhere, ethics and eschatology appear in close relation. But the close relationship is explainable and quite legitimate theologically. For example, Paul asserts that, "faith works (ἐνεργουμένη) through love" (Gal 5:6b). Logically then if love comes via faith it is patently inconceivable that one who practices the opposite of love, that is, enmity, and thus evidently has no faith, could inherit the kingdom. Similarly for Peter, it is only because believers have been "born again" through the Word of God that they are now able to truly love each other and do away with traits contrary to enemy love (1 Pet 1:22–2:1). "The priority of divine saving work is stressed in each case."[105]

---

[99] Cf. also Rom 12:14, 17; 1 Cor 4:12; 1 Thess 5:15.

[100] Ibid., 61.

[101] I.e., "Do not repay evil for evil or abuse for abuse, but on the contrary bless" (1 Pet 3:9; cf. Matt 5:44; Luke 6:28).

[102] See ibid., 61, 123–24.

[103] Dillow, *Servant Kings*, 86, interprets κληρονομίαν in 1 Pet 1:4 as the millennial kingdom in contrast to salvation/deliverance from hell. However Dillow is surely incorrect since Peter uses three synonyms in vv. 3-5, each clearly preceded by the preposition εἰς to describe the eschatological salvation that awaits all those who have been born again. Believers have been regenerated εἰς ἐλπίδα ζῶσαν . . . εἰς κληρονομίαν . . . εἰς σωτηρίαν ἑτοίμην ἀποκαλυφθῆναι ἐν καιρῷ ἐσχάτῳ. The inheritance is nothing more and nothing less than the "living hope" and the "*salvation* ready to be revealed in the last time."

[104] Piper, 'Love Your Enemies,' 124–28.

[105] Ibid., 61: "As in Jesus' teaching there is a reward for loving your enemies, but it is not a reward of mere human achievement." On the question of enemy love being a condition to enter the kingdom see Piper's excellent discussion on 76–80.

Forgiveness in Matthew 18:21-35

The parable of the "unmerciful servant" (NIV) is linked together by ἀφίημι in vv. 21, 27, 32, and 35, and the term ἀδελφός forms an inclusio with vv. 21 and 35.[106] Hence the subject of the parable is *forgiving* a *brother*. The need for the parable probably first arose out of Jesus' instruction concerning disciplining a brother. The scenario presented in v. 15 involves a "brother" (ἀδελφός) who "might sin" (ἁμαρτήσῃ) against another brother. Recalling this scenario Peter questions Jesus in v. 21: "How many times shall my *brother* (ἀδελφός) *sin* (ἁμαρτήσει) against me and I will *forgive* (ἀφήσω) him?" Hence the terms "brother" and "sin" provide a link between the instructions on discipline in vv. 15-20 and Peter's question on *forgiveness* in v. 21. Peter's question on forgiveness in turn provides a link with the ensuing parable in vv. 23-35.[107] Thus the parable provides a warning (v. 35) to those who fail to forgive a wayward brother that subsequently repents (or not?) and desires to be reinstated.[108] However in its immediate context the parable provides follow up instruction to Peter's question concerning how often he should forgive a sinning brother.

Peter's question betrays his incorrect, though thoroughly Jewish,[109] thinking concerning the matter. He wonders if "up to (ἕως) seven times" is enough (v. 21) as if there is a limit to the amount of times one may forgive a sinning brother.[110] Jesus' reply (note again the use of ἕως) may be taken as "seventy seven times" or "seventy times seven" (v. 22). Either way His point is the same: forgiveness is unlimited.[111] It doesn't matter how many times a brother might sin against you; forgive him every time (cf. Luke 17:3-4).[112] But to merely tell someone to practice forgiveness ad infinitum is not enough. Jesus must instruct Peter on the theology of forgiveness, that is, forgiveness

---

[106] D. Hermant, "Structure littéraire du 'Discours communautaire' de Matthieu 18," *Revue Biblique* 103 (1996) 85; see also Davies and Allison, *Matthew*, 2:750–51.

[107] See ibid., 86.

[108] Petri Luomanen, *Entering the Kingdom of Heaven: A Study on the Structure of Matthew's View of Salvation* (Tübingen: Mohr, 1998) 258.

[109] Cf. e.g., Gen 4:15; Lev 16; 26:18; Prov 24:16; 4Q511.2.35; Str-B 1:795–97.

[110] Bruner, *Matthew*, 656.

[111] Davies and Allison, *Matthew*, 2:793: "both numbers amount to the same thing. One is not being commanded to count but to forgive without counting."

[112] A similar dialogue appears in *The Gospel of the Nazaraeans* §13: "'If your brother has sinned in word against you and has made satisfaction, forgive him up to seven times a day.' Simon, his disciple, said to him, 'Seven times?' The Lord answered saying, 'Verily I say to you: until seventy times seven!'"

toward a (Christian) brother[113] is based on the fact that God has forgiven those in His kingdom (cf. Matt 18:23a).[114]

Thus the parable explains further the reason (note διὰ τοῦτο in v. 23) why forgiveness is to be unlimited. Jesus compares the kingdom of heaven to a king "who desired to settle accounts with his slaves" (v. 23). One debtor (ὀφειλέτης) was brought to him who owed an "incalculable"[115] amount of money (v. 24). However he was unable to pay (ἀποδοῦναι) so the master (ὁ κύριος) ordered that he and his whole family be sold along with their possessions to repay the debt (v. 25). The slave (ὁ δοῦλος) begged (πεσὼν . . . προσεκύνει): "Be patient with me and all things I will repay to you" (μακροθύμησον ἐπ' ἐμοί, καὶ πάντα ἀποδώσω σοι) (v. 26). The master responded with compassion (σπλαγχνισθεὶς) and released (ἀπέλυσεν) him and *forgave* (ἀφῆκεν) him the debt (v. 27).

The parable moves onto a new scene. This same slave (note ὁ δοῦλος ἐκεῖνος) found one of his fellow slaves (συνδούλων) who owed (ὤφειλεν) him one hundred denarii. He coerced him to repay what he owed (v. 28) but he was unable. He begged (note again πεσὼν . . . παρεκάλει) for patience: "be patient with me and I will repay you" (μακροθύμησον ἐπ' ἐμοί, καὶ ἀποδώσω σοι) (v. 29). However unlike his master this slave had no patience and evidently no compassion for "he did desire" (ὁ δὲ οὐκ ἤθελεν) to forgive. Instead of releasing his fellow-slave—as he himself had been released (ἀπέλυσεν) in v. 27—he departed (ἀπελθὼν)[116] and cast the slave into prison *until* (ἕως)[117] he paid what he owed (v. 30).

Except for the size of the debt of course the second slave's situation is strikingly similar to that of the first. Both are slaves (note σύνδουλος in vv. 28-29). Both are debtors (vv. 24, 28: ὀφειλ–) who are unable to repay (vv. 25, 29: ἀποδ–). Both beg (v. 26: πεσὼν οὖν ὁ δοῦλος προσεκύνει αὐτῷ λέγων; cf. v. 29: μακροθύμησον ἐπ' ἐμοί, καὶ ἀποδώσω σοι) for patience so that they might find the means to pay what they owe (vv. 26, 29: μακροθύμησον ἐπ' ἐμοί, καὶ . . . ἀποδώσω σοι). No doubt these similarities serve to show the enigmatic not to mention horrifying nature of the first slave's response to his fellow slave's dilemma. The fact that the amount, a

---

[113] Here ἀδελφός is more likely to refer to a Christian brother (Davies and Allison, *Matthew*, 1:782; Carter, *Matthew and the Margins*, 367; contra, BDAG, 19; see the discussion above on Matt 5:21-26).

[114] Bruner, *Matthew*, 657: "the parable gives the foundation of a *theology* of forgiveness to support the *ethic* of forgiveness just now required of Peter; the parable will illustrate why Jesus can require infinite forgiveness of us—namely, because we have been infinitely forgiven."

[115] BDAG, 661: "zillions of talents" (μυρίων ταλάντων).

[116] Note the play on words with ἀπέλυσεν in v. 27.

[117] Cf. Peter's question in v. 21: ἕως ἑπτάκις.

hundred denarii, is a mere ripple in the ocean compared to the zillion talents makes this slave's response even more deplorable. The following table highlights the comparisons:

Table 16: A Comparison of the Slaves in Matthew 18:21-35

First Slave	Second Slave
One owed zillions of talents. εἷς ὀφειλέτης μυρίων ταλάντων (v. 24).	One . . . who owed him one hundred denarii. ἕνα . . . ὃς ὤφειλεν αὐτῷ ἑκατὸν δηνάρια (v. 28).
Then falling prostrate, the slave said to him, "be patient with me, and I will repay you everything." πεσὼν οὖν ὁ δοῦλος προσεκύνει αὐτῷ λέγων· μακροθύμησον ἐπ' ἐμοί, καὶ πάντα ἀποδώσω σοι (v. 26).	Then falling his slave exhorted him saying, "be patient with me, and I will repay you." πεσὼν οὖν ὁ σύνδουλος αὐτοῦ παρεκάλει αὐτὸν λέγων· μακροθύμησον ἐπ' ἐμοί, καὶ ἀποδώσω σοι (v. 29).
Being compassionate the master released his slave and forgave him his debt. σπλαγχνισθεὶς δὲ ὁ κύριος τοῦ δούλου ἐκείνου ἀπέλυσεν αὐτὸν καὶ τὸ δάνειον ἀφῆκεν αὐτῷ (v. 27).	But he did not desire [to forgive his slave], but going out he threw him into prison until he might pay back the debt. ὁ δὲ οὐκ ἤθελεν ἀλλὰ ἀπελθὼν ἔβαλεν αὐτὸν εἰς φυλακὴν ἕως ἀποδῷ τὸ ὀφειλόμενον (v. 30).

That virtually identical situations can produce completely divergent responses causes the other slaves grief so they report it to their master (v. 31). The master calls the slave whom he forgave and addresses him: "You evil slave" (δοῦλε πονηρέ) (cf. 25:26). He responds emphatically focusing the slave's attention on the size of the debt: "All that debt (πᾶσαν τὴν ὀφειλὴν) I forgave (ἀφῆκά) you because you exhorted me" (v. 32). This slave had been forgiven a sizeable debt that should have spurred him on to a similar response when he encountered his fellow-slave. This is the point of v. 33 and the whole parable. It is the theology behind Jesus' reply to Peter. It is the reason brothers should forgive brothers ad infinitum irrespective of how many times they might be on the receiving end of their sin. The forgiven slave should have shown mercy (ἐλεῆσαι) to his fellow slave (σύνδουλόν) as also the master showed mercy (ἠλέησα) to him (v. 33). The master's response in v. 34 is in marked contrast to his first response in v. 27. Rather than being compassionate (σπλαγχνισθεὶς) this master is now angry (ὀργισθείς). Rather than releasing (ἀπέλυσεν) this slave he hands him over (παρέδωκεν). Rather than receiving mercy this slave will now be tortured by merciless jailers (βασανισταῖς).[118] And rather than being forgiven (τὸ δάνειον ἀφῆκεν αὐτῷ) this slave is now obligated to repay "all the debt" (ἕως οὗ ἀποδῷ πᾶν τὸ ὀφειλόμενον). These similarities and differences are compared in the table below:

Table 17: A Comparison of the Master's Responses in Matthew 18:31-35

The Master's First Response (Matt 18:27)	The Master's Second Response (Matt 18:34)
And being compassionate. Σπλαγχνισθεὶς δὲ.	And being angry. Καὶ ὀργισθεὶς.
The master released that slave. ὁ κύριος τοῦ δούλου ἐκείνου ἀπέλυσεν.	His master handed him over to torturers. ὁ κύριος αὐτοῦ παρέδωκεν αὐτὸν τοῖς βασανισταῖς.
And he forgave him his debt. αὐτὸν καὶ τὸ δάνειον ἀφῆκεν αὐτῷ.	Until he might repay everything he owed. ἕως οὗ ἀποδῷ πᾶν τὸ ὀφειλόμενον.

Jesus gives the lesson of the parable in v. 35 with particular reference to v. 34 (οὕτως καὶ) and the fate of the unforgiving slave. The characters of the parable are now made clear. The king or the master is—surprisingly—God.[119] The slave who was forgiven an incalculable debt represents every person who has been forgiven by God. His attitude towards a fellow slave pictures a brother unwilling to forgive a fellow brother who sins against him (vv. 15, 21) in spite of the fact that he himself has experienced God's incalculable forgiveness. The warning is chilling. God will do to each individual what the master did to the unforgiving slave if they do not sincerely—that is, from the heart (ἀπὸ τῶν καρδιῶν)[120]—*forgive their brother.* Unforgiveness is unacceptable in God's kingdom (cf. v. 23). Forgiveness is to be practiced ad infinitum. God

---

[118] Ibid., 168.

[119] Surprising according to Warren Carter, "Resisting and Imitating the Empire: Imperial Paradigms in Two Matthean Parables," *Interpretation* 56 (2002) 262–68: based on Matthew's negative portrayal of kings (2:4-8, 16-18; 6:29; 10:18; 14:1-12; 17:24-27; 20:25-28) and 18:23b-26 Carter suggests that the tyrant and fickle king of this parable is deliberately contrasted with Matthew's faithful (1:1-17) and gracious God (5:45). Yet the king's final act of punishing the unforgiving slave is now said to *resemble* what God will do to those who do not demonstrate forgiveness—"suddenly a similarity is established" (268).

[120] BDAG, 508.

has shown *compassion* on sinners and *released* and *forgiven* their *incalculable debt*. Hence the *beneficiary* of forgiveness should also become the *benefactor*.

The Relationship between Forgiveness and Salvation in Matthew 18:21-35

This passage perhaps like no other demonstrates that "Salvation in Matthew (and Mark and Luke) is by sheer mercy apart from a *prior* condition of good works."[121] Notice the terms that can be applied to God in this parable. God is patient (v. 26), compassionate (v. 27), and merciful (v. 33). He releases people from the enormity of their sin and forgives them from what they would otherwise owe (v. 27).

Notice also the terms used to describe the recipients of God's lavish forgiveness (vv. 26, 29). These recipients recognize their helplessness before God. The term πεσὼν (πίπτω) expresses humility (v. 26; cf. 2:11; 4:9),[122] προσεκύνει (προσκυνέω) denotes "one's complete dependence on or submission to a high authority figure" (18:26; cf. 8:2; 9:18; 15:25)[123] and παρεκάλει (παρακαλέω) here (v. 29) conveys the sense of "implore" (cf. also 8:31).[124] This sheds light on Mary's declaration in Luke 1:50, now quite understandable, "His mercy is from generation to generation *to those who fear Him*." This kind of attitude is exhibited in one who is "poor in spirit" (Matt 5:3) and "humble as a child" (18:4). It is evident in Peter who, after being confronted by the miraculous power of Jesus, fell (προσέπεσεν) before the knees of Jesus, and said, "Depart from me for I am a sinful man" (Luke 5:8). This attitude is also seen in the sinful woman who stood before Jesus' feet, wet His feet with her tears and kissed His feet (7:38). Tax collectors and sinners display such an attitude but yet it is strikingly absent among the religious scribes and Pharisees (Luke 15:1-2). Furthermore it is those who humbly beg for mercy that will receive it (Matt 9:27; 15:22; 17:15; 20:30, 31; Luke 18:13-14) while those who do not perceive they need it will not (18:11-12). After all it is not those who are righteous who need a doctor and recognize their need for God's forgiveness but sinners who are sick (Matt 9:12-13 par.). However to wait until the afterlife to beg for mercy is too late (Luke 16:24-26). This leads us to an important observation regarding the relationship between forgiveness and eternal salvation. In the parable of the unmerciful slave

---

[121] Bruner, *Matthew*, 660 (emphasis mine). "Prior" meaning pre-conversion works.
[122] BDAG, 815.
[123] Ibid., 882.
[124] Ibid., 765.

God's forgiveness *precedes* the slave's forgiveness of his brother.[125] Patently forgiveness does not earn one a place in eternity.

However it is also clear in this parable (see 18:35) that there is a relationship between God's forgiveness and man's.[126] God will not forgive those who do not forgive others. The parable recalls Jesus' words in 6:14-15: "If you do forgive men their trespasses, your heavenly Father will also forgive you. But if you not forgive men [their trespasses], neither will your Father forgive your trespasses" (cf. Mark 11:25).[127] The warning of Matthew 6:15 anticipates the warning of 18:35.[128] The only difference between the two is that v. 35 has an "ecclesial" (cf. vv. 15-18) as opposed to a "universal" focus.[129] Furthermore the outcome for those who are unforgiving is expressed differently. 6:15 states what God will *not* do. He will not forgive. Matthew 18:35 states what He will do. He will condemn.[130] Expressed positively or negatively both express the same point: God will treat the unforgiving person with the same unforgiving attitude (cf. 7:2; Gal 6:7). There "are accountability and punitive consequences for ignoring God's will."[131]

What though will these "punitive consequences be?" How exactly will God treat those who refuse to show mercy and forgiveness to others? The imagery from Matthew 18:34 suggests nothing less than "the eternal damnation to be meted out at the final judgment"[132] or in the words of one commentator, "hellfire."[133] There are several reasons why this is so. First, τοῖς βασανισταῖς connotes "torturers."[134] The βασαν– word group often occurs in the context of eternal judgment (cf. esp. Luke 16:23, 28; Rev 14:10, 11;

---

[125] Piper, *'Love Your Enemies,'* 60.

[126] William Klassen, *The Forgiving Community* (Philadelphia: Westminster, 1966) 149–52.

[127] Sirach 28:2: "Forgive your neighbor the wrong he has done, and then your sins will be pardoned when you pray."

[128] Martinus C. De Boer, "Ten Thousand Talents: Matthew's Interpretation and Redaction of the Parable of the Unforgiving Servant (Matt 18:23-35)" *CBQ* 50 (1988) 221.

[129] Ibid.

[130] Ibid.

[131] Carter, "Resisting and Imitating the Empire," 268.

[132] De Boer, 221, 229; Davies and Allison, *Matthew*, 2:803: "eschatological judgment"; contra Dillow, *Servant Kings*, 384: "Temporal relationships are in view. If we fail to forgive our brother from the heart, God will bring severe divine *discipline* on us in time and withhold temporal forgiveness for fellowship in the family" (emphasis mine). However Dillow uses 1 John, *not* Matthew, to buttress his argument. Second, he begins from a theological, not an exegetical, framework. That is, he argues that salvation is based on works and therefore "ultimately throws the burden of achieving our final destiny back on us" (383).

[133] Keener, *A Commentary on the Gospel of Matthew*, 461.

[134] See W. Mundle, "Torment," in *NIDNTT*, 3:856; Rev 20:10.

20:10).¹³⁵ Matthew 8:29 is especially telling. Confronted with the power of Jesus some demons ask, "Have you come here to torture (βασανίσαι) us *before the time* (πρὸ καιροῦ)?" There is little doubt that by using the phrase πρὸ καιροῦ the demons are thinking of the eschatological judgment that awaits the devil and his angels (25:41).¹³⁶ Thus eternal punishment is in view in 18:34.¹³⁷ Second, the future tense of the verb ποιήσει (Matt 18:35) indicates final judgment¹³⁸ (cf. also 21:40; Mark 12:9; Luke 18:8). Third, the label "evil slave" (δοῦλε πονηρέ) (Matt 18:32) is reversed to designate the unfaithful steward in 25:26 (πονηρέ δοῦλε) whose eternal destiny is "outer darkness where there will be weeping and gnashing of teeth" (v. 30). This is a common description in Matthew (see also Luke 13:28) for hell, the place of eternal torment¹³⁹ (see 8:12; 13:42, 50; 22:13; 24:51; 25:30; cf. Ps 112:10; Luke 6:25b).¹⁴⁰ In conclusion there seems little doubt that Matthew 18:34-35 (cf. also 6:14-15; Mark 11:25) is ultimately referring to eschatological forgiveness with eternal consequences.¹⁴¹

---

[135] Gundry, *Matthew*, 375: "The giving of the king's debtor to 'the torturers' stands for consignment to the punishment of hell."

[136] The phrase πρὸ καιροῦ also occurs in 1 Cor 4:5 to denote the eschatological *time* of judgment at the Lord's coming (cf. Matt 16:3; 1 Peter 5:6). See BDAG, 498.

[137] Marius Reiser, *Jesus and Judgment: The Eschatological Proclamation in Its Jewish Context*, trans. Linda M. Maloney (Minneapolis: Fortress, 1997) 279; Sim, *The Gospel of Matthew*, 139: the "eschatological usage of the verb in [Matt] 8:29 corresponds precisely with the meaning of the nominal cognate in 18:34."

[138] Davies and Allison, *Matthew*, 2:803.

[139] Sim, *The Gospel of Matthew*, 139-40; Carson, "Matthew," 203; see also Reiser, *Jesus and Judgment*, 236-39.

[140] Contra Zane C. Hodges, *Grace in Eclipse: A Study on Eternal Rewards* (Dallas: Redención, 1985) 89-90; Dillow, *Servant Kings*, 385-96. Dillow's (and Hodge's) suggestion that the place of weeping and gnashing of teeth is a place for carnal Christians is hardly convincing since Matt 24:51 makes it plain that also in this place will be "*the* hypocrites." In Matthew ὑποκριτής, in all but possibly one instance (7:5, but even here doubtful), refers to unbelievers (note esp. 23:13). They are invariably made up of those of the Jewish leadership (15:7; 22:18; 23:13, 15, 23, 25, 27, 29, 51; cf. also 6:2, 5, 16). It is these hypocrites that Matthew almost certainly has in mind in 24:51 given the presence of the article and the proximity of v. 51 to chapter 23 (cf. also 6:2, 5, 16). Furthermore in 13:41-42 those who go to the place of "weeping and gnashing of teeth" are those who commit *lawlessness,* who in Matthew experience eternal separation from Christ (7:23). Finally, in 13:41-43, 49, those who are *righteous* are distinguished from those who do lawlessness and the wicked. Only the former groups go into eternal life in 25:46. It therefore seems highly unlikely that the latter group might have any share in eternal life in chapter 13.

[141] See also Sim, *The Gospel of Matthew*, 138-39. Furthermore, the sheer size of the debt suggests repayment was highly unlikely and therefore the imprisonment would have been permanent.

Forgiveness in the Rest of the New Testament

Of course now we are faced with somewhat of a theological conundrum. If God is patient, compassionate, merciful, and forgiving, how is it that He will not act in this way toward those who are not so patient, compassionate, merciful and forgiving? Is it not a contradiction in terms to suggest that God's forgiveness is conditional upon mans' (cf. 6:14-15)?[142] It may be that for some there is no satisfactory way to resolve this tension. Nevertheless the tension here is really no different from a believer's responsibility to forgive on the one hand (18: 21-35) and to correct sin on the other (vv. 15-20).[143] Without this tension one could become a pacifist or antagonist, neither of which are biblical.[144] Evidently if God's character is compassionate, patient, merciful, and forgiving, then those who belong to His kingdom must also exhibit the same qualities. Those who do not cannot expect to participate in His kingdom. After all Paul does say, "Behold then the kindness and severity of God: severity toward those who have fallen, but kindness toward you, *if you continue*[145] *in His kindness*; otherwise you also will be cut off" (Rom 11:22).[146] This does not suggest that forgiveness can be earned; this parable teaches quite clearly that it cannot (see above). However the Bible leaves no doubt that the unmerciful will not receive God's mercy and vice versa when it comes time for judgment (see esp. Matt 25:31-46). Proverbs 17:5 (LXX): "the one who is compassionate will be shown mercy (ἐλεηθήσεται)" (cf. 14:21). Matthew 5:7: "Blessed are those who are merciful (οἱ ἐλεήμονες) for they will be shown mercy" (ἐλεηθήσονται). James sums things up in 2:13: "Judgment (κρίσις) is without mercy (ἀνέλεος) to those who do not show mercy (ἔλεος); mercy (ἔλεος) triumphs over judgment (κρίσεως)."[147] James demonstrates the seriousness of the situation by linking judgment with mercy. Although not directly apparent in v. 13, 4:12 clarifies the nature of the judgment, that is, eschatological judgment vis-à-vis heaven and hell[148] (cf. esp. Matt 10:28; 25:31-46). This certainly fits with what we have observed

---

[142] This is Dillow's (*Servant Kings*, 383) concern.

[143] Davies and Allison, *Matthew*, 2:793.

[144] Jerome Rausch, "The Principle of Nonresistance and Love of Enemy in Mt 5, 38–48," *CBQ* 28 (1966) 31–41.

[145] That is, "if you *practice* God's kindness." For this use of ἐπιμένω see Rom 6:1; 1 Tim 4:16.

[146] Reiser, *Jesus and Judgment*, 279.

[147] Cf. Tob 4:10: "almsgiving delivers from death and keeps you from going into the Darkness."

[148] Cf. Buist M. Fanning, "A Theology of James," In *A Biblical Theology of the New Testament*, ed. Roy B. Zuck and Darrell L. Bock (Chicago: Moody, 1994) 425.

concerning the close relationship between ethics and eschatology in the NT as a whole. I shall discuss this more in chapter eleven.

It may be that we are still caught in a 'theological' conundrum but all that I have said in the aforementioned paragraph does not contradict anything that Jesus Himself taught. In fact it fits in well with His teaching on judgment for judgment and measure for measure (7:2). Matthew 18:35 is then a fundamental teaching of Jesus: in the same way that one treats others God too will treat that person *in the final judgment*. Therefore it is with all seriousness and urgency that Jesus' hearers are urged to be merciful as God is merciful (Luke 6:36; cf. 1 John 4:11). This is exegetically consistent. God's people must forgive as He has forgiven them. Far from being a contradiction in terms, failure to forgive "creates an intolerable inconsistency at the very point where the kingdom is to manifest itself: in the community of the redeemed, living in a fallen world."[149] In other words, one cannot receive and experience God's unlimited grace—as demonstrated to the first servant—and not in turn *want* to show that grace to others.[150] Furthermore, one cannot be the recipient of such grace, treat others without mercy and still expect to receive divine grace (cf. e.g., 2 Kgs 24:4; Amos 5:2-3, 6-7, 10-12, 16-20, 27; Zech 7:18-14).

Finally, by going over ground already covered we may approach the relationship between treating others and salvation from another angle. Matthew 7:21 states that it is only those who do the *will* of God that will enter the kingdom of heaven. We have already observed that the core of God's will in Matthew consists of *mercy* (9:13; 12:7; cf. Hos 6:6; see chap. 6). Working backwards then we can see that the NT's teaching on judgment and mercy is really quite consistent with Matthew 7:21. Those who, like the evil slave, do not demonstrate mercy are not at the same time doing the Father's will—and those who do not do God's will are not able to enter the kingdom (cf. 18:23-25). They do not exhibit the surpassing righteousness (5:20; cf. vv. 21-48) necessary to enter. As an aside, this explains why Jesus excludes them from membership in His (spiritual) family (12:49-50). Here we are not far from the lessons of the Good Samaritan (esp. Luke 10:36).

---

[149] Donald A. Hagner, *Matthew 14–28*, WBC, ed. David A. Hubbard and Glenn W. Barker, vol. 33B (Dallas: Word, 1995) 541; see also Robert Farrar Capon, *The Parables of Grace* (Grand Rapids: Eerdmans, 1988) 40–50.

[150] James D. G. Dunn, *Jesus Remembered*, vol. 1, Christianity in the Making, (Grand Rapids: Eerdmans, 2003) 589–92.

Some Concluding Comments

These passages may be some of the hardest to understand theologically although they are some of the easiest to explain, in my opinion, with respect to the relationship between works and salvation. Quite simply, at judgment time people will be treated in the same way they have treated others and the consequences will be eternal. There are various ways in which we could explain this relationship. One is that Jesus adheres to a measure for measure type principle and somehow this is not at odds with His initiating grace and forgiveness.[151]

Another way to explain this relationship is to look at the NT on the subject of love and salvation. Jesus' teaching is in line with this and presents no problems. We have already observed that for Jesus, mercy, justice, faithfulness (Matt 23:23), and love (22:37-39; Mark 12:30-33; Luke 10:27) are the most important elements of the Law. It is not difficult to see how James could come up with a statement concerning God's judgment of the unmerciful (Jas 2:13). Although some do argue that James (and Jesus) is not discussing matters pertaining to eternal salvation the supporting evidence is scant. The early church evidently carried on this tradition to the point that we could well be excused for concluding that they believed love (including here qualities such as mercy and forgiveness) to be the defining mark of a Christian. John writes at length to make the point that love is the difference between believers and unbelievers (John 13:35; cf. also 1 John 2:9-11; 3:10, 14-15, 17; 4:7-8, 12, 20-21). Indeed for John, like Matthew and James, it is love perfected in his readers that gives them confidence on the *Day of Judgment* (4:17;[152] cf. 2:28; Matt 7:21-23; 18:33-35; 25:31-46; Jas 2:12-13). Paul believes that "faith working through love" is what matters (Gal 5:6; cf. 6:7-10; 1 Cor 13:13). The writer of Hebrews expresses confidence in his readers' salvation because they have demonstrated love to the saints (Heb 6:9-10). True religion for James consists of showing concern for orphans and widows (Jas 1:27), showing no partiality (2:1-4), and attending to the physical needs of others (vv. 15-16). Peter states that, "love covers a multitude of sins" (1 Pet 4:8).[153] Jude urges

---

[151] On the *responsibilities* that salvation brings vis-à-vis "public" relationships see *What Does It Mean To Be Saved: Broadening Evangelical Horizons of Salvation*, ed. John G. Stackhouse Jr. (Grand Rapids: Baker, 2002). This book is a timely reminder that salvation is not just a public affair, though this is not to deny that there are personal dimensions to salvation, e.g., 117.

[152] A believer stands confident at the judgment because he has God's love within him (1 John 4:16) though for John one who has God's love in him also loves others (esp. 3:17). On 1 John 4:17 see Colin G. Kruse, *The Letters of John*, PNTC, ed. D. A. Carson (Grand Rapids: Eerdmans, 2000) 166–67.

[153] What is not clear however is "whose sins are covered?" For the various options see the commentaries. James appears to have understood the phrase as eternal salvation (Jas 5:20).

his readers to "keep themselves in the love of God while they await the mercy of our Lord Jesus Christ into eternal life" (Jude 21). The next passage in this study gives unflinching support to this tradition.

11

The Role of *Judgment* in Salvation

Then the King will say to those on His right, 'come who are blessed by My Father, inherit the kingdom which has been prepared for you from the foundation of the world. For I was hungry and you gave Me (food) to eat; I was thirsty and you gave me (water) to drink; I was a stranger and you received Me as a guest; I was poorly dressed and you clothed Me; I was sick and you visited Me; I was in prison and you came to Me' . . . Then He will say to those on His left, 'depart from Me accursed ones into the eternal fire prepared for the devil and his angels. For I was hungry and you did not give Me (food) to eat; I was thirsty and you did not give me (water) to drink; I was a stranger and you did not receive Me as a guest; I was poorly dressed and you did not clothe Me; I was sick and in prison and you did not visit Me' . . . and they will go into eternal punishment and the righteous will go into eternal life (Matt 25:34-36, 41-43, 46).

The Sheep and the Goats: Salvation by Works?

IN one sense the Sheep and the Goats scene is very straightforward.[1] The Son of Man judges "all the nations" on the basis of their treatment of the least of Jesus' "brothers." Those who have been benevolent receive eternal life and vice-versa. Straightforward though this passage may appear, it certainly has not suffered from lack of examination. Questions concerning the identity of "all the nations" (v. 32) and "the least of these My brothers" (v. 40), have engendered a plethora of literature.[2] Yet in spite of a long history of interpre-

---

[1] Note D. A. Carson, "Matthew," in *EBC*, ed. Frank E. Gaebelein and J. D. Douglas, vol. 8 (Grand Rapids: Zondervan, 1984) 518: "Almost everyone praises the simplicity . . . of the passage."

[2] Some of the more recent articles include, Eugene W. Pond, "The Background and Timing of the Judgment of the Sheep and the Goats," *Bsac* 159 (2002) 201–20; idem, "Who Are The Sheep and Goats in Matthew 25:31-46?" *Bsac* 159 (2002) 288–302; idem, "Who Are 'The Least' of Jesus' Brothers in Matthew 25:31-46?" *Bsac* 159 (2002) 436–48; John Paul

tation³ it is still being said that, "there is no present consensus regarding the meaning."⁴

The passage is especially significant for our study since even a casual glance reveals an ostensive relationship between works and salvation.⁵ In fact the Spanish theologian Juan Maldonado (AD 1533–83) wrote over half a millennium ago, "If there were no other passage but this, it would be clear that eternal life is given not only after works but because of works, and is therefore truly and properly a reward."⁶ It is somewhat surprising that more has not been said concerning this relationship in the passage's 1700 years of interpretation. Such discussions not surprisingly have largely been confined to the sixteenth century.⁷ Here a range of views can be found. Ulrich Zwingli (AD 1484–1531) maintained that salvation could not be by works since it was

---

Heil, "The Double Meaning of the Narrative of Universal Judgment in Matthew 25:31-46," *JSNT* 69 (1998) 3–14; Graham Foster, "Making Sense of Matthew 25:31-46," *Scottish Bulletin of Evangelical Theology* 16 (1998) 128–39; Robert L. Thomas, "Jesus' View of Eternal Punishment," *The Master's Seminary Journal* 9 (1998) 147–67; Kathleen Weber, "The Image of the Sheep and the Goats in Matthew 25:31-46," *CBQ* 59 (1997) 657–78.

³ Sherman W. Gray, *The Least of My Brothers, Matthew 25:31-46: A History of Interpretation*, Society of Biblical Literature Dissertation Series, ed. J. J. M. Roberts, vol. 114 (Atlanta: Scholars Press, 1989), surveys the history of interpretation on this passage beginning with the apostolic fathers up until the 1980's. However, it is not until the fourth and fifth centuries that Gray finds any substantial interpretation of this passage still giving it 1700 years of critical examination. For a more recent survey of interpretation see, Ulrich Luz, *Das Evangelium nach Matthäus*, vol. 3, Evangelisch-Katholischer Kommentar zum Neuen Testament, ed. Norbert Brox et al. (Zurich: Benziger, 1997) 521–30.

⁴ Heil, "The Double Meaning," 3; cf. also John R. Donahue, "The 'Parable' of the Sheep and the Goats: A Challenge of Christian Ethics," *Theological Studies* 47 (1986) 13; Graham N. Stanton, *A Gospel for a New People: Studies in Matthew* (Edinburgh: T. & T. Clark, 1992) 207. Gray, *The Least of My Brothers*, 255, notes for the twentieth century thirty-two "variously nuanced positions" vis-à-vis the identity of "all nations" and "my brothers."

⁵ Cf. Craig S. Keener, *A Commentary on the Gospel of Matthew* (Grand Rapids: Eerdmans, 1999) 604: "the passage explicitly declares that this judgment determines people's *eternal* destinies"; Victor Kossi Agbanou, *Le Discours Eschatologique de Matthieu 24–25: Tradition et Rédaction*, Études Bibliques, vol. 2 (Paris: Lecoffre, 1983) 171: "L'objet essentiel de cet enseignement est la pratique de l'amour dans le quotidien de la vie ordinaire: l'amour du prochain explique l'être-chrétien, la suite du Christ, en même temps qu'il détermine le sort futur de chacun"; H. Benedict Green, *The Gospel According to Matthew in the Revised Standard Version: Introduction and Commentary*, The New Clarendon Bible (NT), ed. H. F. D. Sparks (Oxford: Oxford University Press, 1975) 207: "The context makes clear that the basis of the judgement is their [i.e., the righteous] actions and not membership of the Christian community"; J. Ramsey Michaels, "Apostolic Hardships and Righteous Gentiles: A Study of Matthew 25: 31-46," *JBL* 84 (1965) 27: "This is clearly a reference to specific works of love ... but having eternal consequences."

⁶ Citation taken from Gray, *The Least of My Brothers*, 201.

⁷ See ibid., 191–240, 344.

faith in Christ that produces the works.[8] Similarly John Calvin (AD1509-64) admitted that the kingdom is a reward for good works but these works are empowered by God's grace so salvation is still by grace.[9] Against the reformers Willem Hessels van Est (AD 1542-1613) insisted that works were necessary for salvation.[10] Cornelius Otto Jansen (AD 1585-1638) took a more conciliatory view suggesting that God predestines people to receive the kingdom but they cannot do so apart from meritorious works.[11]

Though modern scholars have been enamored with more pressing issues the tension between works and salvation has not gone completely unnoticed[12] as Francis Beare's comments well illustrate. In "this whole passage there is no trace of a doctrine of the forgiveness of sins, or of the grace of God. The righteous are invited to enter into the Kingdom because they have shown themselves worthy by their kind deeds, not because their sins are forgiven. There is no trace of a saving *faith* . . . There is no mercy shown to the accursed."[13] Hence David Hill ponders in his commentary, "One might be disposed to ask of this story the questions: 'Does acceptance of Jesus Christ by faith count for nothing at the end?' and 'Is the Matthean Gospel at variance with Paul?'"[14] Indeed one might be inclined to think so reading Michael Green: "It looks dangerously like justification by works, the very antithesis of Paul and Augustine and Luther."[15] Though to Victor Agbanou vv. 31-46 is much more than appearance: "puisse parler ici d'une 'théologie matthéenne de la justification par les oeuvres.'"[16] And what are we to dare make of Roger Mehl's comment declaring that this passage is "Le sommaire de l'Evangile"?[17]

---

[8] Ibid., 202.

[9] Ibid., 206.

[10] Ibid., 210.

[11] Ibid., 219.

[12] On this tension cf. C. Leslie Mitton, "Present Justification and Final Judgment: A Discussion of the Parable of the Sheep and the Goats," *ExpTim* 68 (1955–56) 46–50; see also Ulrich Luz, *The Theology of the Gospel of Matthew*, trans. J. Bradford Robinson, New Testament Theology, ed. James D. G. Dunn (Cambridge: Cambridge University Press, 1995) 131–32.

[13] Francis Wright Beare, *The Gospel According to Matthew* (San Francisco: Harper & Row, 1981) 496–97.

[14] David Hill, *The Gospel of Matthew*, New Century Bible Commentary, ed. Ronald E. Clements and Matthew Black (Grand Rapids: Eerdmans, 1981) 330.

[15] Michael Green, *Matthew for Today: Expository Study of Matthew* (Dallas: Word, 1988) 242; cf. also R. T. France, *Matthew*, TNTC, ed. Leon Morris (Grand Rapids: Eerdmans, 1989) 355.

[16] Agbanou, *Le Discours Eschatologique*, 171.

[17] Roger Mehl, "La catholicité de l'église: Commentaire des déclarations de l'Assemblée oecuménique d'Upsal," *Revue d'histoire et de philosophie religieuses* 48 (1968) 369.

Comments such as these, along with a plain reading of Matthew 25:31-46, raise the question as to whether salvation here is gained by works[18] (cf. 23:23) independent of one's confession that Christ is Lord (cf. 7:21-23)?[19] Is this judgment offered as a kind of "amnesty" for those who have never heard the gospel?[20] Or does it merely validate a faith decision already made[21] in which case the criterion for eternity is more evidential than causative?[22] The place to begin is a brief summary of the passage.

The Sheep and the Goats: Context and Summary

The discourse of the sheep and the goats[23] is a concluding response to the disciples' question concerning the sign of Jesus' coming and the end of the age (συντελείας τοῦ αἰῶνος) (24:3; cf. 13:39, 40, 49; 28:20). The disciples learn that timing is not so much the issue (vv. 36, 42; 25:13) but character: they are to be watchful (vv. 4, 42; 25:13), steadfast (v. 13) and prepared (v. 44). Three parables exhort readers to be wise and faithful (24:45–25:30). Each parable ends with a warning variously worded but amounting to the same thing: the eternal destiny of the unfaithful is hell (24:51; 25:10-12, 30).[24] They will find the door to the kingdom of heaven shut (v. 10).

---

[18] Cf. e.g., J. A. T. Robinson, "The 'Parable' of the Sheep and the Goats," *NTS* 2 (1955–56) 231: "Commentators, taking the title [οἱ δίκαιοι] seriously, have been much stretched to prove that it does not teach a doctrine of justification by works!"

[19] Francis Watson, "Liberating the Reader: A Theological-Exegetical Study of the Parable of the Sheep and the Goats (Matt 25.31-46)," in *The Open Text: New Directions for Biblical Studies*, ed. Francis Watson (London: SCM, 1993) 72–79; cf. also Leonardo Boff, *Jesus Christ Liberator: A Critical Christology for Our Time*, trans. Patrick Hughes (Maryknoll, N.Y.: Orbis, 1978) 95.

[20] Frederick Dale Bruner, *Matthew: A Commentary* (Dallas: Word, 1990) 928; cf. Daniel J. Harrington, *The Gospel of Matthew*, Sacra Pagina Series, ed. Daniel J. Harrington, vol. 1 (Collegeville, Minn.: Liturgical, 1991) 359–60.

[21] Craig L. Blomberg, *Matthew*, NAC, ed. David S. Dockery, vol. 22 (Nashville: Broadman, 1992) 376; Beare, *The Gospel According to Matthew*, 493; cf. Hill, *The Gospel of Matthew*, 331.

[22] Carson, "Matthew," 521.

[23] With the exception of Matt 25:32-33 most scholars agree that vv. 31-46 is not a parable. Cf. e.g., Blomberg, *Matthew*, 375; Robinson, "The 'Parable' of the Sheep and the Goats," 225; Carson, "Matthew," 518; France, *Matthew*, 354; Hill, *The Gospel of Matthew*, 330; though contra Gray, *The Least of My Brothers*, 352; Warren Carter, *Matthew and the Margins: A Socio-Political and Religious Reading*, JSNTSup, ed. Stanley E. Porter, vol. 204 (Sheffield: Sheffield Academic, 2000) 181; Leon Morris, *The Gospel According to Matthew*, PNTC, ed. D. A. Carson (Grand Rapids: Eerdmans, 1992) 633; Donahue, "The 'Parable' of the Sheep and the Goats," 9–10.

[24] Cf. the similar fate of the goats in Matt 25:41 and 46 (ibid., 12).

Frequent reference is also made to the coming of the Son of Man (24:27, 30, 37, 44). Verses 27 and 37 describe the nature of His coming,[25] v. 44 the timing, and v. 30 what will take place at His coming. Matthew 25:31 resumes this portion (24:30-31) of the discourse.[26] Hence the sequence of events appears to be:

1. Tribulation (v. 29).[27]

2. The Son of Man (ὁ υἱὸς τοῦ ἀνθρώπου) witnessed by all humanity,[28] comes (ἐρχόμενον) in power and glory (δόξης) (v. 30).

3. He will then send out His angels (ἀγγέλους) who will gather the elect (v. 31; cf. 2 Thess 2:1).

After the intervening exhortations to faithfulness, 25:31a then recaps: "and whenever the Son of Man (ὁ υἱὸς τοῦ ἀνθρώπου) comes (ἔλθῃ) in His glory (δόξῃ) and all the angels (ἄγγελοι) with Him." The next event in this sequence is now introduced in v. 31a and sets the scene of judgment to follow:

4. Then (τότε) He will sit upon His glorious throne (v. 31b).

Hence what follows is the eschatological judgment performed subsequent to the coming of the Son of Man at the end of the age. To be judged

---

[25] Note ὥσπερ γὰρ . . . οὕτως ἔσται ἡ παρουσία τοῦ υἱοῦ τοῦ ἀνθρώπου (Matt 24:27, 37).

[26] It is remarkable how easily Matt 25:31-46 resumes 24:30-31. From vv. 4-31 Matthew delineates and describes the events leading up to the end. Verse 32 clearly marks a break in the discourse with the expression μάθετε τὴν παραβολήν alluding to the fact that for those who are watchful of "all these things" (described in vv. 4-31) the nearness of the end will be evident (vv. 32-35). This in effect answers the disciples' original question in v. 3 although it must be qualified. The encouragement that readers may detect the nearness of the παρουσια must be balanced with the fact that no one knows when this will be (vv. 36-44). This in turn gives rise to a series of another three parables illustrating the need to be faithful until the Son returns (vv. 45–25:30). 24:32–25:30 are strikingly different from 24:4-31 in that the former focuses on exhortation while the latter focuses on events. 25:31-46 resumes the events section not leading up to the end but of the end. For a discussion concerning the progression, themes and outline of Matt 24–25 see Warren Carter and John Paul Heil, *Matthew's Parables: Audience-Orientated Perspectives*, The Catholic Biblical Quarterly Monograph Series vol. 30, ed. Michael L. Barré et al. (Washington, D.C.: The Catholic Biblical Association of America, 1998) 177–209. Agbanou, *Le Discours Eschatologique*, 175: Matt 25:31-46 "juxtapose à la parabole des talents sans d'autre transition que ῞Οταν δέ. Seul le cadre eschatologique du jugement déjà suggéré dans les paraboles précédentes peut valablement rendre compte de cette soudure."

[27] Εὐθέως δὲ μετὰ τὴν θλῖψιν.

[28] Αἱ φυλαὶ τῆς γῆς.

are "all the nations" (πάντα τὰ ἔθνη) (v. 32)²⁹ who will be gathered before the Son of Man. Although some have suggested that nations as opposed to individuals are in view³⁰ this is unlikely since the neuter πάντα τὰ ἔθνη becomes the masculine αὐτούς indicating individuals (cf. also 28:19).³¹ It is these individuals who are separated from one another (cf. 13:49).³² The scene calls to mind the way a shepherd would separate sheep from goats (cf. Ezek 34).³³ The sheep go to the right and the goats to the left (Matt 25:33).

Those on the right are said to be blessed (εὐλογημένοι) (v. 34) and righteous (δίκαιοι) (vv. 37, 46). Their destiny is to inherit the kingdom (v. 34) and go into eternal life (v. 46; cf. 13:43). The reason (γάρ)³⁴ for this judgment is that they have responded compassionately to the least of Jesus' brothers (τούτων τῶν ἀδελφῶν μου τῶν ἐλαχίστων) (25:35-40).³⁵ Those on the left are told that they are cursed (κατηραμένοι). Their sentence is to the eternal fire (v. 41) and eternal punishment (v. 46). The reason (γάρ) given is that they did not respond compassionately to Jesus' brothers (vv. 42-45). Both groups are surprised, not at the judgment or even the reason for the judgment, but that in attending or failing to attend to the needs of Jesus' brothers they were in fact doing so, or not, to Jesus (vv. 39, 44).³⁶

---

²⁹ I shall address the identity of πάντα τὰ ἔθνη below.

³⁰ E.g., Lewis Sperry Chafer, *Systematic Theology*, vol. 4 (Dallas: Dallas Seminary, 1947–48; reprint, Grand Rapids: Kregel, 1993) 6: "The issue is one regarding what nations will be chosen to enter Israel's Messianic kingdom on the earth."

³¹ Blomberg, *Matthew*, 376; Robert H. Mounce, *Matthew*, NIBC, ed. W. Ward Gasque, vol. 1 (Peabody, Mass.: Hendrickson, 1985) 235–36; Agbanou, *Le Discours Eschatologique*, 184. The same phenomenon occurs in Matt 28:19 (μαθητεύσατε *πάντα τὰ ἔθνη*, βαπτίζοντες *αὐτούς* . . . διδάσκοντες *αὐτούς* . . .) where it is clear that the baptizing and teaching is to be of *individuals* and not of national groups (Donald A. Hagner, *Matthew 14–28*, WBC, ed. David A. Hubbard and Glenn W. Barker, vol. 33B [Dallas: Word, 1995] 887; cf. Gundry, *Matthew*, 512).

³² In Matt 13:49-50 it is the angels that will do the separating; here in 25:32 it is the Son of Man who does the separating. However in spite of the difference they are most likely the same judgment. Both occur at the "end of the age" (συντελεία τοῦ αἰῶνος; cf. 24:3); both involve separating the "righteous" (δικαίων; cf. 25:37); both involve "the fire" (τοῦ πυρός; cf. v. 41) of hell as the destination for the unrighteous where there "will be weeping and gnashing of teeth" (cf. 24:51; 25:30).

³³ In Ezek 34 the nature of the judgment appears slightly different to that of Matt 25:31-46. In Ezekiel the leaders of Israel ("shepherds") are judged for not having cared for their flock (of Israel): they have not cared for the sick and the injured (34:2-10). In addition the flock will be judged, "between one sheep and another, and between rams and goats" (vv. 17, 20, 22).

³⁴ Gundry, *Matthew*, 513; Carter, *Matthew and the Margins*, 495.

³⁵ I will discuss the identity of Jesus' ἀδελφῶν below.

³⁶ On the basis that the sheep are surprised many have suggested that these people are anonymous Christians (e.g., W. D. Davies and Dale C. Allison, Jr., *A Critical and Exegetical Commentary on The Gospel According to Matthew*, vol. 3, ICC, ed. J. A. Emerton, C. E. B.

The Identity of "All the Nations" and "The Least of These My Brothers"

The key interpretive issues in this passage are the identity of "all the nations" (v. 32) and "one of the least of these my brothers" (v. 40 cf. v. 45). Of the number of interpretations offered[37] most scholars limit the choice to two: 1) all people are judged on the basis of how they have treated *all people in need* (the universalist interpretation); 2) all people are judged on the basis of how they have treated *the church* (the particularist interpretation).[38] It has been suggested that the difference between these two options is tantamount to a difference between salvation by works and salvation by faith.[39]

WHO ARE "ALL THE NATIONS" (MATT 25:32)?

There are six main views,[40] 1) All humanity, that is, Jew, Gentile, Christian, and non-Christian,[41] 2) All non-Christians—Jew and Gentile,[42] 3) All Christians—Jew and Gentile,[43] 4) All Gentiles—Christian and non-

---

Cranfield, and G. N. Stanton [Edinburgh: T. & T. Clark, 1997] 428). However the surprise is not that they receive the kingdom but that in being merciful they had in fact ministered to Jesus (Blomberg, *Matthew*, 377; Hagner, *Matthew 14–28*, 744; cf. also Foster, "Making Sense of Matthew 25:31-46," 135).

[37] See Gray, *The Least of My Brothers*.

[38] Graham N. Stanton, *A Gospel for a New People: Studies in Matthew*. Edinburgh: T. & T. Clark, 1992, 209; Foster, "Making Sense of Matthew 25:31-46," 128–39.

[39] D. Marguerat, *Le jugement dans l'evangile de Matthieu* (Geneva: Labor et Fides, 1981) 486; contra Bruner, *Matthew*, 914; and Donahue, "The 'Parable' of the Sheep and the Goats," 8.

[40] For the different interpretations offered by twentieth century authors on πάντα τὰ ἔθνη Gray, *The Least of My Brothers*, 257–67; see also Davies and Allison, *Matthew*, 3:422.

[41] Most scholars today, e.g., Carter, *Matthew and the Margins*, 493; Davies and Allison, *Matthew*, 3:422–23; Luz, *Das Evangelium nach Matthäus*, 531; Hagner, *Matthew 14–28*, 742; Gundry, *Matthew*, 511; Blomberg, *Matthew*, 376; Morris, *The Gospel According to Matthew*, 635; Bruner, *Matthew*, 2:915; Carson, "Matthew," 521; Agbanou, *Le Discours Eschatologique*, 184; Hill, *The Gospel of Matthew*, 331; Alistair I. Wilson, *When Will These Things Happen?: A Study of Jesus as Judge in Matthew 21–25*, Paternoster Biblical Monographs, ed. David F. Wright et al. (Carlisle, U.K.: Paternoster, 2004) 244.

[42] Stanton, *A Gospel for a New People*, 212–14; Gray, *The Least of My Brothers*, 358.

[43] Victor Paul Furnish, *The Love Command in the New Testament* (London: SCM, 1973) 79–84; U. Wilckens, "Gottes geringste Büder - zu Mt 25, 31–46," in *Jesus und Paulus: Festschrift für Werner Georg Kümmel zum 70 Geburtstag*, ed. E. Earle Ellis and Enoch Grässer (Göttingen: Vandenhoeck & Ruprecht, 1975) 363–83.

Christian,[44] 5) Non-Christian Gentiles,[45] 6) All Gentiles who are alive at the *rapture* of the church.[46]

We must of course wrestle with Matthew's use of πάντα τὰ ἔθνη elsewhere in His Gospel[47] although even elsewhere there is no consensus.[48] In my mind though the context of Matthew 25:31-46 indicates that all humanity, Jew and Gentile, is in view.[49] First, it is difficult to see Matthew excluding Jews from 24:9 (cf. v. 7), 14, and 28:19. He gives no indication in the preceding discourse that Jews are excluded. The gospel of the kingdom will be preached throughout the *whole inhabited world* (ὅλῃ τῇ οἰκουμένῃ) as a witness πᾶσιν τοῖς ἔθνεσιν (24:14). Presumably the "whole inhabited world" includes Jews. When the Son of Man comes *all the tribes of the earth*

---

[44] David C. Sim, *The Gospel of Matthew and Christian Judaism: The History and Social Setting of the Matthean Community*, Studies of the New Testament and its World, ed. John Barclay, Joel Marcus, and John Riches (Edinburgh: T. & T. Clark, 1998) 221.

[45] Harrington, *The Gospel of Matthew*, 356, 358; J. Lambrecht, "The Parousia Discourse: Composition and Content in Mt. 24–25," in *L'Évangile selon Matthieu: Rédaction et théologie*, Biblotheca Ephemeridum Theologicarum Lovaniensium, ed. M. Didier, vol. 29 (Gembloux: Duculot, 1972) 334; J. M. Court, "Right and Left: The Implications for Matthew 25:31-46," *NTS* 31 (1985) 229; Green, *The Gospel According to Matthew*, 206.

[46] This view dates back (as far as I can tell) to J. N. Darby see *The Collected Writings of J. N. Darby*, ed. William Kelly, vol. 2 (n.p., n.d.; reprint, Sunbury, Pa.: Believers, 1971) 79–80; vol. 10 (n.p., n.d.; reprint, Sunbury, Pa.: Believers, 1972) 374, and has been taken up by dispensationalists; see, e.g., Thomas, "Jesus' View of Eternal Punishment," 153, 155; John F. Walvoord, *Matthew: They Kingdom Come* (Chicago: Moody, 1974) 201; see also idem, "Christ's Olivet Discourse on the End of the Age: The Judgment of the Nations," *BSac* 129 (1972) 307–15; and recently Eugene W. Pond, "Who Are The Sheep and Goats in Matthew 25:31-46?" *BSac* 159 (2002) 288–302.

[47] The term ἔθνος occurs fifteen times in Matt (4:15; 6:32; 10:5, 18; 12:18, 21; 20:19, 25; 21:43; 24:7 [x 2], 9, 14; 25:32; 28:19) and is qualified by πᾶς four times (24:9, 14; 25:32; 28:19). By itself ἔθνος usually means a people group in the general sense (Karl Ludwig Schmidt, "ἔθνος," in *TDNT*, 369; BDAG, 276).

[48] Cf. e.g., John P. Meier, "Nations or Gentiles in Matthew 28:19?" *CBQ* 39 (1977) 94–102 ("all nations" is universal); contra D. R. A. Hare and D. J. Harrington, "'Make Disciples of All the Gentiles' (Mt 28–19)," *CBQ* 37 (1975) 359–69.

[49] This interpretation however is not without its problems. It is quite possible that Matt 19:28 alludes to a separate judgment for Israel in which case a separate judgment for Gentiles in 25:31-46 would make good sense. See Hare and Harrington, "Make Disciples of All the Gentiles," 359–60; Stanton, *A Gospel for a New People*, 213; cf. also George Gay, "The Judgment of the Gentiles in Matthew's Theology," in *Scripture, Tradition, and Interpretation*, ed. W. Ward Gasque and William Sanford LaSor (Grand Rapids: Eerdmans, 1978) 199–215. Further support for this could be marshaled from 21:43, a significant parallel to 25:31-46: "the kingdom of God will be taken away from you and will be given to ἔθνει who do its fruit." However "Gentile" need not be in view here since the abdication of the kingdom does not involve the Jewish nation as a whole just its leadership (Carson, "Matthew," 454). Second, the focus here is not so much ethnic as it is ethics (Carter, *Matthew and the Margins*, 429–30).

(πᾶσαι αἱ φυλαὶ τῆς γῆς) will see Him (v. 30; cf. 25:31). And it is hard to believe that making disciples of πάντα τὰ ἔθνη (28:19) excludes Israel (cf. Acts 1:8).[50]

Second, earlier judgment scenes in Matthew suggest *all* people will be judged (cf. 7:21-23; 16:27).[51] Third, the three preceding parables (24:45–25:30) address the fate of *all* people[52] suggesting the judgment cannot be confined to unbelievers.[53]

Who are Jesus' Brothers (Matt 5:40)?

The main views are, 1) Christian disciples in general,[54] 2) Christian missionaries specifically,[55] 3) Tribulation Jews,[56] 4) Tribulation Jews *and* Gentiles

---

[50] Weber, "The Image of the Sheep and the Goats," 676, suggests that Matt 25:31-46 should be read on the level of *story* (i.e., as understood by the original characters) and *discourse* (i.e., as understood by Matthew's readers). As a story "all nations" refers to all humanity since πᾶς is used throughout Matthew's Gospel to refer to Jesus' *universal* authority (cf. 4:8; 3:15; 26:39, 42; 28:18, 19; 24:30). "To understand πάντα τὰ ἔθνη in 25:32 as less than universal in scope is to vitiate a key christological motif, the pivotal demonstration of the Son of Man's full authority so often proclaimed in Matthew's Gospel." As discourse "all nations" refers to all Christians (cf. v. 32 = the flock of God).

[51] Hagner, *Matthew 14–28*, 742; Donahue, "The 'Parable' of the Sheep and the Goats," 15; contra Pond, "Who Are the Sheep and the Goats?" 299, argues that Matthew's judgment cannot refer to the great white throne judgment in Revelation 20.

[52] Cf. esp. Matt 24:51; 25:12, 30 with vv. 41, 46a, and 24:46; 25:21, 23 with 25:34, 46b.

[53] As Lamar Cope, "Matthew 25:31-46 'The Sheep and the Goats' Reinterpreted," *Novum Testamentum* 11 (1969) 32–44, suggests. Donahue, "The 'Parable' of the Sheep and the Goats," 13: "The literary context is thus strong evidence that the disciples are to see themselves involved in the drama of the final judgment."

[54] Carter, *Matthew and the Margins*, 496; Stanton, *A Gospel for a New People*, 214–17; Thomas G. Long, *Matthew*, Westminster Bible Companion, ed. Patrick D. Miller and David L. Bartlett (Louisville, Ky.: Westminster John Knox, 1997) 286; Hagner, *Matthew 14–28*, 744–45; Morris, *The Gospel According to Matthew*, 639; Harrington, *The Gospel of Matthew*, 358 ("either missionaries or ordinary Christians"); Gray, *The Least of My Brothers*, 358; France, *Matthew*, 357–58; Carson, "Matthew," 520; George Eldon Ladd, "The Parable of the Sheep and the Goats in Recent Interpretation," in *New Dimensions in New Testament Study*, ed. Richard L. Longenecker and Merrill C. Tenney (Grand Rapids: Zondervan, 1974) 197–99.

[55] Luz, *Das Evangelium nach Matthäus*, 539; Blomberg, *Matthew*, 378; Gundry, *Matthew*, 514; Court, "Right and Left," 229; Michaels, "Apostolic Hardships and Righteous Gentiles," 27–38.

[56] Thomas, "Jesus' View of Eternal Punishment," 155–56; Walvoord, *Thy Kingdom Come*, 201; J. Dwight Pentecost, *Things to Come: A Study in Biblical Eschatology* (Findley, Ohio: Dunham, 1958; reprint, Grand Rapids: Zondervan, 1964) 418–20.

(believers),[57] 5) Anyone in need—Christian or not.[58] Of the two issues in this passage this one is, to my way of thinking anyway, the easier since Matthew's use of ἀδελφός in certain contexts clearly refers to disciples (see above). View 3 is unlikely since Jesus never refers to the Jews as brothers.[59] Essentially then what is left is a choice between Christians or all needy people. We have already seen that "brother" in Matthew can basically mean the same as "neighbor" (5:22, 23, 24, 47; 7:3, 4, 5; see chap. 10) so it is not out of the question that the same could be in view here. We should also note that what is not in dispute is whether Christians should respond compassionately to *all* people in need. The answer is clearly yes (e.g., Matt 5:43-48; Luke 10:25-37). However I am not convinced that Matthew 25 teaches this. I understand Jesus' brothers to be Christian missionaries taking the gospel of the kingdom as a witness to all the nations in the midst of opposition (cf. 24:14).[60] The following reasons, in my opinion, point strongly to this view.

First, the literary and conceptual links between 25:31-46 and chapter 10 suggest the final judgment should be understood against a missionary context.[61] The parallels are evident. Most notably Jesus sends out the disciples completely dependent on the aid of others (vv. 9-10). The way the disciples are received will indicate people's reception of the gospel (vv. 11-14). Those who do not receive them will be sorry on "the day of judgment" (v. 15). The disciples are warned that they will be treated badly (vv. 16-18, 21-23). Yet they are to be encouraged for it is "the Spirit of your Father" who will speak in them (v. 19-20; cf. 25:40, 45). Such missionary activity will continue until the Son of Man comes (v. 23)[62]—presumably to judge people's responses and

---

[57] Eugene W. Pond, "Who Are 'The Least' of Jesus' Brothers in Matthew 25:31-46?" *Bsac* 159 (2002) 436–48.

[58] Agbanou, *Le Discours Eschatologique*, 191; Bruner, *Matthew*, 922; Hill, *The Gospel of Matthew*, 331; J. A. Grassi, "'I was Hungry and You Gave Me To Eat,' (Matt 25:35ff): The Divine Identification Ethic in Matthew," *Biblical Theology Bulletin* 11 (1981) 81–84.

[59] Contra Thomas, "Jesus' View of Eternal Punishment," 155–56: the "brothers" in Matt 12:46-50 were Jews. However, this misses the point of v. 50, which says, "For (γάρ) whoever does the will of my Father in heaven is My brother and sister and mother." It might well be that they were Jewish but Jesus explains (γάρ) they are brothers not because they are Jewish but because they do the will of God. The focus is ethical not ethnic. See Ladd, "The Parable of the Sheep and the Goats," 195–97, and his critique of this view (i.e., brothers = Jews).

[60] H. J. Genthe, "Wer sind die geringsten Brüder? Zur Auslegung von Matthäus 25:40," *Die Zeichen der Zeit* 51 (1997) 189; cf. Wilson, *When Will These Things Happen?* 245,

[61] Petri Luomanen, *Entering the Kingdom of Heaven: A Study on the Structure of Matthew's View of Salvation* (Tübingen: Mohr, 1998) 188–89; Michaels, "Apostolic Hardships and Righteous Gentiles," 27–29; Eung Chun Park, *The Mission Discourse in Matthew's Interpretation.* WUNT, ed. Martin Hengel und Otfried Hofius, vol. 81 (Tübingen: Mohr Siebeck, 1995) 161–62; cf. also Stanton, *A Gospel for a New People*, 229.

[62] It has been said that Matt 10:23 is one of the most difficult verses in the entire NT (Carson,

thus separate the sheep from the goats. All will be made known eventually (v. 26) *at the judgment*.[63] Hence they are not to fear men but God who will be the one who determines people's eternal destinies (v. 28). Thus everyone who confesses Jesus[64] before men, Jesus will do the same before His Father in heaven (v. 32) and vice-versa for those who do not confess in Jesus (v. 33). Confession and reception of Jesus' messengers are closely linked for the one who receives a disciple receives Jesus also (v. 40). Those who do so will receive a righteous (δικαίου) reward (v. 41). Any one who gives a cup of cold water to *one of these little ones* (ἕνα τῶν μικρῶν τούτων) will in no way lose his reward (v. 42). The reward mentioned here is explicated in 25:46.[65]

Although the mission outlined in chapter 10 was first restricted to the Twelve it is clear that by the end of Matthew's Gospel Jesus has in mind all disciples (28:18-20). Taking the gospel to all nations (24:14) is a fulfillment of the great commission, which gives wider application to 25:31-46. All Christians are missionaries in that sense and therefore brothers.[66]

In addition to chapter 10 supporting the identity of Christians (missionaries) with "brothers" is the use of the term ἀδελφός in Matthew. The term is used by Jesus to designate those who are committed to Him (12:46-50; 25:40; cf. 23:8).[67] Furthermore, that all Christians are included in chapter 25 is indicated by the qualifier ἐλάχιστος, a term that Matthew uses elsewhere to refer to disciples (18:6, 10; cf. vv. 4-5) and encompasses *all* (cf. 5:19; 11:11)

"Matthew," 250). This is not the place to discuss this matter in any amount of detail but I shall give the various views (cf. ibid., 250–53). Many suggestions have been made as to when this verse is fulfilled: 1) Within the disciples' generation; 2) at or soon after the Resurrection; 3) the AD 70 judgment on Jerusalem; 4) the Second Coming. The last interpretation seems to be the least problematic (cf. 24:30; 25:31; 26:64). The problem of unfulfilled prophecy rests on the assumption that the disciples finished their mission and this is nowhere indicated. The disciples are commanded to go out (10:5-6) and yet they are never said to return (cf. Mark 6:30; Luke 10:17). This suggests that the pre-Pentecost mission to Israel never ended. In line with the Great Commission in Matt 28:19 it still continues (so also Acts 1:8). "Hence the application of 10:23 to the *parousia* could not, from the Matthean perspective, result in an unfulfilled prophecy" (Davies and Allison, *Matthew*, 2:190).

[63] Note 1 Cor 4:5: "Do not judge anything before the time until whenever the Lord comes who will also bring to light the hidden things of darkness and will bring to light the intentions of hearts, and then the praise will come to each one from God" (cf. also *2 Bar.* 83.1-8, esp. v. 3; see Carter, *Matthew and the Margins*, 240).

[64] Lit.: "Everyone then who confesses in me before men" (Matt 10:32).

[65] Park, *The Mission Discourse*, 162. See the discussion in chapter ten on reward vis-à-vis Matt 5:46.

[66] Carson, "Matthew," 519; Donahue, "The 'Parable' of the Sheep and the Goats," 25; Ladd, "The Parable of the Sheep and the Goats," 199.

[67] See BDAG, 18. The term is also used to designate the Twelve in Matt 28:10.

In sum, Christians (i.e., brothers) are called to take the gospel to all nations (i.e., the sheep and the goats). They will meet trouble and hardship along the way (cf. also 2 Cor 11:23-29).[68] Some will accept them and their message (i.e., the sheep) and some will reject them (i.e., the goats). Either way one's response to the messenger will be *indicative* of one's response to the person of Jesus.[69] All will be made known on judgment day.[70]

The Relationship between Judgment and Salvation: Matthew 25:31-46 and the Rest of the New Testament

The coming of the Son of Man in glory with His angels recalls a similar scenario to that portrayed in 16:27 (cf. also 19:28; 24:30).[71] In fact there are good reasons for suggesting that for Matthew, 25:31 and 16:27 are the same event. First, in spite of some minor verbal differences the scenes depicted in the first part of each verse are essentially the same.[72] The basic elements are present in both—the Son of Man comes in glory with angels.[73] Second, in

---

[68] On the parallels between 2 Cor 11:23-29 and Matt 25:35-36 see Michaels, "Apostolic Hardships and Righteous Gentiles," 32–36.

[69] Ibid., 29, offers Acts 16:30-34 as an illustration of what Matthew has in mind in 25:35-46. The Philippian jailer asks Paul and Silas what he must do to be saved (Acts 16:30) to which they respond, "Believe upon the Lord Jesus Christ" (v. 31). The jailer later attends to their wounds and then is baptized along with his household (v. 33). He feeds the two missionaries and the text adds that they were joyful since they had believed (πεπιστευκώς: perfect tense) in God (v. 34). We should also take note of James' use of Matt 25:35-36 to illustrate 'faith without works' in James 2:15-16 (cf. also Jas 1:27).

[70] Along these lines see Donahue, "The 'Parable' of the Sheep and the Goats," 3–31. This interpretation has been rejected on the basis that the "sheep" and the "brothers" are clearly distinct but also that τὰ ἔθνη is never used to refer to Christians (Stanton, *A Gospel for a New People*, 214; Cope, "Matthew 25:31-46," 37). However this is somewhat of a moot point if it is kept in mind that at one point all sheep were in fact unbelievers. All were at one point confronted with a messenger and message of the gospel (cf. also ibid., 14). After all, believers are urged to do good to all but especially towards other believers (Gal 6:10). It is therefore quite scriptural for a believer to be a benefactor and beneficiary at the same time as is well illustrated in the parable of the Good Samaritan. In other words, not only are believers neighbors but they are also to be neighbors. Heil, "The Double Meaning," 3–14, makes a similar point. His thesis is that there are two levels of meaning in Matt 25:31-46. Believers are the righteous sheep that look after the needy brothers yet they are at the same time needy.

[71] Lambrecht, "The Parousia Discourse," 331; Agbanou, *Le Discours Eschatologique*, 176; Robinson, "The 'Parable' of the Sheep and the Goats," 226; Blomberg, *Matthew*, 376; France, *Matthew*, 356; Gundry, *Matthew*, 511; Donahue, "The 'Parable' of the Sheep and the Goats," 11.

[72] Wilson, *When Will These Things Happen?* 166, 240–41; Hagner, *Matthew 14–28*, 741.

[73] Cf. Matt 16:27 and 25:31:

16:27: ὁ υἱὸς τοῦ ἀνθρώπου ἔρχεσθαι ἐν τῇ δόξῃ τοῦ πατρὸς αὐτοῦ μετὰ τῶν ἀγγέλων αὐτοῦ.

the Gospels the presence of the Son of Man with angels indicates judgment[74] (Matt 13:41;[75] Mark 8:38; Luke 9:26; 12:8; cf. also Deut 33:2; Zech 14:5; 2 Thess 1:7). Third, although there are few to no verbal similarities in the second part of the verse the conceptual links suggest the same event. The temporal framework is the same in both instances.[76] Most noticeable is the use of τότε to indicate that after the Son of Man has come *then* judgment. *Then* He will give to each one according to his work (16:27). *Then* He will sit upon His glorious throne (25:31). The throne imagery in v. 31 clearly indicates a judgment scene (cf. esp. Matt 19:28; Luke 22:30; Rev 20:4, 11-13; *1 Enoch* 61.8;[77] 62.1-3;[78] 69.27). These factors suggest that what Matthew has articulated in a few words in 16:27 (cf. Ps 62:13; Prov 24:12; Sir 35:22) he has illustrated in more detail in 25:31-46. The separation of the sheep and the goats is a visual[79] of each one being recompensed according to his work.[80] This leads me to make the following comments regarding the relationship between works and salvation in this passage.

First, it seems clear that at the coming of the Son of Man there will take place a universal judgment.[81] All humanity will be judged and recompensed on the basis of their works (cf. Matt 12:37; Acts 17:31). Respective eternal

---

25:31: ἔλθῃ ὁ υἱὸς τοῦ ἀνθρώπου ἐν τῇ δόξῃ αὐτοῦ καὶ πάντες οἱ ἄγγελοι μετ' αὐτοῦ.

[74] Cf. Robinson, "The 'Parable' of the Sheep and the Goats," 227–28.

[75] On the parallels between Matt 13:24-30, 37-43 and 25:35-40 see ibid., 233–34; cf. also Donahue, "The 'Parable' of the Sheep and the Goats," 11.

[76] Both verses indicate the coming of the Son of Man to be future (Matt 16:27: μέλλει γὰρ . . .; 25:31: Ὅταν δὲ . . . [the indefinite pronoun fits with the fact that no one except the Father knows the time of His coming, 24:36]) followed by a scene of judgment (16:27: καὶ τότε . . .; 25:31: τότε . . .).

[77] "He placed the Elect One on the *throne of glory*; and he shall judge all the works of the holy ones in heaven above, weighing in the balance their deeds."

[78] "Thus the Lord commanded the kings, the governors, the high officials, and the landlords and said, 'Open your eyes and lift up your eyebrows—if you are able to recognize the Elect One!' The Lord of the Spirits has sat down on the *throne of his glory*, and the spirit of righteousness has been poured out upon him. The word of his mouth will do the sinners in; and all the oppressors shall be eliminated from before his face. On the day of judgment, all the kings, the governors, the high officials, and the landlords shall see and recognize him—how he sits on the *throne of his glory*, and righteousness is judged before him, and that no nonsensical talk shall be uttered in his presence."

[79] Davies and Allison, *Matthew*, 3:418: Matt 25:31-46 is "a word-picture" of the last judgment.

[80] Hagner, *Matthew 14–28*, 741: "the remainder of 16:27, 'and he will render to each according to his work,' is, of course, the point of the present parable concerning the sheep and the goats"; cf. also P. C. Böttger, "Recompense," in *NIDNTT*, 135–36.

[81] Wilson, *When Will These Things Happen?* 244.

destinies will be assigned at this point. Now no one denies that believers will be judged on the basis of their works (cf. e.g., 2 Cor 5:10) although some contend that what is at stake is not one's eternal destiny but rewards.[82] However, as we saw in chapter 10, a careful examination of the key passages reveals that the view is not well documented in the NT.[83] Matthew 16:27 is sometimes appealed to but as we have seen this is not a judgment concerning rewards but eternal destiny.[84] John also anticipates a future judgment (cf. John 5:25-28) when "all who have done good will go into the resurrection of life and those who have done evil into the resurrection of judgment" (v. 29).[85] Paul, along with Matthew 16:27, cites Psalm 62:12 and Proverbs 24:12 (ἀποδώσει ἑκάστῳ κατὰ τὰ ἔργα αὐτοῦ) acknowledges a future time when God will judge all people on the basis of their works (Rom 2:6).[86] Those who persevere in doing good will receive eternal life (v. 7) while those who obey unrighteousness will receive wrath (v. 8). The NT ends with the same expectation that Jesus is coming soon and His reward is with Him "to

---

[82] For a detailed articulation of this view see Joseph C. Dillow, *The Reign of the Servant Kings: A Study of Eternal Security and the Final Significance of Man* (Miami, Fla.: Schoettle, 1992) 1992; see also more recently Paul N. Benware, *The Believer's Payday: Why Standing before Christ Should Be Our Greatest Moment* (Chatanooga: AMG, 2002); Robert N. Wilkin, *The Road to Reward: Living Today in Light of Tomorrow* (Irving, Tex.: Grace Evangelical Society) 2003.

[83] Craig L. Blomberg, "Degrees of Reward in the Kingdom of Heaven?," *JETS* 35 (1992) 159–72; Thomas R. Schreiner and Ardel B. Caneday, *The Race Set Before Us: A Biblical Theology of Perseverance and Assurance* (Downers Grove, Ill.: InterVarsity, 2001).

[84] Dillow, *Servant Kings*, does not discuss Matt 16:27.

[85] Cf. though Zane C. Hodges, "Those Who Have Done Good—John 5:28-29," *BSac* (1979) 158–66: "John 5:28-29 views men from the vantage point of the world to come" (p. 164). In other words, John views people from their eternal—not earthly—state. I am not opposed to this truth though I disagree that it is taught here. Hodges argues that John does not view these "individuals in whom an admixture of good and evil has existed during all their earthly career" (ibid.). True John acknowledges that believers sin (1 John 1:8) but this does not mean that their *earthly* lives cannot be summed up as having done "good." Furthermore John often distinguishes between believers and unbelievers from an "earthly" vantage point on the basis of their works (cf. e.g., John 3:20; 1 John 3:6,10; 2 John 11; cf. also 1 John 2:9-11, 17; 3:14-15). However, most telling is John's teaching on judgment. Hodges argues that believers have already been judged (John 5:24) (ibid., 161). This is true but elsewhere John urges his readers to remain (μένετε) in Christ so that (ἵνα) they might have confidence and not be ashamed at His coming (1 John 2:28), which coincides with the day of *judgment* (4:17; as in John 5:29-30). Remaining and fruit bearing are closely associated (John 15:1-6; see my discussion on this passage in chap. 9) suggesting that works do play a part in one's confidence when Christ returns to judge; see Donald G. Bloesch, *The Last Things: Resurrection, Judgment, Glory* (Downers Grove, Ill.: InterVarsity, 2004) 68–70.

[86] That this judgment is future is evident from Rom 2:3 ("do you think O foolish man . . . that you *will* escape the judgment of God") and v. 5 ("but according to your stubbornness and unrepentant heart you are storing up for yourself wrath in the day of wrath and revelation of the righteous judgment of God").

give to each one as is his work" (ἀποδοῦναι ἑκάστῳ ὡς τὸ ἔργον ἐστὶν αὐτοῦ) (Rev 22:12).[87] There are of course other passages that I could list (e.g., Rom 14:10-12; 2 Cor 5:10; 2 Thess 1:6-10; Rev 20:11-13)[88] although doing so would cause a deluge of issues to surface concerning judgment beyond the scope of this study.

Excursus on James 2:21-26

I need to give some mention here to James 2:21-26 since this passage, in my opinion, most likely explicates Matthew's teaching on the last judgment. Since I have already looked at James' use of σῶσαι in chapter five I shall not take the time to review it here. Needless to say it is clear that James 2:14 is speaking of eschatological and eternal salvation. Of interest to us now is James' teaching on justification by works in vv. 21, 24-25.

James insists that Abraham was justified (ἐδικαιώθη) by works *subsequent* to offering (aorist participle: ἀνενέγκας) Isaac on the altar (v. 21). From here James is able to make his main point: "*You see* (ὁρᾶτε) a person is justified by works and not by faith alone" (v. 24; cf. v. 25). Significant of course is that Paul uses the same terms to teach the converse (Rom 4:2-3). How is it that both can use the same material and arrive at seemingly contrary conclusions? In spite of the debate surrounding this passage many scholars now agree that James and Paul complement rather than contradict each other.[89]

The point of reconciliation is that Paul and James are writing from different *perspectives*. Though their terminology may be the same Paul is writing against *pre*-conversion works whereas James is promoting *post*-conversion works.[90] Paul condemns the works of all humanity (Rom 3:9-10) whereas James encourages works from those who have faith in Jesus Christ (Jas 2:1). Paul is concerned about people who claim to have works yet have no faith (Rom 9:31; 10:3; Phil 3:4) whereas James is concerned about people who claim to have faith yet have no works (Jas 2:14, 18). Thus Paul calls for faith apart from works whereas James calls for a manifestation of faith (δείκνυμι in vv. 18b; 3:13) in the form of works.[91] To put it another way, Paul in his teach-

---

[87] Cf. also Sir 35:22; *T. Levi* 3.2; *Ps. Sol.* 9.5.

[88] Cf. Hagner, *Matthew 14–28*, 742.

[89] See James D. G., Dunn, *Unity and Diversity in the New Testament: An Inquiry into the Character of Earliest Christianity* (Philadelphia: Westminster, 1977) 251–52.

[90] Douglas J. Moo, *The Letter of James*, PNTC, ed. D. A. Carson (Grand Rapids: Eerdmans, 2000) 42–43; Paul A. Rainbow, *The Way of Salvation: The Role of Christian Obedience in Justification* (Waynesboro, GA: Paternoster, 2005) 79–88.

[91] See Ebbie Smith, "Unraveling the Untangled: Perspectives on the Lingering Debate

ing on justification is talking about works as he does in Ephesians 2:9—"not by works." James in his teaching on justification is talking about Paul's works in v. 10: "created in Christ Jesus to do good works, which God prepared beforehand, in order that we might walk in them." James is addressing a scenario where there is no walking.

If little else is clear it is clear that Paul and James cannot be speaking about the same justification. Paul means justification as an *entry* point into salvation whereas James evidently means justification at some point subsequent to entry. The question is at what point of a believer's experience is one justified? There is much that I could discuss here but since this is secondary to our study my only concern is to state my interpretation.[92] In all probability James is speaking of Paul's justification as an acquittal or declaration of righteousness,[93] not as the entry point of salvation but the end point, that is, final justification at the future judgment (cf. Isa 43:9; 45:25; 50:8).[94]

Judgment (κρίσις) is a predominant theme in James and eschatology plays an important role[95] (1:10-11; 3:1; 4:11-12; 5:1-12). In fact the expression "our glorious Lord Jesus Christ" in 2:1 conveys an eschatological framework.[96] "Glory" indicates Christ's "exalted position to which He ascended after His crucifixion and resurrection"[97] (cf. Phil 3:21) and in the NT often holds eschatological significance (e.g., Rom 5:2).[98] It is associated with Christ's Second Coming (e.g., Matt 24:30; Tit 2:13; 1 Pet 4:13), which involves judgment. We should be careful not to miss the connection ("glory") with Matthew 16:27 and 25:31. All this is to say that James 2:1 is speaking

---

Concerning *Works* and Grace in James and Paul," *Southwestern Journal of Theology* 43 (2000) 43–55.

[92] For a good discussion of the issues see ibid., 37–43.

[93] Cf. BAGD, 197.

[94] See Moo, *The Letter of James*, 42, 134; also Rainbow, *The Way of Salvation: The Role of Christian Obedience in Justification* (Waynesboro, Ga.: Paternoster, 2005) 79, 213–23.

[95] This fact is well documented. George Eldon Ladd, *A Theology of the New Testament*, ed. Donald A. Hagner, rev. ed. (Grand Rapids: Eerdmans, 1993) 636. See also G. K. Beale, "Eschatology," in *DLNTD*, 336; Andrew Chester and Ralph P. Martin, *New Testament Theology: The Theology of the Letters of James, Peter, and Jude*, ed. James D. G. Dunn (Cambridge: Cambridge University Press, 1994) 16–45.

[96] Peter H. Davids, *The Epistle of James: A Commentary of the Greek Text*, NIGTC, ed. I. Howard Marshall and W. Ward Gasque (Grand Rapids: Eerdmans, 1982) 107. There is debate over the genitive τῆς δόξης in Jas 2:1. I take it as genitive of quality, not unknown to James (cf. 1:25 ἀκροατὴς ἐπιλησμονῆς); see ibid., 106–7.

[97] Buist M. Fanning, "A Theology of James," In *A Biblical Theology of the New Testament*, ed. Roy B. Zuck and Darrell L. Bock (Chicago: Moody, 1994) 426.

[98] BAGD, 203–4.

of final judgment.[99] This is further confirmed by the warning a little later in v. 13, "For judgment (κρίσις) is without mercy to the one who has shown no mercy."

The following table highlights the essential points of difference between Paul and James:

Table 18: Paul *versus* James

James	Paul
Combating a *decreased* emphasis on works (e.g., 1:22-27; 2:1-4, 6, 15-17; 3:10; 4:1-4, etc).	Combating an *increased* emphasis on works (e.g., Rom 3:27–28; 9:31-32; 10:2-3).
The context is *post*-conversion (e.g., 1:3).	The context is *pre*-conversion (e.g., Rom 1:18–3:20).
Justification occurs at the *final* judgment (cf. 1:10-11; 2:12-13; 3:1; 4:11-12; 5:1-12).	Justification is the *initial* transfer of a person from being in Adam to being in Christ (e.g., Rom 3:20-24).

Thus the evidence suggests that James' justification is a reference to the eschatological judgment associated with the Second Coming, the outcome of which concerns eternal salvation. Two things confirm this. First, James' entire concern is expressed in 2:14: faith without works cannot save—in the eschatological sense—someone eternally (v. 14).[100] The three important elements to his argument are "faith" (πίστις), "works" (ἔργα), and "save" (σῶσαι). The first two of these elements are repeated in v. 24, while σῶσαι is presumably replaced by "justified" (δικαιοῦται). This makes sense since James uses βλέπεις (v. 22) and ὁρᾶτε (v. 24) to ensure his readers understand that this is his *main point*. In other words, v. 24 is merely a positive restatement of v. 14. This is made clear in the following table:

Table 19: "Save" in James 2:14 Restated as "Justified" in 2:24

James 2:14		James 2:24
"If someone claims to have *faith* (πίστιν) but *works* (ἔργα) he does not have; is that faith able to *save* (σῶσαι) him?"	=	"You see that a man is *justified* (δικαιοῦται) by *works* (ἔργων) not from *faith* (πίστιν) only."
Faith	=	Faith
Works	=	Works
Save	=	*Justified*

---

[99] Davids, *The Epistle of James*, 107.

[100] Moo, *The Letter of James*, 124; see chapter five above.

Second, James is obviously familiar with Matthew's teaching on eschatological judgment. He utilizes material from Matthew 25:35-36 (in Jas 2:15-16) and has evidently drawn on Jesus' words in Matthew 12:33-35 in his exposition on the tongue in James 3.[101] What is striking is that in Matthew 12:36 Jesus makes reference to the "day of judgment" (ἡμέρᾳ κρίσεως) when all men will give an account for what they have spoken (as in Jas 2:12). Jesus finishes by saying that "from your words you will be *justified* (δικαιωθήσῃ) and from your words you will be condemned" (Matt 12:37). Clearly Jesus knows of a justification that will take place in the "day of judgment" and it is likely James is speaking of the same judgment, that is, all people will be judged on the basis of their works vis-à-vis their eternal destiny.[102]

The Relationship between Judgment and Salvation: Matthew 25:31-46 and the Rest of the New Testament (continued)

Second, what this shows—and we have seen this many times already—is that there is a strong relationship between ethics and eschatology in Matthew[103] and the NT in general.[104] However this does not mean that Matthew or any other NT writer knows nothing of grace or faith in relation to salvation. Indeed for Matthew the kingdom of heaven belongs to the "poor in spirit" (5:3). It is not the righteous (δικαίους) that Jesus calls but sinners (9:9-13). God's elect will not be condemned (15:13).[105] Those who are in the kingdom have received God's forgiveness (18:23-27) and grace (20:1-16). Tax collec-

---

[101] E.g., note that Jesus talks about a good tree producing good fruit and vice-versa (Matt 12:33). What one says is the result of what's in the heart (v. 34). Thus the manifestation of good and evil are simply the product of what is inside a person (v. 35). Likewise, in the context of speaking about the tongue, James argues that fresh water and salt water cannot flow out of the same spring (3:11). Similarly, a fig tree cannot produce olives and a grapevine cannot produce figs (v. 12). The point is that speech is a product of what's inside (cf. v. 13).

[102] A major objection to this view is that Abraham and Rahab do not illustrate a final justification but a justification within history. The aorist participles—ἀνενέγκας (Jas 2:21) and ὑποδεξαμένη (v. 25)—are taken as temporal, i.e., Abraham and Rahab were justified *when* "he offered"/"she received" (NRSV). But these participles literally translated read, "having offered"/"having received" (see ibid., 135–36). Hence the time of justification is not specified. All that is said is that "offering"/"receiving" are prior to justification (D. Edmond Hiebert, *The Epistle of James: Tests of a Living Faith* [Chicago: Moody, 1979] 192).

[103] Weber, "The Image of the Sheep and the Goats," 674, notes that twenty-five percent of Matthew links behavior and eternal destiny. Matt 3:1-12; 5:3-12, 17-20, 21-26, 43-48; 6:1-4, 5-15, 16-18; 7:1-6, 15-20, 21-23, 24-28; 8:5-13; 10:5-15, 16-25, 32-33, 34-39, 40-42; 11:20-24; 12:22-32, 33-37, 36-43, 44-50; 16:21-28; 18:1-5, 21-35; 19:16-30; 20:1-16; 21:28-32; 22:1-14; 23:1-36; 24:3-14, 45-51; 25:1-13, 14-30, 31-46; 26:17-25.

[104] Note e.g., the passages cited above (e.g., Rom 2:6-8, etc.).

[105] See Carter, *Matthew and the Margins*, 319; Bruner, *Matthew*, 917.

tors and prostitutes are going into the kingdom of God before the religious leaders (21:31). These passages illustrate the priority of the work of God. They also illustrate something that seems to be prevalent throughout the NT. *When the focus is on the beginning of salvation God's initiative is highlighted (e.g., grace, calling, election, etc). But when the focus is on the end of salvation the works of individuals are emphasized (e.g., 16:27; 25:31-46; John 5:28-29; Rom 2:6-8).*[106] Some passages are not so clear such as Matthew 5:20 but his widespread emphasis on works and judgment indicate that he is most certainly speaking eschatologically[107] as in 25:34 (cf. also 7:21). Thus it is at the judgment, *not before*, that the *righteous* will enter the kingdom (25:37, 46). But prior to this time entrance is for sinners.

Third, Matthew does not neglect the earlier phase of salvation entirely in his judgment scene for he uses οἱ εὐλογημένοι to describe the sheep who are blessed (25:34). The perfect tense points to a decision already passed while the passive indicates that the righteous had nothing to do with being blessed (cf. 15:13).[108] *God* has blessed them.

Fourth, if I am correct in viewing chapter 10 as the background to the Sheep and the Goats then it is clear that one's eternal destiny in 25:46 is not independent of confession in Jesus. In 10:32 Jesus states that before He will acknowledge[109] anyone before His Father at the judgment (10:15; cf. Rev 3:5)[110] they must confess *in* Him (ἐν ἐμοί).[111] That is, they must make a

---

[106] Cf. also 2 Cor 5:10; 11:15; 2 Tim 4:14; 1 Pet 1:17; Rev 2:23; 20:12-13; 22:12. We see this principle articulated clearly in John 5:24-29. Concerning judgment now, those who have faith in God have eternal life and no longer come into judgment (v. 24). Yet it is those who have done good that will go into resurrection of life (v. 29). We find the same in Paul. One is justified apart from works (Rom 3:20–4:25) yet it is those who have persevered in doing good who will receive eternal life at judgment day (2:7).

[107] Carter, *Matthew and the Margins*, 143; Davies and Allison, *Matthew*, 1:500. Undoubtedly this is how we should interpret Paul when he says, "those who practice such things—sexual immorality, impurity, sensuality, idolatry, sorcery, enmities, strife, jealousy, anger, disputes, dissensions, factions, envy, drunkenness, carousing—will not inherit the kingdom of God" (Gal 5:19-21; cf. Eph 5:5; 1 Cor 6:9-10; outside of Paul cf. Heb 13:4; Rev 21:8; 22:15).

[108] Cf. Luz, *Das Evangelium nach Matthäus*, 535, "'Gesegnete meines Vaters' impliziert den im damaligen Judentum selbstverständlichen Prädestinationsgedanken."

[109] Cf. BDAG, 709.

[110] Luke 12:8 has, "Whoever confesses in Me before men, the Son of Man will also confess in Him ἔμπροσθεν τῶν ἀγγέλων τοῦ θεοῦ." The presence of angels suggests an eschatological judgment scene (i.e., Matt 25:31-46). Cf. BDAG, 709; Otto Michel, "ὁμολογέω," in *TDNT*, 5:208; Carter, *Matthew and the Margins*, 241–42; Davies and Allison, *Matthew*, 2:216: "Matthew will probably have thought of Jesus sitting on a throne at the last judgement."

[111] The phrase ἔμπροσθεν τῶν ἀνθρώπων in context probably indicates that this confession takes places in the human courts of Law (cf. Matt 10:17-20) whereas the phrase ἔμπροσθεν τοῦ πατρός μου τοῦ ἐν τοῖς οὐρανοῖς suggests a heavenly court (v. 26) (Mounce, *Matthew*,

binding promise (ὁμολογεῖν) (cf. esp. 14:7).[112] Conversely those who do not confess in Him will be denied eternal life[113] (Matt 10:33; cf. 7:23; 25:12).

Fifth, the Sheep who enter the kingdom and receive eternal life are also described as "righteous" (δίκαιοι) (25:46, 37). Elsewhere in Matthew Jesus makes it clear that only those who do the will (θέλημα) of God will enter the kingdom of heaven (7:21; cf. 12:50; 21:31). Doubtless then the δίκαιοι have done the *will* of God (cf. 5:20 and 7:21), which as we have seen is essentially expressed in only two places in Matthew, 9:13 and 12:7: "I (θέλω) desire *mercy* and not sacrifice." It is the absence of this that leads Jesus to deride the Pharisees (23:23). They appear "righteous" (δίκαιοι) and yet on the inside they are full of hypocrisy and "lawlessness" (ἀνομίας) (v. 28; cf. 7:23) and are thus unable to enter the kingdom of heaven (23:13). For Matthew then to be righteous is the opposite of hypocrisy and lawlessness.[114] If one is to enter the kingdom inner rectitude must be apparent which in Matthew only comes through conformity to the Law which is tantamount to being properly related to Jesus since He transcends the Law (cf. 5:21-48). These two strands—treatment of others and relationship to Jesus— come together in a summation of the Law[115] (22:40; cf. Rom 13:9-10; Gal 5:14): "love God, love your neighbor" (Matt 22:37, 39). Presumably to do the one is to do the other (cf. esp. 1 John 4:20-21).[116] At this point we are back to Matthew's description of the Sheep and the Goats and not far from Luke's Good Samaritan

---

97–98; Hill, *The Gospel of Matthew*, 194; Davies and Allison, *Matthew*, 2:215–16).

[112] Cf. Michel, "ὁμολογέω," 5:208: "In this context ὁμολογεῖν denotes an act of proclamation in which the concrete relation of man to Jesus is expressed in binding and valid form."

[113] That believers and unbelievers are in view in Matt 10:32-33 is suggested by v. 28: fear "Him who is able to destroy both soul and body in Gehenna"; contra Dillow, *Servant Kings*, 428, 485–86.

[114] Most scholars recognize that righteousness in Matthew constitutes conformity to God's will, itself delineated in the Law (see S. McKnight, "Justice, Righteousness," in DJG, 413–14). Though cf. also Donald A. Hagner, "Law, Righteousness, and Discipleship in Matthew," *Word and World* 28 (1998) 364–71.

[115] Cf. also William R. G. Loader, *Jesus' Attitude Towards the Law: A Study of the Gospels*, WUNT, no. 2, ed. Martin Hengel and Otfried Hofius, vol. 97 (Tübingen: Mohr/Siebeck, 1997) 265–66.

[116] See *A Theology of Liberation: History, Politics, and Salvation*, ed. and trans. Caridad Inda and John Eagleson (Maryknoll, N.Y.: Orbis Books, 1973) 196–203. However, I should qualify this statement. I am not saying that merely loving one another is a *replacement* for loving God as if all one has to do is love others and one has loved God. This would be akin to taking James 2:14-26 and saying that all one has to do is have works and one automatically has faith. Neither of these notions is biblical. We should not forget such biblical exhortations aimed at directing our affections toward God. I am thinking of words (esp. in the Psalms) like desire, hunger, thirst, delight, enjoy, etc.

parable. The righteous ones are those who have acted mercifully toward Jesus' emissaries but in doing so they have also demonstrated, not without confession, their acceptance of Jesus himself.[117] The Goats on the other hand have shown themselves to be unrighteous by their failure to show mercy to Jesus' brothers. They are cursed, though not because of their works per se, but because of their unmerciful actions toward Jesus. Their lack of mercy has merely served to demonstrate their rejection of Him (again see 1 John 4:19-20).[118]

Summary

In sum, the coming of the Son of Man marks a time of retribution for all humanity. Matthew 25:31-46 depicts such a time occurring at the end of the age (cf. Acts 17:31). Matthew's missionary discourse in chapter 10 provides the background for understanding the passage with its allusions to persecutions and imprisonment, the coming of the Son of Man and judgment, the identification of the messenger with Jesus and their reception by others. The relationship between works and salvation in Matthew 25:31-46 is certainly not causative since elsewhere Matthew places priority on grace, election, forgiveness and confession. However it is clear that salvation in v. 46 is eschatological and works— particularly works of mercy—are definitive since they reflect the will of God and His Law summed up in love for God and one's neighbor. The two are inextricably linked only insofar as one cannot be practiced without the other. Hence all humanity can legitimately be judged on the basis of how they have treated brothers since it is a *direct* reflection of their attitude toward Jesus.

---

[117] This is indeed what we see in 1 John 4:20-21. One cannot say one loves God and yet hate one's *brother*. Likewise, the Goats could not say they love God and yet had shown no mercy to Jesus' brothers.

[118] The identification of Jesus with His brothers is well documented elsewhere (Matt 18:5; Luke 10:16; Acts 9:5; cf. also Matt 1:23; 28:20).

12

Summary, Conclusion, and Some Final Thoughts

At the very outset of this book I stated that in the Synoptic Gospels there are many passages that appear to teach a direct relationship between works and salvation (Matt 5:20, 21-26, 43-48 par.; 7:21-23; 10:22; 18:21-35; 19:17-21 pars.; 24:13 par.; 25:34-46; Luke 10:27-28). It has therefore been my contention that for Jesus, "works" play a significant role in determining where one spends eternity. I believe that the passages we have investigated only serve to confirm this. There will still be objections though; the same ones that were raised in chapter one no doubt. I will now respond—one last time—in greater detail to the objections raised there.

Another Look at the Objections to this Book

Response to "The Synoptic Material is Pre-Cross"

One of the major objections I have encountered in writing this book has been the contention that the Synoptic Gospels have little to teach us on matters concerning salvation since these three books are pre-cross. If we want such teaching, it is claimed, we must turn to John or Paul. I could not disagree more. This is one reason I have devoted considerable space in the latter half of this study to investigating what NT writers outside the Synoptic Gospels have to say on this subject. We have found, *without exception*, that Jesus' teaching on the role of works in salvation can be found in every NT writer outside the Synoptic Gospels.

However, more striking than this is the fact that Jesus' teaching on *specific* themes such as entrance requirements for the kingdom, discipleship, endurance, treatment of others, and eschatological judgment, can be widely found outside the Synoptic Gospels. In fact I suspect that this post-Pentecost teaching can in most, if not all, cases be traced back to Jesus Himself. But surely this only makes sense since the disciples were commanded to teach *all* that Jesus had taught them (Matt 28:20; cf. 5:19). Therefore we are merely seeing the evidence of obedience to this command among the rest of the NT writers. It seems very reasonable to suggest that Jesus' teaching on works and salvation provided the seedbed of thought for later teaching on the same subject in the epistles. After all it is only natural that Jesus, the foundation and corner stone upon which the church is built (Eph 2:20-21), should speak authoritatively on matters concerning works and salvation. In my opinion the pre-cross argument simply does not hold true. Why else include instruction on church discipline (Matt 18:15-20) and global evangelization (28:18-20) if it has no relevance for the church today?

Response to "Theological Sophistry"

Joseph Dillow has argued that the conditions for discipleship are contradictory to the demands of the gospel and amount to nothing more than "serious heresy" if imposed on the gospel. I shall say some more regarding discipleship below but here I shall address this objection directly. In my opinion it is very difficult to see a distinction between Jesus' call to discipleship and the gospel for the following reasons. First, in order to become a disciple Jesus declares that one must renounce all one's possessions (Luke 14:33). Though Zacchaeus did not renounce all he had he certainly was willing to renounce all if it was necessary. The point is that Zacchaeus demonstrated discipleship life commitment and is said to have received *salvation* (19:9). Second, Jesus' reply to the would-be disciple wanting to bury his father—"let the dead bury their own dead" (Matt 8:21-22; Luke 9:59-60)—is an indication that the man had a choice. He could choose to return home to bury his father and thus be *dead* spiritually and eternally or he could choose to follow Jesus and *live* spiritually and eternally. The choice was between eternal salvation and eternal death, not between discipleship and some lower form of believing. Third, Jesus calls His disciples "little ones" (Matt 10:42) or alternatively "children" (18:6, 10, 14). Significant then is Jesus' statement that to enter the kingdom of heaven one must become like children (v. 3). In other words one must become like a disciple. Fourth, in John 12:46 Jesus states, "Everyone who *believes* in Me does not remain in darkness." John 8:12 is very similar except instead of "believe" John uses the verb ἀκολουθέω. Hence "follow" and "believe" mean the same thing—at least for John. Fifth, the disciples understand the Rich Young Ruler's refusal to sell all he had and follow Jesus as a failure to be saved. This is confirmed by the fact that the disciples have done what the rich man failed to do. They have *followed* Jesus (Matt 19:27 pars.)

and so are promised *eternal life* (Matt 19:29 pars.). It seems quite clear from these passages that to become a follower or disciple of Jesus is at the same time to become a believer in Jesus.

Response to "Back Loading the Gospel"

Before I address the specific issue of "back loading" I would like to address again the issue of method. Occasionally throughout this book I have had cause to note resistance to my thesis simply because John, Paul, or Acts 16:30-31, do not teach it. First of all I do not agree that John, Paul or Acts provide the kind of solace needed to dismiss the Synoptic teaching. It seems to me that to argue in this kind of fashion is to never let the Synoptic Gospels speak for themselves. Why must we interpret Matthew, Mark and Luke through the eyes of John or Paul? Or why must we discard what the Synoptic writers say because John, Paul or Luke might say something different? Surely these books were read on their own terms. Furthermore, most first century believers would not have had the luxury of reading Romans along side Matthew. I made the point in chapter one: our exegesis must govern our theology not the other way round. If our exegesis is at odds with our theology—and if we are confident in our exegesis—then maybe we should begin making changes to our theology rather than searching for solace in the likes of Paul, John, or Acts. Though I am under no illusion that I myself may not have fallen victim to the same kind of criticism—as no doubt we all do from time to time—I do not believe I have approached any of these passages from anything other than an exegetical standpoint.

In response then to the charge of back loading the gospel I would make the following points. First, it must be remembered that Jesus did not say to His disciples that it was possible for them to enter the kingdom on their own merit. Quite the opposite, it is impossible for any person to enter the kingdom. Yet with God it is possible (Matt 19:26 pars.). Unless one has the enabling power of God it is quite clear that no one can enter the kingdom.[1] Yet at the same time it is palpable that righteousness is required to enter the kingdom (5:20; 25:34, 37, 46). These two facts are not contradictory at all. Rather they are quite complementary. The righteousness required to enter the kingdom is only possible via the enabling power of God.[2] It is vital that

---

[1] John Piper, *'Love Your Enemies': Jesus' Love Command in the Synoptic Gospels and in the Early Christian Paraenesis*, SNTSMS, vol. 38 (Cambridge: Cambridge University Press, 1979) 77: "An *indispensable* condition for entrance into the Kingdom is the power of God"; see Joel B. Green, *Salvation,* Understanding Biblical Themes (St Louis, Mo.: Chalice, 2003).

[2] This is correctly observed by Donald Hagner, *The Jewish Reclamation of Jesus: An Analysis and Critique of Modern Jewish Study of Jesus* (Grand Rapids: Zondervan, 1984) 170: followers of Jesus receive via the rule of God in their lives "a transformed nature."

we keep these two truths together. Back loading the gospel would be a valid criticism *if* I was arguing that the righteousness required for entering the kingdom originated within man himself. Yet it is clear that such pharisaic righteousness will not admit anyone into the kingdom. One must have righteousness that surpasses the Pharisees and this kind can only originate with God (5:3, 20). Thus the priority of God's work is still maintained.

Second, I have often made mention of the close relationship between ethics and eschatology not only in the Synoptic Gospels but the entire NT. It is this kind of thinking that has engendered the label "back loading the gospel." It is claimed that most of the passages that teach a close relationship between ethics and eschatology are said to be speaking of something other than salvation and eternal life. Either reward is in view (e.g., 16:27) or another dispensation (e.g., 10:22; 25:31-46). Hence to argue that these passages refer to salvation, it is claimed, is to load the gospel with additional requirements at the backend as it were—hence the label "back loading the gospel." I have argued that this is not the case. Nowhere is this better illustrated than Matthew's Gospel. At the end of every one of Matthew's five discourses Jesus teaches judgment by works and the judgment in each case applies to eternal salvation (7:24-27; 10:40-42; 13:47-50; 18:32-35; 25:31-46). It will not do to argue that 10:40-42 and 18:32-35 are referring to another judgment since the remaining three passages clearly speak of eternal salvation. Unless other evidence is forthcoming —and I have argued that it is not—one must assume that Matthew has deliberately structured the end of his discourses to all make the same point: in order to enter the kingdom one must exhibit surpassing righteousness (so 5:20).

It appears then that 5:20 is a central verse for not only understanding the SM but also Matthew's entire Gospel. If this is the case Matthew simply develops the idea of surpassing righteousness. In 5:20 we are told that one who wants to enter the kingdom must exceed the righteousness of the Scribes and the Pharisees. The SM as a whole indicates that this kind of righteousness is internally rather than externally motivated. Jesus is not speaking of righteousness as a gift since the subsequent antitheses (vv. 21-48) define the greater righteousness required and clearly the focus is on attitude and conduct. The greater righteousness is given further definition in a synonymous saying in 7:21: "Not everyone who says to Me 'Lord, Lord,' will enter into the kingdom of heaven but only those who do the will of My Father who is in heaven." And then in 13:42-43, 49-50, Jesus declares that at the end of the age it is the righteous who will spend eternity with God while the wicked will be in hell. Evidently wickedness here is not a gift! Matthew's doctrine of righteousness comes to fruition in 25:31-46 where the last judgment presumably describes in greater detail what has already been stated in 5:20. This is surely the case since 25:34, 40, 46, indicate that it is the righteous who inherit the *kingdom* prepared for them before the foundation of the world. The terms "kingdom" and "righteous" make this a clear parallel to 5:20. Though in 25:31-46 we are simply given more detail of not what it means to be righteous—this is aptly spelled out in the SM—but what it looks like to enter the kingdom and conversely what it looks like to be rejected. The parallel with 7:21-23 and 25:31-46 is also striking. In chapter 25 those who are righteous at the last judgment are those who have shown mercy to Jesus' brothers. In 7:21 only those who do the will of the Father will enter the kingdom. In Matthew to do the Father's will is to be merciful (9:31; 12:7). The parable of the weeds of the field (explained in 13:36-43) also closely parallels 25:31-46 since both take place at the end of the age (cf. also vv. 47-50). Matthew 18:21-35 further describes the surpassing righteousness required to enter the kingdom since anyone who does not treat his/her brother with mercy will spend eternity in hell (cf. Jas 2:13). Mercy, righteousness, the Father's will and entering the kingdom/eternal life are clearly intertwined.

Therefore these passages are key to understanding Jesus' view on the role of works in salvation and admission requirements to heaven. The last judgment scene in Matthew 25:31-46 brings to full expression 5:20; 7:21; 13:41-43, 49-50, and 18:21-35. Surpassing righteousness, doing the Father's will and showing mercy are precisely what the Pharisees lacked (see 23:11). It may be significant that this kind of teaching is predominant in Matthew though as we have seen, Mark and Luke reflect similar thinking.

This is surely how we are to understand Paul's statements in 1 Corinthians 6:9-10, Ephesians 5:5 and Galatians 5:19-21 concerning the kind of people who will not inherit the kingdom of God. To argue that "inherit" in these instances means something more than receiving eternal life (e.g., Dillow, Hodges)—as if these people will not inherit the kingdom but they will still have eternal life—cannot be supported from any text. It is patently clear that for Paul all believers are heirs (Rom 8:17;[3] Gal 3:29; 4:7; cf. too Eph 1:14).

Hence the objection that I have back loaded the gospel is, I believe, unfounded. The label itself is completely unwarranted. Rather than back loading the gospel I have merely amplified and explained it—though I have only recited what the text says at this point and little more. Little in the way of interpretation is needed to understand the basic gist of these texts.

---

[3] It will not do to argue that since "children of God" in Rom 8:17 only applies to Christians who are led by the Spirit (v. 14) only those who are "spiritual" are heirs. Paul clearly thinks that all believers are "sons of God through faith in Christ Jesus" (Gal 3:26) and therefore *every* believer is an heir (v. 29).

The Role of Works in Salvation in Church History

In chapter two we looked at the views throughout church history concerning the role of works in salvation. All but one of these views insists on some relationship between works and salvation though all maintain that salvation is by God's grace. Yet even Augustine, often described as the Doctor of Grace, categorically states that Paul nowhere states that salvation is by faith alone. He maintains that works do not save anyone but at the same time no one can be saved without them. But works originate with God and therefore it is wrong to speak of works-righteousness in any sense in spite of their indispensability.

For Thomas Aquinas justification is God's gift and initiates the salvation process. In order for this process to continue grace must be infused via the sacraments so that works may ensue and eternal life merited. Eternal life is therefore a reward but not altogether in the sense that we might think of reward today since, like Augustine, works can only be produced by grace.

Close to Aquinas are the proponents of the *via moderna* who insist that one must initiate their salvation by *facere quod in se est* at which point grace is infused. This puts one in a state of grace apart from which there is no salvation. Eternal life is dependent on whether one continues in this state of grace—made possible by continuing in *facere quod in se est*.

For both Martin Luther and John Calvin works contribute nothing to justification. Yet salvation is not limited to justification. Luther could even speak of justification as a journey. A believer is declared righteous at the outset but he is also in the process of becoming righteous. Calvin on the other hand differentiates between justification and sanctification though sanctification is justification's inevitable result. All in all for the Reformers works are not the cause of salvation but the natural and inevitable consequence.

According to James Arminius God will preserve the believer who continues to trust in Christ. Though the Christian who does not continue in faith can subsequently forfeit his or her salvation. This is the essential difference between Arminius and the Reformers: the former says that salvation is lost whereas the latter insist it was never present.

John Wesley speaks of two justifications: initial and final. The former occurs at the outset of the Christian life by faith whereas the latter occurs at the end and is by works. The final justification merely provides a testimony to one's initial justification.

The salvation-discipleship view, as I have called it, presents a more recent understanding of the relationship between works and salvation and sees salvation, whether viewed initially or entirely, as apart from works altogether.

A Christian who has works demonstrates that he is a disciple. On the other hand the absence of works demonstrates carnality, dead faith, the failure to abide, etc. Paul in 1 Corinthians 3 describes the eternal consequences of this latter group. These people will be saved but only as through fire. Their works will be burned up since the Spirit did not produce them. The only thing these people will lose is their reward.

If I were to align myself with anyone of these views it would be Augustine. I certainly agree with him that man is utterly dependent on God for salvation and any subsequent good work. Yet it is true that Paul never teaches salvation by faith alone if we understand salvation as a broad term. Though he does say that we are saved "not by works" (Eph 2:9). But Paul is talking about *pre-conversion* works. We should not misunderstand Augustine's statement concerning salvation not being by faith alone. Augustine is not thinking of initial justification. But nor is he thinking of a kind of salvation that is *merited*. If *post-conversion* works are necessary for salvation faith is necessary for these works to occur (Gal 5:6; Eph 2:8-10). Thus Augustine would say that faith—more properly grace—is *always* the first cause. He places a lot of emphasis on the notion that the works necessary for eternal life originate only with God (John 15:5). This is something that I have also emphasized. Augustine rightly distinguishes between pre-conversion and post-conversion works. No NT writer ever says that the latter do not save only the former (see Augustine on Eph 2:8-10). I also agree with his understanding of the last judgment. All humanity will be subject to judgment vis-à-vis eternal salvation (see esp. Matt 25:31-46). In the last analysis the decision as to who is saved will be made not on the basis of faith but works. Though we must remember *once again* the origin of these works—God's grace. Hence at judgment time God will indeed crown not so much our works but His own gifts.

It is difficult to know what to make of Aquinas or the *via moderna*. That justification initiates the salvation process and works can only come from grace are appropriate remarks on their own. Though I am not convinced on their understanding of the sacraments. Even though Biel and Ockham dismissed *facere quod in se est* as anything other than God's grace the notion does not fit with the beginning of salvation. Rather it sounds more akin to Luke's "strain every nerve to enter the kingdom of God" (Luke 13:24)—a comment that concerns eschatological salvation.

I am in agreement with Luther and Calvin's teaching on works and justification. Luther is careful in his articulation of the role of works in salvation though he is clear. I agree with him theologically that works are not the cause of one's salvation but the result; although I am not convinced that this is the best way to always describe this relationship. I shall discuss this further below. Luther appears to steer clear of Matthew 25:31-46 and disliked James

2:14-26 evidently because they clashed with Paul's justification by faith apart from works. I align more with Calvin here who did not see these passages as a threat. According to Calvin many passages in the NT teach the reception of eternal life on the basis of works (Matt 16:27; cf. also 5:12; 25:34; Luke 6:23; John 5:29; Rom 2:6; 1 Cor 3:8; 2 Cor 5:10). Eternal life is therefore the consequence of works. He can even speak of works as the cause of salvation though they are the inferior cause. On this point I am in total agreement.

I do not have a problem with Arminius' teaching on works and salvation as a whole. I understand his point vis-à-vis a failure to endure being tantamount to losing one's salvation though I will argue below that I do not ultimately agree with him.

With respect to Wesley's expression of works and salvation I find him very much in line with my own observations. His teaching on two justifications, in my opinion, aligns very much with Matthew 12:37; 25:31-46; Romans 2:5-13, and James 2:14-26. I cannot fault Wesley on this point. In fact I find his observations here very helpful and instructive for understanding the general relationship between works and salvation, not only in Jesus' teaching but also in the NT epistles. That there are two justifications is not a contradiction but rightly understood they complement each other.

I have probably said enough regarding the salvation-discipleship view (a.k.a. "free-grace"). Needless to say that out of all the views I find this one to be the least biblical. At the heart of our disagreement seems to be our understanding of salvation and what constitutes a disciple. We obviously disagree exegetically on many passages and I have tried to point out these disagreements where they occur although as I have already mentioned I cannot interact on every debatable point.

The Role of Works in Salvation in Judaism

Since the time of the Reformation scholars have by and large assumed, based on statements in Paul, that Judaism taught salvation by works. This view was propounded by Luther and perpetuated by Ferdinand Weber, Emil Schürer, Paul Billerbeck, and Rudolf Bultmann. Though the predominant view it did have its critics. Finally in 1977 E. P. Sanders, in his *Paul and Palestinian Judaism,* suggested that Judaism knew nothing of works-righteousness and was in fact always a religion of grace and could be described as covenantal nomism. Subsequent study in the Jewish sources has shown that Sanders has a point and no one it seems is willing to return completely to the view of Luther and others. However studies have also shown that Sanders' position is too simplistic. Many now agree that ancient Judaism was far more complex than what Sanders suggests and it is indeed possible to speak of salvation by works and grace in Judaism.

With this final conclusion I am in complete agreement. The NT seems to affirm both. Paul insisted that salvation has always been by faith at least in the OT since Abraham was justified by faith. Yet in the Synoptic Gospels the Rich Young Ruler and the Good Samaritan present themselves as two examples of Jews who evidently held to a works-righteousness mentality. The discrepancy is probably the result of a combination of a disjunction between theology and practice and a change in salvation history. For Paul one could only be justified by faith in Christ and therefore anyone trying to gain justification through any other means was wrong.

I do not believe that Sanders has articulated the relationship between works and salvation in Judaism appropriately. He has, in my opinion, fallen into the same trap that many also fall into with the NT. That is, thinking of salvation as an entry point. Judaism has a lot to say about righteousness and the end of the age and I doubt whether this relationship can merely be explained as "maintaining" one's salvation.

I certainly do not think that such a relationship exists in the NT. In fact the close relationship between righteousness and the end of the age in Judaism appears to be analogous to some of Jesus' teaching. In both Judaism and the Synoptic Gospels "works" are a pre-requisite to entering the eternal state. However this raises the question as to why Paul and Jesus deride the Jews for a similar kind of works mentality. The only suitable answer appears to concern divine enabling. In other words, the Judaism of Jesus and Paul's day was condemned for self-righteousness. Whereas Paul viewed works as originating with the Spirit, Jesus viewed works as originating within a relationship to Himself and submission to His Father. In Paul the only works that enable one to inherit the kingdom and have eternal life are the "fruit of the Spirit" (Gal 5:16-25; Rom 8:4-14). For Jesus the only works that are acceptable to gain entry into the kingdom are those done out of love and mercy. But even love and mercy are rooted in trust in God. Thus ultimately one must be completely dependent upon God (Matt 5:3) rather than one's own accomplishments. These things are evidently what set the religious leaders apart from the surpassing righteousness described in the SM. In Paul God's grace produces works within a believer (Tit 2:11-12). Likewise for Jesus, the demands of the SM are preceded by grace in the form of beatitudes.

"Works" in the New Testament

It is not uncommon for many believers to view works in a negative light since Paul has so much to say against them in Romans and Galatians, not to mention Ephesians 2:8-9—a hallmark passage. In fact we could almost be excused for thinking that works are the antithesis of grace and faith. However we must keep in mind that in Romans, Galatians, and Ephesians 2:8-9, Paul is speaking of pre-conversion works and these are of a totally different character to post-conversion works (see esp. v. 10). "The new way of salvation does not entail the exclusion of righteous ποιεῖν along the lines of quietism: faith itself is indeed the obedience which renounces all boasting about what it does. What Paul means by faith, then, is not the rejection of works but a very special way of understanding works."[4] The NT knows of two kinds of works: good and evil. The significant point is that neither are invisible (1 Tim 5:25). Also significant is what makes them different. What distinguishes a righteous work from an evil work is their origin. The works of the unsaved are dead (Heb 6:1) whereas God will not neglect those works performed for Christ's sake (v. 10). In the Gospel of John evil works originate with the devil (John 8:41) while good works originate within a saving relationship with Jesus (15:1-6) (so Augustine).

This point needs elaboration for it is crucial to understanding the role of post-conversion works in the NT. Jesus said in John 15:5, "Apart from Me you can do nothing." This is something that every NT writer believes without exception (Acts 1:8; Eph 2:10; Phil 2:13; Heb 13:21; Jas 1:5; 1 Pet 3:16; Jude 16–19). Such statements do not however occur with the same amount of frequency and explicitness in the Synoptic Gospels. They are more or less inferred (cf. Matt 5:3; 19:26; Mark 10:27; Luke 18:27). This may be one reason Jesus' teaching on salvation sometimes appears so "legalistic"—although a select reading of Paul could reveal the same observation (e.g., Rom 2:6-8, 13; 1 Cor 6:9-10, Eph 5:5, Gal 5:19-21; 6:8-10). Taken at face value Jesus believes one must have works—or righteousness—to enter the kingdom. As a rule *we are not told how this is to occur*, just that it must. It is only by looking at His teaching as a whole that we can conclude that these works are impossible apart from divine enabling. The thrust of Jesus' message is "Repent for the kingdom of God is near." Underlying then the whole notion of participating in God's kingdom is submission to God's rule and of course faith in Jesus (Mark 1:15). The demands of the SM can only be met by those who in effect acknowledge their inability to meet those demands; blessed are the poor in spirit. Yet meet them they must. It is no good to reduce Jesus' demands to nothing more than an enticement to cause someone to see their inability. The demands are real but they can only be attained through relationship with Jesus. Presumably this is what contributes to the surpassing righteousness in Matthew's SM.

---

[4] Thomas R. Schreiner, *The Law and its Fulfillment: A Pauline Theology of Law* (Grand Rapids: Baker, 1993) 219.

It is important when reading the NT then to take note of what kind of works are in view. Are they pre-conversion or post-conversion works? Post-conversion works are of utmost importance to James and Peter for example. Even Paul views them as indispensable for those who are saved (Eph 2:10). Yet when it comes to pre-conversion works the NT writers, like Luther, agree that they have no role to play in one's relationship before God. Why the difference in emphases? Presumably because pre-conversion works by their nature originate apart from God and therefore are contrary to God's saving purposes. Post-conversion works on the other hand originate in relationship to Jesus and are produced by the Spirit. They are a demonstration of God's power in the life of a believer and therefore are not only to be encouraged but also are to be expected. To therefore suggest that post-conversion works have no role to play in one's salvation is to completely misunderstand Paul's emphasis. He is not talking about pre-conversion works.

Furthermore, it is vital that we remember that *post-conversion* works are not antithetical to either grace or faith. Paul argues in Galatians 5:6 that what matters most is faith that produces love. Faith that does not manifest itself in love is no faith at all. It is the dead faith that James speaks of (Jas 2:14-16) and typifies the faith of demons (v. 19). Grace also should not be viewed as an opponent to post-conversion works for the latter cannot happen without the former. Classic in this regard is Titus 2:11-13. Here Paul insists that grace teaches us to say no to all sorts of ungodliness and enables us to live godly and righteous lives. Hence for Paul where hatred and ungodliness are present faith and grace are absent (cf. Rom 6:1).

"Salvation" in the New Testament— And a Look at the Question: Can One Lose One's Salvation?

When salvation is spoken of we often think of what believers have been delivered *from*. This is all well and good though it is only half the meaning of salvation. Salvation is never one sided. Salvation is not only deliverance from, it is deliverance *to*: whether it is salvation from sickness *to* health, enmity *to* peace, the devil *to* God, sin *to* righteousness, or death *to* life. The essential idea is that when God saves people He delivers them from one relationship and places them into another.

Given the *loose* way in which salvation is spoken of today as an entry point into the Christian life it is significant that the NT rarely (though not exclusively) uses the salvation word group to refer to the past event of regeneration. More often than not the salvation word-group is used to refer to future or eschatological salvation. Paul is no exception. Furthermore, the NT writers understand salvation much more broadly describing it from a variety of temporal perspectives and in a variety of ways. Nowhere is this better illustrated than in Jesus' encounter with the Rich Young Ruler recorded in all three Synoptic Gospels. Throughout the NT a number of terms may be used to describe one's salvation at different points. For example, the beginning may be described as entering the kingdom, life, justification, sanctification, salvation, redemption, reconciliation, and conversion. The present can be referred to as discipleship, following Jesus, life, eternal life, perfection, and salvation. While the end may be spoken of as hope, justification, sanctification, glory, salvation, inheritance, kingdom, eternal life, and perfection.

For Jesus and indeed it seems the entire NT, salvation is a pilgrimage. This explains why Jesus urges people to *follow* Him. John exhorts his readers to *remain*. Luke in Acts speaks of *The Way* as the life of salvation as if it is a path to be traveled. Paul's readers have entered into a *walk*; in Hebrews readers are urged to *run the race*; and Peter's readers are addressed as *pilgrims*. What this indicates is that salvation is never complete until eternity. This doubtless explains the warnings and exhortations to endurance and the tension that modern day readers feel concerning eternal security and loss of salvation. It does not seem that these types of questions bothered the NT writers like they do us today. If salvation is something that is yet to be completed then to speak of losing one's salvation is technically a contradiction in terms for one cannot lose what they have not yet attained.[5] We must simply endure until the end. Or as Paul put it, we must work out our salvation "with fear and trembling" (Phil 2:12). The modern day notion of "once saved always saved," reveals more our incorrect thinking on salvation than it does anything the NT writers taught. Of course what this statement often means is that once someone has made a profession of faith they are always saved. Yet James would certainly not subscribe to such a doctrine (Jas 2:14). Now this is not to say that any NT writer would argue that once someone has received the Spirit they could then lose it. I happen to think that this would be incomprehensible to any NT writer at a theological level. Salvation is a now-but-not-yet deal and although believers have not yet attained complete salvation they have it now. Otherwise why would Paul speak of the Spirit as a down payment of our inheritance (Eph 1:14)? Why would Paul speak of some of the Corinthians

---

[5] Paul A. Rainbow, *The Way of Salvation: The Role of Christian Obedience in Justification* (Waynesboro, Ga.: Paternoster, 2005) 247, may allude to this truth in saying: "That we are 'saved' requires careful qualification . . . Our salvation is in progress and is partly a matter of hope. We have advanced to the middle period between the two moments of justification, the latter of which is pending. We are not yet glorified. Our certainty that we are 'saved' will be absolute only when we find ourselves in the state of glory with the process of salvation behind us."

being disciplined in order that they might not be (eternally) condemned with the world (1 Cor 11:32; cf. 5:5)? It is my belief that such statements incontrovertibly teach that the salvation yet to be attained in eternity is secure right now though not complete.

However we must remember that the NT does not address its readers at a *pure theological* level most of the time. Their writings are motivated by pastoral concerns. Practically speaking no NT writer, as far as I can tell, bestows assurance on any individual concerning his or her salvation. This is the Spirit's job (Rom 8:16). The best the NT writers can do is express confidence that one is and will be saved (Heb 6:10). Thus at a practical level, that is, based on what they can see, they must urge their readers to endure for it is only by holding fast to one's original confession that anyone can be saved in the end (see esp. Heb 4:14; 10:23).

What then do we do with passages like Romans 8:31-39 that teach that nothing can ever separate us from the love of Christ? First, I am aware that not all believe that this passage teaches the eternal security of the believer. This is not the time or place to discuss this. Nor is it tremendously important at this juncture. My point here is that there are, in my view, passages that appear to teach the eternal security of believers. How—and can we—reconcile such passages with what I have been describing vis-à-vis the necessity for endurance in salvation? I think the point of reconciliation here is one of perspective. Passages such as 8:31-39 look at things from God's perspective. We might say that He knows who are His. However there are also passages—especially John 15:1-6; 1 Corinthians 15:2; Colossians 1:23; Hebrews 3:6, 14—that teach the possibility of forfeiting salvation through lack of endurance. These passages appear to teach anything but eternal security. However in these instances the perspective in view is not God's but ours. The NT writers do not know for sure those who are God's. Hence in a pastorally appropriate way they urge their readers on to endurance.

We might therefore ask: if one failed to endure did they lose their salvation? Perhaps we could say from man's perspective they did—or not, depending on how we define salvation. If we define salvation as something practical that someone enters into, becoming involved in the Christian community, gaining a taste for things pertaining to God, serving God, etc., then clearly *they have lost* something. However if we think of salvation in more theological categories as new birth, the deposit of the Holy Spirit, God's election, etc., then I am more inclined to suggest that salvation was never entered into in the first place. There may have been the appearance of salvation (1 John 2:19), however evidently it did not stand the test of time. In other words their salvation was in appearance only (Luke 8:13); they believed in vain (1 Cor 15:2); they received God's grace in vain (2 Cor 6:1); they demonstrated that they were never part of the Christian community (1 John 2:19); they were deceived (Jas 1:16). I believe it is textually accurate to speak in these categories.

We must remember though that this is from *God's* perspective. That is, such people did not lose their salvation, they simply never had it—irrespective of any faith profession they might have made (see again John 2:23-25; 8:30-46; cf. also Acts 8:13, 18-24). From man's perspective the faith profession gives the appearance of salvation and thus one may be tempted to think—on the basis of passages such as Romans 8:31-39—that salvation is secure; however this would be erroneous thinking. This kind of "once-saved-always-saved" mentality is not what Paul, Jesus or anyone else had in mind.[6]

The Role of Works in Salvation in the Synoptic Gospels

What Must One Do to Enter the Kingdom?

If anyone claims that Jesus did not hold to a close relationship between works and salvation they must contend with clear teaching to the contrary in Matthew 5:20 and 7:21. One objection might be that these verses apply to the eschatological kingdom and do not apply to eternal life (e.g., Govett, Dillow). However this argument cannot be sustained in light of the reference to entering life in v. 13, which is clearly to be understood alongside 5:20 and 7:21. This is confirmed by the reference to "Gehenna" in 5:22, and again in vv. 29-30, which simply clarifies what it means to not enter the kingdom in v. 20. Furthermore eternal life and the kingdom are equated in the story of the Rich Young Ruler and in Matthew's last judgment scene in 2:34 and 46. It is clear that eternal life and the kingdom cannot be separated as if separate requirements were needed to enter.

The point hardly needs repeating but I must reiterate it all the same. I am not saying that one must be righteous in order to join Jesus up front as it were. This is to again confuse pre-conversion works with post-conversion works. Jesus calls *sinners* to repentance not the righteous. However when judgment day comes (7:22-23) it will not be sinners who enter into the kingdom but the *righteous*. This distinction is important to make for it is only once anyone is in a relationship with Jesus that they are able to produce the kind of righteousness required to make it into the eschatological kingdom (i.e., post-conversion works). This does not mean that one is self-righteous but neither does it mean that one simply has righteousness as a gift from God.

---

[6] For further reading on this subject one should see ibid., 240–48.

The righteousness required is described primarily in Matthew's antitheses. That said however it is not true that such righteousness emerges outside the realm of divine enabling for it is *impossible* for anyone to enter the kingdom apart from God (Matt 19:26 pars.). One must be living under the rule of God—expressed through "repent for the kingdom is near.") One must recognize one's own helplessness to produce this kind of righteousness—expressed through "blessed are the poor in spirit" and "become humble like a child." We must also remember that those who enter the kingdom will in fact call Jesus "Lord, Lord," (7:21). But this confession will be accompanied by doing the Father's will (cf. Jas 2:14-26). So it is completely wrong to say that Jesus (and the OT for that matter) teaches any form of works-righteousness—if by that we mean *our* works merit eternal life.

In order to understand the nature of surpassing righteousness we must take into account the similar declaration in Matthew 7:21. One who is surpassingly righteous is evidently one who does the Father's will. Failure to do the Father's will and thus be righteous will disqualify one from entering into the kingdom (remember that to enter into the kingdom is tantamount to entering into life [v. 13]). In Matthew God's will is centered in Hosea 6:6 and so is typified in those who demonstrate love and mercy. It is these qualities that are at the core of each of the antitheses (Matt 5:21-48) and it is precisely what the Pharisees lacked (23:23). All this suggests that Jesus believed love and mercy to be a key, if not the key, to surpassing righteousness.

What Must One Do to Have Eternal Life?

The Rich Young Ruler

Crucial to understanding the role of works in salvation in the Rich Young Ruler is a proper understanding of the rich man's attitude toward wealth and salvation. For most Jews to divest oneself of wealth was to divest oneself of God's blessing. This is evident when the disciples ask, "Who then can be saved?" Hence what Jesus was in effect asking the ruler to do was *trust* completely in Him as the only avenue to blessing. Why Jesus asked the ruler if he'd kept the Law is a little more difficult. My suspicion is that Jesus is merely giving the stock Jewish answer for anyone wanting to enter life. However the irrefutable point is that what counts in the end is not keeping the Law but doing what Jesus says (cf. Matt 5:17-48). Furthermore, what Jesus says *surpasses* the commandments and thus He asks nothing more of the Rich Young Ruler than what is stated in 5:20: surpassing righteousness is necessary to enter the kingdom.

The Good Samaritan

In order to understand why Jesus told the lawyer to "go and do" we must understand that for Jesus to love God and love your neighbor are virtual synonyms (1 John 4:20a; cf. Matt 5:23-24; 25:40, 45). The rest of the relationship between works and salvation is explained by the fact that the lawyer is thinking of salvation at the end of the age of which *doing* must precede (so 7:21).

The Role of Discipleship in Salvation

It is popular to think of discipleship as some kind of arduous commitment only met by the spiritually elite (see Matt 11:28-29). It is not surprising that many evangelicals now teach a distinction between being a disciple and merely being a Christian. The NT, in my opinion, teaches no such distinction. In other words there are not two categories of relationship to Jesus.

The reason of course it is not popular to equate salvation with discipleship is because the conditions of discipleship appear to be a "work." However this is incorrect for two reasons. First, the conditions for discipleship graphically display what it means to repent and believe in the gospel. One who submits to the conditions of discipleship also places complete confidence in Jesus. *The nature of faith, the gospel, and the kingdom, demand nothing less.*

The second reason that discipleship cannot be considered a work is because discipleship is not defined only by its conditions. The Gospels paint a very realistic picture of what it looks like to be a disciple and it is not always marked by remarkable commitment. In fact believing disciples[7] can be a mixed bag spiritually and it is wrong to conclude that a disciple must live above a certain spiritual criteria. Not even the Twelve lived up to this. The same is true of the rest of the NT. Paul urges his readers in Ephesians 4:1 to live up to their call. Clearly he recognizes a gap, or the potential for a gap, between their call and the reality of Christian living. This is why he uses the imperative. We must keep in mind that in reality there is often a gap between our call to discipleship and the way in which we live out our call.

The Role of Endurance in Salvation

There seems no other way to describe the role of endurance in salvation in the Synoptic Gospels than to say that endurance is a *condition* for eternal and eschatological salvation. The salvation in view is clearly not physical for otherwise Jesus' warnings against death would be farcical. Neither is the salvation

---

[7] I use the qualifier *believing* since not all disciples are Christians but all Christians are disciples.

limited to the future Tribulation as if the command to endure only applies to future Tribulation Christians. Jesus' warnings in Matthew 10 are carried out in Acts and all are commanded to take the gospel to the world by the end of Matthew (Matt 28:19-20). Certainly the early church understood endurance to be a defining mark of every believer in Christ. Hence even if it can be argued that the endurance sayings in the Synoptic Gospels do not apply to the church today, there are plenty of passages in the rest of the NT that do (cf. John 15:1-6; Rom 2:7; 1 Cor 15:1-2; Col 1:22-23; 2 Thess 1:4-5; 1 Tim 4:16; 2 Tim 2:12; Heb 3:6, 14; 4:14; 10:23; Jas 1:12; Rev 2:10).

It is vital that we understand what endurance actually is for it is easy to over-exaggerate its meaning. Fortunately the context in each case provides adequate clues. Negatively it means staying free of deception and sin and not denying Jesus. Positively it involves continuing to confess Jesus in times of persecution and suffering. We see both these aspects well documented throughout the NT.

It is also important to understand that endurance does not contradict the gospel—it amplifies it. No one will be saved in the end if they do not continue to believe in Jesus Christ (1 Cor 15:1-2). Faith is an essential component to endurance (2 Thess 1:4-5). However as is true of NT saving faith, enduring faith will express itself in obedience to God (1 Tim 4:16; Rev 14:12). Yet to really understand what endurance is all about we must look at the two people who are held up as models of endurance—Jesus (in Hebrews) and Job (in James). By examining their lives we can deduce that endurance evidently excludes such things as questioning God, acknowledging pain and anguish, wanting to give up, and sadness. At the core of endurance is hanging on to God and remaining faithful to Him even though every bone and muscle in the body might want to abandon Him. That's endurance; it's also trust.

The Role of Treating Others in Salvation

Given our observations elsewhere concerning the idea of loving God equating to loving one's neighbor, it is not surprising that there is a very strong relationship between the way in which someone treats others and their eternal destiny. Quite simply, at judgment time people will be treated in the same way they have treated others. Those who have lived with unresolved anger, evidently viewed as a perpetual and unrepentant problem, do not exhibit the surpassing righteousness required to enter the kingdom and thus are subject to the fires of hell (Matt 5:21-26). Similarly those who do not love their enemies not only share the character of unbelievers but also their eternal destiny (vv. 45-47; Luke 6: 32-35). Finally those who do not forgive others will also not be forgiven by God. Their destiny is hell (18:34-35; cf. 6:14-15).

While these passages evidently teach that God's final treatment of man is dependent upon man's final treatment of his fellow man we should not forget that Jesus in fact taught that at judgment time a measure for measure type principle would be implemented. Whatever problems we have with this theologically it is clear that this is what the text teaches. One may argue whether in fact eternal salvation is in view though there is no doubt that God's treatment of man is dependent upon man's treatment of others in the end. This is simply what the text says and somehow we must assume that this is not at odds with God's grace and forgiveness.

Whatever problems this may cause, this kind of teaching does not contradict the NT teaching on love as a whole. Jesus' teaching is very much in line with other NT writers. Most notable is James 2:12, "Judgment is without mercy to the one who has shown no mercy." John clearly believes love to be the defining mark of a Christian since it is what distinguishes a believer from an unbeliever (John 13:35; 1 John 2:9-11; 3:10, 14-15, 17; 4:7-8, 12, 20-21). He even says that love is what gives us confidence on the day of judgment (4:17). This is right in line with Matthew 7:21-23 where doing the will of the Father, that is, mercy, admits one into the kingdom. We see this taught explicitly in 25:31-46 and we could cite many other passages (Gal 5:6; 6:7-10; Heb 6:9-10; Jas 1:27; 2:1-4, 15-16; 1 Pet 4:8; Jude 21). Clearly there is a close relationship between love/mercy/treatment of others, and salvation in the NT, to the degree that where love is absent so too is salvation.

The Role of Judgment in Salvation

Matthew 25:31-46 simply *illustrates* the preceding discussion. In the final judgment when the Son of Man judges all humanity He will separate the sheep from the goats. The sheep are the righteous and have shown mercy to Jesus' brothers (Christians). The goats have not. The sheep inherit the kingdom and enter into eternal life. The goats do not. Once again in the words of James, "judgment is without mercy to those who have shown no mercy but mercy triumphs over judgment." Since mercy reflects the will of the Father, Matthew 25:31-46 merely elucidates 7:21-23.

In order to understand and interpret this passage (25:31-46) one must note the parallel with Matthew's missionary discourse in chapter 10. This suggests that this judgment should be understood against a missionary context though not necessarily Christian "missionaries" per se (see 28:18-20). One's response to the Christian messenger will be indicative of one's response to Jesus. All will be revealed at the judgment (Matt 10:26). Matthew 16:27 is another important parallel indicating that this and 25:31 are in all probability the same event. Hence the separation of the sheep and the goats is a visual illustration of each one being recompensed according to his work (cf. Acts 17:31).

That there will be a future judgment on the basis of works vis-à-vis eternal salvation is well documented in the NT. John writes that, "all who have done good will go into the resurrection of life and those who have done evil into the resurrection of judgment" (John 5:29). Paul, along with Matthew 16:27, cites Psalm 62:12 and Proverbs 24:12 to teach that in the future God will judge all on the basis of their works (Rom 2:6). Those who persevere in doing good will receive eternal life (v. 7) while those who obey unrighteousness will receive wrath (v. 8).

It is my opinion that the troublesome James 2:14-26 passage teaches judgment on the basis of works. James' point is clear: the absence of works will not save anyone *in the end*. Though the meaning of salvation is debated the evidence is lacking for anything except eternal salvation (cf. esp. 4:12 and Matt 10:28). With this is mind James' justification by works makes complete sense as a restatement of the same thought. He simply replaces "save" with "justification" but his point is the same.

This leads me to believe that Matthew's last judgment scene (Matt 25:31-46) is James' salvation/justification by works (note esp. Jas 2:15-16 par. Matt 25:35-36) although I have not explored this here (cf. also Rom 14:10-12; 2 Cor 5:10; 2 Thess 1:6-10; Rev 20:11-13; 22:12). Thus we may legitimately speak of salvation by works though what I mean of course is eschatological salvation by works.

Some Final Thoughts

Did Jesus Teach Salvation By Works?

So did Jesus teach salvation by works? We have clearly seen that indeed He did. However we must remember to carefully define our terms. If by salvation we mean 'conversion' and something akin to Paul's justification by faith; and if by works we mean works prior to conversion and thus originating from ourselves then it is clear—Jesus did *not* teach salvation by works. If however we mean final or eschatological salvation and post-conversion works originating from God Himself then, yes, Jesus *did* teach salvation by works—in the same way that James taught *justification by works*. The answer—yes or no—depends on what perspective of salvation we are speaking about. This is exactly the tension we see for example between James 2 and Romans 4. Both apostles use the same terminology—"justification" and "works"—and yet both apostles argue *different* conclusions. Paul says that no one is justified by means of works; James says that we are. They are simply speaking from different perspectives. Both are correct.

Eschatological salvation then, in the Synoptic Gospels, is indeed by works. But we must remember—also in the Synoptic Gospels—that it is *impossible* for anyone to enter into the kingdom. Thus Jesus is—and must be—the One who calls, since with God "all things are possible." He alone can get the camel through the eye of the needle. Only those who are poor in spirit are blessed and enter into the kingdom. Thus Jesus calls sinners only. All this points to the *priority* of God's grace. By priority I mean that even conversion is not possible apart from God's call. It follows that works—works that save—are not possible unless God enables them. Hence those who enter into eternal life have been blessed *by God* and enter into something prepared *by God* (Matt 25:34). We must remember in this regard that Jesus' words to the disciples concerning the impossibility of man entering the kingdom refer primarily to the *eschatological* kingdom. Thus, even though works are necessary for salvation, the works themselves are only possible "with God." Works then are, as we saw in chapter two from John Calvin, "inferior causes." The possession of eternal life, says Calvin, "is by means of good works . . . eternal life [is] a consequence of works." We can rightly say then along with Augustine that at the time of final salvation God will "crown not so much thy merits, as *His own gifts*."

Explaining the Role of Works in Salvation in the Synoptic Gospels

It is not uncommon to express the role of works in salvation along the following lines: works are the *evidence* of a salvation already begun. I agree with this statement theologically and believe it can be defended exegetically from many passages in the NT (cf. e.g., Matt 7:15-20; John 13:35; Acts 26:20; 2 Thess 1:4-5; Heb 3:14; Jas 2:14-26; 3:13; 1 John 2:19; 3:14). However this does not appear to be the primary way the Synoptic Gospels describe this relationship. Rather in these writings it is probably more accurate to speak of works as the *condition* for final salvation or entrance into the eschatological kingdom. (But remember that by "works" we mean *post-conversion* works!). By condition we mean that if (post-conversion) works (e.g., endurance, love, mercy, forgiveness) are not present then final salvation will not be granted. When Jesus says that one's righteousness must exceed that of the scribes and the Pharisees in order to enter the kingdom of heaven (Matt 5:20) He means if this kind of righteousness is absent one will not be able to enter. Righteousness is a prerequisite for entering the kingdom. For the Rich Young Ruler to enter the kingdom Jesus required him to sell all he had and give it to the poor. His failure to do so meant he was denied entrance and salvation. Jesus patently made doing a requirement for the lawyer who wanted to know how to inherit eternal life. The converse of "the one who endures until the end will be saved" is "the one who does not endure until the end will not be saved." Endurance is a condition for final salvation.

Understanding the Role of Works in Salvation

It will no doubt be puzzling to some as to how and why Jesus can hold to this kind of relationship, that is, works as a condition to final salvation. There are six factors at least that account for this relationship.

First, Jesus understands salvation to be more than just an historical entry point. Salvation is submission to God's rule—His kingdom—now and entrance into His eschatological kingdom or eternal life in the future. Thus where Paul is primarily speaking out against *pre*-conversion works Jesus is endorsing *post*-conversion works. Therefore passages that appear to contradict Paul do not in fact contradict him at all.

Second, since the works that admit one into the kingdom are post-conversion works they are also necessarily produced or enabled by the power of God. One does therefore not gain admittance in the end by one's own works as if they were somehow meritorious. The surpassing righteousness originates from God Himself (cf. 2 Cor 3:18). Once again this is patently different from Paul's saying in Ephesians 2:9: "not from works in order that no one might boast." These kinds of works (pre-conversion works) belong to man (cf. v. 8). They are what the Pharisees boast in (Luke 18:9-12) and do not admit anyone entry into the kingdom of God (Matt 7:22). However the "good works" that Jesus requires bring glory to God in heaven (5:16). They surpass the self-righteousness of the Pharisees and are a pre-requisite for entering the kingdom.

Third, it follows that for Jesus, works are the evidence of one's relationship to God (7:15-23 par.). The outward manifestation of evil is merely a reflection of one's heart (15:17-20 par.). This is significant since God evidently views the outward manifestations of men and women as legitimate criteria for judgment (12:37). However this does not mean that every so-called good work is worthy of eternal life (cf. 7:22-23) lest anyone think they can deceive God. This is the reason why only Jesus will judge humanities' works (cf. 7:1). People may deceive people but they will not deceive God (Gal 6:7-8).

Fourth, even though works are necessary for salvation Jesus and the Synoptic writers do not mean sinless—or even something similar—perfection. Kingdom entrants are to ask their Father to forgive their debts. This assumes that they have debts to be forgiven. They are to *continually* exhibit an attitude of repentance, indicating that they have something to repent of. Entailed in this is recognizing their spiritual poverty, mourning over their sin and hungering and thirsting for righteousness. These are not 'one-time' events but continual. Logically then those who are 'being saved' also have things to repent of; there are areas in which they are impoverished; there is sin to mourn over and there is *still* righteousness to hunger and thirst for. How do we reconcile this shortfall in righteousness with claims that believers are to be righteous when they enter eternity? Zane Hodges suggests it is because righteousness at the gate of eternity is viewed from an eternal perspective. I suggest, from the evidence in the Synoptic Gospels, that the righteousness is being viewed as a *pattern of life*. In other words momentary lapses into anger, impatience, un-forgiveness, etc. do not exclude one from the kingdom as if what was required was letter of the law type "perfection" in every sense of the word—not as Matthew 5:48 speaks of it. We have an example of "a pattern of life" in Romans 4 where Paul comments on Abraham's faith. Paul states, citing Genesis 15:6 (in Rom 4:3), that Abraham believed God's promise that he would father a son at the age of ninety-nine. Paul isolates Abraham as a *model* of the kind of faith that qualifies one to be declared righteous. Especially worthy of note are Paul's later words in verse 20 regarding Abraham: "He did not waver in unbelief but was strengthened in his faith." Yet the Genesis accounts at some points do not indicate such a strong faith. In fact there are times when it seems that Abraham did *not* believe God (cf. esp. Gen 16:1-4; 17:15-18; cf. also 18:10-12). Evidently Paul is not interested in momentary lapses of faith; such lapses occur even in the likes of Abraham—and Job as we have seen. Rather Paul is interested in characterizing[8] "the basic pattern and direction of Abraham's life, which was ultimately typified by trust in God, not by doubt."[9] Of course in the Synoptic Gospels the disciples themselves are classic examples of this kind of tension.

Fifth, Jesus identifies with others—mostly His own people it seems (Matt 10:40; Luke 10:16; cf. Acts 9:4-5). Therefore how one treats another person is a direct reflection of one's attitude toward Jesus (Matt 25:40, 46). We are not given any explanation for this phenomenon though presumably it is due to the fact that men and women have been made in the image of God and believers especially have the presence of God dwelling within them. Since one's attitude to Jesus is seen in the treatment of others, qualities such as love and mercy are a legitimate indicator of one's relationship to God.

Sixth, Jesus apparently believes that judgment should be fair and consistent. We might call this proportional recompense or measure for measure

---

[8] Note the use of the aorist, ἐπίστευσεν and διεκρίθη, in Rom 4:3 and 20, respectively.

[9] Thomas R. Schreiner, *Romans*, BECNT, ed. Moisés Silva, vol. 6 (Grand Rapids: Baker, 1996) 238.

(Matt 7:1-2 par.). This seems especially important in understanding the relationship between treatment of others and salvation. One cannot expect to treat others poorly without being subject to judgment. In the same way they have treated others God will also treat them on judgment day.

Bibliography

Primary Works

The Apostolic Fathers. Translated by Kirsopp Lake and edited by G. P. Goold. Vol 1. The Loeb Classical Library. Cambridge, Mass.: Harvard University Press, 1912. Reprint, 1977.

The Babylonian Talmud. Edited by I. Epstein. London: Soncino Press, 1964–90.

The Fathers of the Church: A New Translation, ed. Ludwig Schopp. Vols. 1–6. New York: Cima, 1947–48.

The Fathers of the Church: A New Translation, ed. Joseph Deferrari. Vols. 7–42. New York: Fathers of the Church, 1949–61.

The Fathers of the Church: A New Translation, ed. Joseph Deferrari. Vols. 43–64. Washington, D.C.: The Catholic University of America Press, 1962–69.

The Fathers of the Church: A New Translation, ed. Bernard M. Peebles. Vols. 65–67. Washington, D.C.: The Catholic University of America Press in association with Consortium Press, 1971–72.

The Fathers of the Church: A New Translation, ed. Hermigild Dressler. Vols. 68–72. Washington, D.C.: The Catholic University of America Press, 1977–82.

The Fathers of the Church: A New Translation, ed. Thomas P. Halton. Vols. 73–103. Washington, D.C.: The Catholic University of America Press, 1983–2002.

Aquinas, St. Thomas. *Summa Theologica.* Translated by Fathers of the English Dominican Province. 5 vols. London: Benziger Brothers, 1911. Reprint, Allen, Tex.: Christian Classics, 1981.

Aristotle. *The Metaphysics.* Translated by Hugh Tredennick and edited by T. E. Page et al. Vol. 1. The Loeb Classical Library. Cambridge, Mass.: Harvard University Press, 1933. Reprint, 1956.

Arminius, James. *The Works of James Arminius.* Translated by James Nichols. 3 vols. Grand Rapids: Baker, 1986.

Augustine. *Sermons on Selected Lessons of the New Testament.* A Library of Fathers of the Holy Catholic Church, Anterior to the Division of the East and the West. 2 vols. Oxford: John Henry Parker, 1844.

Biel, Gabriel. *Epithoma pariter et collectorium circa quattuor sententiarum libros.* Tübingen: Otmar, 1501.

———. Sermones dominicales de Tempore et de Sanctis per totum
annum, etc. n.p. 1519.

Bullinger, Heinrich. *De gratia dei iustificante nos propter Christum, per solam fidem absq operibus bonis, fide interim exuberante in opera bona libri IIII.* Zurich: Ex Officina Froschoviana, 1554.

Calvin, John. *Selected Works of John Calvin: Tracts and Letters*, ed. Henry Beveridge and Jules Bonnet. 7 vols. Grand Rapids: Baker, 1983.

———. *Institutes of the Christian Religion*. Translated by Henry Beveridge. 2 vols. Grand Rapids: Eerdmans, 1975.

Catholic Church. *Catechism of the Catholic Church*. Mahwah, N.J.: Paulist Press, 1994.

Charlesworth, James H., ed. *The Old Testament Pseudepigrapha*. 2 vols. New York: Doubleday, 1983–85.

Dio Chrysostom. *Dio Chrysostom*. Translated by J. W. Cohoon and edited by T. E. Page et al. Vol. 1. The Loeb Classical Library. Cambridge, Mass.: Harvard University Press, 1932. Reprint, 1961.

———. *Dio Chrysostom*. Translated by H. Lamar Crosby and edited by T. E. Page et al. Vol. 4. The Loeb Classical Library. Cambridge, Mass.: Harvard University Press, 1946. Reprint, 1956.

Diodorus, Siculus. *Diodorus of Sicily*. Translated by C. H. Oldfather and edited by T. E. Page et al. Vol. 1. The Loeb Classical Library. Cambridge, Mass.: Harvard University Press, 1933. Reprint, 1946.

Elliott, J. K. *The Apocryphal New Testament: A Collection of Apocryphal Christian Literature in an English Translation*. Oxford: Clarendon, 1993.

García Martínez, Florentino, ed. *The Dead Sea Scrolls Translated: The Qumran Texts in English*. 2d. ed. Translated by Wilfred G. E. Watson. New York: E. J. Brill, 1996.

Glas, John. *The Works of Mr. John Glas*. 5 vols. Perth: R. Morison & Son, 1782.

Herodotus. *Herodotus*. Translated by A. D. Godley and edited by T. E. Page et al. Vol. 2. The Loeb Classical Library. Cambridge, Mass.: Harvard University Press, 1921. Reprint, 1963.

Isocrates. *Isocrates*. Translated by Larue Van Hook and edited by T. E. Page et al. Vol. 3. The Loeb Classical Library. Cambridge, Mass.: Harvard University Press, 1945. Reprint, 1961.

Josephus. *Completed Works of Josephus: New Updated Edition*. Translated by William Whiston. Endinburgh: William P. Nimmo, Portland Coates, 1867. Reprint, Peabody, Mass.: Hendrickson, 1987.

———. *The Life Against Apion*. Translated by J. Thackeray and edited by G. P. Goold. Vol. 1. Loeb Classical Library. Cambridge, Mass.: Harvard University Press, 1926. Reprint, 1976.

———. *Jewish Antiquities*. Translated by Ralph Marcus and edited by G. P. Goold. Vol. 7. The Loeb Classical Library. Cambridge, Mass.: Harvard University Press, 1933. Reprint, 1986.

Kee, Howard Clark, ed. *The Cambridge Annotated Study Apocrypha: New Revised Standard Version*. Cambridge: Cambridge University Press, 1994.

Lombardo, Gregory J. *St. Augustine on Faith and Works*. Ancient Christian Writers: The Works of the Fathers in Translation, ed. Walter J. Burghardt and Thomas Comerford Lawler, vol. 48. New York: Newman Press, 1988.

Luther, Martin. *Luther's Works*. Vols. 1–30 ed. Jaroslav Pelikan, vols. 31–55 ed. Helmut T. Lehmann. Philadelphia: Muhlenberg Press, 1955.

———. *D. Martin Luthers Werke: Kritische Gesamtausgabe*. Vol. 22. Weimar: Hermann Böhlaus Nachfolger, 1929.

Neusner, Jacob. *Sifre to Deuteronomy: An Analytical Translation*. 2 vols. Brown Judaic Studies 98, 101. Atlanta: Scholars Press, 1987.

———. *The Mishnah: A New Translation*. New Haven: Yale University Press, 1988.

Philo. *Philo*. Translated by F. H. Colson and G. H. Whitaker and edited by T. E. Page et al. Vol. 2. The Loeb Classical Library. New York: G. P. Putnam's Sons, 1929.

Plato. *Laches, Protagoras, Meno, Euthydemus.* Translated by W. R. M. Lamb and edited by T. E. Page et al. Vol. 2. The Loeb Classical Library. Cambridge, Mass.: Harvard University Press, 1924. Reprint, 1962.

———. *Laws.* Translated by R. G. Bury and edited by T. E. Page et al. Vol. 11. The Loeb Classical Library. Cambridge, Mass.: Harvard University Press, 1926. Reprint, 1961.

Plutarch. *Moralia.* Translated by Harold North Fowler and edited by T. E. Page et al. Vol. 10. The Loeb Classical Library. Cambridge, Mass.: Harvard University Press, 1936. Reprint, 1960.

Sandeman, Robert. *Discourses on Theron and Aspasio: Addressed to the Author.* Edinburgh: Sands, Murray, Donaldson, and Cochran, 1759. Reprint, New York: John S. Taylor, 1838.

Schaff, Philp. *The Creeds of Christendom.* Vol. 2. New York: Harper & Brothers, 1877. Reprint, Grand Rapids: Baker, 1977.

Tertullian. *Tertullian's Homily on Baptism.* Edited and translated by Ernest Evans. London: SPCK, 1964.

———. *On Penance and Purity.* Ancient Christian Writers, ed. Johnannes Quasten and Walter J. Burghardt, trans. William P. Le Saint, vol. 28. Westminster, MD: Newman Press, 1959.

Wesley, John. The Works of John Wesley. 1st ed., 1872. London: Wesleyan Conference, 1872. Reprint, Grand Rapids: Zondervan, 1958.

Zwingli, Huldrych. *Sämtliche Werke: Einzig vollständige Ausgabe der Werke Zwinglis unter Mitwirkung des Zwingli-Vereins Zürich herausgegeben.* Corpus Reformatorum. Zürich: Theologischer Verlag, 1982–91.

Secondary Works

Agbanou, Victor Kossi. *Le Discours Eschatologique de Matthieu 24-25: Tradition et Rédaction.* Études Bibliques, vol. 2. Paris: Librairie Lecoffre, 1983.

Aland, Kurt. *Synopsis of the Four Gospels.* 10th ed. Stuttgart: Biblia-Druck, 1993.

Aldis, W. H. *The Message of Keswick and Its Meaning.* London: Marshall, Morgan & Scott, n.d.

Althaus, Paul. *The Theology of Martin Luther.* Translated by Robert C. Schultz. Philadelphia: Fortress, 1966.

Anderson, H. George, T. Austin Murphy, and Joseph A. Burgess, eds. *Justification by Faith.* Lutherans and Catholics in Dialogue, vol. 7. Minneapolis: Augsburg, 1985.

Arand, Charles P. *That I May Be His Own: An Overview of Luther's Catechisms.* Saint Louis, Mo.: Concordia, 2000.

Attridge, Harold W. *A Commentary on the Epistle to the Hebrews,* Hermeneia, ed. Helmut Koester. Philadelphia: Fortress, 1989.

Avemarie, Friedrich. *Tora and Leben: Untersuchungen zur Heilsbedeutung der Tora in der frühen rabbinischen Literatur.* Texte und Studien zum Antiken Judentum 55. Tübingen: Mohr Siebeck, 1996.

———. "Erwählung und Vergeltung: Zur optionalen Struktur rabbinischer Soteriologie." *New Testament Studies* 45 (1999) 108–26.

Barabas, Steven. *So Great Salvation: The History and Message of the Keswick Convention.* Westwood, N.J.: Fleming H. Revell Company, 1952.

Barnard, Leslie W. "To Allegorize or not to Allegorize." *Studia Theologica* 36 (1982) 1–10.

Barnett, Paul. *The Servant King: Reading Mark Today.* Sydney: AIO, 1991.

Barrett, C. K. "The Background of Mark 10:45." In *New Testament Essays: Studies in Memory of Thomas Walter Manson 1893–1958*, ed. A. J. B. Higgins. Manchester: Manchester University Press, 1959, 1–18.

———. *A Critical and Exegetical Commentary on The Acts of the Apostles*. International Critical Commentary, ed. J. A. Emerton, C. E. B. Cranfield, and G. N. Stanton, 2 vols. Edinburgh: T. & T. Clark, 1994.

Bauer, Walter, William F. Arndt, and F. Wilbur Gingrich. *A Greek-English Lexicon of the New Testament and Other Early Christian Literature*. Revised by F. Wilbur Gingrich and Frederick W. Danker. 2d. ed. Chicago: University of Chicago Press, 1979.

———. *A Greek-English Lexicon of the New Testament and Other Early Christian Literature*. Revised and edited by Frederick William Danker. 3d. ed. Chicago: University of Chicago Press, 2000.

Bavaud, G. "La doctrine de la justification d'après Calvin et le Concile de Trent." *Verbum Caro* 22 (1968) 83–92.

———. "La doctrine de la justification d'après Saint Augustine et la Rèforme." *Revue des études augustiniennes* 5 (1959) 21–32.

Baziou, J.-Y. "Quand le salut vient à l'Église par l'étranger." *Spiritus* 170 (2003) 45–54.

Beale, G. K. *The Book of Revelation: A Commentary on the Greek Text*. The New International Greek Testament Commentary, ed. I. Howard Marshall and Donald A. Hagner. Grand Rapids: Eerdmans, 1999.

Beare, Francis Wright. *The Gospel According to Matthew*. San Francisco: Harper & Row, 1981.

Beasley-Murray, G. R. *Jesus and the Kingdom of God*. Grand Rapids: Eerdmans, 1986.

———. *Gospel of Life: Theology in the Fourth Gospel*. Peabody, Mass.: Hendrickson, 1991.

Becker, J. C. *Paul the Apostle, the Triumph of God in Life and Thought*. Philadelphia: Fortress, 1980.

Benware, Paul N. The Believers' Payday: Why Standing Before Christ Should Be Our Greatest Moment. Chattanooga: AMG, 2002.

Berkhof, L. *The History of Christian Doctrines*. Grand Rapids: Eerdmans, 1953.

Berkouwer, G. C. *Faith and Perseverance*. Studies in Dogmatics. Grand Rapids: Eerdmans, 1958.

Best, Ernest. *Disciples and Discipleship: Studies in the Gospel According to Mark*. Endinburgh: T. & T. Clark, 1986.

Best, Thomas F. "The Apostle Paul and E. P. Sanders: The Significance of Paul and Palestinian Judaism." *Restoration Quarterly* 25 (1982) 65–74.

Betz, Hans Dieter. *The SM: A Commentary on the SM, Including the Sermon on the Plain (Matthew 5:3–7:27 and Luke 6:20-49)*. Hermeneia: A Critical and Historical Commentary on the Bible, ed. Adela Yarbro Collins. Minneapolis: Fortress, 1995.

Bjork, William G. "A Critique of Zane Hodges' *The Gospel Under Siege*: A Review Article." *Journal Evangelical the Theological Society* 30 (1987) 457–67.

Blass, F., and A. Debrunner. *A Greek Grammar of the New Testament and Other Early Christian Literature*. Translated and revised by Robert W. Funk. Chicago: The University of Chicago Press, 1961.

Blauvelt, Jr., Livingston. "Does the Bible Teach Lordship Salvation?" *Bibliotheca Sacra* 143 (1986) 37–45.

Bloesch, Donald G. *The Last Things: Resurrection, Judgment, Glory*. Downers Grove, Ill.: InterVarsity, 2004.

Blomberg, Craig L. *Matthew*. New American Commentary, ed. David S. Dockery, vol. 22. Nashville: Broadman, 1992.

———. "Degrees of Reward in the Kingdom of Heaven?" *Journal of the Evangelical Theological Society* 35 (1992) 159–72.

Bock, Darrell L. "Jesus as Lord in Acts and in the Gospel Message." *Bibliotheca Sacra* 143 (1986) 146–54.

———. A Review of *The Gospel According to Jesus*, by John F. MacArthur. *Bibliotheca Sacra* 146 (1989) 21–40.

———. *Luke 1:1–9:50*. Baker Exegetical Commentary on the New Testament, ed. Moisés Silva, vol. 1. Grand Rapids: Baker, 1996.

———. *Luke 9:51–24:53*. Baker Exegetical Commentary on the New Testament, ed. Moisés Silva, vol. 2. Grand Rapids: Baker, 1996.

———. "The Kingdom of God in New Testament Theology." In *Looking into the Future: Evangelical Studies in Eschatology*, ed. David. L. Baker. Grand Rapids: Baker, 2001, 28–60.

Boehmer, Heinrich. *Road to Reformation: Martin Luther to the Year 1521*. Translated by John W. Doberstein and Theodore G. Tappert. Philadelphia: Muhlenberg Press, 1946.

Boer, Martinus C. de. "Ten Thousand Talents: Matthew's Interpretation and Redaction of the Parable of the Unforgiving Servant (Matt 18:23-35)." *Catholic Biblical Quarterly* 50 (1988) 214–32.

Boerma, C. *The Rich, The Poor - and the Bible*. Philadelphia: Westminster, 1978.

Boers, Hendrikus. "Polarities at the Roots of New Testament Thought." In *Perspectives on the New Testament: Essays in Honor of Frank Stagg*, ed. Charles H. Talbert. Macon, GA: Mercer University Press, 1985, 55–75.

Boff, Leonardo. *Jesus Christ LiberatOre.: A Critical Christology for Our Time*. Translated by Patrick Hughes. Maryknoll, N.Y.: Orbis Books, 1978.

Boisset, J. "Justification et sanctification chez Calvin." In *Calvinus Theologus: Die Referate des Congrés Européen de recherches Calviniennes*, ed. W. H. Neuser. Neukirchen-Vluyn: Neukirchener Verlag Neukirchen-Vluyn: Neukirchener Verlag des Erziehungvereins, 1976, 131–48.

Bolster, George R. "Wesley's Doctrine of Justification." *The Evangelical Quarterly* 24 (1952) 144–55.

Borchert, Gerald L. *Assurance and Warning*. Nashville: Broadman, 1987.

Borgman, Brian. "Rethinking a Much Abused Text: 1 Corinthians 3:1-15." *Reformation and Revival* 11 (2002) 71–93.

Bosch, David J. "Evangelism and Social Transformation." *Theologia Evangelica* 16 (1983) 43–55.

Braaten, Carl E., and Robert W. Jenson, eds. *Union With Christ: The New Finnish Interpretation of Luther*. Grand Rapids: Eerdmans, 1998.

Brockwell, Jr., Charles W. "John Wesley's Doctrine of Justification." *Wesleyan Theological Journal* 18 (1983) 18–32.

Brooke, George. Review of *Paul and Palestinian Judaism*, by E. P. Sanders. *Journal of Jewish Studies* 30 (1979) 247–50.

Brown, E. "The Meaning of Perfection in Matthew." *Unitarian Universalist Christian* 53 (1998) 24–30.

Brown, Francis, S. R. Driver, and Charles A. Briggs. *A Hebrew and English Lexicon of the Old Testament with an Appendix containing the Biblical Aramaic*. Oxford: Clarendon, 1951.

Brown, Jeannine K. *The Disciples in Narrative Perspective: The Portrayal and Function of the Matthean Disciples*. Academia Biblica, ed. Saul M. Olyan and Mark Allan Powell, no. 9. Atlanta: SBL, 2002.

Brown, Raymond E. *The Gospel According to John*. The Anchor Bible, 2 vols. Garden City, N.Y.: Doubleday, 1970.

Bruce, A. B. *Training of the Twelve*. Endinburgh: T. & T. Clark, 1871. Reprint, Grand Rapids: Kregel, 1971.
Bruce, F. F. *Hard Sayings of Jesus*. Downers Grove, Ill.: InterVarsity, 1983.
Bruner, Frederick Dale. *Matthew: A Commentary*. Dallas: Word, 1990.
Bultmann, Rudolf. *Essays, Philosophical and Theological*. Translated by James C. G. Greig. The Library of Philosophy and Theology. London: SCM, 1955.
———. *Theology of the New Testament*. Translated by Kendrick Grobel. 2 vols. London: SCM, 1955.
———. *Existence and Faith: Shorter Writings of Rudolf Bultmann*. Translated by Schubert M. Ogden. London: Hodder and Stoughton, 1960.
———. *The History of the Synoptic Tradition*. New York: Harper and Row, 1963.
Burge, Gary M. *The Anointed Community: The Holy Spirit in the Johannine Tradition*. Grand Rapids: Eerdmans, 1987.
Burnaby, John. *Amor Dei: A Study of the Religion of St. Augustine: The Hulsean Lectures for 1938*. London: Hodder and Stoughton, 1938.
Burroughs, Jeremiah. *The Rare Jewel of Christian Contentment*. London: Peter Cole, 1648; Edinburgh: Banner of Truth, 1964; Reprint, 1979.
Byrne, Brendan. *'Sons of God' - 'Seed of Abraham': A Study of the Idea of the Sonship of God of all Christians in Paul against the Jewish Background*. Analecta BibliCalif.: Investigationes Scientificae in Res Biblicas, 83. Rome: Biblical Institute Press, 1979.
Caird, G. B. Review of *Paul and Palestinian Judaism*, by E. P. Sanders. *Journal of Theological Studies* 29 (1978) 538–43.
———. *New Testament Theology*. Edited by L. D. Hurst. Oxford: Clarendon, 1994.
Cameron, Euan. *The European Reformation*. Oxford: Clarendon, 1991.
Capon, Robert Farrar. *The Parables of Grace*. Grand Rapids: Eerdmans, 1988.
Carroll, John T. "Sickness and Healing in the New Testament Gospels." *Interpretation* 49 (1995) 130–42.
Carson, D. A. *Divine Sovereignty and Human Responsibility: Biblical Perspectives in Tension*. New Foundations Theological Library, ed. Peter Toon. Atlanta: John Knox, 1981.
———. "Matthew." In *Expositors Bible Commentary*, ed. Frank E. Gaebelein and J. D. Douglas. Grand Rapids: Zondervan, 1984.
———. *The Gospel According to John*. Grand Rapids: Eerdmans, 1991.
———. "Reflections on Christian Assurance." *Westminister Theological Journal* 54 (1992) 1–29.
———. *Exegetical Fallacies*. 2nd ed. Grand Rapids: Baker Books, 1996.
———, Peter T. O'Brien, and Mark A. Seifrid, eds. *Complexities of Second Temple Judaism*. Vol. 1. Grand Rapids: Baker, 2001.
Carter, Warren. *Households and Discipleship: A Study of Matthew 19–20*. Journal for the Study of the New Testament Supplement Series, 103, ed. Stanley E. Porter (Sheffield: Sheffield Academic Press, 1994).
———. "Matthew 4:18-22 and Matthean Discipleship: An Audience-Orientated Perspective." *Catholic Biblical Quarterly* 59 (1997) 58–75.
———. John Paul Heil. *Matthew's Parables: Audience-Orientated Perspectives*. The Catholic Biblical Quarterly Monograph Series 30, ed. Michael L. Barré et al. Washington, D.C.: The Catholic Biblical Association of America, 1998.
———. *Matthew and the Margins: A Socio-Political and Religious Reading*. Journal for the Study of the New Testament Supplement Series, ed. Stanley E. Porter, vol. 204. Sheffield: Sheffield Academic Press, 2000.
———. "Resisting and Imitating the Empire: Imperial Paradigms in Two Matthean Parables." *Interpretation* 56 (2002) 262–68.

———. *Matthew: Storyteller, Interpreter, Evangelist*. Revised edition. Peabody, Mass.: Hendrickson, 2004.
Chafer, Lewis Sperry. *He that is Spiritual: A Classic Study of the Biblical Doctrine of Spirituality*. Revised edition. Philadelphia: Sunday School Times, 1918; Reprint, Grand Rapids: Zondervan, 1967.
———. *Systematic Theology*. 8 vols. Dallas: Dallas Seminary Press, 1947–48. Reprint, Grand Rapids: Kregel, 1993.
Chaffin, R. F. "The Theme of Wisdom in the Epistle of James." *Ashland Theological Journal* 29 (1997) 23–49.
Chantry, Walter J. *Today's Gospel: Authentic or Synthetic?* London: Banner of Truth, 1970.
Chenu, M. D. *Introduction A L'etude de Saint Thomas D'Aquin*. Paris: Librairie Philosophique J. Vrin, 1950.
Chester, Andrew, and Ralph P. Martin. *New Testament Theology: The Theology of the Letters of James, Peter, and Jude*. Cambridge: Cambridge University Press, 1994.
Chin, Moses. "A Heavenly Home for the Homeless: Aliens and Strangers in 1 Peter." *Tyndale Bulletin* 42 (1991) 96–112.
Chrisope, T. Alan. *Jesus is Lord: A Study in the Unity of Confessing Jesus as Lord and Savior in the New Testament*. Hartfordshire, England: Evangelical Press, 1982.
Clark, Francis. "A New Appraisal of Late Medieval Nominalism." *Gregorianum* 46 (1965) 733–65.
Clucas, Robert S. "The Neighbour Questions." *Theologia Evangelica* 17 (1984) 49–50.
Cocoris, G. Michael. *Lordship Salvation—Is it Biblical?* Dallas: Redencíon Viva, 1983.
Coenen, L., E. Beyreuther, and H. Bietenhard, eds. *The New International Dictionary of New Testament Theology*. English translation edited by C. Brown. 4 vols. Grand Rapids: Zondervan, 1975–86.
Colijn, Brenda B. "Salvation as Discipleship in the Gospel of Mark." *Ashland Theological Journal* 30 (1998) 11–22.
Collins, John J. *The Apocalyptic Imagination: An Introduction to Jewish Apocalyptic Literature*. 2d ed. Grand Rapids: Eerdmans, 1998.
Collins, Kenneth J. "Twentieth-Century Interpretations of John Wesley's Aldersgate Experience: Coherence or Confusion?" *Wesleyan Theological Journal* 24 (1989) 18–31.
———. "A Hermeneutical Model for the Wesleyan Ordo Salutis." *Wesleyan Theological Journal* 19 (1984) 23–37.
Compton, Bruce R. "Persevering and Falling Away: A Reexamination of Hebrews 6:4-6." *Detroit Baptist Seminary Journal* 1 (1996) 135–67.
Conzelmann, Hans. *An Outline of the Theology of the New Testament*. The New Testament Library, ed. Alan Richardson et al., trans. John Bowden. London: SCM, 1969.
Cope, Lamar. "Matthew 25:31-46 'The Sheep and the Goats' Reinterpreted." *Novum Testamentum* 11 (1969) 32–44.
Cothenet, Edouard. "Le réalisme de l'espérance chrétienne selon 1 Pierre." *New Testament Studies* 27 (1981) 564–72.
Court, J. M. "Right and Left: The Implications for Matthew 25:31-46." *New Testament Studies* 31 (1985) 223–33.
Courtenay, William J. "The King and the Leaden CoInd.: The Economic Background of 'Sine Qua Non' Causality." *Traditio: Studies in Ancient and Medieval History, Thought, and Religion* 28 (1972) 185–209.
Cranfield, C. E. B. *The Gospel According to Saint Mark*. Cambridge Greek Commentary Series, ed. C. F. D. Moule. Cambridge: Cambridge University Press, 1959.
———. *The Epistle to the Romans*. International Critical Commentary, ed. J. A. Emerton, C. E. B. Cranfield, and G. N. Stanton, 2 vols. Edinburgh: T. & T. Clark, 1979.

Crenshaw, Curtis I. *Lordship Salvation: The Only Kind There Is: An Evaluation of Jody Dillow's "The Reign of the Servant Kings" and Other Antinomian Arguments.* Memphis, Tenn.: Footstool Publications, 1994.

Crespy, Georges. "The Parable of the Good Samaritan: An Essay in Structural Research." *Semeia* 2 (1974) 27–50. (Originally published as "La parabole dite: 'Le bon Samaritain.' Recherches structurales," *Etudes Théologiques et Religieuses* 48 [1973]: 61–79, trans. John Kirby).

Cubie, David L. "Perfection in Wesley and Fletcher: Inaugural or Teleological?" *Wesleyan Theological Journal* 11 (1976) 22–37.

———. "Placing Aldersgate in John Wesley's Order of Salvation." *Wesleyan Theological Journal* 24 (1989) 32–53.

Culpepper, R. Alan. *Anatomy of the Fourth Gospel: A Study in Literary Design.* Philadelphia: Fortress, 1983.

Cunliffe-Jones, Hubert, ed. *A History of Christian Doctrine: In Succession to the Earlier Work of G. P. Fisher Published in the International Theological Library Series.* Philadelphia: Fortress, 1978.

Dabney, Robert Lewis. Discussions. Edited by C. R. Vaughan. Vol. 1. Richmond: Presbyterian Committee of Publication, 1890–92.

Dahl, Nils A. "Paul and Palestinian Judaism: A Comparison of Patterns of Religion." *Religious Studies Review* 4 (1978) 153–58.

Davids, Peter H. *The Epistle of James: A Commentary of the Greek Text.* New International Greek Testament Commentary, ed. I. Howard Marshall and W. Ward Gasque. Grand Rapids: Eerdmans, 1982.

Davies, Brian. *The Thought of Thomas Aquinas.* Oxford: Clarendon, 1992.

Davies, W. D. *Paul and Rabbinic Judaism: Some Rabbinic Elements in Pauline Theology.* 4th ed. Philadelphia: Fortress, 1980.

Davies, W. D., and Dale C. Allison, Jr. *A Critical and Exegetical Commentary on The Gospel According to Matthew.* International Critical Commentary, ed. J. A. Emerton, C. E. B. Cranfield, and G. N. Stanton, 3 vols. Endinburgh: T. & T. Clark, 1997.

Derrett, J. Duncan M. "Paul as Master-builder." *Evangelical Quarterly* 69 (1997) 129–37.

Dibelius, Martin. *James: A Commentary on the Epistle of James.* Hermeneia, ed. Helmut Koester, trans. Michael A. Williams, and rev. Heinrich Greeven. Philadelphia: Fortress, 1976.

Dillow, Joseph C. *The Reign of the Servant Kings: A Study of Eternal Security and the Final Significance of Man.* Miami: Schoettle, 1992.

Donahue, John R. "The 'Parable' of the Sheep and the Goats: A Challenge of Christian Ethics." *Theological Studies* 47 (1986) 3–31.

———. "Who Is My Enemy? The Parable of the Good Samaritan and the Love of Enemies." In *The Love of Enemy and Nonretaliation in the New Testament*, ed. William M. Swartley. Studies in Peace and Scripture. Louisville, Ky.: Westminster/John Knox, 1992, 137–56.

Donaldson, Terrence, *Paul and the Gentiles: Remapping the Apostle's Convictional World.* Minneapolis: Fortress, 1997.

Drovdahl, Robert R. "Myth of Becoming; Myth of Being." *Christian Education Journal* 13 (1992) 25–32.

Dumas, André. "Une fin créatrice de ses moyens: l'insouciance du coeur." *Recherches de Science Religieuses* 68 (1980) 321–36.

Dunn, James D. G. *Unity and Diversity in the New Testament.* Philadelphia: Westminster, 1977.

———. "The New Perspective on Paul." *Bulletin of the John Rylands University Library* 65 (1983) 95–122.

———. *Romans 1–8*. Word Biblical Commentary, ed. Bruce M. Metzger, David A. Hubbard, and Glenn W. Barker, vol. 38A. Dallas: Word, 1988.

———. "Works of the Law and the Curse of the Law (Galatians 3:10-14)." In *Jesus, Paul and the Law: Studies in Mark and Galatians*. Louisville, Ky.: Westminster/John Knox, 1990, 215–36.

———. *Jesus' Call to Discipleship*. Understanding Jesus Today, ed. Howard Clark Kee. Cambridge: Cambridge University Press, 1992.

———. *Jesus Remembered*. Vol 1, *Christianity in the Making*. Grand Rapids: Eerdmans, 2003.

Duroux, Benoit. "Aspects psychologiques de l' 'analysis fidei' chez S. Thomas d'Aquin." *Freiburger Zeitschrift für Philosophie und Theologie* 2 (1955) 148–72.

Edwards, James R. *The Gospel According to Mark*. Pillar New Testament Commentary, ed. D. A. Carson. Grand Rapids: Eerdmans, 2002.

Eno, Robert B. "Some Patristic Views on the Relationship of Faith and Works in Justification." *Recherches Augustiniennes* 19 (1984) 3–27.

Erickson, Millard J. "Lordship Theology: The Current Controversy." *Southwestern Journal of Theology* 33 (1991) 51–55.

Evans, Craig A. "How are the Apostles Judged? A Note on 1 Corinthians 3:10-15." *Journal of Evangelical Theological Society* 27 (1984) 149–50.

———. *Luke*. New International Biblical Commentary, ed. W. Ward Gasque. Peabody, Mass.: Hendrickson, 1990.

———. Jesus' Ethic of Humility. *Trinity Journal* 13 (1992) 127–38.

Fanning, Buist M. "A Theology of James." In *A Biblical Theology of the New Testament*, ed. Roy B. Zuck. Chicago: Moody, 1994, 417–35.

Fee, Gordon D. *The First Epistle to the Corinthians*. New International Commentary on the New Testament, ed. Gordon D. Fee. Grand Rapids: Eerdmans, 1997.

Fine, H. A. "The Tradition of a Patient Job." *Journal of Biblical Literature* 74 (1955) 28–32.

Finnis, John. *Aquinas: Moral, Political, and Legal Theory*. Oxford: Oxford University Press, 1998.

Flusser, D. "A New Sensitivity in Judaism and the Christian Message." *Harvard Theological Review* 61 (1968) 107–27.

Forbes, Greg. "Children of Sarah: Interpreting 1 Peter 3:6b." *Bulletin for Biblical Research* 15 (2005) 105–9,

Foster, Graham. "Making Sense of Matthew 25:31-46." *Scottish Bulletin of Evangelical Theology* 16 (1998) 128–39.

Fowl, Stephen. "Receiving the Kingdom of God as a Child: Children and Riches in Luke 18ff." *New Testament Studies* 39 (1993) 153–58.

Fox, F. Earle. "Biblical Theology and Pelagianism." *The Journal of Religion* 41 (1961) 169–81.

France, R. T. *Matthew*. Tyndale New Testament Commentaries, ed. Leon Morris. Grand Rapids: Eerdmans, 1989.

Freedman, D. N. et al., eds. *The Anchor Bible Dictionary*. 6 vols. New York: Doubleday, 1992.

Funk, Robert W. "The Good Samaritan as Metaphor." *Semeia* 2 (1974) 74–81.

Furnish, V. P. *The Love Command in the New Testament*. London: SCM, 1973.

Garland, David. E. *1 Corinthians*. Baker Exegetical Commentary on the New Testament, ed. Robert W. Yarbrough and Robert H. Stein. Grand Rapids: Baker, 2003.

Gaventa, Beverly Roberts. "Comparing Paul and Judaism: Rethinking our Methods." *Biblical Theology Bulletin* 10 (1980) 37–44.

Gay, George. "The Judgment of the Gentiles in Matthew's Theology." In *Scripture, Tradition, and Interpretation*, ed. W. Ward Gasque and William Sanford LaSor. Grand Rapids: Eerdmans, 1978) 199–215.

George, A. *Études sur l'oeuvre de Luc*. Paris: Gabalda, 1978.
Gerrish, B. A. *Grace and Reason: A Study in the Theology of Luther*. Oxford: Clarendon, 1962.
Gerstner, John H. *Wrongly Dividing the Word of Truth: A Critique of Dispensationalism*, 2nd ed. Edited by Don Kistler. Morgan, PA: Soli Deo Gloria, 2000.
———. "Aquinas was a Protestant." *Tabletalk* 18 (1994) 13–15, 52.
Gilson, Etienne. *History of Christian Philosophy in the Middle Ages*. New York: Random House, 1955.
Godfrey, W. Robert. "Reversing the Reformation," *Eternity* 35 (1984) 26–28.
Goppelt, Leonhard. *Theology of the New Testament*. Edited by Jürgen Roloff and translated by John E. Alsup. Vol. 1. Grand Rapids: Eerdmans, 1981.
———. *Theology of the New Testament: The Variety and Unity of the Apostolic Witness to Christ*. Edited by Jürgen Roloff and translated by John E. Alsup. Vol. 2. Grand Rapids: Eerdmans, 1982.
Govett, Robert. *Entrance into the Kingdom: Or Reward According to Works*. Miami: Conley & Schoettle, 1978.
Gowan, Donald E. "Wisdom and Endurance in James." *Horizons in Biblical Theology* 15 (1993) 145–53.
Grassi, J. A. "'I was Hungry and You Gave Me To Eat,' (Matt 25:35ff) The Divine Identification Ethic in Matthew." *Biblical Theology Bulletin* 11 (1981) 81–84.
Graves, Mike. "Luke 10:25-37: The Moral of the 'Good Samaritan.'" *Review and Expositor* 94 (1997) 269–75.
Gray, Sherman W. *The Least of My Brothers, Matthew 25:31-46: A History of Interpretation*. Society of Biblical Literature Dissertation Series, ed. J. J. M. Roberts, vol. 114. Atlanta: Scholars Press, 1989.
Green, E. M. B. *The Meaning of Salvation*. Philadelphia: Westminster, 1965.
Green, H. Benedict. *The Gospel According to Matthew in the Revised Standard Version: Introduction and Commentary*. The New Clarendon Bible (New Testament), ed. H. F. D. Sparks. Oxford: Oxford University Press, 1975.
Green, Joel B, Scot McKnight, and I. Howard Marshall, eds. *Dictionary of Jesus and the Gospels*. Downers Grove, Ill.: InterVarsity, 1993.
———. *The Gospel of Luke*. New International Commentary on the New Testament, ed. Gordon D. Fee. Grand Rapids: Eerdmans, 1997.
———. *Salvation*. Understanding Biblical Themes. St Louis, Mo.: Chalice Press, 2003.
Green, Michael. *Matthew for Today: Expository Study of Matthew*. Dallas: Word, 1988.
Grosheide, F. W. *Commentary on the First Epistle to the Corinthians*. New International Commentary on the New Testament, ed. F. F. Bruce. Grand Rapids: Eerdmans, 1953.
Grudem, Wayne. "Perseverance of the Saints: A Case Study from Hebrews 6:4-6 and the other Warning Passages in Hebrews." In *The Grace of God, the Bondage of the Will*, ed. T. Schreiner et al., vol. 1. Grand Rapids: Baker, 1995, 133–82.
Gullerud, C. M. "U.S. Lutheran–Roman Catholic Dialog on Justification by Faith: An Examination." *Journal of Theology* 24 (1984) 19–24.
Gundry, Robert H. "Grace, Works, and Staying Saved in Paul." *Biblica* 66 (1985) 1–38.
———. *Mark: A Commentary on His Apology for the Cross*. Grand Rapids: Eerdmans, 1993.
———. *Matthew: A Commentary on His Handbook for a Mixed Church under Persecution*. 2d ed. Grand Rapids: Eerdmans, 1994.
Gundry-Volf, Judith M. "The Least and the Greatest: Children in the New Testament." In *The Child in Christian Thought*, ed. Marcia J. Bunge. Grand Rapids: Eerdmans, 2001, 29–60.
Guthrie, Donald. *New Testament Theology*. Downers Grove, Ill.: InterVarsity, 1981.
———. *New Testament Introduction*. 4th ed. Downers Grove, Ill.: InterVarsity, 1990.

Gutiérrez, Gustavo. *A Theology of Liberation: History, Politics, and Salvation*. Edited and translated by Caridad Inda and John Eagleson. Maryknoll, N.Y.: Orbis Books, 1973.

Hagner, Donald A. "Salvation, Faith, Works." *The Reformed Journal* 29 (1979) 25–27.

———. "Paul in Modern Jewish Thought." In *Pauline Studies*, ed. Doanld A. Hagner and Murray J. Harris. Grand Rapids: Eerdmans, 1980, 143–65.

———. *The Jewish Reclamation of Jesus: An Analysis and Critique of Modern Jewish Study of Jesus*. Grand Rapids: Zondervan, 1984.

———. "Paul and Judaism: The Jewish Matrix of Early Christianity: Issues in the Current Debate." *Bulletin for Biblical Research* 3 (1993) 111–30.

———. *Matthew 14–28*. Word Biblical Commentary, ed. David A. Hubbard and Glenn W. Barker, vol. 33B. Dallas: Word, 1995.

———. "Law, Righteousness, and Discipleship in Matthew." *Word and World* 28 (1998) 364–71.

Hall, Christopher. "What Evangelicals and Liberals Can Learn from the Church Fathers." Plenary address at the Evangelical Theological Society. Valley Forge, PA: 2005.

Hannah, John D. "The Meaning of Saving Faith: Luther's Interpretation of Romans 3:28." *Bibliotheca Sacra* 140 (1983) 322–34.

Hare, D. R. A., and D. J. Harrington. "'Make Disciples of All the Gentiles' (Mt 28–19)." *Catholic Biblical Quarterly* 37 (1975) 359–69.

Harrington, Daniel J. *The Gospel of Matthew*. Sacra Pagina Series, ed. Daniel J. Harrington, vol. 1. Collegeville, Minn.: Liturgical Press, 1991.

———. "The Rich Young Man in Matthew 19:16-22: Another Way to God For Jews?" In *The Four Gospels*, ed. F. Van Segbroeck et al., vol. 2. Belgium: Leuven University Press, 1992.

Harris, Murray J. *Slave of Christ: A New Testament Metaphor for Total Devotion to Christ*. New Studies in Biblical Theology, ed. D. A. Carson, no. 8. Downers Grove, Ill.: InterVarsity, 1999.

Harrison, Everett F. "Must Christ Be Lord To Be Savior? No." *Eternity* 10 (1959) 14, 16, 48.

Harrison, W. *Arminianism*. London: Duckworth, 1937.

———. *The Beginnings of Arminianism to the Synod of Dort*. London: University of London Press, Ltd., 1926.

Hartin, Patrick J. "Call to Be Perfect through Suffering (Jas 1:2-4) The Concept of Perfection in the Epistle of James and the SM." *Biblica* 77 (1996) 477–92.

Heick, Otto W. *A History of Christian Thought*. Vol. 1. Philadelphia: Fortress, 1965.

Heil, John Paul. "The Double Meaning of the Narrative of Universal Judgment in Matthew 25:31-46." *Journal for the Study of the New Testament* 69 (1998) 3–14.

Hellerman, Joseph H. "Wealth and Sacrifice in early Christianity: Revisiting Mark's Presentation of Jesus' Encounter With The Rich Young Ruler." *Trinity Journal* (2000) 143–64.

Hengel, Martin. *The Charismatic Leader and His Followers*. Edited by John Riches and translated by James C. G. Greig. Endinburgh: T. & T. Clark, 1996.

Heniz, Johann. *Justification and Merit: Luther vs. Catholicism*. Berrien Springs, MI: Andrews University Press, 1984.

Henry, Carl F. H. "Justification: A Doctrine in Crisis." *Journal of the Evangelical Theological Society* 38 (1995) 57–65.

Héring, J. *The First Epistle of Saint Paul to the Corinthians*. London: Epworth Press, 1962.

Hermant, D. "Structure littéraire du 'Discours communautaire' de Matthieu 18." *Revue Biblique* 103 (1996) 76–90.

Hicks, John Mark. "Election and Security: An Impossible Impasse?" Paper presented at the Evangelical Theological Society. Colorado Springs: 2001.

Hiebert, D. Edmond. *The Thessalonian Epistles: A Call to Readiness*. Chicago: Moody, 1971.

———. *The Epistle of James: Tests of a Living Faith*. Chicago: Moody, 1979.
Hill, David. *Greek Words and Hebrew Meanings: Studies in the Semantics of Soteriological Terms*. Cambridge: Cambridge University Press, 1967.
———. "False Prophets and Charismatics: Structure and Interpretation in Matthew 7:15-23." *Biblica* 57 (1976) 327–48.
———. *The Gospel of Matthew*. New Century Bible Commentary, ed. Ronald E. Clements and Matthew Black. Grand Rapids: Eerdmans, 1981.
Hirsch, E. D. *Validity in Interpretation*. New Haven: Yale University Press, 1967.
Hodges, Zane C. *The Hungry Inherit: Refreshing Insights on Salvation, Discipleship, and Rewards*. Chicago: Moody, 1972.
———. "Those Who Have Done Good — John 5:28-29," *Bibliotheca Sacra* 136 (1979) 158–66.
———. *The Gospel Under Siege: Faith and Works in Tension*. 2nd ed. Dallas: Redención Viva, 1981.
———. *Grace in Eclipse: A Study on Eternal Rewards*. Dallas: Redención Viva, 1985.
———. *Dead Faith: What Is It? A Study on James 2:14-16*. Dallas: Redención Viva, 1987.
———. *Absolutely Free!: A Biblical Reply to Lordship Salvation*. Grand Rapids: Zondervan, 1989.
———. Review of "A Review of *The Gospel According to Jesus*," by Darrell L. Bock. *Journal of the Grace Evangelical Society* 2 (1989) 79–83.
———. *The Epistle of James: Proven Character Through Testing*. Edited by Arthur L. Farstad and Robert N. Wilkin. Irving, Tex.: Grace Evangelical Society, 1994.
———. *Harmony With God: A Fresh Look at Repentance*. Dallas: Redención Viva, 2001.
Horbury, W. "Paul and Judaism." *Expository Times* 90 (1979) 116–18.
Horsley, Richard A. "Ethics and Exegesis: 'Love Your Enemies' and the Doctrine of Nonviolence." In *The Love of Enemy and Nonretaliation in the New Testament*, ed. William M. Swartley. Studies in Peace and Scripture. Louisville, Ky.: Westminster/John Knox, 1992, 72–101.
Ingelaere, Jean-Claude. "La 'parabole' du Jugément Dernier (Matthieu 25:31-46)." *Revue d'Histoire et de Philosophie Religieuses* 50 (1970) 23–60.
Johnson, Luke T. *Sharing Possessions: Mandate and Symbol of Faith*. Overtures to Biblical Theology, ed. Walter Brueggemann and John R. Donahue, vol. 9. Philadelphia: Fortress, 1981.
———. *The Letter of James*. Anchor Bible, ed. W. F. Albright and David Noel Freedman. Vol. 37A. New York: Doubleday, 1995.
Johnson, S. Lewis, Jr. "How Faith Works." *Christianity Today* 33 (1989) 21–25.
Johnson, W. Stanley. "Christian Perfection as Love for God." In *Christian Ethics: An Inquiry into Christian Ethics from a Biblical Theological Perspective*, ed. Hynson, Leon O., and Lane A. Scott. Wesleyan Theological Perspectives, ed. John E. Hartley and R. Larry Shelton, vol. 3. Anderson, Ind.: Warner Press, 1983, 97–113.
Jones, Bruce W. "More about the Apocalypse as Apocalyptic." *Journal of Biblical Literature* 87 (1968) 325–27.
Jones, Peter Rhea. "The Love Command in Parable: Luke 10:25-37." *Perspectives in Religious Studies* 6 (1979) 224–42.
Julian, Ron. *Righteous Sinners: The Believer's Struggle with Faith, Grace, and Works*. Colorado Springs: NavPress, 1998.
Julicher, Adolf. *Die Gleichnisreden Jesu*. Tübingen: 1910; Nachdruck, Darmstadt: Wissenschaftliche Buchgesellschaft, 1963.
Kaiser, Walter C., Jr. "The Old Testament Promise of Material Blessings and the Contemporary Believer." *Trinity Journal* 9 (1988) 151–69.

Käsemann, Ernst. *The Wandering People of God: An Investigation of the Letter to the Hebrews*. Translated by Roy. A. Harrisville and Irving L. Sandberg. Minneapolis: Augsburg, 1984.

Keener, Craig S. "Luke." In *The IVP Bible Background Commentary: New Testament*. Downers Grove, Ill.: InterVaristy, 1993.

———. *A Commentary on the Gospel of Matthew*. Grand Rapids: Eerdmans, 1999.

Kelly, J. N. D., *Early Christian Doctrines*, 5th ed. New York: Harper & Row, 1958. Reprint, New York: Continuum, 2000.

Kelly, William, ed. *The Collected Writings of J. N. Darby*. Vol 2. No publisher; no date. Reprint 1971.

———. *The Collected Writings of J. N. Darby*. Vol 10. No publisher; no date. Reprint 1972.

Kendall, R. T. *Once Saved, Always Saved*. Chicago: Moody, 1983.

King, Nicholas. Review of *Paul and Palestinian Judaism: A Comparison of Patterns of Religion*, by E. P Sanders. *Biblica* 61 (1980) 141–44.

Kirk, J. A. "The Meaning of Wisdom in James: Examination of a Hypothesis." *New Testament Studies* 16 (1969) 24–38.

Kisker, Scott. "Justified but Unregenerate? The Relationship of Assurance to Justification and Regeneration in the Thought of John Wesley." *Wesleyan Theological Journal* 28 (1993) 44–58.

Kisner, Gerald D. "Jesus' Encounter with the Rich Young Ruler and Its Implications for Theology and Development." *The Journal of Religious Thought* 49 (1992–93) 81–6.

Kittel, G., and G. Friedrich, eds. *Theological Dictionary of the New Testament*. Translated and edited by G. W. Bromiley. 10 vols. Grand Rapids: Eerdmans, 1964–76.

Klassen, William. *Forgiving Community*. Philadelphia: Westminster, 1966.

———. *Love of Enemies: The way to Peace*. Overtures to Biblical Theology, ed. Walter Brueggemann and John R. Donahue, vol. 15. Philadelphia: Fortress, 1984.

———. "'Love Your Enemies': Some Reflections on the Current Status of Research." In *The Love of Enemy and Nonretaliation in the New Testament*, ed. William M. Swartley. Studies in Peace and Scripture. Louisville, Ky.: Westminster John Knox, 1992, 1–31.

Klausner, J. "Christian and Jewish Ethics." *Judaism* 2 (1953) 16–30.

Kolb, Robert, and Timothy J. Wengert, eds. *The Book of Concord: The Confessions of the Evangelical Lutheran Church*. Translated by Charles Arand et al. *Smalcald Articles* by Martin Luther. Minneapolis: Fortress, 2000.

Kruse, Colin G. *Paul, The Law, and Justification*. Peabody, Mass.: Hendrickson, 1996.

———. *The Letters of John*. Pillar New Testament Commentary, ed. D. A. Carson. Grand Rapids: Eerdmans, 2000.

Kümmel, Werner Georg. *The Theology of the New Testament According to its Major Witnesses: Jesus-Paul-John*. Translated by John E. Steely. Nashville: Abingdon, 1973.

Kvalbein, Hans. "Go therefore and make disciples . . . The Concept of Discipleship in the New Testament." *Themelios* 13 (1988) 48–53.

Ladd, George Eldon. *The Presence of the Future: The Eschatology of Biblical Realism*. Grand Rapids: Eerdmans, 1974.

———. "The Parable of the Sheep and the Goats in Recent Interpretation." In *New Dimensions in New Testament Study*, ed. Richard L. Longenecker and Merrill C. Tenney. Grand Rapids: Zondervan, 1974, 191–99.

———. *A Theology of the New Testament*. Revised edition by Donald A. Hagner. Grand Rapids: Eerdmans, 1993.

Lambrecht, J. "The Parousia Discourse: Composition and Content in Mt., 24-25." In *L'Évangile selon Matthieu: Rédaction et théologie*, Bibliotheca Ephemeridum Theologicarum Lovaniensium, ed. M. Didier, vol. 29. Gembloux: Duculot, 1972, 309–342.

———. "The Sayings of Jesus on Nonviolence." *Louvain Studies* 12 (1987) 291–305.

Lampe, G. W. H. "Christian Theology in the Patristic Period." In *A History of Christian Doctrine: In Succession to the Earlier Work of G. P. Fisher Published in the International Theological Library Series*, ed. Hubert Cunliffe-Jones. Philadelphia: Fortress, 1978.

Laney, J. Carl. "Abiding is Believing: The Analogy of the Vine in John 15:1-6." *Bibliotheca Sacra* 146 (1989) 55–66.

Lang, G. H. *Firstborn Sons, Their Rights and Risks.* London: Samuel Roberts, 1936. Reprint, Miami Springs: Conley & Schoettle, 1984.

Lawler, Michael. "Grace and Free Will in Justification: A Textual Study in Aquinas." *The Thomist* 35 (1971) 601–630.

Laws, Sophie. "The Doctrinal Basis for the Ethics of James." *Studia Evangelica* 7 (1973) 299–305.

Leith, John H. *John Calvin's Doctrine of the Christian Life.* Louisville, Ky.: Westminster/ John Knox, 1989.

Lenski, R. C. H. *The Interpretation of St. Luke's Gospel.* Columbus, Ohio: Wartburg, 1946.

Lescelius, Robert H. *Lordship Salvation: Some Crucial Questions and Answers Including a Reply to "So Great a Salvation" by Charles Ryrie and "Absolutely Free!" by Zane C. Hodges.* Asheville, NC: Revival Literature, 1992.

Lindstöm, Harald. *Wesley and Sanctification.* Stockholm: Nya Bokförlags Aktiebolaget, 1946.

Loader, William R. G. *Jesus' Attitude Towards the Law: A Study of the Gospels.* Wissenschaftliche Untersuchungen zum Neuen Testament, no. 2, ed. Martin Hengel and Otfried Hofius, vol. 97. Tübingen: Mohr Siebeck, 1997.

Lodahl, Michael E. "'The Witness of the Spirit': Questions of Clarification for Wesley's Doctrine of Assurance." *Wesleyan Theological Journal* 23 (1988) 188–97.

Lohse, Bernard. *Martin Luther's Theology: It's Historical and Systematic Development.* Translated and edited by Roy A. Harrisville. Minneapolis: Fortress, 1999.

Long, Thomas G. *Matthew.* Westminster Bible Companion, ed. Patrick D. Miller and David L. Bartlett. Louisville, Ky.: Westminster/John Knox, 1997.

Louw, J. P. and Eugene A. Nida, eds. *Greek-English Lexicon of the New Testament Based on Semantic Domains.* New York: United Bible Societies, 1988.

Lundström, Gösta. *The Kingdom of God in the Teaching of Jesus: A History of Interpretation from the Last Decades of the Nineteenth Century to the Present Day.* Translated by Joan Bulman. Edinburgh and London: Oliver and Boyd, 1963.

Luomanen, Petri. *Entering the Kingdom of Heaven: A Study on the Structure of Matthew's View of Salvation.* Tübingen: J. C. B. Mohr, 1998.

Luz, Ulrich. *Matthew 1–7: A Commentary.* Translated by Wilhelm C. Linss. Minneapolis: Augsburg, 1989.

———. *Das Evangelium nach Matthäus.* Vol. 3. Evangelisch-Katholischer Kommentar zum Neuen Testament, ed. Norbert Brox et al. Zurich: Benziger, 1997.

———. *The Theology of the Gospel of Matthew.* Translated by J. Bradford Robinson. New Testament Theology, ed. James D. G. Dunn. Cambridge: Cambridge University Press, 1995.

———. *Matthew 8–20: A Commentary.* Hermeneia: A Critical and Historical Commentary on the Bible, ed. Helmut Koester, trans. James E. Crouch. Minneapolis: Fortress, 2001.

MacArthur, John F., Jr. *The Gospel According to Jesus.* Panorama City, Calif.: Word of Grace, 1988.

Maddox, Randy L. "Responsible Grace: The Systematic Perspective of Wesleyan Theology." *Wesleyan Theological Journal* 19 (1984) 7–22.

Marcus, Joel. "Entering into the Kingly Power of God." *Journal of Biblical Literature* 107 (1988) 663–75.

Marguerat, D. *Le jugement dans l' Evangile de Matthieu*. Geneva: Editions Labor et Fides, 1981.
Marshall, Christopher D. *Faith as a Theme in Mark's Narrative*. Society for New Testament Studies Monograph Series, ed. G. N. Stanton, vol. 64. Cambridge: Cambridge University Press, 1989.
Marshall, I. Howard. "Preaching the Kingdom of God." *Expository Times* 89 (1977) 13–16.
———. *The Gospel of Luke: A Commentary on the Greek Text*. New International Greek Testament Commentary, ed. I. Howard Marshall and W. Ward Gasque. Grand Rapids: Eerdmans, 1978.
———. *Kept by the Power of God: A Study of Perseverance and Falling Away*. 3d ed. Carlisle: Paternoster Press, 1995.
———. "Salvation, Grace and Works in the Later Writings in the Pauline Corpus." *New Testament Studies* 42 (1996) 339–58.
Martens, Allan. "Salvation Today: Reading Luke's Message for a Gentile Audience." In *Reading the Gospels Today*. McMaster New Testament Studies, ed. Stanley E. Porter. Grand Rapids: Eerdmans, 2004.
Martin, Ralph P. "Salvation and Discipleship in Luke's Gospel." *Interpretation* 30 (1976) 366–80.
———., and Peter H. Davids, eds. *Dictionary of the Later New Testament and its Developments*. Downers Grove, Ill.: InterVarsity, 1997.
Matlock, R. Barry. "A Future For Paul." In *Auguries: The Jubilee Volume of the Sheffield Department of Biblical Studies*, ed. David J. A. Clines and Stephen D. Moore. Journal for the Study of the Old Testament Supplement Series 269, ed. David J. A. Clines and Philip R. Davies. Sheffield: Sheffield Academic Press, 1998, 143–83.
Mattill, A. J. *Luke and the Last Things: A Perspective for the Understanding of Lukan Thought*. Dillsboro, NC: Western North Carolina Press, 1979.
McDermott, John M. "Jesus and the Kingdom of God in the Synoptics, Paul, and John." *Eglise et Théologie* 19 (1988) 69–91.
McDonald, James I. "The Concept of Reward in the Teaching of Jesus." *Expository Times* 89 (1978) 269–73.
McGrath, Alister E. *Iustitia Dei: A History of the Christian Doctrine of Justification*. 2d ed. Cambridge: Cambridge University Press, 1998.
———. *Reformation Thought: An Introduction*. Oxford: Basil Blackwell, 1988.
———. "Justification in Earlier Evangelicalism." *Churchman* 98 (1984) 217–28.
———. "The Anti-Pelagian Structure of 'Nominalist' Doctrines of Justification." *Ephemerides Theologicae Lovanienses* 57 (1981) 107–19.
McKnight, Scot. "The Warning Passages of Hebrews: A Formal Analysis and Theological Conclusions." *Trinity Journal* 13 (1992) 21–59.
———. *A New Vision for Israel: The Teachings of Jesus in National Context*. Grand Rapids: Eerdmans, 1999.
———. *Turning to Jesus: The Sociology of Conversion in the Gospels*. Louisville, Ky.: Westminster/John Knox, 2002.
McQuilkin, J. Robertson. "The Keswick Perspective." In *Five Views on Sanctification*. Grand Rapids: Zondervan, 1987, 151–83.
Mehl, Roger. "La catholicité de l'église: Commentaire des déclarations de l'Assemblée oecuménique d'Upsal." *Revue d'Histoire et de Philosophie Religieuses* 48 (1968) 367–72.
Meier, John P. "Nations or Gentiles in Matthew 28:19?" *Catholic Biblical Quarterly* 39 (1977) 94–102.
Merrill, Eugene H. "A Theology of the Pentateuch." *A Biblical Theology of the Old Testament*, ed. Roy B. Zuck. Chicago: Moody, 1991.

Metzger, Bruce M. *Textual Commentary on the Greek New Testament*. 2d ed. Stuttgart: German Bible Society, 1994.

Michaels, J. Ramsey. "Apostolic Hardships and Righteous Gentiles: A Study of Matthew 25: 31-46." *Journal of Biblical Literature* 84 (1965) 27–37.

Michel, A. "Purgatoire." In *Dictionnaire de Théologie Catholique: contenant l'exposé des Doctrines de la Théologie Catholique leurs Preuves et leur Histoire*, ed. A. Vacant, E. Mangenot, and É. Amann, vol. 13. Paris: Librairie Letouzey et Ané, 1936, 1163–326.

Mitton, C. Leslie. "Present Justification and Final Judgment: A Discussion of the Parable of the Sheep and the Goats." *Expository Times* 68 (1956) 46–50.

Moloney, Francis J. *The Gospel of John*. Sacra Pagina 4. Collegeville, Minn.: Liturgical Press, 1998.

Montefiore, C. G. *Judaism and St. Paul*. London: Max Goschen, 1914.

Moo, Douglas J. "'Law,' 'Works of the Law,' and Legalism in Paul." *Westminster Theological Journal* 45 (1983) 73–100.

———. "Jesus and the Authority of the Mosaic Law." *Journal for the Study of the New Testament* 20 (1984) 3–49.

———. "2 Peter and Jude." In *The NIV Application Commentary: From Biblical Text . . . To Contemporary Life*. The NIV Application Commentary Series, ed. Terry Muck. Grand Rapids: Zondervan, 1986.

———. "Paul and the Law in the Last Ten Years." *Scottish Journal of Theology* 40 (1987) 287–307.

———. *James*. Revised edition. Tyndale New Testament Commentaries. Grand Rapids: Eerdmans, 1987.

———. *The Epistle to the Romans*. New International Commentary on the New Testament, ed. Ned B. Stonehouse, F. F. Bruce, and Gordon D. Fee. Grand Rapids: Eerdmans, 1996.

———. *The Letter of James*. Pillar New Testament Commentary, ed. D. A. Carson. Grand Rapids: Eerdmans, 2000.

Moore, D. Marselle. "Development in Wesley's Thought on Sanctification and Perfection." *Wesleyan Theological Journal* 20 (1985) 29–53.

Moore, George Foot. "Christian Writers on Judaism." *Harvard Theological Review* 14 (1921) 197-254.

———. *Judaism in the First Centuries of the Christian Era: The Age of the Tannaim*. 3 vols. Cambridge, Mass.: Harvard University Press, 1944.

Morris, Leon. *New Testament Theology*. Grand Rapids: Zondervan, 1986.

———. *Luke*. Tyndale New Testament Commentaries, ed. Leon Morris. Grand Rapids: Eerdmans, 1974. Reprint, Grand Rapids: Eerdmans, 1989.

———. *The Gospel According to Matthew*. Pillar New Testament Commentary, ed. D. A. Carson. Grand Rapids: Eerdmans, 1992.

Mounce, Robert H. *Matthew*. New International Biblical Commentary, ed. W. Ward Gasque. Peabody, Mass.: Hendrickson, 1985.

Neander, August. *General History of the Christian Religion and Church*. Translated by Joseph Toplady. Vol. 4. 2d ed. American ed. Boston: Crocker & Brewster, 1851.

Neill, Stephen, and Tom Wright. *The Interpretation of the New Testament: 1861–1986*, 2nd ed. Oxford: Oxford University Press, 1988.

Net Bible: New English Translation. Spokane, WN: Biblical Studies Press, 1998.

Neusner, Jacob. "Comparing Judaisms." *History of Religions* 18 (1978) 177–91.

———. *Ancient Judaism: Debates and Disputes*. Chico, Calif.: Scholars Press, 1984.

———. *Paradigms in Passage: Patterns of Change in the Contemporary Study of Judaism*. Studies in Judaism, ed. Jacob Neusner et al. Lanham, MD: University Press of America, 1988.

Bibliography

———. *Judaism and Its Social Metaphors: Israel in the History of Jewish Thought.* Cambridge: Cambridge University Press, 1989.

———. *Judaic Law from Jesus to the Mishnah: A Systematic Reply to Professor E. P. Sanders.* South Florida Studies in the History of Judaism 84. Atlanta: Scholars Press, 1993.

Nickelsburg, George W. E., Jr. *Resurrection, Immortality, and Eternal Life in Intertestamental Judaism.* Harvard Theological Studies, vol. 26. Cambridge, Mass.: Harvard University Press, 1972.

Noll, Mark A. "John Wesley and the Doctrine of Assurance." *Bibliotheca Sacra* 132 (1975) 161–77.

Noll, Stephen F. "The Good Samaritan and Justification by Faith." *Mission and Ministry* 8 (1990) 36–37.

Nolland, John. *Luke 1-9:20.* Word Biblical Commentary, ed. David A. Hubbard and Glenn W. Barker, vol. 35A. Dallas: Word, 1989.

———. *Luke 18:35-24:53.* Word Biblical Commentary, ed. David A. Hubbard and Glenn W. Barker et al, vol. 35C. Dallas: Word, 1993.

Nygren, Gotthard. *Das Prädestinationsproblem in der Theologie Augustins.* Göttingen: Vandenhoeck & Ruprecht, 1956.

Oberman, Heiko A. *Masters of the Reformation: The Emergence of a New Intellectual Climate in Europe.* Cambridge: Cambridge University Press, 1981.

———. *The Harvest of Medieval Theology: Gabriel Biel and Late Medieval Nominalism.* Cambridge, Mass.: Harvard University Press, 1963.

O'Brien, P. T. "Justification in Paul and Some Crucial Issues of the Last Two Decades." In *Right with God: Justification in the Bible and the World*, ed. D. A. Carson. Carlisle: Paternoster, 1992, 69–95.

———. *The Letter to the Ephesians.* Pillar New Testament Commentary, ed. D. A. Carson. Grand Rapids: Eerdmans, 1999.

Olivier, Daniel. *Luther's Faith: The Cause of the Gospel in the Church.* Translated by John Tonkin. Saint Louis, Mo.: Concordia, 1982.

O'Meara, Thomas F. "Thomas Aquinas and Today's Theology." *Theology Today* 55 (1998) 46–58.

———. "Grace as a Theological Structure in the *Summa theologiae* of Thomas Aquinas." *Recherches de théologie ancienne et médiévale* 55 (1988) 130–53.

Osborne, Grant R. "Soteriology in the Gospel of John." In *The Grace of God, The Will of Man*, ed. Clark H. Pinnock. Grand Rapids: Zondervan, 1989, 243–60.

Ozment, Steven E. *Age of Reform: an Intellectual and Religious History of Late Medieval and Reformation Europe.* New Haven: Yale University, 1980.

Packer, J. I. "History Repeats Itself." *Christianity Today* 33 (1989) 22.

Park, Eung Chun. *The Mission Discourse in Matthew's Interpretation.* Wissenschaftliche Untersuchungen zum Neuen Testament, ed. Martin Hengel und Otfried Hofius, vol. 81. Tübingen: Mohr Siebeck, 1995.

Patte, Daniel. "Jesus' Pronouncement About Entering the Kingdom Like a Child: A Structural Exegesis." *Semeia* 29 (1983) 3–42.

Paxson, Ruth. *Rivers of Living Water: How Obtained — How Maintained: Studies Setting Forth the Believer's Possessions in Christ.* Chicago: Moody, 1918. Reprint, Chicago: The Bible Institute Colportage Ass'n, 1941.

Peace, Richard V. *Conversion in the New Testament: Paul and the Twelve.* Grand Rapids: Eerdmans, 1999.

Pelzer, Auguste. "Les 51 articles de Guillaume Occam censurés, en Avignon, en 1326." *Revue d'histoire ecclésiastique* 18 (1922) 240–70.

Bibliography

Pentecost, J. D. *Things to Come: A Study in Biblical Eschatology*. Findley, Ohio: Dunham, 1958. Reprint. Grand Rapids: Zondervan, 1964.

———. *Design For Discipleship: Discovering God's Blueprint for the Christian Life*. Grand Rapids: Zondervan, 1971. Reprint, Grand Rapids: Kregel, 1996.

Peterson, David. *Hebrews and Perfection: An Examination of the Concept of Perfection in the 'Epistle to the Hebrews'*. Society for New Testament Studies Monograph Series, ed. R. McL. Wilson and M. E. Thrall, vol. 47. Cambridge: Cambridge University Press, 1982.

Pfurtner, Stephen. *Luther and Aquinas on Salvation*. Translated by Edward Quinn. New York: Sheed and Ward, 1964.

Piper, John. *'Love Your Enemies': Jesus' Love Command in the Synoptic Gospels and in the Early Christian Paraenesis*. Society for New Testament Studies Monograph Series, vol. 38. Cambridge: Cambridge University Press, 1979.

———. *The Pleasures of God: Meditating on God's Delight in Being God*. Portland: Multnomah, 1991.

———. *The Purifying Power Of Living By Faith In . . . Future Grace*. Sisters, Ore.: Multnomah, 1995.

Pond, Eugene W. "The Background and Timing of the Judgment of the Sheep and the Goats." *Bibliotheca Sacra* 159 (2002) 201–20.

———. "Who Are The Sheep and Goats in Matthew 25:31-46?" *Bibliotheca Sacra* 159 (2002) 288–302.

———. "Who Are 'The Least' of Jesus' Brothers in Matthew 25:31-46?" *Bibliotheca Sacra* 159 (2002) 436–48.

Przybylski, Benno. *Righteousness in Matthew and His World of Thought*. Cambridge: Cambridge University Press, 1980.

Radmacher, Earl D. *Salvation*. Swindoll Leadership Library, ed. Charles R. Swindoll and Roy. B. Zuck. Nashville: Word, 2000.

Rainbow, Paul A. *The Way of Salvation: The Role of Christian Obedience in Justification*. Waynesboro, GA: Paternoster, 2005.

Räisänen, Heikki. *Paul and the Law*. Philadelphia: Fortress, 1986.

Rausch, Jerome. "The Principle of Nonresistance and Love of Enemy in Mt 5, 38-48." *Catholic Biblical Quarterly* 28 (1966) 31–41.

Reiser, Marius. *Jesus and Judgment: The Eschatological Proclamation in Its Jewish Context*. Translated by Linda M. Maloney. Minneapolis: Fortress, 1997.

Reymond, Robert L. "Dr. John H. Gerstner on Thomas Aquinas as a Protestant." *Westminster Theological Journal* 59 (1997) 113–21.

Richardson, Peter, and Stephen Westerholm. *Law in Religious Communities in the Roman Period: The Debate Over Torah and Nomos in Post-Biblical Judaism and Early Christianity*. Studies in Christianity and Judaism, ed. Peter Richardson, vol. 4. Ontario: Wilfrid Laurier University Press, 1991.

Ridderbos, H. M. *Matthew*. Bible Student's Commentary, trans. Ray Togtman. Grand Rapids: Zondervan, 1987.

Rieger, Hans-Martin. "Eine Religion der Gnade: Zur 'Bundesnomismus,' - Theorie von E. P. Sanders." In *Bund Tora: Zur theologischen Begriffsgeschichte in alttestamentlicher, frühjüdischer und urchristlicher Tradition*, ed. Friedrich Avemarie und Hermann Lichtenberger. Wissenschaftliche Untersuchungen zum Neuen Testament, ed. Martin Hengel und Otfried Hofius, vol. 92. Tübingen: Mohr, 1996.

Robinson, J. A. T. "The 'Parable' of the Sheep and the Goats." *New Testament Studies* 2 (1956) 225–37.

Roy, Steven C. "New Wines and Old Wine Skins? The Relationship of Evangelical Thinking on Spiritual Formation and Theological Models of Sanctification." Paper presented at the Evangelical Theological Society. Valley Forge, PA: 2005.

Ryrie, Charles C. *So Great Salvation: What it Means to Believe in Jesus Christ*. Wheaton: Victor, 1989.

———. *Balancing the Christian Life*. Chicago: Moody, 1969.

Saarnivaara, Uuras. *Luther Discovers the Gospel: New Light Upon Luther's Way from Medieval Catholicism to Evangelical Faith*. Saint Louis, Mo.: Concordia, 1951.

Saldarini, A. J. A Review of *Paul and Palestinian Judaism*, by E. P. Sanders. *Journal of Biblical Literature* 98 (1979) 299–300.

Sanders, E. P. *Paul and Palestinian Judaism: A Comparison of Patterns of Religion*. London: SCM, 1977.

———. *Paul, the Law and the Jewish People*. Philadelphia: Fortress, 1983.

Sandmel, Samuel. "Paul and Palestinian Judaism: A Comparison of Patterns of Religion." *Religious Studies Review* 4 (1978) 158–60.

Schelkle, Karl Hermann. *Theology of the New Testament: Salvation History — Revelation*. Translated by William A. Jurgens. Vol. 2. Collegeville, Minn.: Liturgical Press, 1971).

Schlatter, D. A. *Der Evangelist Matthäus: seine Sprache, sein Ziel, seine Seibständigkeit: Ein Kommentar zum ersten Evangelium*. Stuttgart: Calwer Verlag, 1963.

Schleck, Charles A. "St. Thomas on the Nature of Sacramental Grace." *The Thomist* 18 (1955) 1–30, 242–78.

Schnackenburg, Rudolf. *The Gospel According to St John*. Vol. 2. New York: Crossroad, 1982.

Schoeps, H. J. *Paul: The Theology of the Apostle in the Light of Jewish Religious History*. Translated by Harold Knight. Philadelphia: Westminster, 1961.

Schreiner, Thomas R. "Is Perfect Obedience to the Law Possible? A Re-examination of Galatians 3:10." *Journal of the Evangelical Theological Society* 27 (1984) 151–60.

———. "Israel's Failure to Attain Righteousness in Romans 9:30-10:3." *Trinity Journal* 12 (1991) 209–20.

———. *The Law and Its Fulfillment: A Pauline Theology of Law*. Grand Rapids: Baker, 1993.

Schreiner, Thomas R., and Ardel B. Caneday. *The Race Set Before Us: A Biblical Theology of Perseverance and Assurance*. Downers Grove, Ill.: InterVarsity, 2001.

Schürer, Emil. *A History of the Jewish People in the Time of Jesus Christ*. Translated by Sophia Taylor and Peter Christie. Vol. 4. New York: Charles Scribner's Sons, 1896.

Schweizer, Eduard. *The Good News According to Matthew*. Translated by David E Green. Atlanta: John Knox, 1975.

Scofield, C. I. *The Scofield Reference Bible*. New York: Oxford University Press, 1967.

Seifrid, Mark A. "Blind Alleys in the Controversy Over the Paul of History." *Tyndale Bulletin* 45.1 (1994) 73–95.

———. "The 'New Perspective on Paul' and its Problems." *Themelios* 25 (2000) 4–18.

———. *Christ, Our Righteousness: Paul's Theology of Justification*. New Studies in Biblical Theology, ed. D. A. Carson, no. 9. Downers Grove, Ill.: InterVarsity, 2000.

Shank, Robert. *Life in the Son: A Study of the Doctrine of Perseverance*. Springfield, Mo.: Westcott, 1961.

Shanor, Jay. "Paul as Master Builder: Construction Terms in First Corinthians." *New Testament Studies* 34 (1988) 461–71.

Shepherd, Massey H. "The Epistle of James and the Gospel of Matthew." *Journal of Biblical Literature* 75 (1956) 40–51.

Sidebottom, E. M. "'Reward' in Matthew 5:46, etc." *Expository Times* 67 (1956) 219–20.

Sim, David C. *The Gospel of Matthew and Christian Judaism: The History and Social Setting of the Matthean Community*. Studies of the New Testament and its World, ed. John Barclay, Joel Marcus, and John Riches. Edinburgh: T. & T. Clark, 1998.

Smith, Ebbie. "Unraveling the Untangled: Perspectives on the Lingering Debate Concerning Works and Grace in James and Paul." *Southwestern Journal of Theology* 43 (2000) 43–55.

Smith, Harmon L. "Wesley's Doctrine of Justification: Beginning and Process." *The London Quarterly and Holborn Review* 33 (1964) 120–28.

Smith, Jay E. "The New Perspective on Paul: A Select and Annotated Bibliography." *Criswell Theological Review* 2 (2005) 91–111.

Smith, Robert. "Justification in 'the New Perspective on Paul." *The Reformed Theological Review* 58 (1999) 16–30.

Sproule, John A. "Parapesontas in Hebrews 6:6." *Grace Theological Journal* 2 (1981) 327–32.

Stackhouse John G., ed. *What Does It Mean To Be Saved: Broadening Evangelical Horizons of Salvation*. Grand Rapids: Baker, 2002.

Stanton, Graham N. "Salvation Proclaimed: Matthew 11:28-30: Comfortable Words?" *Expository Times* 94 (1982) 3–9.

———. "The Origin and Purpose of Matthew's SM." In *Tradition and Interpretation in the New Testament: Essays in Honor of E. Earle Ellis*, ed. Gerald F. Hawthorne and Otto Betz. Grand Rapids: Eerdmans, 1987, 181–92.

———. *A Gospel for a New People: Studies in Matthew*. Edinburgh: T. & T. Clark, 1992.

Stegner, William Richard. "The Parable of the Good Samaritan and Leviticus 18:5." In *The Living Text: Essays in Honor of Ernest W. Saunders*, ed. Dennis E. Groh and Robert Jewett. Lanham, MD: University Press of America, 1985, 27–38.

Stein, Robert H. "Interpretation of the Parable of the Good Samaritan." In *Scripture, Tradition, and Interpretation*, ed. W. Ward Gasque and William Sanford LaSor. Grand Rapids: Eerdmans, 1978, 278–95.

———. *Luke*. New American Commentary, ed. David S. Dockery, vol. 24. Nashville: Broadman, 1992.

Stendahl, Kristen. *Paul Among Jews and Gentiles: And Other Essays*. Philadelphia: Fortress, 1963.

Stephens, W. P. *The Theology of Huldrych Zwingli*. Oxford: Clarendon, 1986.

Stott, John R. W. "Must Christ Be Lord To Be Savior? Yes." *Eternity* 10 (1959) 15, 17–8, 36–37.

Strack, H. L., and P. Billerbeck. *Kommentar zum Neuen Testament aus Talmud und Midrasch*. 6 vols. Munich: Beck, 1922–61.

Strange, Roderick. *The Catholic Faith*. Oxford: Oxford University Press, 1986.

Studor, Basil. *Trinity and Incarnation: The Faith of the Early Church*. Translated by Matthias Westerhoff and edited by Andrew Louth. Collegeville, Minn.: Liturgical Press, 1993.

Talbert, Charles H. *Reading the Sermon on the Mount: Character Formation and Decision Making in Matthew 5–7*. Colombia, SC: University of South Carolina, 2004.

TeSelle, Eugene. *Augustine The Theologian*. London: Burns & Oates, 1970.

Thielman, Frank. *From Plight to Solution: A Jewish Framework for Understanding Paul's View of the Law in Galatians and Romans*. Supplements to Novum Testamentum, ed. C. K. Barrett, A. F. J. Klijn, and J. Smit Sibinga 61. Leiden: E. J. Brill, 1989.

Thiselton, Anthony C. *The First Epistle to the Corinthians*. New International Greek Testament Commentary, ed. I. Howard Marshall and Donald A. Hagner. Grand Rapids: Eerdmans, 2000.

Thomas, Robert L. "Jesus' View of Eternal Punishment." *The Masters Seminary Journal* 9 (1998) 147–67.

Bibliography

Tiessen, Terrance L. *Who Can Be Saved? Reassessing salvation in Christ and World Religions*. Downers Grove, Ill.: Intervarsity Press, 2004.

Townsend, Michael J. "Christ, Community and Salvation in the Epistle of James." *Evangelical Quarterly* 53 (1981) 115–23.

Trinkaus, Charles, and Heiko A. Oberman, eds. *The Pursuit of Holiness in Late Medieval and Renaissance Religion*. "Nominalism and Late Medieval Religion" by William J. Courtenay. *Studies in Medieval and Reformation Thought*, ed. Heiko A. Oberman et al., vol. 10. Leiden: E. J. Brill, 1974, 26–59.

Van Elderen, Bastiaan. "Another Look at the Parable of the Good Samaritan." In *Saved By Hope: Essays in Honor of Richard C. Oudersluys*, ed. James I. Cook. Grand Rapids: Eerdmans, 1978, 109–19.

Van Unnik, W. C. "L'usage de σωζειν 'sauver' et des dérivés dans les Évangiles synoptiques." In *Sparsa Collecta: The Collected Essays of W. C. Van Unnik*, vol. 1. Supplements to Novum Testamentum, ed. W. C. Van Unnik et al. Leiden: E. J. Brill, 1973.

Von Loewenich, Walther. *Luther als Ausleger der Synoptiker*. Forschungen zur Geschichte und Lehre des Protestantismus, ed. Ernst Wolf, series 10, vol. 5. Munich: Chr. Kaiser, 1954.

Wainwright, Geoffrey. "Perfect Salvation in the Teaching of Wesley and Calvin." *Reformed World* 40 (1988) 898–909.

Walker, Williston. "The Sandemanians of New England." In *Annual Report of the American Historical Association for the Year 1901*. 2 vols. Washington, D.C.: Government Printing Office, 1902.

Wall, Robert W. *Revelation*. New International Biblical Commentary, ed. W. Ward Gasque. Peabody, Mass.: Hendrickson, 1991.

Wallace, Daniel B. *Greek Grammar Beyond the Basics*. Grand Rapids: Zondervan, 1996.

Walvoord, John F. *The Revelation of Jesus Christ*. Chicago: Moody, 1966.

———. *Matthew: They Kingdom Come*. Chicago: Moody, 1974.

———. "Christ's Olivet Discourse on the End of the Age: The Judgment of the Nations." *Bibliotheca Sacra* 129 (1972) 307–15.

Wanamaker, Charles A. *The Epistles to the Thessalonians*. New International Greek Testament Commentary, ed. I. Howard Marshall and W. Ward Gasque. Grand Rapids: Eerdmans, 1990.

Ward, Roy Bowen. "The Works of Abraham: James 2:14-26." *Harvard Theological Review* 61 (1968) 283–90.

Watson, Francis. "Liberating the Reader: A Theological-Exegetical Study of the Parable of the Sheep and the Goats (Matt 25:31-46)." In *The Open Text: New Directions for Biblical Studies?*, ed. Francis Watson. London: SCM, 1993, 57–84.

Watson, N. M. "Justified by Faith, Judged by Works . . . ?" *New Testament Studies* 29 (1983) 209–21.

Watson, Philip. "Erasmus, Luther, and Aquinas." *Concordia Theological Monthly* 40 (1969) 747–58.

Wawrykow, Joseph P. *God's Grace and Human Action: 'Merit' in the Theology of Thomas Aquinas*. Notre Dame, Ind.: University of Notre Dame Press, 1995.

Weber, Ferdinand. *Jüdische Theologie auf Grund des Talmud und verwandter Schriften*. Leipzig: Dörffling & Franke, 1897.

Weber, Kathleen. "The Image of the Sheep and the Goats in Matthew 25:31-46." *Catholic Biblical Quarterly* 59 (1997) 657–78.

Wessel, Walter W. "Mark." In *Expositors Bible Commentary*, ed. Frank E. Gaebelein and J. D. Douglas. Grand Rapids: Zondervan, 1984.

Westerholm, Stephen. "Letter and Spirit: The Foundation of Pauline Ethics." *New Testament Studies* 30 (1984) 229–48.

———. *Israel's Law and the Church's Faith: Paul and His Recent Interpreters*. Grand Rapids: Eerdmans, 1988.

Wilckens, U. "Gottes geringste Büder - zu Mt 25, 31-46." In *Jesus und Paulus: Festschrift für Werner Georg Kümmel zum 70 Geburtstag*, ed. E. E. Ellis and E. Grässer. Göttingen: Vandenhoeck & Ruprecht, 1975, 363–83.

Wilkin, Robert N. *Confident in Christ: Living By Faith Really Works*. Irving, Tex.: Grace Evangelical Society, 1999.

———. *The Road to Reward: Living Today in Light of Tomorrow*. Irving, Tex.: Grace Evangelical Society, 2003.

Wilkins, Michael J. *The Concept of Disciple in Matthew's Gospel: as Reflected in the Use of the Term Μαθητής*. Supplements to Novum Testamentum, ed. C. K. Barrett and A. F. J. Klijn. Leiden: E. J. Brill, 1988.

———. *Following the Master: A Biblical Theology of Discipleship*. Grand Rapids: Zondervan, 1992.

Wilkinson, Bruce. *Secrets of the Vine: Breaking Through to Abundance*. Sisters, Ore.: Multnomah, 2001.

Willis, John R. *A History of Christian Thought: From Apostolic Times to Saint Augustine*. Hicksville, N.Y.: Exposition Press, 1976.

Willis, S. "The Good Samaritan: Another View." *Expository Times* 112 (2000) 92.

Willis, W. ed. *The Kingdom of God in 20th-Century Interpretation*. Peabody, Mass.: Hendrickson, 1987.

Wilson, Alistair I. *When Will These Things Happen?: A Study of Jesus as Judge in Matthew 21–25*. Paternoster Biblical Monographs, ed. David F. Wright et al. Carlisle, U.K.: Paternoster, 2004.

Wink, Walter. "Neither Passivity nor Violence: Jesus' Third Way (Matt. 5:38-42 par.)." In *The Love of Enemy and Nonretaliation in the New Testament*, ed. William M. Swartley. Studies in Peace and Scripture. Louisville, Ky.: Westminster/John Knox, 1992, 102–25.

Wright, N. T. *The Climax of the Covenant: Christ and the Law in Pauline Theology*. Minneapolis: Fortress, 1992.

Young, Norman H. "The Commandment to Love Your Neighbor as Yourself and the Parable of the Good Samaritan (Luke 10:25-37)." *Andrews University Seminary Studies* 21 (1983) 265–72.

Unpublished Works

Bing, Charles C. "Lordship Salvation: A Biblical Evaluation and Response." Ph.D. diss., Dallas Theological Seminary, 1991.

Blaising, Craig Alan. "John Wesley's Doctrine of Original Sin." Ph.D. diss., Dallas Theological Seminary, 1979.

Huang, Caleb Tzu-Chia. "Jesus' Teaching on 'Entering the Kingdom of Heaven' in the Gospel According to Matthew: (Interpretation of Selected Texts in Matthew's Gospel Including also Several Parables)." Ph.D. diss., Concordia Seminary, 1986.

Ketcham, Donald Louis. "The Lordship Salvation Debate: Its Nature, Causes, and Significance." Ph.D diss., Baylor University, 1995.

Page, Homer Ausburn, Jr. "An Investigation of the Concept of Reward in the Gospel of Matthew." Ph.D. diss., New Orleans Baptist Theological Seminary, 1991.

Pagenkemper, Karl E. "An Analysis of the Rejection Motif in the Synoptic Parables and its Relationship to Pauline Soteriology." Ph.D. diss., Dallas Theological Seminary, 1991.

South, Thomas Jacob. "The Response of Andrew Fuller to the Sandemanian View of Saving Faith." Ph.D. diss., Mid-America Baptist Seminary, 1993.
Wilson, George Todd. "Entering the Kingdom in the Theology of Matthew." Ph.D. diss., The Southern Baptist Theological Seminary, 1971.

Subject Index

A

Abraham, 100–101, 103, 203, 233, 271
   Covenant with, 80n73, 97n175, 137, 140
   Faith of, 42, 205, 323, 336
   Works of, 74, 128, 308, 311n102
Actions. See Works
Acts (Bible), 113, 224–25, 331
   see also under Salvation; Works
Adam and Eve, 105
Adherence, 221–22, 225
Adoption, 50n252, 51
Adultery, 22n24, 236n92
Agbanou, Victor K., 296
Age to Come, 142, 160, 193, 205, 208
   see also End of the Age
Allegiance, 222, 225
Allegories, 213–14
Allison, Dale C., 288n132
Althaus, Paul, 45n221
Ambrose, 21
Anger, 67, 129, 155, 157, 161, 196, 260–67, 331, 336
Antinomianism, 20, 41, 69, 111
Antitheses, 171, 267, 318, 329
   see also Sermon on the Mount
Apollos, 278–79
Apostasy, 8, 22n24, 51, 53, 54n281, 55, 69, 114n259, 251
Apostles, 222–24, 226–27, 229, 234, 244, 304, 330
   see also Disciples/Discipleship; and individual Apostles
Aquinas, Thomas, 29–34, 68–69, 320–21
Aristotle, 221n4
Arminius, James, 8n34, 51–55, 60n329, 69, 320, 322

Assurance, 8, 16, 54n281, 67–68, 105, 168
   Aquinas on, 34
   Arminius on, 52, 55, 61
   Calvin on, 50n253
   Lack of, 23, 210
   New Testament on, 327
   Wesley on, 60–61
Atonement. See Repentance; Sinners/Sins, Atonement for
Augustine. See Faith; Grace; Justification; Merit; Salvation; Works; Works-Salvation Relationship
Avemarie, Friedrich, 73n7, 93–96, 109

B

Baptism, 21–24, 26, 136n11, 156, 299n31
Barrett, C. K., 123
Bauckham, Richard, 114n259
Bavaud, G., 46
Beare, Francis W., 296
Beatitudes, 26n61, 182–83, 240, 272n65, 276n84, 277, 323
   see also Sermon on the Mount
Behavior, 48n243, 49n249, 167, 177, 182, 198
Belief. See Faith
Believers, 200, 218n148, 305n70
   Discipleship of, 222–28, 330n7
   Endurance of, 249–50, 253, 257
   Judgment of, 68, 122n43, 127, 303, 307
   Life of, 48n243, 53–54, 57, 281, 332
   Salvation of, 69, 114, 152, 157, 163, 319n3
   Sonship of, 271, 273, 319n3

Believers (continued)
  Works of, 130–31, 323, 325
  Works of God as, 60n330, 124–27, 336
  see also Christianity/Christians; Unbelievers
Bible, 41, 208, 249–50, 258, 290
  Interpretations of, 4n13, 13–14, 17
  see also New Testament; Old Testament; *and individual Books*
Biel, Gabriel, 34–38, 321
Billerbeck, Paul, 76, 94, 108, 322
Blind Man, Parable of, 205n92, 206
Borchert, Gerald L., 152–53
Borgman, Brian, 280n96
Brothers, 302–5
  Forgiveness of, 260–65, 283–86, 319, 332
  Love for, 197, 227–28, 294, 299
Brown, Jeannine K., 7
Bruce, E. F., 5n20
Bullinger, Heinrich, 47
Bultmann, Rudolf, 13, 76–77, 108, 322
Burroughs, Jeremiah, 152–53
Byrne, Brendan, 111n248

C

Calling, 119, 126, 334
  see also Disciples/Discipleship, Jesus' call to; Sinners/Sins, Jesus' call to
Calvin, John, 8n34, 30, 44, 46–51, 60n329
  see also under Justification; Salvation; Works; Works-Salvation Relationship
Camel and Needle, 191–92, 206, 334
Caneday, Ardel, 151–53, 248
Carson, D. A., 93, 96–107, 109, 110
Carter, Warren, 202n73, 286n119
Certainty. See Assurance
Chafer, Lewis Sperry, 3–4, 12n49, 62–63, 299n30
Charity, 26, 31, 201n69
  see also Love; Poor, giving to
Children, Becoming like, 64, 145, 166, 183–85, 187, 205–6, 224, 227, 287, 316, 319n3, 329

Children, Becoming like (continued)
  see also Humility
Christianity/Christians, 70, 156, 292, 300–305
  Born-again, 8, 24, 282
  Carnal, 61n334, 63–65, 66n354, 67, 251n30, 277–81, 289n140, 321
  Committed, 9, 24n42, 64, 177n39, 179, 251–52
  Discipleship of, 9, 227–28, 321, 330n7
  Evangelical, 3, 5, 152
  Fruits of, 31, 256–57, 278
  Judaism vs., 75–76, 78, 84, 113–15, 172n19
  Life of, 23–24, 31n104, 39, 43–48, 159–61, 164, 336
  Requirements for, 10–13, 68, 168, 332
  Salvation of, 38, 40, 134n2, 152, 255, 277–79, 327–28
  Works by, 20, 28, 49n245, 125, 128, 130–31, 227, 295n5
Church
  Early, 235n91, 251, 278–82, 292, 316–17, 331
  Temple of, 115, 218n148
  Works-salvation relationship in, 10n43, 16-17, 19–70, 122, 300, 320–22
Clement of Rome, 21
Colijn, Brenda B., 238n98
Collins, Kenneth J., 55n292
Commandments, 48n243, 58, 79n59, 95–96, 103–4, 120, 123, 208
  Eternal life through, 188, 190, 193–211, 329
  Keeping of, 7, 41, 42n196, 50n253, 55, 119n27, 250, 253, 258–59
  see also Law
Commitment, 64, 99, 101, 221–23, 226–27, 230, 234, 238–39, 242, 316, 330
Compassion, 26, 167, 180n63, 214n125, 284–87, 290, 299, 303
Condign merit, 33n124, 36n150, 38, 48n243, 69
Confession, 27, 39, 40n175, 54n286, 97n175, 176–78, 187

Subject Index   365

Confession (continued)
    Jesus and, 246–47, 251–53, 277, 297, 304, 312–14, 329, 331
Confidence, 192, 218, 231, 251–52, 327, 330, 332
Contrition. *See* Repentance
Conversion, 23n37, 28n73, 152, 153n11, 157n132, 326
    Forgiveness at, 21, 52, 175
    Jesus' call to, 149n86, 220, 230, 232, 240, 334
    Luther and, 39
    Paul and, 71, 83
    Salvation as, 3n7, 8n31, 146, 164, 167, 237, 245–46, 252–53, 333
    Wesley and, 55
    Works and, 12, 68, 127, 129n80, 227
Corinthians (people), 60n330, 63, 158, 278–80, 326–27
Council of Jerusalem, 12
Council of Trent, 29, 30n96, 50n253, 68
Covenant, 35–36, 39n168, 48n243, 69, 160, 194n33, 198n54, 213n122
    Abraham and, 80n73, 97n175, 137, 140
    Israel and, 11, 76n36, 86, 87n113, 107, 109, 139–40
    Judaism and, 79, 82–84, 97–99, 104–7, 110–12, 114–15
Covenantal nomism, 81–84, 87, 89n126, 90–93, 96–98, 104, 109, 111–12, 114, 322
Crimes, 26n60, 263–64
    see also Commandments, Keeping of; Sinners/Sins
Cross, taking up, 224, 229, 240, 247–48
    see also Disciples/Discipleship
Cubie, David L., 55n292

D

Dabney, Robert Lewis, 280n96
Damnation. See Hell; Punishment, Eternal
David (King), 102, 137
Davids, Peter H., 202n72
Davies, W. D., 78, 108, 288n132
Death, 113n254, 122n43, 129n81, 134–35

Death (continued)
    Deliverance from, 21, 157, 325
    Physical, 157, 241n115, 243, 245–46, 249–50, 316
    Spiritual, 145
Deeds. *See* Works
Deification, 21n14
Deliverance, 135, 137–40, 161n157, 163, 325
Demons, 117, 155–56, 237n96, 289
    see also Satan
Destiny, Eternal. *See* Life, Eternal
Destruction, Eternal. *See* Punishment, Eternal
Devil. *See* Satan
Dillow, Joseph C., 7n29, 11–12, 64, 65, 66n354, 67n360, 140n31, 151n98, 228n45, 230n60, 238n99, 251n30, 282n103, 288n132, 289n140, 316, 319, 328
Dio Chrysostom, 221n9
Disciples/discipleship, 5, 8–10, 117n11, 261n10, 302–4, 326
    Jesus' call to, 134–35, 208, 220, 223, 226–34, 316, 330
    Mission of, 121–22, 254–57, 275, 277, 316, 336
    Requirements for, 144–46, 150, 184–85, 200, 207n97, 208–11, 228–34, 237–38, 247–48, 314–16
    Salvation and, 12, 156, 164, 167–68, 189, 192–93, 209, 220–41, 316, 330
    see also Salvation-Discipleship
Dispensationalists, 61n332
Divine intervention, 13n53, 22
Doing, 118–20, 128–29, 215–19
    see also Works
Donahue, John R., 305n70
Dunn, James D., 85n104, 87n113
Duns Scotus, 29n82

E

Election
    Grace and, 54, 110, 112, 311–12, 314

Election (continued)
    Judaism and, 78n50, 80–84, 85n104, 89, 91n137, 94, 103–5, 111n248, 114, 166
        Salvation and, 54, 162, 298, 327
        Works as proof of, 42, 48n243, 50
Elijah, 234
Eliphaz, 203
Elisha, 234
End of the Age, 166, 216, 244, 297–99, 314, 318–19, 323, 330
    see also Age to Come
Endurance, 127, 128–29, 258, 315, 326–27
    Salvation through, 1, 11n47, 27, 161, 168, 172n16, 181, 202n72, 238, 242–59, 322, 330–31, 334–35
    see also Perseverance
Enemies
    Deliverance from, 137, 163, 325
    Love for, 196, 212n116, 213n121, 260, 262–63, 267–73, 282, 331
Enns, Peter, 114
Ephesians (Bible), 1, 124, 126, 158, 324
Epistles, 3n10, 113n253, 153, 157–63, 224–25, 253, 316
    see also New Testament; *and individual Epistles*
Esau, 110
Est, Willem Hessels van, 296
Eternity. *See* Kingdom; Life, Eternal
Ethics, 219, 239, 282, 291, 301n49, 303n59, 311, 318
Evangelistic strategy, 146, 189, 195–96, 204, 218–19, 234n87, 316, 330
Evil, 28n75, 45, 100–101, 104–5, 175n25, 268, 282
    Ceasing, 58, 60n330, 124, 131n91, 161, 289n140
    Punishment of, 27, 97n176, 110, 264, 318–19
    Surpassing, 26n61, 196n43, 265–66
    Works of, 121–22, 324, 335
Exegesis, 13–14, 17, 79–80, 317
Exiles, 98, 109, 140n27
Exodus (Bible), 113n253, 139–40
Exorcism, 148n84
Ezra, 114n259

F

Facere quod in se est, 35–38, 39n168, 68–69, 320, 321
Faith
    Aquinas on, 29–34
    Arminius on, 52–55, 69
    Augustine on, 22–28, 68, 321
    Calvin on, 46–51
    Endurance and, 248, 250–51, 253, 331
    Fruits of, 12, 50n253, 56–57, 177, 277
    Gospels on, 326–27, 330
    James on, 27n64, 49, 59, 67, 128, 236–37, 305n69, 310
    John on, 27n64, 237n96, 254–57, 316
    Lack of, 48n243, 55, 226–27
    Love and, 45, 46n228, 225, 238, 282, 325
    Luther on, 39–46, 73–74
    Matthew on, 254–55
    New Testament on, 205–7, 218n48, 326
    Paul on, 3, 12, 20, 27n64, 59, 72, 77–80, 83, 86–87, 108–9, 113, 124, 126, 131n91, 151n98, 184, 200, 225, 238, 257n51, 321–22, 324–25, 333–34, 336
    Reformers on, 39–51
    Salvation through, 1–4, 61n333, n334, 70, 135–36, 147, 156, 165, 167, 209, 230–32, 235–38, 296–97, 300, 312n106, 328
    Synoptic Gospels on, 236–37, 320
    Testing of, 250–51
    Wesley on, 55–61
    Works and, 20–21, 23–24, 27, 64, 125, 129, 133n99, 162, 207n96, 258, 305n69, 310, 321, 324
    see also God, Faith in; Jesus Christ, Faith in
Faithfulness, 172, 173n21, 240n112, 242, 292, 297–98, 331
Family, Forsaking, 25, 169, 207n97, 226, 235, 237, 247–48
    see also Hatred, Family
Father. *See* God

Fee, Gordon D., 281
Fire. *See* Gehenna; Hell
Flusser, D., 172n19
Forgiveness
    Judaism on, 78n54, 82–83, 98, 101–5, 283
    Lack of, 167, 331, 336
    New Testament on, 22n24, 29, 56, 83–92, 152n105, 290–92
    Salvation and, 283–92, 314, 334
    see also God, Forgiveness by; Sinners/Sins, Forgiveness of
Fowl, Stephen, 205n92
Free will, 16, 25n50, 107n241
    Aquinas on, 29n90, 32n113, 33n119, 34n130
Friends, 254, 263, 265
Fruits, 36, 50, 56–58, 119n22, 121–22, 169, 278
    Good, 27n54, 40, 42, 44, 46n228, 287, 311n101
    Lack of, 67n360, 176, 186, 256–57

G

Galatians (Bible), 1, 11n46, 74, 83, 133, 323–24
Garden of Eden, 110
Gehenna, 110, 142, 148, 185, 241, 260, 264, 266, 313n113, 328
    see also Hell
Gentiles, 78n50, 80, 112, 124n56, 270, 300–303
    Faith of, 55, 87
    Righteousness of, 74, 268, 274
    Salvation for, 83, 138
Gerrish, B. A., 39n168, 40n172
Gerstner, John, 7
Gifts. *See* God, Gifts of
Glas, John, 61n333
Glorification, 50, 66n354, 159, 163–64, 196n42, 326, 335
God
    Dependence on, 22–23, 182, 187, 195
    Faith in, 26–27, 49, 160, 170, 258
    Forgiveness by, 1, 7, 26, 34n127, 52, 98, 101–3, 114, 286–90, 311–12, 331–32, 335–36

God *(continued)*
    Gifts of, 21n14, 25n50, 28, 39, 50n252, 51, 56n295, 68, 107, 115, 156, 187n93, 198, 203, 320, 328–29
    Glory of, 118, 121n38, 122n41, 131, 335
    Grace of, 3n8, 9n40, 21, 28, 32–33, 36n150, 78n50, 89, 195, 206, 239, 291–92, 296, 311–12, 321, 323, 327, 332, 334
    Jesus' relationship with, 56, 121–22, 154–55, 168
    Judgment by, 109, 122n43, 130, 176, 184n81, 198, 252, 263n16, 279
    Justification by, 20–22, 30, 37, 44–45, 59, 205–6
    Kindness of, 257n51, 270, 271–72, 290–91
    Love for, 1, 35, 38, 83, 188, 195, 211, 216–19, 268, 313–14, 330–31
    Man's relationship with, 31, 50, 55–56, 66n354, 68–69, 79, 98–99, 132, 139–40, 162–63, 173, 182n75, 202, 207, 217–18
    Mercy of, 26, 34, 49n246, 50–51, 80n73, 81–83, 97–102, 104–7, 110, 111n246, 137, 157, 186, 239, 290–91
    Obedience to, 12n49, 20, 25n50, 27–28, 48, 50n253, 54–55, 58, 99, 114n259, 120, 124, 126, 193–211, 224, 250, 258–59, 331
    Perfection of, 170, 270, 272
    Power of, 16, 34–36, 38, 55, 115, 125, 149, 155, 168, 186, 210n106, 232, 317–18, 324, 334–35
    Promises of, 43n211, 57n301
    Righteousness of, 129, 203, 225, 266
    Salvation by, 4, 21, 120–21, 123, 138–39, 161, 162n166, 186–87, 193, 204, 206, 208, 232, 321
    Servants of, 137, 139, 163, 279–80
    Sons of, 268, 270–74, 276–77, 319n3
    Will of, 21, 33, 74, 117, 119, 166, 169, 171–83, 186–87, 196, 215, 277, 291, 303n59, 313, 318–19, 329, 332

God (continued)
  Works of, 25, 120–21, 124–25, 129, 177, 186, 225, 312
  Wrath of, 67, 157, 266–67
Godliness, 47, 203, 238–39, 251, 325
  see also Ungodliness
Goodness, 26n61, 28n75, 45n219, 50n252, 51, 76n36, 80n73, 100–102, 105, 121–22, 190, 268, 270
Good Samaritan, 6n22, 110, 173n20, 211–18, 291, 305n70, 313–14, 323, 330
Gospels, 2, 5n20, 63–65, 80, 189, 230, 281
  Back-loading, 12–13, 317–20
  Discipleship in, 224–25, 226, 228
  Endurance in, 246n16, 251, 253
  Judaism in, 18, 88n118, n121, 113
  Preaching of, 150, 194, 204–8, 242–43, 252, 301, 303–6, 316, 331
  Truth of, 61n333, n334
  see also Synoptic Gospels
Govett, Robert, 328
Grace
  Aquinas on, 29–34, 68–69
  Arminius on, 52–55
  Augustine on, 24n44, 25, 38, 68, 320–21
  Calvin on, 49n245
  Free, 61–68, 78n50, 150n92, 322
  Judaism on, 9, 17, 78n50, 84–87, 88n117, 89–111, 113–14, 166, 322–23
  Luther on, 40n175, 43n211, 44, 74
  Ockham on, 36–38, 69
  Paul on, 90, 126, 184, 325
  Reformers on, 39–51
  Salvation through, 1–4, 6, 22, 23n34, 70, 113, 163, 186n92, 195, 292, 296, 311–12, 314, 320, 323
  Wesley on, 55–61
  Works and, 25, 28, 125, 324–25
  see also God, Grace of
Graves, Mike, 214n125
Gray, Sherman W., 295n3
Green, H. Benedict, 295n5
Green, Joel B., 152–53
Green, Michael, 296
Gregory of Rimini, 38

H

Hagner, Donald A., 88n118, n121, 89n125, 90, 108, 111n246
Harrington, Daniel J., 200n60
Hatred, 240, 260, 267, 325
  Disciples, 242–43, 246, 254
  Family, 11, 167–68, 229, 230, 238n99
  see also Families, forsaking
Healing, 135–36, 147n79, 163, 206–7, 325
Hearing, 13, 67, 119, 128, 131, 161
Heaven, 64, 143–44, 147, 149, 151–52, 188, 191, 193, 200, 205–6, 209n101, 276, 284
  see also Kingdom; Life, Eternal
Hebrews (Bible), 127n67, 181, 251–53, 258
  see also under Salvation
Heil, John Paul, 305n70
Hell, 161, 196n44, 289
  Deliverance from, 12, 56, 69, 151, 243n2, 282n103
  Eternity in, 3, 67, 152, 178n50, 290, 297, 299, 318–19, 331
  see also Gehenna
Hellerman, Joseph H., 188, 235n91
Hengel, Martin, 234n85
Herodotus, 221n5
Hill, David, 296
Hirsch, E. D., 14
History, divine intervention in, 13n53, 22
Hodges, Zane C., 2n4, 5n20, 8n33, 61n334, 64, 144n53, 161, 208–10, 228n46, 230n60, 237n96, 238n99, 239, 241, 289n140, 307n85, 319, 336
Holiness, 30n92, 46, 48–49, 54, 56–59, 69, 137, 139, 181, 252
Holy Spirit, 48, 110n243, 156
  Fruits of, 42n201, 60, 110n243, 114–15, 129n81, 186, 323
  Grace of, 33–34, 48, 57n301, 156–57, 254
  Indwelling of, 21, 41, 46n228, 50–51, 63, 66n354, 67n360, 115, 125, 131n90, 133, 160, 218n148, 251n30
  Works of, 56n295, 78n57, 122n41, 324, 326–27

Hope, 31, 34, 128, 159, 161, 163, 282n103, 326
Humanity, 301, 306, 308, 314, 321, 332
Humility, 50n250, 145n63, 161, 179, 183–85, 187, 206, 238, 274, 287
see also Children, Becoming like
Hypocrisy/Hypocrites, 76n36, 172, 276, 289n140, 313

I

Immortality. *See* Life, eternal
Individualism, 107
Initiation, 228
Integrity, 47–48, 50n252, 124
Intellectual assent, 61n333, 70
Intention, 78, 265n29, 280n96
Isaac, 103, 128, 140, 203
Isaiah, 147, 149–50, 182n72
Isocrates, 221n6
Israel
    Covenant with, 11, 76n36, 86, 87n113, 107, 109
    Deliverance of, 137–40, 147, 149, 163
    Election of, 78n50, 81–83, 91n137, 94, 98–99, 103–4, 114–15
    Judgment of, 299n30, 301n49, 302

J

Jacob, 97n175, 103, 140, 203
Jailor's question, 1, 230n60, 305n69
James
    Paul vs., 3n10, 10, 25, 59, 129n80
    Writings of, 44n212, 65, 67, 214, 249–50, 252, 258, 266, 290, 292
    see also under Faith; Justification; Salvation; Works
Jansen, Cornelius Otto, 296
Jesus, 213n122
    Crucifixion of, 12, 56, 87, 120, 121n38, 127, 159n148, 280–81, 309
    Denial of, 226, 246–47, 254
    Endurance of, 258, 331
    Faith in, 1, 29, 40–42, 47–48, 52–53, 63–64, 67, 69, 83–84, 87, 145,

Jesus (continued)
    151–52, 160–61, 250–59, 277, 296–97, 308, 314, 316, 319n3, 323–24, 330–31
    Following, 9, 12, 25, 66n354, 144–46, 163–64, 169, 185, 192–93, 196, 199n58, 209–10, 220–41, 316, 326
    God's relationship with, 56, 121–22, 154–55, 168
    Grace of, 46, 113–14
    Judaism vs., 2n4, 112–14, 167, 271
    Judgment by, 27–28, 335
    Kingdom of God as, 88n118, 135, 148n85, 210–11
    Love and, 218, 225, 229n40, 327, 332
    Man's relationship with, 132, 144n53, 198, 214n125, 218n148, 257, 289n140, 313–14, 324–25, 328, 336
    Mercy of, 45–46, 52, 292–93
    Messiah as, 13n53, 78–80, 88n118, 92n142, 138, 168
    Mission of, 137–38, 150, 179, 229
    Obedience to, 169, 201, 204–5, 208, 219, 222, 261, 302n50
    Passion of, 30–31, 189, 214n125, 241n115
    Paul vs., 1, 3, 11
    Resurrection of, 115, 150, 162n166, 163, 186, 241n115, 309
    Return of, 9, 27–28, 117n11, 159, 184n82, 241, 244–45, 289n136, 297–98, 304n63, 305–10, 314
    Salvation through, 1–3, 15, 21–22, 55, 59, 61n334, 64–65, 120, 136–37, 139–41, 150, 154, 156–57, 162n166, 205–6, 228, 232, 238n98, 240, 244, 324, 328
    Warnings by, 246–47, 331
    see also under Justification; Life, Eternal; Works; Works-Salvation Relationship
Jews, 214n125, 268, 300–303
Job, 203, 258, 331, 336
John, writings of, 13n53, 15, 65, 113n254, 197, 217, 253–54, 292, 307, 332

John, writings of (continued)
    see also under Faith; Salvation; Works;
        Works-Salvation Relationship
John the Baptist, 138, 221–23
Josephus, 101, 221n7, 233, 265n29
Josiah (King), 217
Judah, 114
Judaism, 55, 203–6, 218, 221, 283
    Christianity vs., 75–76, 78, 172n19,
        200n60, 289n140
    First-century, 9n40, 75, 81, 85, 88,
        90n130, 140n27, 244
    Hellenistic, 77–79, 80n72
    Jesus vs., 2n4, 112–14, 167, 271
    Paul vs., 11, 124n56
    Rabbinic, 77–78, 81n75, 82, 88,
        92n140, 94, 101, 109, 215–16
    Sander's assessment of, 80–92
    Second Temple, 96–107
    Tannaitic, 91n137, 101–3
    see also under Forgiveness; Grace;
        Life, Eternal; Merit; Obedience;
        Righteousness; Works-Salvation
        Relationship
Judas, 55, 226, 247
Jude, writings of, 27n64, 130–31, 162–63, 292–93
Judgment, 66, 79n59, 128–29, 155, 168, 264, 266
    Criteria for, 6, 196n44, 331–32, 335–37
    Eschatological, 52, 126, 133,
        161n157, 176–78, 184n81, 185,
        244, 256–57, 276, 288n132,
        289–91, 294–315, 332–33
    see also God, Judgment by; Jesus,
        Judgment by; Sheep and Goats,
        Parable of
Jülicher, Adolf, 213
Justice, 24n43, 33, 102, 172, 173n21, 272n65, 292
Justification, 16, 61n334, 66n354, 67, 156, 164, 216, 326
    Aquinas on, 29–30, 33n117, 68
    Arminius on, 52–55, 57n307
    Augustine on, 22–28, 36n144, 43, 296
    Calvin on, 46–51, 69, 320, 321–22
    James on, 49, 308–10, 333–34

Justification (continued)
    Jesus on, 58, 311
    Judaism on, 89n126
    Luther on, 39–46, 49, 69, 73, 75, 296, 320, 321
    Medieval teachings on, 47n235
    Ockham on, 35–38
    Patristic teachings on, 19–22
    Paul on, 1, 3, 12, 20, 22, 24, 39–40,
        43, 44n212, 48–49, 58–59, 71–
        72, 77, 79–80, 83, 86–87, 108–9,
        111n247, 124, 129n80, 131n91,
        151n98, 157–58, 185, 187–88,
        196n42, 197, 205–6, 239, 296,
        308–11, 312n106, n107, 321,
        323, 333–34
    Reformers on, 39–51, 56n295, 61n333, 69
    Wesley on, 55–61, 69
    see also Faith; God, Justification by;
        Salvation; Sanctification; Works

K

Keeping, 120
    see also Commandments, Keeping of
Kendall, R. T., 66n354, 67
Keswick model, 61n332
Kingdom, 10n43, 24n41, 155–57, 242–43, 282n103, 330
    Entrance into, 12, 114, 119, 146–51,
        166–87, 252, 260, 263–64,
        266n35, 273–77, 290–91,
        296–97, 311–13, 315–19, 321,
        323–24, 332, 334–35
    Of God, 193, 225, 232, 244–45, 247, 248n24, 251–52
    Inheritance of, 1–3, 54, 65–67, 104,
        126, 159–60, 163–64, 267, 282, 294
    Jesus as, 88n118, 115, 135
    see also Heaven; Life, Eternal; Salvation
Kings, Matthew's treatment of, 286n119
Kruse, Colin G., 9n40, 85n104, 89, 108

L

Ladd, George Eldon, 147n79
Law, 20, 42n196, 292, 336
   Jesus' transcendence of, 170–71, 177, 194n33, 198–99, 261, 313
   Judaism on, 72, 74–84, 86–87, 89–91, 93–96, 99–103, 106–9, 112, 114n259, 115, 233, 234n85
   Obedience to, 9n40, 32n112, 40, 49n247, 58, 171–72, 173n21, 193–211, 214–18, 329
   Paul on, 10, 71, 111n246, 113n254, 159–60n148
   Works of, 24n43, 41, 43, 57n306, 92n142, 124, 129n80
   see also Commandments
Lawlessness, 117, 119, 173–74, 177, 180n63, 187, 242, 289n140, 313
Lawyer's question, 1, 167, 173n20, 211, 214–16, 230n60, 335
Learning, 221–22, 239
Lepers, 147n79
Life, 10, 26n61, 48, 64, 282
   Christian, 23–24, 31n104, 39, 43–45, 159–61, 164, 336
   Eternal, 10, 21–24, 30–33, 64, 76, 188–219, 239, 249n26, 250–51, 256, 276, 289, 297–99, 325–26 (*see also* Salvation)
   Aquinas on, 29–34, 68–69
   Arminius on, 52, 55
   Augustine on, 68
   Calvin on, 49n247, 51
   Jesus on, 141–52, 166–87, 317
   John on, 154–55
   Judaism on, 80n73, 94–96, 99, 100–101, 105, 110, 143
   Luther on, 40n172, 44
   Ockham on, 36, 69
   Paul on, 78n50, 157–59, 175
   Requirements for, 7, 41, 119n27, 120, 235–41, 319, 328–30
   Works and, 2–4, 6, 12n49, 24–25, 28, 50–51, 260–94, 306–7, 311–16, 321–22, 328, 331–35
   Loss of, 222–24, 229, 247–48
   Physical, 154–55, 161, 193, 241, 245
Lohse, 43n211

Lordship Salvation Debate, 5, 8n31, 16, 61–62
Love, 60n330, 199–201
   Faith and, 45, 46n228, 225, 238, 282, 325
   God and, 35, 38, 51, 78n50, 83, 186, 188, 195, 211, 216–19, 268, 313–14, 330–31
   Lack of, 172–74, 242, 246
   Mercy and, 329, 332, 336
   Salvation through, 1, 167, 195, 208, 211–12, 260, 292, 330, 334
   Works of, 23, 27n64, 41, 121n38, 126, 128–29, 143, 295n5, 323
   see also Enemies, Love for; Neighbors, Love for
Luke, writings of, 6, 113, 214, 228n45, 242–45, 268–70
   see also under Faith; Justification; Salvation; Works; Works-Salvation Relationship
Luomanen, Petri, 3n8
Luther, Martin, 7n27, 14, 38, 39–46
   Calvin vs., 44, 48–49
   Judaism vs., 72–77, 79–82, 85, 88, 93, 108, 111
   Roman Catholics vs., 2n4, 89
   see also under Justification; Righteousness; Salvation; Works; Works-Salvation Relationship

M

MacArthur, John F., 2n4, 5n20, 61n334
Maldonado, Juan, 295
Man, 25, 34, 36, 45, 63–65, 190, 262, 265–67
   see also God, Man's relationship to; Jesus, Man's relationship to
Mark, writings of, 236, 242–44, 287, 317, 319
Marshall, I. Howard, 8n34, 9n40, 53n273, 135n7, 136n11
Mary, Virgin, declaration of, 137, 287
Matthew, 13n53
   Writings of, 6, 200–201, 226, 233, 239–40, 266, 273–77, 317, 330
   Forgiveness in, 283–92

Matthew (continued)
    Judgment in, 275–76, 294–314, 318–19, 328, 333
    Love in, 268–70, 292
    Missionary discourse in, 242–46, 257, 314, 332
    see also under Faith; Righteousness; Salvation
McDermott, John M., 149n86
McGrath, Alister E., 20n7, 21n14, 23n37, 25n50, 34n133, 36n144, 37, 39n168, 42n197, 47n235, 56n295
McKnight, Scot, 240
Meekness, 182, 184, 187n93
Mehl, Roger, 296
Mercy, 182, 184, 206, 231
    Judgment and, 128–29, 290–91, 310
    Lack of, 172–74, 285–87, 296
    Love and, 329, 332, 336
    Works of, 2, 6, 26, 167, 211–13, 216–18, 313–14, 319, 323, 334
    see also God, Mercy of; Jesus, Mercy of
Merit, 187
    Aquinas on, 31–34, 68, 320
    Augustine on, 24, 25n50, 28, 115, 198, 321, 334
    Calvin on, 49
    Judaism on, 76n36, 78n50, n57, 79n61, 85n104, 89n126, 91n137, 92, 102–3, 105–7
    Luther on, 40, 44, 46
    Ockham on, 35–36
    Paul on, 85n103
    Salvation and, 6, 9n40, 21–22, 248, 317, 329
    Works and, 4n11, 12n49, 50n252
    see also Condign merit
Messiah, 13n53, 78–80, 88n118, 92n142, 138, 168
Michaels, J. Ramsey, 295n5
Middle Ages, 31n106, 33n124, 36n144, 37–38, 39n171, 48n243
Ministers, 278–81
Miracles, 13n53, 117, 118n15, 119, 122n42, 177
Mishnah, 89n125, 91n137, 272n65
Missionaries, 302–4
Montefiore, Claude G., 77, 79, 80n72, 81n75, 108

Moo, Douglas J., 129n80
Moore, George Foot, 78, 81n75, 93, 108
Morality, 119n24, 124, 184
Moses, 102, 104, 113n253, 124n56, 194, 199, 213n122
Murder, 22n24, 261, 265–67

N

Nations, 243, 294, 299n30, 300–302, 304
    see also Humanity
Neighbors, 261n10, 303, 305n70
    Love for, 1, 128, 188, 199, 208, 211–12, 215–19, 267, 270, 313–14, 330–31
Neusner, Jacob, 92n140
New Testament, 63–65, 67, 223–27, 266–67, 270–73, 277–82, 330
    Endurance in, 249–59, 330–32
    Eternal life in, 7n29, 53–54
    Forgiveness in, 22n24, 29, 56, 83–92, 152n105, 290–92
    Interpretations of, 3n10, 43n211, 81n75, 82n82
    Judaism in, 112–15
    see also under Faith; Salvation; Works
Noll, Mark A., 60n329
Nominalism, 34–38

O

Obedience, 159n148, 179, 190, 227
    Faith and, 41n188, 324
    Judaism on, 72, 76, 81–82, 85n104, 87n116, 89, 94–96, 97n175, 102–7, 109–10, 111n248
    Justification and, 42, 49
    Paul on, 78, 83–84
    Salvation through, 6, 59, 65, 66n354, 67
    see also Commandments, Keeping of; God, Obedience to; Law, Obedience to
Ockham, William of, 34–38, 69, 321
Old Testament, 79n61, 90, 109, 201n71, 203, 233, 250, 267, 329
    see also under Salvation

Origen, 20, 213n122
Orthodoxy, 21, 22
Osborne, Grant R., 54n281
Ozment, Steven E., 37n150, 39n168, 48n243, 49n249, 50n252

P

Parables, 213–14
Pardon. *See* Forgiveness
Partakers, 65–67, 251–52
Pastoral Epistles, 1, 133
Patience, 182n73, 253, 287, 290, 336
Patristic period, 19–38
Paul, 213n121, 305n69
    James vs., 10, 25, 59, 129n80
    Jesus vs., 1, 3, 11
    Judaism vs., 2n4, 17, 71–115
    Writings of, 66n354, 90, 224–25, 251–52, 266, 277–82, 290, 292, 330
    see also under Faith; Grace; Justification; Righteousness; Salvation; Works; Works-Salvation Relationship
Peace, 137, 163, 272n65, 273, 282, 325
Pelagianism/Pelagius, 2n, 20n7, 25n50, 34n133, 35–38, 48n243, 69
Penance. *See* Repentance
Pentecost, 11, 122n42
Pentecost, J.D., 64n341
Perfection, 50n251, 143, 164, 170, 173n21, 270, 272–73, 326
    Eternal life and, 149, 151, 159–61, 188, 191, 193–94, 199–202, 208
    Sinless, 131n92, 200, 335–36
Persecution, 177, 181–84, 260, 267, 271, 273, 331
    Disciples and, 242–43, 252, 254, 275
Perseverance, 8, 34n130, 52–55, 61n334, 65, 66n354, 67, 333
    see also Endurance
Peter
    Denial of Jesus by, 226, 246–47, 254
    Writings of, 12, 27n64, 111n247, 112, 192, 249–50, 252, 282, 287, 292
    see also under Salvation; Works

Pharisees, 88n118, n121, 113n254, 117–20, 148n85, 221–23, 263, 271, 287
    Righteousness of, 24, 166, 170–74, 231, 266n35, 274, 313, 318–19, 329, 334–35
Philip (Apostle), 254
Philippians (people), 125, 208
Piety, 76n36, 80, 203, 234n85, 274
Pilgrimage, Salvation as, 142–44, 146, 151–53, 159n146, 162–64, 167, 225, 228, 246, 320, 326
Piper, John, 8n31, 201n71, 276n84, 277, 282
Plato, 221n3
Poor, Giving to, 1, 188, 191, 200, 204, 206, 208-9, 231
Poor in Spirit, 119, 177, 179–87, 198, 287, 311, 324, 329, 334
Poverty, 203, 207, 336
Practice, 120
    Theology and, 7–9, 109, 110, 127, 323
Prayer, 60n330, 97–98, 100–101, 103–4, 206, 260, 267–68
Predestination, 12n49, 24n44, 50–51, 52n269, 54n281, 107, 126, 227–28, 296
Presumption, 34, 50n252
    see also Theology, Presuppositions in
Prodigal Son, 231
Prophesying, 117, 177
Prophets, 139, 163, 213n122, 268
    False, 175–76, 242, 246
    Persecution of, 271, 275
Prostitutes, 184–85, 187, 312
Protestantism, 3n9, 9, 30n92, 39, 43n211, 48n243, 57n307, 72
Psalms, 97–98, 109, 180
Punishment, 6, 32, 76n36, 102–3, 114n259, 263
    Eternal, 2, 48n243, 152, 169, 178, 244–45, 254–55, 257, 264, 288–89, 294, 299
Purgatory, 263n16
Purity, 49, 170, 182, 184
Pythagoras, 221n6

Q

Quietism, 324
Qumran community, 107, 109

R

Race, salvation as, 127, 159–61, 165, 225, 326
Rahab, 311n102
Räisänen, Heikki, 86n112
Ransom, 140, 150, 241
Reconciliation, 148, 157–58, 265, 326–27
Redemption, 137, 139–40, 157–58, 163–64, 245, 326
Reformation/Reformers, 3n9, 17, 23n37, 30, 38–52, 47, 69
  see also under Justification; Works
Regeneration, 21, 46–48, 50, 161, 164, 325, 327
Religion, 20, 76, 79n61, 128, 292
Repentance, 35, 39, 60–61, 67n360, 182–85, 240, 251n30, 336
  Fruits of, 58, 119n22, 237
  Judaism on, 75, 78, 82–84, 97–98, 102–3, 105, 107, 114
  Lack of, 66, 196n44
  By Peter, 247
  Salvation through, 11n46, 41, 138, 144n55, 147–49, 156, 160, 169, 179, 230–32, 324, 328–30
  Works and, 22n24, 122, 123–24
Resurrection, 43n211, 312n106
  Final, 27–28, 96, 101–2, 105, 110n243, 333
Revelation, receipt of, 63
Revelation (Bible), 122, 155, 181, 182n74, 250, 252
Rewards
  Calvin on, 50–51
  Heavenly, 36n144, n150, 64, 67, 193n27
  Judaism on, 95–96, 99, 101–3, 107, 268
  Loss of, 66–68, 321
  Salvation as, 5, 9, 16, 143n49, 244, 273–77, 282

Rewards *(continued)*
  Works and, 32, 70, 126, 133, 270, 280–81, 295–96, 304, 307
Rich Young Ruler, 1, 6n22, 7, 26–27, 49n247, 64, 110, 119n27, 120, 141–52, 164, 188–93, 230n60, 234–35, 316, 323, 326, 328, 329, 334–35
Righteousness, 20–21, 181–83, 268, 277
  Aquinas on, 33n117, 68
  Calvin on, 30, 48–49
  Judaism on, 78, 80n73, 84, 87n117, 89n126, 94, 96, 98–100, 103–7, 114n259, 203n83
  Lack of, 197, 239, 267, 297, 333
  Luther on, 30, 39, 40n175, 42, 43n211, 44–45, 73–75, 320
  Matthew on, 208, 271, 287, 289n140, 311–14
  New Testament on, 113, 137–39, 161, 163, 197–98, 282, 324
  Paul on, 10, 71, 83–84, 92n142, 121n41, 157, 159n145, 205, 238, 309, 325
  Rerformers on, 47–48, 56n295
  Salvation through, 142, 175, 185, 216, 281–82, 294, 295n5, 296, 299, 317–18, 328, 332, 336
  see also Pharisees, righteousness of; Surpassing righteousness; Works-Righteousness
Roman Catholicism, 2n4, 29, 40n175, 43n211, 69, 72, 75, 81, 162n166
Romans (Bible), 1, 74, 83, 133, 317, 323–24
Roy, Steven C., 4
Ryrie, Charles C., 10n43

S

Sacraments, 30, 38, 39, 40n175, 68, 320
Sacrifice, 98, 172, 210–11, 222–24, 313
  see also Self-sacrifice
Sadducees, 204
Saints, 27, 50, 52–53, 259, 292
Salvation, 19–70, 89, 92, 193
  Acts on, 135, 146, 156–57, 164, 326
  Aquinas on, 29–34
  Arminius on, 52–55, 69

Salvation (continued)
  Augustine on, 22–28, 34n133, 153, 320–21
  Bible on, 140n31, 152–53, 165, 248n24, 322
  Calvin on, 46–51, 153, 296, 320
  Definitions of, 14–15, 17, 116, 134–38, 150–53
  Discipleship and, 12, 156, 164, 167–68, 189, 192–93, 209, 220–41, 316, 330
  Endurance and, 242–59
  Eschatological, 31, 59–60, 131, 133, 136–37, 141, 148n85, 149, 152, 155–59, 161–63, 167, 174–75, 184n82, 185–87, 196, 216, 219, 230n59, 238–39, 244, 248, 251, 255, 260, 270, 282, 294–314, 316, 318, 321, 325, 328, 330–34
  Faith and, 1–4, 11, 61n333, n334, 67, 70, 135–36, 147, 156, 165, 167, 209, 230–32, 235–38, 296–97, 300, 312n106, 328
  Forgiveness and, 287–90
  Grace and, 1–4, 6, 22, 113, 320, 323
  Hebrews on, 155, 159–61, 225, 326
  James on, 134n3, 136, 141–52, 161–62, 196n43, 281, 287, 326, 333–34
  John on, 10, 11n46, 154–56, 163, 228n46, 230, 315, 326
  Judaism on, 71–115, 196, 218
  Loss of, 8, 17, 53n273, 66, 244, 255, 325–28
  Love and, 1, 167, 195, 208, 211–12, 260, 292, 330, 334
  Luke on, 134n3, 136–38, 141–52, 225, 239, 287, 321, 326
  Luther on, 39–46, 75, 82, 153, 320
  Matthew on, 5n15, 6n23, 136, 139, 141–52, 162, 175, 185, 187, 273–77, 287
  New Testament on, 10–11, 134–65, 167, 216, 225, 239, 290, 292, 305–15, 323–28
  Ockham on, 35–38
  Old Testament on, 1, 138, 140n31, 149–50, 323

Salvation (continued)
  Paul on, 1, 3–4, 23–25, 53–54, 71–72, 78n50, 79, 80n72, 83–84, 87n116, 115, 126, 157–60, 163–65, 175, 183n76, 196n42, 197, 208, 238–39, 315, 319, 320-21, 323, 325–26, 328
  Personal, 34n127, 114–15
  Peter on, 131n91, 135, 162–63, 181, 225, 326
  Physical, 134–35, 147n79, 153n110, 161, 167, 243
  Present, 59–60, 137, 138, 152, 156–59, 163
  Reformers on, 39–51
  Requirements for, 26–27, 188–219, 248–49, 252–53, 294, 324, 329–30, 332
  Spiritual, 135–36, 147n79, 167, 244
  Synoptic Gospels on, 1–18, 134–53, 156–57, 160, 164, 166–67, 186, 209, 216, 230n60, 238, 324, 326
  Treatment of others and, 260–93
  Via moderna on, 35–38, 39
  Wesley on, 55–61
  see also God, Salvation by; Jesus, Salvation through; Kingdom, Entrance into; Life, Eternal; Works-Salvation Relationship
Salvation-Discipleship, 61–70, 153, 320–22, 330–31
Sanctification, 4–5, 30–31, 61n332, 151n98
  Calvin on, 48, 49n249, 69
  Judaism on, 77
  Justification and, 16, 23n37, 30–31, 43, 61n332, n334, 151n98, 152, 156, 164, 320, 326
  Paul on, 157–58, 160
  Wesley on, 56n295, 57n301, 58n316, n317
Sandeman, Robert, 61n333
Sanders, E. P., 9, 16–17, 72–73, 80–92, 99, 101, 104–5, 107, 108, 110–12, 114, 166, 322–23
Satan, 135–36, 213n122, 289, 294
  Deliverance from, 148n84, 325
  Relationship to, 132, 163, 177
  Sons of, 173, 254, 257, 271

Satan (continued)
  Testing by, 53, 250
  Works of, 121, 125, 130, 324
  see also Demons
Schoeps, H. J., 79, 80n72, 108
Schreiner, Thomas R., 6, 7n27, 8n33, 91, 93, 108, 151–53, 210n106, 248
Schürer, Emil, 76, 108, 322
Scotism, 29n82
Scribes, 117–20, 233, 263, 271, 287
  Righteousness of, 166, 170, 173n21, 266n35, 274, 318, 334
Scriptures, 13–14, 17, 26–27, 50–51
  see also individual Scriptures
Second Coming. *See* Jesus, Return of
Security, eternal, 2, 8, 16–17, 24, 34, 53–55, 65, 168, 326–27
Seifrid, Mark A., 93, 108, 152n105
Self-sacrifice, 64, 208, 209n101, 229, 238n99, 240
Selling all, 12, 64, 119n27, 144, 146, 167, 188, 191–211, 218, 235, 240, 316, 334–35
Sermon on the Mount (SM), 168–86, 196n44, 201, 208, 215, 265–68, 273–77, 282, 318–19, 323–24
Servants, 6–7, 26, 53, 137, 139, 163, 184, 279–80, 283–92
Service, 26n61, 224–25, 234n86
Shank, Robert, 7n27, 8n34, 53, 54, 55
Sheep and Goats, Parable of, 6, 7n27, 28, 166, 173, 180n66, 218, 294–314, 332
Sickness, 135, 163, 183, 325
Silas, 1, 305n69
Simeon, 138
Sinners/sins, 6, 24n42, 25n50, 38, 66–67, 113n254, 131n92, 203, 213n122, 236n92, 268, 270–71
  Atonement for, 35–36, 81–83, 114, 154–55, 159n148, 163, 182, 231, 240n112, 336
  Cycle of, 39, 40n175, 54–55, 69, 103
  Deliverance from, 40n172, 48, 121n41, 184–85, 238n99, 244, 325, 331
  Forgiveness of, 12n49, 21–22, 29, 46, 56–58, 60–61, 135–36, 138, 147, 152n105, 156, 178n48, 214n125, 283, 296, 328

Sinners/sins (continued)
  Jesus' call to, 150, 175, 187, 197, 225, 311–12, 334
  Judaism on, 97–101, 103–6, 110
Slaves, 184, 224–25, 227, 254, 284–86, 289, 291
  see also Servants
Socrates, 221n9
Son of Man. *See* Jesus Christ
Sonship, 268, 270–74, 276–77, 319n3
Sophistry, theological, 11–12, 316–17
Soteriology. *See* Salvation
Souls, salvation of, 39, 48, 99n191, 100–101, 140, 161, 163, 243, 266
Spirit. *See* Holy Spirit
Stendahl, Krister, 6, 7n27, 79–80, 108
Stephens, W. P., 46n228
Strack, Hermann, 76, 88
Submission, 179, 222, 232, 280, 287, 323–24, 335
Suffering, 161, 181, 214n125, 243, 252, 258, 331
Surpassing righteousness, 166–67, 196, 199–200, 208, 264–66, 318–19, 323–24, 331
  Eternal life through, 177–83, 186–87, 260, 274–75, 277, 291, 329, 334–35
Synod of Dort, 51
Synoptic Gospels, 11, 115, 168, 207, 228n46, 257, 276, 315–16, 330–31
  see also under Salvation; Works; Works-Salvation Relationship

T

Talbert, Charles H., 182n73, n75
Tax collectors, 184–85, 187, 206, 225, 231, 268, 270, 274, 287, 311–12
Teachers/teaching, 118n15, 119, 131, 221–25, 280, 299n31
Temptation, 53, 242, 249–50
Tertullian, 21–22
TeSelle, Eugene, 23n34, 24n44
Testing, 249–52, 278
Theology
  Medieval, 38, 39n171, 48n243
  Practice and, 7–9, 109, 110–12, 323

Theology (continued)
  Presuppositions in, 13–14, 34, 36n144
  Prosperity, 203, 206
  see also Exegesis
Thessalonians (people), 181, 183n76, 251
Thief on the Cross, 60n325
Thomas (Apostle), 254
Thomism, 29–38, 68, 320
Tiessen, Terrance L., 186n92
Torah, 76n36, 78–79, 84, 86n112, 95–96, 99, 110, 114n259, 173n21
Traditions, Jewish, 233–37, 265, 316
Transformation, 26, 44, 48, 58
Transgressions. *See* Sinners/Sins
Treatment of Others, 170, 260–94, 299–300, 303–4, 313–15, 331–32, 336–37
Tribulation, 243n2, 244, 246, 250–52, 298, 302, 331
Tröger, Karl-Wolfgang, 241n15
Trust
  God, 179, 182n73, 231, 323, 336
  Jesus, 128, 204–7, 209n101, 218, 234–37, 320, 329
Truth, 50n250, 124

U

Unbelievers, 9, 132, 249n26, 257, 268, 292, 331–32
  Judgment of, 53, 122n43, 302, 313n113
  see also Believers; Faith, Lack of
Unfaithfulness, 53, 240n112
Ungodliness, 29n90, 131n90, 203, 325
  see also Godliness
Unmerciful servant, 6–7, 26, 283–92
Unrighteousness, 239, 297

V

Vengeance. *See* Anger
Via moderna, 34–38, 39, 68–69, 320, 321
Virtues, 30, 50n250
Von Loewenich, Walther, 7n27

W

Walk, Salvation as, 63, 165, 225, 227, 326
Wawrykow, Joseph P., 33n121, n123
Way, Salvation as, 164, 225, 326
Wealth, 179, 191–92, 194–95
  Salvation and, 136, 146–47, 202–7, 210, 218, 235–37, 329
Weber, Ferdinand, 75–76, 81, 93–94, 108, 111, 302n50, 322
Wesley, John, 55–61, 69, 153, 320, 322
Westerholm, Stephen, 87n117, 90–91, 93, 108
Westminster Confession of Faith, 12n49, 50n253
Wickedness. *See* Evil
Wilkin, Robert N., 11n46, 226n40, 234n87, 243n2, 246n16, 248n24, 253n34
Will, 24n44, 32
  see also Free will; God, Will of
Wisdom, 118, 126, 129–30, 280–81, 297
Word, 14, 67, 118–19, 128, 131–32, 161, 251–52, 266, 282
Works, 12, 31, 220
  Acts on, 123–24, 133, 317
  Aquinas on, 29–34
  Arminius on, 52–55
  Augustine on, 24n44, 25, 38, 198, 213n122
  Calvin on, 46–51, 198, 321
  Conversion and, 12n49, 42, 44, 57–59, 114, 126, 133, 187, 308, 321, 324–25, 328, 333–35
  Definitions of, 14–15, 17, 133, 167
  Endurance and, 246n16, 254
  Faith and, 20–21, 27, 64, 125, 129, 133n99, 162, 207n96, 237, 258, 305n69, 310, 321, 324
  Grace and, 25, 28, 125, 324–25
  James on, 118n17, 128–30, 132–33, 310, 325
  Jesus on, 41, 118n15, 120–21, 124, 131, 315–16
  John on, 120–22, 132–32, 332
  Judaism on, 90, 99–109
  Justification by, 22n26, 277, 296, 306–8, 333

Works (continued)
  Of love, 23, 27n64, 41, 121n38, 126, 128–29, 143, 295n5, 323
  Luke on, 1, 118n17, 120, 123
  Luther on, 6, 39–46, 133, 321, 325
  Matthew on, 3n8, 117n11, 118n17, 184, 333
  New Testament on, 116–33, 321–25
  Ockham on, 35
  Paul on, 40n174, 54, 79, 80n72, 83–84, 86–87, 86n112, 124–27, 132–33, 160, 237, 251, 253, 324–25, 333, 335
  Pelagius on, 37
  Peter on, 123, 130–31, 133, 325
  Reformers on, 39–51, 61n333, 320, 322
  Synoptic Gospels on, 6, 117–20, 126, 132–33, 219, 323
  Wesley on, 56–61
  see also Fruits; God, Works of; Mercy, Works of
Works-righteousness, 20n7, 123, 157, 320, 328–33
  Jesus on, 6n22, 214, 219
  Judaism on, 80n72, 99–103, 105–10, 322–24
Works-Salvation Relationship, 1–18, 23–24, 61n334, 67–70, 119, 121, 123, 127, 131n91, 132, 248, 288n132, 292–93, 300, 312, 334–37
  Augustine on, 2n4, 22–28, 36n144, 52, 68, 115, 334
  Bible on, 3, 8, 11, 16–17
  Calvin on, 52, 334
  In Church history, 19–70, 320–22
  James on, 11, 14, 124, 181, 334
  Jesus on, 5, 7, 11, 15, 17, 46n228, 166–87, 197–98, 204, 214, 315–16, 319, 322, 328, 333–35
  John on, 317, 333
  Judaism on, 5n20, 16, 17, 71–115, 166–67, 185–86, 322–23
  Luke on, 317, 319
  Luther on, 39–47, 52, 73–75, 322
  Matthew on, 277, 294–314
  New Testament on, 5n20, 14–15, 18, 112–13, 168, 185–86, 316, 318, 322, 333, 334–35

Works-Salvation Relationship (continued)
  Paul on, 9–10, 14, 110, 317
  Reformers on, 69
  Synoptic Gospels on, 2–5, 12, 15–18, 40, 110, 113, 167, 220, 315–18, 334–36

Y

Yahweh, 138–40
Young, Norman H., 213n121

Z

Zaccheus, 136, 138, 144, 204n90, 205n92, 231, 316
Zacharias, 137, 139
Zealots, 221n9
Zephaniah, 104
Zwingli, Huldrych, 46n228, 47, 295–96

Scripture Index

Old Testament

Genesis
2:16-17, 135
4:5-8, 265
4:15, 283n
13:2, 203
15:6, 78, 205, 336
16:1-4, 336
17:15-18, 336
18:10-12, 336
22:1, 250
22:12, 250
23, 233
26:12-15, 203
30:43, 203
39:4, 234n

Exodus
2:23-25, 139
3:7-10, 139
3:12, 139n
3:16 LXX, 140
3:16-22, 139
3:17 LXX, 140
4:31 LXX, 140
6:2-9, 139
6:7, 139
7:16, 139n
8:1, 139n
9:1, 139n
9:13, 139n
10:3, 139n
10:7, 139n
10:26, 139n
13:19 LXX, 140
19:1-15, 139
19:4-6, 139n
20:12, 95
20:12-16, 190
20:13, 261
20:20, 250
23:11 LXX, 179n
24:13, 234n
28:25, 234n
28:43, 234n
29:30, 234n
30:20, 234n
32:34 LXX, 140
33:11, 234n
33:14, 240
38:25 LXX, 140

Leviticus
16, 283n
18:5, 90, 94, 94n, 95, 95n, 96, 196n, 215, 215n
19:10 LXX, 179
19:17, 267
19:18, 211, 267, 267n, 268, 270
23:22 LXX, 179
26, 76n, 109
26:18, 283n
26:40-5, 98
26:40-42, 97n

Numbers
3:6, 234n
3:31, 234n
11:28, 234n
27:17, 176n

Deuteronomy

4:5-6 LXX, 129
4:23-29, 102
5:16, 95, 96
5:16-20, 190
7:6-11, 78n
8:2, 250
8:18, 203
9:26, 149
10:8, 234n
21:5, 234n
22:7, 95, 96
24:19 LXX, 179
27, 266
28, 76n
28:1-14, 203
28:25-26, 233
28-29, 109
28:47-48, 203
30:1-5, 98
30:1-10, 97n
30:11-20, 196n
30:15-18, 90
31:6, 115
32:4-6, 102
33:2, 306
33:9, 234

Joshua

1:1-2, 234n

Judges

2:22, 250
3:4, 250

1 Samuel

2:7 LXX, 179n
2:8 LXX, 179n
2:11, 234n
2:18, 234n
3:1, 234n
22:28 LXX, 179n

2 Samuel

19:7, 267

1 Kings

1:20, 235
8:46, 78n
14:10-11, 233
19:19-21, 234
19:21 LXX, 234n

2 Kings

6:15, 234n
23:10, 264
24:4, 291
24:14 LXX, 179n

1 Chronicles

22:9-10, 272n

2 Chronicles

7:14, 135
32:31, 250
33:1-20, 97n

Ezra

9:1-10:17, 109

Nehemiah

9:6-37, 97n

Esther

1:20 LXX, 179n
9:22 LXX, 179n
13:15 LXX, 149

Job

1:21, 258
1:22, 258
2:10, 258

Scripture Index   381

Job (continued)
3:1-12, 258
3:13:26, 258
4:7, 203
6:2, 258
6:10, 258
6:11, 258
6:30, 258
7:3, 258
7:7, 258
7:11, 258
7:20, 258
9:2-20, 258
9:21, 258
10:1, 258
10:18-19, 258
12:10-25, 258
13:15, 258
13:21, 258
14:14-17, 258
15:4, 203
15:29, 203
16:7-14, 258
16:19-21, 258
17:9, 258
19:21, 258
19:25-27, 258
21:4, 258
23:2, 258
23:10-12, 258
23:11-12, 258
23:14-16, 258
26:6-14, 258
27:2-6, 258
28:23-28, 258
29:12 LXX, 179
30:11, 258
42:7-8, 258

Psalms

1:1-3, 146n, 203n
7:2 LXX, 139n
9:18 LXX, 179n
9:23 LXX, 179n
9:30 LXX, 179n
9:35 LXX, 180n
11:6 LXX, 180n

Psalms (continued)
13:6 LXX, 180n
14 LXX, 124
14:2 LXX, 123
19:7-8, 14
24:16 LXX, 180n
33:7 LXX, 180n
34:10 LXX, 179n
34:13-17, 282
37, 187
37:1, 182n
37:3-5, 182n
37:7-9, 182n
37:11, 182, 182n
37:34, 182n
37:40, 182n
39 LXX, 147
40:9-10, 147
41:1, 135
41:17 LXX, 180
47, 149
48:8 LXX, 241
49:7-9, 140
49:8-9, 241
51, 97n
62:12, 307, 333
62:13, 306
68:30 LXX, 180n
69:6 LXX, 180n
71:4 LXX, 180
71:12 LXX, 180
71:13 LXX, 180n
78:8 LXX, 180n
87:10 LXX, 180n
95 LXX, 147
96:1-13, 147
103:3, 135, 176n
106:41 LXX, 180n
107:5-9, 182
108:22 LXX, 180n
112:3, 146n, 203
112:10, 289
119:18, 14
119:35, 14
130:8, 140n
139:13 LXX, 180n
139:21-22, 267
147:3, 135

Proverbs

2:22 LXX, 179n
6:23, 196n
10:15, 146n
10:15-16, 203n
10:16, 146n
13:18, 146n, 203
14:31 LXX, 180n
15:6, 146n, 203n
17:5 LXX, 180n, 290
19:7 LXX, 179n
19:17 LXX, 180n
20:9, 78n
24:12, 306, 307, 333
24:16, 283n

Ecclesiastes

7:20, 78n

Isaiah

3:14-15 LXX, 179n
5:8-10, 195n
10:1-3, 195n
10:2 LXX, 179n
19:22, 135
22:4 LXX, 247n
26:19, 135
29:18, 135
29:19 LXX, 179n
35:5-6, 135
38:16-17, 135
40:3-5, 138
40:6, 138
40:9-11, 147
41:14, 139
42:7, 135
43:9, 309
43:14, 139
43:16-18, 139
44:24, 139
45:25, 309
50:8, 309
52:7, 150
52:7-10, 147
52:9, 140

Isaiah (continued)
55:7, 230n
57:15, 181
61:1 LXX, 180
61:1-11, 147
61:2-3 LXX, 182
61:6 LXX, 182

Jeremiah

3:12, 230n
3:14, 230n
3:22, 135, 230n
16:4, 233
22:16, 217
30:7, 65n
31:18, 32
60:21, 94

Ezekiel

15, 257
18:12 LXX, 179n
19:12, 257
20:11, 90
22:6-31, 195n
22:19 LXX, 179n
27, 195n
34, 176n, 299, 299n
34:2-10, 299n
34:17, 299n
34:20, 299n
34:22, 299n
40:46, 234n
42:14, 234n
43:19, 234n
44:11-12, 234n
44:15-17, 234n
44:19, 234n
44:27, 234n

Daniel

4:24 LXX, 148n
4:28 LXX, 148n
12:2, 216
12:2-3, 142n

Hosea

6:1, 230n
6:6, 172, 173n, 186, 291, 329
14:4, 135

Joel

2:32, 112

Amos

2:6-7, 195n
2:7 LXX, 179n
4:1 LXX, 179n
5:2-3, 291
5:6-7, 291
5:10-12, 195n, 291
5:11 LXX, 179n
5:16-20, 291
5:27, 291
8:4 LXX, 179n
8:4-8, 195n

Habakkuk

2:14, 78

Zechariah

7:18, 291
13:9, 250
14:5, 306

Malachi

2:4-5, 196n

New Testament

Matthew

1:1-17, 286n
1:2, 261n
1:11, 261n
1:21, 136, 185n, 271
1:23, 314n
1:24, 118n

Matthew (continued)
2:4-8, 286n
2:6, 176n
2:8, 183
2:9, 183
2:11, 183, 287
2:13, 183
2:14, 183
2:16-18, 286n
2:20, 183
2:21, 183
2:34, 328
2:42, 233n
2:46, 328
3:1-12, 311n
3:2, 148, 149, 149n, 179, 182n, 231n
3:3, 118n
3:8, 119n, 121n, 176n, 230, 231n, 237
3:8-12, 257
3:10, 119n, 254
3:11, 231n, 311n
3:12, 311n
3:13, 311n
3:15, 302n
3:43, 143n, 196n
3:47, 143n, 200n
3:48, 201n
4:1, 250
4:8, 302n
4:9, 287
4:15, 301n
4:17, 149, 149n, 169, 179, 182n, 231n
4:17-25, 182, 182n
4:18, 261n
4:18-22, 169, 169n, 222, 222n, 229n
4:19, 118n, 144n, 223
4:20, 169n, 192, 229
4:21, 175, 261n
4:22, 169n, 192, 229
4:23, 169
4:23-25, 177
4:25, 169
5:1, 169, 169n, 223n
5:1-2, 222
5:1-6, 183n
5:2, 169n

Matthew (continued)
5:3, 115, 119, 132, 148n, 149, 168, 169, 177-178, 178n, 179–81, 183-84, 186, 187, 187n, 198, 208, 276n, 287, 311, 318, 323, 324
5:3-4, 195
5:3-9, 183
5:3-13, 311n
5:4, 182, 187n
5:4-9, 178n, 276n
5:5, 182, 184, 187, 187n
5:6, 174, 182, 187n
5-7, 197
5:7, 182, 184, 275, 290
5:7-9, 183n
5:8, 182
5:9, 182, 272n, 273, 277
5:10, 148n, 149, 168, 169, 177, 178, 178n, 181–83, 184, 276n, 277
5:10-12, 267
5:11, 183, 184, 268, 276n
5:11-12, 275
5:12, 50, 178n, 268, 273, 322
5:13-14, 183
5:13-16, 275
5:16, 118, 273, 335
5:17, 261, 261n, 268
5:17-19, 171
5:17-20, 198, 199, 311n
5:17-48, 329
5:18-19, 194n, 198n
5:19, 119n, 185n, 265, 304, 316
5:20, 24, 24n, 27n, 166, 167, 169, 170, 171–75, 177, 178, 178n, 179, 182n, 183, 186, 187, 187n, 191, 196, 198, 200, 230n, 239, 260, 264, 266n, 267, 273, 274, 275, 276, 291, 312, 313, 315, 317, 318, 319, 328, 329, 334
5:21, 261, 267
5:21-22, 175, 196n, 264n
5:21-26, 263–66, 284n, 311n, 315, 331
5:21-42, 200
5:21-47, 170, 173n
5:21-48, 171, 187n, 194n, 196, 198n, 199, 260, 291, 313, 318, 329
5:22, 196n, 260, 261, 262, 263, 263n, 264n, 265, 266n, 303, 328
5:22-24, 261n

Matthew (continued)
5:23, 119, 263, 303
5:23-24, 262, 262n, 265, 330
5:23-25, 262n
5:23-26, 262, 265
5:24, 263, 303
5:25, 148n, 263
5:25-26, 262, 266
5:26, 148n, 263, 264, 264n
5:27, 303
5:27-30, 197n
5:28, 148n, 196n
5:28-29, 185
5:29, 175, 178n
5:29-30, 328
5:30, 148, 175, 178n, 196n
5:31, 261
5:32, 118n
5:33, 261
5:36, 118n
5:38-42, 267–82, 269n
5:38-48, 290n
5:39-40, 268n, 269
5:40, 302–5
5:41-47, 200
5:43-47, 173n
5:43-48, 202n, 267–82, 303, 311n, 315
5:44, 196n, 282n
5:44-45, 260
5:45, 268, 270, 271–73, 286n
5:45-47, 331
5:46, 118n, 268n, 273, 274, 275, 276n, 277
5:46-47, 268
5:47, 118n, 261n, 274, 276, 303
5:48, 143, 170, 173n, 191n, 196n, 199, 200, 201, 268, 270n, 272, 273, 336
5:56, 263n
6:1, 171, 173n, 273
6:1-2, 274
6:1-4, 311n
6:1-8, 177n
6:1-18, 170, 196n
6:2, 276, 289n
6:4, 273, 274
6:5, 274, 276, 289n
6:5-15, 311n
6:6, 273, 274

Matthew (continued)
6:7, 268, 276
6:8, 273
6:9, 272
6:10, 149, 172n, 178
6:13, 138
6:14-15, 1, 5n, 26, 58, 273, 288, 289, 290, 331
6:15, 288
6:16, 274, 276, 289n
6:16-18, 311n
6:18, 273, 274
6:19-21, 143
6:19-34, 170
6:20, 276
6:20-24, 179, 236
6:24, 199, 207, 225
6:25-34, 207n, 237n
6:26, 273
6:29, 286n
6:32, 268, 273, 301n
6:33, 171, 171n, 179
7:1, 335
7:1-2, 263, 337
7:1-6, 176, 311n
7:1-12, 170
7:2, 288, 291
7:3, 303
7:3-5, 261n
7:4, 303
7:5, 289n, 303
7:7, 58
7:11, 27n, 273
7:12, 118n
7:13, 177, 178, 194n, 328, 329
7:13-14, 142n, 169, 179, 187, 191n, 238
7:14, 142, 184, 190n, 194n, 276
7:15, 175
7:15-20, 176, 176n, 177, 311n, 334
7:15-23, 176n, 335
7:16-20, 176
7:17, 46n, 119n, 169
7:18, 119n
7:19, 119n, 176, 176n
7:20, 45, 121n

Matthew (continued)
7:21, 117, 119, 166, 169, 171, 172, 173n, 174, 176, 177, 179, 182n, 183, 186, 187, 196, 197, 215, 276, 291, 312, 313, 318, 319, 328, 329, 330
7:21-23, 175–77, 297, 311n
7:22, 117n, 119, 177, 178, 335
7:22-23, 328, 335
7:23, 117, 119, 169, 172, 174, 176, 176n, 178, 191, 216, 219, 247, 276, 277, 289n, 292, 302, 313, 315, 319, 332
7:24, 119, 197n, 208
7:24-27, 170, 178, 276, 318
7:24-28, 311n
7:26, 119, 208, 263
7:28-8:1, 169n
7:29, 171, 261
7:33, 247
8:1, 169
8:2, 287
8:4, 194n, 198n
8:5-13, 207, 236, 311n
8:6, 183
8:8-9, 118n, 194n
8:8-10, 231
8:9, 118n, 224
8:10, 230
8:11-12, 148
8:12, 289
8:13, 231
8:18-22, 236n
8:19, 230, 233
8:19-22, 233
8:19-27, 226, 227
8:21, 169n, 223n, 226
8:21-22, 145, 222, 233, 236, 316
8:22, 144n, 234n
8:23, 223n
8:25, 135, 135n, 148, 161n, 227
8:26, 227, 236n
8:27, 227
8:29, 264, 289, 289n
8:31, 287
9:2, 183, 224n
9:9, 144n, 222
9:9-13, 311
9:10, 223n
9:10-11, 268

Matthew (continued)
9:11, 223n
9:12-13, 287
9:13, 171, 172, 174, 175, 197, 291, 313
9:14, 223n
9:18, 183, 287
9:19, 223n
9:20-22, 207, 236
9:21, 135, 161n
9:21-22, 135n
9:22, 135, 161n
9:22-24, 231
9:27, 287
9:28, 118n
9:31, 319
9:36, 184
9:37, 223n
10, 242, 244, 331
10:1, 223n, 229
10:1-5, 244
10:1-23, 239n
10:2, 261n
10:5, 268, 301n
10:5-6, 304n
10:5-15, 311n
10:6-7, 148, 242
10:7, 149, 149n, 179, 275
10:7-8, 177
10:9, 243
10:9-10, 303
10:11, 243
10:11-14, 303
10:13, 243
10:14, 242, 275
10:15, 254, 303, 312
10:16, 242
10:16-18, 303
10:16-25, 311n
10:17, 264
10:17-19, 242
10:17-20, 247, 312n
10:18, 254, 286n, 301n
10:19-20, 254, 303
10:21, 243, 261n
10:21-23, 303
10:22, 2, 5n, 27, 65n, 136, 230n, 242, 243, 244, 251, 252n, 254, 315, 318
10:22-23, 181n

Matthew (continued)
10:23, 242, 244, 245, 248, 254, 303n, 304n
10:24, 254
10:24-25, 169n, 223n
10:26, 242, 304, 312n, 332
10:28, 148, 161, 239n, 241, 243, 244, 254, 290, 304, 313n, 333
10:31, 242
10:32, 247, 251, 304, 304n, 312
10:32-33, 242, 244, 246, 247, 248, 311n, 313n
10:33, 247, 254, 304, 313
10:34-39, 311n
10:35-37, 145
10:37, 25, 229n, 234, 247
10:37-39, 239n, 242
10:38, 229, 229n, 247
10:39, 229, 240, 241, 242, 243, 244, 247
10:40, 254, 275, 304, 336
10:40-42, 248, 275, 276, 276n, 277, 311n, 318
10:41, 275, 304
10:41-42, 242, 244
10:42, 145, 223n, 304, 316
11:1, 222, 223n
11:2, 118n, 223n
11:2-5, 135
11:2-6, 168
11:11, 145, 145n, 185n, 304
11:12, 149, 168, 239n
11:15, 180
11:19, 114, 118, 225, 268
11:20-21, 231n
11:20-24, 184, 311n
11:21-24, 239n
11:23, 184
11:28, 184
11:28-29, 239, 240, 330
11:28-30, 240n
11:37-39, 222
12:1-2, 222, 223n
12:1-14, 239n
12:2, 118n
12:3, 118n
12:7, 172, 174, 291, 313, 319
12:8, 194n, 198n, 222
12:12, 118n

Matthew (continued)
12:16, 118n
12:18, 301n
12:21, 301n
12:22-32, 311n
12:28, 148, 149, 168
12:29, 148n
12:33, 311
12:33-34, 311n
12:33-35, 311n
12:33-37, 311n
12:35, 311, 311n
12:36, 67, 311
12:36-37, 58
12:36-43, 311n
12:37, 306, 311, 322, 335
12:41, 231n
12:44-50, 311n
12:46-47, 261n
12:46-50, 303n, 304
12:48-50, 261n
12:49, 223n
12:49-50, 291
12:50, 119n, 172, 172n, 223n, 224n, 313
13:10, 223n
13:11, 147n
13:16-17, 168
13:21, 249
13:23, 119n
13:24-30, 257, 306n
13:26, 119n
13:27-28, 225n
13:28, 118n
13:32, 145
13:36, 223n
13:36-43, 257, 319
13:37-43, 306n
13:38-39, 268
13:39, 297
13:40, 254, 297
13:41, 119n, 178, 197n, 306
13:41-43, 289n, 319
13:42, 264, 289
13:42-43, 318
13:43, 174, 178n, 187, 198, 275, 299
13:44, 143, 144n, 196, 210
13:47-50, 276, 318

Matthew (continued)
13:49, 174, 175n, 187, 198, 275, 289n, 297, 299
13:49-50, 299n, 318, 319
13:50, 264, 289
13:55, 261n, 271
13:58, 118n, 236n
14:1-12, 286n
14:2, 117n, 125n
14:3, 261n
14:7, 313
14:12, 223n, 234, 235
14:15, 223n
14:19, 223n
14:20, 135
14:21, 27n, 183, 290
14:22, 223n
14:26, 223n
14:28-29, 226
14:30, 135n, 161n
14:31, 236n
15:2, 223n
15:7, 289n
15:8-9, 265
15:12, 223n
15:13, 311, 312
15:17-20, 335
15:21-28, 207, 236
15:22, 287
15:23, 223n
15:25, 287
15:26, 183
15:32-33, 223n
15:36, 223n
15:38, 183
16:3, 289n
16:5, 223n
16:8, 236n
16:13, 223n
16:16-19, 183
16:20-21, 223n
16:21, 150, 225
16:21-28, 311n
16:22-23, 183
16:23, 184
16:24, 144n, 146n, 223n, 229, 229n
16:25, 229

Matthew (continued)
16:27, 9, 24, 50, 67, 117n, 118n, 197n, 302, 305, 305n, 306, 306n, 307, 307n, 309, 312, 318, 322, 332, 333
17:1, 261n
17:4, 118n, 184
17:6, 223n
17:10, 223n
17:12, 118n
17:13, 223n
17:15, 287
17:16, 223n
17:17, 226
17:18, 183
17:19, 223n
17:20, 226
17:24-27, 184, 286n
18, 145
18:1, 223n
18:1-5, 183, 185n, 311n
18:3, 145, 147, 166, 183–85, 191, 224n, 316
18:3-4, 187
18:4, 145n, 184, 287, 304
18:5, 185, 304, 314n
18:6, 145, 224n, 304, 316
18:6-9, 184, 185, 185n
18:8, 142, 178, 184n, 185n
18:8-9, 142, 185, 190n
18:9, 142, 178, 184n, 185n
18:10, 145, 304, 316
18:14, 145, 172n, 316
18:15, 261n, 286
18:15-18, 288
18:15-20, 283, 290, 316
18:17, 268
18:21, 261n, 286
18:21-25, 53
18:21-35, 7, 282, 283–89, 315, 319
18:23, 284, 286
18:23-25, 147n, 291
18:23-26, 286n
18:23-27, 311
18:23-32, 225n
18:23-35, 26, 288n
18:24, 284
18:25, 284
18:26, 284, 287

Matthew (continued)
18:27, 284, 285, 287
18:27-31, 311n
18:28, 284
18:28-29, 284
18:29, 287
18:30, 284
18:31, 285
18:32, 285, 289
18:32-35, 276, 318
18:33, 285, 287
18:33-35, 292
18:34, 264, 285, 286, 288, 289n
18:34-35, 260, 289, 331
18:35, 118n, 119n, 260, 261n, 286, 288, 289, 291
19:3, 250
19:7, 190n
19:10, 223n
19:13, 223n
19:13-15, 183
19:14, 205, 224n
19:16, 110, 119n, 141, 142, 189, 189n, 202n
19:16-17, 49n, 120, 184
19:16-22, 141, 196n
19:16-30, 188, 311n
19:17, 41, 142, 143, 143n, 178, 188, 190, 191n, 194, 200, 201, 202n
19:17-21, 315
19:18-19, 190
19:19, 201n
19:20, 189n, 194, 199, 206n
19:21, 1, 26, 143, 144, 180, 180n, 188, 191, 191n, 199, 200, 201, 276
19:22, 189, 189n, 191, 202
19:22-24, 201n
19:23, 147, 147n, 191, 200, 223n
19:23-24, 141, 180, 183
19:23-25, 148
19:24, 147, 147n, 191
19:25, 136, 137, 146, 191, 203, 223n
19:26, 119, 132, 146n, 186, 187, 187n, 191, 192, 195 204n, 210n, 317, 324, 329
19:27, 150, 192, 192n, 316
19:28, 148, 192, 193n, 301n, 305, 306

Matthew (continued)
19:29, 142, 151, 192, 192n, 193, 197, 261n, 317
19:29-30, 193
19:30, 193
20:1, 2, 8, 117n
20:1-16, 311, 311n
20:5, 118n
20:12, 118n, 119n
20:15, 118n
20:17, 223n
20:19, 301n
20:20-21, 271
20:24, 261n
20:25, 301n
20:25-28, 286n
20:26, 184
20:27, 184
20:28, 140, 184
20:30, 287
20:31, 287
20:32, 118n
21:1, 223n
21:6, 118n, 223n
21:13, 118n
21:15, 118n
21:20, 223n
21:21, 118n, 236n
21:23, 118n
21:24, 118n
21:27, 118n
21:28-32, 311n
21:31, 119n, 178n, 183, 184, 185, 312, 313
21:32, 171
21:34, 147, 172n
21:34-36, 225n
21:36, 118n
21:38-39, 271
21:40, 118n, 289
21:43, 119n, 301n
21:45-46, 271
21:46, 222
22:1-14, 66n, 148, 311n
22:2, 118n
22:3-10, 225n
22:8, 229
22:13, 289

Matthew (continued)
22:15, 271
22:15-16, 222
22:16, 223n
22:18, 250, 289n
22:24-25, 261n
22:36, 194
22:37, 313
22:37-39, 292
22:37-40, 265
22:39, 313
22:40, 313
23, 113n
23:1, 169n, 223n
23:1-36, 311n
23:3, 117, 117n, 119, 119n, 120
23:4, 88, 88n, 239n
23:5, 118, 118n
23:8, 261n, 304
23:11, 184, 319
23:12, 184
23:13, 172, 183, 185n, 276, 289n, 313
23:15, 118n, 264, 276, 289n
23:17, 263
23:23, 118n, 171, 172, 173n, 174, 194n, 198n, 289n, 292, 297, 313, 329
23:24, 191n
23:25, 289n
23:25-28, 174n
23:26, 230
23:27, 289n
23:28, 171, 172, 174, 313
23:29, 289n
23:31, 271
23:33, 264, 276
23:51, 289n
24, 242, 244
24:1, 223n
24:2, 242
24:3, 223n, 297, 298n, 299n
24:3-14, 311n
24:4, 175
24:4-5, 246
24:4-23, 242
24:4-31, 298n
24:5, 175
24:5-9, 246
24:6, 245

Matthew (continued)
24:7, 301, 301n
24:9, 242, 243, 301, 301n
24:10, 242, 246
24:11, 175, 242, 243, 246
24:12, 172, 177, 242, 246
24:13, 11n, 65n, 136, 242, 244, 245, 246, 315
24:14, 245, 301, 301n, 303, 304
24:19, 178
24:22, 134, 135n, 161n, 178
24:24, 175
24:27, 298, 298n
24:27-31, 244
24:29, 178, 298
24:29-31, 181
24:30, 298, 302, 302n, 304n, 305, 309
24:30-31, 298, 298n
24:31, 298
24:32, 298n
24:32-35, 298n
24:36, 178, 306n
24:36-44, 298n
24:37, 298, 298n
24:40-41, 244
24:44, 298
24:45-25:30, 297, 298n, 302
24:45-51, 311n
24:46, 118n, 302n
24:51, 244, 276, 289, 289n, 297, 299n, 302n
25, 7, 276, 303
25:1-12, 148
25:1-13, 311n
25:2-3, 263
25:8, 263
25:9-10, 303
25:10, 244, 297
25:10-12, 297
25:11-14, 303
25:12, 247, 302n, 313
25:13, 297
25:14-30, 225n, 311n
25:15, 303
25:16, 117
25:16-18, 303
25:19-20, 303
25:21, 302n

Matthew (continued)
25:21-23, 303
25:23, 302n, 303
25:26, 285, 289, 304
25:28, 304
25:29, 58
25:30, 244, 289, 297, 299n, 302n
25:31, 31, 298, 302, 304n, 305, 305n, 306, 306n, 309, 312, 332
25:31-35, 275
25:31-46, 5n, 6, 27n, 28, 166, 177, 180n, 185, 216, 219, 241, 244, 275n, 276, 290, 292, 294n, 295n, 296, 297, 297n, 298n, 299n, 300n, 301, 301n, 302n, 303, 303n, 304, 305-8, 311, 311n, 318, 319, 321, 322, 332, 333
25:32, 294, 299, 299n, 300-302, 301n
25:32-33, 297n
25:33, 299
25:34, 50, 51, 66n, 147n, 148, 168, 173, 230n, 239n, 244, 275, 276, 299, 302n, 312, 317, 319, 322, 334
25:34-36, 294
25:34-46, 2, 115, 197, 198, 315
25:35-36, 305n, 311
25:35-40, 299, 306n
25:35-45, 277
25:35-46, 305n
25:36, 297
25:37, 173, 299, 299n, 312, 313, 317
25:39, 299
25:40, 31, 118n, 119n, 218, 261n, 294, 300, 303, 304, 319, 330, 336
25:41, 178, 264, 289, 297n, 299, 299n, 302n
25:41-43, 294
25:42, 297
25:42-45, 299
25:44, 176, 299
25:44-46, 11, 162
25:45, 118n, 217, 218, 300, 303, 330
25:46, 66n, 142, 147n, 173, 174, 178n, 184, 187, 197, 230n, 244, 275, 289n, 294, 297n, 299, 302n, 304, 312, 313, 317, 319, 336
25:47-50, 319
26:1, 223n
26:8, 223n

Matthew (continued)
26:10, 117
26:12, 118n
26:13, 118n
26:17, 223n
26:17-25, 311n
26:18, 118n, 223n
26:19, 118n, 223n
26:25, 222
26:26, 223n
26:28, 185n
26:29, 178
26:35-36, 223n
26:38, 189n, 258
26:39, 145, 258, 302n
26:40, 223n
26:42, 172n, 302n
26:45, 223n
26:55, 228n
26:56, 223n
26:59, 264
26:64, 304n
26:70, 247
26:72, 247
26:73, 118n, 145
26:74, 247
26:75, 247
27:22, 118n
27:23, 118n
27:40, 134, 135n, 161n
27:42, 135n, 136, 139, 161n
27:42-43, 139
27:46, 258
27:49, 134, 135n, 161n
27:64, 223n
28:7, 223n
28:8, 223n
28:10, 224, 224n, 261n, 304n
28:13, 223n
28:14, 118n
28:15, 118n
28:16, 223n
28:18, 302n
28:18-20, 304, 316, 332
28:19, 268, 299, 299n, 301, 301n, 302, 302n, 304n
28:19-20, 146, 244, 331
28:20, 120, 297, 314n, 316

Mark

1:4, 231n
1:14-15, 115, 147, 232
1:15, 148, 149, 168, 179, 230, 231n, 324
1:18-20, 192
2:5, 135, 207, 224n, 236
2:15-16, 223n
2:17, 150, 197
2:18, 222, 223n
2:23, 223n
2:27, 198
3:4, 118n, 134, 135, 135n, 161n
3:7, 223n, 230
3:8, 118n
3:9, 223n
3:14, 118
3:35, 119n, 224n
4:10, 225
4:11, 147n
4:18-19, 207
4:26, 149
4:27-28, 149
4:29, 149
4:31-32, 149
4:32, 119n
4:34, 223n
4:40, 226, 236n
5:18-19, 223
5:19, 118n, 235
5:20, 118n
5:23, 135, 135n, 161n
5:28, 135n, 161n
5:31, 223n
5:32, 118n
5:34, 135, 135n, 161n, 223
5:36, 231
6:1, 223n
6:6, 236n
6:12, 231n
6:14, 125n
6:16, 134n
6:21, 118n
6:26, 189n
6:29, 223n
6:30, 119, 304n
6:35, 223n
6:41, 223n

Mark (continued)
6:45, 223n
6:52, 226
6:56, 135, 135n, 161n
7:2, 223n
7:5, 223n
7:5-13, 235
7:6, 88, 88n
7:8-9, 14
7:9, 120
7:12, 118n
7:13, 118n
7:17, 223n, 225
7:18, 226
7:19, 198
7:37, 118n
8:1, 223n
8:4, 223n
8:6, 223n
8:10, 223n
8:17-21, 226
8:21-22, 222
8:27, 223n
8:29, 226
8:33, 226
8:33-34, 223n
8:34, 146n, 229, 229n
8:34-35, 241n
8:34-38, 117n
8:35, 137n, 229, 241
8:35-38, 241
8:36, 241
8:37, 140, 241
8:38, 9, 241, 306
9:5, 222
9:14, 223n
9:18, 223n
9:28, 223n
9:31, 222, 223n
9:32, 226
9:34, 226
9:39, 118n
9:41, 145
9:43-47, 264
9:47, 148, 183
10:10, 223n
10:13, 223n
10:13-15, 183

Mark (continued)
10:14, 205
10:14-15, 224n
10:15, 141, 183
10:17, 119n, 141, 189, 189n
10:17-22, 141
10:17-30, 147n
10:17-31, 188
10:18, 190
10:19, 190
10:20, 190, 190n, 194
10:21, 144, 188, 190, 191, 191n
10:22, 189, 189n, 191, 203
10:23, 147, 147n, 191
10:23-24, 141
10:24, 147, 191n, 203, 223n, 224n
10:24-25, 183
10:25, 147, 191
10:26, 136, 137, 146, 191, 192, 203, 204n
10:27, 132, 146n, 191, 192, 195, 210n, 324
10:28, 150, 192, 192n
10:29, 192, 192n
10:30, 142, 151, 193
10:31, 193
10:32, 226
10:35, 118n
10:36, 118n
10:38-39, 226
10:43-45, 224
10:45, 140, 150
10:46, 223n, 271
10:46-52, 207, 236
10:52, 135, 135n, 161n
11:1, 223n
11:3, 118n
11:5, 118n
11:14, 223n
11:21, 222
11:22, 236n
11:23, 231
11:23-24, 231n
11:25, 288, 289
12:9, 289
12:30-33, 292
12:33, 198, 265
12:34, 149n

Scripture Index 393

Mark (continued)
12:38-40, 280
12:43, 223n
13, 244
13:1, 223n
13:5-6, 246
13:6-9, 246
13:7, 245
13:9, 264
13:12, 243
13:13, 65n, 136, 242, 244, 245, 246
13:20, 134, 135n, 161n
13:21, 231
13:22, 246
13:26-27, 244
13:34, 117
14:12-13, 223n
14:14, 223n
14:16, 223n
14:25, 148
14:32, 223n
14:45, 222
14:49, 228n
14:50, 226
14:66-72, 226
15:7, 118n
15:8, 118n
15:30, 134, 161n
15:30-31, 135n
15:31, 136, 161n
16:7, 223n
16:16, 136n

21:28, 117

Luke

1:6, 123n
1:13, 271–73
1:25, 118n
1:38, 224n
1:45, 231
1:47, 137
1:48, 224n
1:49, 118n
1:50, 287
1:51, 118n
1:54-55, 137
1:68, 118n, 139

Luke (continued)
1:68-70, 137
1:69, 140
1:70, 140
1:71, 137, 140, 229n
1:72, 137
1:72-73, 140
1:74, 137, 138, 140
1:74-75, 140
1:75, 137, 139
1:77, 137, 140, 140n
1:79, 137
2:11, 138
2:26, 138
2:27, 118n
2:29, 224n
2:30, 138
2:31, 138
2:32, 138
2:38, 140
3:3, 124, 138, 231n
3:4, 58
3:8, 114, 144n, 231n
3:8-14, 124, 230
3:9, 58
3:13, 120n
4:18, 180, 180n
4:18-19, 137n, 150
4:21, 168
4:23, 118n
4:43, 150
5:8, 287
5:20, 147
5:27-32, 114
5:30, 223n
5:31-32, 148n
5:32, 175, 197, 231n
5:33, 222
6:1, 223n
6:9, 134, 135n, 161n
6:13, 223n
6:17, 223n
6:20, 180, 207, 223n
6:21, 273
6:22, 229n
6:23, 50, 273, 322
6:24, 207
6:25, 273, 289

Luke (continued)
6:27, 268
6:27-28, 213n
6:27-30, 269
6:27-35, 267–82
6:28, 282n
6:29-30, 268n
6:31, 270
6:32-33, 270, 276n
6:32-34, 270
6:32-35, 331
6:35, 260, 268, 270, 271, 273
6:35-36, 213n
6:36, 173n, 270, 270n, 272, 273, 291
6:37, 197n
6:37-38, 273
6:40, 223, 223n
6:43, 46n, 57
6:46, 119n
6:47, 119n
7:2, 224
7:11, 223n
7:18, 223n
7:29, 118n
7:34, 225
7:36-50, 114, 207, 236
7:38, 287
7:48, 136
7:50, 136, 223
8:9, 223n
8:10, 147n
8:12, 135n, 136, 161n, 231
8:13, 183, 231, 251, 252, 327
8:14, 207, 235
8:21, 119, 224n
8:22, 223n
8:25, 236n
8:27, 156n
8:27-10:52, 156n
8:36, 135, 135n, 161n
8:48, 135, 135n, 161n, 223
8:50, 135, 135n, 161n, 231
9:14, 223n
9:16, 223n
9:18, 223n
9:23, 146n, 228n, 229
9:23-26, 117n
9:24, 229

Luke (continued)
9:24-25, 148
9:26, 306
9:33, 156n
9:40, 223n
9:43, 223n
9:51-24:53, 216n, 217n, 233n
9:54, 223n
9:57, 233n
9:57-58, 233
9:57-62, 233
9:59, 233n
9:59-60, 145, 233, 316
9:60, 234n
9:61-62, 234
10:7, 117n
10:9, 149n
10:11, 149n
10:13, 231n
10:16, 218, 219, 314n, 336
10:17, 304n
10:23, 223n
10:25, 110, 119n, 211, 214, 215, 217
10:25-28, 1, 5n, 188, 212
10:25-37, 167, 212n, 214n, 218, 303
10:26, 211, 214
10:26-27, 195
10:26-28, 194
10:27, 199, 211, 212, 214, 265
10:27-28, 315
10:28, 119n, 211, 213n, 214, 215, 217
10:29, 118n, 211, 212n, 213, 216, 267
10:30, 211
10:30-36, 212
10:31, 211
10:32, 156n, 211
10:32-33, 211n
10:34-35, 211
10:36, 211, 291
10:37, 119n, 211, 213, 213n, 215, 217, 292
10:52, 156n
11:1, 222, 223n, 225
11:9, 36
11:20, 148
11:29-32, 148n
11:32, 231n
11:52, 148n

Luke (continued)
12:1, 223n
12:5, 264
12:8, 306, 312n
12:15, 142
12:16-21, 207
12:22, 223n
12:28, 236n
12:33, 143
12:42-43, 53
12:43, 53n
12:44, 53
12:45, 53n
12:46, 53, 53n
12:57-59, 263
13:1-5, 135, 203
13:3, 230, 231n
13:5, 231n
13:14, 117
13:23, 136, 137
13:23-24, 238, 240
13:24, 159n, 239, 321
13:25-30, 238
13:26-27, 176n
13:27, 117, 175n, 239
13:28, 289
13:29, 148
14:13, 180
14:14, 197n
14:15, 148
14:15-24, 114
14:16-24, 148
14:25, 229
14:26, 229, 234, 239n
14:27, 229, 229n
14:33, 144, 223n, 316
15:1-2, 114, 287
15:7, 230, 231n
15:10, 231n
15:17, 231, 231n
15:18-21, 231
15:19, 118n
16:1, 223n
16:8, 118n
16:9, 26n
16:13, 225
16:16, 147, 168, 198
16:19-31, 207

Luke (continued)
16:20, 207n
16:23, 288
16:24, 207n
16:24-26, 287
16:25, 142
16:28, 288
16:30, 231n
16:31, 230
17, 148n
17:1, 223n
17:3-4, 231n, 283
17:5-6, 236n
17:7-10, 224n
17:14, 147n
17:15-19, 207, 236
17:19, 135, 135n, 147, 161n, 223
17:20-21, 168
17:21, 148, 148n, 168, 210
17:22, 148n, 223n
17:22-37, 148n, 149n
17:23, 148n
17:24, 148n
17:26, 148n
17:30, 148n
17:31, 148n
17:33, 148n
17:34, 148n
17:35, 148n
17:36, 148n
17:37, 148n
18, 205
18:1-8, 206
18:7, 118n
18:8, 118n, 289
18:9, 144n, 230n, 231
18:9-12, 335
18:9-14, 206
18:11-12, 216, 287
18:13, 231, 231n
18:13-14, 239, 287
18:15, 141, 223n
18:15-17, 183, 206
18:16, 205
18:16-17, 147, 224n
18:17, 64, 183, 239
18:18, 119n, 141, 189, 189n
18:18-23, 141

Luke (continued)
18:18-30, 188, 205n, 206
18:19, 46n, 190, 190n
18:20, 190
18:21, 194
18:22, 64, 144, 188, 190n, 191, 191n, 206, 235
18:23, 189n, 203, 206
18:24, 147, 147n, 191
18:24-25, 141, 183
18:25, 147, 191, 216
18:26, 136, 137, 146, 192, 203, 226
18:27, 132, 146n, 191, 192, 195, 210n, 239, 324
18:28, 150, 192n, 216
18:29, 192, 192n
18:30, 142, 151, 193
18:31-32, 216
18:31-34, 206
18:35-24:53, 245n
18:35-43, 205n
18:37, 216
18:42, 135, 135n, 161n
18:42-43, 223
19:1-9, 206, 230
19:1-10, 114, 192, 204n
19:3, 206n
19:5, 231
19:6, 231
19:7-9, 231
19:8, 138, 144, 206, 235
19:9, 138, 144, 206, 316
19:10, 136, 138, 150, 205n
19:15, 225n
19:16, 215
19:20, 215
19:23, 120n
19:29, 223n
19:37, 223n
19:39, 223n
20:45, 223n
21, 244
21:7, 243
21:8-12, 246
21:12-19, 181n
21:13, 243
21:16, 243, 245
21:17, 246

Luke (continued)
21:18, 65n, 244
21:19, 242, 243, 245, 246
21:20-24, 243
21:22, 243
21:24, 243
21:25-28, 243
21:27, 245
21:28, 139n, 245
21:31, 168, 245
21:36, 243
22:11, 223n
22:19, 118n
22:23, 120
22:28-30, 168
22:30, 148, 306
22:39, 223n
22:46, 223n
23:15, 120
23:35, 135n, 136, 161n
23:37, 134, 135n, 161n
23:39, 135n, 136, 161n
23:41, 120
23:42, 168
23:42-43, 149
23:48, 231n
24:19, 118
24:21, 140
24:25, 231
24:47, 231n

John

1:12, 273
1:14, 218n
1:29, 256n
1:35, 223n
1:37, 223n
1:49, 222
2:2, 222, 223n, 226
2:11, 254
2:11-12, 222, 223n
2:16, 256n
2:17, 223n
2:22, 223n
2:23, 237n, 254
2:23-24, 154
2:23-25, 257, 328

John (continued)
2:25, 190, 207, 234
3:1-12, 254
3:3, 66n, 150n
3:5, 24, 24n, 27n, 150n
3:6, 41
3:16, 155
3:17, 154
3:20, 307n
3:21, 121
3:22, 222, 223n
3:25, 223n
3:36, 154
4:1, 223n
4:1-27, 222
4:2, 223n
4:8, 223n
4:14, 155
4:27, 223n
4:31, 222, 223n
4:33, 223n
4:34-38, 120
4:39-42, 254
4:50, 254
4:53, 254
5:1-18, 254
5:8-12, 256n
5:12, 154
5:17-21, 120
5:20-21, 122n
5:24, 54n, 154, 185n, 307n
5:24-29, 185n
5:25-28, 307
5:28-29, 28, 123n, 185n, 216, 307n, 312
5:29, 27, 50, 115, 123n, 197n, 307, 322, 333
5:29-30, 307n
5:36, 120
5:36-40, 120
6:3, 223n
6:6, 250
6:8, 223n
6:12, 223n
6:13, 250
6:14, 254
6:16, 223n
6:22, 223n
6:24, 223n

John (continued)
6:25, 222
6:27, 256
6:27-29, 120
6:28-29, 128n
6:29, 121
6:35, 182n
6:39, 155
6:40, 155
6:44, 32
6:47, 154
6:50-51, 155
6:51, 155
6:53-58, 155, 155n
6:54, 155
6:56, 256
6:58, 155
6:60, 254
6:60-61, 223n, 226
6:66, 223n, 226, 254
6:66-69, 226
6:68, 254
6:69, 226
6:70-71, 226
7:3, 223n
8:12, 145, 230, 316
8:23, 154
8:28, 222
8:30, 256
8:30-46, 257, 328
8:31, 223n, 237n, 254, 256
8:33, 114
8:35, 256
8:39, 114, 121, 131n, 144n, 271
8:41, 121, 271, 324
8:44, 121, 257, 271
8:51, 54, 155
8:52, 155
8:59, 256n
8:67-69, 222
9:1-2, 203
9:1-3, 135
9:2, 222, 223n
9:3-4, 120
9:3-7, 120
9:27-28, 223n
9:28, 114, 223n
9:41, 14

John (continued)
10:4, 27
10:7, 142n
10:9, 142n
10:10, 154
10:18, 256n
10:24, 256n
10:25, 120
10:27, 54
10:27-29, 54n
10:28, 155
10:28-29, 54
10:32, 120, 121
10:37, 120
10:38, 120
11:7-8, 223n
11:8, 222
11:11, 225
11:12, 135n, 161n, 223n
11:24-26, 155
11:25-26, 155
11:26, 155
11:39, 256, 256n
11:41, 256, 256n
11:48, 256, 256n
11:54, 223n
12:4, 223n
12:16, 223n
12:25, 154
12:27, 135n, 161n
12:46, 145, 155, 230, 316
12:47, 154
12:48, 155
13:5, 223n
13:8, 247
13:22, 223n
13:23, 223n
13:31-35, 121n
13:35, 223n, 292, 332, 334
13:38, 247
14, 218
14:2, 155n
14:6, 142n
14:9, 218n, 254
14:10, 120, 256
14:11, 120
14:12, 121, 122, 122n
14:12-17, 121n

John (continued)
14-15, 132
14:20, 121, 122
14:22, 226
14:23, 121, 155n, 218n
14:37, 226
15, 65, 121, 122n
15:1-6, 53, 63n, 121n, 254n, 255, 256, 307n, 324, 327, 331
15:1-7, 27
15:4, 46n, 254
15:5, 24, 32, 121, 132, 181n, 186, 195, 198, 208, 321, 324
15:6, 65, 121n, 254, 256, 257
15:7, 122n
15:8, 121n, 223n
15:9, 121n
15:9-10, 121n
15:10, 121n
15:12, 121n
15:13, 121n
15:13-15, 225
15:15, 254
15:17, 121n
15:18-19, 254
15:20-16:4, 181
15:20-21, 254
15:24, 120
15:26, 254
15:27, 254
16:7, 122n
16:17, 223n
16:22, 256, 256n
16:27, 225
16:29, 223n
16:30, 226
17:1-5, 120
17:3, 27n, 142, 154
17:4, 120
17:12, 55, 155, 194n
17:15, 256, 256n
17:18, 223
17:21, 121
18:1-2, 223n
18:2-5, 226
18:10, 226
18:15-17, 223n
18:15-18, 226

Scripture Index 399

John (continued)
18:17, 254
18:19, 222, 223n
18:25, 223n, 247, 254
18:25-27, 226
18:27, 247, 254
18:36, 238n
19:15, 256, 256n
19:26-27, 223n
19:31, 256, 256n
19:38, 223n, 226, 256, 256n
20:1, 256
20:1-2, 256n
20:2, 256
20:2-4, 223n
20:4-10, 256
20:8, 223n, 254
20:10, 223n
20:13, 256, 256n
20:15, 256, 256n
20:17, 224n
20:18-20, 223n
20:19, 226
20:25-26, 223n
20:25-29, 254
20:28, 222
20:30, 223n
20:31, 154, 254
21:1-2, 223n
21:4, 223n
21:7, 223n, 247
21:8, 223n
21:12, 223n
21:14, 223n
21:15-17, 225, 247
21:20, 223n
21:23-24, 223n

Acts

1-2, 122n
1:3, 150n, 157
1:5-9, 122n
1:6, 157
1:7, 157
1:8, 132, 181n, 198n, 302, 304n, 324
1:26, 223
2:1-4, 122n

Acts (continued)
2-3, 12
2:18, 225n
2:21, 156
2:21-41, 122n
2:38, 156, 230
2:44, 236n
2:44-45, 235n
2:47, 156
3:19, 124, 156
3:21, 157
3:25, 114
3:26, 124
4:4, 156
4:9, 135n, 156, 161n
4:12, 156, 207
4:32, 146n, 236n
4:32-37, 235n
5:14, 146n, 156
5:21, 264
5:22, 264
5:31, 156
5:31-32, 124
5:38, 123
6:1, 146n
6:2, 146n
6:7, 146n
7:22, 113n, 123
7:25, 139
8:12, 150n, 156
8:13, 328
8:15, 156
8:17, 156
8:18-24, 328
8:20, 156, 178
8:22, 124
8:36, 156
8:38, 156
9:1, 146n
9:2, 146n
9:4, 218
9:4-5, 336
9:5, 314n
9:10, 146n
9:25, 146n
9:26, 146n
9:35, 156
9:36, 123, 132n, 146n

Acts (continued)
9:38, 146n
10:15, 112
10:28, 112
10:35, 123, 123n, 127n
10:38, 135
10:43, 156
10:44-46, 156
10:47-48, 156
11:3, 123
11:14-15, 156
11:15, 156
11:17, 156
11:18, 156
11:21, 156
11:24, 156
11:26, 146n
11:29, 146n
13:10, 156
13:12, 156
13:38, 156
13:39, 156
13:46, 156
13:48, 156
13:52, 146n
14:9, 135n, 156, 161n
14:15, 156
14:20, 123, 146n
14:21, 146n
14:22, 146n, 150n, 157, 181
14:26, 123
14:28, 146n
15, 12
15:2, 223
15:3, 156
15:8, 156
15:10, 123, 146n
15:11, 156
15:19, 156
15:38, 123
16:1, 146n
16:7, 156, 225n
16:30, 1, 305n
16:30-31, 317
16:30-34, 305n
16:31, 1, 156, 202, 230n, 305n
16:33, 156, 305n
16:34, 305n

Acts (continued)
17:30, 156, 230n
17:31, 306, 314, 333
18:23, 146n
18:25, 156
18:26, 156
18:27, 146n
19:1, 146n
19:2, 146n, 156
19:8, 150n, 156
19:9, 146n
19:30, 146n
20:1, 146n
20:16, 270
20:21, 230n
20:25, 156
20:29, 230n
20:30, 146n
20:32, 156, 157
21:4, 146n
21:16, 146n
22:3, 80n
22:16, 156
23:6, 271
24:15, 157
24:25, 157
25:26, 270
26:18, 156
26:20, 123, 123n, 124, 156, 237, 334
26:22, 334
26:28, 146n
27:20, 135n, 156, 161n
27:31, 156, 161n
27:34, 156
28:17, 156
28:23, 150n, 156
28:31, 150n, 156
31, 135n

Romans
1:1, 225n
1:5, 237n
1-11, 183n
1:12, 125n
1:16, 115, 158, 186
1:17, 24, 113
1:18, 267

Romans (continued)
1:19, 266
1:29, 267
2:3, 307n
2:5, 197n, 307n
2:5-8, 197n, 216
2:5-13, 322
2:6, 24, 50, 118n, 307, 322, 333
2:6-7, 115, 126
2:6-8, 311n, 312, 324, 333
2:7, 251, 307, 312n, 331, 333
2:7-8, 157
2:8, 307, 333
2:10, 126
2:12-16, 216
2:13, 43n, 49n, 58, 83, 91, 158n, 197, 324
2:19, 114
3:1, 63
3-4, 3n, 12
3:8, 26n
3:9-10, 308
3:20, 41, 124
3:20-4:25, 312n
3:21, 92n
3:21-4:25, 205
3:23, 158n
3:24, 1
3:27, 124n
3:28, 1, 24, 40, 124, 124n
3:31, 111n
4, 11, 109, 124n, 336
4:1-5, 1
4:2, 124n
4:2-3, 308
4:3, 336, 336n
4:4, 24
4:18, 205n
4:18-21, 205
4:20, 205n, 336, 336n
4:21, 205n
5:1, 1
5:2, 309
5:3, 251
5:9, 157, 158n
5:9-10, 158
5:10, 157, 158n
5:20, 26n, 124n

Romans (continued)
6, 57
6:1, 290n, 325
6:1-14, 121n, 126
6:12, 54n
6:15, 54n
6:16, 54n
6:16-22, 225
6:21, 157n
6:22, 121n, 157n, 158
6:22-23, 157
6:23, 24, 54n, 249n
7, 76, 113n
7:5, 125, 125n
7:6, 130n
7:7-25, 111n
7:10, 91, 196, 196n
8:1, 59n
8:3, 115
8:4-11, 130n
8:4-14, 114, 323
8:6, 54n
8:9, 115, 273
8:9-11, 218n
8:11, 115, 125, 164, 186, 208
8:12-14, 54n
8:13, 54n
8:14, 319n
8:14-15, 273
8:15, 59n
8:16, 164, 224n, 327
8:17, 319, 319n
8:18-27, 129n
8:19, 273
8:23, 158n, 159, 273
8:24, 158n
8:25, 251
8:29, 202, 228
8:30, 50, 196n
8:31-39, 327, 328
8:33, 43n
9, 91n
9:5, 78n
9:8, 164, 224n
9:10-11, 129n
9:10-12, 124n
9:22, 178
9:23, 126n

Romans (continued)
9:26, 273
9:30-10:3, 88n, 113
9:30-31, 89n
9:31, 308
10:3, 171, 308
10:5, 91
10:9, 61n, 158, 158n, 176
10:10, 1, 159n
10:13, 158, 158n
11:5-6, 24
11:6, 124
11:14, 158n
11:15, 157n, 158n
11:20, 257n
11:20-22, 55
11:22, 83, 290
11:28, 78n
12:13, 235n
12:14, 181, 282n
12-16, 183n
12:17, 282n
12:19, 266
13:3, 126n
13:9, 199n
13:9-10, 313
13:10, 126, 177, 199
13:11-12, 157
13:12, 125n, 126
14:10-12, 308, 333
14:17, 150n
14:20, 125
15:4, 251
15:5, 251
15:15-16, 114
15:18, 126
15:26, 180
16:1, 224n
16:23, 224n

1 Corinthians

1:1, 224n
1:2, 158
1:10, 224n
1:11, 279
1:12, 279
1:13, 125n

1 Corinthians (continued)
1:18, 115, 158, 186
1:18-25, 280
1:21, 281
1:24, 115, 186
1:30, 48
2:1-5, 279
2:1-16, 279
2:5, 281
2:14, 63
2:15, 63
2:16, 280
3, 279, 280, 321
3:1, 63
3:1-4, 63n
3:1-15, 277, 277n
3:4, 279
3:5, 278, 279
3:6, 198, 278
3:7, 279
3:8, 50, 278, 322
3:9, 278
3:10, 278
3:10-15, 279n
3:12, 65
3:12-15, 278
3:13, 278, 280n
3:14, 126
3:14-15, 126, 278
3:15, 25, 157
3:16, 115, 218n
3:18-20, 280
4:1, 279
4:3, 279
4:4, 279
4:5, 279, 280n, 289n, 304n
4:6, 278, 279
4:12, 181, 282n
4:14, 224n
4:16, 224
4:17, 224n
4:20, 150n
5:5, 157, 327
6:9, 157
6:9-10, 26n, 66n, 83, 126, 150n, 175, 197, 197n, 312n, 319, 324
6:11, 158
7:5, 250

1 Corinthians (continued)
7:15, 224n
7:23, 227
8:9-13, 227
9:1, 125, 280, 280n
9:5, 224n
9:21, 199
9:25, 159n, 238, 238n, 281
10:33, 158
11:1, 224
11:2, 14
11:23, 14
11:32, 327
12:6, 125n
12:11, 125n
12:31-13:13, 66n
13:2, 22
13:13, 292
13:17, 280
15:1-2, 14, 53, 253, 253n, 331
15:2, 158, 327
15:3-8, 13n
15:10, 46n, 80n, 114
15:15, 150n
15:50, 157
15:58, 278
16:9, 125n
16:12, 224n
16:22, 225

2 Corinthians

1:1, 224n
1:6, 125n
2:15, 158
3:3-18, 114
3:18, 115, 202, 335
4:7, 186
4:7-5:5, 241
4:12, 125n
5:10, 50, 67, 126, 197n, 307, 308, 312n, 322, 333
5:11, 80n
5:19, 56
6:1, 327
6:2, 158
6:13, 224n
6:16, 218n

2 Corinthians (continued)
7:9-10, 182
7:10, 157
7:11, 182
8:9, 180
8:14, 270
9:8, 125, 125n, 126n
10:11, 126
11:15, 118n, 126, 312n
11:23-29, 305, 305n
12:9, 115, 186
12:9-10, 114
12:21, 83

Galatians

1:14, 113
2:2, 279
2:8, 125, 125n
2:10, 180
2:11-14, 111n
2:12, 111n
2:14, 112
2:16, 1, 109, 124
2:17, 111n
2:18, 111n
2:19, 111n
3, 109
3:1-5, 111
3:2, 124
3:5, 125n
3:6-7, 271
3:10, 41n, 88n
3:10-14, 87n
3:11, 1
3:19, 124n
3:24, 1
3:26, 164, 319n
3:26-27, 273
3:29, 319, 319n
4:3, 225n
4:5-6, 273
4:6, 164
4:7, 319
4:8, 225n
4:11, 279
4:19, 224n
4:28, 164

Galatians (continued)
4:29, 181
4:30, 51
4:31, 224n
5:1, 227
5:4-5, 43n
5:5, 159n
5:6, 22, 23, 27n, 42, 46n, 59n, 68, 125, 125n, 200, 208, 237n, 282, 292, 321, 325, 332
5:14, 313
5:16, 125, 130n
5:16-25, 114, 323
5:19, 125n, 126
5:19-21, 26n, 66n, 126, 175, 197, 197n, 312n, 319, 324
5:19-23, 129n
5:20-21, 267, 282
5:21, 54, 66n, 83, 150n, 157
5:22, 121n
5:22-23, 198
5:22-25, 125
5:24, 164
5:25, 66n
6:1, 131n
6:2, 199
6:4, 125n
6:7, 288
6:7-8, 335
6:7-10, 292, 332
6:8, 54n, 157, 175, 198
6:8-9, 197n
6:8-10, 324
6:9, 54
6:10, 236n, 305n

Ephesians

1:4, 126
1:5, 273
1:11, 125n
1:13, 164
1:14, 164, 319, 326
1:18, 51
1:19, 115, 125n, 186
1:19-20, 125, 208
1:20, 125n
2:1, 164

Ephesians (continued)
2:2, 125, 125n, 126, 158, 164
2:3, 164
2:5, 158, 164
2:6, 164
2:7, 164
2:8, 24, 25, 124, 158, 335
2:8-9, 1, 324
2:8-10, 59n, 321
2:9, 124n, 253, 253n, 309, 321, 335
2:9-10, 124
2:10, 132, 158, 164, 181n, 198n, 309, 324, 325
2:13, 164
2:20, 164
2:20-21, 316
2:21, 115, 218n
2:22, 115
3:5, 271
3:17, 125n
3:20, 115, 125, 125n, 186
4:1, 126, 158, 164, 330
4:10-16, 278
4:16, 125n
4:17, 126, 158
4:31, 266
5:1, 224, 224n
5:1-2, 200, 208
5:2, 126, 158
5:5, 126, 150n, 197, 197n, 312n, 319, 324
5:5-6, 66n
5:8, 126, 158, 227
5:11, 126
5:15, 126, 158
5:18, 66n
5:26, 158
5:51, 175
6:8, 126

Philippians

1:1, 225n
1:3, 21n
1:6, 125, 125n, 270
1:28, 157
1:29, 181
2:2, 225n

Philippians (continued)
2:6-8, 229
2:12, 158, 208, 326
2:12-13, 125
2:13, 125n, 132, 151n, 181n, 186, 198, 208, 324
2:15, 224n
2:16, 279
2:25, 224n
3:2, 126
3:4, 308
3:4-7, 83, 113
3:6-15, 80n
3:9, 124
3:20-21, 157
3:21, 125, 125n, 202, 309
4:1, 280

Colossians

1:1, 224n
1:4-8, 253
1:10, 126n
1:13, 150n
1:21, 126
1:21-23, 53
1:22-23, 331
1:23, 253, 253n, 327
1:29, 125, 125n, 238n
2:6, 59n, 253
2:12, 125, 125n
3:8, 266
3:14, 173n
3:17, 126
3:23, 119n
3:24, 51
3:25, 126
4:7, 224n
4:9, 224n
4:11, 150n
4:12, 225n, 238n

1 Thessalonians

1:3, 125
1:6, 224
1:9, 225n
1:10, 157, 157n

1 Thessalonians (continued)
2:12, 150n
2:13, 125, 125n
2:14, 224
2:16, 148n
2:19-20, 280
3:2, 224n
3:3, 181
3:5, 250, 279
3:10, 224n
5:9, 157
5:15, 282n

2 Thessalonians

1:4, 253
1:4-5, 181, 183n, 251, 252, 331, 334
1:5, 150n, 157
1:6-10, 308, 333
1:7, 306
2:1, 298
2:7, 125, 125n
2:9, 125, 125n
2:10, 157
2:13, 125
2:13-14, 157
2:15, 14
2:17, 126, 126n
3:5, 251
3:6, 14

1 Timothy

1:2, 224n
1:5, 22
1:15, 158
1:18, 53
1:19, 53
1:25, 126
2:4, 158
2:8, 266
2:10, 126n
2:15, 135n, 161n
3:16, 10
4:1, 10, 53
4:1-16, 251
4:7-10, 238
4:10, 238n

1 Tiimothy (continued)
4:16, 10, 53, 197n, 258, 290n, 331
5:3-6:16, 238
5:9-15, 53
5:10, 126n
5:25, 126, 126n, 132n, 324
6:9, 178
6:9-10, 53
6:12, 159n, 238, 238n
6:18, 126n
6:18-19, 197n

2 Timothy

1:5, 22
1:8-9, 115, 186
1:9, 1, 118n, 124, 124n, 157
2:5, 281
2:10, 157
2:11-13, 66n
2:12, 55, 250, 331
2:13, 55
2:15, 4, 126
2:21, 126n
2:24, 225n
2:50, 55
3:8, 22
3:12, 181, 183n
3:13-15, 53
3:17, 126n
4:7, 159n, 238n
4:7-8, 238
4:8, 33, 125, 281
4:14, 118n, 126, 312n
4:16, 157
4:18, 126, 157

Titus

1:1, 225n
1:7, 266
1:16, 126
2:7, 126n
2:11-12, 323
2:11-13, 114, 325
2:13, 309
2:14, 126
3:1, 126n

Titus (continued)
3:3, 225n
3:5, 1, 124, 124n, 157
3:7, 157
3:8, 126n
3:14, 126n
3:15, 225

Philemon

1-2, 224n

Hebrews

1:10, 127
1:14, 159
2:1-4, 127n
2:5, 159
2:6, 271
2:10, 159, 159n, 161, 181
2:13, 224n
2:15, 225n
2:18, 159n
3:6, 65n, 127n, 251, 327, 331
3:7-4:11, 127n
3:9, 127
3:12, 251
3:14, 65, 127n, 159, 160, 160n, 251n, 252, 327, 331, 334
4, 65
4:1, 160
4:2-3, 160
4:3, 127, 160
4:4, 127
4:5, 160
4:6, 160
4:9, 160
4:10, 127
4:11, 251
4:14, 128, 160, 253, 327, 331
4:14-15, 159n
5:8, 159n, 258
5:8-9, 181
5:9, 159, 159n
5:11-6:12, 127n
5:11-14, 159n
6:1, 60n, 127, 132, 159, 159n, 160, 161, 198, 202, 324

Hebrews (continued)
6:4, 66, 251, 251n, 252
6:4-6, 53, 127n
6:5, 159
6:6, 66, 127n, 251
6:8, 160n
6:9, 159
6:9-10, 127, 292, 332
6:10, 132, 198, 324, 327
6:11, 159, 160n, 251
6:12, 159, 161, 251, 253
7:11, 159n
7:11-19, 251
7:19, 159n
7:25, 159, 160
7:28, 160n, 181
9:9, 159n
9:9-10, 251
9:11, 160, 160n
9:14, 127, 159n
9:15, 159, 270
9:28, 159
10:1, 159, 159n, 160, 160n
10:10, 160
10:14, 159n, 160
10:19-39, 127n
10:23, 128, 161, 251, 253, 327, 331
10:24, 127
10:26, 66
10:27, 66
10:29, 160
10:32, 127n
10:35, 160, 251
10:36, 127, 127n, 159, 161, 172, 172n, 197n, 251
10:39, 178
11, 160
11:6, 31
11:9, 251
11:33, 123, 127n
12:1, 127, 127n, 159, 161, 252
12:2, 161, 258
12:2-3, 127, 127n
12:3, 258
12:4, 251
12:4-11, 161
12:7, 127n, 252
12:10, 160, 181, 252

Hebrews (continued)
12:11, 181
12:14, 58, 69
12:14-29, 127n
12:22, 160
12:23, 159n, 160
12:28, 159
13:4, 312n
13:5, 115
13:9, 251
13:14, 159, 160
13:17, 280
13:21, 127, 132, 181n, 186, 198n, 224n, 324
13:22, 127

James

1:1, 225n
1:2-4, 128, 173n, 181, 249, 250
1:2-15, 249
1:3, 250
1:4, 128, 128n, 202, 202n
1:5, 130, 132, 181n, 198n, 324
1:6, 231, 236n
1:8, 236n
1:10-11, 162, 309
1:12, 54n, 128, 130n, 162, 181, 197n, 249, 249n, 281, 331
1:13, 250
1:13-15, 249, 249n
1:14-15, 130n
1:14-16, 54n
1:15, 128
1:16, 328
1:17, 46n
1:18, 161
1:19, 128
1:19-20, 161
1:20, 123, 128n, 129, 266, 266n
1:20-21, 265, 266n
1:21, 124, 128, 161, 161n, 162, 266
1:21-23, 128
1:22, 67, 128
1:22-23, 128n
1:22-25, 197, 197n
1:25, 67, 128, 128n, 129, 199, 309n
1:26, 67, 128

James (continued)
1:27, 128, 217, 292, 305n, 332
2:1, 237n, 308, 309, 309n
2:1-4, 292, 332
2:1-17, 128
2:2-3, 180
2:5, 180, 249n, 281
2:6, 180
2:8, 128, 128n, 199, 266n
2:9, 128n, 129
2:12, 128n, 199, 311, 332
2:12-13, 292
2:13, 26, 128, 128n, 162, 290, 310, 319
2:14, 25, 49, 67, 115, 128n, 161, 162, 308, 310, 326
2:14-16, 325
2:14-26, 14, 128, 128n, 129n, 133, 177, 187, 216, 227, 236n, 313n, 322, 329, 333, 334
2:15, 26, 224n
2:15-16, 128, 292, 305n, 311, 332, 333
2:15-17, 11, 162
2:17, 41, 46, 128n
2:18, 128n, 129, 207, 218n, 237, 308
2:19, 23, 49, 128n, 237n, 325
2:20, 41
2:20-26, 128n
2:21, 308, 311n
2:21-22, 22n, 128n
2:21-26, 308–11
2:22, 59n, 310
2:24, 3n, 44n, 49, 115, 310
2:24-25, 308
2:25, 311n
2:26, 67
3, 311
3:1, 280, 309
3:1-12, 128
3:2, 131n, 227
3:12, 128n
3:13, 118n, 128, 128n, 129, 207, 237, 308, 334
3:14-16, 129
3:14-18, 129
3:15, 130
3:15-18, 129n
3:18, 128n
4:1-3, 130

James (continued)
4:4, 236n
4:7, 130
4:8, 36, 68, 236n
4:10, 162
4:10-12, 184
4:11, 128n
4:11-12, 162, 309
4:12, 161, 162, 290, 333
4:13, 128n
4:15, 128n
4:17, 128n
5:1-12, 309
5:3, 162
5:6, 249n
5:7-8, 162
5:9, 162
5:11, 258
5:12, 162
5:15, 128n, 161
5:16, 125n
5:19-20, 67
5:20, 67, 161, 292n

1 Peter

1:1, 162
1:2, 162
1:2-4, 162n
1:3, 163, 163n
1:3-9, 241
1:4, 282, 282n
1:4-5, 131n
1:6, 249
1:6-7, 162n
1:7, 131n, 249, 250
1:9, 131n, 162, 162n, 163, 181, 249
1:10, 163
1:12, 162n
1:13, 131n, 163
1:14, 227
1:15, 130, 130n
1:16, 225n
1:17, 118n, 130, 130n, 162, 312n
1:18, 130n, 131, 163
1:22-2:1, 282
1:23, 163
2:2, 163

1 Peter (continued)
2:12, 130, 130n, 131, 131n
2:14, 131
2:15, 130, 131
2:20, 130, 131
2:21, 181
3:1, 131, 162n
3:1-2, 130n
3:2, 130
3:6, 130, 131, 131n
3:9, 282, 282n
3:10-11, 131n
3:10-12, 282
3:11, 130n
3:12, 282
3:13, 130n
3:14, 181
3:16, 130, 130n, 132, 181n, 198, 324
3:16-17, 131
3:17, 130
3:20, 131
4:7, 131n
4:8, 292, 332
4:13, 131n, 309
4:17-18, 163
4:18, 131n
4:19, 130, 131
5:1, 131n
5:3, 280
5:4, 131n, 281
5:6, 131n, 184n, 289n
5:10, 131n, 224n
5:12, 224n

2 Peter

2 Peter, 14n
1:1, 163n, 225n
1:3, 125
1:4-5, 163
1:10, 42
1:11, 150n
1:13, 163
2:7, 130n
2:8, 130
2:18, 130n
2:20, 163n
2:20-21, 53

2 Peter (continued)
3:2, 163n
3:7, 163
3:11, 130, 130n
3:13, 163
3:15, 163, 224n
3:18, 163n
5:1, 163
5:4, 163
5:10, 163

1 John

1 John, 121n
1:3, 66n, 154
1:6, 197n
1:7, 66, 66n
1:8, 131n, 307n
2:3-4, 27n
2:6, 197n
2:9-11, 292, 307n, 332
2:10, 121n
2:10-11, 155
2:17, 154, 172, 172n, 307n
2:18, 113n
2:19, 257, 327, 328, 334
2:27-28, 257
2:28, 227, 292, 307n
3, 57
3:2, 202, 224n
3:3, 66n
3:5-6, 57
3:6, 66n, 155, 307n
3:6-9, 54n, 238n
3:7, 66n
3:8, 121
3:8-9, 60n
3:8-10, 271
3:9, 57
3:10, 121n, 173, 197, 227, 292, 307n, 332
3:11, 121n
3:12, 121
3:14, 121n, 154, 334
3:14-15, 292, 307n, 332
3:15, 196n, 267n
3:17, 217, 292, 292n, 332
3:18, 121n

1 John (continued)
4:7, 121n, 200, 208
4:7-8, 271, 292, 332
4:10, 154
4:11, 291
4:12, 292, 332
4:16, 292n
4:17, 265, 292, 292n, 307n, 332
4:19-20, 314
4:20, 195, 217, 219, 330
4:20-21, 292, 313, 314n, 332
5:4, 156n
5:20, 154

2 John
11, 121, 307n

3 John
10, 121
15, 225

Jude
Jude, 14n
1, 225n
1:3, 163n
1:25, 163n
4, 53
12, 53
15, 130
16-19, 131, 132, 181n, 198n, 324
21, 293, 332

Revelation
1:1, 225n
1:9, 181
2:2, 122
2:3, 249
2:4, 122
2:4-5, 122
2:5, 122
2:6, 122
2:7, 156
2:9-10, 181
2:10, 243, 245, 249n, 250, 281, 331

Revelation (continued)
2:10-11, 249
2:11, 156, 250
2:17, 156
2:19, 122
2:20, 225n
2:22, 250
2:23, 118n, 122, 312n
2:26, 122, 156
3:1, 122
3:2, 122
3:5, 156, 312
3:8, 122
3:10, 250
3:10-12, 249
3:11, 281
3:12, 156
3:15, 122
3:17, 180
3:20, 36
3:21, 156
7:3, 225n
7:10, 155
7:14, 181
7:16, 182n
9:20, 122
9:20-21, 250
11:15, 150n
11:18, 123n
12:10, 150n, 155
14:4, 229n
14:10-11, 288
14:12, 250, 252n, 253, 258, 259, 331
14:12-13, 122
16:11, 122
17:8, 156, 178
17:11, 178
18:6, 118n, 122
19:1, 155
19:5, 225n
20:4, 181, 250, 306
20:7-15, 250
20:10, 288n, 289
20:11-13, 306, 308, 333
20:12, 118n, 122n
20:13, 118n, 122, 197n, 312n
20:15, 156
21:7, 156, 273

Revelation (continued)
21:7-8, 197n
21:8, 312n
21:27, 197n
22:3, 225n
22:6, 225n
22:12, 67, 122, 197n, 308, 312n, 333
22:15, 197n, 312n

Old Testament Aprocrypha

2 Baruch
2 Baruch, 107, 109, 114
3:9, 196n
14.12, 106
24.1, 78n
44.14, 78n, 106
44.15, 106
51.2, 106
51.3, 106
51.7, 106
75.5, 106
78.6-7, 106
83.1-8, 304n
84.8-11, 106
85.13, 264
85.15, 106n

1 Esdras
1 Esdras, 98n
1:23, 98
1:47-51, 98
5:49, 98
7:6-15, 98
8:74-80, 98, 109

4 Ezra
4 Ezra, 77n, 90, 109, 114
3:1-2, 244
7:6-14, 178
7:26-36, 264
8:32, 105

4 Ezra (continued)
8:33, 105
8:35-6, 105
12:34, 105
14:30, 196n
14:34, 105

1 Maccabees
6:49, 272n
6:58, 272n
11:51, 272n
13:57, 272n
14:11, 272n

2 Maccabees
1:4, 101n, 272n
6:18-7:40, 101n

Prayer of Azariah
1:78, 81, 99

Prayer of Manasseh
7, 97–98
8, 103
9-15, 97–98

Sirach
15:17, 76n
22:24, 265
27:30-28:11, 266n
28:2, 288n
28:5, 265n
28:6, 273n
28:11, 265
29:11-13, 75
31:3-10, 203–4
35:22, 306, 308n
48:11, 216

Tobias
4:10, 290n
6:15, 233n

Wisdom

2:13, 272n
2:16, 272n
5:5, 272n

Talmud and Rabbinic

b.Aboda Zarah

10, 110
10b, 110
10c, 110
17b, 75n
20b, 110, 110n

m.Abot

1:17, 197
2.7 A and B, 94n, 95n, 196n, 216n
3.15, 76n, 102
3.17, 102
4.9, 102
4.11, 103
4.16, 216n
4.22, 102
5.8-9, 76n, 102
5.19, 216n

b.Baba Batra

8b, 75n
9a, 75n

m.Berakot

3.1, 233n

y.Berakot

7.1, 95
10a, 267n
28b, 77n, 78n, 216n
55b, 191b

b.Hullin

142a, 96

b.Kerithot

7a, 80n

b.Ketubbot

67b, 75n

m.Makkot

3.15, 95
3.16, 76n

m.Pe'ah

1.1, 272n

y.Pe'ah

1.1, 76n, 110
1.30, 110
1.31, 110
1.32, 110
1.32.a, 110
1.32.b, 110
1.32.e, 110

b.Qiddusin

36a, 272n

b.Sanhedrin

99a, 110
101a, 78n

m.Sanhedrin

10.1, 94

t.Sanhedrin

13.3, 80n

b.Shab
31a, 79n
153a, 77n

b.Sebu'ot
13a, 80n

Sota
7b, 216n
9.15, 110n

m.Yoma
8.9, 103

Tg.Neof.Leviticus
22:31, 103

Tg.Neof.Deuteronomy
9:4-5, 103

Mek.Exodus
15.1, 79n

Genesis Rab.
22.6, 96
35.2, 78n

Exodus Rab.
2.5, 78n
15.3-5, 78n

Deuteronomy Rab.
2.24, 80n

Sifra Ahare Mot
8.10, 94n, 95
8:11, 95n

Sifre Deuteronomy
26, 80n
307, 102
307.3, 102n

Old Testament Pseudepigrapha

Life of Adam and Eve
27.2, 105
28.4, 105
29.3, 105
31.4, 105

Ahiqar
137, 203n

Apocalypse of Abraham
15.6, 257

Apocalypse of Zephaniah
2.8-9, 105
7.1-7, 104
7.8, 100n, 104
7.9, 104
8.5, 100, 104
10.10-11, 105
11.1-6, 105
37.2, 105, 106, 106n

1 Enoch
27.1-2, 264
41.1, 100
54.1-6, 264
58:2, 142n
61.8, 100, 306
62.1-3, 306
69.27, 306
89.12-27, 176n
89.12-90:42, 176n

1 Enoch (continued)
90.26, 264
92.4-5, 80n

2 Enoch

2 Enoch, 100, 100n
44:5, 99
49:2, 99
49:2-3, 100n
52:15, 99

Joseph and Aseneth

Joseph and Aseneth, 99n
8.5, 99
8.9, 99
11:10, 99, 99n
15.5, 99
16.16, 99
19.5, 99
21.13-14, 99
21.21, 99

Jubilees

1.5, 104
1.15, 230
1.18, 104
1.20, 104
1.21, 104
1.23, 230
15.32-34, 80n
41.24, 114

Midrash Psalms of Solomon

41.8, 267n
104.27, 267n

Psalms of Solomon

Psalms of Solomon, 109
1:46-47, 97n
3:12, 142n
5:16-17, 203n–204n
9.5, 308n
9.16-19, 80n

Psalms of Solomon (continued)
13:11, 142n
14.2, 196n
14.10, 142n

Sybilline Oracles

1.100-3, 257
2.292-310, 257

Testament of Abraham

A11, 100
A12.1, 100
A12.4, 100
A12.5, 100
A12.10, 100
A12.11, 100
A12.12-14, 100
A12.13, 100
A12.15, 100
A12.17-18, 100
A13.3, 100
A13.4, 100
A13.5, 100
A13.6, 100
A13.8, 100
A13.9, 101
A13.10-11, 101
A13.14-15, 101
A13.18, 100, 101
B9, 100

Testament of Dan

1:3-2:5, 265
5.3, 216n

Testament of Issachar

5.2, 216n
7.6-7, 216n

Testament of Levi

3.2, 308n
13.5, 78n

Testament of Naphtali
8.5, 78n

Testament of Simeon
2:6-13, 265

Other Non-canonical

Gospel of the Nazaraeans
Gospel of the Nazaraeans, 195
13, 283n

1QH
6.8-10, 80n
11.29-32, 80n
15.13-19, 80n
18.21-22, 80n

1QM
14:7, 180

1QS
1-2, 107
1.7, 107
2.25, 107
3.3, 107
3.7-9, 107
3.15-16, 107
3.18-25, 80n
11.11, 107
11.17-18, 107

4Q
393 1-2.ii.2-4, 97n
504 4.6-7, 97n
511.2.35, 283n

www.ingramcontent.com/pod-product-compliance
Lightning Source LLC
Chambersburg PA
CBHW052128010526
44113CB00034B/1021